ABOUT THE AUTHOR

Peter Hain's childhood was spent in apartheid South Africa, a period that came to an end when his parents were forced into exile in 1966.

A leader of the Anti-Apartheid Movement and the Anti-Nazi League in Britain during the 1970s and 1980s, Hain obtained degrees at Queen Mary College, London, and the University of Sussex. He was elected Labour MP for Neath in 1991, having been a Young Liberal until 1977. In government he served as Secretary of State for Wales and Northern Ireland, as Secretary of State for Work and Pensions and as Leader of the Commons. He was also Europe Minister, Foreign Minister and Energy Minister. He chaired the UN Security Council, and negotiated international treaties curbing nuclear proliferation and banning the conflict-inducing trade in blood diamonds.

Author of a popular recent biography of Nelson Mandela, *Mandela* (2010), Hain has written numerous books and pamphlets and appears widely on radio and television, as well as being an experienced public speaker.

Married with two sons and four grandchildren, he is a keen football, rugby, cricket and motorsport fan.

OUTSIDE IN
PETER HAIN

Biteback Publishing

First published in Great Britain in 2012 by
Biteback Publishing Ltd
Westminster Tower
3 Albert Embankment
London
SE1 7SP

This paperback edition published in 2012
Copyright © Peter Hain 2012

All other photos from the personal collection of Peter Hain.

ISBN 978-1-84954-410-8

10 9 8 7 6 5 4 3 2 1

A CIP catalogue record for this book is available from the British Library.

Set in Garamond and Placard by Namkwan Cho
Cover design by Namkwan Cho

Printed and bound in Great Britain by
CPI Group (UK) Ltd, Croydon, CR0 4 YY

For Elizabeth with love and thanks

'If political change was easy, it would have been achieved a long time ago. Stick there for the long haul.'

Walter Hain, to his son Peter in 1965

CONTENTS

PREFACE

This is the story of an 'outsider' turned 'insider': anti-apartheid militant to Cabinet Minister, serving twelve years in Labour's government between May 1997 and May 2010.

I first found myself in the public eye in 1965 aged fifteen unexpectedly delivering the reading at the funeral of an anti-apartheid friend who had been hanged in Pretoria. Then in Britain, from the age of nineteen, political notoriety led to two extraordinary Old Bailey trials and being sent a letter bomb. Thirty years later I was sworn in as a Privy Counsellor by the Queen.

This is intended as a readable rather than erudite book, from struggle and protest in the 1960s and 1970s to negotiating the 2007 Northern Ireland settlement. Hopefully the reader will enjoy the fun as well as the sadness, the highs and the lows, the achievements and the setbacks of an unusual political life. My aim has also been a book that has durable interest, giving a sense of what the noble calling of politics can be like, and an insight into modern government based upon contemporaneous notes and dictated recordings – an independent account of Labour in power from neither a 'Blairite' nor a 'Brownite' perspective.

I am very grateful to my wife Elizabeth Haywood for her dedicated, detailed and frank comments on the drafts, and to my parents Walter and Adelaine Hain for their observations, their courage in the anti-apartheid struggle and a lifetime's support. My wonderful sister Sally Hain painstakingly downloaded and transcribed the majority of recordings, with assistance from Cari Morgans and Matt Ward. My former government political advisers Phil Taylor and David Taylor commented expertly on the whole draft; Frank Baker, Sarah Lyons, Glynne Jones, Andre Odendaal, John Underwood and Phil Wyatt advised on parts. My agent Caroline Michel gave invaluable advice throughout, as at its conception did Gail Rebuck. My thanks to them all.

Hopefully, when they are old enough to read it, Harry, Seren, Holly and Tesni Hain will discover their unusual hinterland and perhaps also be inspired to make a difference as their Grandad always strove to do.

Peter Hain
Ynysygerwn, Neath, July 2012

CHAPTER ONE

FREEDOM STRUGGLE

'Ah, Peter, return of the prodigal son!' Nelson Mandela beamed, welcoming me to his Johannesburg home in February 2000.

Although on an official government visit, in a sense I was also being welcomed to *my* 'home' – to South Africa, the panoramic, sunshine country of my childhood, as the first ever British Minister for Africa to be born on that continent.

Ten years earlier, with Mandela still in prison I remained banned from entering South Africa – a legacy of my anti-apartheid campaigning – and I wasn't an MP then, still less a government minister. And ten years before *that*, I had never even considered being an MP: I was more steeped in extra-parliamentary protest and activism, the roots of which lay earlier in my South African-born parents' brave anti-apartheid work when I was a boy.

As I settled onto his sitting room sofa for our discussions, my Foreign Office officials taking notes, all of us enjoying the thrill of being in the great man's presence, I was barely three years into a ministerial life in the Labour governments of Tony Blair and Gordon Brown; it would last a further nine years, seven as a member of the Cabinet.

Although we had met a number of times before, it was always special to be in his presence. A humble icon without an ounce of self-importance or arrogance, he had a unique aura: a sense of deep tranquillity and gentleness with everyone, yet also a worldly shrewdness that made you feel simultaneously at ease and in awe.

A twinkle in his eye, Mandela – or *Madiba* (his clan name), used by those close to him – courteously poked fun at the elegant British High Commissioner, Dame Maeve Fort, who had arranged the meeting; he was especially taken with English ladies – the Queen included. But soon we moved on to talk about African policies, including his efforts as a mediator in the civil conflict in Burundi. Then, the meeting over, we walked out together in the bright summer's day to a battery of television cameras, photographers and journalists gathered under the trees in his front garden, his hand resting on my shoulders, in part affectionately, in part because (now aged eighty-one) he found walking increasingly difficult.

Even ten years after his release from prison, and having meanwhile served as President for five years and then stepped down, Mandela's saintliness remained. 'I wanted to welcome my friend Peter Hain,' he said, generous to a fault. 'He was a noted supporter of our freedom struggle and we thank him for that. Except for people like Peter, who was a leader of the anti-apartheid movement, I might not be standing here, a free man today, and our people would not be free.'

It was a proud and almost magical moment for me, standing alongside the global giant who inspired such universal affection and admiration. He had been imprisoned on Robben Island under the old apartheid regime when, as a teenager in England, I was first denounced in South Africa as 'Public Enemy Number One'. My crime was leading successful campaigns to stop all-white South African sports tours from 1969.

Now aged fifty, I was feted as a returning VIP, not just from the days of the freedom struggle, but representing the government of the old colonial power, the United Kingdom – which in past decades I had vigorously attacked for its complicity in sustaining apartheid, denouncing as weasels its Africa Ministers.

But the journey to become a British Cabinet Minister started a long time before my years as a militant anti-apartheid protester. My transition from outsider to insider began as a son of Africa.

‡

My life as a young boy in South Africa effectively ended with a close family friend being hanged by the apartheid government.

And the beginning of that end really began, I suppose, when the Security Police took my mother and father away in the middle of the night. Although I was aged eleven, unusual things had been happening to our family for a while, and my anti-apartheid parents had warned me that this might happen, making plans for my Gran (who lived nearby) and our black maid Eva Matjeka to look after us. I was their eldest child, used to taking responsibility and to looking after my younger brother Tom, then aged nine, and my two small sisters Jo-anne and Sally, aged six and four.

Still, when a hand shook me awake in our Pretoria home in May 1961, I couldn't help being frightened. As my eyes opened there was a familiar friend, Nan van Reenen, a kindly middle-aged lady, anxious in the gloom: 'Peter, your parents have been put in jail,' she said gently, holding my hand.

I was drowsy, confused: what was happening? Where were they? They might never come back – what on earth would I do? Then: mustn't panic, mustn't let my parents down, stay calm, carry on.

Nan told me how, with fellow Liberal Party activists Maritz van den Berg and her son Colyn, they had been putting up posters in support of the 'Stay-at-home' protest called by Nelson Mandela when the Security Police turned up and detained them.

We checked to see that the others were still sleeping, she tucked up on our living room sofa, and I went back to bed and tried to close my eyes, worrying and wondering what lay ahead of us and how my even younger brother and sisters would react when they awoke.

Before she left in the morning Nan and I told them what had happened. The girls were wide eyed, and Tom very quiet. They did not cry but all of us knew that tears were being held back. Although I had no idea what was coming next, I felt I had to look after them somehow. I didn't think of myself as the young boy I was, just that I needed to do what had to be done.

Gran soon came over and moved in – though not Grandad, who (I later learnt) took a dim view of it all. Eva quietly took charge and ensured everything went as smoothly as possible, and one of my parents' activist friends, Anita Cohen, brought a huge meringue cake round to cheer us up.

It seemed almost normal to me that they had been detained, because we had become used to our telephone being tapped, to Special Branch surveillance of our house in the Pretoria suburb of Hatfield, and to police suddenly raiding and searching our house.

Our family was close knit and somehow my parents had managed to keep up a caring family life amidst all the trauma of their increasing participation in the resistance to apartheid. Despite being on the receiving end of a police state where basic human rights had virtually disappeared, I remember a blend of the ordinary and the extraordinary in our day-to-day lives, a mixture of excitement, stress, shock, and yet lots of family fun and togetherness too.

Dad took time to teach his boys about cricket, to come and watch us play in school teams, and take us to club football matches and motor races. He made space to help with my homework and to discuss my emerging interest in what they were doing in politics. Amidst all the persistent political pressure and crises she faced, Mom, incredibly, was also always there for us and looked after the family home. She was the fulcrum of both their political activism and our family life, somehow balancing both. I never recall feeling that their activism came ahead of their children. In fact I still feel privileged to have had the best parents in the world.

Very little was made of their arrests by our teachers or our friends, as we were well looked after, and life went on. These sort of things happened, and Mom and Dad would be out soon, we were reassuringly told. But it still seemed an age before they were released, and my mother kept the letter I wrote to her.

'Gran and Eva are looking after us well but we are missing you a lot,' it said in clear, careful writing.

I must have blanked out my worries and emotions – doubtless a characteristic that was to stand me in good stead later on – because I do not recall it being a terrible episode. But six-year-old Jo-anne was in retrospect reaching for comfort in wanting to feel her mother near her when she modified a petticoat she had always loved Mom wearing. It had layers of stiff net which made her skirts stick out, rather like a modern day crinoline. There was a thin nylon section, from waist to hip before the netting and Jo-anne cut holes in this, so that she could wear the petticoat with her arms through the holes. We all yelled at her that she would get into 'big trouble' when Mom and Dad got back. But we were wrong – of course she didn't.

They had been the first people to be detained without charge under a new Twelve-Day Law aimed at rising political dissent, which allowed for detention without trial. My father and his two male comrades Colyn and Maritz were taken off to share a cell in Pretoria Local jail where conditions were not bad. But he was concerned throughout about my mother with whom he had no contact until they were released – an anxiety increased when he almost immediately received a letter in prison from his municipal employer sacking him.

Mom had been locked up alone in a large echoing hall in Pretoria Central Prison, in which white women detainees had been held during the 1960 Emergency. Reverberating up the stairwell, she could hear the screams of black women prisoners being assaulted. She also found the wardresses flesh-creeping and intimidating, especially when they deliberately came to watch her having a bath; so much so that she decided to wash in a hand basin where it was more private. Although comforted that our Gran would be caring for us with Eva, she nevertheless worried continuously about her children – though she never revealed her real predicament and fears until many years later.

Before the twelve days kicked in, they had been held for the maximum two days while the police searched in vain for evidence to bring charges. Mom had secretly chewed up and spat out the one piece of incriminating evidence that could have led to charges – a leaflet urging people to go on strike and stay at home – quickly managing to do this just as the Special Branch first turned up. Told about this later, I was rather taken with her ingenuity, having recently seen my first James Bond film, *From Russia with Love*.

Much as they tried, the Special Branch could not find anything to bring a prosecution, and after the fourteen days were completed my parents had to be released. I hadn't known about the exact timing, and so it was a great relief to walk home from school with my brother Tom and sister Jo-anne and unexpectedly see my Dad strolling along to meet us with my little sister Sally in her favourite perch on his shoulders. Four-year-old Sally had been frightened when she first saw him because he had grown an unfamiliar beard in prison. But Jo-anne, especially close to her father, looked up from chatting to a school friend, had a rush of happiness and ran across the road to be scooped up for a huge hug.

The immense joy of family reunion was, however, tempered by my father's forced unemployment. Losing his job was a big financial blow. Yet somehow we struggled through financially with the help of a donation from an anonymous Liberal Party member. Until he was offered a temporary post by a Party member two months later, we had to survive living on account at local shops. I remember the understanding of shopkeepers as I signed for essential items in the chemist or grocery store – an experience which made me even more determined than before. I was not going to be beaten down by anyone, ever – and certainly not by our enemies.

But soon my parents were in action again – and life settled back to its abnormal normality.

‡

None of my white cousins or school friends experienced anything like this, for they were conventional English-speaking white South Africans. And, intriguingly, so by origin were my parents. My mother Adelaine was descended from the English 1820 Settlers and my father Walter from Scottish immigrants who had left Glasgow after the 1914–18 World War. As a nineteen-year-old, he had been wounded in action fighting with the Allies in Italy in 1944. I was actually born a British subject (and remained so) in 1950 in Nairobi, Kenya, where my father had been working on his first job after graduating from Witwatersrand University in Johannesburg as an architect.

Our stay there didn't last long because my Dad was offered a new job back in South Africa. When I was aged about fifteen months my parents daringly drove an old car several thousand miles down the African continent, home to South Africa; deliberately, they hadn't informed their own parents, expecting disapproval. But they were delighted that I learnt to walk on the way, though occasionally envious as I munched my food, sometimes when they had run out of money to feed themselves. Well into the four-week journey I was apparently reluctant to leave the car since it had become 'home'. I slept on the back seat and Mom and Dad slumped on the front seats at night. Amidst numerous tyre punctures, breakdowns and mishaps in the African bush, they had throughout friendly help from inquisitive locals amazed at seeing white people out on their own in the heart of Africa.

As I grew up, first in Natal for a few years, and then mainly in Pretoria from 1954, our lifestyle, at least to begin with, was a conventional one in the 1950s and 1960s for a white family of moderate means. My father worked, my mother ran the home. We were not well off, but we were able to live in a comfortable, rented detached house set in ample grounds. A black maid lived separately in a room with toilet and shower next to the garage – the usual servant's accommodation.

Until I was about eight, my parents' social circle was typical. We would visit relatives and friends and they would visit us. It was a happy, carefree and secure childhood, with the weather and the space for outdoor activities. Pretoria in those days was easy going and my brother and I were able to roam without restriction with our friends on bicycles and in soap box cars we built ourselves. And, every December, the two rear bench seats of our Volkswagen minibus were turned into a bed for the 700-mile overnight trip to my maternal grandparents' home on the banks of the Kowie River, at the pretty little seaside town of Port Alfred in the Eastern Cape. There we spent our Christmas holidays, fishing off the jetty or spending long lazy days on the broad sandy beaches and swimming freely in the warm waters of the Indian Ocean.

‡

The process of making South Africa such a very pleasant place in which a white boy could grow up had begun some 300 years earlier, when the first permanent settlers from Europe landed at what became Cape Town in 1652. In the centuries that followed, their descendants and followers remorselessly colonised the rest of the land to the east and north, pushing the indigenous black tribes into remote and less hospitable areas.

British settlement increased after Britain in 1806 annexed the strategically important Cape, later triggering conflicts with the Afrikaans-speaking whites descended from early Dutch, German and French Huguenot settlers. Two bloody 'Boer Wars' occurred, during which 26,000 Afrikaner women and children died in British concentration camps. All this spawned a fierce nationalism in Afrikaners, deeply resentful of their English-speaking compatriots. Eventually South Africa was granted independence in 1910.

Throughout this period and afterwards, racist, white dominance increased until the hated system of *apartheid* (meaning 'separateness') was instituted from 1948 when the Afrikaner National Party came to power for the first time. Pro-Nazi during the Second World War, the 'Nats' (my parents called them) quickly ushered in probably the worst racist tyranny the world has ever witnessed.

Apartheid affected everything. I had to go to a whites-only school, travel on a whites-only bus, play sport with and against whites alone, live in a whites-only area, sit on a whites-only park bench and observe my parents voting in whites-only elections.

As a teenager I remember vividly my Dad showing me the legislation which statutorily defined 'whiteness' in terms which for me perfectly captured the Orwellian character of apartheid:

A white person means a person who –

(a) in appearance is obviously a white person and who is not generally accepted as a Coloured person; or

(b) is generally accepted as a white person and is not in appearance obviously not a white person.

‡

My mother had lived until aged nineteen on the outskirts of Port Alfred, close to a Coloured* family and with Africans of the Xhosa tribe passing her door en route to the town. Two of her school teachers – one apparently a communist – had commented in different ways to her that everyone should be treated equally, and she remembered being struck that, instead of being inferior, Paul Robeson, the black American singer-actor, was hugely impressive in one of his Hollywood films when she saw it at the local cinema. Her father was prominent in the Eastern Cape branch of the mainly English-speaking United Party, which was led by the wartime hero and Prime Minister Jan Smuts, and she sometimes accompanied him to public meetings.

On one occasion she was to startle her father by challenging the visiting United Party MP about something he had said at a meeting when he stopped by later at their home for a meal. She had also worked for the town's community newssheet (to which her Dad, active on local issues, contributed). She typed it and staffed the office. So she was the more politically aware when, aged twenty-one, she married my father in Pretoria in 1948. Although he had been brought up to question everything and was vigorously anti-establishment by temperament, his parents had never talked politics to him. Despite the fact that they had both been Labour Party members in their youth in Glasgow, they shunned the politics of their adopted country; like most British immigrants they turned a blind eye to the racism and went along with the status quo.

The vast majority of white South Africans continued to live a life thriving off apartheid but curiously insulated from its terrible consequences. Current affairs

---

*   Mixed race, one of four racial groups, the others whites, Africans (blacks) and Asians.

was not taught in schools, and my parents had little knowledge of the mesh of repressive laws that stultified black life. They were barely aware of the African National Congress (ANC) nor of its new emerging leaders in the late 1940s, including of course Nelson Mandela. But, unusually for whites, they did share a respect for blacks. Their eyes had been opened by the more relaxed racial structure they found in Kenya, and also by the warm, friendly face of the Africans they had encountered on their eventful drive back home in 1951.

So a South African friend from Kenya was on fertile ground when he recommended two years later that they be invited to join the newly formed non-racial Liberal Party. They formed a branch with a student, Annette Cockburn, in Ladysmith where we lived at the time and where Tom had been born. There was nowhere else to have the inaugural meeting except in our house, and it was addressed by Alan Paton, author of the renowned *Cry, the Beloved Country*. Elliot Mngadi, later National Treasurer of the Party, remarked: 'This is the first time I've ever come through the front door of a white man's house.' (Blacks acting as servants or gardeners might be allowed in the back door.)

From a young age, I became used to blacks being in our home – not only as servants but as equals and friends. Years later, well after we had moved to Pretoria, where Jo-anne was born, we would visit Party colleagues in one of the black townships that ringed the towns and cities throughout the country. Under apartheid's rigid segregation, town centres were reserved for white residents. It would have been unheard of for any of my white school friends or relatives to do this, just as they would never have considered having blacks as friends rather than servants.

My free-spirited parents, having always wanted to visit Britain, decided they had better do so before their three children were old enough to incur substantial travel costs. Our car was sold to pay for the ocean liner fare, my father arranged for a job in London, and we embarked at Cape Town at the beginning of 1956. Apart from being embarrassingly seasick – once all over a corridor floor while running for a basin – I found it all rather exciting.

But I remember how cold and grey London felt arriving in mid-winter. It seemed so strange, so different. No wide open spaces, no barefoot sunshine any more. Shoes and socks, thick clothes, coats, huddling inside the house to get warm, heavy traffic, big city – and so many people: walking, talking, buzzing, thronging the pavements, everywhere and anywhere I looked.

We lived first in the west London suburb Ealing, where I began school. Then, because the rent was much less, we moved to a tiny cowman's cottage on a farm in Ruckinge overlooking Romney Marsh in Kent. My sister Sally was born there that Christmas, and I recall playing happily on the farm and helping the hay making amidst the excitement of combine harvesters and tractors.

In one spell of very hot weather, we all took our bedding and slept out on the front lawn – that seemed a real adventure – especially when the milk woman surprised us in the early morning.

Soon after they had arrived my parents discovered the liberal newspapers, the *Guardian* and the *Observer,* through which they gained a much better understanding of world affairs than was possible from the parochial and conservative South African media. Great events occurred in 1956: Suez, when the British, French and Israelis attacked Egypt, and the Soviet invasion of Hungary. These made a big impact upon them and they joined progressive British opinion in strongly opposing both.

They also read of tumult in their home country. In August 1956 10,000 women of all races gathered at the seat of government, the Union Buildings in Pretoria, in protest against the extension to women of the hated Pass Laws, which controlled every movement of blacks, who were required to carry an identity document (or 'pass') at all times. That December 156 people – including Nelson Mandela and the entire leadership of the ANC – were arrested for high treason, the following 'Treason Trial' lasting two years before they were acquitted.

Meanwhile apartheid laws such as the Immorality Act (outlawing sexual inter-course between whites and members of any other racial group) were introduced, provoking increasing protests and boycotts by blacks. My parents followed all these events avidly, and became concerned and restive. Late in 1957 when my father's old architectural firm in Pretoria telephoned and asked him to return, they decided to do so, and he flew out alone early in December. We had no car and Mom was left to pack up and travel with four small children, first by bus and train up to London, and then down to Southampton to board an ocean liner.

A fortnight later there was a hum of excited anticipation as the ship pulled into Port Elizabeth docks in the hot summer sunshine. For a seven-year-old boy it seemed an enormous drop from the deck to the quay below where my Dad, whom we had not seen for six long weeks, waited with both sets of grandparents. Holding onto the railings, three-year-old Jo-anne sang over and over again a little song 'Hello, My Daddy'. But I distinctly remember glimps-ing ugly hammerhead sharks circling the hull: a menacing shiver clouded my joy, but I didn't know why.

‡

The city of my childhood, Pretoria, holds strong memories, some fond, some unhappy. With wide streets lined with jacaranda trees, majestically purple in flower, it had white suburbs with detached homes and large gardens kept nicely manicured by black gardeners. The old capital of Afrikanerdom and a bastion of apartheid, it held few progressive instincts. Yet a branch of the Liberal Party had become active by the time we returned there early in 1958, and my parents quickly rejoined.

Their introduction was dramatic. A peaceful women's demonstration against being forced to carry passes in the nearby township of Lady Selborne was broken up by baton-wielding police. Many were injured and when their men folk returned from work feelings ran high. The township was soon in uproar. The local Liberal Party chairman John Brink had driven in to try to restrain the police and, when he failed to return, I remember the drama of my Dad driving out to look for him and being worried as we all waited anxiously for his return. To my relief, he came back soon. But this was because he had met John returning from the township, bloodied, in a windowless car which had been stoned by residents venting their fury at a white intruder, not knowing he was on their side. He only managed to escape when the local ANC organiser Peter Magano recognised him and jumped onto the car bonnet in protection. The blood and shattered glass were terrible, I thought; he could easily have been killed – and Dad too, trying to rescue him. What was happening to us, I wondered?

Then aged eight, the only other time I had been frightened and shocked by the sight of a bloodied face and clothes was when a black boy called Tatius, in his early teens, and allowed to stay in our servant's quarters as a favour, had been set upon by white youths as he walked along a nearby pavement. Apparently they took exception to him penny-whistling, and beat him up 'to teach him a lesson'. He arrived home crying, billowing bloody bruises on his face, his legs and arms raw. It was all too sadly typical of the random, savage cruelty blacks might face. Protests by my Dad to the local police station were greeted with barely hidden contempt, and he angrily wrote a letter to the *Pretoria News*. On publication, his name was duly noted by the Special Branch as somebody new to keep an eye on.

Lady Selborne was unusual in being a mixed-race township with an old British colonial heritage, which meant the normal restrictions on whites visiting did not apply, and my parents were later to become well known there. During the day my mother visited regularly, accompanied by my youngest sister Sally, who was under school age and who would usually be left at the local Tumelong English Mission in a black crèche (unthinkable for a white child) while Mom went about her Party business. The English women running the Mission, Hannah Stanton and Cecily Paget, were Liberal Party members.

From aged eight onward, I occasionally went along too at weekends, sometimes with my brother and two younger sisters as we were too young to be left alone at home. The more we did so the less novel it became, driving through the dusty or muddy tracks and peering at the houses, some ramshackle, others more solid, but all so starkly different from the comfortable white communities in which we and our school mates lived. I remember staring in wonderment then – as I have ever since – at seeing African women hanging out clothing to dry, pristine despite the primitive conditions for washing and the dust swirling around.

My parents were both soon on the Pretoria Liberals' Committee. My mother later became branch secretary, a position she held until she was banned from doing so in 1963. Our rented houses, first in Hilda Street and then in Arcadia Street, saw regular visitors and callers from Liberal members and others, black as well as white. Despite the continuous buzz of activity, my parents ensured that our friends could come around to play, and that we could go to their houses. My brother and I later organised bicycle races through our yard and out via the garage entrance onto the pavement, then back in through the front gate; these sometimes went on for several hours with school friends teaming up in pairs and sharing the cycling as my Mom and Dad acted as race controllers and my small sisters cheered us on. We were also taken regularly to watch motor racing at the Kyalami circuit some thirty miles away on the road to Johannesburg. The nine-hour all-night race was a special treat as I watched my favourite, the British driver David Piper, win every time in his green Ferrari.

Not all of my boyhood was entirely innocent, however. Aged about ten we stole the odd tin of condensed milk from boxes in our house bound for a black township. We occasionally went around at night throwing small stones on the mostly corrugated iron roofs of white homes and then scampered away. We got old clothes, winding them up to look like snakes, then crouched behind our garden hedge and pulled them in the gloom across the pavement so that passing pedestrians – invariably blacks – jumped in fear as we screeched in delight. But one of these pranks rebounded terribly as I remember to this day in shame. With friends we would put a balloon in a plastic bag and leave it lying on the road for one of many cyclists, enjoying from our vantage point on the garage roof how they were startled when it burst as they rode over it. Then we placed a large stone inside an empty-looking bag, and I watched horrified as an old black man crashed against it, all his precious shopping – food and provisions – spewing out over the street. I rushed out of my hiding place to help him gather it up, seeing him weeping and feeling terrible, not least because I knew he was poor. I never did anything like that again.

‡

Mom and Dad had first met and talked in August 1958 to Nelson Mandela, his close comrade Walter Sisulu and other defendants during what became known as the 'Treason Trial'. Held in the Old Synagogue courtroom in Pretoria, many of the accused went outside during the lunch break for food provided in turn by the local Indian community, Liberals and other sympathisers. The charismatic Mandela, my parents told me, was 'a large, imposing, smiling man'. Increasingly their activities crossed over with the ANC, whose Pretoria leader, Peter Magano, became a friend and key contact.

Also in 1958 the Liberal Party launched a weekly news and comment magazine, *Contact*, covering the anti-apartheid struggle. My parents subscribed and Mom later became its Pretoria correspondent. Telling us to 'keep quiet and go and play', she would clatter away on her small Olivetti typewriter, covering Nelson Mandela's trial and other trials until she was banned from doing so. She was a self-trained 'journalist' – but, unlike my Dad, not university educated, having gone to work straight from school as an office clerk. At this time in her early thirties, small, dark haired and pretty in an unaffected way, she cut a diminutive dash as she scurried about organising and harrying the authorities, especially in courts and police stations where blacks were treated worst.

Other political organisations at the time represented the different racial groups – Mandela's ANC for example was mainly for Africans and the Congress of Democrats mainly for whites. The Liberal Party's appeal was based on membership open to all racial groups on an equal basis. Committed to universal franchise, it contained a range of political opinion from socialists to free market liberals; but both its unity and its radicalism sprang from an uncompromising support for human rights and a fierce anti-racism, the principles which above all inspired my parents and became increasingly imbibed by their children.

Many whites in Pretoria remained bitterly opposed to the very existence of the Liberal Party, seeing it as in some respects even worse than the ANC because it contained whites like them. Students at Pretoria University, an Afrikaans-speaking institution, were militantly pro-apartheid and would line up outside Party meetings, shouting slogans and abuse. I remember vividly their noisy, intimidating barracking outside a Party colleague's home as we remained inside and feeling fearful, wondering if they might burst in at any moment, until they finally went away.

By contrast my parents became close friends with many blacks. David Rathswaffo, for example, was a particular family favourite who would call by and take time to swap greetings and stories with me. He had some great one-liners where syntax and grammar got horribly jumbled, to hilarity all round;

he would always say 'can I see you *in camera*?' if he had some confidential information. He also never quite came to terms with telephone tapping. One day, needing to give my mother an urgent message about helping a black comrade who had escaped from the court, David lowered his voice and whispered 'please come, Jimmy has escaped' – as if the whisper might fool those listening in.

David was also a clerk at the Supreme Court in Pretoria, where all the major political trials took place. Until, that was, in 1959 when the government decided that blacks should not carry out such 'responsible tasks', which should be reserved for whites. David was replaced by a white man – whom he had to train for the job – and made redundant.

It was incidents and events like this, part of the staple diet of our daily lives, which meant that from a young age I became politically conscious without being myself politically involved. My Dad used to spend time with me explaining some of the absurdities of reserving better jobs for whites under apartheid: that black decorators could paint the undercoat but not the final coat, that they could pass bricks to white builders but not lay these themselves.

By this time the new Nationalist Prime Minister Hendrik Verwoerd was well into his stride. A more intellectual leader than his predecessors with a total belief in the ideology of apartheid, he had earlier complained that the pre-apartheid system of schooling had misled blacks by showing them 'the green pastures of white society in which they are not allowed to graze'. Soon he would end the attendance of what had been a handful of blacks at the white universities.

In 1959 a prominent Pretoria Liberal and local doctor, Colin Lang, contested the Pretoria East by-election to the Provincial Council as the Nationalists' only opponent. He turned in a creditable performance, with twenty-four per cent of the vote, saving his deposit. Our home was the campaign headquarters. This was my parents' first experience of electioneering and canvassing for a non-racial party amongst the overwhelmingly racist white electorate. I remember, aged nine, helping to leaflet in the tree-lined white suburbs, and finding it fun. Party members came across from Johannesburg to help. One of them, Ernie Wentzel, was a young white lawyer who subsequently became a great family friend. He addressed open-air public meetings from the back of a flat-bed lorry, silencing the bitterly hostile audience's shouts of 'Would you like your sister to marry a Kaffir?' with the response (in a heavy Afrikaans accent): 'Christ man, you should see my sister!' I thought this hilarious and used to enjoy my Dad recounting the tale to friends.

The by-election raised the profile of the Pretoria branch and brought my parents and other key activists to the attention of the authorities. Mom and

Dad were soon helping to produce a monthly newsletter called *Libertas*. It was typed by Mom and printed on a noisy and dilapidated old Gestetner duplicator which stood in a corner of our dining room, its black ink frequently dripping where it shouldn't, and its wax stencils hung up for reuse if needed. I would get roped in to collate the sheets for stapling and helped with pushing it through doors as it was distributed by a team transported in our Volkswagen minibus – all rather exciting, I felt.

‡

In February 1960, just as I turned ten, the British Prime Minister, Harold Macmillan, addressed the South African Parliament, speaking of the 'winds of change' blowing through the African continent, and greatly embarrassing the apartheid government, who had good reason to expect the usual plati-tudes of complicity from Britain my parents had warned me to expect. They were delighted at this international shot-in-the-arm for anti-apartheid forces who felt increasingly alone and isolated in what was by now a full-blown police state.

The speech engendered hope amongst blacks burdened by anger, poverty and frustration, and the ANC called for an economic boycott in protest against the 'passes' blacks had to carry all the time. These identity documents were designed to restrict and control the movement of blacks about the country and, if a black person was outside a designated rural area, they had to be in order and signed by a white employer. On one occasion Mom illicitly signed many passes for men fearing arrest in Lady Selborne.

Then on 21 March 1960, at Sharpeville township south of Johannesburg, policemen sitting in armoured vehicles suddenly opened fire on peaceful protesters, using over 700 rounds and killing sixty-nine men, women and children and wounding over 180 others. Most were shot in the back while running away.

For days afterwards the police laid siege to Sharpeville: food was running short and, explaining the horror of the massacre, my mother told us she had to go and help. I was worried something might happen to her – maybe the police would open fire on her too? So it was a relief when she returned, buoyed up, explaining that, after filling up our minibus with provisions donated through the Liberals, she had stopped for petrol at a service station and asked for the tyre pressures to be checked because 'we are heavily loaded with food for Sharpeville'. The van was instantly surrounded by the black attendants, check-ing the tyres, cleaning the windscreen and then escorting the vehicle onto the highway, with encouraging shouts and whistles.

A state of emergency was declared as riots swept the country and the killings reverberated around the world. The Treason Trial was proceeding in Pretoria and the ANC President, Chief Albert Luthuli, was staying at the house of the Pretoria Liberal Chairman, John Brink, while giving evidence. He publicly burnt his pass on 26 March 1960 and called on others to follow suit. His action coincided with the Government's suspension of the Pass Laws, which my parents heard with great excitement. But Luthuli was arrested, tried and later fined. My Mom had the privilege of being sent to pay the fine and transport him back to the Brinks' home where I remember meeting him. He seemed a grandfatherly figure, silver grey hair and austere but friendly towards a boy who knew little about the detail except that his treatment by the police was plain wrong. Although still only ten, I was by now very conscious that the police were our enemies.

The relaxation of the Pass Laws gave false hope that they were to be abolished. For a short period there was a feeling throughout the country that apartheid was teetering and my parents were excited by the prospect, though my Dad, always a hard-nosed realist, told me that it was a mistake to raise expectations. He was proved right. The Pass Laws were reinstated on 7 April and, worse, the next day the ANC and its break-away, the Pan African Congress (PAC), were banned as unlawful organisations. This was a heavy blow, particularly to the ANC, which for nearly half a century had struggled non-violently against harsh discriminatory laws that in Europe would long before have led to bloody insurrection. Mandela and his colleagues decided they had no alternative but to reorganise the ANC to enable it to function underground, and the PAC adopted the same course.

This period in 1960 was a tense time for our family. Along with some 2,000 anti-apartheid activists, many prominent Liberals were detained and I found it chilling that they included many whom I knew on first-name terms and who had visited our home. Now there was the uncomfortable sense that a bright light was shining on everything we did as a family. For the first time our phone was tapped, our mail intercepted and our house regularly observed by the Security Police. I got used to knowing that harmless phone calls to friends were no longer private. But, with Special Branch cars parked up outside the house, for my brother Tom and me there was also a sense of 'cops and robbers', eerie yet exhilirating.

Then in June Mom was advised that her name had been seen on a list of people to be arrested, that she should leave immediately, and meanwhile go quickly to a home of friends unconnected with the Liberals. We arrived home from school to be told we were going on holiday right away. Although it was a nice surprise, when I (as the oldest) was told the real reason, my mood turned quickly to worry that we might be caught. In Mom's absence I had to ensure clothes and toys were properly packed – though apparently she opened her case later to find far too many underclothes and very little else of use.

My Dad came home from work and we loaded the vehicle, checking there were no Special Branch around, before we drove to collect Mom. She took the wheel and we waved goodbye to him for the fourteen-hour overnight drive to our grandparents' home in Port Alfred. I repeatedly looked back at the road behind and it was a real relief to see that we were not being followed. The tension receded and, on arrival, we quickly settled into the routine of a break by the seaside, albeit (unlike our normal sun-baked holidays) this time in the middle of the South African winter.

My Dad later joined us. It was a criminal offence under the State of Emergency to divulge information on detainees and there was difficulty communicating between areas, so he had been asked to check on the state of the Party in the Eastern Cape Province and Natal. We drove there before returning to Pretoria and I remember Alan Paton's house, The Long View, high up overlooking the hills north of Durban. He was kindly, though a little gruff, to a ten-year-old barely aware of his growing international reputation.

But something he told me made a big impact: 'I'm not an all-or-nothing person, Peter. I'm an all-or-something person.' This was to become a watch-word for my subsequent political activity in which strong principles had not so much to be compromised as to be blended with hard-edged practicalities: the aim achieving concrete goals, not basking in the luxury of purity.

Moustached and fit, Dad was informal and friendly, though strict and severe to any of his children if we ever strayed. Self-discipline and hard work were ethics he instilled in me. 'The things that are really worth achieving are usually difficult to do' was one of his sayings. Another was: 'if it was easy to change apartheid, it would have been done a long time ago; you have to be prepared to stay the course for the long term'. However he also encouraged us to enjoy ourselves and both my parents were popular amongst my friends. Affectionate and close to each other, they became renowned for selflessly look-ing after others. Unwilling to give up on a challenge until all avenues were exhausted, they were always practical and impatient with the petty personality tensions or starry-eyed idealism present in left-wing politics. I was proud of them and these values and attitudes were to become important guides for me in my own political life much later.

‡

We returned from our unscheduled holiday after the country-wide State of Emergency was lifted at the end of August 1960 and the remaining detainees were released. But soon afterwards our home was raided by the Security Police for the first time and statements by people wounded at Sharpeville taken secretly the day after the shootings were seized, never to be seen again. We returned home from school to be told in a matter-of-fact way what had happened. Although I took it in my stride, the house seemed 'dirty' somehow, as if burglars had been through all our stuff.

Whites in the local Liberal Party contributed food parcels for the families of ANC or PAC detainees and I sometimes helped my parents deliver these in our minibus to Pretoria's townships of Lady Selborne, Atteridgeville and Eastwood. Although there was always a certain tension about these missions, I remember also a sense of purposeful enjoyment and accomplishment.

Meanwhile Mom had become known in Pretoria as the person for non-whites to contact whenever anyone fell foul of the police. On one occasion she helped bail a group of women from Soweto, including the mother of Nelson Mandela's close leadership comrade, Walter Sisulu. With the ANC and PAC now illegal, black membership in the Pretoria branch of the Liberal Party – by this time the only legal anti-apartheid group in the city – boomed. There seemed a constant flow of people in and out of the house. Branch meetings were held in our living room with my father and others collecting black and Asian members from their segregated townships and taking them home afterwards.

Amidst the increasing political turmoil surrounding us I was enjoying school life at Hatfield Primary School, where I became Head Prefect. Strict discipline, doing homework conscientiously on time and playing sport virtually every afternoon were the watchwords. Certain teachers, aware of the Hains' growing notoriety, were quietly supportive, as were some of my friends and their parents.

In March 1960 the Treason Trial ended with the acquittal of all defendants. The ANC President, Oliver Tambo, immediately left the country to ensure that the organisation survived outside South Africa. Nelson Mandela went underground before he could be rearrested, and became leader of the ANC armed wing, *Umkhonto we Sizwe* (Spear of the Nation), which he said would perform sabotage with strict instructions not to kill. I recall intense discussions with my father, who was totally opposed to violence. But he did not attack the ANC, and acknowledged to me that the longer apartheid continued the more violence there would inevitably be; that's why we had to persuade apartheid's rulers to change before it was too late.

One morning I woke before dawn, shivering in shock to discover strangers in the bedroom shared with my brother Tom. Who were they? What on earth were they doing? What were they stealing? Were we going to be hurt? Then Mom and Dad realised we had woken and gave us a hug, explaining they were Security Policemen and not to worry. The episode soon turned more incongruous than threatening. I was keen on cars and motor sport, and the men had my scrapbooks culled from my father's weekly car magazines – they were searching in vain for 'incriminating evidence'. Then Jo-anne and Sally called out from bed next door that the cupboard drawer for their panties was being searched – which embarrassed the officers. But they also knocked over the cage of my pet white mouse which escaped only to be pounced on and killed by our cat, which upset us all. I found my mood switching during the search from initial fear to amusement and then outrage.

A few months later, and while still underground, Nelson Mandela called for a three day 'stay-at-home' at the end of May 1961 to protest against all racial laws – in which my parents participated, leading to their arrest. The stay-at-home was a great success on the first day, but it soon fizzled out after massive police intimidation and raids (some 10,000 were detained). The last disciplined, mass non-violent demonstration to be held in the old South Africa was over.

‡

By this time contacts with our relatives had become increasingly strained. Although our wider family was quite close, none of them was at all politically involved. My uncle Hugh was by then the millionaire owner of a construction company and did not want his business affected. When we were holidaying in Port Alfred, we would be invited out on their speedboats and on one occasion I attempted water skiing. We had also been regular visitors to his house to play with our five cousins who were similarly aged, and to swim in their pool. But these invitations suddenly stopped. Mom and Dad tried to explain to us why, shielding how upset they were, especially from my sisters Jo-anne and Sally, who (aged six and four) were far too young to understand why they would no longer be seeing their close cousins, Anne and Liz.

My mother, brought up as a Christian Scientist, now felt estranged: what was Christianity about, she felt, if not to give support and understanding in times of difficulty? Her brother Hugh and sister-in-law were devout Christian Scientists, as were most of her wider family. How could the admirable principles of Christianity be reconciled with apartheid? And how could the sometimes fundamentalist Christians in the Dutch Reformed Church who ran the apartheid government possibly justify the human misery they deliberately inflicted?

I and the younger children used to go to the nearby Christian Science Sunday School and my crunch moment came while my parents were in prison. When I realised that the person teaching us was a police officer, I decided that we were not going any more. I later started to discuss religion with my Dad, always an atheist, gradually coming to the conclusion that I was possibly an atheist too, but probably more of an agnostic.

My aunt Marie Hain meanwhile ran a travel agency in Pretoria and felt obliged to place an advert in the *Pretoria News* saying that her company had no relationship with the Mrs Hain of the Liberal Party – who just happened to be her sister-in-law. Despite the absence of any personal hostility between us, a barrier grew as we moved in different worlds. When life later became extremely difficult and my father was out of a job, our well-off relatives could have helped but chose not to. They remained in all other respects friendly and (within the white framework) decent, caring family folk. It was simply that they were not 'political', we were a gross embarrassment, and they feared it would be risky to be too closely associated – upsetting and difficult to understand, especially for my younger brother and sisters.

Then, in December 1961 *Umkhonto* began a campaign of placing incendiary bombs in government offices, post offices and electrical sub-stations, carrying out 200 attacks in the following eighteen months. When I asked them anxiously about this, my parents were amazed that the ANC were able to place some of these bombs in Pretoria offices, where all government workers, down to the cleaners, were white – until Peter Magano said: 'Don't forget the messenger boys are still black!'

The term 'boy' was patronisingly applied by whites to all black men and, from an early age, I remember castigating friends when they called out to their black gardeners in this way. The spectacle of bumptious white kids casually talking down to greying black grandfathers tending their gardens epitomised for me the daily indignity of apartheid. On one occasion my best friend Dave knocked off the hat of an elderly man and I remember having a real go at him and insisting he picked it up and gave it back – which he sheepishly did.

By 1962 my father, now working in a private architectural practice, had taken over as Chairman of the Pretoria Liberals and so my parents occupied what were effectively the two top positions in the city's only legal anti-apartheid force. As such they became even more prominent targets in this citadel of Afrikanerdom. They seemed to be permanently in the *Pretoria News* and, late in 1962, my father began to write frequent leader page articles for the *Rand Daily Mail*, the country's main liberal newspaper, which made me even more proud.

He also helped me with my essays on current affairs at Pretoria Boys High

School. My favourite teacher, Terence Ashton, remarked that my writing 'seemed remarkably similar to that of W. V. Hain in the *Rand Daily Mail*'. Ashton taught us English and, trying to explain the phrase *persona non grata* to our class said: 'Hain's parents are *persona non grata* with the government because they *think*.' The school had some liberally minded teachers, increasingly aware of my parents' growing role. While they never referred to it, some were quietly sympathetic, my reputation as a hard worker and enthusiastic sportsman perhaps standing me in good stead. The only time I was picked upon was when some boys started calling me 'a communist'; despite being upset, I was determined to ignore them, staring fixedly ahead as if I hadn't heard.

‡

On 5 August 1962, having been seventeen months on the run, Nelson Mandela was finally captured near Howick Falls in Natal, after an informer tipped off the police. Mostly disguised as a chauffeur, he had evaded the authorities and travelled throughout the country organising the ANC underground, with the media dubbing him the 'Black Pimpernel'.*

His trial opened at the Old Synagogue in Pretoria on 22 October and my mother covered it for the Liberal magazine *Contact*. She was often the only one in the white section of the public gallery when Mandela entered each day; after raising his fist in the traditional ANC *Amandla!* salute to the packed black section he would turn and do the same to her, an acknowledgement she found very moving. Nearly thirty years later when she and I met him in the House of Commons in May 1991 she said: 'I don't suppose you remember me.' To which he replied, giving her a great hug: 'How could I forget!'

It was around this trial that I first became properly aware of Nelson Mandela's importance. His beautiful wife Winnie attended the trial each day, often magnificent in tribal dress. Once, when my sisters went with Mom, Winnie bent down and kissed the two little blonde girls, to the evident outrage of the onlooking white policemen repulsed at the spectacle. But, although Mandela's magnetic personality dominated the courtroom, it did not prevent him being sentenced to five years hard labour on Robben Island.

By now the world was beginning to mobilise against apartheid. On 6 November 1962 the General Assembly of the United Nations voted for sanctions against South Africa, and my parents had become friendly with two sympathetic officials in the Netherlands and West German Embassies. We got

---

*   For his story see Peter Hain, *Mandela* (London, Spruce, 2010).

to know them too as our families mixed, and they both mentioned the difficulty of meeting non-whites socially and suggested that the Liberal Party host
gatherings to remedy this. These were held in our house, what became known
as our 'diplomatic parties', for me exciting occasions as I took to spotting the
different models amongst the dozens of cars pulled up on our front drive.

Then our lives took a turn for the worse. In January 1963 my mother was
summoned before the Chief Magistrate of Pretoria and warned to desist from
engaging in activities 'calculated to further the aims of communism'. He was
unable to specify which of her activities fell within this definition and advised
her to write to John Vorster, Minister of Justice, for clarification. The reply
from his office merely repeated the phrase and then stated: 'Should you so
wish, you are of course at liberty to ignore the warning and, if as a result
thereof, it is found necessary to take further action against you, you will only
have yourself to blame.' Aged thirteen, I remember very clearly a daily newspaper cartoon which had Vorster saying: 'Go and find Adelaine Hain, see what
she is doing and tell her she mustn't.'

She was by now spending hours haunting the courts – sometimes dashing
from building to building when 'grapevine' information told of yet another
group of black detainees. She would find out their names, inform the parents
and get legal representation if necessary. Many had been assaulted and tortured.
I remember being distressed when she told me how one young man had been
inflicted with electric shock torture and went completely out of his mind,
staring vacantly into space.

Meanwhile my parents had been excited by John Kennedy winning the
American Presidency and his sympathy for the civil rights movement led by
the charismatic black preacher Martin Luther King. 'There's the answer to white
South African prejudice,' my Dad used to say, 'how can anybody deny King is
a highly intelligent man?' Yet when confronted with this question, whites used
to reply – 'Yes, but he is not like *our* blacks: they really are inferior.' You could
not win with such prejudiced ignorance. (When Kennedy was assassinated on
22 November 1963, I can still remember the moment I saw the shocking news
on billboards in Pretoria; a piece of hope in me died too.)

With Liberal activists like my parents proving increasingly troublesome
to both the Security Police and Ministers, the government set about the
systematic destruction of the Party. In Parliament the Minister of Justice, John
Vorster (detained during the war for his pro-Nazi activities), accused Liberals
of being communists in disguise and tantamount to terrorists. Government
ministers stated in Parliament: 'We will have to restrict the Liberal Party.' A
cartoon in the *Pretoria News* of 11 March 1963, titled 'the Scapegoat', had a
goat marked 'Liberal Party' being dragged by a knife-wielding Vorster up a hill

towards a sacrificial pyre at the summit, with Prime Minister Verwoerd and other government luminaries forming an applauding procession behind him.

During 1963 many prominent Liberals throughout the country were banned and the fear of repression increased almost daily. My parents warned me that life was going to get much more difficult as the government extended its police state by introducing the notorious law which increased to ninety days the twelve days for which people could be held without charge (and under which my parents were held in 1961). There was nothing we could do about this because it never occurred to me that they should give up their ideals for a more comfortable life.

Instead I remember clearly the front pages of the main newspapers luridly headlining the 'Rivonia plot', with pictures of all those caught on 12 July. Mandela's close comrades, Walter Sisulu and eight others based underground at Lilliesleaf farm in the Rivonia district just outside Johannesburg, were arrested and charged, and a mood of retribution swept through white communities.

Nelson Mandela was brought back from Robben Island and what was to become known as the Rivonia Trial commenced in Pretoria. Labelled Accused No 1, Mandela concluded his statement with the now famous words: 'During my lifetime I have dedicated myself to this struggle of the African people. I have fought against white domination, and I have fought against black domination. I have cherished the ideal of a democratic and free society in which all persons live together in harmony and with equal opportunities. It is an ideal which I hope to live for and to achieve. But if needs be it is an ideal for which I am prepared to die.'

I read these powerful words aged fourteen, trying to take in their full significance, and aware they were a great inspiration to my parents and all involved in the struggle, for all those found guilty faced the death penalty. In fact, after worldwide pleas for clemency, they were all sentenced to life imprisonment, and in July 1964 Mandela returned to Robben Island, not to be seen or heard in public again for nearly twenty-six years.

‡

The year before, in July 1963, we had moved from Hatfield out to a smallholding at The Willows, to the east of Pretoria. The rented house consisted of two large thatched *rondavels* (circular dwellings) on a terrace well back from the road and at the foot of a *kopje* (small hill). With a small, leaky swimming pool and plenty of space to play, it was wonderful for children. I laid a makeshift cricket pitch which I used to water every evening, and Tom and I used to play football against each other until it was too dark to see the ball.

Our move to The Willows took the Security Police by surprise. It was some weeks before they traced us, during which we escaped their attention for the first time for years. Our telephone had not yet been connected and they were unable to trace us that way. Then one day our maid Eva answered the door to a man who asked her the name of her 'baas'. Eva did her 'dumb Kaffir' routine (with white strangers she always pretended to know nothing and understand less) and he was turning away when my mother went to see what was happening. He saw her, turned back and said that he was looking for a house that he'd heard was for sale. Eva was furious with my Mom for showing herself. 'He is Special Branch', she hissed. 'Now they'll know where we live.' She was right. Thereafter we had the usual Security Police cars parked on the road outside, our phone was speedily connected and tapping resumed.

In September 1963 there was a knock at the door which I answered, quickly joined by my Mom. We were confronted by the same two large Security Police Officers who had arrested my parents in 1961 – Sergeants Viktor and van Zyl (the latter referred to as 'banana fingers' because of his huge hands). I distinctly remember their burly figures framing the door and trying to seem calm and not intimidated even though I felt anything but.

They handed Mom an envelope containing her banning order which ran for five years and limited her to being in the company of not more than one person at a time; restricted her movements to the Pretoria magisterial district; and prohibited her from entering certain specified places such as factories, non-white communities, school or university areas and courts of law. It also required her to report to a police station five miles away every Wednesday. The ban effectively ended her work as Secretary of the Pretoria Liberal Party and stopped any overt political activity whatsoever. It was also unique: for the first time in any banning order she was prohibited entrance to courts. The conclusion was that her practice of haunting the courts to gain representation for political prisoners was the main reason for her ban.

It was hardly unexpected; we had all discussed the possibility for months. But it was still a weird existence, and left her feeling angry and frustrated. She effectively ceased to be a public person and could not be quoted by the media. The restriction on meeting more than one person at a time was near fatal politically. I was dismayed that she could no longer continue with all her good work helping so many stricken people.

She was not even allowed to come into our schools and discuss our progress with teachers – that could only be done standing outside on the pavement, which was just about feasible for the primary school, but not for my high school, standing as it did in the middle of large grounds. It was a blow because she had always taken a very close and active interest in our progress and was well known by our teachers. We had become used to my parents being targeted, but why should *our* schooling be so affected, why did *we* have to be picked on this way? It made me feel even more angry about the growing state restrictions on our freedom as a family.

Gradually however, she adjusted and worked out ways of acting as a contact for political prisoners whose relatives continued to approach her for assistance when they had problems. She seemed to me to be just as active. Although she could no longer participate openly in the life of the Liberal Party, she was kept in touch daily with events by David Rathswaffo, who took over as secretary. He would make a coded telephone call from a call box near the Party office and she would then drive in to a pre-arranged rendezvous.

We began holding our 'diplomatic' parties again, with the Security Police loitering around the gate taking down the registration numbers. Party luminaries such as Alan Paton and Peter Brown attended in addition to Pretoria members. My Mom's ban meant she had to sit in the kitchen and be visited by the guests one at a time; I enjoyed escorting them through for her. It made me feel I was helping her political fight. My younger brother Tom and I also had fun serving drinks under the guidance of a Coloured member, Alban Thumbran, who had been a waiter, while my young sisters Jo-anne and Sally helped with the snacks.

On one occasion I heard a noise just outside. Peering through the window in the dark I was startled to catch a glimpse of someone lurking there, and called out to my Dad 'Special Branch, Special Branch'. As we ran out there was a commotion and a figure began charging noisily up through the bushes and rocks of the dark *kopje*. My Dad, running after his quarry, shouted: 'Peter - bring the gun!' Although I knew this was a ruse as we had no gun, the man ahead must have panicked. Before making off into the night, he picked up a stone and threw it, glancing off a tree right in front of Dad's face. By now the party-goers had spilled out and it all seemed like a bit of a thrill. But the next morning we went up to have a look and found a large gash on the branch, forcibly bringing home to me that what had seemed like an exciting incident could have ended in a terrible family tragedy.

‡

Two friends, Fabian Ribeiro, a black doctor from Mamelodi, and his wife Florence, a sister-in-law of the PAC leader Robert Sobukwe, used to drop in regularly at The Willows. Sometimes their young children came and we would play with them. Unusually for blacks, they were financially very well off, but apartheid drastically restricted the way they could spend their money. They explained to me that they could not own a house in their township, send their children to the school of their choice, or take their family on holiday since there were no resorts for blacks. So they drove a Mercedes and, being a car enthusiast, I would inspect it carefully as we couldn't afford anything like it. They also dressed very well, Florence at the height of fashion. In those days non-whites were not permitted to try on clothes before purchasing, so Florence told me that absurd special arrangements had to be made for her to go into Hamiltons, Pretoria's top clothes shop, after hours so that she could try on her choices without upsetting white customers. (Tragically the Ribeiros were both victims of state-sponsored assassinations: murdered by gunmen outside their home on 1 December 1986, as the Truth and Reconciliation Commission confirmed ten years later.)

Meanwhile, because of his political activities, my father's work opportunities had been restricted to a limited number of private employers who would take him on. We found increasing difficulty in making ends meet. Reluctantly we decided we could no longer afford our maid, Eva Matjeka. So, to everyone's regret, Eva, who had become one of the family, had to leave.

However, her departure had one positive effect: the servant's room was vacant when my mother received a fraught telephone call from David Rathswaffo. Jimmy Makoejane, my parents' PAC friend from Lady Selborne, had escaped from court and come to him for help. Aware that our phone was tapped, she cut him short by saying she would come into town right away, and asked me to look after the other children.

Jimmy had been involved in the 1963 campaign by the PAC underground group, POQO, and had managed to flee. But he had been kidnapped from a train on the Rhodesian border by the Security Police and returned for trial before managing to escape again during a lunch recess; astonishingly he had just walked straight out undetected. Jimmy was dropped off late that night near our house and Dad carefully walked through the surrounding bush, secretly collected him away from the prying eyes of the Special Branch parked at the front gate, and installed him in Eva's empty room. Although I was intrigued to glimpse a black stranger in our kitchen being fed dinner late by my mother and wondered how he had got there, I had learnt not to ask too many questions (and only heard the full story long afterwards in London).

The next day, with Jimmy lying down on the back seat of a friend's car and covered by a rug, Dad drove him out to a nearby train station, attracting no interest from the Security Police who were watching at the gate for our cars. Jimmy got clean away, eventually ending up in Tanzania. But when the Security Police played back their phone tap-tapes, they arrested David, who said that Jimmy had told him he'd been acquitted, had 'borrowed ten bob' and disappeared. They held David for a few days, taking away his epilepsy pills. Fortunately, he told them nothing about my parents' involvement or they would have faced immediate arrest and prosecution.

‡

Enthusiastic about sport, I learnt at first hand the extent to which apartheid infected it. We used to swim regularly at Pretoria's international-standard swimming pool for whites. In 1962 South Africa was involved in lucrative trade deals with Japan and visiting Japanese businessmen were granted 'honorary white' status, allowing them to stay in hotels and enjoy privileges usually confined to whites alone. But this caused consternation when a Japanese visitor was mistaken for a local Chinese and ejected from a bus for whites. A Japanese water polo team came over too and, after initially refusing it access to the pool, Pretoria City Council relented: business before racism. But the decision caused such public uproar that the pool was drained after the team departed so that white customers could have 'fresh' water.

Attending a white state school (it would have been illegal to do otherwise) I had to play in whites-only school or club sports teams, and could not play against black teams. Sport was legally segregated from school right up to national representative level. We also used to watch our home football team, Arcadia, at the Caledonian stadium. (I played in its youth sides.) Partitioned off on the other side of the stadium from whites were non-white spectators, some personal friends. We used to mingle before the match and then separate. As with other sports events, we could not stand together or use the same entrances, toilets or facilities.

Although Arcadia was an all-white team playing in an all-white league, black spectators were amongst the noisiest and most partisan supporters. Then the government introduced proclamations banning non-whites from such major sports events, and our friends could no longer attend. The carnival atmosphere at Arcadia's home matches disappeared. But crowds of blacks still gathered outside, listening to the match. Some of the keenest shinned up to watch from trees adjoining the ground. But this so angered white neighbours that, as I watched in horror and frustration, police dogs were used to drive them from these vantage points, pulling them down bloodied and screaming.

‡

Difficult though life had become for us, it was about to get a great deal more so. Over five days in July 1964 many members of the African Resistance

Movement (ARM) were arrested. Some were friends in the Liberal Party who felt that non-violent means had reached the end of the road and that the sabotage of installations such as power pylons was the only way forward. Others were mostly young white idealists frustrated by the denial of legal and peaceful channels for change. Still others were from the ANC Youth League.

The ARM's first act of sabotage had taken place nearly three years earlier and my parents had themselves been sounded out. But, quite apart from the serious moral questions raised by violence, they considered such action naive and counter-productive, believing it would simply invite even greater police state repression without achieving anything tangible. To protect themselves, those undertaking the sabotage did not resign from the Liberal Party as its rules obliged them to do, and this occasioned considerable acrimony when their activities were eventually revealed. My parents had fraught discussions with close friends and I often talked to my father about his views, which made a big impression on me. He had witnessed the horror of the Second World War at first hand – the German shelling that had wounded him in 1944 in Italy had killed his close friend right next to him in their Apennine trench. The trouble with violence, he insisted vehemently, was that it tended to develop a life of its own. Whatever the intention, once started, it spread automatically. Also there was no way of containing it: even blowing up a remote pylon risked killing an innocent person who might be passing by.

The round-up of ARM members came after the police discovered incriminating documents at the Cape Town flat of the national organiser, Adrian Leftwich, a prominent Liberal. Incredibly, he had kept a record of the entire cell structure of the ARM. Turning state witness, he was later paraded around the country giving evidence against his former comrades. Amongst those arrested was Liberal activist Hugh Lewin, a good friend of ours.

Although we had always managed to live something akin to a normal life, we were now beginning to feel severely hemmed in. Then on 24 July 1964 a bomb exploded on the whites-only concourse of Johannesburg railway station, mortally injuring an elderly lady and severely wounding her young granddaughter.

I remember hearing the news on my bedroom radio and rushing to seek reassurance from my parents, not really thinking that they would be involved but needing to hear them say so. They were both very upset, my father sounding off against the 'idiots who did that sort of mindless thing'. Whoever was responsible had better not come to him for help, he told me grimly.

A few days later, Ann Harris and her six-week-old son David turned up unexpectedly at our home in The Willows, telling us that her husband John had been arrested and was being held in Pretoria Local prison. My parents had met John and Ann a few years earlier when they were new Johannesburg

Liberal Party members. Both were teachers. John shared my Dad's interest in sport, cars and motor racing (rather uncommon interests amongst the politically involved). So they got on especially well, as did Ann and my Mom. They visited us in Pretoria, we went to their home, and John went with us to several motor races. We used to go regularly to Grand Prix and major sports car races at Kyalami, near Johannesburg, where our minibus would be parked in Clubhouse Corner and the whole family would watch from its roof.

I always had great fun with John. Once he drove fast around corners with my brother and me in his new car as we shrieked with delighted excitement. I regarded him as my friend too, and not simply one of my parents' adult circle. He was a real enthusiast for whatever happened to be the current one of his many interests. And he was very competitive too, hating to be beaten when we played table tennis. He had a position on just about everything and loved an argument, disagreeing passionately with anybody who wanted to engage in an opposing point of view. Yet he bore no grudges, and when the argument was over, he would be joking and laughing again.

My father later told me of a fierce argument between them on a long drive back to Pretoria after a Party meeting in the Cape. John was insistent that, although an act of violence might cause casualties in the short term, in the long term it could save lives if it hastened the end of the violence of apartheid. Like Mandela's ANC had already become, he was deeply frustrated by the inability of young white radicals like him to accomplish anything against a police state that remorselessly crushed all peaceful opposition. He with other Liberal friends was attracted to the African Resistance Movement, and was disappointed that my Dad would have none of it.

When she arrived suddenly at our home, Ann was distraught, explaining how she had been refused permission to see John in Pretoria Local prison. But she had been told that she could bring food for him each day and collect his laundry. Could my parents put him on their list for food parcels? However, as she could not drive and was dependent upon others bringing her the forty miles from Johannesburg for prison visits, Mom and Dad suggested she stayed with us until his release. They assumed that John, who had been under police surveillance after his banning in January that year, could not possibly have been involved in the station bombing and would be released in a week or so.

So my sisters Jo-anne and Sally gave up their bedroom for the adjoining playroom and Ann and baby David moved in. But instead of a short stay, they were to be with us for nearly eighteen months and became part of the family. Helping look after and play with David as he grew from baby to toddler, including changing his nappies, was a formative experience for a teenage boy, and was to help me as a father more than a decade later.

Life revolved around a daily visit to the gaol by my mother and Ann, taking food to John, Hugh Lewin, and others who were all held incommunicado under the ninety-day law. The extra housework occasioned by a tiny baby, coupled with the daily 25-mile round trip to the prison, transporting children to and from school and my father to and from work, meant that it became difficult to cope without help. Mom contacted Eva, who was without a job, and she took up residence again.

‡

Ann's arrival at our house changed our lives forever. The station bomb had thrown the white community into a frenzy. Never before had whites been attacked in this way, and the security services were quick to exploit the resulting panic, giving us extra attention.

I was sure John would be out soon. But after a while, when all the other ARM detainees had been visited by relatives, and Ann still had heard nothing, my parents began to realise that there was something seriously amiss. Then, in John's laundry, they noticed a blood stain on a shirt. After his lawyer made enquiries a menacing member of the Security Police turned up with a letter for Ann – frightening ten-year-old Jo-anne, who worried that her Mom was going to be arrested again and came running in, saying through her tears 'I didn't cry in front of him'.

The letter was the first direct communication Ann or the lawyers had received from John. He wanted to reassure her that he had cut himself shaving – and he joked that he was unused to wet shaving as he'd had to hand in his electric shaver. In reality, of course, he was still bleeding from horrendous beatings, including a broken jaw and damaged testicles. The letter somehow did not ring true for Ann, who suspected, rightly, that he had been forced to write it, and she was dreadfully stressed.

My mother meanwhile was ingeniously engaged in receiving and passing messages to her friends in detention. She regularly washed their clothes and noticed a dirty handkerchief with a large 'C' in ink on it. Racking her brains, she recalled that lemon juice could be used as invisible ink. So she ironed it and found a message. Thereafter she developed other methods: taking the pith out of an orange and gluing it back after inserting a message inside; or after cooking a whole onion sliding a note between the leaves to be covered as it cooled. These were never discovered and formed an invaluable communications route.

However, as John's detention continued my mother began to suspect that he must have had some connection with the station bomb. Even by the standards of the security constraints we normally operated under (phone tapping and not knowing whether rooms in our home were bugged), it was a particularly awkward period for my parents to communicate. I was worried about my friend being in jail especially when it became evident he had been badly beaten, but remained unaware of the extent of John's involvement.

Then, a month after the explosion, the old lady, Mrs Ethel Rhys, tragically died (her twelve-year-old granddaughter, Glynnis Burleigh, was maimed for life), and John was charged with murder. Ruth Hayman, a Liberal Party friend and John's lawyer, was then able to see him for the first time, finding him in a terrible state; he had only been charged after his jaw, which had been wired up, had mended enough for him to be presentable in court.

By now Ann had admitted to my parents what she had known all along: that John was indeed responsible for the bombing and, once he was charged on 14 September, they told us. I could not believe it. How had he done this? It was shocking, and I felt numb – not so much betrayed as confused. I discussed it over and over again with my Dad.

He like my Mom was equally upset and I could sense their torn feelings. Although condemning without qualification what he had done, my parents remain convinced John never intended to harm anybody. He had meant it as a spectacular demonstration of resistance to tightening state oppression. Indeed he had telephoned a fifteen-minute warning to both the station police and two newspapers, urging that the station concourse be cleared. This was not done and the result was devastation on the station and the pretext for the government to enforce an even more oppressive regime.

My parents told me at the time that they strongly suspected ignoring John's warning was deliberate, and this was confirmed years later. A former security informer, Gordon Winter, stated in his book *Inside Boss* that the decision not to use the station loudspeaker system to clear travellers from the concourse had gone up through the notorious head of the Security Police, H. J. van den Bergh, to the Justice Minister, John Vorster.

For my parents there was less a dilemma about where their duty lay – to their close friend John and his family – than a sombre realisation of the likely serious consequences for our family. 'We have to stand by Ann and give what help we can to John in prison,' they insisted. Aged fourteen I did not fully comprehend just how grave it would be for us. For me it seemed like another dark twist in a pattern of life which had got steadily tougher over the years.

Having long been targets for the local security forces my parents were now principal targets for the whole state and its compliant media. Instead of being one of many enemies, it was almost as if we were *the* enemy and I became only too aware that the white community of which we were part had now completely turned on us. The harassment became vitriolic. Our house was now under continuous surveillance, with Security Police cars parked on the road outside twenty-four hours a day. As we left we would be tailed – on one occasion even when Tom and I rode down to the nearest shops on our bikes. If I had thought too much about it, I would have been terrified, but I was determined to follow my parents in carrying on as normally as we could, trying not to be cowed.

Raids on our home also became more regular. Once I cycled the five miles home from school to find Security Police turning over the house and searching through my school books and papers. Mom looked understandably upset and I glared at them, determined not to be intimidated and to stand up for her. But then their menacing presence took a comic turn. A young officer had discovered a list of star names which constituted my own chosen 'World XI' cricket team. It included Gary Sobers, Wes Hall, Richie Benaud and even South Africa's Graeme Pollock, like me a left-handed batsman and my idol. But the names were listed at random and I had attached numbers indicating positions in the batting order. The officer thought he'd found a coded list and rushed excitedly to show it to his captain, who, after a quick glance, told him not to be a damned fool. I felt like laughing out loud, but sensed their embarrassment and didn't want to provoke any of them in the brittle atmosphere. One up to us: the kind of small victory which kept up spirits then, and later on whenever we recounted the story.

Meanwhile another Liberal friend, Maritz van den Berg, had been detained under the ninety-day law on 29 July and held in Pretoria Local prison for a month before being unconditionally released. It was soon obvious that he had spoken freely because others were immediately pulled in for questioning. One of them, Alban Thumbran, was released again almost at once and telephoned to warn us 'Maritz is singing like a bird'. This was to be the signal for messages to be relayed, by various covert means, to as many people as my parents thought might need to know.

One party colleague, Derek Cohen, was only contacted after Mom had thrown off pursuing Security Police vehicles in an exciting manoeuvre with all of us children in the car providing cover for her as if on a routine family outing. She pulled up at traffic lights in the lane indicating left, then suddenly jumped the lights and tore rightward, leaving the tailing vehicle blocked by oncoming traffic from following her. We drove straight to our friend's house, and he immediately left on the next plane for London. Shortly afterwards the Security Police called round looking in vain for him.

In September 1964, my father was visited at his office and handed a banning order with a special clause inserted. The same day I opened our front door to a burly Security Police figure who handed my mother an addendum to her ban, personally signed by the Minister of Justice, John Vorster. It contained a similar new clause giving them special permission to communicate with each other. This was exceptional: as a married couple they had to be given an Orwellian exemption from the normal stipulation that banned persons were not allowed to communicate in any way.

His banning was clearly a reprisal for providing support to the hated John Harris and his family. It meant that my parents had no flexibility any more for their political activity. My mother could not act behind the scenes for my Dad because he too was barred from doing anything.

So they coopted me as something of a surrogate. From then on, aged fourteen, I became increasingly active in a liaison role, taking and passing messages to individuals with whom they were prevented from communicating, such as journalists and other banned people, so helping them to continue much of their political work behind the scenes. It was something I enjoyed because I was helping them and believed in their cause even if I was not up to scratch on all the detail. It was also quite exciting – and sometimes scary, as I worried that, if this subterfuge were to be discovered, they might be arrested for breaking their bans. I idolised my parents. Although they never once pressured me to assist them, I felt it the natural thing to do so. Stereotypical adolescence – resentment of and rebellion against parents apparent in friends and school mates – somehow passed me by.

Another consequence was that my father – who had often come to see me playing cricket or rugby on school fields on his way home from work – was now barred from doing so, except when a game was near enough to the school fence and he could pull up on the road and look over. Seeing him there always gave me a boost, although I had trouble trying to explain to my uncomprehending team mates why he couldn't come over, as they had never even heard of a banning order.

‡

Their bans meant that neither of my parents was able to attend John Harris's trial in Pretoria, which began on 21 September 1964 – though they gave as much support as they could from the outside. To their shock, Harris's co-conspirator, John Lloyd, another friend and Liberal Party member, was to be the main prosecution witness, and it became vital to get news to Lloyd that if he gave evidence John Harris would be sentenced to death. Mom, who knew Lloyd's girlfriend, was able to smuggle such a message in to him and establish from her that he had received it.

Now the emotional stress became increasingly nightmarish, for Lloyd ignored this warning. At the trial he did not merely give evidence in corroboration of John's own confession (which would have carried a life sentence for manslaughter), but damningly went much further. My parents were aghast as Lloyd insisted that John's act was pre-meditated murder. John consistently denied this and police testimony in court confirmed that he had indeed telephoned a warning to the railway police and urged them to clear the concourse, in order to avoid injuring anyone.

Nevertheless it became obvious that the judge accepted Lloyd's version with fatal consequences for John. My parents were distraught as they described the savage turn of events. I arrived back after school to find Ann increasingly tearful and Mom trying to console her while herself feeling much the same. They were all desperate and I did not know what to do – nothing at all, it seemed could be done. We were being sucked inexorably towards an horrendous end.

From the outset Lloyd was kept away from the others. When they were all transferred to Pretoria Local gaol at the end of July, he was housed on his own at a Pretoria police station, allowed frequent visits from his mother and given proper bedding with sheets. Evidence at the trial showed that Harris and Lloyd had been the only ones in their ARM cell still at liberty after the main arrests. The two had discussed a number of projects to 'make a big splash' to show that their ARM organisation had not been destroyed as the Justice Minister, John Vorster, had boasted on the radio. Amongst these were the bomb at Johannesburg station, a bomb in an underground car park and bombs in the private post boxes at Pretoria Post Office, all to be carried out on 24 July. John Harris was to carry out the first and Lloyd the other two.

However, Lloyd (the flatmate of fellow ARM member Hugh Lewin, who had been arrested on 9 July) was himself detained on 23 July, the day before John carried out his part of their project. It was not established whether the security services thereby had advance notice of the station bomb, but Lloyd's initial statement to the police mentioning John Harris, and his proposal to plant a bomb at a station, was made at 12.45 p.m. on 24 July, nearly four hours before the explosion. It may therefore have been that the security services had even greater forewarning than John himself gave. But, like the decision to ignore the latter, it suited their purposes to allow the bomb to explode as an excuse for the clampdown which then followed.

When it came to his judgment, the judge stated that Lloyd's evidence incontrovertibly proved that John indeed had 'an intention to kill' and so was guilty of murder. There was no other evidence of the character necessary to sustain a capital offence and John's wife Ann, who had been present in court throughout, was now faced with the hideous inevitability of her husband facing the gallows. Although brave, she was inconsolable at home that night, as we all waited for sentence to be passed. My younger brother and sisters had been shielded from just how desperate John's predicament was, but my parents had kept me fully apprised throughout, so I recall being numb, trying all the time to imagine some escape route for John and us all. Tormented, I couldn't think of one.

The Judge reconvened the court on 6 November 1964, my Mom waiting for Ann outside, parked on her own so that she did not break the terms of her banning order and find herself mixing with more than another person. In the waiting crowd – quite extraordinarily, his young son with him – was the hangman, there to bear witness as he ghoulishly sized up his promised victim. The executioner was not disappointed as John was formally sentenced to death by hanging – the first white in the struggle – an outcome cheered by the government-controlled media.

Mom, deeply upset and shaking, came home as quickly as possible to speak to us ahead of anyone else, Ann blankly staring ahead, and going straight to her bedroom. My twelve-year-old brother Tom (who like me was a great fan of John's) went completely white with shock, and my still younger sisters (seven and nine) could hardly take it in. I was stunned: although I had been conditioned to expect it, now the dreadful reality sank in. But, surely, somehow, we could do something, I wondered frantically?

‡

During the next five months the shadow of the noose hovered over us. Mom and Dad were involved in frantic efforts to save John's life. When his legal appeal on 1 March 1965 failed – because no additional evidence was forthcoming – they rushed about helping organise clemency appeals. Ann and John's father flew down to Cape Town for an interview with the Minister of Justice, John Vorster, which proved predictably pointless. Petitions from a range of public figures were presented and the matter was even raised in the British Parliament.

A week after John's sentence four more ARM members stood trial in Pretoria including Hugh Lewin, who was jailed for seven years. My mother used to stand behind the court building each day to catch a glimpse of Hugh being driven in, and they would exchange waves. Again – and although he had promised not to give evidence – the main prosecution witness in Hugh's case was John Lloyd. (The best man at Hugh's wedding, Adrian Leftwich, was also a state witness.)

Afterwards, Lloyd was released as part of an immunity deal by which he avoided being charged as an accomplice and soon afterwards left with his mother for Britain, where a job awaited him. Ensconced safely there, a friend, Jill Chisholm, flew over to ask him to assist in John Harris's appeal by retracting his 'intention to kill' evidence. But he refused and instead threatened to tell the South African Security Police that she was 'trying to get him to perjure himself'. Then John's lawyer, Ruth Hayman, also well known to Lloyd as a fellow Liberal, flew over. Lloyd initially agreed to a draft affidavit retracting his evidence, promising to return in the morning to sign it. But he failed to do so. After a third similar encounter, with Randolph Vigne, another ARM member who had escaped to Britain, he eventually signed only a watered-down, anodyne statement which was forwarded to the State President – but it was too little and too late. Lloyd even ignored Ann's final desperate cable – 'I plead for John's life with the conviction that he and your friends would have done it for you.'

‡

A grim sense of foreboding enveloped us all. However, for good secrecy reasons, I knew nothing about one episode while John Harris was being held on death row. He managed to convey a message to Ann that he had been approached by a warder who wanted to help him escape. At great personal risk, and from the outset highly suspicious of a set-up designed to trap them, my parents decided to help Ann. But, after weeks of tense and contorted dealings with the warder, including posting him over £1,000 (a huge amount then), with Mom insisting that Ann had elastoplast stuck discreetly over her fingertips so as to cover her prints, the plot collapsed. It had been a Security Police trap from the beginning.

There seemed nothing anybody could do, and after a date was set for the execution (1 April 1965), I had found myself imagining acquiring a helicopter, or summoning up a James Bond, to get John out somehow. I went to sleep the night before the execution still trying to think of something fresh to change what, deep down, I knew was unchangeable.

The grisly, medieval ritual of being hanged by the neck until dead weighed heavily. Some years before we ever imagined personally knowing somebody involved, I recalled vivid discussions with my father about his total opposition to capital punishment, and descriptions of the brutal violence of the act: a trap door opening underneath, the sudden jerk of the body, jack-knifing as the neck bore all the weight and broke, blood spouting. This was all about to happen to our friend – my friend.

John was due to be hanged at dawn, and I remember waking unusually early, as the moment arrived, finding Ann and my parents already up, waiting as still and silent as the darkness outside. Immediately our phone rang and the caller asked to speak to Ann. My mother refused, recognising the familiar voice of a Security Police officer who went on to say mockingly, 'Your John is dead.'

My strong memory is of being overwhelmed by a sort of blank hopelessness and deep anger. Like my parents I hadn't condoned what he had done; on the contrary we had bitterly condemned it both before and after we knew he was responsible. But, under any civilised system, he would have continued to devote his life to teaching children and never have been involved in the subversion which ended his life so grotesquely.

My father and our barrister friend, Ernie Wentzel, had previously asked permission from the Prison Kommandant for the body to be released for cremation. This was not a normal procedure and, to everyone's surprise, it was granted and a service was arranged at Pretoria Crematorium for half past seven that same morning, just a few hours after his execution. (Ernie thought that the permission was given so the Security Police could monitor who would attend). As banned persons my parents required permission to go and this was duly given – again surprisingly.

But no sooner were their spirits raised than they were dashed. My father's request to read the main address was refused at the last moment. That night it was too late to ask anyone else, and there would not have been many people willing or able to undertake a task that invited notoriety amidst a febrile white public and media mood which had been baying for blood. I remember coming across my parents who were consoling Ann crying in the garden as the sun set, not knowing what to do. When I saw her, I felt frustrated and deeply sorry. So I said somewhat lamely, 'Can I help?' I wasn't quite sure how, but Ann turned, her face lighting up.

I was quickly shown a copy of the typed two-page funeral address my father had prepared according to Ann's wishes, and reflecting John's strong atheist convictions. Dignified yet uplifting, it began with a Shakespearean sonnet, and continued with John Donne's

> *No Man is an Island, entire of itself. Every man*
> *is a piece of the continent, a part of the main.*
> *Any man's death diminishes me,*
> *Because I am involved in mankind.*
> *And therefore send not to know for whom*
> *the bell tolls – it tolls for thee.*

From the Bible was Matthew's 'Blessed are they which are persecuted for right-eousness sake', and Ecclesiastes 'To everything there is a season', which was on a frequently played album of ours sung beautifully by Judy Collins. The songs were the Battle Hymn of the Republic, concluding with 'We Shall Overcome', immortalised at the time at American civil rights and peace demonstrations by Joan Baez. John's last brave words – we learnt later from a prison priest in attendance – were to sing 'We Shall Overcome' as the noose was tightened around his neck, the trap door opened below his feet, and the last breath was torn from him.

Aged fifteen, dressed in my school blazer and tie, I found myself ushered up to the raised lectern before the assembled congregation, waiting as the coffin was carried through. I spotted a small boy in his school shorts, my twelve-year-old brother Tom, inserting himself amongst the bearers who in turn had grabbed hold of the coffin from prison warders and police. The number and variety of people, apart from relatives, who attended the funeral was deeply moving: the chapel was full, including non-whites unusually allowed in to attend a white funeral. But it was something of a blur for me as I glimpsed many friends – Liberal Party members from both Pretoria and Johannesburg, people from the townships and even members of the diplomatic corps. All knew that by attending their names would be diligently recorded by the Special Branch officers outside.

Although the ceremony had been carefully prepared, and I had only to read out the address distributed to all who attended, I had never spoken from any platform before and had always avoided school plays or performances, being quite a private, undemonstrative and rather shy boy. The occasion made me even more nervous. Grown white men were crying and our black maid Eva was sobbing heart-wrenchingly out loud. As I began, I trembled, my voice seeming not to want to come out. I had a stage fright moment wondering whether I could carry it off. But fortunately that passed immediately.

The proximity of the coffin a yard to my left, containing the body of a friend hanged only two hours earlier, made the ordeal especially unnerving. It had been explained to me how I needed to press a button to take the coffin away. But in the middle of the service I almost panicked, realising that I hadn't been told when exactly to do it. The last thing I wanted was to get that wrong. But then, while singing the Freedom Rider's song 'We Shall Overcome', I thought this must be it: what seemed a totally irrevocable step as the coffin moved eerily away out of sight, John's body to be cremated.

I stepped down awkwardly to be surrounded by a tearful Ann and proud parents, my small brother and little sisters huddled together. Embarrassingly, people kept coming up and thanking me. I thought I was just doing what anybody would have done, and it all seemed over almost before it had begun. But I tried to glare at the Special Branch as we left to show I wouldn't be intimidated by their presence and, an hour later, was back at school, having missed the first lesson. I slipped into the classroom, my favourite teacher Terry Ashton giving me a sympathetic but unobtrusive welcome. Although the school had been warned I would be late, none of my classmates knew the reason until a report with my photograph appeared in the papers the following day.

‡

The station bomb was a pivotal event. It was exploited both to increase repression and systematically to discredit and destroy the Liberal Party. In 1965 the period for which people could be held without charge was extended from 90 to 180 days; two years later it was to become indefinite. The Liberals' magazine, *Contact*, closed after its fifth editor was banned and Alban Thumbran, the Coloured member to whom my parents were especially close, was also banned. Ruth Hayman, John Harris's lawyer and my parents' friend and legal mainstay, was banned and house-arrested. Our battered old Volkswagen minibus, for years effectively the Pretoria Liberals' main transportation, was stolen in circumstances which pointed to Security Police responsibility; it was eventually found months later in Hartebeesport dam west of Pretoria after the water level had fallen drastically in a drought.

By now my father's continued employment as an architect who specialised in hospital design was threatened. He had been out of work for two months after his arrest in 1961. Then he had a temporary job in Johannesburg before being taken on by a Pretoria firm which, amongst other commissions, carried out the design of hospitals for the Transvaal provincial government. But soon after his ban the firm was told that if they continued to employ him, they would no longer receive any government work. So he had to resign, and opened his own office. But local work dried up and, although he had a few commissions of his own for projects outside the Pretoria magisterial district (to which his ban confined him), permission for him to leave Pretoria to inspect and survey the sites was refused by the Minister of Justice. The word went out in the profession in Pretoria that private architectural firms would get no work if they employed him.

So, with great sadness and even greater reluctance, my parents, who had no private means, decided they had no alternative but to leave their country for one in which Dad could obtain work. He wrote to the firm in London that had employed him in 1956 and was immediately offered a job. He then accepted a friend's generous offer of rented accommodation in a flat above his home in Putney, south west London.

It was a traumatic decision for all of us. My father, then aged forty-one, knew his already badly disrupted architectural career would be further undermined. Both my parents were leaving the country of their birth which they loved and for which they had sacrificed many of the comforts and privileges of white life. They were also leaving their parents, relatives and close friends. I, my brother and sisters were also leaving our friends for a future unknown. We didn't want to do it, and resisted the idea until we were told it was inevitable.

One small consolation was that, on inspecting a map of London, my brother and I discovered that Chelsea's football stadium, Stamford Bridge, was near our new home; the team was doing well at the time and we became fans. I was able to book cheap tickets for the World Cup football finals, so there was something exciting to look forward to. We also talked of seeing cricket at Lord's and motor races at Silverstone and Brands Hatch – places of awe to a young 'colonial' boy like me.

Friends raised the finance for our passages on a Union Castle liner from Cape Town. Dad was eligible for a British passport because his father had been born in Glasgow and my mother was eligible as she had married him before 1951. I was British, having been born in Kenya, and my sister Sally had been born in Britain. This left Tom and Jo-anne, and the British Embassy helpfully registered them, so that we all had British documents.

However, the Security Police were unaware of all this and, when my parents applied for permission to leave the Pretoria area they were obstructive, until it was pointed out that we had British passports and had already been issued with departure permits. The latter were then withdrawn and replaced with one-way exit permits, which prohibited my parents from returning to South Africa and withdrew their citizenship. In the typically bloody-minded manner of the local bureaucracy, permission to leave Pretoria was then delayed until the last moment – at one point it looked as though we would have to delay our departure.

I went with my brother and sisters to a farewell party in the Liberal Party offices, representing our parents whose ban prevented them from being present. It was a sad yet joyous occasion and everyone there treated us as surrogates for the absent parents they held in such high and affectionate regard. My parents departed with heavy hearts. There was no glory going into exile: they felt intensely guilty at leaving friends and colleagues behind, though simultaneously relieved that the all-consuming pressure under which our family had been living for the previous three years would now be eased. They wrote a press release which had to be issued in my name and which I wrote out by hand (because their bans still prevented them from saying anything publicly themselves). It urged whites to change before it was too late.

On 14 March 1966, the tears flowed as many of our friends, together with my grandparents and Party stalwarts, came to Pretoria railway station to see us off on the first leg of our journey to Cape Town, a thousand miles away; the banned Alban Thumbran stood waving alone at the end of the platform. We would never see my grandfather or Alban again. Waiting on the platform at Johannesburg station as the train passed through were more Party members to say farewell and shower us with parting gifts. Although deeply upsetting, I with the other children found our departure also exciting: the train journey was novel and so was the waiting ship.

We were all just making the best of it, as we always had through the years of increasing adversity. Looking back, I must have been toughened by the various experiences thrust upon me. I had learnt to cope, and also perhaps to blank out the inevitable emotion of those experiences, to 'move on', telling myself nobody and no group would get the better of me. Although I was quietly angry about what had happened to us, I knew far, far worse had happened to others. But I didn't feel a 'victim', and I didn't feel damaged.

Nevertheless, Mom and Dad later freely admitted being more worried about me than their other children, because I had been more exposed, and was at a critical moment in the final years of my high school career. In retrospect, Tom, Jo-anne and Sally variously found adjusting to their new life in England much more difficult than I did. And there was to be a shockingly salutary indictment of the psychological pressures people like us had been through. A friend, the same age as me, and whom I looked up to as an extremely bright school student and a very talented young cricketer to boot, abruptly committed suicide a year after coming into exile in London at the same time. Nobody who knew him could find an explanation except in the turmoil of his parents' involvement in the struggle and their enforced departure from their homeland.

‡

After leaving the train at Cape Town docks, we were carefully watched by the Special Branch to ensure my parents complied strictly with the terms of their permission to leave by going straight onto the ship. Then we steamed out of the old docks into the heaving Cape rollers, and I could see Robben Island, grim behind the cold spray, trying to picture Nelson Mandela and his comrades incarcerated in their harsh isolation. Behind, we were leaving a South Africa in which the powers of darkness were very much in the ascendant. The principal liberation movement, the ANC, was outlawed and in disarray; its leaders were in gaol; its military wing *Umkhonto* seemingly crushed. Other resistance groups had similarly been banned or paralysed. The Liberal Party was badly damaged by the banning of its main activists (and two years later new legislation forced it to disband).

When asked later why they had – so unusually for whites — sacrificed a wonderful life for their beliefs, my parents would play down their role: 'We only did what we felt we had to do.' Others might say they were an ordinary couple who did extraordinary things.

Our departures had been marked by talk that we would be back one day to savour the freedom of a new South Africa. But these were only the ritual exchanges of close comradeship. We had no illusions. The apartheid state seemed immortal. We were going for good, my father always made clear.

As it transpired, however, we were destined to join others in exile in what was to become a decisive era of international struggle against apartheid. But I had not the faintest idea as our beloved South African coast disappeared from sight, that within three years I would find myself playing a significant role in that struggle.

CHAPTER TWO

DIRECT ACTION

'It would be a mercy for humanity if this unpleasant little creep were to be dropped into a sewerage tank. Up to his ankles. Head first.' So wrote the celebrated right-wing newspaper editor Sir John Junor, catching perfectly the sense of outrage provoked in certain quarters by my militant anti-apartheid protests and radical views from the late 1960s onward.

But the teenager arriving in England in April 1966 was oblivious to this future notoriety. Southampton docks loomed, chilly and misty in the early morning as the ship was piloted in to its berth. After our enjoyable two-week voyage, the weather was a dank contrast to the heat which had accompanied us most of the way, and which continued to envelope our sunny homeland.

Being served by a friendly Spanish waiter in the ship's restaurant was a treat because eating out was not something our family had ever been able to afford. We had found ourselves on the same trip as our prosperous black doctor friend, Fabian Ribeiro, and his wife Florence. Both Catholics, they were on a pilgrimage to Lourdes, the only way as blacks they could get permission to take a holiday. Their presence on board was much to the astonishment of white passengers who had never encountered blacks doing that sort of thing before: holidays were what whites did. They were especially incredulous when, at a fancy-dress evening, my father and Florence went jauntily dressed in their pyjamas labelled 'The Immorality Act' (the apartheid law banning both mixed-race marriages and mixed-race sex). Fabian and our friend Ann Tobias, who was also on the trip, went as President Nkrumah of Ghana and his Egyptian wife. My parents always had a sense of fun and informality alongside their serious anti-apartheid activity.

We arrived the day after Labour's huge general election victory and election posters were still on display. But, aged sixteen, I was more struck by watching television for the first time and going to see our favoured football club, Chelsea.

We concentrated upon building a fresh life on the assumption that we were never going back. As we were to discover, many South African exiles in Britain then lived a kind of limbo existence – waiting to return. That was their choice and their dream. But my parents were determined to put down roots, to get involved in the community, and to make a new future. We must not be outsiders: Britain was now our home, they made clear to me. Although they became active in the Anti-Apartheid Movement almost immediately, regularly meeting other exiles including old friends, it took a while before we were thrust into hyper-activism again.

On the curious advice of our English landlord, an ex-Communist Party member, Tom and I were recommended to enrol at what turned out to be the local state grammar school, Emanuel, in Battersea, and we arrived with my father for an interview. The head teacher, lugubrious and ruddy faced with whiskers, seemed rather a toff. 'Would you like to write an essay, boy?' he asked. 'No thank you very much, Sir', I replied, putting a literal interpretation on the very English phrase 'would you like', and not recognising it for the polite instruction it actually was.

The school's culture was a world away from Pretoria Boys High. There seemed to be plenty of wasted time, the school day spreading out from nine in the morning until nearly four o'clock in the afternoon and what seemed to me too many free periods and an over-long lunch break. I was used to starting by eight, working hard, and then ending by one-thirty, either to travel home for lunch or to leave plenty of time for sport and homework. But I managed to escape joining the Combined Cadet Force by claiming (falsely I fear) that I had not done that sort of thing before.

Placed into 'Lower 5 General' – the bottom-performing class of the year – it was suggested I spend an additional year there catching up with the curriculum for the 'O' level exams the other boys my age were sitting in six weeks' time. I baulked at losing a year like that and, against official school advice, resolved to enter the exams anyway, paying a special fee for late entrance. It was very hard work for a couple of months, because I was far behind the whole curriculum. But, using excellent revision and exam techniques successfully learnt in Pretoria, spotting likely questions and boning up intensively on areas of my strength in each subject, I was able to assemble sufficiently high marks across my areas of expertise in each exam to offset questions where I was either weak, or in some cases knew nothing whatsoever. My pass grades awarded in all ten 'O' levels entered – which included Afrikaans – were creditable though not as high as in my previous school.

Meanwhile the teacher who squeezed in careers advice between teaching history and supervising the Combined Cadet Force, asked me: 'What do you want to do, boy?'

'Don't really know, Sir,' I replied.

'In that case you will be an engineer,' he decided. My school future was planned: 'A' levels in physics, applied maths and pure maths, and catching up on curriculum gaps.

That summer Tom and I went to see the visiting West Indies cricket team play England in three test matches. It was awesome going to Lord's, the venerable home of English cricket, and then to the Oval and Trent Bridge, and to watch English legends like Colin Cowdrey and Tom Graveney who had been figures of distant wonderment back in South Africa where I was a keen but second-rate left-handed batsman and spin bowler, noted for catches close up to batsmen. We were especially excited by West Indies players like Gary Sobers, Wes Hall and Lance Gibbs, never having seen these black legends perform before. Then there was the extraordinary sight of Basil D'Oliveira, a Cape Coloured, who was selected that year as an English Test player, having been barred from playing for his own South Africa because he wasn't white. We were also able to go to Wembley with bargain World Cup football tickets we had purchased back in Pretoria, and I was lucky enough to win a ticket in the draw for the final between West Germany and England. Standing next to a Tottenham Hotspur fan at the so-called 'Geoff Hurst' end of Wembley, I cheered on my new country to an exciting and historic victory.

I settled down phlegmatically into my new existence, albeit missing my old one. But Tom found adjustment much more difficult, escaping from home and school until he was eventually discovered and experimenting with cannabis. My parents later freely admitted it was painful coping with the free-spirited behaviour and sexual mores of 1960s London youth, especially for their two girls Jo-anne and Sally – a far cry indeed from the semi-Calvinism of South African family life. Additionally, I had brought with me a naive colonial schoolboy image of England: all royals, pomp and ceremony with cricket on village greens. So it was startling to discover the extent of poverty and shabbiness that still pervaded so many parts of London. I read my Dad's *Guardian* for the sport and increasingly the politics, and it was an eye opener watching leading politicians being questioned on television, and seeing top quality current affairs programmes like *World in Action* and *Panorama* – a stark contrast to the state-controlled propaganda of South African radio and the deference to the select group of favoured white apartheid politicians allowed on it.

‡

About a year after arriving, I decided to join the Anti-Apartheid Movement. It had been formed in 1959, in response to a call from then ANC President Albert Luthuli for an international boycott movement which gathered momentum after the 1960 massacre at Sharpeville.

By late 1967 and early 1968, when I was seventeen going on eighteen (and still at school in my final year doing my 'A' levels), I gradually became more politically involved, following current debates, and avidly discussing with my father topical issues like the Vietnam War, joining him in becoming hostile to American intervention. In Britain there had been huge anti-bomb marches in the late 1950s and early 1960s organised by the Campaign for Nuclear Disarmament, and direct action tactics were adopted by its militant offshoot, the Committee of 100. When we arrived, similar protests were growing against the Vietnam War, and Tom and I went on the big demonstration in Grosvenor Square in October 1968, witnessing violent clashes between police and protesters determined to storm the US Embassy. London had been eerily boarded up as we marched from Victoria Embankment to Mayfair. The fervour of the time resonated in its chants: 'London, Paris and Berlin – we shall fight, we shall win!' And 'Hey, hey, LBJ, how many kids have you killed today?' (LBJ, of course, being the US President Lyndon Baines Johnson, later to refuse to seek a second term, a man broken by the war.)

I also grew angry about the failure of Harold Wilson's Labour government to deal firmly with the illegal rebellion by the white minority in Rhodesia. Their leader, Ian Smith, had made a Unilateral Declaration of Independence to maintain their racist rule. The campaign against UDI was being organised by the Anti-Apartheid Movement and I began to attend more of its meetings. Partly because of what I felt was the Labour government's abject timidity on Rhodesia, partly because of our connection to the South African Liberal Party, and partly because the British Young Liberals were then a vibrant, irreverent force for radicalism, I decided to join the latter, aged seventeen.

But that wasn't at all straightforward. Although my parents had joined the local Liberals in Putney where we lived, there was no youth branch. So, in order to join, I had to form one. It was daunting, but I warmed to the notion of setting up something myself rather than joining an established body as an outsider. Two others were recommended to me, Miranda, an attractive girl my age, and Mike, an older trainee accountant. We divided up the officer posts between us. I ended up as chairman, discovering a zest for organisation probably instilled by observing my parents, and the Young Liberals' radical politics quickly took over my life.

It led me into an exciting culture of left-wing ideas. Young Liberal leaders, expert at attention grabbing, had appropriated for themselves the term 'Red Guards' from Mao's recent 'Cultural Revolution' in China and called for a 'cultural revolution' in their senior Party and in Britain as a whole. The YL movement's energy and flair for publicity, together with its continual pamphleteering and campaigning, provided an ideal crash course in political education. I started reading left-wing books and pamphlets voraciously, and was taught how to draft press releases, deal with the media and how to organise. We also supported militant, though non-violent, direct action where necessary, emulating the wave of protest and civil rights demonstrations in America, and university student sit-ins.

Aged eighteen going on nineteen, politics was already in my blood. But my belief in socialism really crystallised around 1968–9 – the years of the Paris uprising, of student agitation throughout Europe and the US, of the Soviet invasion of Czechoslovakia, and of anti-Vietnam War protests. A 'new left' had emerged, iconoclastic and just as opposed to capitalism as to Stalinism: 'Neither Washington nor Moscow' – our slogan was for a 'bottom up' social-ism rather than a 'top down' one, popular participation not state bureaucracy, workers' control not nationalisation: these were the watchwords, and the more radical Young Liberals like me called ourselves 'libertarian socialists'. We were immersed in an exciting ferment of new and radical ideas shaped by the passionate debate in teach-ins, conferences, demonstrations and sit-ins.

But, by the 'sex, drugs, rock and roll' folklore of the late 1960s, I must have cut a rather boring figure. Girls interested me, but short-term relationships didn't. I was deeply anti-drugs and never touched the stuff; in total frustration, a fellow Young Liberal once tried to stuff a cannabis spliff into my mouth. I wasn't interested in drink and barely followed the pop charts, in stark contrast to Tom, who got caught up in the bohemian youth culture of the late-1960s.

Instead, an increasingly busy political activism dominated my life. However, I had been instilled with a hard-work ethic, both by my parents and at school, and so managed to get three good 'A' levels and to be accepted for a year's engineering student apprenticeship that preceded a mechanical engineering degree course at London University's prestigious Imperial College, starting in October 1969. This after turning down an opportunity to apply for Oxford, having frustratingly travelled up and searched for what I had been told was 'Maudlin' College; how could that pronunciation possibly apply to the actual 'Magdalen' College? I did not take to the upper-class snobbery of Oxford – though, in later years became a regular speaker at student meetings there.

As apartheid moved up the political agenda, a number of leading Young Liberals early in 1968 formed a 'Southern Africa Commission' (SAC). This brought together members with an interest in the area and, although I had only joined the YLs in Putney a few months before, I quickly came into contact with national YL leaders. As the only ex-South African involved, I found myself propelled into modest prominence which was to bring me into close touch with leaders of the wider Anti-Apartheid Movement and, in October, I was encouraged to stand and was elected to its National Executive Committee.

One of my first activities with SAC was setting up a 'Medical Aid for Southern Africa' appeal in 1968 to assist the ANC and other liberation movements. Many people sympathetic to, or actually involved in, anti-apartheid movements would not associate themselves with guerrilla activity, but would back medical aid. I visited the ANC's London office and held discussions with, amongst others, Thabo Mbeki, recently a student at the University of Sussex and thirty-one years later the President of his country. With the help of my mother, we typed up and printed on a second-hand Gestetner duplicating machine (similar to her old one in Pretoria) copies of a pamphlet supporting the medical aid appeal, my father doing the artwork for the cover.

I hitch-hiked with the Putney YL secretary Miranda 250 miles up to my first national Young Liberal conference in Scarborough in April 1968. We booked into cheap rooms and I later wondered wistfully about pretending not to notice her romantic overtures. Instead I immersed myself in the conference excitement, meeting the leadership stars and soaking up the politics. We seemed part of a big change. I was called to the rostrum to make a brief speech in favour of a resolution supporting the ANC's liberation struggle. But, despite the radicalism of the YLs, it was narrowly defeated, after strong appeals by pacifists.

I was by instinct and conviction resolutely opposed to violence. For me violence was no academic matter: I had seen too much of it in South Africa. But the predicament of those resisting apartheid convinced me that the ANC was justified in adopting guerrilla tactics. With all democratic and legal channels blocked, I was persuaded by those like Nelson Mandela who had argued there was no alternative, and started advocating the cause of the ANC and its sister liberation groups fighting racist regimes in southern Africa.

However, my support for the ANC's guerrilla struggle was never to be confused with support for 'terrorism'. The vital distinction is that the violence of guerrilla movements is directed against the oppressive apartheid state whereas the violence of terrorists such as Al Qaeda is directed indiscriminately against innocent bystanders. Although the distinction did sometimes become blurred, as on the few occasions when sabotage carried out by the ANC unintentionally caught bystanders, I believed that it nevertheless remained valid and important – and a foundation for building political solidarity.

A violent strategy by resistance movements can only be justified when, as was the case with European countries invaded by Hitler during the Second World War, or with a contemporary tyranny like apartheid, all other means have been exhausted with no viable alternative. To deny people the right to resist such tyrannies violently is to deny them their humanity and to acquiesce in their oppression. When the crunch comes, all the pacifist can do is to bear moral witness, dying bravely as the guns fire, the bombs go off or the tanks roll in.

‡

I had always been very keen on sport and even much later when a Cabinet Minister still often turned to the sports pages of a newspaper first. So I instinctively saw the importance of anti-apartheid work in sport, which might otherwise have appeared an unusual choice for political protest, at best peripheral, at worst eccentric. I understood the white South African psyche: they were sports mad, Afrikaners especially fanatical about rugby. Whether it was participation in the Olympics or a cricket tour, international sport gripped the white nation as nothing else – and, importantly, granted them the international respectability and legitimacy they increasingly craved as the evil reality of apartheid began to be exposed by horrors such as the Sharpeville massacre. Moreover it was easier to achieve success through practical protest against sports links than it was to take on the might of either international capital or military alliances and secure trade or arms boycotts. Victories in sport were crucial during a period when internal resistance was being smashed and it was extremely hard to come by external successes. Soon we began achieving these.

That this was an issue absolutely central to the ideology of white domination was demonstrated with devastating clarity in the ruling National Party daily newspaper, *Die Transvaler*, on 7 September 1965. Arguing that 'the white race had hitherto maintained itself in the southern part of Africa' because 'there has been no miscegenation', its editorial continued:

> The absence of miscegenation was because there was no social mixing between White and non-White ... If they mix on the sports field then the road to other forms of social mixing is wide open ... With an eye to upholding the white race and its civilisation, not one single compromise can be entered into – not even when it comes to a visiting rugby team.

Countless statements could be quoted by top rugby, cricket, sports or government figures justifying racism in sport on the most spurious and blatant basis. Some resorted to extraordinary sophistry, almost word for word those which Hitler and his fellow Nazis used to exclude Jews from pre-World War Two German teams. Others resorted to plain fantasy. Attempting to justify the omission of blacks, a white swimming official said in 1968: 'Some sports the African is not suited for. In swimming the water closes their pores and they cannot get rid of carbon dioxide, so they tire quickly.'

In 1965 the Anti-Apartheid Movement had organised low-key placard-carrying pickets outside each ground on the South African cricket tour to Britain. But the whole question was suddenly elevated in 1968 over whether the

coloured South African Basil D'Oliveira, by then a top and regular English Test
player, should be selected for the English cricket tour to South Africa that year.

Following weeks of seedy manoeuvring and high drama, D'Oliveira was
first offered £40,000 to declare himself unavailable by a South African-based
representative of the cigarette company Rothmans. Then, to everyone's astonishment, he was omitted from the touring party. The distinguished cricket
journalist John Arlott wrote: 'No one of open mind will believe that he was left
out for valid cricketing reasons.' And, it transpired decades later, Doug Insole,
the chairman of the selectors, had been in touch with the South Africans
beforehand to be told D'Oliveira would not be welcome.

However, after weeks of raging controversy, D'Oliveira was finally included
when the Warwickshire all-rounder Tom Cartwright withdrew with a shoulder
injury.* Then came a dramatic new twist. Pretoria refused to accept D'Oliveira's
selection. 'It's not the England team. It's the team of the anti-apartheid movement,' the South African Prime Minister Vorster preposterously blustered, and
the tour was then cancelled, provoking universal outrage in Britain.

Yet, even after this unprecedented veto of their tour by the apartheid
government, the English cricket authorities brazenly announced in January
1969 that they would proceed with the scheduled 1970 cricket tour to Britain
by a white South African team. Anticipating this decision, I had drafted a
motion which SAC approved in January 1969 pledging 'ourselves to take direct
action to prevent scheduled matches from taking place unless the 1970 tour
is cancelled'. The motion got a small mention in *The Times* and it was sent to
the cricket authorities. (I had not tried to get it through the AAM National
Committee as it was cautious and conservative on the question of direct action,
in retrospect understandably so since this might have jeopardised its broader
following – though I found it frustrating at the time.)

The previous year I had been introduced to those in exile in London running
the South African Non-Racial Olympic Committee (SAN-ROC) in which our
late friend John Harris had been involved (his passport had been withdrawn
as he tried to board a plane to argue internationally for Olympics expulsion).
SAN-ROC had been successful in getting white South Africa suspended from
the Olympics for the first time in 1964, and in May 1969 it held a public
meeting in London where I raised from the floor the question of direct action
to stop the tour. The former Robben Island prisoner Dennis Brutus was in

---

* Ironically, Tom was one of my constituents when I was elected MP for Neath in 1991 and
my teenage son Jake was coached under his supervision. We became friends and he told
me in 1995 that he had always been unhappy about the idea of going on tour, that pressure
had been put on him to accept despite the fact that it was known to Lord's he was injured,
and that he withdrew out of conviction – not simply for the publicly quoted explanation.

the chair and very supportive, as was his colleague Chris de Broglio. Sports apartheid protests in Britain up until that time had been symbolic: holding up banners outside sports grounds. These had been impressive and vital stages in the process of mobilising awareness. Indeed they still had an important role to play. But the new dimension which I was the first to advocate was direct action: physically disrupting the very events themselves and thereby posing both a threat and a challenge which could not be ignored by the sports elites who had been impervious to moral appeals and symbolic protests.

It was the product of that unique late-1960s era in which I had been caught up. I was inspired to adopt tactics of non-violent direct action to confront sports apartheid from student sit-ins like that at Hornsey College of Art in 1968, worker occupations, and squats in empty houses. It was not enough simply to bear witness, I felt.

A new more militant movement gathered momentum alongside the AAM which maintained the discreet, sometimes uneasy, distance which I respected as necessary to its more conventional role. A private tour by an all-white South African club side sponsored by a wealthy businessman, Wilf Isaacs, experienced the first-ever taste of direct action against cricket anywhere. At the opening match in the Essex town of Basildon in July 1969, I led a group of Young Liberals onto the pitch. I had contacted a dozen or so beforehand and planned our intervention, gathering as spectators at the small club ground, having tipped off journalists. Play was interrupted for over ten minutes until police dragged us, limp, off the field, with photographs and stories in the media gaining attention for this novel tactic. Subsequent tour matches in Oxford and at the Oval, south London, saw even greater and more successful disruptions, organised by local anti-apartheid groups.

Also that July, on the opening day of a Davis Cup tennis match in Bristol between white South Africa and Britain, I travelled down with two Putney Young Liberals, Helen Tovey and Maree Pocklington, young women like me in their late teens. We planned our protest on the drive down, not knowing quite what to expect, tense and worried as we arrived and purchased tickets. Taking our seats separately we waited until I signalled and then ran onto the court, on this occasion disrupting play for the first time in an international event in front of live television coverage, causing consternation which was widely reported in the media. We were carried off and taken to the local police station before being released after perfunctory questioning. It was my first taste of a police cell – ironically, my parents later remarked, a British rather than a South African one. Later in the three-day tournament, play was further disrupted by an invasion and flour bombs were thrown onto the court in protests organised by the Bristol Anti-Apartheid group.

Because sport was being targeted by direct action, the protests were highly newsworthy with, as I had anticipated, publicity for each encouraging others. A crucial feature was that these events were taking place across the country and action could be initiated locally, which meant the emerging movement was characterised by considerable local autonomy and spontaneity. A network soon fell into place and, with active encouragement by Dennis Brutus and Chris de Broglio of SAN-ROC, we decided to launch the Stop The Seventy Tour Committee (STST) at a press conference in September 1969. It had broad support, from the AAM and the United Nations Youth, to the National Union of Students, Christian groups, and young communists, Trotskyites and Liberals. A Reading University student, Hugh Geach, was secretary and, aged nineteen, I was pressed by Dennis Brutus, Chris de Broglio and others into a leadership role, and found myself acting as press officer and convenor of the committee (later encouraged to assume the chair). It was daunting because I had anticipated being more of a foot soldier supporting more experienced and illustrious figures to lead the campaign.

I gave a pledge at the press conference that there would be 'mass demonstrations and disruptions throughout the 1970 cricket tour' – more out of hope and a determination to lead from the front, because there was no national organisation as such in place; I was confident it would emerge, just as the local activity had begun to gather pace in the previous few months. Indeed the public threat was deliberately pitched to be newsworthy and therefore to capture the sense of interest needed to galvanise a big movement. I also promised demonstrations against the Springbok rugby tour which, we had realised rather belatedly, was due to start in six weeks' time. The aim was to use it as a dummy run to build a campaign capable of stopping the following summer's cricket tour. Looking back, I recall a fearless innocence, part exhilarating and part just getting on with what I felt had to be done: I was determined to win a decisive battle against the evil of apartheid and more convinced perhaps than anybody else we could achieve that through non-violent direct action.

That September, I spoke for the first time at the Liberal Party's annual conference in Brighton, urging support for direct action. I wasn't a natural or experienced orator and it was a little nerve-racking. My photograph appeared in national newspapers and I was invited by the then producer of the Thames TV evening news show, Frank Keating, to go back up to London and do my first television interview; he subsequently became a noted sports journalist. None of this fazed me: I just took one step at a time, unsure whether I could manage the next one, but then finding indeed that I could – and quite successfully. It did not change me much as a person, still quite shy and modest, living at the family home, though gaining experience with a growing public profile. My South African roots and still-strong accent enabled me to speak authoritatively in the anti-apartheid cause.

Through all this I had been spending a year as a student engineering apprentice where I learnt at first hand practical mechanical engineering at the west London company CAV, a subsidiary of Lucas Industries, and was ready to begin my university course. But, since my involvement first surfaced in the media in the summer, the South African press had begun to take an increasing interest, and I formed good relationships with several London-based journalists. Their regular reports rapidly elevated me to the status of a 'hate' figure in my old home: called 'Public Enemy Number One'. The fact that 'one of their own' had turned against them provoked stories about me 'taking revenge' for the treatment of my parents. Back in South Africa a young Pretoria 'insider' was being transformed into an ogre 'outsider'.

The STST campaign had hardly been publicly launched than I received a welcome indication of its potential impact in the form of a registered letter date marked Pretoria October 1969 from the South African Minister for the Interior. It informed me that my right as a British citizen to enter the country without an 'alien's temporary permit' or visa had been withdrawn. (In fact I had no intention of returning nor had I indicated any desire to do so.) Around the same time, my old Pretoria Boys High School head, Desmond Abernethy, arrived in London and sought me out, courteously pressing me to stop my activities. While I was at school he had been quietly, albeit distantly, sympathetic as my parents' notoriety grew. It was a strange encounter, because I had been used to obeying his dictates; head teachers in those days were both revered and feared. But now he found himself unable to persuade his formerly well-behaved pupil, as I politely declined his request. The sense that he was doing his duty was confirmed by a newspaper story reporting his mission back in South Africa.

On the back of growing excitement and publicity, the campaign simply took off. Our modest family flat in Gwendolen Avenue, Putney, became the headquarters address and 'office'. There was no administration as such. Volunteers turned up to help and Mom quickly assumed the crucial role of unofficial dogsbody, fielding phone calls, coordinating information and helping with correspondence – well versed from her Pretoria days in running an organisation. Dad came home from work to write leaflets and background briefs. Suddenly, in a reversal of roles from our life in South Africa, I had become the front person; but I could not have done this without their constant support in the background.

My public threats of direct action against the rugby tour and confident predictions we could stop the cricket tour generated widespread publicity. I found myself being regularly interviewed on television and radio, using the guidance and experience I had gained through the Young Liberals to deal with the press on a daily basis. This coincided with the start of my mechanical engineering course at Imperial College, to which I cycled daily. Decades before the era of mobile phones, I used to spend lunch breaks with homemade sandwiches in a phone box talking to journalists and local organisers through messages relayed from my mother at home where the phone rang incessantly. Aged nineteen going on twenty, life was both everyday student wrestling, increasingly despondently, with thermo-dynamics, and exhilarated national protest leader.

‡

Meanwhile a mass movement was snowballing, locally based, largely spontaneous, and usually focused around student unions, though involving trade unions, local branches of the Anti-Apartheid Movement, socialists, radicals, liberals, independents, trade unionists and the churches.* It was predominantly, though by no means exclusively, young and soon took the Springbok rugby tour by storm.

The opening match, against Oxford University in October 1969, was switched after strong opposition from both the college authorities and students who sprayed weed killer on the ground and threatened to wreck the match. The new venue was kept secret to avoid demonstrations but Bob Trevor, a friendly Welsh sports journalist (and Labour Party member) with the London *Evening News*, had promised to phone us immediately the press were informed. At 9.30 the night before, our phone rang and his familiar voice said: 'Twickenham, 3 p.m' I immediately relayed the news to the Oxford Committee Against Apartheid and around the country where coaches of demonstrators waited: over 1,000 rushed to the ground and we all purchased tickets, grouping together in the main stand. The match took place under siege, with pitch invasions and constant hostile chanting. Midway through I spotted an opening in the police cordon and tried to jump over the spectator fence, but was immediately grabbed, carted out and dumped on the pavement. Sensationally, the mighty Springboks lost, clearly unnerved by the atmosphere.

The tour organisers could not have played more into our hands. Switching the first fixture from Oxford at the last minute attracted front page lead stories on the morning of the match and set the scene for the remaining games of the 25-match tour. Local organisers suddenly realised they were part of a mass

---

* For an account see Peter Hain, *Don't Play with Apartheid* (London, Allen & Unwin, 1971).

national movement and each of the matches saw demonstrations of varying sizes. Several of the biggest set piece confrontations were at the home of the English Rugby Union, Twickenham. As it lay within easy reach of central London, we were able to get 2,000 inside for the first scheduled match in late November – some 'disguised' by cutting their hair or wearing Springbok rosettes – and a similar number outside. I was one of over a hundred demonstrators who managed to climb over the fence surrounding the pitch and outwit the police. Play was stopped for over ten minutes until we were carried off and summarily ejected from the stadium.

The week before, in Swansea, there had been the most brutal confrontation of the entire tour. A Wales Rejects Apartheid Committee had been formed with widespread support from all walks of life. But in south Wales – a socialist stronghold with an honourable tradition of international solidarity going back at least to the Spanish Civil War – rugby fanaticism came first. At Swansea, there were ugly scenes as police threw 100 peacefully invading demonstrators back from the pitch and deliberately into the clutches of 'stewards' who promptly handed out beatings. One demonstrator's jaw was broken and he nearly lost an eye. Others, including women, were badly assaulted. Journalists from papers like *The Times* not supportive of the demonstrations nevertheless condemned the 'viciousness' of the police and stewards.

Looking back over forty years later, we were possessed of a fearless idealism. I never worried overly about potential repercussions – possibilities of violence against me, threats of prosecution, or the very personal fury I increasingly attracted. Morality was on our side, our cause was just, our militancy necessary.

By now white South Africa was apoplectic. An Afrikaans government-supporting paper, *Die Beeld*, stated in an editorial: 'We have become accustomed to Britain becoming a haven for all sorts of undesirables from other countries. Nevertheless, it is degrading to see how a nation can allow itself to be dictated to by this bunch of left-wing, workshy, refugee, long-hairs who in a society of any other country would be rejects.'

The police and rugby authorities got wise to our tactics, and in Northern Ireland (itself in turmoil following civil rights protests) the match was cancelled for security reasons. Elsewhere matches were made all-ticket and security inside massively increased so that police stood shoulder to shoulder around the pitch facing spectators. In Cardiff all pretence at a normal rugby match was abandoned as barbed wire was put up around the field. In blue-rinse conservative Bournemouth the match had to be abandoned because the open ground there could not be defended.

Our tactics changed as well. We knew that the STST campaign had by now been infiltrated (including at a national level). My home telephone number was tapped – a familiar though uncomfortable experience we thought had been left behind in Pretoria. So we established an 'inner group' of some of my most trusted and experienced activists – several older than me who had years before participated in nuclear disarmament direct action demonstrations. It was called the Special Action Group and worked on clandestine projects under the leadership of London dentist Mike Craft and experienced activist Ernest Rodker. It booked Rosemary Chester, a vivacious young woman, into the team's London hotel in Park Lane. (Decades later she became Lady Kirkwood, wife of the former Liberal MP Lord Archy Kirkwood.) Rosemary slipped through the hotel in the early hours gumming up the players' door locks with solidifying agent so they had to break down the doors to get out on the morning of the pre-Christmas international match at Twickenham. Another attractive girl, a student involved in the campaign, became a 'Mata Hari', deputed to chat up the players. She struck up a friendship with one Springbok at Bristol and back in London they met again. He and some colleagues agreed to go with her to a 'reception party' we had organised. But when she went to collect them after the post-match festivities she discovered her man was completely drunk and interested only in groping her.

Michael Deeny, an STST activist who worked in the City, turned up in a smart suit, politely told the driver of the team's coach waiting outside their London hotel that he was wanted inside, slipped into his seat and chained himself to the steering wheel. The team restlessly paced around the hotel foyer as a long delay ensued while police eventually found a metal cutter, Deeny meanwhile having been subjected to a mauling. Later at the match at Twickenham, protesters evaded the heavy police cordon. Two of my Putney Young Liberal friends Mike Findlay and Peter Twyman had practised their plans in our back garden, running and quickly attaching themselves to a broomstick with handcuffs we had purchased. Unlike other protesters they were dressed in jacket and tie. We had acquired special ringside seats in front of the security cordon and, at a pre-arranged moment, they suddenly burst out, running to evade furious pursuers, one just managing to chain himself to the goalposts. Play was interrupted until he was cut free. Orange smoke pellets were also thrown amongst the players, which, as well as disrupting play, produced dramatic television and newspaper pictures.

At the last Twickenham match in late January 1970, we distributed packets of powdered dye to selected protesters which turned black on contact with dampness. These were thrown onto the pitch so that the Springboks, rolling on the wet grass, were smeared with black stains to chants from protesters on the terraces of 'paint them black and send them back'. As I walked to the turnstiles to enter the ground, I was faced with the police commander, John Gerrard, who jocularly said: 'Now Mr Hain, you wouldn't be doing anything silly like taking a packet of dye in with you?' To which I replied, discomforted that he might search me: 'Now, you know I wouldn't do a silly thing like that.' He waved me through, the packet safely in my pocket, later to be hurled on the turf. There seemed something of a mutual respect between Gerrard and me, as if senior police officers like him were wary of martyring me as they enforced security; however, other demonstrators were often dealt with very harshly.

Wherever the team went, resting, training or playing, it was under siege. Over Christmas, two months into the tour, the players took a step inconceivable in the annals of Springbok history and voted to go home. But the management, under political pressure, ordered them to stay. The tour finally staggered to an end, with the players bitter and unsettled. For the vice captain, Tommy Bedford, it proved a cathartic experience. Within a year he publicly stated I should be listened to, not vilified, and praised our objectives. Although his response was a relatively isolated one in South Africa, it signalled the huge and destabilising impact of our campaign.

For the first time, the Springboks, accustomed to being lionised as perhaps the leading national rugby team in the world, had instead been treated as pariahs. They were no longer faced merely with what they habitually dismissed as the spluttering of 'misguided liberals and leftists' while they retreated to the warm hospitality of their rugby hosts. This was something of quite a different order. Anti-apartheid opponents had now shown a physical capacity to threaten the Springboks' ability to tour in the old way.

The reaction amongst the black majority in South Africa was, however, diametrically different. After their release many years later, both Nelson Mandela and Govan Mbeki told me that on Robben Island news of the demonstrations had given all the political prisoners there an enormous morale boost; Mbeki said it had also brought a smile to their faces when they learnt that 'the son of the Hains' was leading the campaign. A close friend of my parents, Hugh Lewin, was then in the fifth of his seven years in Pretoria Central with a news black-out imposed. He described how reports had leaked through his warders, Afrikaner rugby fanatics to a man. First they started swearing to each other about the '*betogers*' (demonstrators). Initially confused, Hugh began to piece it together and realised something big was getting to them. Gradually the truth seeped out. He and his fellow 'politicals' were thrilled. For him the *coup de grâce* came when the warders began moaning about 'that bastard Peter Hain' – though he found it difficult to match his recollection of a well-behaved boy in his early teens with the monster apparently responsible for these dreadful events. Hugh claimed to have detected in the quality of their soup served up on a Saturday evening how successful the demonstrators had been in disrupting that afternoon's game: the poorer the soup, the more successful the demonstration!

The saturation coverage given to the campaign in the South African media reached parts of South African life that no other boycott campaign was able to, because most white South African men cared about sport first and foremost. The huge psychological and political impact was well illustrated by banner headlines greeting the return home of a Springbok canoeing team in February 1970: 'NO DEMONSTRATIONS!' It had come, canoed and then gone, in virtual secrecy – we certainly never got to hear of it. But the team's captain was very clear about the reasons for their 'success' at an ecstatic homecoming reception: 'Most demonstrators are hippies and hippies don't like water – that's why we weren't worried by them.'

‡

The campaign had meanwhile taken over my life. Although I attended lectures and tutorials as required, I had lost all interest in my mechanical engineering degree course, and was barely keeping up with the work. The sheer elation and effort involved in leading STST was all-consuming, but I had also grown disillusioned with academic engineering studies that seemed a world away from my enjoyable year in industry. I was also changing fast as a person and becoming clearer about what I did and did not want to do. Only afterwards informing my worried parents, I quietly applied to switch degrees and was accepted elsewhere within London University at Queen Mary College to study economics and political science. The head of the department, Maurice (later Lord) Peston, told me decades later that the university authorities had unsuccessfully tried to pressure him to block my admission.

The rugby tour had provided the movement with a perfect springboard from which to plan direct action to stop the cricket tour, due to start at the beginning of May 1970. But opposition, coordinated by the Anti-Apartheid Movement, went much wider. The churches, led by the former England cricket captain and Bishop of Woolwich, David Sheppard, urged cancellation. The Commonwealth Games, due to take place in Edinburgh that summer, also became an important lever. SAN-ROC's international expertise and contacts were put to good use as it was privately pointed out to African and Asian countries that they would be in an intolerable position participating in the Games at the same time as an apartheid cricket tour was under siege elsewhere in Britain.

Then, late in the night on 19 January 1970, demonstrators simultaneously raided fourteen of the seventeen county cricket club grounds. All were daubed with paint slogans. In addition a small patch in the outfield of Glamorgan's Cardiff ground was dug up and weed killer was sprayed on Warwickshire's Birmingham ground. Pre-planned telephone reports from each small, tight group poured in throughout the night to the Press Association news agency and to my home. In the morning the coordinated protest dominated the radio bulletins and there were screaming headlines with photos in the evening papers and television programmes and the following day's national newspapers.

The impact of the protests was principally psychological: a devastating shock to the cricket authorities and a surprise to almost everyone. The widespread strength of the movement had been starkly revealed in an operation seemingly carried out with almost military precision. More than this, the fear at the back of the cricket authorities' mind – and probably shared by most others – had suddenly been realised: the spectre of a cricket tour collapsing amidst damaged pitches and weed killer was conjured up and began to crystallise.

Speculation was rife, especially as it was not clear who was responsible. The Anti-Apartheid Movement denied all knowledge. People inevitably accused STST – as it alone had the organisational capacity necessary to mount the raids – but I said that the STST national committee had not authorised or approved the action, thereby distancing us from it. The only national figure to give the raids full backing was the Young Liberal chairman, Louis Eaks, who attracted headlines and dominated the air waves when he said 'some Young Liberals had been involved' (which was accurate as far as it went, though he had no involvement or prior knowledge himself). In truth it was indeed a covert operation by key STST activists executed from the centre with deadly efficiency and effect.

Within weeks, 300 reels of barbed wire arrived at Lord's and most county grounds introduced guard dogs and security. The pressure on the cricket authorities grew. West Indies cricket leaders angrily denounced the tour. There was speculation that African, Asian and Caribbean countries would withdraw from the Edinburgh Commonwealth Games. One by one, a range of public bodies came out against the tour and there was talk of trade unions taking industrial action. Some Labour MPs, including the AAM's vice chairman, Peter Jackson, said they would join sit-down pitch invasions. The chairman of the government-sponsored Community Relations Commission, Frank Cousins, told the Home Secretary that the tour would do 'untold damage' to race relations.

On the 12 February the governing body, the Cricket Council, met at Lord's, which I managed to infiltrate, attempting to enter their press conference until spotted by officials who ushered me out – but not before I had glimpsed an extraordinary sight: the pitch eerily surrounded by barbed wire, silhouetted in the snowy night. Lord's, the magisterial home of international cricket, looked for all the world like a concentration camp, symbolising the torment which had torn asunder this most dignified and graceful of games.

The Cricket Council issued a sombre statement explaining that the tour had been cut drastically to just twelve matches from its original schedule of twenty-eight. Further it was to be played on just eight grounds instead of the original twenty-two and artificial all-weather pitches would be installed as an additional security precaution. It was a striking decision, on the one hand indicative of the bunker-like obstinacy of Lord's and the reactionary ideology which prevailed there, on the other hand testimony to the growing power of the campaign. I denounced the decision, quipping that we might rename ourselves 'The Stop The Seventy *Half* Tour campaign'.

However events also took a more serious turn. The Conservative Shadow Attorney General, Sir Peter Rawlinson, attacked the Labour Home Secretary, James Callaghan, for remaining 'neutral' and thereby 'acknowledging the licence to riot'. Rawlinson also called for an injunction to be taken out against me, insisting my public statements threatening to stop the tour constituted a direct incitement to illegal action. After Cabinet documents were made public thirty years later (and, ironically, when I was a serving Labour government Minister), it was also revealed that Ministers had discussed whether or not to prosecute me, with the Home Secretary James Callaghan in favour.

At the time I had been privately warned by a friendly solicitor that my open advocacy of disruptive protests made me extremely vulnerable to a charge of conspiring unlawfully because the then conspiracy laws provided a catch-all basis for curbing radical political action. Although thanking him for the warning, I pressed on regardless of the personal risk of a prosecution and likely prison sentence. There was no question of doing anything else in my mind. Our whole strategy was predicated upon being open about our disruptive plans because it was public knowledge of our planned direct action which constituted our prime tactical weapon. The threat of direct action held the key to our strategy to get the tour stopped in advance, and as its author, I was determined to carry it through regardless.

‡

During February and March the campaign mushroomed. Action groups to complement those established during the rugby tour sprang up throughout the country. The AAM was deluged with offers of help and its membership shot up. About a hundred enquiries a day by phone and letter poured into our home, which remained the STST headquarters; my mother was almost permanently on the phone and the family flat was filled with volunteers and callers. The Labour Prime Minister, Harold Wilson, publicly opposed the tour for the first time. The West Indian Campaign Against Apartheid Cricket was launched after the leading black activist Jeff Crawford had contacted me; I felt this introduced an important extra dimension which fused our campaign with the battle against racism in British society.

Meanwhile SAN-ROC, through the Supreme Council for Sport in Africa, consolidated the basis for a Commonwealth Games boycott. Trade unions came out against the tour: television workers and journalists threatened a media black-out, and radio's 'voice of cricket', John Arlott, announced he would not do the ball-by-ball commentaries for which he was internationally renowned. Mike Brearley (later to be one of England's most successful cricket captains) took the courageous step of speaking at STST's national conference.

Opposition was by now reaching right into the establishment. Leading public figures, including David Sheppard, formed the Fair Cricket Campaign, (FCC) whose vice chairman was the senior Conservative Sir Edward Boyle. Though explicitly committed to lawful, respectable methods and publicly deliberately distant from STST's methods, which it opposed, the FCC was privately friendly. Through a mutual contact I was invited for a confidential meeting with its leaders which I undertook not to disclose, arriving to an atmosphere courteous but edgy. However, we quickly found cordial common ground when I said I was relaxed if they felt it necessary to criticise our militancy, but it would be best if we both refrained from arguing publicly with each other since we had a common objective (to stop the tour) and a common enemy (apartheid). Arguing amongst ourselves would merely play into the hands of our opponents. David Sheppard especially saw the sense of this immediately, and we agreed to stay in touch and keep our contacts confidential. Apart from having good relations, the enormous advantage from my standpoint was in having a 'spectrum of protest', from STST's militancy, through the AAM's conventional pressure group profile and its very effective links into the labour movement, and SAN-ROC's expert international lobbying, to this impeccable respectability: there was now a very broadly based opposition to the tour which I knew was essential for victory. It also reflected my antipathy to the debilitating sectarianism I had witnessed over the previous couple of years of radical activism. Although STST's direct action powered the whole campaign, it could have been isolated without a great hinterland of broad public support, and I was at pains to stake out a non-sectarian position, refusing to criticise the more moderate groups and understanding their concerns about our militancy.

Meeting these establishment figures was interesting in another way. As the radical, by now somewhat notorious, outsider, dressed in his habitual jeans and anorak, here I was in a posh Kensington drawing room of suits and erudite accents. Perhaps because I had not been brought up in Britain's deeply stratified and class-ridden society, I did not feel at all awkward about this – instead rather intrigued, which I sensed also went for those to whom I was introduced. They all seemed decent well-meaning people – though perhaps rather naive in considering that letters to *The Times* and words in well-placed ears might stop the tour.

My casual dress was by now a personal badge. I did not possess a suit and never wore a tie; smart for me was what in modern parlance would be called 'smart casual'. So in major television studio interviews I would typically wear a trademark polo shirt or maybe light polo neck jersey with open jacket. Anything smarter would have been 'selling out' my radicalism. My hair was longish and curly, compared with shoulder-length hair and beards then the norm amongst radical males, I was clean cut: in retrospect perhaps I was doing my own thing and making my own statement. Indeed by the radical, student, hippie standards of the late 1960s and early 1970s I was awkwardly unfashionable, only struggling into flared trousers a couple of years after everyone else had been wearing them and they were about to go out of fashion. I didn't do trendy.

However, some could not cope with my polite but firm informality. Arriving mid-afternoon in February 1970 for a set-piece televised debate at the Oxford Union in my anorak, jacket and polo shirt, standing waiting on the station platform was the preposterous sight of the Union's secretary in a dinner jacket and bow tie. And then at the end of a heated and excellent debate, our opponents fiddled the vote, requiring a recount the next day when it transpired we had won, the media meanwhile delightedly reporting that we had lost. (Thank God I hadn't chosen Oxford for my degree.)

At Durham University – a sort of aspiring Oxford for upper-class debutantes where the Union Society officers were even more pretentious – my informal dress caused minor pandemonium. I arrived in the early evening after several days touring around the North East speaking at political meetings dressed in standard anorak and polo shirt, grip bag in hand. 'We will show you to your room, Sir,' a Jeeves-like older man said, taking an inscrutable look at me. 'Thank you,' I replied, surprised at having a room at all. A little weary, I lay down on my back for a doze. Half an hour later there was a knock on the door and Jeeves squinted in. 'Oh, you are not changed yet, I'll be back in a few minutes.' Before I could respond he closed the door and scurried away. It was getting towards the time of the debate, in which I was due to lead the case for stopping apartheid sports tours.

Eventually he came back, looking aghast. 'You *still* haven't changed?'

'No, *these* are the only clothes I have!' It was clear I was inadvertently break-ing all the rules. But the debate was about to start and I was the star guest, albeit the sole speaker not in the dinner jacket nobody had warned me about. If I *had* been, at least the organisers would have had the choice of uninviting me. The debate went well with a majority of the audience clearly on my side, but the *pièce de résistance* of the whole absurd occasion was a silver service dinner afterwards, clearly the evening's highlight for the Union officers, as they got out cigars. To my bewilderment a silver mechanism on wheels came chuntering around the long table towards me, passing by each dinner guest in turn. What on earth *was* it? Apparently, I was being offered a glass of port. So this was how the upper classes were trained.

By April, the campaign's momentum was still accelerating. The Prime Minister, Harold Wilson, said that people 'should feel free to demonstrate against the tour', though he specifically criticised our plans for disruptive protests. The British Council of Churches also called for peaceful demonstra-tions. The Queen announced that neither she nor any member of the Royal family would make the traditional visit to the Lord's test match, and the South Africans would not receive the traditional invitation to Buckingham Palace. Then, with the tour just six weeks away, the Supreme Council for Sport in Africa announced that thirteen African countries would definitely boycott the Commonwealth Games if the tour went ahead; Asian and Caribbean coun-tries soon followed, raising the prospect of a whites-only Games in Edinburgh running alongside a whites-only cricket tour. Sparked off by local direct action, the campaign had provoked an international diplomatic and political furore.

The Anti-Apartheid Movement played a crucial organisational role, both as a participant in STST and in its own right. Its indefatigable and formidable executive secretary, Ethel de Keyser, worked herself into the ground. An AAM poster caught the public's imagination and was widely published in the press. Under the caption 'If you could see their national sport you might be less keen to see their cricket', it showed a policeman beating defenceless blacks in Cato Manor township outside Durban.

Plans went ahead to blockade the team in at Heathrow Airport. Thousands of tickets were being bought up by local groups (the games had been made all-ticket). Secret plans were being executed by the tightly run STST Special Action Group, which privately consulted me throughout. Its members had ingeniously discovered the existence of an old underground train tunnel running right underneath Lord's cricket ground with a disused but still functional air shaft which could facilitate a dramatic entry – potentially by hundreds of activists.

But, although much activity was nationally coordinated by STST, local groups operated quite independently. This was partly by design – to avoid acting like a conspiracy – and partly a product of the way the movement had evolved. There was also a considerable degree of individualistic autonomy in the campaign. People were quite literally doing their own thing. I opened our front door one day to be faced by two bright-eyed if somewhat zany youths who were model aeroplane buffs. They excitedly told me of their plans to buzz the pitch during play from their aunt's flat, which overlooked Lord's. There were reports from all over the country of other novel protest methods. Some individuals were breeding armies of locusts which they planned to let free on the turf. Others acquired small mirrors with which they intended to blind the batsmen. Newspapers had a field day reporting a series of such stories, and I was blamed for just about everything, regardless of whether or not I had any prior knowledge or involvement.

By now I was very much at the eye of a huge political storm, learning all the time while leading, and having to play daily media demands by instinct, only too aware that saying the wrong thing could be calamitous but equally resolved to stick to our chosen course, come what may. I was increasingly the target of hate mail and threats to my safety or life – something familiar to our family from our Pretoria days where the danger had been very real by comparison with what here seemed like the rantings of assorted nutters. But if the pressure on me individually was huge, at least I had the security of my close family and rock-solid loyalty of the activists around me and the movement beyond for which I had become the figurehead.

The combination of sport, race and direct action had a toxic potency for many on the right in Middle England. Amongst some a cricket tour to England stopped by 'radical agitators' seemed equivalent to the loss of empire, as revealed in letters sent by members to the Marylebone Cricket Club (MCC).[*] One labelled me and STST as a 'complete negation of all this country stands for', another saw the MCC in standing against us as 'the last bastion of what remains of the British way of life'. I was denounced as a 'dangerous anarchist and communist', the writer – blissfully unaware that the two ideologies were at loggerheads – noting that if they can 'smash this tour they will turn to other things'. Another described the STST campaign as 'persistent mob pressure and an attempt at neo-communist rule'.

---

[*] Thanks to Theo Barclay, 'A Search for Stability? Upper Middle Class Attitudes to Immigration and Race Relations Between 1968 and 1970, Seen through Public Reaction to the Stop the Seventy Tour Campaign' (BA Hons Dissertation, Brasenose College, Oxford, 2010).

Despite the much greater storm around *them*, the cricket establishment held firm. In mid-May, with the first match just three weeks away, they were invited to meet the Home Secretary. James Callaghan was by now very concerned at the likely threat to public order, and the government was also deeply embarrassed by the impending collapse of the Commonwealth Games. After an unfruitful exchange in which he urged cancellation, Callaghan said he 'detected a lurking belief that they are a lonely band of heroes standing out against the darkening tide of lawlessness'. Certainly, the Cricket Council's members reflected old-worldly, far-right political beliefs. And both they and our other critics were now making their stand on defending the rule of law against our alleged illegality. But immediately after the meeting there came a decisive and unexpected boost to anti-apartheid forces. SAN-ROC's patient work had paid off and South Africa was finally expelled from the Olympics.

The following week events scrambled to a climax. It became clear that the Prime Minister was about to call a general election, and there was a notable shift in opinion. E. W. Swanton, cricket correspondent of the conservative *Daily Telegraph*, and Ted Dexter, the former England captain and one-time Conservative Party parliamentary candidate, both urged cancellation. The Cricket Council met in emergency session, with widespread media predictions the tour would be off. Though hopeful, I was sceptical that they would cave in, something nagging away at me to this effect. And, indeed, the Council meeting ended still defiant – though perversely effectively conceding our case for the very first time by announcing a new policy that there would be no future tours until South African teams were selected on a multi-racial basis. It was as if they hoped this switch would sugar the pill of their stubborn refusal to be 'bullied' as many of their diehards saw it.

But still the drama was not over. The Home Secretary asked to see them again and now formally requested cancellation. Another hurried meeting was arranged at Lord's and, on this occasion, the decision was indeed final. At long last, the tour was off, cricket's leaders bitterly complaining they had no option but to accede to what they interpreted as a government instruction – in reality a face-saving excuse for their humiliation. From their sordid manoeuvrings over Basil D'Oliveira to their astonishing decision to proceed with the 1970 invitation to the South Africans, even after their own tour there had been stopped by the apartheid government, they seemed to me impervious to the modern world.

My own delight was tempered by intense relief that what would certainly have become an ugly series of skirmishes had thankfully been avoided. In the weeks leading up to the cancellation I had become increasingly worried about the dangers of violence. For me the direct action strategy was designed to succeed because of the *threat* it posed. Although I would certainly have carried it through, I would have taken no pleasure in doing so. Others involved, however, saw things differently and some were even a little disappointed that the impending confrontation had been averted, either because they believed it would have benefited their own political factions or because the sudden absence of a campaign to execute had left a rather large gap in all our lives.

Some wanted STST to continue in an unspecified form with its own distinctive and now highly successful brand of direct action. But I was very clear that it could and should not. Of course lessons must be learnt from its tactics and applied elsewhere. But it had been set up for a very specific purpose and that purpose had been fully achieved. To continue would inevitably contaminate that achievement and I believed that the same level of success was not sustainable. In any case there was an established organisation, the Anti-Apartheid Movement, into which energy should be channelled. Its membership had more than doubled during the campaign (ironic, since, very early on, some of its leaders – anxious that they could not control STST – had been to see me, urging dissolution of the organisation and its incorporation into AAM, which I politely but firmly rebuffed). Leadership, I had learnt, requires leading and taking decisions which might not be universally popular within the ranks, like my announcement the very same evening that we stopped the tour that we would wind up STST and encourage all our supporters to join the AAM.

'Hain stopped play' was the cricketing headline in a sympathetic feature in the *Guardian* newspaper. But the right-wing press trumpeted darkly about 'anarchy', 'lawlessness' and the threat to England's civilisation. A campaign whose nine-month gestation was in the minds of a few people had now won with mass support. STST had emerged as one of the very few British protest groups to have completely achieved its objectives.

For the first time in ten long bitter years since Sharpeville, black South Africans and whites involved in the resistance had something to cheer about. For them, it was a clarion call in the wilderness, a flash of light in the dark. There were people abroad prepared to risk a great deal in standing up for their rights. From the Cape Reserve in our home town of Pretoria came a simple but moving cable from our activist friends Poen Ah Dong, Alban Thumbran and Aubrey Apples, who had waved us goodbye in 1966: 'And so say all of us.' (To have said anything more explicit would have invited police attention.) Messages of congratulation poured in. There were ecstatic celebrations as disbelieving supporters absorbed the full extent of their momentous achievement.

And the link to the wider anti-apartheid campaign could not have been made clearer than by Moses Garoeb, a leading freedom fighter in the South West African People's Organisation (SWAPO), when he told me that STST had been an 'inspiration' to SWAPO cadres in the African bush as they heard the news on their radios. I replied that it was the dedication and sacrifices of people like them which inspired us to campaign even more vigorously.

It had always been the contention of apologists for sports links that maintaining contact provided a channel for encouraging whites to see how the rest of the world lived and so breed more liberal attitudes. This was pure fantasy, for during all the decades of so-called 'bridge building', apartheid in sport had actually become more entrenched, and I was always convinced that an effective sports boycott would deliver a decisive blow. And so this proved. Hardly had the cricket tour been stopped than top South African cricketers, one after the other, tumbled out to condemn apartheid in sport. Never before had they spoken out like this. Peter Pollock, the fast bowler who had been due to tour and who hadn't previously opposed apartheid in sport, was forthright. A week after the cancellation he told the Johannesburg *Sunday Times*: 'Sports isolation stares South Africa in the face, and to creep back into the laager is no answer. Sportsmen who genuinely feel there should be multi-racial sport should say so.'

‡

Nine months before I had been virtually unknown outside anti-apartheid and Young Liberal circles. Now I was a national public figure attracting both idolatry and infamy. Having appeared in television news and current affairs programmes, I was widely recognised when out and about, my privacy a thing of the past. Aware of adulation from supporters, I came to appreciate that this could be accompanied (sometimes simultaneously) by jealousy. All this attention was somewhat bemusing but simply came with the territory: a consequence of the leadership role into which I had been propelled. I remained in many other respects still the same person, quite conventional, solidly rooted in my family, hard working and happy. To some contemporaries my lifestyle was 'boring' because I was too busy to socialise much and shunned the media celebrity circuit. Fame was not something I had sought, although I quickly realised that it brought both opportunities and obligations to pursue the politics and the values to which I was fiercely committed.

Meanwhile, encouraged by STST's success, the Australian Campaign Against Racialism in Sport (CARIS) now focused upon the mid-1971 Springbok rugby tour to Australia and – in an uncanny repeat – a cricket tour due to start in October. I was invited to support the campaign and left for Sydney on a 31-hour flight after successfully sitting my first-year university exams. I had never flown such a long distance before, and enjoyed an unexpected visit to the cockpit after the captain had spotted my name and invited me up to join him for a fascinating few minutes. We were over Vietnam at the time and it seemed surreal imagining fighting still being waged in that torn and tortured land six miles down below me. This was my first experience of the modern air traveller traversing lands of conflict, poverty and despair, out of sight, out of mind, taking off from peace and security and landing back within it as if everything going on underneath was on another planet.

The plane circled down over Sydney early in the morning, with a fine view of its harbours and beaches. It was two days before the arrival of the Springboks on 24 June 1971 and, after meeting my expectant new comrades, including my opposite number, Peter MacGregor, I went straight into a press conference. For the next two weeks there was a vigorous schedule of media appearances, speaking engagements and private tactical briefings – with no intervals for coping with jet lag. In Brisbane I was taken to the field where the match was due to be played. It was completely open, with no visible defences, and there, in a television interview which was repeated for days afterwards, I said that it 'would be a piece of cake' to stop the match. It was later switched to a more secure venue – a first victory for the campaign.

The Springboks began in conservative Perth but the campaign was able to achieve something which had eluded us in Britain when trade unions promised to boycott the servicing of planes, and both the major domestic airlines decided they would not carry them. So the team had to fly 1,700 tiring miles to Adelaide cramped into a series of chartered light aircraft, the seven-hour flight three times longer than the regular airline. I flew in on a scheduled flight from Brisbane to speak at a huge meeting in the Central Methodist Church, finding the excellent response I received reminiscent of the days of STST. My message was clear: just as in Britain the cricket tour would be stopped and the rugby one so badly disrupted that it would be the last. Over 1,000 demonstrators besieged the Adelaide match. There were interruptions to play and I watched from outside as smoke flares were let off under the floodlights. The police and stewards lashed out indiscriminately, even arresting the mild-mannered Australia correspondent of *The Times*, an English gent to a tee.[*]

The campaign gathered pace and at student union meetings I described some of the tactics STST had deployed and encouraged activists to follow suit, delighting them with amusing tales of our ingenuity and of sports apartheid's incongruity. The environment and radical spirit was very similar to Britain eighteen months earlier, except that the distances between venues were so

---

[*] See his book on the campaign: Stuart Harris, *Political Football* (Melbourne, Gold Star Publications, 1972).

huge it was not feasible to bus in large numbers of demonstrators as we had done. Another difference, readily apparent, was the lower threshold at which violence was triggered, usually by the police.

In Melbourne armed guards with dogs patrolled the venue. At a rally attended by 5,000, I was greeted enthusiastically, saying that the campaign was 'well on the way to emulating the success that we achieved in Britain'. I went on: 'We are seeing a concentration camp-type atmosphere building up and I welcome that. It strips this tour of all its pretensions.' The demonstrators then set off to the ground, where 650 policemen with truncheons and horses started to wade into the march. The *Sydney Morning Herald* reported the next day: 'Many Victorian policemen took the law into their own hands.'

The resulting violence was sickening. Even after the match, as we walked peacefully away, police on horseback charged us and we fled terrified in all directions – it was to prove my most frightening experience in decades of demonstrating. It had been a tense day in another respect. That morning calls had been made to the media purportedly from a right-wing assassin threatening to shoot me, so I was constantly peering around, knowing all too well, however, that there would be no way of preventing such an attempt – if indeed it was for real, rather than the hoax I suspected but could not ignore.

By the time I left after two weeks, which included visits to Canberra and Sydney, the campaign was in full swing. I had enjoyed again both the company of so many committed people and enthusing young activists. One evening in Sydney, briefing a private gathering on some of the more covert of STST's methods, an attractive blonde student, Verity Burgmann, caught my eye. Her charismatic sister Meredith was a veteran Vietnam demonstrator, and in a few snatched minutes as we drove between destinations Verity and I were drawn to each other. We promised to keep in touch by letter, but it wasn't until she visited a relative in London months later that we became close, and she subsequently took the big step of arranging to study at the London School of Economics. We had much in common – our beliefs, our commitments, our deep interest in radical politics.

Back in Australia, meanwhile, on 8 September 1970, one month after the battered Springboks had departed, the legendary cricketer Sir Donald Bradman, announced as chairman of the Australian Cricket Board of Control that, 'with great regret', the cricket tour had been cancelled. The Australian campaigners were jubilant – job done, like STST.

It was another decisive blow against apartheid sport. Within months I was invited to give evidence to the United Nations Special Committee Against Apartheid. It was my first visit to New York, flying quickly in and out with not a chance to see the sights, apart from a tour of the UN building, including the

Security Council chamber which meant such a lot to me. Not for the first time, and to my regret decades later, I failed to take the opportunity to spend some leisure time there: politics came first and there was more work to do back home.

‡

If we had succeeded with cricket, rugby remained a more difficult nut to crack. We had been able to stop tours coming from abroad, but it was very difficult to prevent teams visiting South Africa and, despite opposition, England went ahead with their tour in 1972. By this time we had formed the Stop All Racist Tours campaign (SART) of which I was chair. A group of demonstrators disrupted the England training session in Twickenham. We also arranged for the team coach to be hemmed in at their hotel in Richmond prior to their departure for Heathrow Airport. Just before the coach was due to leave, we called the fire brigade, which descended on the hotel in force. Additionally we requested several skips to be brought, ostensibly to take away rubbish, but in fact to block the team's departure.

We were unable to stop this tour and the one by the British Lions in 1974. Prior to the latter's departure I was one of a dozen people who broke through security and staged a rooftop occupation of the Rugby Union's offices at Twickenham. However, the Labour Foreign Minister, Joan Lestor, a stalwart of the Anti-Apartheid Movement, instructed the British Embassy to withdraw the usual courtesy facilities for a visiting national side from the Lions. In a futile last-minute attempt we demonstrated at the Lions' London hotel and occupied its reception area, forcing the hotel management to persuade the captain, Willie John McBride, to meet me. A giant of a man from Northern Ireland, it quickly became clear there was no earthly chance of a meeting of minds. In a polite enough exchange we just talked past each other: the Lions were going, regardless, imperiously indifferent to their complicity in sports apartheid. Out there they played whites-only teams, and returned in triumph unbeaten, their dazzling play with legendary Welsh quarter backs sweeping all aside. Afterwards much was made of the support they had from black and Coloured fans, but the latter always backed anybody against the hated white Springboks; more significant was the realisation amongst South Africa's white rugby fraternity that their now much more limited scope for international competition was damaging their own previous omnipotence. The Lions returned to face a demonstration at a Heathrow Airport hotel reception. My young sister Sally managed to throw a flour bomb which burst on the shoulder of the former Conservative Prime Minister Edward Heath, who was there to greet the team. Hypocritically, I felt, the Labour Sports Minister, Denis

Howell, who had opposed the tour, also attended, ostensibly to welcome their sporting success.

By now barred from Britain, the Springboks were harried wherever they managed to go abroad. In 1973 we had also occupied the forecourt of a London hotel in which the visiting New Zealand rugby team were staying, in a protest against the Springbok tour scheduled for New Zealand later in the year. That tour saw an epic series of battles spearheaded by my New Zealand opposite number, Trevor Richards, who inspired mass opposition, the protests bitterly dividing the society, including within families. In 1974 I was asked to visit France for several days to join the campaign there against a visiting South African rugby side. I spoke no French and translators helped me at meetings and with the media. Although the protests were relatively muted – the otherwise strong French left seemingly bemused by the mixture of politics and rugby – it was an important first in taking the battle into France where the campaign against apartheid was much weaker, and the organisers felt my presence had raised the profile of the campaign.

‡

In 1970, the *Financial Times* had reported on South Africa shortly after the stopping of the cricket tour: 'Is it purely coincidental that the stepping up of the anti-apartheid campaign in Britain and America during the past year or so has been accompanied by a sharp falling off in the inflow of capital into the country? Those who follow these matters are convinced it is not.'

After our success, those centrally involved in STST launched the Action Committee Against Racialism in July 1970, specifically to apply direct action tactics elsewhere. It was a small activist group and we discovered that a South African trade centre was scheduled to open in central London's St Martin's Lane, financed by the South African government, whereupon I wrote to the estate agents warning that the premises would become the target 'for an intensive campaign of demonstrations'. The threat received extensive publicity and we copied the letter to surrounding shops and offices, provoking paranoia through the property complex in which it was to be located. We followed this up with a noisy picket. Shortly afterwards the front doors of the complex were gummed up with solidifying agent. Then a few days later smoke flares were let off in the lifts during the lunch hour; amidst the frenzy that there might be a fire, the fire brigade was called. On each occasion the press were alerted and the estate agents informed. A week later the firm acting for the organisers of the trade centre announced that they had shelved plans to take a showroom in London.

I also joined Anti-Apartheid Movement protests against Barclays Bank, which had an extensive South African subsidiary and maintained the discriminatory staff wages and customer arrangements characteristic of apartheid; it bankrolled the South African economy, so underpinning apartheid. A 'Boycott Barclays' campaign spread across Britain, and eventually the bank took the extraordinary step of pulling out of South Africa entirely, signifying another major success for the Anti-Apartheid Movement.

Meanwhile as part of a consumer boycott, I helped orchestrate militant tactics in high-street supermarkets. Protesters plastered black and white stickers on South African goods with a skull and crossbones marked 'DANGER – PRODUCT OF APARTHEID'. We also filled carriers and trolleys with all the South African produce we could find, had the bill rung up at the till and then suddenly 'discovered' that the contents were all South African and refused to pay, leaving cashiers and managers with angry customers queuing up in frustration as the resulting chaos was sorted out. The boycott movement was by now spreading internationally and in 1974 I spoke at a major international conference in Holland focused on South African produce. It was organised by the Dutch anti-apartheid movement, which had been running a successful boycott of South Africa's Outspan oranges.

Meanwhile Verity and I had gone our separate ways, and I had begun going out with Pat Western, a friend of my sister Jo-anne. In early February 1975, washing my old Volkswagen Beetle, I pondered our future. Probably time to get married, I thought. I looked at my diary, as usual full up with political commitments stretching way ahead, discovering the only Saturday free was the very next one. Pat, taken aback to be phoned at her work, was fortunately free and agreeable too. Surprising relatives who wrongly suspected she was pregnant, we were married at a hastily arranged ceremony at Wandsworth Register Office on 8 February – jostling press photographers determined to snap us with me, tieless in my leather jacket, bang in front of the register office door labelled No. 10.

‡

With political resistance suppressed, and the sports boycott now near universal, by the mid 1970s sport became the territory inside South Africa in which the ideological battle over apartheid was fought. The ANC encouraged black sports organisations under the South African Council for Sport (SACOS) to become part of the resistance. Meanwhile the authorities attempted to coopt certain black sportsmen and they were permitted to play against white teams in certain controlled circumstances. But these public-relations gestures did not alter the fundamental structure of sports apartheid: both legislatively and practically it remained intact from school to national level.

In parallel with the regime's new 'cooption strategy' internally, I was placed in the novel position of being courted by my opponents. Having anticipated that this might happen, I had developed a response which focused single-mindedly upon sport. We had won the original argument for a boycott on the basis that South African sport was organised on race, not on merit. To middle-ground opinion it could be presented as an argument about sport – which in turn legitimised political intervention in an area which would otherwise have been seen as taboo. If, through ending sports segregation, it could be shown progress was being made, I did not want us to be forced back upon the argument that we would not budge until the whole structure of apartheid was abolished, because that would have placed anti-apartheid forces in the position of having to justify singling out South Africa as against other countries with tyrannical regimes that did not poison their sport.

So, early in 1977 I had determined on a strategy of proposing changes in the law which might 'exempt' sport from apartheid. It might well be fanciful to imagine this actually occurring – how in practice could a black citizen be treated equally while engaged in sport, but then leave the stadium and resume a life still rigidly regulated by apartheid? But the argument neatly placed white South Africans once more on the defensive and was deliberately intended to do so. In this stance I had the full support of the SAN-ROC leaders Dennis Brutus and Chris de Broglio, who knew the sports world inside out. However, I was privately criticised in some anti-apartheid circles whose argument was that you could not have 'normal sport in an abnormal society'. Although agreeing entirely with this as a *principle*, I was convinced it was not a *political strategy* for anti-apartheid forces to retain the near-universal sports boycott we had achieved through direct action protests and successful international lobbying, and I managed to win a carefully negotiated policy position after a difficult debate at an annual meeting of the Anti-Apartheid Movement. I also held discussions with the Labour Minister of Sport, Denis Howell, and on 8 February 1977 drafted some notes for his department.

‡

Because the number was not publicly listed, my home phone very rarely rang with an unfamiliar call, and that evening in spring 1977 was a curiosity.

'Craven, South Africa,' the guttural voice said resolutely. 'I would like to talk. Will you meet me?' He almost choked on the request as if hating himself for having to ask a favour at all.

South Africa's 'Mr Rugby', Danie Craven, had been a bitter opponent during the Stop The Seventy Tour campaign. Chief spokesman for the Springboks, he had regularly denounced me and our rugby tour demonstrations, often in the most lurid terms. So, for him to call personally was astounding to say the least.

Was this some kind of manipulative stunt, I immediately wondered? The South African propaganda machine had been busily courting world opinion with all manner of ruses. On the other hand, in newspaper interviews with white South African journalists, I had been deliberately indicating that, if *sports apartheid* was abolished, there might be a basis for the country's *sports isolation* to end. Perhaps Craven was responding to these?

I was warily courteous. What was the purpose? Would a meeting be strictly private? Having partly satisfied myself on these points, I agreed. Others in my position might well not have done so – it was treating with the enemy after all – but I felt instinctively it was the right thing to do. However, his suggestion of a venue next to the South African Embassy was not acceptable – only if he came to the small ground floor flat in Putney which my wife Pat and I had purchased.

In the early evening the following day, he arrived in a taxi and apprehensively knocked at our front door. Watching through our front window, I spotted a companion of his peering out of the taxi as it sped off. I was apprehensive too, satisfying myself he was alone with no heavies or media in tow before opening the door.

He came in distrustfully, brusquely declining the offer of tea or coffee, seemingly unsure whether to be aggressive or to return my respectful politeness. Gradually he thawed. Was it correct, as he had heard, that I wasn't really 'anti-rugby' or 'anti-sport'?

Yes, I replied – indeed I was a bit of a sports nut, had played lots of cricket, football and even some rugby in Pretoria as a schoolboy. I had never been 'anti-South African sport' but 'anti-apartheid sport'. Why had I not been allowed by law to play with or against black boys in the school or club teams of my youth?

We circled around each other, Craven part bristling, part reasonable, appealing to me that youngsters he was renowned for grooming into great players were being thwarted by the absence of international competition to benchmark themselves against as Springboks had always done so successfully before the boycott. So I suggested that we left 'politics' to one side and talked about changes that would be required in the way sport was played and organised in South Africa to warrant lifting the boycott. He warmed to that. Surely Craven would agree with me that the aim would be to make sport truly non-racial – that is, free of all apartheid restrictions – even if these remained in other spheres of life? It turned the tables neatly on his still simmering suspicion that I remained 'anti-rugby'. He agreed, and said that he wanted to move faster but the government was blocking the way.

I responded by producing the list of reforms I had been formulating. These included fully integrated club and school sport and a multi-million programme immediately to improve black sports facilities and opportunities. He did not demur. There also had to be changes in a variety of laws which affected sport. These included suspension of the old Pass Laws which meant sportsmen or women had to have prior permission to play at 'away' venues outside the municipal areas to which their pass confined them.

There were a dozen or so such pieces of apartheid legislation directly affecting the conduct and organisation of sport just as they determined every other aspect of society. However improbable it might be to conceive of sport as some kind of non-apartheid oasis within the country, I knew full well that for Craven it was highly significant: for these purposes, I was not demanding the entire abolition of the apartheid edifice, merely that sport was exempt from it. In return the boycotts could be lifted and Craven could get his beloved Springboks on the world stage again. I also told him he should talk to the ANC and black sports groups inside the country, for their consent and participation was crucial, not mine. If they still said 'no' to lifting the boycott, then that was that. (My whole strategy was to force whites like Craven to treat with the people they were oppressing.)

Craven took my list of reforms away with him. We had got on increasingly well as our talk proceeded from the initial stiffness. Underneath his gruff Afrikaner assertiveness was a traditional, well-mannered gentleman. I rather liked him and sensed the feeling was mutual. He even presented me with a Springbok team tie which I placed surreptitiously at the bottom of a drawer: the gift remained a secret, could even have been misinterpreted as a sign of betrayal, so deep were hostilities at the time. We both respected the confidentiality of the meeting, old enemies, old ogres, finding some common cause perhaps? Although I wasn't under any illusions, I was convinced that, at some point, politics would have to take over from protest, and the meeting was a highly significant signal that white sports leaders were beginning to recognise that they had to change and change fundamentally or their desperation to return to world sport would never be fulfilled.

‡

Then on 9 August 1977, the former South African Test cricket captain Ali Bacher, who had been due to lead the cancelled 1970 tour to Britain, also beat a path to my door. Acting as an emissary for the white South African Cricket Association, he aggressively sought to persuade me that things were changing for the better and we should call off the boycott. I did not agree, and our exchanges were acrimonious compared with the down-to-earth honesty and warmth of Dr Craven. It confirmed what my father had always told me: Afrikaners rather than English-speaking whites would ultimately be the ones to be won over when a settlement with the black majority finally occurred.

Meanwhile, the then editor of the liberal *Daily Dispatch*, Donald Woods, had arrived in London acting as go-between for further discussion. Despite his anti-apartheid inclinations and his growing reputation as an opponent of the system, Donald had been extremely hostile to the STST campaign seven years before. He had been used in television interviews (as was another, even more prominent, liberal South African, Helen Suzman) to criticise our campaign and especially its direct action strategy; like most white South Africans, he could not stomach attacks on their sport and accused us of 'law breaking'. However, he was becoming progressively radicalised, especially through his friendship with the black consciousness leader Steve Biko.

As a daily newspaper editor, Donald Woods had extensive contacts with Cabinet Ministers and had been asked by Piet Koornhof, then Sports Minister, to find out as discreetly as possible whether I, together with Chris de Broglio and Dennis Brutus, might be prepared to negotiate an end to the sports boycott in return for the dismantling of apartheid in sport. Koornhof was taking a considerable risk: if news of the initiative leaked, it could be used against him by his more conservative opponents in the National Party who would be horrified at the thought of talking to the likes of us.

We were initially suspicious. Why was Donald carrying messages from the government we were seeking to destroy? But, he assured us, there was nothing to lose by testing Koornhof's sincerity and his ability to deliver. In return we insisted that, while we might present a set of proposals, progress would depend upon Koornhof negotiating internally with SACOS leaders. An agreement could not be made unilaterally by international anti-apartheid leaders. Indeed we had no authority from our movements for doing so. At the same time, I was clear that we had to keep up the momentum – to push out a boat of proposals and see where it sailed.

So on 22 June 1977 I drew up a confidential memorandum agreed with Chris and Dennis for a 'Proposed South African Sports Summit'. As conditions for our attendance at such a summit, we insisted that: passport restrictions, bannings and harassment of non-racial sports officials must end; the government should declare an official moratorium on all sports tours for two years while the sports system was reorganised; a non-racial sports policy must be implemented including the full integration of club and school sport, repealing of all racist legislation in so far as it affected sport, merging separate sports groups into single democratic organisations, and having non-racial overseas

touring sides. If these conditions were agreed in advance and in full, our statement concluded, 'we would be prepared to accept an invitation from SACOS
to attend a formal meeting. If implemented we would be prepared publicly to
recommend dropping the boycotts and demonstrations, to take effect at the
end of the moratorium period, subject to satisfactory progress having been
made in establishing a non-racial sports structure.'

Donald Woods later wrote: 'When I handed Dr Koornhof the letter from
Hain and the others he pondered it at length before looking up to say: "We can
meet these conditions. We can do a deal. There are certain aspects of it that will
be very difficult, but I am sure we can do it." Arrangements were discussed for
me to meet Koornhof for secret negotiations in Switzerland in August 1977. But
before flying back from South Africa to discuss this with me, Woods was phoned
by Koornhof and asked to meet the head of BOSS (South African Bureau for
State Security), General H. J. van den Bergh. 'HJ' warned that Koornhof was
going too far, too fast, and that *he* would like to meet me in Paris instead. But
Woods was by now becoming a target for the government that had asked him to
act as an interlocutor. He was subsequently banned and had to flee the country
following the murder in police custody of his friend Steve Biko. He decided
against putting this proposition to me and I only learnt about it some years later.*

However, I was quite content with the outcome. Though intrigued by
Koornhof's overtures, I hadn't expected anything to come of them. On the
one hand I was determined to formulate a reasoned response which could be
publicly defended and which put whites, desperate to regain world participation, under pressure. On the other hand, I was equally determined not to
compromise our position, especially since a major advance had only just been
secured at the summit meeting of Commonwealth country leaders in Scotland.
On 15 June 1977 they unanimously adopted the Gleneagles Agreement, under
which each government pledged for the first time to take every practical step
to discourage sports links with South Africa.

In the years that followed, as part of the lobbying operation then being
undertaken by white sports leaders and officials, various South African newspapers invited me to visit 'and to see for myself'. Although I knew perfectly well
what was going on inside the country, I did not want to be seen to be unreasonable. Again despite criticism from others in the Anti-Apartheid Movement,
and to the horror of my parents fearful for my safety, I said I would be happy
to visit, to see and to talk. But, on one condition: that a government Minister

*   For his account of this episode, see Donald Woods, *Asking for Trouble* (London, Victor
    Gollancz, 1980). The copy he gave me is inscribed: 'To Peter whom I met on the road
    to Damascus.'

wrote to me in advance withdrawing the ban on my entry first imposed in October 1969 and guaranteed my safety. Otherwise, how could I simply fly in? As I expected, the letter never came – to my immense relief.

But the seeds we had sown did eventually come to fruition. There was an extraordinary, but again secret, meeting set up in October 1988. In Harare, Zimbabwe, Danie Craven and his close colleagues met a top ANC delegation led by Thabo Mbeki. After two days of talks, they reached agreement that the ANC would press for the ban on the Springboks to be lifted if rugby was reorganised on a fully non-racial basis. Thabo Mbeki indicated a softening in the ANC's old position, stating that while the boycott should be maintained against racist institutions in South Africa, non-racial organisations had to be treated differently – a concession on the old position that apartheid in its entirety had to be abolished before sports links could be resumed. But with the ANC illegal, the meeting was highly controversial. Within eighteen years of stating at the time of our Stop The Tour campaign that he would never have a black in his side, Craven, as the leading sports figure in South Africa, had moved, first to talk to me in 1977, and finally in 1988 to do the previously unthinkable and treat with the ANC – still regarded by most whites as the 'terrorist' arch-enemy.

If Craven had been allowed to implement his agreement with the ANC, it would have been an historic step forward. But he was blocked, both within his own rugby board and by the government, which condemned him for 'plunging politics knee-deep into rugby' and spelt out 'the negative consequences of this kind of action for South Africa in its fight against terrorism'. South Africa's President, P. W. Botha, publicly condemned Craven, insisting that the ANC was wrapping itself in a cloak of piety 'in order to stab you in the back with a dagger'. Sport, Botha added, was part of the ANC's terrain of 'subtle subversion' and 'there are still politically blind moles in this country who fail to see this'.

Although many anti-apartheid activists were privately equally unhappy with the ANC's initiative, I was always supportive. As Nelson Mandela was to show in political negotiations leading to the overthrow of apartheid, the ANC was extremely sophisticated – sometimes too much so for activists schooled in the harsh and necessary arts of 'no compromise'. In reality our position had actually been strengthened by the ANC's demonstration of flexibility at Harare, for it revealed to the world that all the blockages were from white South Africa. But, from now onward, sport – instead of being an important means of confronting whites with the realisation that they had no alternative but to change – became a means of offering them a glimpse of a new post-apartheid South Africa in which their beloved sports tours could resume.

CHAPTER THREE

UNDER ATTACK

One Saturday morning in June 1972 a letter bomb suddenly appeared at the breakfast table at our family home in Putney. My usual pile of mail was being opened by my fourteen-year-old sister Sally, having some fun as she was helped by six-year-old David, son of John Harris. 'What's this?' Sally asked. I looked up, horrified to see an explosive device. Recessed into a thick sheet of balsa wood were hideous metal cylinders and terminals with wires protruding.

We sat transfixed, expecting it to explode, seconds seeming like ages.

Yet nothing happened. So, not really knowing if this was wise but anxious to get it clear of the home, I warily picked up the device and carried it gingerly outside, covering it with a dustbin lid. My mother called the police and ten minutes later a uniformed constable appeared and stood guard.

'What are you doing here?' the constable was asked by Beryl, a neighbour, as she put rubbish out, still in her gown and slippers.

'There's a bomb here, lady.'

She scampered terrified indoors.

Soon the Metropolitan Police's anti-terrorist bomb squad – on red alert at the time for IRA bombings in London – arrived, lights flashing and sirens blaring, swarming all over our house. They were friendly but formal, and I couldn't help noting that, for the very first time, I was being protected by the police and security services, not targeted by them. They made the device safe and took it away for investigation, asking us to maintain media silence; odd, I thought, normally terrorist threats are widely publicised.

Everything had happened so suddenly that the deadly implications were only now beginning to settle in – a sickening churn in my stomach; I had always accepted I was a target and had received many threats over the years, by letter, telephone, or in person. 'Green ink' letters came in almost weekly, most repellently racist and sexually twisted, threatening all manner of nasty ends to my life. Anonymous phone calls pledging I would be maimed or killed were also frequent. Just after the cricket tour was stopped, I was confronted on London's Hungerford Bridge by an angry, foul-mouthed racist who loosened the leash on his snarling dog, encouraging it to leap at me, fangs bared as I backed away quickly, relieved that he did not bite me. Another time, a fascist pulled a knife on me in a pub until he was hustled away by a friend, more burly and street-wise than me.

Special Branch officers later told me the bomb was powerful enough to have blown us all up and our terraced house as well. How apartheid supporters would have enjoyed, not just our elimination, but that of John Harris' small son David too. A small electrical fault – caused by the gap between the spring-loaded contacts having been wrongly adjusted – stood between us and oblivion. The envelope was postmarked Vienne, in France, and attached to the inside was a plastic disc which had been inserted between metal, spring-loaded contacts on the device. The disc remained behind when the package was removed from its envelope, closing the contacts and completing the circuit.

In practice there was very little that could be done to protect myself against the South Africans who had one of the world's most ruthless secret services with a grim record of eliminating both internal and external opponents. A number of anti-apartheid activists had been killed by letter bombs sent by BOSS, the South African Bureau for State Security, established in 1969. BOSS's 'Z-squad', set up explicitly to wage such terrorist attacks, took the final letter in the alphabet because it specialised in final solutions: assassination of apartheid's enemies.

One of the first victims was Dr Eduardo Mondlane, the President of the Mozambique liberation movement, FRELIMO, whom I had met in London in 1968 when organising the Medical Aid Fund for the liberation struggle. A likeable, highly educated and impressive figure, he was shockingly killed a year later in Tanzania in 1969 when a letter bomb exploded as he opened it on his desk. In 1982 a friend, the writer and ANC activist Ruth First, was similarly assassinated in her study at the Eduardo Mondlane University in Maputo, in the by now liberated Mozambique. Ruth – wife of the ANC's underground commander, Joe Slovo – had, while living in London, been a leading figure in the Anti-Apartheid Movement (AAM), and one of the most supportive of my leadership of STST.

The letter bombs were part of South Africa's response to the growing internationally-based resistance to apartheid. Liberation movements were on constant alert as their leaders became targets for assassination, their offices in foreign cities bombed and burgled, their leading figures shot, and their camps in the African bush attacked by fighter planes. Anti-apartheid demonstrators were also harassed and the AAM's London headquarters broken into. There was also a great deal of cooperation and outright collusion between South African security services and those of Western governments like Britain's, as was evident during the Stop The Seventy Tour campaign, in which there were several instances of *agents provocateurs* deliberately inciting violence, one of whom was followed back to the South African Embassy.

Before the 1969-70 rugby tour started, BOSS printed a leaflet signed 'The

Vigilantes' stating that 'counter protest cells' had been established all over the country. It appeared to come from loyalist rugby supporters and warned that any left-wing protesters who interrupted play would be 'carried off and walloped'. The leaflet was distributed to national newspapers and *The Times*, amongst others, reported it. During the rugby tour, BOSS distributed a press release from a hoax group, the 'Democratic Anti-Demo Organisation', which threatened to spray demonstrators with red paint and cover them with feathers. At the time I was very suspicious of the provenance of these initiatives, but it emerged that BOSS was responsible only in 1981, in a book by the former South African agent and journalist Gordon Winter.[*] For instance, a Mr Peter Toombs, whom I remember well, had launched an 'Anti-Demonstration Association' from his house in Oxfordshire in 1969 and, according to Winter, had previously completed paid assignments for the South Africans. His 'organisation' had no members on the ground, but he seemed well connected and was put up to oppose me in TV interviews.

And, within hours of the cricket tour being cancelled, Gordon Winter's BOSS handler in London asked him to prepare a detailed report on me and on each one of the activities undertaken by the STST campaign. Winter wrote that it was to be used to 'pin me to the wall'.

‡

Immediately after the 1970 tour was stopped, I faced a private prosecution for criminal conspiracy by an eccentric English barrister and parliamentary draughtsman, Francis Bennion. Private prosecutions, though virtually unknown, had apparently played a role over the centuries, and Bennion's initiative was soon backed by the right-wing Society for Individual Freedom (then with close links to British intelligence). Gordon Winter was instructed by BOSS to help and pass over his material on me. This he did, liaising initially with the pro-Pretoria Gerald Howarth, its general secretary (who entered Parliament in 1983 as a hard-right Conservative close to Margaret Thatcher).

In June 1971, the 'Hain Prosecution Fund' was launched to raise £20,000 for Bennion's venture. Howarth was its treasurer and Ross McWhirter its chairman. These two, together with Winter, respectively provided links with the hard right, MI5 and BOSS. Bennion flew to South Africa to raise money and BOSS circulated subscription lists through the South African civil service, in what was described in the South African media as the 'Pain for Hain' campaign – a title which also caught on amongst right-wing circles in Britain where donations

---

[*]   Gordon Winter, *Inside Boss* (London, Penguin, 1981).

were also solicited. Bennion let it be known that he had tried to persuade the Director of Public Prosecutions to take over the case – as the law could have allowed. But, even though the Attorney General, Sir Peter Rawlinson, when in opposition had called for me to be charged, now in government over a year later, he was no longer interested. The new Conservative administration may well have been happier for it to proceed privately, because legal precedent also enabled the DPP to take it over and then drop it.

At Heathrow Airport in June 1971, just as I was about to depart for the campaign against the Springbok rugby tour in Australia, two plain-clothes Metropolitan Police officers served me with a summons for criminal conspiracy. They were affably officious, even smirking: with an air of 'nothing really to do with us, guv, but we are pleased all the same'. They must have been monitoring my whereabouts because, although my campaign visit had been pre-publicised, details of my flight had not. The timing was transparent: to try to dissuade me from flying out. Although momentarily confused at what was happening, recalling how anti-apartheid friends in South Africa had often been stopped from flying abroad, I was not going to be intimidated. However, I had not really thought through the consequences, and so was relieved to be phoned when I returned by Larry Grant, legal officer of the National Council for Civil Liberties, who had read widespread media coverage of the conspiracy summons. He offered to represent me because the NCCL was concerned about the way conspiracy charges were being brought at the time to suppress political dissent.

The case became something of a *cause célèbre* and I was relieved when volunteers organised a 'Peter Hain Defence Fund' to assist with costs not covered by the legal aid to which I was entitled as a student. Mike Steele, the former Liberal Party press officer, now a parliamentary reporter, coordinated the fund and attracted a range of prominent people, including Liberal peer Lord Avebury, Labour MP Neil Kinnock and my supporter from STST days David Sheppard, now Bishop of Liverpool. Initially, the case seemed more of an irritating inconvenience, absorbing a great deal of time and energy which could have been much more productively spent on political activity. I also saw it as an attack on my fight against apartheid – a political trial, rather like other ones radical activists faced during this period of high protest and youth unrest. But by the time I was introduced to my lawyers, Michael Sherrard QC and Brian Capstick, I realised it was very serious indeed. At our first 'conference' in their legal chambers, they both stressed that the way the conspiracy law was framed at the time undoubtedly made me very vulnerable. Sherrard, leafing through a copy of my recently published book about the STST campaign, *Don't Play with Apartheid,* quietly explained it could be construed as an admission of guilt; it was soon evident my lawyers considered they had a hell of a battle on their hands to prevent me going to prison.

I had turned up for the conference as usual in casual though neat clothes, never before having entered the cloistered confines of the Temple, the traditional London citadel for the country's top barristers, which slopes down from the Strand to the Thames embankment. I was curious about how this part of the legal establishment operated. Their chambers were lined with bookshelves containing rows of formidable legal tomes amidst a bustling atmosphere of formality and aloofness. However, the two barristers became increasingly informal and friendly as time went on, closer to me in Sherrard's case than he had ever been to a client, he admitted.

Soon the case was up and running with 'committal proceedings' to determine whether the evidence justified a fully fledged trial: a week's hearing at Bow Street Magistrates' Court in October 1971. I decided to wear a jacket and borrowed a tie from my father so that I could less easily be typecast as the rebel. This was an opportunity for the stipendiary magistrate to test the prosecution case, my lawyers advising it was highly likely I would be committed for trial at the Old Bailey and that we should keep our powder dry and hold back on our defence. Their predictions proved accurate as a parade of witnesses appeared in the small court, my book triumphantly produced as the equivalent of the smoking gun with my fingerprints all over it.

Four counts of conspiracy were levelled against me, covering the sit-down at Bristol tennis court, the interruption of the Wilf Isaacs cricket match, disruption of the rugby tour and the stopping of the cricket tour. I was charged with conspiring with 'others unknown' – even though many were well known, or could at least have been easily identified. Laid at my door were literally hundreds of individual actions (one tally revealed over 900) across the entire United Kingdom (which for these purposes, strangely, included the Republic of Ireland because of the match played in Dublin). They included trespass, breaches of the peace, intimidation, violence against people and property, and the antique offence of 'watching and besetting' which had been directed at highway robbers and vagrants: nobody could explain to me how or why it was being applied to stopping sports matches in the late twentieth century.

Although some of these individual 'particulars' were not criminal offences, when prefixed with 'conspiracy', they were transformed into crimes. I found myself in an *Alice in Wonderland* world where words were simply reinterpreted to suit the purposes of the prosecutors. The law on conspiracy, I quickly learnt, was ancient in origin, dating from 1304, and over the years judges had used their discretion with enthusiasm to enlarge its scope.* For example, in 1969–70 when I was running on sports pitches or helping organise others to do so, 'an agreement to commit a civil trespass' was then 'not indictable', as a leading legal textbook put it; that is to say, I could have been sued by the owners of sports grounds but not prosecuted. But in 1972 a judge declared in a case of student protesters who occupied the Sierra Leone Embassy that, because this involved a matter of 'substantial public interest', conspiracy to trespass was after all a criminal offence. Despite the fact that this declaration came some two years after our protests (though conveniently just before my trial), it was still applied to me retrospectively, defying one of the cardinal rules of British law. When the lawyers later disputed this on appeal, Lord Justice Roskill cheerily responded: 'Hain would not have done it had it not been a matter of public interest.' The judges might well have said in my case: 'We don't like what he was up to, interfering with our enjoyment of cricket, tennis and rugby, and we shall find a way of reinterpreting the law to stop him doing it.'

‡

The trial took place in August 1972 and lasted four weeks (fortunately during my university vacation). Because of renovation works at the Old Bailey, it was transferred to the Royal Courts of Justice, a venerable palace of winding corridors, spires and ermine. I had never before been to, let alone been a defendant in, such a grand court and was struck by the pompous procedure, and the unctuous bowing and scraping before the judge. As he entered, bewigged, robes flowing behind and held by an usher, an official would shout 'Silence! Be upstanding in court!' Once, with the judge midway to his seat, the official suddenly shouted for a second time: 'Stand up there in the back row!' We all turned around, curious, the judge cocking an eye. A little old lady plaintively called back: 'But I am just short!'

As the trial began, the courtroom became like a theatre with everyone playing to the audience: barristers in comic attire, long black robes and yellowing white wigs perched incongruously on their heads, always studiously courteous, but sometimes cuttingly sarcastic; judge sitting on high, remote and dominating; defendant sticking out like a sore thumb.

However, I did get what turned out to be my only concession during the entire trial from the judge, Bernard Gillis, who was transparently hostile:

---

* See Peter Hain, *Political Trials in Britain* (London, Allen Lane, 1984), chapter 7; Robert Hazell, *Conspiracy and Civil Liberties* (London, Bell, 1974); and Robert Spicer, *Conspiracy* (London, Lawrence and Wishart, 1981).

I was allowed as a 'person of good character' to sit in the well of the court alongside my lawyers, not in the dock. I was also allowed out on bail to leave with my family and friends during the lunch break and to go home overnight rather than be detained, relieved that the toiletries and change of clothes I had brought with me on the opening day proved unnecessary.

Due to the enormous list of activities and offences involved, it took seven minutes for the clerk of the court to read out the charges against me. Then the jury was sworn in: nine white men, one white woman, a black man and an Asian man. My lawyers had explained how they had several opportunities to challenge members of the jury as they took the stand in order to avoid a composition that might be packed against me for some reason (the prosecution had the same right). This was a hit-and-miss process and after one of the challenges, one woman turned around in disbelief saying: 'What's wrong with *me*?' Very aware my fate was in their hands, I stared intently, as each one took the oath and sat down: would they be fair, even sympathetic, or hostile? Outside the court we had studiously to avoid each other; on one occasion I found myself embarrassingly alone with one juryman as we stood pretending not to notice each other at either end of a row of urinals.

As expected, my book, *Don't Play with Apartheid*, proved to be the main evidence against me and the trial involved lengthy textual analysis and argument about it. The prosecution was opened by Owen Stable QC, a large portentous figure whose father, the retired judge Sir Wintringham Stable, had over two years before during the STST campaign written a letter to the *Daily Telegraph* calling for me to be prosecuted for conspiracy. This family 'heirloom' was now carried forward by his son who asserted: 'Hain and his friends tried to set themselves above the law.' He then embarked upon a day-and-a-half-long opening speech, referring to my 'fertile, trouble-making propensities' and insisting that the 'very future of English civilisation' was at stake.

Although in English law one is supposed to be innocent until proved guilty, the reverse applied in my case. This was because, as a judge in an earlier conspiracy trial had determined, 'conspiracy can be affected by a wink or a nod without a word being spoken'. Basically, if it could be shown (as it was pretty easy to do) that I had advocated direct action and played a leading role in the overall movement, then I was guilty of conspiracy – even if I had nothing to do with the individual acts carried out by those 'others unknown'. The only way I could prove I was *not* responsible was by calling some of those who *were*. For example, Peter Jordan was a school teacher who on 31 December 1969 ran on the pitch in Bristol and sprinkled tin tacks. Although I had nothing to do with it and strongly disapproved because of likely injuries to players, I was charged with conspiracy for this action too. Tracking Jordan down via his address in a newspaper report of his arrest at the time and calling him as a witness was the only way I could prove we had never met or communicated: and that, in his own words, 'it was a spontaneous act'.

The 1969–70 Springbok captain, Dawie de Villiers, was flown over from Johannesburg to give evidence, as was the private cricket tour sponsor, Wilf Isaacs. But they were only able to describe the events and could not directly implicate me. The prosecution's star witness was to be Gordon Winter, who later confessed he had all along been working for BOSS while London correspondent for the South African *Sunday Express*. (Other journalists refused to cooperate.) But, at the last minute, he 'turned'. Nearly ten years later he revealed he was instructed by BOSS to maintain his cover for a more important task – smearing the then Liberal leader, Jeremy Thorpe. We were expecting him to provide the most telling evidence, as he had been ubiquitous: appearing at all the demonstrations, and always popping up with notebook and camera to hand. So much so that we always suspected he might have BOSS links, especially as he had been implicated in some odd events while living for a while in South Africa.

But, when called for the prosecution, and to our utter astonishment, Winter switched under questioning into becoming a virtual defence witness, alleging that Bennion's team had asked him only for selective photographs showing the demonstrators in a bad light. Giving me a large wink from the witness box – which I found disconcerting and embarrassing – he ostentatiously pulled out a wad of photos showing police attacking demonstrators. (One officer was actually convicted in 1974 for planting a knife on a black demonstrator.) Winter also emphasised the defence's reliance upon my role as a spokesperson for the campaign, rather than as head conspirator and organiser of all the demonstrations, which the prosecution wanted to prove in order to find me guilty of conspiracy. His evidence was extremely astute; he argued that I had been 'elected by the press' as STST's chairman, which was partly true as I had never been formally appointed but simply assumed the role to general consent. We were startled at his unexpected helpfulness, which came without reason or explanation.

The court proceedings dragged on and on as Owen Stable tried – mostly unsuccessfully – to squeeze out any direct link to my involvement. His cast of witnesses were able only to describe what had happened at the various sports events, with no evidence to implicate me directly. Even Police Commander John Gerrard was fairly neutral about my participation, appearing almost a reluctant witness. I sat and took notes, occasionally suggesting a line of cross-examination to my lawyers. At lunch intervals we adjourned to the court canteen with my family, girlfriend Verity Burgmann and solicitor Larry Grant to discuss progress. Periodically after the day had concluded I trooped across the road to the Temple for a 'conference' with my lawyers.

Two weeks into the trial, it was crystal clear that the prosecution were relying almost exclusively on my book as a self-confession of guilt. Their last witness was Wilf Wooller, the right-wing, colourful sporting character from Wales who in media interviews had always denounced me in the most personal and extravagant terms; he was a joy to have as an opponent in BBC interviews as I never allowed myself to be provoked by his offensiveness and as a result the audience were invariably more sympathetic to me. His opening greeting when we met face to face for the first time during the STST campaign was: 'I hope to see you behind bars before the tour is out. And I really mean that.'

‡

However, the oppressive, catch-all, nature of the law on conspiracy meant it was almost impossible to prove my innocence and my lawyers recommended I should not go into the witness box, because I would in all probability have convicted myself. Although certainly not guilty of over ninety per cent of the particulars with which I was charged, I was nevertheless guilty of coordinating and organising action to disrupt and stop the various sports events and tours. Michael Sherrard, my experienced Queen's Counsel, considered Judge Bernard Gillis was after an exemplary prison sentence, and was especially concerned that he would be unable to answer a likely question from the judge as to what 'exactly was my defence in law'. It appeared there was no answer to this, in which case my defence would collapse instantly. However, I could not be asked that question because I was not a lawyer.

So, at a conference in chambers, and unusually with my worried parents specifically invited, it was finally decided that I should effectively 'sack' my barristers and defend myself. By conducting my own case I could appeal directly to the jury on a basis of justice not to convict me. Through making opening and closing speeches for the defence and through examining witnesses, I would be talking to the jury without being cross-examined in the witness box.

When the prosecution case concluded, Michael Sherrard announced to the court that 'on my client's instructions' my barrister team was withdrawing from the case. He cheerily added – expressly as a warning to the judge – 'we will be watching from the pavilion'. It was a dramatic moment and I couldn't help enjoying the fact that both Owen Stable and Judge Gillis were dumbfounded. As the experienced *Sunday Times* journalist Derek Humphry reported, the prosecution were 'flabbergasted, as their preparation for the case had been on the certainty that Hain would have to give sworn evidence'. Judge Gillis made clear his extreme unhappiness too and tried to persuade me to change my mind, especially about not giving evidence myself. Humphry added: 'Lawyers said later that Judge Gillis came close to using improper pressure on Hain by his constant attempts to persuade him not to defend himself and his attempts to alter Hain's decision not to go into the witness box.'

It was nevertheless a daunting task. I had no legal training. I was on my own facing the bewigged might of the prosecuting team, with only my solicitor, Larry Grant, and his assistants, Yvette Gibson and young trainee barrister (and years later famous QC) Geoffrey Robertson, sitting below me in the well of the court.

Geoffrey had quickly provided a very good draft for my opening statement on the defence case, though I had to curb his rolling prose and penchant for outrageous wit. Initially nervous when I rose to deliver it, I soon got into my stride, by now an experienced public speaker, though addressing the court was something else entirely. Soon, however, taking my own defence seemed the most natural and obvious thing to have done, because it made explicit what had previously only been implicit in the rarefied atmosphere of the court. Instead of the political issues at stake being submerged in legal niceties, they could now be teased out through my own advocacy. What's more, my destiny was in my own hands. I was fighting for my freedom. I also saw it as part of fighting the anti-apartheid cause, as my conviction could have opened the way for other South African-inspired prosecutions.

I told the court that I 'stood broadly by' what I had written in *Don't Play with Apartheid*, but insisted that it had not been written 'as a confession'. There had been no lawyer vetting every sentence in anticipation that it would be transformed from something written for readability into a legal document in which the interpretation of even the most casual sentence was liable to land me up in prison. Although it clearly exasperated Judge Gillis, my mention of 'prison' was pre-meditated in order to alert the jury, who we rather doubted would have wanted that outcome, however tempted they were to convict me.

I emphasised my total opposition to violent protest and insisted that I was honest and open about my role and objectives. I had never hidden my commitment to non-violent direct action – indeed had publicly proclaimed it. This was no sinister, covert conspiracy. STST was disarmingly open and candid. Furthermore, I pointed out: 'The campaign was a loose movement. It was not a rigid organisation. We had no generals. We had no apparatus through which to conspire.' It was quite ludicrous to charge me with nearly a thousand offences committed the length and breadth of the British Isles. Moreover it was oppressive to frame the conspiracy charge in such a way that, if I was found guilty of one particular offence, I was guilty of the lot. The jury's verdict would be given only on each of the four counts rather than their contents. This was iniquitous because, even if the jury found I was not guilty of hundreds of offences in each of the four conspiracy counts, there was no way of the judge knowing this when he passed sentence. They might decide I was guilty only of the trivial offences or those which were strictly non-violent, but the judge might assume guilt for the most violent offences. However, the iniquities of the then law on conspiracy meant that it was the *conspiracy* which mattered, rather than the particular actions or offences. And since there clearly was an organisation of which I was the leading public figure, this made my defence an uphill battle.

We had lined up a series of activists from across Britain to testify that they had organised local protests – from scattering tin tacks and digging up cricket pitches, to demonstrations outside the grounds – quite independently of me. But, as they confirmed that they had never met or talked to me, the prosecution objected and Judge Gillis became increasingly testy, until eventually I was stopped from putting questions. We had an increasingly tense battle as he repeatedly interrupted me, sometimes legitimately when my inexperience showed and I found myself putting a question to a witness incorrectly in such a way that it was 'leading' towards a particular answer. However, on other occasions Judge Gillis was simply aggressive, reflecting his deep unhappiness at the manner in which I was evidently – and observers thought persuasively – getting my case across to the jury. Once when I overstepped the mark and cheekily called Owen Stable 'My Learnt Friend' (the cosy parlance used between barristers in court), Gillis gave me a severe ticking off. 'Mr Hain, you are not Learnt. You must not say that again.' I apologised profusely, maintaining my posture of polite innocence which always seemed to irritate him even more; I wondered if he might have preferred me to be rude and raucous and therefore more of a caricature protestor.

The defence witness subject to the most hostile cross-examination was Ethel de Keyser, the indomitable executive secretary of the Anti-Apartheid Movement, herself a South African exile. She was asked 218 questions by the prosecution for hours spread over two days and, despite being on the receiving end of a QC skilled at tying up witnesses in knots, she never flinched. With almost uncanny precision she skipped deftly between his barbs, her composure never ruffled. She looked carefully at several STST campaign bulletins giving details of upcoming demonstrations, but said she had never seen one before, which meant they could not be presented as evidence before the jury. So effective was her performance that Stable was unable to make any use of her evidence in his final address to the jury.

But her appearance was notable for another reason. When Stable began asking her about the AAM's annual general meeting in October 1969, he seemed remarkably well informed, and it became apparent he was working from a transcript of a tape recording made at the meeting. This must have been done secretly because the AAM itself only recorded minutes of decisions and reports in the normal way. The prosecution must have felt they had a trump card because I had spoken of STST's direct action plans at that meeting. If Ethel de Keyser had been able to confirm Stable's account of the meeting, then the prosecution would have got admitted as evidence before the court whatever transcript Stable was reading from. This would have included my contribution and been their first direct evidence to support the conspiracy charges. But the AGM was three years before and she was frankly unable to recall points of detail about what had been said in over six hours of reports, discussion and debate, especially since she was not a stenographer but had been busily engaged behind the scenes, making sure the day went smoothly. Stable would not reveal in court the source of the tape recording. But we had good reason to believe it was the South African security services, suspected by the AAM of regularly infiltrating meetings and bugging and also breaking into its headquarters.

After Ethel's appearance, which was designed to show that the AAM operated autonomously from STST as a perfectly legal and open organisation, we took stock as a team and decided not to call a queue of other witnesses, some of them outside already waiting to give evidence and disappointed to be told they were no longer needed. (My mother and the Special Action Group coordinator Mike Craft deliberately sat there so that the prosecution thought they would be called when we had no intention of doing so.) With a hostile judge and the possibility when cross-examining defence witnesses of producing ricochet ammunition to the prosecution, the danger was of unintentionally serving up new evidence against me. Other than my book, the prosecution had very little evidence of my culpability – not of course that they needed very much under the conspiracy laws.

So we proceeded to the final stages of the defence case, the conclusion of which was deliberately planned. We had dispensed with any conventional etiquette between defence and prosecution lawyers in which they typically inform each other of developments; for me this was 'war'. The Labour MP Peter Jackson was stopped by the judge while he answered a question confirming his publicly stated intention to run onto cricket pitches – again, quite independently of me. Anticipating a similar reaction to the appearance of the imposing and be-robed Colin Winter, Bishop-in-Exile of Damaraland, South West Africa, I had prepared my response. His evidence was duly blocked before a battery of objections. I protested that legal procedures were being used to stop me from mounting my own defence properly and abruptly announced that in these circumstances, although we had plenty of witnesses ready to be called, I had no alternative but to close my case.

Judge Gillis was evidently disconcerted; he could see perfectly well how the jury would view me as a victim. So was Owen Stable, who – caught completely by surprise – immediately had to begin his closing statement. It was a delicious moment as he stumbled into his speech with the prosecutor's nightmare, a weekend break, intervening. Eventually, after an over-long and boring summary of the prosecution case, Stable, eyeing up the jury, finally concluded with a flourish: if I were let off, it would be 'an incitement to politically inspired law breaking' on such a massive scale – by for example homeless families occupying empty properties, Jews protesting at the Russian ballet, Palestinians disrupting performances by Israeli artists – that England's green and pleasant civilisation would be under dark and dangerous threat. All that stood in the path of these terrible and alien forces was the jury.

‡

Meanwhile over the weekend I had drafted my own closing speech, using Geoffrey Robertson's construction of the argument to underpin my own instincts. I too relied upon my book and tried to establish it was not the transparent confession the prosecution were pretending. Addressing the jury, I took two days, dissecting all the evidence to prove it was an open, honest campaign in which I had never sought to hide my role or objectives. This was a 'scapegoat prosecution' in a 'politically motivated' trial. I also reminded jurors of the honourable tradition of non-violent direct action – from Chartists and suffragettes demanding the vote in Britain, to Gandhi over independence for India and black Americans demanding civil rights in the USA. Every sentence, every word had to be judged carefully for I knew only too well how my freedom depended upon the jury.

Throughout my speech I was repeatedly interrupted by Judge Gillis – another departure from court convention, which allowed closing speeches to be delivered without challenge. It was not as if what I was saying was legally or procedurally wrong – my legal team ensured that. Judge Gillis simply seemed determined to derail me. His laborious, three-day, summing up was, legal observers believed, so biased as to constitute a basis for appeal should I be convicted.

After a weekend break, he sent the jury out at 10.35 a.m. on Monday 22 August 1972. I watched each one rise and be guided out by ushers, wondering who might support me and who might not. Conscious I could be sent to prison, I had packed a few clothes and toiletries. Although I had been on bail for the proceedings – able to go out at lunchtimes and home overnight – I was then taken down and confined to the cells below the court to await my fate. A canteen meal intervened as the hours dragged by, other inmates in for 'proper' crime intrigued about my presence. They seemed to think it was all rather a joke, which was hardly my attitude. Locked back in my cell, the tension grew. There was nothing to do but wait, my mind going around in circles. Larry Grant came in to pass the time and we discussed possible outcomes. What could be going on in the jury room? Then he left me on my own again. Time dragged even more.

Finally there was a jangle of keys and a warder said the court was reconvening, I assumed for the verdict. This time I was shown ominously into the dock. At 4.21 p.m., nearly six long hours after the twelve jurors had first retired, they all looked strained, the foreman nervously announcing that they could not agree on any of the four conspiracy counts. A frisson swept through the now packed courtroom, the press section now bulging, and my spirits rising a little at this unexpected development. But what would happen next?

Judge Gillis informed them solemnly that he would now accept a majority verdict 'if ten of you are in agreement' and I was taken back down. On my own again, the tension was now unbearable as yet another hour went by. Conflicting thoughts swirled around in my head, one minute hopeful, the next worried that a majority verdict might make a conviction easier.

Then at last I was taken upstairs. At 5.57 p.m. the jury trooped back in and in vain I studied each face intently, desperate for a clue. But they all looked glum. 'Have you now been able to reach a verdict?' Judge Gillis asked. The foreman rose. 'Yes,' he replied. I was guilty on the third count, the peaceful Davis Cup tennis court sit-down at Bristol – by far the least serious of the counts and the one where I was most culpable as charged.

But then came a dramatic twist. Pressed hard by the judge, the foreman stated that they could not agree on any of the remaining three counts. There were gasps of relief from spectators and smiles all round. I was overcome with both elation and vindication. The judge and prosecutors looked absolutely thunderous. As the *Sunday Times* reported: 'It was evident that Hain had succeeded in going over the heads of the prosecution and the judge and influencing the majority of the jury with his political philosophy.' I managed to confirm later that the two black jurors held out even against my conviction over the tennis court disruption. They were joined by others in refusing to convict on the much more serious and imprisonable rugby and cricket tour counts.

In the absence of a retrial (which the prosecution hastily confirmed they would not request), the judge then directed that 'verdicts of not guilty be recorded in Counts 1, 2 and 4'. He ticked me off, fined me £200 and I was free to go. So there it was: all the huge panoply and expense of a month-long trial and I now had a criminal conviction for sitting on a tennis court for a couple of minutes. I was elated, hugging my parents, Verity and my legal team, and delivering a defiant series of interviews to journalists, television crews and photographers jostling outside.

By this time, I was aged twenty-two and more drained than I had ever been before. The 'Pain for Hain' prosecution failed in its fundamental objective: to remove me from a leadership role in the anti-apartheid struggle. And the verdict was greeted with widespread disappointment in the white South African media. But it certainly succeeded in diverting my time and energies from the political arena to the courtroom. One way and another it took several months out of my active political life – a minor consolation perhaps for those who wanted revenge for the defeat inflicted on them in 1970.

Notwithstanding the verdict, however, England's green and pleasant civilisation remained intact.*

‡

The next visible attack on me came in the form of an expensive 3,000-word smearsheet, 'The Hidden Face of the Liberal Party'. It used various reports of my anti-apartheid activities taken viciously out of context. There were lurid photographs of the 1964 station bomb in Johannesburg for which our friend John Harris was hanged, implying that as a fourteen-year-old I was somehow responsible. Hundreds of thousands of copies were distributed in key parliamentary seats (including my home constituency of Putney) where the Liberals might have been expected to do well in the October 1974 election.

Contained in the broadsheets (one was also produced on the Labour Party, with a joint print run of about three million) were the by now familiar themes of the hard right: extremism in the Liberals and Labour and allegations of subservience to Moscow. They were published by the Foreign Affairs Publishing Company, which had close links with white South Africa, British intelligence and the CIA. In view of the huge production costs the broadsheets must have been financed by the South African intelligence services and indeed fitted an emerging pattern of disinformation, destabilisation and disruption.

---

*   For an account of the case see Derek Humphry (ed.), *The Cricket Conspiracy* (London, National Council for Civil Liberties, 1973).

During the 1970s, South Africa's Information Department moved well beyond the normal bounds of foreign information and propaganda, with the active blessing of the Prime Minister, John Vorster, who, over ten years before, had signed my parents' banning orders. In close cooperation with the head of BOSS, General H. J. van den Bergh, they mounted 138 secret projects, spending tens of millions of pounds. They sponsored front organisations, spread disinformation and secretly financed newspapers at home and abroad. Hundreds of people were victims of their nefarious activities.

One of their projects was the Committee for Fairness in Sport (CFS), established in 1973. Funded by wealthy white South African businessmen, and with money laundered through the Information Department, it undertook a programme of expensive newspaper advertisements featuring photographs of black and white athletes competing together in specially staged, one-off events (the underlying structure of sports apartheid remaining unchanged). There was also a well-oiled public relations drive, part of which included flying over a black South African journalist, Leslie Sehume, to confront anti-apartheid leaders and to call for support for British Lions and New Zealand rugby tours to South Africa.

Sehume had a much publicised half-hour debate with me on BBC television in April 1974 and his role symbolised a fresh tactic. The sports editor of the black Johannesburg newspaper *The World*, he was represented as the 'true' voice of the black majority. Previously I had faced only white opponents in media interviews and having a black opponent was designed to put me on the defensive: who did I think I was, an outsider dictating to a black South African like Sehume? He was plausible (even acknowledging that people like me had helped 'accelerate change'), received some favourable coverage in the right-wing press in Britain, and was feted by British apologists for apartheid. But he was a transparent 'Uncle Tom'. While in London for several weeks, he held forth from a luxurious apartment in London's Waldorf Hotel which was about as far apart from his readers in black townships at home as it was possible to get.

In a melodramatic and doubtless pre-meditated line he told me during our television debate: 'If you returned to South Africa now, you would be stoned out of the country – by blacks, not whites.' Powerful stuff and widely reported, but unfortunately for him not true. It was immediately denounced by his newspaper, *The World*. Although careful not to endorse our boycott strategy (for it remained illegal to advocate sanctions and boycotts), an editorial in the paper took 'the strongest exception to Mr Sehume's remarks' and in an accompanying page-long article reported the views of a range of black sports and civic leaders. Norman Middleton, president of the South African

Soccer Federation, spoke for most when he said Sehume was being 'used to exploit his own people' and added: 'Peter Hain would be welcomed to South Africa as a hero because he is a fighter for the blacks.' After a similarly controversial trip a year later to New Zealand, Sehume was sacked by *The World* and ended up officially on the payroll of the CFS and therefore indirectly an employee of the South African government.

‡

However, the attacks came not only from the apartheid state and their mainstream British allies. In 1971 I was the principal speaker at a Young Liberal meeting in a small Lincolnshire market town, Melton Mowbray. The small community hall was packed as I was welcomed and rose to address the gathering as I had become accustomed to doing.

But, hardly had my speech begun than there was a sudden commotion on the floor of the hall, pandemonium, screams and chairs flying as a menacing group of men terrified the audience who fled, some crying, out of the door. I was stuck at the front on the stage, recognising the ringleader, Colin Jordan of the British Movement (BM), an avowedly Nazi organisation, his wreckers milling around the floor.

It was obvious from their taunts that I was their target, and I had to do something. I muttered to the chairman 'Get a car at the front door', and he melted away, the BM supporters menacingly pointing and shouting at me. I knew instinctively that if I displayed any weakness they would be after me like a pack of hounds.

There was a pause as we eyed each other up. Seconds felt like hours. I was terrified but dared not display this: any weakness would invite attack. But there were no exits. What should I do? A sixth sense guided me and, as if on automatic pilot, I stepped down from the stage and walked deliberately but not arrogantly right through their middle. The fascists seemed thrown, drawing back. Then they realised I was through and a few chased after me, lunging and catching my arm with a painful blow as I escaped into the waiting car. I was away, heart pounding, and worrying that one of the enemy might also jump on the late train to London. (Nobody did so.)

Four years later, in Hemel Hempstead in 1975, there was a similar fascist attack by National Front supporters when I was again the main speaker at a Young Liberal meeting. It was over before it had begun, the meeting wrecked, the audience fleeing in terror, the fascists fortunately for me melting away. And then as a Labour parliamentary candidate in 1986, a party meeting we had organised in Roehampton College was also broken up by the National Front. The organiser, it was later revealed, had a conviction for grievous bodily harm – but again, despite aggressive barracking and threats directed my way, I escaped any physical harm.

‡

Meanwhile, South Africa had introduced conscription to perform active military duties along the country's borders which were being threatened by Mandela's ANC and other liberation forces. This led to growing alienation, and an increasing number of young whites, including young Afrikaners, began doubting whether apartheid was worth fighting, and maybe dying, for. A white underground group called *Okhela* – the Zulu word for 'spark' – had been formed in 1972, and aimed to mobilise dissident whites on an undercover basis. In its commitment to raising 'white consciousness', *Okhela* saw its role in parallel with the growing Black Consciousness movement inside South Africa led by Steve Biko.

In 1977, I received via the then executive secretary of the Anti-Apartheid Movement, Basil Manning, a covert approach to meet two members of *Okhela*. At their insistence, we talked in my car in London ostensibly to avoid any surveillance. Large, clean-cut, fit young Afrikaners, they described the group's aims and appealed to me to join them. Although I replied that I would be happy to offer support, I explained that my most effective contribution to the struggle was as an anti-apartheid activist in Britain. However, they persisted and, in what I felt was an attempt to make me feel guilty at not being willing to lay myself on the line in the guerrilla struggle, tried to press me to travel to one of the frontline states and be infiltrated into South Africa. I expressed my lack of enthusiasm and was privately unimpressed at what seemed a particularly foolhardy escapade. I was also suspicious: there was something about their demeanour which did not ring true. So I said I would think about it, and that they should contact me in a few weeks' time.

Although I never heard from them again, there was a revealing sequel to this mysterious episode. After the exposure in 1980 of the 'master spy' Craig Williamson as a captain in the South African security services – he had successfully operated in London in the 1970s posing as an anti-apartheid exile – the two men were also revealed as double agents who had infiltrated *Okhela*.

‡

On Friday 24 October 1975 I had finished drafting a chapter for my political science doctoral thesis at The University of Sussex in our small Putney flat. But

I needed a new typewriter ribbon and drove quickly down to the stationers W. H. Smith in nearby Putney High Street to buy one. On returning, I was in the middle of a lunch snack with my wife Pat when she got up from the kitchen table to answer a ring at the door and returned to announce that there were some policemen who wished to see me.

One of the officers asked if that was my car outside, as he pointed to our blue Volkswagen Beetle. Yes, I told him. Had I been out in it recently? Yes, I said, to buy typewriter ribbons, immediately recalling I had parked illicitly on a yellow line and feeling guilty. Well, they would just like me to go with them down to the police station.

Pat, who had begun to look rather uneasy, said she would like to go with me, but this seemed unnecessary. It shouldn't take longer than twenty minutes, the officer told us categorically. There seemed no reason for me to be uncooperative.

Only when he refused to let me finish eating my sandwich, and followed close on my heels as I went to collect my jacket and glasses, did I begin to feel that there was something awry. Exactly what was it all about, I asked? Couldn't it be discussed here? No – I would only find out when I got to the station.

The atmosphere had grown highly confused. The police were crowding into our doorway. Was I being arrested, I asked. If so, what was the charge? I would only go if I was given a proper explanation. In that case he would have to arrest me, he said. My change of manner had obviously put him out. He turned to have a quick discussion with his colleagues – then another police-man called out: 'Snatch at Barclays.'

Snatch at Barclays Bank? What on earth could this have to do with me? Pat, at my side, giggled nervously. You must be joking, she told them. My mind had become jumbled: parking tickets, policemen, bank snatch, me. Events had ceased to make sense.

There was obviously a mistake somewhere, but it could not be anything that would take long to sort out. So I followed them down the path and was startled to see that there, parked in the road, were several squad cars and a 'black Maria' police van together with a further dozen policemen and policewomen.

One of the officers insisted on driving my car down to nearby Wandsworth police station and I was ushered into the back seat of the nearest police vehicle. As we pulled away the officer sitting beside me reached for a microphone and spoke into it: 'The suspect has been arrested. Everything's under control.'

In my growing confusion I turned to him. Me, a 'suspect'? Had I been arrested, then, without knowing it? No, not really, he replied. It was just normal procedure. All would be explained when we got to the station. There was nothing else he could tell me.

‡

Being charged with a crime you have not committed and know nothing about is bad enough for any citizen. Being charged with a bank snatch a few hundred yards from my home in the most bizarre circumstances plunged me into a world that would have done Franz Kafka's *The Trial* proud. Except that it was most certainly for real and seemingly did not happen by accident.[*]

Quite unbeknown to me, almost exactly as I was getting into my car to drive down to buy the typewriter ribbon, a man roughly my age and of roughly my appearance snatched a bundle of five pound notes totalling £490 from a cashier in the Upper Richmond Road, Putney, branch of Barclays Bank – a bank which had been a target for anti-apartheid protesters including me. He ran down the High Street, pursued by several bank staff who were joined by four boys from Putney's Elliott School. He then ran up a side street, Oxford Road, turned round obligingly, said 'Alright, here you are then', tossed the money back, and disappeared.

Minutes later I drove down the very same street towards the High Street and pulled up outside W. H. Smith. As I got out of the car, oblivious to what had gone on, several of the schoolboys – twelve years old – noticed me, thought I resembled the thief they had just been chasing and reported my car registration number to the police.

After arriving at Wandsworth police station I was soon subjected to an interrogation, two detectives verbally hustling me: it was obvious I was the type to steal money, quite in character in view of my past record of protest; I was a 'troublemaker', which equalled a 'criminal'; of course I had snatched the money from the bank, why not come clean and admit it? I was both dazed but also angry at their aggressive insinuations. 'This must be a fit-up!' I exclaimed. One of the investigating detectives belligerently told me: 'You have caused a lot of trouble with your protests and we are going to make this charge stick on you.'

Locked up in a cell for the rest of the day, a confusing swirl of thoughts increasingly mesmerised me as the long hours dragged by, nothing happening, no explanations, nobody to speak to. What made it worse was I had not the slightest idea about the theft. How had it happened? How on earth had I been picked up? What was all this really about? I got bouts of jitters as fright overcame me. It was difficult because it was so unreal. My world had turned upside down.

I began to wonder whether perhaps I *had* done it. Perhaps I *was* a bank

---

[*] See Peter Hain, *Mistaken Identity* (London, Quartet, 1976).

robber? For a moment I considered the possibility that I had 'flipped' –
but then what had I done with the money I was supposed to have stolen?
Occasionally I paced up and down the cell, peering at graffiti through the dim
light. There was a scribble on the wall: 'Am I guilty or not guilty? – somebody
please tell me.' Whoever had written that rather reflected my own distraught
frame of mind.

After eleven hours in detention – and on the basis only of statements by
two of the four boys – I was eventually charged in the early hours of the
Saturday morning with snatching the money, despite vehemently protesting
my innocence. I didn't even know which branch of Barclays had been the
scene of the crime (there were then two in central Putney several hundred
yards apart). Fingerprints (including a fresh one) on the money did not match
mine and there was no other evidence upon which to charge me.

I arrived home shell shocked. Later that day the police leaked the news to
the media and I found myself facing 'HAIN IN BANK THEFT' headlines
in the Sunday papers. There was another twist on the Monday when an identification parade was scheduled. The police leaks had ensured huge publicity,
and my photograph was on the front page of the London *Evening Standard*
above a caption: 'Peter Hain, due to appear on an identification parade
today'. Bank staff later confirmed in court that copies of the newspaper had
been in their office and that they had read it before attending the parade.

As I stood nervously in line, the cashier from whom the money had been
snatched walked past and then straight back to me, placing her hand on my
shoulder. She was Mrs Lucy Haines, a slight, nervy, grey-haired woman, probably in her late fifties, and I had never seen her in my life before (variations
on my surname were another quirky feature of the case). Although none of
the other bank witnesses (including those who had chased the thief at close
quarters) did so, the police now had a 'positive identification' to corroborate
that of the two twelve-year-olds who had reported my car number.

Later that evening, however, came about the only break I got in six miser-
able months during which the case consumed my life and because of which
I had virtually to abandon my doctoral thesis. Terry MacLaren, the oldest of
the schoolboys, who it turned out had refused to go along with his friends
to report my car number, was watching the ten o'clock news that night on
television and saw me pictured outside the police station after the parade.
'That's not the man. They've got the wrong one,' he told his Dad. Many if
not most other fathers would have told their young son to shut up and mind
his own business and few boys would have been as strong willed as fourteen-
year-old Terry. But, fortunately for me, his father contacted my solicitor the
next day.

‡

Intrigued by the bizarre nature of the case, journalists, political acquaint-
ances and others began discussing whether I had been set up by BOSS, the
South African security service. But, frustratingly for me, direct evidence
was absent.

Then on 3 February 1976, two months before the trial was due to start, a
Mr Kenneth Wyatt rang my parents' home saying he wanted to talk to me
about my case. Wary when I rang him back that it might be yet another crank
call, I pressed him. He appeared calm and offered to come and see me the
following day, arriving on time, a large, bespectacled, shambling figure, quiet,
almost diffident, and conspiratorially concerned that his car might have been
followed.

I had never met or heard of Wyatt before. Although he talked in a disjointed,
rambling fashion, his manner was open and reasonable and gave no grounds
for supposing that he was either unbalanced or devious. At the suggestion of
my solicitor John Dundon, I took notes as he began by saying that he might
not be believed because he had been in the pornography business, and had
been convicted to serve two years for distributing pornographic material.

He then said he had been approached by a group headed by a Mr Fred
Kamil, formerly a security officer with the South African-based conglomer-
ate Anglo-American – a corporation which specialised in diamond mining,
amongst other things – and told to contact and inform me that the bank theft
had been carried out by a South African agent specially flown over to Britain
for the job.

Wyatt delivered his account quite flatly without emotion or hype, explaining how information about my case had reached Kamil through his contacts
with Anglo-American's extensive security service, which worked closely with
BOSS. One of Kamil's contacts in South Africa accidentally came across a
confidential dossier in BOSS headquarters containing a plan to discredit leaders of the Liberal Party, including me and the Party leader, Jeremy Thorpe. A
document in the dossier stated that the operation against me had gone successfully and 'action against Thorpe is going according to plan'.

According to Wyatt, the South Africans wanted to see a permanent Tory
government in Britain and they believed that damaging the Liberal Party by
discrediting its leadership would ensure a Tory victory at the polls.

Wyatt further maintained that one of Kamil's female intelligence contacts
had come across a photograph at BOSS's Johannesburg headquarters of
an agent who was my 'double', and who had left South Africa for Britain
in August 1975, returning at the end of October (the bank theft took place

on 24 October). The agent had since gone to ground but not before boasting to colleagues that he had been given a bonus of £50,000 for a 'very successful project'.

After he had left I was both excited and disorientated. The facts of the bank theft case simply did not add up and I instinctively suspected a South African plot. But, a few weeks before the start of my trial, I did not want to be accused of desperately alleging this when there was no direct evidence. Instead I arranged for Wyatt to repeat his story to the BBC journalist Roger Courtiour, who was making a television documentary on my case.

However, a fortnight later, some people were charged with conspiracy to extort £1 million from the Anglo-American Corporation, Kenneth Wyatt one of them. In court it became clear that everything Wyatt had told me about Kamil and his group was true. It emerged that Fred Kamil had worked briefly for British intelligence and then fruitfully for Anglo-American. However, he lost his job in 1970 after a dispute over £500,000 which he claimed was owed to him.

In a desperate attempt to get this money, in May 1972 he tried to hijack a South African Airways Boeing which he believed was carrying a relative of the Anglo-American head, Sir Harry Oppenheimer. When the plane landed in Malawi, he was arrested and imprisoned for eleven years. He only served less than a third of the sentence, however, and was released in unusual circumstances with the assistance of the South African authorities. Still maintaining that he was owed the full £500,000, he went to Spain and hired Wyatt and four others to try and extort the money from Anglo-American officials in London.

Then events took an even more extraordinary turn. Several weeks earlier the male model Norman Scott publicly broke allegations that Jeremy Thorpe had an affair with him.* But I was tipped off shortly afterwards that the *Daily Mirror* was about to publish a story about South African attempts to discredit Thorpe and informed him by telephone. The *Mirror,* which had been investigating my case, was reporting that Gordon Winter had been promoting these same allegations about Thorpe two years before. I told Thorpe of the belief in anti-apartheid circles that Winter was a BOSS agent.

I now decided to write a confidential memorandum describing the Wyatt approach and handed it to the Liberal leader at his home on 24 February. To my surprise, he said that the Labour Prime Minister, Harold Wilson, would be interested, picked up the phone, rang 10 Downing Street and despatched

---

* Wyatt's visit took place a week after these allegations surfaced. Four months later Thorpe resigned and in 1979 was tried and acquitted of conspiracy to murder Scott. His three co-defendants did, however, admit to a conspiracy.

the memo there right away. (Within ten days Winter, by now back in South Africa, was handed a copy of my memo in Johannesburg by the head of BOSS, surmising it had reached him via British Intelligence, since the memo was still strictly confidential.)

Meanwhile I was contacted by a London-based American academic, Dan Hughes, a go-between for a young British doctor, Diane Lefevre. Although extremely nervous and vague about substantiating details of the Wyatt allegation, she was anxious to reinforce its general validity. In several separate instances she was remarkably well informed. For example, amongst my often bizarre mail, I had received anonymously in an envelope postmarked Johannesburg a photograph dated 1964. It pictured Gordon Winter swimming with Sir Harry Oppenheimer's daughter Mary, in the pool at the Oppenheimer home in Johannesburg. We had not mentioned it to anyone else, but now Dr Lefevre asked me whether I had received it.

According to Gordon Winter, the photo was sent by the head of BOSS, H. J. van den Bergh, anxious to promote rumours that Anglo-American, not BOSS, was behind the plot against the Liberal Party. Winter stated that Diane Lefevre infiltrated the Kamil group for a section of British intelligence hostile to apartheid. When Wyatt and his co-conspirators were eventually tried and convicted at the Old Bailey in 1977, it was alleged in court that Dr Lefevre was a British intelligence agent; she denied this but was never able to explain her role. (Wyatt was imprisoned, evidently much to his surprise: he had told journalists beforehand that he would be 'protected'.)

Then on 9 March 1976, Harold Wilson, briefed by MI6 officers, astonished the House of Commons when he answered a 'planted' question from Labour MP James Wellbeloved, who maintained close connections with British intelligence. 'I have no doubt at all, there is strong South African participation in recent activities relating to the leader of the Liberal Party,' he said, adding there had been 'very strong and heavily financed private masterminding of certain political operations'. This South African participation, he stated, was 'based on massive resources of business money and private agents of various kinds and various qualities'. Later he also referred specifically to 'the Hain case'. This set the media off in pursuit of more details. My memo to Thorpe became public knowledge, Wyatt was widely interviewed and new, even stranger, actors soon appeared on the stage.

However, I remained frustrated that Wyatt and Lefevre could be discredited if called as witnesses in court. We even had to bear in mind the possibility that their appearance might have been designed to achieve precisely that and thereby weaken what was a strong defence. So I had to remain content at fighting for my innocence within the rules of a conventional criminal trial,

while strongly suspecting that I was really the victim of a much larger South
African plot.

‡

For two full weeks at the end of March and into April 1976 the Queen *v.* Peter
Hain played to a packed house in the Old Bailey's court number 8. Between
twenty and forty reporters sat in: 'The largest number since Christine Keeler,'
an usher remarked nostalgically. One eyewitness gave evidence that the thief
was 'South African' in appearance. And the prosecution tried half-heartedly
to suggest that, since I had been active in the campaign to get Barclays Bank to
withdraw from South Africa, I might have staged the theft as a political protest.
Otherwise South Africa hardly received a mention in the proceedings.

There were no surprises in the prosecution evidence – except that in court it
seemed if anything even flimsier. The unreliability – at times incongruity – of
identification evidence featured throughout. As the *Sunday Times* reported:

> A confusing picture has emerged of the culprit as a sharp-featured, dark-eyed
> man, sometimes wearing spectacles, sometimes not, aged between twenty-three
> and thirty and anything from 5 feet 10 inches to 6 feet 2 inches in height, of
> medium build, very skinny, quite slim, with a long face, very drawn and white,
> of normal complexion but needing a shave, a very 'sallow' complexion with a
> darkish tinge, foreign looking, possibly Spanish, Egyptian or 'Afrikaans', not
> foreign, with black curly hair worn collar length, not very long fluffy hair reach-
> ing just below the ears, shortish wavy brown hair with ginger tints, wearing light-
> blue jeans and dark trousers as well as a white check shirt, a blue check shirt, a
> cream shirt with puffed sleeves, a light shirt with dark stripes, a cream waistcoat
> made of thick velvet wool, white tennis shoes and brown suede 'Hush Puppies'.

The prosecutor, Michael Corkery, opened on the basis that it had been a 'spur-of-
the-moment theft'. He called Mrs Lucy Haines, the cashier who had picked me
out on the identification parade. But, far from being damning, she was hesitant,
saying she had seen the thief only for a 'split second' and at one point was seemingly unable to pick me out in court – even though I was sticking out in the dock
like a sore thumb. She also confirmed she had seen me periodically on television
well before the theft took place, and in the newspaper just before the parade.

Apart from the twelve-year-old schoolboys – whose evidence was embarrassingly inconsistent – and the cashier, no other witness was able to identify
me: not even the bank's accountant, Timothy Hayne. He had led the half-
mile chase behind the thief, told the court that he knew my face well from

television and the newspapers and said I was not the man. None of the police officers called could implicate me. The photofit picture was nothing like me. The fingerprint analyst confirmed that my prints had not been on any of the notes – though there was a fresh 'unknown' print on the top note.

Nevertheless identification evidence remained a compulsive curse: once the finger had been pointed at me, I faced a conviction and had virtually to prove my innocence. Fortunately, Terry MacLaren – whom my solicitor John Dundon described as 'a witness in a million' – was remarkably composed, fluent, and compellingly convincing. He said the other boys had been behind him throughout the chase – sometimes up to thirty yards. Terry added that he had got a clear sight of the thief initially some thirty feet across Putney High Street, and later during the chase as he had turned back to glance several times at his pursuers. He also described with astonishing accuracy what had happened when I went in to shop at W. H. Smith, including my having greeted a friend there. And he described in detail the differences between me and the thief.

The trial and the build-up to it imposed a much bigger strain on me and my family than the conspiracy case over three years before which had been a straightforward political trial. This one challenged my honesty and presented me as some sort of clumsy criminal. So I felt emotion welling up when my highly skilled QC, Lewis Hawser, pointed out the string of contradictions in the case against me.

Hawser laid out for the jury 'the whole picture as it must be presented by the prosecution' to sustain a guilty verdict:

Peter Hain leaves his house to buy typewriter ribbons. He must park his car behind Oxford Road somewhere. He walks to the bank – over a quarter of a mile – so that would take five to seven minutes. He cases the joint, spends three to five minutes waiting to snatch the money, snatches it and is involved in a tiring chase.

He dodges down Oxford Road, gets in his car and then drives back along the very road down which he has been chased by a man from the bank and some boys. All this within five minutes. He must have passed in his car the four boys who had chased him. He parks right in front of the boys, gets out, goes into Smith's. He doesn't rush to buy the typewriter ribbons as fast as possible – in any case he could have bought them from Surrey Typewriters in Putney Bridge Road without retracing his route – he reads a magazine. He behaves quite normally and looks relaxed within five minutes of a very tiring chase. He then goes home, lunches, doesn't change his clothes. The police come and he volunteers that he had been to Smith's. Members of the jury, the bare bones of the story just don't hang together. This is a classic case of mistaken identity.

Then came yet another remarkable twist. The judge, Alan King-Hamilton, was a member of the Marylebone Cricket Club and I was its *bête noire* during the Stop The Tour campaign. I was reliably informed later by senior members of the legal profession that he had been keen to try the case and that court administrators were equally happy to give it to him. In a quite extraordinary summing up, he suggested without any substantiation that my wife Pat, my mother and a family friend, Vanessa Brown, may have been untruthful alibi witnesses (not even the prosecution had made that allegation). He also introduced a ridiculous new hypothesis – that I had put on a jumper when I got back to the car since the thief wasn't wearing one – which he then had to withdraw under joint challenge from defence and prosecution, the latter worried that it compromised their case. His open hostility to the defence shocked even the most experienced lawyers and was the talk of the Bar for some time. At best he might have confused the jury and at worst he raised serious doubts in their minds as to my innocence.

Perhaps that helped explain what then followed: not an instant verdict at all. Wondering about my fate, held in the hands of 'twelve men and women good and true', I was taken down stairs to the cells where I had mixed during lunch breaks with other defendants to whom I was a real curiosity. 'How's it going then, Peter?' they would say each day. 'Has the judge thrown it out yet?' None of them believed I was guilty, which I can't say was my view of them: most seemed veterans of the criminal process.

After five long and tense hours, during which the jury were called back and advised to reach a majority verdict, they quickly returned. I was led back upstairs to discover my fate, my senses dulled. 'Not guilty,' the foreman stated emphatically. But the sheer relief his words engendered hardly registered with me because pandemonium had broken out. The public gallery erupted with cheers and clapping. There were calls of 'order, order' as bewildered ushers rushed about. The floor of the court was alive as the people seemed to take over. The judge who had ruled his fiefdom for two weeks had finally lost control. I couldn't hear what he was trying to say amidst the smiling, hugging jumble of people, as I struggled to curb my emotions. Then I was out of the dock at last and into the warm comfort of my family. After gaining control of myself, I spotted through the crowd some members of the jury filing out. I stepped forward to thank them, and they smiled somewhat shyly. Justice done – despite the police, despite the judge – and despite the South African security services behind this 'Putney plot'.[*]

---

[*]   See my book *A Putney Plot?* (Nottingham, Spokesman, 1987).

‡

As played out in court, it seemed a straightforward, though classic, case of mistaken identity. But I could not afford to become obsessed with it. The case was traumatic enough and at the time I met other mistaken identity victims who had been so consumed by their injustice that their lives were virtually destroyed; so I resolved to get on with mine.

Nevertheless the South African connection would not go away. A month after my acquittal, on 17 May 1976, a Mr Frederick Cheeseman rang the office of the Liberal Chief Whip, David Steel MP, claiming to be an ex-intelligence officer with some information about a smear campaign against the Party. When interviewed by Steel's aides he claimed he had been visiting BOSS headquarters in Pretoria in September 1974 when he was shown a series of dossiers profiling leading Liberal and Labour figures which were to be used as the basis for a smear campaign. After extensive reading of the documentation he provided, and checks on his identity with security services across the world by the BBC television journalists Barrie Penrose and Roger Courtiour, who had been investigating the South African angle, the BBC *Nine o'Clock News* ran the story as a lead exclusive, and other media followed it.

However, a day later, Cheeseman did a complete *volte face*. In an exclusive interview with the *Daily Express*, he claimed to be a hoaxer: a Walter Mitty character on the dole. This effectively killed investigations into the possible role of BOSS and other intelligence operatives in my case, that of Jeremy Thorpe and possibly those of other Liberal and Labour politicians. A few years later it emerged that Cheeseman, far from being bogus, was an intelligence agent on active service – and remained so.*

A former British intelligence officer, Colin Wallace, told me when I interviewed him in 1987: 'The Colonel Cheeseman saga is known in intelligence circles as the "double bubble" because it contains a second dimension in deception and not only deflects attention from the main target, but also "bursts", leaving the investigator doubting everything he has uncovered so far. I have no doubt that Penrose and Courtiour did get quite close – possibly too close – to the truth and various deceptions were put into action to discredit their investigations.'

Although the Putney bank theft may have appeared an isolated event, a bizarre one-off, it coincided with an extraordinary period in British politics in 1974–6 during which there was a concerted drive to establish a new right-wing

---

* Confirmed by, amongst others, Barrie Penrose and Roger Courtiour, *The Pencourt File* (London, Secker & Warburg, 1978).

dominance in Britain. This contained a number of different threads which converged into a common purpose and which others subsequently analysed.[*]

By the mid-1970s key sections in the British establishment had become increasingly alarmed at what they believed was a leftward political drift in Britain, and had taken steps to reverse this. The escalating crisis in Northern Ireland, the growth of the left in both the trade unions and the Labour Party, successful extra-parliamentary protest and direct action such as STST, trade union and student militancy – all were seen to pose a major threat.

Many on the right believed they really were faced with 'the end of civilisation' in Britain as they had known and controlled it. In 1972 striking miners using flying pickets had emerged victorious against the Conservative government of Edward Heath, Britain's energy supply then heavily dependent upon coal. At Saltley Gate coke depot in Birmingham, then the nation's main supply of coke for gas and power stations, 15,000 picketing miners proved too much for the police, who were forced to close the gates. The miners' success horrified conservative forces, who viewed it as a 'seditious victory' for trade union power over the state and felt the country was staring into an abyss of anarchy.[†] Their fears turned almost to panic when the Tory government suffered a series of further defeats at the hands of the trade unions, most notably following another miners' strike in the winter of 1973–4. After imposing a three-day working week to limit energy demand, Edward Heath called an election on the theme 'Who Governs Britain?' He lost, Labour formed a minority government in February 1974 and then won a small majority in an October general election.

With all of these events causing considerable disquiet, the right now began to go on the offensive. There was a move within the Tory Party against Edward Heath, who was felt to be too liberal, and he was eventually replaced in 1975 by Margaret Thatcher. The Thatcherites began strengthening their hold over the Conservative Party and relied upon various research organisations and pressure groups which were found to have clear links with British intelligence. Amongst these were the Institute for the Study of Conflict, the Society for Individual Freedom (which had helped sponsor my 1972 prosecution) and the National Association for Freedom (which BOSS helped fund).

At another level activity was less open. In 1971, with the crisis escalating in Northern Ireland, the British Army established an 'Information Policy Unit' which it officially denied existed but which became an instrument of

---

[*]   See especially Stephen Dorril and Robin Ramsay, *Smear!* (London, Fourth Estate, 1991).

[†]   Keith Jeffrey and Peter Hennessy, *States of Emergency* (London, Routledge & Kegan Paul, 1983), p. 235.

'disinformation' and 'black propaganda'. Its leading operative was a local army information official, Colin Wallace, who became senior information officer at the Army HQ outside Belfast between May 1968 and February 1975. When he left the service in 1976 after a distinguished career, Wallace provided detailed evidence on 'psychological operations' – or 'psy-ops' as they were known in the trade – including establishing front organisations and organising paramilitary projects.

However the distinction became increasingly blurred between 'legitimate' targets such as the IRA or the Protestant paramilitaries, and 'illegitimate' targets in Britain. By 1973 Wallace and his colleagues were working very closely with the British security services on 'British' rather than 'Irish' intelligence work. The 'Irish crisis' had come to be merged with what they perceived to be a 'British crisis'. What began as counter-terrorist project in Ireland widened significantly to cover intelligence work on, and psy-ops against, all manner of activity which had nothing to do with Irish affairs, and certainly nothing to do with terrorism. Wallace confirmed that, over the years, his psy-ops work was steadily widened to cover figures and groups on the left in British politics – and here 'left' was defined in very broad terms indeed to cover anybody not identifiably on the hard right, including members of the Labour and Liberal Parties, and even 'liberal' Tories.

Amongst the people who were targets in this process were Edward Heath, Harold Wilson and Jeremy Thorpe, who between them headed all three major democratic parties in Britain at the time. Wallace confirmed that Heath was a target because he was regarded as 'too weak', Wilson because he was the main alternative to rule by the right, and Thorpe because the Liberals might become influential enough to block the return of a new, rightist Conservative government. (Much the same prognosis of course with which Kenneth Wyatt had first approached me in 1976; and in 1977 the Liberals did conclude a formal pact to sustain in power a Labour government which had lost its slim majority in the House of Commons.) Evidence of a plot involving elements in the British and South African security services to disrupt the Liberal and Labour Parties was confirmed in 1987 by the retired MI5 agent Peter Wright.[*]

Amongst the many people Colin Wallace recalled being asked to monitor and sift intelligence upon was me. Although I had paid a brief visit there in February 1972 as chair of the Young Liberals, I had done very little political work on Ireland. But this was not the point, as Wallace told me early in 1987: 'We saw you as an important target in the long term. You were clearly on your way up in politics. Through your anti-apartheid activities and your

---

[*] See Peter Wright, *Spycatcher* (Melbourne, Heinemann, 1987).

involvement in radical campaigns, you had offended many people on the right and it was important to neutralise you.' The information on 'indigenous' British figures like me on Wallace's psy-ops target list was provided by MI5. The list included otherwise impeccably respectable individuals such as Liberal peer Lord Avebury, who was a target simply because he had headed the 'Peter Hain Defence Fund' for my 1972 conspiracy charge.

A former MI5 intelligence officer, Cathy Massiter, confirmed in a TV documentary in March 1985 that a fundamental shift of emphasis occurred between 1970 and 1984 when she was in the service. From being a counter-espionage organisation aimed at hostile foreign powers, MI5 switched towards a domestic surveillance organisation. She found herself being directed to monitor individuals in CND and leading trade unionists. The F Branch in MI5 expanded enormously to cover these domestic targets. Apart from tapping phones and maintaining surveillance, MI5 infiltrated individuals into various groups and organised illegal burglaries of target houses and offices. (Amongst many others, my own phone was tapped and there was evidence of infiltrators in the various anti-apartheid, anti-racist and political campaigns in which I had been active.)

When Labour came back to power, the attention of Wallace and his colleagues became even more directed at domestic British politics. Wallace recorded that MI5 was particularly anxious because it believed Labour would phase out internment without trial in Northern Ireland, withdraw from the European Economic Community, succumb to growing trade union power and left-wing influence, establish greater control over the intelligence services, and introduce a Freedom of Information Act. Significantly, MI5 was also concerned Labour would take tougher action against South Africa and the illegal Smith regime in Rhodesia – thus 'encouraging Marxist influence in southern Africa'.

Wallace added: 'Most of my work during this period was being used by others for totally unconstitutional ends.' He explained that this created an atmosphere in which he and his colleagues found it steadily more difficult to distinguish between, for example, a suspected IRA bomber and a British anti-apartheid activist. Information on both was being fed across his desk. Both appeared on target lists and in his security files. Both represented a common threat and both therefore were legitimate targets.

Wallace spoke quietly and authoritatively during our meeting in 1987, his wife having made us a cup of tea in their modest house in Arundel, Sussex. The way in which intelligence information could be abused was evident in his contemporaneous files in which it was eerie seeing my name appearing. For example there was a cutting from the *Irish Press* dated 7 February 1972 which described Russian reaction to the events on 'Bloody Sunday' the previous week when the army killed unarmed civilians in the Northern Ireland city Derry. Russian journalists working for TASS and *Pravda* were quoted in the article. Wallace had underlined their names and noted alongside the cutting: 'KGB – link to Labour activists. See also Bloody Sunday Commemorative vigil Peter Hain. Hain's family deported SA 1966 for Communist activity.' (As a leaflet in Wallace's file confirmed, I was one of the sponsors of that 1973 vigil.)

Fifteen years after the files had been prepared and twelve years after my bank theft arrest, Wallace described to me this technique as 'guilt by tenuous association'. I was just one of many to whom it was applied. A false entry on MI5 records about my parents' 'communist activity' provided a pretext for my name to be associated first with Soviet communism and then back full circle to Irish terrorism. As Wallace also confirmed, it is not hard to envisage how, on this basis, action to discredit me could be rationalised by members of the security services. Wallace not only stated that he worked closely with MI5 and the CIA but confirmed (as Gordon Winter had done) that both these agencies then worked with BOSS.

‡

Meanwhile there was some discussion in senior military circles as to whether the armed forces should intervene in British politics, possibly by organising a coup. Field Marshall Lord Carver, Chief of Defence Staff in 1974, later acknowledged that such discussion had occurred amongst 'fairly senior officers', but said he personally 'took action to make certain that nobody was so stupid as to go around saying those things'. In 1974–5 private 'citizens armies' were being prepared by retired military figures. They included General Sir Walter Walker (until 1972 Commander-in-Chief of NATO's Northern Command in Europe) and Colonel David Stirling (known for his wartime exploits in the Special Air Service). The purpose, as Stirling expressed it, was to 'provide on a volunteer basis the minimum manpower necessary to cope with the immediate crisis following a general strike or a near general strike in the knowledge that the government of the day must welcome our initiative'. Stirling's group, GB75, and Walker's group, Civil Assistance, were covertly assisted by British intelligence officers, whether acting officially or freelancing.

One of Civil Assistance's Kent area coordinators was Lieutenant Colonel Frederick Cheeseman, who had surfaced publicly in May 1976 as the source of the South African plot allegation. Also involved in this activity were Ross McWhirter and George Young. Both had close links with British intelligence and both were key figures in the Society for Individual Freedom, which was connected to my 1972 conspiracy prosecution.

Harold Wilson told the BBC's Penrose and Courtiour: 'I am not certain that for the last eight months when I was Prime Minister I knew what was happening, fully, in Security.' During this period – spanning summer 1975 to his resignation in spring 1976 – he had become more convinced of an earlier suspicion that there was 'a very right-wing faction' in MI5 which had sought to smear him and others in his administration. In 1978 the author Chapman Pincher, a right-winger with extremely good intelligence sources, wrote: 'The undermining activities which Wilson complained of were not only genuine but far more menacing than he revealed. Certain officers, inside MI5, assisted by others who had retired from the service, were actually trying to bring down the Labour Government."

Colin Wallace stated that what Wilson had called 'this mafia faction' numbered at least forty agents. He added: 'Information supplied by the CIA to MI5 was used to justify a number of in-depth investigations into Harold Wilson's activities and those of other Labour MPs/supporters to find out if sufficient "hard evidence" could be gathered to wreck the Labour Party's chances of gaining power.' When the investigations failed to uncover anything of value, elements within the Security Service, supported by others in Whitehall including former members of the intelligence and security services, embarked upon a disinformation campaign to achieve the same objective.

Perhaps the most significant supporting evidence came from Peter Wright. He was a leading, if not the leading, member of this MI5 group in the mid-1970s in the F4 and F6 branches of the service. In his 1987 book *Spycatcher* he confirmed the validity of the earlier and quite separate accounts given by Wallace and Pencourt.

Over the bank theft case, the interests of this British hard right and the South Africans coincided. Peter Wright testified that the MI5 faction was openly sympathetic to white South Africa during the height of the Cold War because it was seen as an ally against 'international communism'. Colin Wallace corroborated this, adding that information was regularly 'traded' between MI5 and BOSS. Even joint operations were carried out where the agencies shared common objectives.

‡

---

*   Chapman Pincher, *Inside Story* (London, Sidgwick & Jackson, 1978). For confirmation that elements in MI5 and the CIA sought to discredit Wilson and bring down the Labour Government see David Leigh, *The Wilson Plot* (New York, Pantheon Books, 1988).

Consequently, in framing me on the Putney bank theft, BOSS would have had the active or tacit support of members of the rightist MI5 group. This would have given BOSS both the 'cover' and operational back-up necessary. Assistance from MI5 agents would also have opened up channels to ensure I was linked to the crime.

Quoting his former London 'handler' – later to be BOSS's head in the Transkei – Gordon Winter reported that a BOSS agent had been watching my home in a parked car with a walkie-talkie radio. When I left to go shopping the agent alerted the real thief to act. This man had a criminal record and immediately after committing the theft was flown to Paris and then to South Africa to start a new life. (This account is uncannily similar to that given quite independently by Kenneth Wyatt.) According to Winter the only minor slip-up was that the individual's hair had been styled to resemble mine whereas I had by coincidence changed my hairstyle only shortly before the event. Winter adds that immediately after the theft BOSS arranged for Scotland Yard to be called to link me to the crime. The caller told the Yard to check on Special Branch files where they would find I had campaigned actively against Barclays' involvement in South Africa, and had once actually taken part in a picket outside the very same Putney branch of the bank (this was true).

How does this account square with the facts? First, the intervention of the schoolboys must have been unplanned: they were clearly no part of any BOSS plot. But then their role was confined purely to implicating me through reporting my car number. Similarly, the local police force need not have been a party to the plot: they came into the picture only from the time my name was reported as a suspect. Second, one interpretation of the thief's behaviour (as reported by nearly a dozen eyewitnesses) is fully compatible with the role of a BOSS operative. About twenty minutes before I left the house, one of the cashiers had spotted the thief behaving suspiciously; she later told the court that he must have been 'casing the joint'. He had peered through the window and come into the bank.

Other witnesses reported seeing what they assumed was the same man in the area even before this. Uncannily, nearly an hour before the theft, one witness, Elizabeth Forshaw, spotted a man while she was shopping in Putney High Street: 'I saw a familiar face, and immediately I thought it was Peter Hain ... Suddenly, when he was within a few feet I did not think it was Peter Hain. Before I was absolutely convinced, but when he came within two or three feet I knew it wasn't him.' (She explained that she was particularly interested in people she had seen on television and knew what I looked like.) After the theft, the thief turned round while running from his pursuers and threw the money back – not the behaviour of someone desperate for the money but maybe that

PETER HAIN

of someone keen to allow witnesses to see his face since everybody accepted that he resembled me.

Third – and perhaps most significant – is the evidence of a phone call to Scotland Yard. Winter stated that this originated from a tip-off by BOSS. However, an anonymous phone call to Scotland Yard from a BOSS agent implicating me would be far less effective than one channelled through an authoritative intermediary in MI5. Neither Winter nor BOSS could have been aware of one fact which was never made known outside the very few most intimately involved in my defence team. This was an unexplained incident which both confused and intrigued my solicitor, John Dundon – so much so that he later made a separate statement about it in front of a solicitor colleague. At one point during my detention, while Dundon was in the police station waiting to see me, the officer in charge of the investigation referred obliquely to telephone conversations with senior officers in Scotland Yard, and to important evidence gained thereby. The Wandsworth detective hinted that this evidence was being weighed in the decision on whether or not I should be charged. But he would not elaborate. Neither Dundon nor I could make any sense of it at the time. He was convinced that something more was involved than simple consultations with Metropolitan Police chiefs over a potential political embarrassment if a mistake was made in charging a public figure. But he had no proof and so had no basis for pursuing it.

If BOSS (or perhaps a British intelligence source) did phone the Yard as Winter described then this could be the elusive factor in those key hours when the decision was finally made to proceed against me. It would make sense of Dundon's conversation with the detective, of the lengthy delay while consultations took place, and of the relative importance which the detective attached to those consultations. With knowledge of police procedures it is not hard to see how, to the investigating officers, 'evidence' via Scotland Yard could seem important corroboration for local evidence gathered quite independently – especially since that local evidence (the sum total of which at this stage came from two of the schoolboys alone) was extremely thin.

Colin Wallace told me he had established through a then serving British intelligence officer the contents of a record held by the security services in London. According to him, it stated that the Metropolitan Police were tipped off by MI5 almost immediately after the bank theft that I was responsible. This tip-off occurred *before* the schoolboys implicated me by reporting my car number. Wallace said the security service record confirmed BOSS's involvement. The record also showed there was an earlier attempt to set me up some weeks before, but this failed to implicate me sufficiently. (I was completely unaware of this at the time. However, just before my trial my solicitor was shown statements from a witness who saw me on TV and had reported to police I looked like the thief in a bank snatch across the river from my home at Fulham one month before the Putney theft.)

Once my arrest had been accomplished, however, it seems that a section of MI5, or more likely MI6, wanted the South African plot to be known through a source which could not be traced back. The two intelligence services were also known to have quite different political attitudes towards South Africa. MI6 tended to be more anti-apartheid, reflecting Foreign Office policy. By contrast, MI5 – particularly Peter Wright's faction – were actively pro-South Africa, reflecting their Cold War, anti-communist priority which virtually 'equated anybody not blue with being red', in Colin Wallace's words.

BOSS had a history of disrupting anti-apartheid activity in Britain and it was logical for them to frame me for the bank theft. A 'deniable operation', like many others across the world at the height of apartheid, the real crime remained conveniently unsolved and, frustratingly for me, the real bank thief was never identified.

CHAPTER FOUR

LIBERALS, ORWELL AND LABOUR

'**D**o you really hate cricket?' Momentarily caught unawares I quickly explained that I loved the game, had played it, still did so albeit intermittently. Ted Geaney, a decent, self-taught Liverpudlian, steeped in the labour movement but also a member of my old foe, the Marylebone Cricket Club, asked me just about the last question I had prepared for. He was head of research for the Union of Post Office Workers, and I was being interviewed at its south London headquarters in August 1976 for the post of his assistant.

Seven years before this, however, my wider political participation, mainly through the Young Liberals, had continued. Having been elected to its National Executive at Easter 1969, I was elected national publicity officer the following year, now a nationally known political figure through the Stop the Seventy Tour campaign and the most prominent Young Liberal.

The movement was a combination of youthful Liberal Party members – 'junior' Liberals – and others like me who had been drawn in through the radical verve and libertarian socialism of the mid-to-late 1960s. On the right tended to be Party loyalists, on the left those like me for whom the YLs were a vehicle for transforming British politics; there was a constant tension between the two wings. Although I was in the youth section of a mainstream political party, I never saw myself as a 'party politician' then, being mildly contemptuous of the genre and in a more or less constant struggle against the Party leadership and bulk of the membership which I saw as too right wing. They saw me as too much trouble, though there was some respect and even affection, especially for my continuing anti-apartheid activities.

Having served as a national officer, I was encouraged to stand for the YL leadership in 1971, the left-wing candidate with broad support and a high profile. But then, as if out of nowhere, a rival appeared: Chris Green, who had not been active in the YLs and few seemed to have heard of. A decent enough guy with an upper-middle-class accent, it was soon apparent that the Party establishment was behind him, the Liberal leader Jeremy Thorpe, covertly and sometimes not so covertly, using the resources of his office to drum up support for Green.

Young Liberal members appeared where none had existed, phantom names and YL branches took their place on voting lists and, suddenly, I was no longer the favourite: once again the outsider. It was a tough battle, and there were times when I wondered whether it was all worth it. I had never been desperate for the YL leadership and I was not really adept at factional or plotting politics. But since people had asked me, I felt I could make a difference. In the event, I scraped home to acclamation at the annual conference in Plymouth, the vast majority of delegates behind me and the media fascinated: I was driven back home by an older YL colleague, listening to news of my election and interviews on BBC radio.

However, within weeks, I was invited to dinner at Thorpe's flat near Westminster, his housekeeper cooking, as I politely declined wine (I hardly drank at all in those days). It was as if there had been no plot to defeat me as we discussed the future of the Party and how we might work constructively together.

I threw myself into the YL leadership, enjoying the role, though only too aware that the movement remained a coalition between radicals like me and Party loyalists. Our conferences, always over Easter at seaside towns, often agreed daring policies ahead of their time, such as support for the Palestinian cause and abortion on request. Several national journalists usually attended in search of political stories at a quiet news time, including Chris Moncrieff, later doyen of the Parliamentary Press Gallery and legendary political editor for the Press Association. He always managed to get headlines out of our utterances. Standing for re-election for a second year at the YL's Morecambe conference in 1972, I was photographed by the media working on my speech amidst damp windswept deck chairs by the beach.

I encouraged a series of ideological initiatives during my two years as chairman, including a pamphlet of essays called *Scarborough Perspectives*, published to coincide with the parent Party's annual conference at that seaside resort in 1971. My own essay explored my strengthening belief in 'libertarian socialism'. The Liberal student leader Lawrence Freedman (many years later a respected professor of war studies) contributed a thoughtful piece. A colleague, Simon Hebditch, wrote about 'anarcho-syndicalism', the newspapers causing a fuss by covering the most lurid ideas and infuriating the Party leadership. There was a huge row at the Party conference and peace had to be brokered to prevent the leadership moving to expel us. But we were not setting out simply to embarrass leading Liberals as some alleged. As YL leader I was passionate about our ideas and the imperative for radicalising the Liberal Party and changing society.

The following year we published the *Harle Syke Declaration*. A 2,000-word statement of our libertarian socialist philosophy, the text of which I had drafted, it was amended and negotiated over a weekend at the modest Lancashire village of the same name, parental home to one of our officers, Gordon Lishman, many years later to be director of the charity Age Concern. His mother helpfully fed a dozen or so YLs including me who slept on floors and used the single bathroom. I had conceived the idea from the 'Haslemere Declaration', published in 1968, a radical creed against world poverty and for domestic reform.

In the June 1970 general election I had issued a statement on behalf of Putney Young Liberals advocating voting Labour because the Putney constituency was so marginal between Labour and Tories. It understandably caused some bad feeling in the local Liberal Party but the sitting Labour MP, Hugh Jenkins, considered it helped him to hold the seat, despite an unexpected Tory victory sweeping Edward Heath into No. 10.

During the campaign I had been shopping down Putney High Street as Heath swept by on the back of an open Land Rover. A crowd had gathered to hear him speak outside the local Conservative headquarters, and on a whim I walked over. More out of mischief than anything else I began an impromptu heckle. Quickly, middle-aged Tory women turned on me, snarling venomously. Soon I was surrounded by police constables giving me some protection – a novel experience. The women were not letting up, however, and through the officers' legs repeatedly kicked me on the shins, as if getting revenge for the stopping of the cricket tour the previous month. 'Gangster! Communist! Law breaker, destroying England's sport! You nasty little man! Get back to South Africa!' they screamed as I was hustled away.

I was involved in another, albeit quite different, row involving Edward Heath four years later, after I had stepped down as Young Liberal chairman, my two-year term having ended. The winter of 1973–4 had been stormy, with petrol rationing after soaring global oil prices, a three-day week for industry and then a miners' strike. Heath called an impromptu election on the theme 'Who Governs Britain?' But he lost it – though no party had an overall majority, the Liberals having polled well (including for the first time in Putney, where I helped organise the campaign, dubbed by the candidate as 'the secret agent' to avoid possible controversy over my role). Heath told the media he had telephoned Jeremy Thorpe, asking him up from his constituency of North Devon to see whether they could form a coalition.

There was consternation in the Liberal Party. YLs like me had supported the miners and we were having no truck with the Tories. So I issued a press statement saying: 'We did not campaign to keep a Tory government in office.' It got widely covered, other Liberal figures chipping in with similar views. Meanwhile – having leapt over a fence behind his house to escape

journalists – Thorpe was in the dark travelling up by train on the long journey to London: these were the days long before mobile phones. He was
ambushed by television cameras and reporters at Paddington station asking
him to comment on my statement.

The Party clearly would not wear a deal and, instead of being the first Liberal
in generations to be in government, Thorpe's ambitions were thwarted. Heath
resigned and Harold Wilson formed a minority Labour government and, for
the first time I was on first-name terms with several government Ministers,
whom I knew from their activities in the Anti-Apartheid Movement.

‡

By this time I was a postgraduate student in political science at the University
of Sussex, having completed my London university course in July 1973, gaining a first-class degree – which provoked a tongue-in-cheek letter from a
friend, the Liberal peer Lord Avebury, to the *Daily Telegraph* arguing that its
readers would be relieved to hear the news. The paper's letters column had
for years been filled with denunciations of me as 'a student layabout' who
was 'protesting at taxpayer expense'. But my good news instead provoked
further fulminations about how the standard of degrees had self-evidently
collapsed.

However, both my under- and postgraduate degrees had given me the
opportunity to read much more widely, from Karl Marx to John Stuart Mill,
and from modern advocates of participatory democracy to practitioners of
community action. Having organised direct action protests I found myself
studying political theorists of civil disobedience. The same was true of
my broader political ideas and experiences. Other students were studying
what made politics tick, while I came from the world of politics to study what
academics and writers made of it all. On this occasion I, not the others, was the
'insider'. But the more I studied and read, the more my ideas, developed first
in the environment of radical political activism, began to deepen and become
more rounded, reflected in a book I wrote at the time, *Radical Regeneration:
protest, direct action and community politics.*

I remained a strong direct actionist, cool about much other protest action.
Of course symbolic protest – for instance the huge march in London to
support miners involved in the epic 1984–5 strike in Britain or demonstrations
to demand Nelson Mandela's release – is often very necessary, and frequently
all that can be done to promote a cause. But far too often – and especially in

* Quartet Books, London, 1975.

student circles at the time – protest seemed to me to be for effect rather than for results.

While at the University of Sussex, I organised a group of activists, including some from the newly formed Friends of the Earth, to protest against the huge juggernaut lorries which were then becoming prevalent in freight haulage. Our objective was a switch to rail as the more environmentally friendly means of transport. In both London and Sussex small groups of protesters descended on juggernauts parked up for the night and drilled holes in their tyres, immobilising them, a perfectly non-violent and safe form of direct action. Yet I could not persuade a meeting of the Sussex Students Union to support this action, objections ranging from the fact that I was a Young Liberal to that 'it was not central to the class struggle'. This sort of vacuous posturing was unfortunately typical of left-wing student politics.

Several years later – and after I had left university – similar arguments clouded the Anti-Nazi League, which I helped found and launch in 1977, becoming its national spokesman. It was criticised by some on the left who did not think the ANL's focus on the proven Nazi ideas of the National Front leaders and many of its members was the correct way to approach the problem, arguing instead that it had to be done within a broad 'anti-*racist*' rather than 'narrow' anti-*Nazi* context. Others were opposed because the Socialist Workers Party had a leading role, and the SWP had a history of sectarian battles with rivals on the left and of exploiting single-issue campaigns to recruit its members.

My attitude was straightforward. I did not agree with the SWP's politics, but at least they were prepared to act with some verve and determination. Just as with STST before, I was interested in practical and effective action, not sectarianism or the niceties of left-wing theology which often amounted to little more than posturing. The NF at the time was a serious problem. In the mid-1970s they had pushed the Liberals into fourth place in parliamentary by-elections and in the 1977 Greater London Council elections polled fully 10 per cent. Just as significant, they had attracted some following amongst disaffected working-class youngsters unable to get a job, and there was something of a fashion for Nazi insignia and regalia amongst 'skinheads', working-class youth who menacingly shaved their heads and wore heavy boots. Wherever the NF was active there was also a disturbing inevitability about rises in local racist violence and intimidation.

Yet, despite good intentions to oppose the NF, trade union and Labour Party activity had no impact because it was organised in a traditional way that never touched the problem. Similarly, existing left-wing anti-racist groups were having no real impact on the ground where it mattered.

In the ANL we had a simple philosophy. The problem had to be tackled with real urgency. What mattered was *unity in action* against the National Front, not endless theorising or repetitive meetings to discuss what might be deemed a 'more coherent' left-wing or anti-racist approach. An imaginative, radical, new strategy was required, even if that meant appearing to muscle in on territory claimed by more established anti-racist organisations (as some alleged at the beginning had happened with STST). Nothing was working and a new approach was imperative. Not for the first time, I found myself in the 'getting on with it' camp.

The ANL – probably the first such protest group to achieve this – fused anti-racist politics with the popular youth culture of the day, thereby gaining a wider audience that would not have touched a conventional political campaign with a barge pole. Working-class youngsters swung behind the ANL in a way that had never been achieved before. The contribution of rock music, or to be more precise, the punk and reggae music of the late 1970s, was crucial. 'Rock Against Racism' national carnivals and local gigs involved huge numbers of people and were organised jointly with the ANL. Anti-racist politics remained deadly serious, but for the first time it could also be fun. (What heresy! traditional leftists said at the time, as they claimed to be busying themselves in earnest 'class warfare'.) Another contributory factor to its success was the self-organisation implicit in the campaign. Rather like STST, supporters were actively encouraged to do their own thing in a way that they felt would relate best to their own environment. Thus we had 'Teachers Against the Nazis', 'Students Against the Nazis', 'Miners Against the Nazis', even 'Vegetarians Against the Nazis' and 'Skateboarders Against the Nazis', each with their own badges and leaflets, each taking their own initiatives and involving their own people. Within a year of its launch the Anti-Nazi League had mobilised hundreds of thousands across the country either to act within their own peer groups, workplaces, schools, colleges or local communities, or to join together at local and national events.

Wherever the National Front tried to demonstrate or leaflet, they were opposed by the ANL, and also denied platforms to spread their hate. This confrontation strategy was highly controversial – a denial of free speech, critics argued. Sometimes (though by no means always) it resulted in violent clashes, the most terrible when the ANL activist Blair Peach was killed by a police officer in Southall, west London, in April 1979. I attracted some criticism for the policy of confrontation, even though when I was present or able to do so, I always used my influence to urge restraint. Our position was that we would mass to prevent the NF swaggering through black or Jewish communities and causing violence as a result. It was up to the police or local councils to prevent the NF marching and meeting – then there would be no opportunity for confrontations, either with opposing ANL demonstrators, or with local residents fearful of the presence of Nazis in their neighbourhoods. Lessons had been drawn from when the Blackshirts, led by Oswald Mosley and targeting Jewish communities, were physically stopped by left-wing activists in Cable Street in London's East End in October 1936.

In the event, such was the power we mobilised that within a few years the National Front was put out of business, and one of its leaders, Martin Webster, publicly admitted that the ANL had caused this.* Nevertheless some anti-racist traditionalists and left-wing fundamentalists continued to assert that the focus on Nazism was too narrow, and that instead the challenges were ones of class and race. To me all this was *déjà vu*. It smacked almost exactly of the *contre-temps* I had in 1969–70, for example, with the 'revolutionary socialist' student leader Tariq Ali over the Stop The Tour campaign. He criticised the campaign because it was 'not confronting capitalism'. If we had dug up cricket or rugby pitches or burnt down stadiums, then that would indeed have been an attack on private property, which Marxists saw as the foundation of capitalism. Similarly many on the 'revolutionary' left argued that demonstrators should confront the police outside rugby grounds because that was 'confronting the state', rather than getting inside and disrupting matches as we did. Activists like me were indulging in *bourgeois* tactics – and that was not for *real* leftists, still less *real* revolutionaries.

I was impatient with such specious sophistry. Although I was proudly part of the left, my background, my Young Liberal roots (to many quixotic) and my impatience with traditionalists meant I was often seen as an impertinent outsider. Many within the left also continued to frustrate me with what I saw as their armchair posturing. I wasn't really interested in whether or not our non-violent direct action perfectly fitted some contemporary Marxist paradigm, still less whether it was accompanied by the 'correct' jargon. I was preoccupied with a less exalted concern: the best way to defeat apartheid, and our sports protests were at the time indisputably that. None of our leftist critics came anywhere near achieving such concrete results, though their fiery rhetoric kept them on a self-satisfying high. And this was to reinforce in me again Alan Paton's belief in 'all or something' – not 'all or nothing'. That was to become my watchword as I picked my way between the byways and subways of radical politics and protest – and also very much later on in my parliamentary and governmental career.

---

*   For the story of the Anti-Nazi League, see Dave Renton, *When We Touched the Sky* (Cheltenham, New Clarion Press, 2006).

‡

During the period from 1968 to 1975, I listened to arguments between Marxists and anarchists, socialists and liberals, and I read the burgeoning literature of the contemporary New Left voraciously: Noam Chomsky, E. P. Thompson, Raymond Williams, Ralph Miliband, and many more American and British writers. But it was George Orwell, a writer of the left from a different era, that seemed to set all this in a more grounded, more mature and historic perspective in *Homage to Catalonia*.

I recall it less as the classic it was on the barbarous Spanish Civil War of the 1930s, and more as a personal discovery by Orwell of how his democratic socialist instincts were sharpened and shaped by the buffeting swirl of ideological clashes and bitter struggles within the inspirational resistance to Franco's fascism in Spain. Orwell describes how the left, which led this resistance, was typically divided between anarchists, syndicalists, communists, Trotskyites, socialists and liberal republicans. As he witnessed the heroism and the horror, the passion and sometimes the ulterior purposes of these competing groups, he experienced both all that is best, and all that is worst, about the left.

The best was the extraordinary bravery and dedication of the Spanish left to resist Franco. Volunteers like Orwell who joined the international brigades made incredible sacrifices for the cause, poorly trained yet fighting and often dying for their anti-fascist beliefs in a foreign land. The Spanish left also lit a fervent flame for community socialism with their agricultural cooperatives and worker collectives.

The worst was the bitter sectarianism between communists, Trotskyites and anarchists, and how this crippled the overall resistance, their own ideological objectives and party interests thwarting the left unity desperately necessary to defeat the enemy. In the case of the communists, their continuing allegiance to Moscow when Stalin and Hitler were manoeuvring towards a pact led to betrayals of fellow members of the resistance.

Trotskyites in some ways came out better in Orwell's eyes, though they too were on the receiving end of his penetrating criticism that relied not so much on invective as a bluntness which I found refreshing. Orwell was never one for bullshit – and the left would be a lot healthier if his writ even today ran right across its politics. He was contemptuous of posturing, of striking up positions so as to be seen to follow whatever was deemed at the time the acceptable 'line'. Equally he had no time for adventurism or the tendency of the Trots, both in Spain at the time and more contemporarily, to pose 'transitional demands' incapable of being satisfied but which, from their point of view, could 'expose' left-wing opponents as betraying the faith. (Some of this damaging dogma also infected the Labour Party's left, as I was to experience in the 1980s). However, I did not read *Homage to Catalonia* as some dry textbook, but instead a gripping narrative, climaxing in the internecine firefight in Barcelona where the left helped defeat itself, and thereby opened the door to Franco's murderous victory and equally murderous rule.

Like Orwell's, the socialism that I had come to believe in during the first ten years of my life in Britain was instinctively 'libertarian' rather than 'statist', favouring democracy and liberty rather than central control and bureaucracy. And like his, my politics were determinedly non-sectarian, committed to the broadest possible unity for practical action towards progressive objectives. His book helped define an enduring set of beliefs that were to guide me through more than forty years of political life, both outside and inside government.

Furthermore, both my reading of political history and my participation in extra-parliamentary action convinced me that it could be a vital force for change – but not as some kind of syndicalist substitute for democratic government. The 1970 South African tour would not have been stopped without our direct action campaign, but it was actually cancelled at the request of the Home Secretary. On the other hand the then Labour government had no answer to the rise of the National Front from the mid-1970s; instead the extra-parliamentary activity of the Anti-Nazi League was required to defeat the NF.

Extra-parliamentary protest and action helped to create the foundations of democratic government in Britain, as the campaigning by Chartists for universal franchise, and suffragettes for votes for women, graphically demonstrated. But once a democracy had been created such action was an essential means of pressuring and thereby complementing democratic government. My radical youth outside conventional politics and government was never insurrectionary and that is why I had, by belief and temperament, kept open the door to operating inside the parliamentary system as well.

‡

From 1973, researching for my three-year doctoral thesis in political science at the University of Sussex, I read increasingly widely, becoming more and more persuaded of the socialist case, though comfortable enough in the Young Liberals for the time being at least. Throughout this time I remained a leading anti-apartheid activist as well. Alongside work on my doctoral thesis on neighbourhood councils and public participation, I was able to do some part-time teaching through tutorials, which I enjoyed immensely. But, after two years of research, just as I was beginning to type up a draft of the first chapter of my thesis in October 1975, the mistaken identity bank theft case hit me and turned my life upside down. The effort to clear my name absorbed most of my time and destroyed my final year's work programme; my funded course having ended, I needed to find a job.*

I had spotted an advert for a research officer post at the Union of Post Office Workers in the left-wing weekly the *New Statesman*. The union's office was a few miles from where we lived, convenient since our first baby was imminent, the salary was good, and I had been increasingly attracted to the labour movement. However I had few illusions about my employability: I was notorious, had just been acquitted of robbing a bank, a case which generated headlines, and I was regarded as troublemaker.

The interview confirmed all my fears. Tom Jackson, the well-rounded general secretary, a genial, popular public figure and jazz fan with a handle-bar moustache, welcomed me into his spacious office, smiling. Then he came straight to the point. 'Why should I appoint a bloody Liberal?' he asked.

'A very good question, I can well understand why you ask,' I replied. 'But some Young Liberals like me always were socialists. I find myself more and more interested in the trade union movement and the Labour Party, and I would like to work for you.'

He hadn't quite expected my disarming answer and the interview then took a different tack. Apart from Ted Geaney's cricket question, our discussion became about why Jackson should bother to create a lot of trouble for himself by appointing me. Others he was interviewing were well qualified too. He could have a quiet life and choose one of them. By the end of our allotted time, and reflecting afterwards, I felt I should just save him all the nuisance, do him a favour, and withdraw. Driving back home and then discussing it with my wife Pat, I was inclined to do just that. But inertia set in.

The evening drew on into the night and then the phone rang. 'Peter, I am going to take a chance. You have got the job,' Tom Jackson boomed. It transpired they had discussed the appointment going around in circles for hours afterwards and he had eventually gone back to talk it over with his partner Kate. Both surprised and delighted, I thanked him profusely.

However, the next day, I had to disappoint him by phoning up to apologise for postponing our first proper meeting: Pat had gone into labour. It was long and tough for her, over eighteen hours during which I mopped her brow and faithfully carried out her instructions to insist she have as natural a birth as possible, certainly not to be artificially induced as the hospital doctors wanted.

---

* I was only able to complete the thesis four years later in my own spare time, amidst work, politics and bringing up two young sons, obtaining a Master of Philosophy degree, revised as a book: *Neighbourhood Participation* (London, Temple Smith, 1980).

They were not best pleased. But the result was the most magical moment of my life: witnessing the birth of my first child, Sam, choking back the emotions because South African boys like me didn't do tears.

Six weeks later, we took him along to what was to be my last Liberal Party annual conference in Scarborough. Delegates cooed over the tiny baby who gurgled away happily as he was humped from the back of the conference auditorium, to fringe meetings and cafes, returning at night to a damp bed and breakfast, which was all we could afford.

‡

There was a bit of rumbling in the union when it became known that I was their new assistant research officer. A special conference in Brighton was due a couple of months after the interview and Tom Jackson made a point of walking me around the conference floor making introductions, an outsider to their world.

It was a great job for me and I worked for the union for fully fourteen years, later taking over as head of research when Ted Geaney retired. I was both conscientious and scrupulous about keeping my high profile political activism separate from my relatively modest role within the organisation. They in turn allowed me plenty of freedom outside and sometimes inside working hours. It just meant I had to work doubly hard to become an insider, both physically and politically. It was never a problem for me to show due deference to the national officers and members I served and, once that was clear to them, they were happy to have me. Tom Jackson's choice had been vindicated, ironically to some since he was seen as being on the right of the labour movement and I was seen as a left-wing activist.

Some of the characters were larger than life. Maurice Styles, still an active member of the Communist Party as Jackson had been in his youth, represented the bulk of the union's members: 120,000 postmen (there were hardly any postwomen in those days). A tubby and amiable cockney, he was well schooled in political history, his bluff demeanour concealing a shrewd operator who could be as tough as anybody when he needed to be. Perhaps because he was more political than many of his colleagues in the national leadership, we got on very well.

Part of my role was to do the background research for negotiations over pay and conditions. Meticulous analysis and calculations went on for weeks before meetings during the big annual showdowns, when figures, facts and arguments were traded. Finally, both sides rolled up their sleeves, drew back from the brink and invariably did a deal, making me wonder about the ritual of all the voluminous analysis followed by detailed argumentation during grinding meetings.

A case in point was an exhaustive study into the pay and conditions of doorkeepers. Post Office officials had produced reams of material which we dutifully checked and counter-checked, disputing some external comparators, accepting others. Finally, after a couple of years of exchanges, came the crunch meeting. Maurice and I went along to the old Post Office Headquarters, a cavernous colonial building in St Martin's Le Grand, just behind St Paul's Cathedral. I was armed with my calculator, and there was a bright but nervously hesitant official fronting for management. It quickly became apparent we were being stalled over obtuse points and their pay arguments were way off the mark. The usually patient and polite Maurice finally snapped, to my astonishment pulling out his own calculator – one I had never seen before. He banged away on it, then paused and stared at the equally amazed officials opposite. 'You are taking the piss,' he barked. 'Don't insult me with those figures of yours. We are off.' He gathered his papers as if to leave and I hastily followed suit.

The nervous official stuttered in fright: 'Can we have an adjournment?'

'Just don't waste my time coming back with the same old nonsense,' Maurice replied gruffly, stabbing at his calculator.

The managers trooped out and I turned incredulous. 'Don't worry about the calculator,' he winked, showing me a blank screen as he pressed the keys, 'I bought it at a Communist Party jumble sale and it's never worked.' When the meeting resumed, we got a fair deal.

On another occasion, when national pay negotiations were on the brink of a breakdown, a postal strike looming, the union's pay negotiating team was at full strength, with the Post Office's then chairman, Ron Dearing, present, leading the management team as a signal of how serious it was. As the argument raged to and fro across the table, tension rising, suddenly the door burst open and an elderly tea lady bustled in with a trolley. Visibly embarrassed, Dearing turned, urging her to withdraw for a while, his senior officials desperately seeking to hustle her out.

'No way,' she replied. 'Tea's at 3.10 on the dot – always is, come sun or rain.'

'But I am the chairman of the Post Office!' Dearing beseeched her.

'Don't care who you are, duck. Teatime's teatime,' she stated emphatically, as she clattered around handing out the cups and distributing biscuits.

Negotiations over pay and conditions were frequently tense and periodically ended in strikes or disputes. Hardly had I joined the union than there was a serious industrial dispute at Grunwick, a small film-processing company in north-west London. In the August heat wave of 1976 workers, fed up with

bad conditions and poor pay, walked out. Their strike became a focal point
for the labour movement because repeated attempts to obtain recognition for
the trade union of their choice (APEX, the union of which I and every other
UPW employee was a member) failed: normal procedures against an obdurate
employer led nowhere. Picketing of the firm escalated into bitter confrontations between trade unionists and the police, aggressive tactics by the elite
Special Patrol Group inflaming the atmosphere with over 500 arrests. Soon the
dispute became a national controversy. The right saw it as a symbol of all that
was wrong with Britain under the Labour government of the time, the left the
abject failure of even the pro-union laws Labour had implemented.

Sharing the anger at the exploitation of low-paid workers, mostly women,
I joined thousands of others on demonstrations to support the pickets after
volunteers from UPW headquarters were provided with a coach and encouraged to do so. Sometimes I made my own way there early in the morning.
It became a national *cause célèbre*. Even Labour Cabinet Minister Shirley
Williams appeared on the picket line in solidarity, attracting howls of outrage
from Conservatives and their supporting newspapers.

Quickly, however, our own union became embroiled. Grunwick's lifeblood
was the mail service – the conduit for receiving film and returning photographs –
and London postmen refused to handle their business. Postal workers had always
thought they had the right to strike, indeed had exercised it during a seven-week
pay dispute in 1971, and on several other occasions going back to 1921.

But an ultra-right group, the National Association for Freedom (comprising
many of the elements behind my 1972 conspiracy trial), sought an injunction
against the union for a breach of the 1953 Post Office Act, and I was immediately involved in researching the background. It transpired that an ancient
offence was being exploited. This went back to 1710 when the Post Office had
been established under the reign of Queen Anne. At that time mail coaches
and mail workers were regularly attacked by footpads and highwaymen, and it
was made an offence 'wilfully to detain or delay' any packet or letter. The same
wording was to be found in the 1953 Act and the 1863 Telegraph Act, obviously
intended to apply to criminals, not to trade unionists.

The injunction was not resolved because the Grunwick dispute went to
(ultimately unsuccessful) arbitration and the UPW suspended its action.
However, within weeks the UPW was back in court on similar grounds – and
this time I was the trigger. Late in 1976 a circular had come in from the UPW's
international postal and telecommunications federation, urging support for a
week's boycott of mail and telecommunications to South Africa as part of an
international protest against apartheid. It landed on my desk with a request
for advice from Tom Jackson and I went to his office. He didn't need much

persuading, still smarting from the Grunwick injunction. 'Let's take them on, Peter,' he said. I could also detect a twinkle in his eye – a union leader depicted by the left as 'right wing' at the head of a great cause.

I helped draft the necessary documents for Tom to obtain authorisation from the union's National Executive, which he duly did, and drafted a press release announcing the reasons for refusing to handle traffic to and from South Africa, thrilled that I was fortuitously able to assist the anti-apartheid struggle, albeit in the studiously backroom role to which I purposely held. (In the prurient media climate of subsequent decades my relative anonymity would surely have been exposed, perhaps to become a divisive issue for the union.)

However the planned boycott soon attracted headlines and the bile of the right. The UPW, a moderate trade union, had inadvertently stumbled into the middle of the growing confrontation about the legitimacy of the Labour government in the eyes of its right-wing opponents. The Freedom Association this time obtained a successful injunction in January 1977 against the union from the celebrated right-wing judge Lord Denning, after the (Labour) Attorney General, Sam Silkin, had refused its request. Nine months later, reviewing this and the Grunwick case, Denning remarked: 'By and large I hope we are keeping the [Labour] government in order.' And, on his role and that of his senior colleagues, he added: 'We have ways and means of getting around the law.'* His comment and the episode summed up my own experience: that the much-vaunted impartiality of the British legal system was fiction.

‡

In those days if you posted a letter in the early morning, first class to another address within the same town or city, it would invariably arrive second post later in the day. That was nearly my undoing, upstaging a carefully planned but obviously sensitive switch in my party membership from Liberal to Labour.

By 1977, a year into my job as trade union researcher, I felt increasingly comfortable within the labour movement, attending the union's conferences and getting involved in its political and policy work as an affiliate of the Labour Party. With a friend and YL colleague, Simon Hebditch, who had been a vice chairman when I was national chairman, I also began going to conferences of the Nottingham-based Institute for Workers Control and read the influential left-wing Labour newspaper *Tribune* each week.

I was increasingly resolved to join Labour. But I had been a Young Liberal for nearly ten years and a member of the Party's national executive for some

---

* See Peter Hain, *Political Trials in Britain* (London, Allen Lane, 1984), p. 97.

of that time as well. I still felt ties of loyalty to many Liberals who had been very supportive, especially in times of difficulty such as the conspiracy and bank theft trials. I had friends, young and old, in the Party and was on good terms with the then leader, David Steel, whose campaign the previous year to succeed Jeremy Thorpe I had supported when most fellow radicals in the Party had backed his rival, the talented but mercurial John Pardoe. My parents were also active Liberals and I knew they would be unhappy.

As a figure with a high profile, I could not make the switch in some anonymity (as other YL colleagues at the time had been doing and continued to do later). So, in strict confidence, Simon Hebditch and I made our preparations as best we could. First we went to see Neil Kinnock – the fiery Welsh Labour MP and later Party leader – who had been a stalwart anti-apartheid campaigner and was good enough to be one of the main figures in a support campaign around my conspiracy and bank theft trials. He and his wife Glenys welcomed us warmly to their modest family home in south-west London one evening. Neil gave some good advice and promised to help. He suggested I appear at the *Tribune* rally at the Labour conference in Brighton and promised to speak in confidence to the editor, Dick Clements.

Next we went to see the Cabinet Minister Tony Benn, then the rising leader of Labour's left. He was an inspirational figure for young radicals like me and I had by chance met him some years before since my parents knew his secretary. His vision of the Labour Party attracted me. A few months before I had sent him a book review I had written for a newspaper where I was critical of Ramsay MacDonald, the Labour leader who in 1931 had defected and formed a national government. Benn had handwritten a friendly note back. Now he proffered support and also gave good advice in his rambling but engaging home in Bayswater. He treated us to a tour of the library in his basement, packed full of labour movement material going back generations. In retrospect it was ironic that these two Labour giants, Benn and Kinnock, worked together to back me when, just a few years later, they were engaged in mutual hostilities over the struggle for Labour's future.

As I was to find over the years, trust is a vital but rare value in politics. I was hugely dependent on them both, people I hardly knew. A maelstrom of passionate principle, jealousy, rivalry, pettiness and personality swirls amongst members of any political party and it was comforting to realise that our respect was self-evidently mutual and they both adhered strictly to the confidential basis for my intended transition.

Nearly two decades later, when a number of Conservatives switched to Labour under Tony Blair I always made a point of seeking them out because I knew what they must have gone through: a potent mixture of anxiety and guilt on the one hand, hope and conviction on the other, overhung with concern about the reception from new colleagues. For my part, the motivation was entirely idealistic. As a libertarian socialist, I was drawn to the more radical spirit then rising in Labour, one absent to my late 1960s generation when I had first got involved in British politics.

Various accusations were bandied against me. Some Liberals said my move was for career reasons, some Labour people said the same. The truth was I had been on a journey to my natural political home. It was nothing to do with a 'career' – at the stage I had never thought of being an MP for example. I was a big fish in the small Liberal pond, about to be a small, somewhat insecure, albeit very well-known one in the large Labour pond. Although the great majority in Labour were very welcoming, others never fully accepted me, decades later still hanging a 'former Liberal' tag around me, usually behind my back.

But the careful plans for newspaper articles and welcoming statements from Kinnock and Benn were nearly all upstaged by the damnably efficient first-class post. I felt an obligation to leading Liberals in both the national Party and the Putney branch to inform them personally.* So I typed up and posted about twenty letters, popping them into the letter box early in the morning, hoping they would reach the recipients the following day just before our mid-morning statement on joining Labour was due to be issued. However, the Putney Liberal officers received theirs the same day, informed the national Party headquarters and soon a spoiling operation began with leaks to the media, whose incessant phone calls I ignored. A frantic twenty hours followed with hurried calls to Kinnock and Benn on how best to manage the tobog-ganed announcement, including a planned article for the *Guardian*, where Simon and I explained our reasons for the switch.

With headlines in the papers and news spreading fast around political circles, a prepared call was made to the secretary of Putney Labour Party to say a new member wanted to sign up as soon as possible. That evening I knocked on the door of Phyllis Courtney, who, to my relief, smiled in welcome. 'Thought it might be you,' she twinkled, handing me a form to sign and receiving my subscription. She and her husband Peter were to become not just party colleagues but good friends – the very best of the Labour grass roots, straight and true. My nightmare had been: what if the local Party had rejected me? That was by no means impossible, given the stroppy character of some constituency

---

* My parents, to whom I had been and remained extremely close – and whom I had only informed very late – were especially insistent about communicating with the Putney Liberals, in which they were busy activists. They were distressed about my move – though some five years later switched to Labour as well and, increasingly over the years, became Putney Labour stalwarts.

parties at the time and the then Party constitution which vested the power to refuse membership in local parties. Fortunately for me – Neil Kinnock having made some judicious exploratory enquiries – that seemed unlikely in Putney's case. By coincidence the Party's general committee was due to meet that same evening and, much to my relief, approved my membership.

Two weeks later I was thrown somewhat naively into the cauldron of my first Labour conference. When Neil Kinnock first suggested speaking at the annual *Tribune* rally I had no idea about just how big an event this was, the prestige of speaking and the jealousy my appearance would create. For left-wing figures it was a prized and much-sought-after slot. Perhaps in retrospect I should have talked about the Anti-Apartheid Movement and the Anti-Nazi League and how these movements chimed with the socialist values I shared in common with those at the rally. Instead of which I spoke about my belief in libertarian socialism. Although there was generosity from the platform and from many in the packed audience of well over a thousand, there was also resentment amongst others who gave me a good heckling. Used as I was to the political rough and tumble, that did not worry me too much, and I was exhilarated by fine speeches, especially from Tony Benn and Neil Kinnock. Another was from Jimmy Reid, leader of the famous sit-in at Upper Clyde Shipbuilders in 1971, and a former Communist who had also just switched to Labour.

My real embarrassment was not being pre-warned about the traditional singing of the emblematic 'Red Flag', which marked the close of the rally. So when the whole platform rose and joined the audience in a rousing rendition of its lyrics, I mumbled along, my stilted performance inevitably making the late television coverage. The next morning's papers also had a bit of fun at my expense. (However, my discomfort was nothing like that of the right-wing Conservative Secretary of State for Wales, John Redwood, who represented an English constituency. In 1995 he was widely lampooned for an excruciating performance rolling his eyes and whistling during the Welsh national anthem, 'Land of My Fathers', at the end of a Welsh Tory conference. He hadn't bothered to learn the words.)

Meanwhile, however, many Putney Labour members went out of their way to welcome me, including Mike Gapes, the national Party's student officer and subsequently a Labour MP, and Greg Dyke, recent candidate for the Greater London Council and subsequently director general of the BBC. I reciprocated by throwing myself into local activism, deliberately not seeking Party positions or limelight, writing local newsletters then foreign to Labour but successful amongst Liberal practitioners of community politics.*

---

*   See Peter Hain (ed.), *Community Politics* (London, John Calder, 1976).

Within a few years I had formed a group of close Party friends in Putney, sharing a busy social and political life – many having young children like us (my second son Jake was born in 1978). We helped ensure Putney Labour became a vibrant, campaigning local Party renowned for new ideas and committed to activism. That was in stark contrast to many other Constituency Labour Parties who practised what I mischievously termed the *resolutionary* politics of endless meetings where activists talked only to themselves and believed the 'class struggle' was advanced mainly by passing resolutions demanding (often impossible) positions of the leadership whose historic role was to betray the rank and file.

Labour, I discovered, was very good at talking to itself within a party structure which was admirably democratic from top to bottom but also insufferably bureaucratic. Constituency Parties often had very little relationship with their local communities. Some were run by right-wing caucuses suspicious of fresh blood: people trying to join would be told 'membership is full up' and turned away. Others might be able to join but be either frozen out or turned off by boring meetings dominated by a few self-obsessed people, dedicated in their own way to the Party, but intolerant of new ideas. Still others, comprising a significant albeit minority section of the Party's left, operated in an almost Leninist fashion, intolerantly shouldering others aside.

I wrote two pamphlets for the labour movement publishers Spokesman, who had been associated with the great socialist philosopher and peace activist Bertrand Russell. Both advocated a more radical, campaigning, Labour Party which opened out and involved local communities.* At local Party meetings around the country, I illustrated my case with an anecdote audiences always laughingly enjoyed, recognising the awkward, all-too typical, symbol of their own Party's behaviour. After warming them up by saying I was sure their own Party was quite different from all the others – meetings always stimulating, and plenty of political and policy debate – I would tell this tale: 'A local branch secretary looked down his membership list, discovered a member who hadn't attended for years and years, knocked on her door and asked: "Why weren't you at the last branch meeting?" To which came the reply: "If I'd known it was the *last* branch meeting I'd have been there to celebrate!" My sons Sam and, when he was older, Jake would accompany me selling pamphlets at the back of the hall, and usually my standard jokes went down well. But in one cold hall with a glum audience huddled together, Sam was the only one to respond, his small voice cackling shrilly. 'I have heard you speak so often I know when to laugh now, Dad,' he said afterwards.

---

*   Peter Hain and Simon Hebditch, *Radicals and Socialism* (Nottingham, Spokesman, 1978); Peter Hain, *Refreshing the Parts that Others Cannot Reach* (Nottingham, Spokesman, 1980).

Well before my boys joined me on these speaking tours, I was phoned in the summer of 1980 with an unexpected offer: 'Would you like to visit China?' I didn't really know what to say. My sons were still small – aged four and two – and it would be an extra burden on Pat, who in any case had to cope with my hyper-activism. Also there was the cost: the air fare, which we could not afford. So I declined politely. Several more calls, with successive offers to reduce my contribution until it was zero, and I was left with little excuse, finding my name added to the quaintly entitled 'Noted Persons Delegation' from Britain's Society for Anglo Chinese Understanding.

The three week visit gave me both a fascinating insight into post-Mao China,* and a sense of its huge global potential. Others on the delegation were all around double my age, eminent professors and Sino experts, including Ramsay MacDonald's daughter Sheila Lochead, with whom I got on well. Then sprightly in her seventies, she told me tales of life as a young girl in No. 10. When we were first introduced she had described herself as 'Malcolm MacDonald's sister'. I immediately thought of the Newcastle United and England footballer of the same name and blurted this out to general hilarity, the rest of the learnt group well aware her brother was a distinguished former British Ambassador to China.

‡

Within months of joining Labour I also joined the Labour Co-ordinating Committee, a new pressure group associated with Tony Benn which advocated a more left-wing, democratic, participatory Labour Party. Welcomed into the LCC and encouraged to stand for its Executive, I soon became part of an activist-based movement for change in my new Party. I was happy to put the work in, utilising the skills and experience of my previous ten years, finding it exciting and absorbing, with no regrets at all about having moved political homes.

Before each annual conference in 1978, 1979 and 1980 there would be caucus meetings, often at Tony Benn's house. He and his vivacious, highly political wife Caroline would provide some beer and wine, even though they were teetotal themselves. There we would plan for victory against the 'forces of reaction', mostly centred on the Party leadership of Jim Callaghan. Our main demands for change were that the Party leader should be elected by the whole Party and not just MPs; that MPs should be subject to periodic reselection

---

* I later wrote a political thriller which in part drew upon my impressions, *The Peking Connection* (London, Lawrence & Wishart, 1995).

by their local parties; and that the manifesto should be drawn up with the participation of the Party's National Executive.

By 1980, all of these democratic reforms were eventually won after set-piece battles repeatedly waged at the conferences, rank and file members increasingly in no mood to accept the old ways. The leader had traditionally been able simply to veto policies for inclusion in the election manifesto. Some MPs had become self-serving, right wing and remote from the constituency parties which had first chosen them. And Party members had no influence over who should be their leader, traditionally chosen by MPs alone. All of these changes, which seemed so momentous at the time, were later accepted as normal, although some of the original content was sensibly modified: for instance, on the leadership, membership decision by one-person-one-vote, rather than by local party or trade union caucuses.

The high noon and also the nemesis of this radical phase came at the 1981 Party conference in Brighton, where our standard bearer, Tony Benn, was defeated for the deputy leadership by the centre-right Denis Healey with only the narrowest of margins. Immediately after the nail-biting drama when the result was declared to the conference, I remember disagreeing with some colleagues on the LCC Executive who were already talking of repeating the contest the following year as the rules would have permitted. 'We cannot go through all this again,' was my instant reaction: the Party was badly split and, as important, the left was split. Neil Kinnock and many fellow Tribune MPs had refused to back Benn; the contest, spread over several months, had been at once stimulating and hugely divisive. Aghast at what they were experiencing, a group of prominent former Cabinet Ministers – Roy Jenkins, Shirley Williams, David Owen and Bill Rodgers – damagingly defected to form their own new party, the Social Democrats, later to join an electoral alliance with the Liberals.

A significant section of the Party's left believed in fighting on through the structures, from local constituency party and trade union branches up to the annual conference, with the aim eventually of taking over on a genuinely left-wing programme with an authentically left-wing leadership under Tony Benn. Although I was still motivated by much of the idealism behind all this, I had become increasingly estranged from the intolerance of this emerging left. I also believed that any victory by long march through the party's institutions would be a hollow one, fearing that opponents would become alienated and the Party's support would narrow rather than deepen. This latter argument – revolving around the relationship between activists and voters – had always been more important to my socialist politics than to some others on Labour's left, and now was to be progressively even more so. Very much in agreement was Robin Cook, the Scottish MP and member of Tribune, bright with a laconic wit, who began to work ever more closely with us.

The split within the Party's left – symbolised by the developing enmity between Benn and Kinnock – started to play itself out within the Labour Co-ordinating Committee, where two camps appeared, a 'soft' and a 'hard' left. I found myself at the radical end of the former, and was pressed to stand as vice chairman against the incumbent, Audrey Wise MP (with whom I had worked closely since joining the Party), at the 1982 annual general meeting held in Newcastle. To some, my victory signified a move away from being a Bennite pressure group, pure and simple, to one which was to play a key role in mobilising activists for a broader, more popular, politics that could one day propel Labour back into office.

‡

In more recent times I was struck by being asked for advice on a 'political career' – as if politics was a 'career' like any other one: you might choose politics to earn a living rather than accountancy or insurance or the law.

'But politics is not just a job, it's a mission,' I would respond. *Why* do you want to get involved? For career self-advancement? Or because of your beliefs and values, your commitment to make a difference, to change society? It had never occurred to me that I would end up having a 'career' in politics. I was a campaigner, fighting for justice. Protest and, more and more I accepted, party politics, was the mechanism for delivering that. It wasn't an end in itself. It wasn't – or at least shouldn't be – a conduit for self-promotion.

In over forty years in politics, my role evolved. It was never planned. I never set out to be an MP, still less to be a government Minister. That hasn't made me better than others who set out to make a political career for themselves – just different. Even when I ended up near to the very top of the Cabinet I had a very different perspective, albeit by then also from within the Westminster bubble.

When Putney's first ever Labour MP, Hugh Jenkins,[*] was defeated in the 1979 election, having served since a famous victory in 1964 when seemingly half the acting world flooded into the constituency to back him, it didn't occur to me I might be selected as the parliamentary candidate.

But, at the end of 1980, when the process of selecting a candidate was formally triggered, I was unexpectedly approached by a respected ward secretary, one of those many selfless party servants, a young mum to be, Kelly

---

[*]   See his book of interviews with some of the Party's activists: *Rank and File* (London, Croom Helm, 1980).

Marchant. What made it surprising was one of the favourites, an able local councillor with a long track record in the Party, was in her own ward, where he could have anticipated backing. 'Why not have a go?' she said. 'You will have plenty of support, you could really energise the Party.'

That was probably true, I reflected, having reluctantly promised her to at least think about it. After all I *was* a campaigner. That was bread and butter to my politics. The role would give me a platform for my ideas. I had worked hard locally for the Putney Party, including acting as Hugh Jenkins's assistant election agent. I would also enjoy taking on the obnoxious new Tory MP, David Mellor, extremely able, but who specialised in being offensive to just about everyone, some in his own party and family included. *Private Eye* described him as 'about as likeable as a mouthful of Brylcreem'. But Labour had then bounced back in the polls after a bad 1979 defeat by Margaret Thatcher. If we actually won Putney I would become an MP – and I wasn't at all sure about *that*. Also I remained notorious. Right-wing opponents would fight a venomous campaign. I might not be electable. Anyway I was just three years a Party member, surely they wouldn't have me? But Kelly wouldn't give up, and a group of friends in the Party also encouraged me. So I decided to give it a go.

I had stood for, and won, internal Party elections before. But campaigning for myself to become *the* candidate was different. The issue was *you* in a way I had not really encountered before, the whole Party's identity projected through its would-be MP, its future support dependent upon the level of the candidate's appeal. I wore the suit and tie I had only occasionally donned for funerals or union negotiating sessions at Post Office headquarters, and addressed ward and trade union selection meetings which had the right to make nominations. My central message was about the campaigning party Labour needed to be in Putney and also about the radical policies we required.

My support gathered momentum and enthusiasm. Then came the packed final selection meeting in a community hall in spring 1981 which each of the short-listed candidates addressed in turn before awaiting the verdict in a pub nearby. The bottom candidates fell out, their votes transferred, and we were shepherded back in to be told I had won. Although I had gained respect throughout the local party for my work, I now felt totally accepted, suddenly elevated as the de facto leader of the Putney Party, a clear and popular winner over the two favourites, who, with their camps, were generous in response after what had been a hard-fought but comradely contest. I had stumbled onto the road which would eventually lead me from protest organiser into Parliament.

During the next two years I worked hard to build a successful campaign organisation so that, by the time Margaret Thatcher called the general election for early May 1983, we were well prepared. The national Party headquarters described ours as Labour's best constituency campaign in the country. For nearly four weeks I was driven around in a trade union-supplied car from morning to dusk, meeting and speaking to as many voters-as I could, with an enthusiastic team of activists. By now in my mid-thirties, I enjoyed real ale and wine, but had resolved deliberately not to touch a glass of alcohol for the entire campaign even though we would typically adjourn at the end of an evening's campaigning to the nearest pub.

The constituency was emblazoned with red 'Hain Labour' posters, outnumbering the blue Tory ones by four to one. Our leaflets were everywhere. Where we encountered voters who were either not at home or who said they were 'doubtful', we went back again and again on a crusade to persuade. We invented what we called 'blitz canvassing': a small team with me the whole time knocked doors ahead and called me over when somebody was in, to maximise voter-contact. I was constantly running between front doors down streets or along tower block corridors. Once a week our central organising team would gather for a late meal at the home of an activist couple, Pat and Rob Dark, to consider progress and plot strategy. We called a big public meeting, addressed by Neil Kinnock and myself, electrifying an audience of several hundred.

It was exhilarating. Campaigning was my forte and I loved it. We had a passionate band of activists, students from around nearby campuses poured in, and people were despatched to preach the gospel. The actress Julie Christie, like me a supporter of the Campaign for Nuclear Disarmament, joined us. So did another leading actress, Glenda Jackson, and Bill Owen of the popular television series *Last of the Summer Wine*. We would take over Putney High Street and festoon shoppers with Hain-Labour stickers. Once, when we were allocated a big open-topped bus by the Party HQ, we paraded triumphantly down the High Street, spotting our Tory opponent David Mellor, who cut a lonely and forlorn figure shopping on the pavement. He had became a government Minister by then, yet childishly stuck his tongue out at us, in a parody of his odious reputation.

The only dampener came when Jill Craigie, wife of Labour leader Michael Foot, appeared with their famed dog Dizzie chaotically in tow. Although she was a bit of a hit in the High Street, back at our campaign office she worried me when she asked at the top of her voice in front of a team of helpers stuffing envelopes: 'Do you think they will attack Michael when we lose?' However, a few days before election day, Robin Cook phoned me to ask if I would support Neil Kinnock as the next Labour leader: absolutely, I replied, pleased that some forward planning was occurring.

But I don't recall any of us considering we might lose in Putney. Indeed, a few days before polling, the BBC reported Putney might be a surprise Labour win against all the odds of what was proving to be Labour's worst national performance in living memory. Somehow we were insulated from the dismal wider picture, and that in retrospect symbolised the malaise in Labour at the time: I had an army of dedicated and decent activists, but clearly the Party's left-wing policies which excited us had little traction with voters. The BBC 'exit poll' after voting closed predicted a Conservative landslide across the country and I arrived at the count in the local town hall with two speeches prepared, for winning or losing, quickly understanding from the bundles of votes that started to pile up and the increasingly gloomy faces of my team that we were doomed. Returning to a friend's house afterwards, I thanked scores of activists gathered to watch the results on TV and to party. I remember huge warmth and also gallons of tears as I assured everyone that I was fine and we would fight on. The following Monday I was back at my desk at union headquarters.

‡

Although many of us felt it was great at the time, Labour's left-wing 1983 election manifesto was subsequently described by Gerald Kaufman, the shrewd former aide to Prime Minister Harold Wilson, as the 'longest suicide note in history'. We had been routed and the Labour Co-ordinating Committee (LCC) led an important post-mortem on the election. Along with a group of others on the left I had come to realise Labour could not continue like this. We had to fashion a new politics which expressed the best spirit of the left but in a way which broadened our appeal.

An immediate choice presented itself after Michael Foot's resignation as Party leader. The LCC with the rest of the 'soft left' backed Neil Kinnock as his successor. Since Tony Benn was ineligible to stand after being defeated at the election in his Bristol seat, the veteran left-wing MP Eric Heffer stood, backed by the 'hard left'. I was recruited to Kinnock's campaign committee and, with the trade unions swinging behind him, he was a runaway winner, beating Roy Hattersley, who, however, also stood and won as his deputy against Michael Meacher, another friend of mine whom the LCC backed. The Kinnock–Hattersley leadership was presented as a 'dream ticket' uniting left and right – but excluding the hard left.

In the latter, Militant was growing in strength and influence. Disciples of Leon Trotsky, Militant followed a strategy of what Trotsky called 'entryism': a group which operated with its own discipline and constitution – effectively a 'party within a party'. Militant members were highly sectarian: if you were not a fellow traveller you were an enemy, especially so if, like the LCC, you were on the left. They viewed figures like me as more of a threat than the old right of the Party because we had a stronger claim to the left than Militant did and appealed to idealistic young people too. After I was chosen to fight Putney again in 1985, Militant organised a meeting in the constituency to attack my candidature – something against the Party's rules: members were barred from attacking properly adopted Labour candidates. On frequent occasions when I was attending a labour movement or anti-racist conference, one of their young supporters would follow me about in an intimidating fashion making threats and shouting 'class traitor'. Militant attracted young people who tended to experience a few years of intense hyper-activism and often burnt themselves out in the process. I found them an especially peculiar group because they did not actively support organisations like the Anti-Apartheid Movement or the Anti-Nazi League; Militant characterised these as 'bourgeois' since they were necessarily broad-based politically rather than explicitly and ideologically socialist.

So when Neil Kinnock moved to expel the group, he had my full support and that of the LCC, though Tony Benn and others on the left violently disagreed – which meant that my own previously close friendship with Benn became frayed. I retained considerable affection and admiration for him, feeling uncomfortable, especially given his support for me in joining the Party. But, as I found over the years, even close friendships in politics – which is such an intense and emotionally driven activity – can be badly damaged by policy or strategy disagreements. Kinnock's initiative began with an explosive attack on the conduct of the Militant cadre which controlled Liverpool City Council in the middle of his leader's speech to the annual Labour conference in Bournemouth in 1985. All of us sitting in the hall knew that it was a defining moment in what was to become Kinnock's relentless and courageous drive to make Labour electable again.

I did not always agree with Neil, however, expressing disappointment in a *New Statesman* article that he had rapidly elevated a talented young MP, Tony Blair, to the front bench when he might have favoured somebody on the soft left; it was symptomatic of what many in the LCC felt was the way Kinnock tacked too much to the right. Tony's wife Cherie, who had been elected to the LCC Executive, told me I was 'mean' to have done this when we sat down together at the next meeting. Although something was made in biographies of Tony Blair about his 'influential' role in the LCC and how this was formative in the modernisation of the Party – a process which he was to complete after becoming leader in 1994 – none of us in the national LCC leadership were aware of it at the time. I recall Tony attending a couple of LCC meetings in Parliament attended by MP supporters, but he did not stand out.

My biggest disagreement was Neil's stance on the great, year-long, miners' strike of 1984–5. The LCC Executive had adopted a position which agreed with Kinnock's view that the miners' leader Arthur Scargill should not have bounced the union into a strike without a proper ballot. But we also agreed with most in the labour movement that the Thatcher government was mounting such a naked and oppressive attack on the miners that they simply had to have our full-hearted support.* We sent a delegation to meet Kinnock and, since I knew him best, I expressed our view in forthright terms which he took rather badly. However, I knew he was torn between loyalty to the mining communities he cherished and represented as an MP, and what he saw as his duty as Party leader.

Along with other Putney Labour Party members I threw myself into repeated fundraising activity for the miners' families. I also travelled up to South Yorkshire, staying over for the night. Early the next morning I was driven around by Scargill's wife Ann to a picket as we dodged tailing police. I also called in at their bungalow in a pit village outside Barnsley as Scargill watched a furore on the national TV news about his chief of staff receiving a controversial donation from Libya's leader, Colonel Gaddafi.

A month later I helped organise a Miners' Families Christmas Appeal with the support of celebrities, trade union leaders and leading politicians including Tony Benn. I had deliberately sought Glenys Kinnock's backing with Neil's obvious enthusiasm. I also persuaded Britain's best-known football manager and Labour voter, Brian Clough, to make the first donation. Since he was coach to Nottingham Forest, and the Nottinghamshire miners had split from their union to work on through the strike, his support was significant and I waved his cheque at our launch press conference. The appeal raised more than £250,000 and had the advantage of being humanitarian, which encouraged donations even from those critical of Scargill's handling of the issue.

When the general election campaign occurred in May 1987 – and despite another excellent local campaign with this time an impressive national one under Neil Kinnock and Peter Mandelson, who had joined the party as communications director – we were again roundly defeated in Putney. My agent, Penny Jones, and other close friends immediately told me the Party needed me in Parliament and I must seek a safe Labour seat elsewhere. This took some contemplation because I had lived there ever since arriving from South Africa over twenty years before. Most close friends lived in the area, my boys went to local state schools and I believed that it was important for candidates to be locally rooted if possible.

---

*   For an analysis see Chapter 9 in my book *Political Strikes* (London, Penguin Books, 1986).

But by now, having devoted the best part of ten years' effort to getting elected, and seeing at first hand the influence MPs could have, I was committed to becoming one myself. It was a wrench to turn my back on Putney and I did not much fancy selling myself elsewhere in the country. But everyone close to me urged it was the right thing to do, and the trade union of which I was a member, the GMB, together with my employer union (by now called the Communication Workers) agreed to back me.

In 1989 unsuccessful forays into two London constituencies, Bethnal Green and Woolwich, and the South Yorkshire one of Rotherham, gave me helpful experience. Then, Michael Foot encouraged me to try in his historic constituency of Blaenau Gwent, previously represented by the founder of the National Health Service and inspirational socialist Nye Bevan. I won the only party branch to have an open contest: Tredegar, the village where Nye was born and where Michael had lived. The other branches invited only the European Member of Parliament Llew Smith to nomination meetings and his supporters deliberately kept me off the final shortlist.

Although that was another disappointment, it was to prove a turning point, the contacts I made in Wales leading me to a next, and this time, successful outcome. But not before I had taken a huge risk in travelling secretly back to South Africa, to feel very much an outsider in what had once been my own country.

CHAPTER FIVE

INTO PARLIAMENT

Were they following us? Surely not – bloody hell, they were.

Spotting the ominous, tailing, white police van took me back with a jolt a quarter of a century to my childhood in Pretoria when we were constantly under surveillance. This time it was in the black township of New Brighton outside South Africa's southern seaside city, Port Elizabeth. At first, others in our car were disbelieving. Then they realised my nervy paranoia was for real: wherever we went, the police van relentlessly followed. It was December 1989 and I was on a secret (and illegal) visit to make a film for Granada Television's then famed documentary programme, *World in Action*.

Our guide, a well-known resistance leader in the Eastern Cape, Mkhuseli Jack, hastily redirected us to the township's dry cleaners. Our British camera crew swiftly hid all their equipment amidst rows of clothing while the women running the place continued to serve their customers as if nothing untoward had happened. Minutes later, the police van pulled up right alongside our car. I crouched rigid in the back, desperately hoping I would not be recognised as the officers curtly engaged the charismatic Mkhuseli, a familiar figure who had recently been imprisoned. He spun them a story to their evident scepticism, my discomfort turning to fright.

Then the programme's producer, the formidable Linda McDougall, confronted the suspicious officers. Displaying her best 'English lady' bravado, she asserted loudly that this was her first time in a township. Why couldn't she travel about freely? Why was she being harassed? This was a country which welcomed tourists, wasn't it? Where was their superintendent? She wanted to complain.

The officers retreated in embarrassment under her torrent, climbed into the van and drove off. It had been a narrow escape and I insisted we abandon the Port Elizabeth leg of our visit – with some regret, not least because the disappointed Linda had intended to drive to nearby Port Alfred, to film me back in the seaside resort where I had spent happy days as a boy on holidays with my grandparents.

The whole idea for the venture had been hers. One of Britain's most original and incisive TV producers, she had suggested to me a year before that I might go back to make a film. At first I had dismissed the very idea. I was banned from returning. It could be very dangerous. Old scores could be settled. New evidence that officially sponsored death squads were responsible for the murder of over fifty anti-apartheid activists – some friends – would make it especially hazardous. Linda retorted that she had filmed eruptions in black townships secretly, surreptitiously entering the country on a train from Zimbabwe or Botswana. But I was well known and doing something similar was fraught with danger. Yet Linda persisted. We met on and off for about a year. The prospect of being able to expose in a television film the still deeply entrenched racism in the sports system was an attractive one. But the logistics of a visit seemed impossible.

Then two things changed. First it was announced that the former England cricket captain Mike Gatting was taking out a 'rebel' England XI cricket tour in early January 1990, organised by Ali Bacher. This could have been the start of a serious breach of the boycott. Second, Linda came up with an ingenious solution. I was to change my name by deed poll and *World in Action* would negotiate a new passport with the authorities as they had done with similar ventures the other side of the Iron Curtain.

I was still very much in two minds about the idea. I now had a family, a job and a mortgage. My wife Pat and my parents were implacably opposed. But I still decided to go ahead (some might argue, putting my politics before my family, as many in the anti-apartheid struggle were forced to do). Only Linda, the programme's senior editors and my immediate family were in the know. In case something happened to me, I warned our sons, Sam aged thirteen and Jake aged eleven, the night before I left that I might be captured if they breathed a word. (They did not.)

I took a week off work, assembled a new identity as a telecommunications businessman (an easy task as head of research for the Communication Workers Union) and was booked on a British Airways flight from Heathrow to Cape Town. My new passport bore the name 'Peter Western-Hain'. Pat's maiden name being Western, this provided a half-plausible reason for the Passport Office. Asking no questions, Larry Grant, my old solicitor friend from the 1972 conspiracy trial, accepted my explanation of a 'gesture to feminism' with obvious scepticism, confidentially making the deed poll arrangements to change my name without being aware of the purpose. We had calculated that the computer check on arrival would not spot the toxic but now hyphenated suffix 'Hain' in the new surname.

The overnight flight out was edgy. Booked in Club Class for the first time, amongst business travellers, wearing a dark suit and ostentatiously reading a *Financial Times* and various telecommunications journals culled from my office, I hoped against hope there would not be a chance encounter with someone who recognised me. We judged that the risk of recognition was slight because nobody would have imagined me going back to a country where I was a known *bête noire*. I also wore glasses normally used only occasionally for long distance and never in public. Exchanging monosyllabic courtesies with the unsuspecting South African businessman in the seat next to me, I discouraged proper conversation, my mood both excited and worried. What would it feel like being back again? Would I get through immigration security? If I was caught, what would happen to me? Normally a good sleeper, I dozed fitfully as the jumbo jet whispered over the African continent of my birth.

The plane stopped over at Johannesburg on the flight to Cape Town and I decided to stay on board rather than risk brushes with officialdom by joining other passengers as they stretched their legs. Unexpectedly, there were familiar old sounds as black cleaners, whistling and chatting cheerily, appeared in the cabin to tidy up before we took off again.

Linda McDougall was waiting at airport arrivals in Cape Town, having travelled out two weeks before to set up interviews and research locations, also under a pseudonym; we had kept in touch clandestinely by phone as she furiously fed meters in public call boxes. As the plane circled down, there was Table Mountain, majestic, covered by a velvet white cloud.

Blinking out into the Cape brightness and feeling hot in my suit, I donned my prescription sunglasses and walked tensely across the tarmac, joining the queue of passengers at immigration control, trying to appear relaxed. An official brusquely examined my passport, then looked up and stared. Was this the moment I would be exposed? Then he uninterestedly muttered 'Purpose of visit?' I replied 'Business' and he waved me through into the unknown.

Then, after all our careful preparation, my luggage wasn't on the carousel at baggage reclaim. I searched desperately, eventually going to enquiries. If I left it, a stray bag turning up might provoke unwelcome interest. On the other hand I was attracting attention to myself as I started filling in a form, almost certain that the clerk was looking quizzically at me.

Suddenly there was a shout. My case had appeared at the other end of the baggage area and I picked it up in relief, walking quickly through to find Linda, frantic with worry. Hardly speaking we jumped into her hired BMW and started driving somewhere, anywhere, as I checked we weren't being followed, remembering how the exiled anti-apartheid poet Breyten Breytenbach was allowed to enter in 1975 while the Security Police followed and picked up all his contacts before he was arrested and imprisoned.

‡

During the following nine days in which we travelled illicitly around the country, I felt I was always on borrowed time. It was eerie – but exhilarating too. I rarely display my emotions but they kept welling up inside, once severely embarrassing me when I burst out crying – something I had never done as an adult before – in front of Linda McDougall and the respected South African journalist Phillip van Niekerk (who had helped research the film and accompanied us). We were flying from Port Elizabeth and I was describing how moving it was to meet vibrant leaders like Mkhuseli Jack and to witness the ANC's distinctive green, gold and black colours being proudly worn so openly. ANC graffiti decorated townships to an extent unimaginable when I was last there in 1966.

While I was interviewing activists who produced a monthly newspaper, *Saamstaan* (Solidarity), in Oudtshoorn, a backwater in the Karoo desert famed for its ostrich farms, the Security Police patrolled busily in cars outside. One of their colleagues was bugging the office and phoned up, issuing threats over the 'shit' being told to 'these foreign journalists'. (Since my name had not been mentioned they were unaware of my presence.) Only four months previously, I was assured, the police would have burst in and rounded us up. Over the past two years they had harassed the paper's sellers, shot one of its journalists, burnt down its offices and restricted its editor, Reggie Oliphant. Yet here was Reggie telling me he had 'unrestricted himself' by talking to us and, though confined to his home between six at night and six in the morning, showing he would not be intimidated by threats, either to his family or his own life. The old certainties of the iron-fist regime were crumbling.

Reggie, who had lost his job as a teacher in 1981 because of his campaigns for non-racial sport, was a fierce opponent of the Gatting rebel tour. Whatever impression of reform was being projected abroad by white cricket officials, he greeted with incredulity the very idea of mixed sport in a remote town like Oudtshoorn. Similarly, in Guguletu, then a squalid Cape township, teachers spoke to me on the only football field, which was covered by an uneven stretch of fine grey gravel littered with glass; they could not give their names for fear of dismissal.

The Cape Flats, a mosaic of townships and squatter settlements to the south east of the city, stretching over miles of flat sand down to the sea, was divided by buffer strips from white suburbs with swimming pools and blooming jacaranda trees. Unemployment was estimated at sixty to seventy per cent. But still the population rose relentlessly beyond a million. People had to put up their own homes – mostly made from old corrugated iron or timber. A lucky few were able to construct brick dwellings. For others home was under black plastic sheets stretched across rickety frames, with cardboard inside to keep out the wind. In the winter, it was wet and cold. In the summer, particularly when the south-easter blew, it was like a dust bath. The sand got in your eyes, in your hair and, it felt like, under your skin too. After a few minutes I was desperate for a warm shower, wondering how on earth the local women could keep motivating themselves to hang out washing scrubbed pristine clean in cold water tubs. Brown's Farm was a squatter settlement where 15,000 people lived in flimsy, hastily erected shacks and where women spent a good part of their day in an exhausting mile-long walk to collect water, struggling across a motorway, several being badly injured over the previous year by busy traffic. The kids there were so dirty and diseased, I couldn't help myself flinching as they gathered round, clutching me for a hug, desperate for warmth and affection.

In Port Elizabeth, Ronnie Pillay and Khaya Majola, top black cricketers with the non-racial South African Cricket Board, told me despairingly how cricket was dying amongst their people because of abysmal facilities. Across the country, for every thousand rand the government spent on sport, just one rand went to blacks; of every hundred cricket fields only fifteen were available for blacks to play on – and most of these of very poor quality. The deliberate repression of non-racial sports bodies outside the white-dominated racial structures continued. When I interviewed him, the president of the Western Cape National Sports Congress, Ngconde Balfour, had only recently emerged from nine months' detention, mostly in solitary confinement.

Apart from that scary episode with the white police van, the trip proved highly successful and we were not detected. None of the interviewees knew I was coming, only that a 'British journalist' wanted to talk to them. Nonetheless, the moment I stepped off the plane at Oudtshoorn, Reggie Oliphant, waiting alongside the runway, claimed he recognised me. (We had never met before.) Most people couldn't believe I was there. Some stared as if seeing a ghost and the burly Khaya Majola had tears in his eyes. Audaciously, we even interviewed Danie Craven at his beautiful rugby headquarters in Stellenbosch. It was risky, but Linda was concerned that there should be some balance in the programme. He reacted in amazement as I walked in on camera: 'Aren't you scared?' he asked (very appropriately). We had counted on his old-fashioned sense of honour in upholding a promise he had made to Linda beforehand not to mention the interview until we had returned safely. To his credit he stuck to this and the meeting made a dramatic moment in the film.

The final hurdle was getting safely out through Johannesburg's Jan Smuts Airport, notorious for its steely security – though the tension obviously got to me because, despite a very smooth flight, I was sick on the plane. Evading a few curious questions about having a tan in the middle of a British winter, we managed to keep the venture secret over Christmas until two weeks later when the film, 'Return of the Rebel', had been edited and was ready for trans-mission. News was simultaneously broken in the London *Guardian* and the South African morning papers. Val Rose-Christie, the white civil rights worker who had shown us round the Cape Flats, was startled on the drive into work to see banner headlines on posters stating 'HAIN WAS HERE'. There were angry questions in the South African Parliament and, when they eventually discovered the 'Western-Hain' connection, the computer system at points of entry was expensively modified.

As an exercise in lifting the protest profile around the Gatting rebel tour, the venture was a triumph. After widespread media attention in Britain, the film got good ratings and video copies were smuggled in and distributed amongst ANC supporters. My predictions that the tour would be disrupted by angry demonstrators helped create a frenzy of interest within South Africa, their media making the link between the STST protests and the opposition likely to be faced by the rebel cricketers. (I had had private talks with some of the organisers about the tactical lessons which could be applied from STST.) The anti-apartheid sports campaign had come full circle. Where direct action had set the seal on tours abroad, now it was about to inflict fatal damage at home – a prospect inconceivable seven years before when there had been another rebel cricket tour, and when political conditions did not permit any protests at all.

At London's Heathrow Airport the departure of the Gatting team was delayed for several hours after an anti-apartheid activist deliberately telephoned a hoax bomb warning. At Johannesburg Airport, dogs, tear gas and batons were used to attack peaceful demonstrators led by Winnie Mandela, showing how worried the authorities were about the growing movement which threat-ened to disrupt and maybe even curtail the rebel tour. The bitterness the tour had provoked amongst the black majority had been seriously under-estimated. The demonstrators – focused around the National Sports Congress, which was aligned to the Mass Democratic Movement inside and the ANC outside – mobilised across the country and the tour quickly degenerated amidst violent police attacks, compounding the greedy, grotesque miscalculation of staging it in the first place.

This was a time of momentous political change. All Nelson Mandela's closest comrades – including Walter Sisulu and Govan Mbeki – had just been released from prison. Negotiations with the government secretly begun from within jail by Mandela were at last bearing fruit. Then suddenly the rebel tour threatened to undo a lot of the goodwill that had been carefully built up. Such was the pressure that, after one of the clandestine negotiating meetings in London then taking place between the ANC and the South African government,* an agreement was initiated to stop the demonstrations in exchange for abandoning the second stage of the Gatting tour. Even the tour organiser Ali Bacher conceded that it had been a mistake, and the humiliated cricket rebels came home prematurely, with payoffs averaging over £100,000.

Following the deal to cut it short, Bacher began to negotiate with the National Sports Congress, to agree upon a democratic, non-racial structure for cricket from school and club level up to national sides. From this followed the establishment of the United South African Cricket Board – the first unified sports group in the country's history – with Bacher's deputy Khaya Majola, a first-class cricketer who for years had spurned inducements to be co-opted into the white sports system. Building upon proposals first put forward to Danie Craven and others thirteen years before, I also proposed a charter for change which if implemented could permit South Africa's readmission to world sport. Our decades-long struggle was at last bearing fruit.

‡

The secret visit had also provided a unique opportunity to make sense of the tumultuous changes about to be unleashed in the country.

Amongst African National Congress leaders like Govan Mbeki (whom I interviewed on camera) downward to activists operating through the United Democratic Front and the Mass Democratic Movement there was a mood of confidence I had not expected. People who had just emerged from long years of detention spoke with determined optimism about their plans for the future and their belief in the inevitability of white rule ending in a negotiated solution.

For its part, white authority seemed rather punch drunk, unsure about the new ground rules. Thus, the press were still banned from carrying Nelson Mandela's picture, but the ANC's colours were worn or displayed openly. Some protests were being permitted, provided they received prior police permission and conformed to tight restrictions. Others were still repressed. At the same time morale amongst previously omnipotent white police had collapsed.

Strikingly the government was being forced to change, not out of desire, but of necessity. The pressure from an increasingly defiant black majority was growing, their trade unions powerful and their consumer muscle threatening white business. Even the very limited foreign sanctions over loans and

---

* See Robert Harvey, *The Fall of Apartheid* (Basingstoke, Palgrave Macmillan, 2003) and the film *Endgame* (2009).

investment had an impact: the economy was in bad shape and whites complained constantly about depressed living standards and low economic expectations. During the visit I was shown a confidential report by a top consortium of white businesses, which argued that an emerging urban crisis threatened the development of a modern economy. It called for the rapid eradication of all apartheid legislation.

Time did seem to be running out for whites-only rule. There seemed a realisation that they no longer had sufficient bullets. But I also sensed that whites were losing their political will to govern in the old way of ruthless force and sometimes outright terror. There were parallels with the still fresh tumult in eastern Europe following Soviet President Gorbachev's reforms and the collapse of the Soviet bloc: the demise of an old order which in East Berlin allowed people to pour buoyantly into Security Police buildings which they had passed by terrified only days before. The armed might of South Africa's police state was still intact and the white political power still immense. But there comes a psychological moment when that doesn't count any more, as had just occurred in Romania with the startling ejection of an old dictator.

Events were moving very quickly. Nelson Mandela was gradually being transformed amongst white commentators from feared ogre to national saviour. Back in London on 2 February 1990, I gripped the chair, hairs standing up on my back, as I watched the live television broadcast of President F. W. de Klerk opening the first session of the new Parliament in Cape Town, the building I had been filmed covertly walking past six weeks before. De Klerk made good his promise of a 'new South Africa' and surprised everyone by boldly announcing the unbanning of the ANC and other outlawed organisations. He also gave notice of the impending release of Mandela and hundreds of other political prisoners. And he declared his readiness to negotiate a new constitution based upon equal rights.

It was simply breathtaking and took some time to sink in. I suppressed a surge of tears, phoning my parents, my mother openly sobbing with joy. Relatives, friends and colleagues phoned each other or chatted excitedly as they gathered in front of televisions or radios. We could hardly believe it. But there was no going back. The new South Africa now beckoned at last.

‡

'Return of the Rebel' propelled me to national attention once again, Linda McDougall (a shrewd political observer) telling me it had been important in reminding people about my past. Although that had not been my motive, she maintained it was pivotal in 'relaunching' me as a national figure at a crucial time in my political life.

A few days after President de Klerk's speech to Parliament, I was in my office early as usual in the morning preparing a quick digest of key newspaper stories for the union's general secretary. Unusually for that time of the day, the phone rang. It was Keith Jones, a Welsh official of the Transport and General Workers Union, who had helped in my attempt for Michael Foot's seat, Blaenau Gwent. 'The MP for Neath has just surprised the local Party by announcing he is standing down. There are no favourites, not at all like Blaenau Gwent. It's wide open. You should go for it.'

So I did, immediately, having learnt the hard way that if you are not in a parliamentary selection contest from the very beginning, it's hard to make up ground. The MP, Donald Coleman, had a low profile and I knew nothing about Neath – except that it was both a Labour and a rugby stronghold, and the Springboks had played there in 1969. But everything started to fall into place. One of the Communication Workers' national officials, Derek Hodgson, was a Cardiff boy and quickly made some calls, especially to Ken Hanbury, the Welsh regional secretary, a selfless activist who lived in the neighbouring constituency and soon got to work for me. The key figure was Terry Thomas, vice president of the South Wales Federation of the National Union of Mine Workers (NUM) during the big strike five years before, when he had famously pledged 'hell would freeze over' before the miners gave in. Now he was the full-time Wales political officer of my union, the GMB. He had helped me in Blaenau Gwent, and also had good contacts in Neath, a traditional mining constituency.

Terry arranged some meetings and I travelled down by train to link up with him four days later, with copies of a leaflet adapted for Neath from the template I had used in other selections. He had fixed for me to meet a small but influential group in the Neath constituency at the Working Men's Club in the town of Pontardawe in the Swansea Valley. Most were miners at the two large local pits, the last ones remaining after the local industry had been decimated by Margaret Thatcher.

Walking into the nearly empty club that Saturday afternoon, 10 February, I was aware it might well be a make or break for me. Every candidate for a constituency selection like this – and especially one like me with no friends or even contacts within the constituency – needs a small team of backers. It was soon evident that the key person present was Howard Davies, a small, wiry former NUM lodge secretary at Blaenant colliery at the time of the big strike. A red-head at the start of the year-long strike, he turned grey with stress by the end. 'Tell me why I should back a former Liberal?' he asked bluntly. After I had replied – fortunately satisfactorily, he later told me – the meeting went well, their initially polite wariness lightening as the conversation continued, the burly Lyn Harper, another miners' official during the strike, characteristically wise-cracking. Most had seen me on the *World in Action* film, Steve Williams, a train driver and union activist, referring to it approvingly.

As we got up to leave, Howard Davies issued another challenge. 'There's a male voice choir concert in my village tonight. There will be lots of people there who will notice you. Do you want to come?' I looked quizzically at Terry. I had intended to catch the train back to London, with Nelson Mandela's release due the next day. I wanted to see it broadcast live and had been asked to do television interviews. On the other hand, this was a big and unexpected opportunity. 'Can I check on practicalities and call you later?'

'OK, but don't leave it too long. It starts in two hours, we can't be late,' Howard replied firmly, telling me weeks later my response was a test. If I came, it would show real commitment. If not – well?

Terry drove me back to his house where we checked train times. A very early train the next day, Sunday, meant I could be in time for the historic Mandela release. His wife hastily cooked sausages which I gulped down – I didn't eat meat but wasn't about to reveal another idiosyncrasy on top of being an outsider, a troublemaker, a former Liberal and an ex-South African. We phoned Howard. I could stay at his house, he had told his flabbergasted wife Elaine. His teenage son would stay with his girlfriend leaving the only available bed for me. I was embarrassed at the trouble they were going to, especially since they had never before had anybody outside their family spend the night in their small property originally built, as most of the homes in villages like this were, by the mine owner.

The chapel in their village of Seven Sisters was packed with several hundred for the early evening concert. I had never seen or heard a male voice choir perform before, and it was captivating. In the interval various people were thanked by the evening's witty chairman, Emyr Lewis, a Labour activist and secretary of the village rugby club, who also welcomed me as 'an important guest', referring to my anti-apartheid campaigning and Mandela's imminent release. Howard had clearly fixed this and was also busy introducing me to those he knew – which seemed to be virtually everyone.

Afterwards Howard, Elaine and I went for a meal in a local pub with Lyn Harper and his wife Cherrill, the evening great fun. Despite my protestations, they insisted on paying for me. Driving back afterwards, crammed into Lyn's old Austin, it suddenly lurched – a flat tyre which Lyn, acutely embarrassed, had to change in the rain, Howard giving him leg-pulling advice. The two were clearly 'characters', with an endless fund of stories from the South Wales Valleys, their experiences as miners, and the big strike. They were also visibly unhappy about what they termed the 'clique' which had run the Neath Labour

Party for years. 'Members living in the Valleys feel excluded, so do younger ones,' they maintained: there was an opportunity for an outsider like me to get support.

I got up at the crack of dawn, Howard generously offering to drive me eight miles down the valley to catch my train, collecting Lyn on the way. It wasn't a problem, they insisted; the first shift down the pit meant they were habitual early risers, though Howard was clearly uneasy about making me a cup of tea, which he claimed his sleeping wife normally did. Reflecting hard on the three-hour journey back I finally took an auspicious – some might say reckless – decision to pull out of another selection which had been going for weeks in the marginal London seat of Dulwich, where I was well placed and had been invited to a clutch of branch nominating meetings over the next few days. Because Dulwich's culture was similar to Putney, I would be more of an insider there; quite the opposite was true in Neath. It was a fateful choice because most seasoned politicos would have said my chances in Neath's close-knit constituency, which, like elsewhere in the South Wales Valleys, could be prone to parochialism and suspicious of outsiders, were zero. I was very torn about letting down those who were working for me in Dulwich, one of whom said bitterly: 'You are making the biggest mistake of your political life.' (Fortunately, it turned out, the opposite was true for me and for Dulwich, who chose a future Cabinet Minister: Tessa Jowell.) But I had been immediately drawn to Neath: something about it – the coal-mining solidarity, the warm people – just felt right. There are life-changing decisions, I had learnt, when you have to follow your instinct. By the time I reached London, I had made up my mind. If Howard and Lyn were prepared to put their faith in me, then Neath it was.

‡

Few who watched on television on 11 February 1990 will ever forget the image of the world's most famous political prisoner, kept out of sight for over a quarter of a century, stepping to freedom through the gates in the fence around Victor Verster prison: it was one of those defining moments in history which many ordinary onlookers will remember forever, recalling exactly where they were and what they were doing. I was back in Putney with my family, hugging each other, tears in our eyes, hundreds of millions of viewers in his country and across the world weeping openly.

With his wife Winnie by his side Mandela walked towards the massed ranks of TV cameras and spectators. Except for his obvious humility and humanity, he looked almost regal, a giant amongst his people. The government had carefully pre-released the first photograph of him for decades, meeting President de Klerk. It had revealed, not the burly bearded freedom fighter in the prime of his life, for decades his image the world over, but a slim, dignified old African statesman with a smile of destiny hovering somewhere between the benign and the all-knowing.[*]

I marvelled at his commanding press conference the next day, staged before 200 of the world's media seated in the sun-drenched garden of the Archbishop of Cape Town, home to the irrepressible Desmond Tutu. Mandela had never appeared on live television; when he had gone into prison there was no television in South Africa. Yes, he had been granted a television set in his last couple of years in prison. But, as someone schooled in both the opportunities and vagaries of the modern media, I found it extraordinary to see that he looked a natural. He was masterful, charming the hard-bitten journalists, who gave him a spontaneous ovation at the end. For days afterwards almost continuous live broadcasts covered his exhilarating appearances, enchanting not just black South Africa but a watching world.

His release was momentous, part of a transformation for which anti-apartheid activists like me had campaigned for years. Unexpectedly, however, it was to have another, much more personal, impact. Almost subliminally, it signalled a process by which I started to be perceived rather differently: instead of being depicted an agitating outsider, I became more accepted by mainstream opinion. Over the next few years, I found myself courteously stopped by total strangers on public transport or in the street – on several occasions people actually crossed the street. The conversation would be brief and invariably went something like this: 'Mr Hain, I just wanted to apologise. I now understand why you did all those protests. I used to think you were just a troublemaker. I realise I was mistaken. Good luck to you.'

‡

Much the same sentiment may have helped me in Neath where the formal procedure of selecting a parliamentary candidate was now in full swing. Back in my office early on the Monday morning after my eventful weekend, I called Howard Davies to discuss what we might do next. 'Don't forget the postal votes,' I reminded him, recalling that in Woolwich the winner had been assiduous in courting older or infirm members and the pile he accumulated

---

[*] For a concise, readable biography of Nelson Mandela, see Peter Hain, *Mandela* (London, Spruce, 2010).

was decisive. 'That was when I realised you were deadly serious, and I'd better be too,' Howard would later say.

The Labour leader, Neil Kinnock, had to remain officially neutral in such contests, but his office let it be known that he was a friend. The process of choosing a candidate was exhaustively democratic. Thirty candidates had applied and I spent nearly three months travelling up and down from London, staying with Howard Davies, Ken Hanbury and, on one occasion, Steve Williams, whose baby son was moved out of *his* bedroom. The Communication Workers were generous with time off work and help with train tickets, though I frequently drove down myself in our battered Volkswagen camper van which doubled as family car. The heating often did not work and I was sometimes frozen, disembarking from the vehicle in scarf, woolly hat and gloves. Once, when I visited a picket line during a strike at a local coal washery, the battery went flat and the pickets had to push the van to start the engine – amidst much leg-pulling banter.

Pat and the boys travelled down with me on a few occasions to meet local people. We stayed in a Travelodge on a couple of nights – not much of a replacement for a planned two-week Easter holiday in Malta which simply had to be cancelled, our money lost. The family had willingly sacrificed this in the wider cause and, Neath being a more traditional, family-orientated community than London for example, their presence was much appreciated and remarked upon; I may have been 'abnormal' in other ways but at least I was a 'normal' family father was the implicit, reassuring message, particularly when one unpleasant untruth circulated that I was some sort of druggie; another preposterous one that I effetely manicured my fingernails.

The Communication Workers put me on their delegation for the annual conference of the Wales Trade Union Congress in the north Wales seaside resort of Llandudno. Terry Thomas, Ken Hanbury and Derek Hodgson ensured I was introduced to as many delegates as possible, especially those with a Neath connection. One, Andy Richards of the Transport and General Workers Union, spontaneously invited me to the Welsh rugby cup final the day after the conference closed. Neath were playing at the legendary Cardiff Arms Park, scene of one of the Springbok matches we had tried to stop. So I changed my plans, once again at short notice, and had an eventful drive with Andy and a couple of others back down through Wales to Neath, at one stage getting lost up a mountain track.

Howard and Elaine put me up for the night, their son again willingly exiting to stay with his girlfriend. At 8.45 in the morning, a beautiful sunny Saturday, Andy, whose bulky frame barely squeezed into his Ford saloon, picked me up outside Howard's house. He dropped me fifteen minutes later with little explanation, suitcase in hand, outside the Green Dragon pub in the village of Cadoxton. What was going on?

'Just taking my car home. I'll be having a few pints with the boys today. Back soon,' Andy said cheerily.

'What do I do?'

'Go into the pub of course! The boys are expecting you. We'll put your case on the coach when it arrives to collect us,' he replied.

'But I can't just walk into a strange pub at this time of the morning,' I protested. 'It's illegal.'

Andy shook his head with an ironic smile. 'You've got a lot to learn, Pete. But don't worry, the boys will see you right.' Then he drove straight off.

I looked around me. There was a churchyard adjoining the small square in front of the pub, houses on either side. All was peaceful, nobody in sight, total quiet, except for a cacophony of birds tweeting away, the curtains on the pub drawn. Feeling extremely uncomfortable I pushed gingerly at the front door which, surprisingly, opened. Still nothing. Then I pushed at an inner door, and it burst open to reveal a noisy crowd of men, women, grandmothers and children bedecked in club scarves. Pints were being knocked back and a cooked breakfast served to general merriment. Nine o'clock in the morning! The licensing laws only permitted opening around midday.

The drinking continued until the coach arrived an hour later, and then in Cardiff before the match. As we got yet another round in I only survived by always topping up my pint of lager with a half (and sometimes replacing it with two bottles of Appletiser, which looked rather similar to lager). Welcome to a south Wales rugby Saturday. Oh – Neath won by the way, and afterwards supporters poured onto the pitch to celebrate, the first occasion since my Pretoria school days that I had been on a rugby pitch legitimately.

I spoke to as many branch officials as I could and was invited to meetings in pit villages and in the main town of Neath itself, my campaign quickly gathering momentum. Local branches of the Mineworkers nominated me, as did other trade unions, and I won the largest number of party branches too. An important staging post was passed: I had achieved more than a third of the total number of nominating organisations and by rule could not be excluded from the shortlist as had happened in Blaenau Gwent.

I may have become the frontrunner, but it was still a tough contest. Up against me for the two final all-member selection meetings were several local candidates with limited support and the former Labour MP for the Essex seat of Thurrock, Oonagh MacDonald, who had emerged as my main opponent. Over two hundred people crowded into the final big meeting in Neath's Victorian Gwyn Hall. Some had still to make up their minds, and this would be the decider so we were taking no chances, my supporters planting their questions. Since I had made a big point of finding a home in Neath, Howard asked Oonagh why she had chosen to live in Twickenham, right on the other side of London many miles from her previous constituency; she floundered.

I was also asked another planted question: 'Do you hate rugby?' Some of my opponents had been putting it about that I did. We wanted to flush it out and I replied to laughter: 'No of course not, I played it at school. It's apartheid I hate and the fact the Springboks are selected on race not merit.' My speech was rehearsed with an impassioned finale. 'I am proud of what I have done in politics – fighting apartheid, stopping racist sports tours, fighting against British Nazis, standing for Labour and fighting the Tories in London. But it would be the proudest day of my life if you chose me in this great Labour community of Neath.'

Howard – always privately frank but incredibly loyal – was delighted with my performance, and hopeful about the outcome. We had to wait nearly a week for the count, as member, trade union and postal votes were checked and included. I travelled down by train wondering what my fate would be and he met me in the early evening to walk to where the declaration would be made. The waiting media, believing I would win, were filming and watching my every move. As the candidates made uneasy small talk, the tension rose. Then the scrutineers walked in, Ali Thomas, another ex-miner and later to be leader of the county council, giving me a large wink. The result was formally announced: I had won, almost on the first ballot, just tipped over by the vote of the engineering workers' union, whose right-wing general secretary, Bill Jordan, I had spoken to beforehand. He hadn't much fancied supporting me and only reluctantly agreed to do so, once the union's own shortlisted candidate had been eliminated in the count as he was always likely to be. 'I am not sure I made the right decision,' he told me later when I thanked him and he realised it had been decisive.

Invited to speak by the shell-shocked Party officers who had all backed other candidates, I delivered a short, deliberately low-key speech which concealed my elation, and then did media interviews. The Welsh media led on the news, their predictable angle that a controversial outsider had won a surprise victory. One friendly trade union official quipped: 'Well, Peter, you may not be Welsh, but at least you are not bloody English!'

I decided my priority would be to reach out to those who had opposed me and build a new unity in the local Party, so quickly set about that task, telling one of my elated left-wing supporters who relished the prospect of clearing out the old guard: 'I am going to have to disappoint you by being very friendly with people you don't like. The MP has to command support across the whole

Party.' Unlike Putney, the result meant I was as good as the next MP for Neath already, such was the size of the Labour majority.

‡

The day after I was selected I began house hunting. One owner opened his front door in astonishment, clutching the local *Evening Post* with my selection reported prominently. 'I was just saying to my wife minutes ago: "Now *there's* a man who will need a new house!"' We managed to find one relatively soon in the former pit village of Resolven up the Neath Valley. But we didn't have much in the way of savings so all we could secure was a crazy mortgage.

I threw myself into working the constituency whenever I could get down from London, at weekends or school holidays, treating this solid Labour seat like a marginal as I had Putney. The local Party hadn't been used to having a campaigner as an MP; my predecessor Donald Coleman was assiduous and respected but traditional. I visited rugby clubs in the evenings, and through Howard got to know the officers of Neath Rugby Club, attending matches and being invited back to have a drink with the committee afterwards. I met pensioners and knocked on doors to introduce myself, well aware there was still an under-current against an outsider – and in this case one with additional baggage. A number of locals had almost identical conversations with me, invariably jocular: 'I'm Labour, Peter,' they would say, 'but I carried you off the pitch at Swansea against the Springboks! You spoiled my afternoon.' When I replied 'I wasn't even present!' they would have none of it. Over the years so many constituents claimed exactly the same thing that I stopped denying it: why spoil a bit of folklore?

It was just as well that I did put in all this groundwork because Donald Coleman tragically and suddenly died of a heart attack in January 1991. Seven months after my selection I was unexpectedly thrust into a by-election, scheduled for 4 April 1991, feeling a heavy responsibility.

An early requirement was to be 'Folletted' as it was known in the Party after Peter Mandelson had insisted Labour representatives broke with tradition to be smartly turned out as part of his 'New Labour' mission. Barbara Follett, parliamentary candidate for Stevenage, wife of the acclaimed novelist Ken, and a fellow ex-South African whom I knew, advised candidates and prominent Labour figures on suitably coloured clothes to coordinate with their complexions and characteristics. I turned up in a dark blue suit, light blue shirt and red tie. 'Perfect!' she said, 'Don't let's waste any more time – but, what about a raincoat? Can't fight a by-election without a raincoat. It's spring. It's Wales. It will pour. You need a decent one, beige will be the best colour. I will drop you off at Burberry in the Haymarket.'

Before I knew it, she was driving me there in her sports car. I didn't really know what a Burberry store was and stumbled through the door surprised to encounter voluminous members of staff almost lined up with helpful advice. Shown downstairs, I found myself quickly taken in hand as various quality raincoats were hung on me. Rather nice, I thought. This had been going on for a while when, suddenly, I remembered: nobody had mentioned the price – obviously not the sort of trivial detail a gentleman need detain himself with. I stole a glance at the labels in shock: £498, £623 – no way! Gulping down an apologetic excuse about needing to rush, I made my exit. A narrow escape. The next day I bought a perfectly serviceable one for £90 at a menswear shop in Neath.

Although Labour was doing quite well in the national polls, there was some nervousness at Party headquarters in London. An official was despatched to do some focus groups. 'You have political form,' he remarked cheerfully. 'But the good news is people see you as a "strong voice" for them.' So our main campaign slogan became 'Peter Hain: A Strong Voice for Us'. Or in Welsh: '*Llais cryf i ni.*' Predictably, the media had only one story in mind: a traditional, rock-solid Labour constituency being 'taken for granted', rebuffing a radical outsider. My opponents exploited the line too, especially Plaid Cymru, who ran an aggressive campaign about me not being Welsh, spreading lies about being 'imposed by London'. There was a right-wing tone to their propaganda; so much, I thought, for their claims to be the 'progressive' and 'left wing' force in Welsh politics.

Had I not met thousands of local people over the previous year, found a home, and had regular campaigning stories on local issues in the local papers, these attacks could have undermined me. They had two competing conse-quences: a minority of Labour supporters were persuaded and mostly voted Plaid, but the majority were resentful, hardening my support. Neil Kinnock, still concerned I was an outsider, was astonished that the Neath rugby players agreed to be photographed with me after a training session which we used in a leaflet under the headline 'The Winning Team'.

Neath Labour Party had never seen a campaign like it. Doors were actually knocked and votes recorded for chasing up on the day; such canvassing, routine in a seat like Putney, was unknown. I rushed about on a relentless schedule morning till night, running between front doors, mostly driven about with Howard Davies and the MP for Pontypridd, Kim Howells, chosen as my offi-cial 'minder'. He was excellent, had been Wales research officer of the NUM during the big strike and had lived locally. He also knew the routine, having been elected in a by-election himself two years before, again in the face of an aggressive Nationalist campaign. Kim, hugely talented and well schooled in Welsh culture and socialist politics, was a veteran of the 1968 era like me. He was a great raconteur and we had tremendous fun, including at his own expense when in the village of Crynant, he refused to go down a couple of streets. 'An old girlfriend down there,' he explained cryptically. But, as with all those close Valley village neighbourhoods, she heard he was around, came rushing out when I knocked on her door, and went off searching for him in vain.

The raincoat came in extremely handy because the weather was awful and campaigning was like vertical swimming. Experienced and proficient at canvassing, with newer activists often sent out with me to observe and gain experience, I had developed my own techniques in Putney. Small but important practices paid off, like always stepping back from a doorway or, if there was a step, moving back down so that the voter never felt threatened or dwarfed. I would also seek out a point of common identity to make small talk or a political point on which we could heartily agree, especially if the conversation was going awkwardly, so leaving with the householder at the very least feeling friendly about the exchange. But on one occasion, in the isolated former pit village of Tairgwaith, my routine caught me out. I had just chatted amicably to a pregnant woman about when her baby was due, successfully leaving a happy voter pledging her support. Next door was another woman with a similarly large bump so I opened the same line of chat. 'But I am just fat!' she exclaimed sourly.

Nevertheless it was heartening to get such ready Labour support on what seemed like every door. But would they turn out to vote, because by-elections traditionally have lower turn-outs? The campaign's highlight was a meeting in the old Neath Town Hall, a vital occasion to boost morale. By-elections are in part about which party has the momentum and, although we were comfortably placed from the outset, this meeting was important in reminding people about our values and creating a sense of both excitement and inevitability about a Labour victory.

Sometimes, however good a speaker is, or however excellent the jokes, nothing can be done to rouse an audience which just sits there passive or even indifferent. On other occasions you just know when a meeting will be great, the room preferably too small rather than leaving the audience rattling around, the temperature warm rather than cold, the chemistry making people feel pleased to be present. From the moment the platform entered the hall, the packed meeting rising spontaneously in applause, I knew it would be a success. Every seat was taken and scores of people stood against each wall, some sitting on the floor alongside the platform.

When it came to my turn I welcomed each of the visiting speakers in Welsh which got an enthusiastic response – a third of my constituents, including Howard, being native Welsh speakers. Fortunately I was able to rouse the audience, getting a massive ovation. The mood was electric and Roy Hattersley, the Party's deputy leader and by-election veteran, remarked afterwards: 'That was the best election meeting I have ever attended.' He went back to London to douse any residual doubt amongst the Westminster cognoscenti, convinced I would sweep home.

Which, fortunately, I did. After running a gauntlet of abuse about being a 'foreigner' from Plaid Cymru supporters lined up outside the count, I went back to the old town hall to greet and thank our great band of activists and supporters who were partying in the early hours. A journey, in a way begun thirty years earlier as a boy in Pretoria, but only really given direction ten years before in Putney, had now reached its destination as a Member of Parliament. But it was to be the start of yet another journey to a fresh destination, also unplanned.

‡

In some respects I might have been better placed than most to make a success of being an MP. Over the years, I had worked with MPs and been a regular at Westminster, in the Anti-Apartheid Movement and as vice chair of the Labour Co-ordinating Committee. Additionally, for the Communication Workers, I had briefed supportive MPs at sessions of a parliamentary Bill committee when Mrs Thatcher's Tories took through legislation to privatise British Telecom.

So I was certainly not in awe of the place, indeed had a healthy scepticism of its rituals and arcane traditions such as senior parliamentary clerks wearing wigs and some male officials breeches and tights. I entered determined not to be absorbed into the comfy establishment as, I had observed, happened to far too many Labour MPs – especially those who began as radicals on the left. I wanted to remain my own person.

Equally, however, I wanted to be effective, to be able to make a real difference. And that meant learning what not to do from Ken Livingstone, the left-wing former Greater London Council leader who had been elected MP for Brent East in 1987. He entered with a huge profile and never really made the effort to be part of the Labour team. Indeed he seemed to go out of his way to make enemies, for instance on one occasion gratuitously insulting Labour MPs from northern England by falsely implying that they spent their evenings either drunk or in brothels. He did not serve on parliamentary Bill committees and was rewarded by being denied his own office for years by Ray Powell, the Welsh Labour whip who allocated them. I entered with a much lower but still large profile, and was conscious of the jealousies that sweep around Westminster. So I resolved try to become an insider – but on my own terms if I possibly could.

Within days of getting elected I readily agreed to serve on the Committee of the Finance Bill, which involved some weeks of solid support for the Labour Treasury team and an occasional foray against the government when backbenchers like me were encouraged to speak. Mostly, we were not. Frankly I hardly understood much of the technical content of the Bill and focused on a few of the bigger issues on which I could speak when allowed in order to get some coverage back in my local papers. Another tour of duty involved sitting upon Statutory Instrument committees, which passed legislative regulations upstairs in committee rooms. These were usually routine, often short, dull and a good opportunity for catching up with constituency correspondence and reading. However I did once have a bit of fun on an SI concerning 'paralytic shellfish' off the Scottish coast, with a short, tongue in cheek, speech demanding to know why Welsh 'paralytic shellfish' were not being given equivalent attention.

On the day I took the oath of allegiance – as an agnostic, affirming rather than swearing on the Bible – a coach load of Party members came up. I was especially pleased that, as we gathered for photographs outside, they held aloft one of the local banners from the miners' strike, 'Women Against Pit Closures'. Neil Kinnock came out to join us and we sang an impromptu Welsh national anthem, which I had carefully learnt soon after being selected in Neath from a tape recording by Howard Davies's wife Elaine.

Howard – whom I had approached to be my agent and case worker during the selection process a year before (the best decision I ever made in this period) – quickly established my constituency office. We had purchased and modernised a tiny derelict property with funds raised overwhelmingly from trade unions, buttressed by some of my own savings and a whip-round by kind friends from Putney. I had been determined to establish a proper advice service, open and welcoming during office hours to act as a community focus both for my activities and for local citizens. Once it was properly established, I handed the building over to the local Party, which was able to have its own property for the first time. Nine years later the Party was able to take out a modest mortgage and purchase a bigger building containing a much more suitable High Street office.

The rebel inside me still struggled to get out, however. A couple of months after my election, the annual civic dinner of Neath Borough Council was due. Howard asked me whether I was going to buy a dinner jacket like every other male attending. 'No way,' I replied, 'it's against my socialist principles.'

'Well, that's a matter for you,' he replied disapprovingly.

A few weeks later he tried again, and still I resisted. 'Well, that's a matter for you,' he repeated, 'But you will regret it.' He was very unhappy, predicting my obstinacy would rebound badly.

Howard never gave up when he had the bit between his teeth. With the date of the dinner fast nearing, he confronted me yet again. 'This is your first major civic event as the MP. You are still new. And you are an outsider. You haven't yet won everyone over. Your enemies will exploit it. I am a miner and I will be wearing one. What makes you think you are so special?'

We had never argued liked this before. I had tried to avoid the issue and he kept forcing me to wrestle with the pros and cons. Howard was very canny, totally loyal – had become my best friend – and watched my back with an intuitive distrust of others whose motives he suspected. What kept nagging away at me was his accusation that I would give offence to my hosts. I had been brought up to be polite. Finally I caved in and bought the bloody dinner suit, special shirt and bow tie. And, having worn it once, it no longer seemed to matter any more. Was this the first sell-out, I wondered?

Recent Labour entrants to the House of Commons like me, or longer-serving ones out of favour with Ray Powell, were clustered in an area of the House of Commons called the Cloisters, where deceased Kings or Queens traditionally lay in state. (In that eventuality, we were informed, we would be unceremoniously cleared out.) A dozen of us had desks, one behind another, in a row in a narrow corridor-like area. Staff would typically sit on a bench opposite our desks, discussing what to do with piles of letters and circulars in the morning post. It was pretty chaotic as other MPs or their staff walked in between us, to and from their own desks.

Experienced and proficient as she was from her days in Pretoria, my mother, now aged sixty-four, had willingly taken a job as part-time secretary. She worked from home and came in regularly on her senior citizen London Underground pass. I was fortunate to have her work for me from the outset for the next eighteen years, conscientious to the point of being over-diligent until she finally retired in 2009, by then aged eighty-two, but still busy and competent.

I was also fortunate to employ from day one a highly experienced and able Westminster researcher, Isobel Larkin; she had worked part time for several Labour MPs and had approached me before the by-election to work full time. Having them both in place meant I was able to making a flying start, instead of being swamped under a pile of mounting correspondence and diary pressures. From this experience I always advised budding or newly elected MPs to take on support staff, either temporarily or permanently, at the very outset. The pressures on new MPs are enormous, not just from constituents but from the daily, unfamiliar, whirl of duties and meetings in Westminster. Some are simply overwhelmed and never really find their feet. Others get buffeted around by competing demands. Even though I had pre-planned considerably, I felt as if I was on a constant treadmill, keen to do my best by Neath and to make my mark in Parliament.

‡

It is a strange place. An MP can spend years and years at the Palace of Westminster and still discover new procedures, new routes, new nooks and crannies, hitherto unknown spaces. Even though I was a young left-winger and he was an old right Labourite, I made an effort to get on reasonable terms with Ray Powell, on occasion asking his advice and making small talk when I saw him – which was difficult because he communicated mainly in grunts. After several months in the Cloisters corridor, I was allocated an office to share with Geoff Lofthouse, a former Yorkshire miner, unassuming, decent and a source of useful advice. The office was in the old Scotland Yard building, Norman Shaw North, and I imagined that some detective or other working on a famous case might have had a desk at the same spot.

Once Ray took me up into what seemed like an attic high up, several floors above the Commons Chamber. 'See that door there?' he pointed. 'One day I was up searching for additional spaces for new offices for MPs with one of the House officials who had a giant ring with a great bundle of keys. I asked him what was behind that door. He said it was a cupboard or something but I was inquisitive.'

Ray gave me a wink. 'The official got pretty cross with me as he searched through his keys for one that would fit, complaining I was wasting his time. Then, eventually, he found the key and opened the door. What a sight! There were neat flats for air raid wardens, beds made up, tinned cans of food, all untouched since the Second World War. I had them allocated for converting to new MP offices.' MPs now each have an office of their own with adequate facilities for staff, often working with them rather than well away as occurred when I was first elected. They have Ray to thank for this because he dedicated his time to improvements in Westminster's ancient and anachronistic facilities.

A working-class man from the south Wales coal valleys, he was a fixer of the old school. Come the annual round of elections to the Labour Shadow Cabinet, Ray would conspiratorially trade favours – such as foreign trips in the gift of the whips, or getting 'slipped' from votes, or the promise of a new or better office – for a ballot paper. He would walk around with a clutch of them in his inside jacket pocket, and fill them in with his own favourites. He never asked me to do this, although he did once express the hope that I 'would do the right thing'. Although I replied 'of course', I actually voted as I was intending to do anyway and simply didn't tell him – just as well, because he would not have approved. Mind you, it was later apparent that if all the promises made by Labour MPs to Shadow Cabinet candidates had been totalled up, they would have been many times the size of the Parliamentary Party. Not everybody told the truth in what was euphemistically termed the 'most sophisticated electorate in the world'.*

Early on, a veteran MP of a quite different character, Tony Benn, kindly offered to give me a guided tour. The highlight was another cupboard where a suffragette campaigning for votes for women had hidden on the night the national census was taken so that she could declare her place of residence as the House of Commons. Tony proudly showed me where he had affixed a plaque of commemoration for this historic event, explaining that Commons officials would not agree to undertake this because it contravened some rule or other. But they would not take it down if Tony commissioned it and screwed it on himself – which he promptly did. In this phase of his political career, Tony was an inspiring teacher of socialist politics, with a commendably punishing schedule of countrywide meetings.

The procedures of the House of Commons remain a perennial mystery, although a series of Labour Leaders of the House in the late 1990s and early 2000s, including me, had them simplified. I resolved right away never to be afraid to ask, even if it might display an embarrassing ignorance. On many occasions, on the back benches or indeed in government, a colleague would mutter: 'Thank goodness you asked that question, Peter, because otherwise I wouldn't have known the answer either.'

I was advised to submit questions for oral answer to a Cabinet Minister every day, even if I had no special knowledge of the subject, because questions were selected by random shuffle and the odds were that you would at least be called once a week if you tabled daily. One subject upon which I did have specialist advice was the Royal Mail, which the Tories planned to privatise. My question was listed quite high in the order and so would be reached, and I decided to ask whether the government had consulted the Queen. Ten minutes before the session began I was walking through the Members' Lobby, where MPs could chat to each other or to reporters, and by chance bumped

---

* In 2011 I strongly urged the new Labour leader, Ed Miliband, to abolish the elections and appoint his Shadow Cabinet like Prime Ministers did their Cabinet. This change was overwhelmingly approved by the Party.

into Mike Steele, a friend from my Young Liberal days who was now a journalist with ITV Wales. I tipped him off about my question, hoping he might cover it. 'But you can't ask that,' he said, alarmed, explaining that Her Majesty could not be referred to in the Chamber in a partisan way. What was I to do? The clock was ticking, my question due, and I anxiously sought advice from an old hand in the Whips' Office, explaining I was still determined to make my point about the Queen. He pondered a moment, suggesting an ingenious solution. And so, recorded in the official record of the Commons for that day is the question from the Honourable Member for Neath asking whether the Minister, before privatising the Royal Mail, would consult 'the person whose head appears upon the stamp'.

Westminster's culture and ethos seemed designed to breed deference to the establishment and to its conservative values. MPs were there on sufferance, given almost obsequious respect at times by House officials and functionaries, but never encouraged to be in charge. Even more so, visitors were deliberately kept in awe of the place. They were called 'strangers' as if they were not citizens – voters in charge of our democracy, voters who had put us in Parliament in the first place. In 2004, when Leader of the Commons, I introduced what was seen as a 'revolutionary' reform to get rid of the traditional term 'stranger'. The visitors' gallery was renamed from 'Strangers' Gallery' to 'Public Gallery' and we abolished a ridiculous procedure under which an MP could disrupt proceedings by putting on a top hat and shouting 'I spy strangers', forcing the gallery to be cleared. This was fiercely resisted by traditionalists, however, and only achieved after a relatively narrow vote. MPs did insist on keeping the name for the bar to which they could take friends or visitors: 'Strangers Bar'. I happily concurred since that was just a traditional label, not a designation of deference.

I was friendly to anyone willing to be friendly to me, sometimes even to those who were not. But one approach really took the biscuit. There were more Tories than Labour and so we were constantly sought out for 'pairing', an arrangement whereby government and opposition MPs register each other as 'pairs', meaning both agree not to vote on certain, second order matters. The right-wing Conservative MP Gerald Howarth brazenly approached me immediately I arrived. He had been one of the organisers of the conspiracy prosecution against me in my 1972 trial and I gave him short shrift. I also recognised, sitting on the Conservative benches opposite, some who as students had worn 'Hang Nelson Mandela' badges in the 1980s when an especially obnoxious period of far-right politics gripped the Federation of Conservative Students. We had been enemies then and, judging from their attitudes, still were. Mandela himself visited Westminster a month after I was elected in May 1991 and I was thrilled to meet him for the first time in Neil Kinnock's office. He was friendly and chatty, full of mischief, yet with inner steel.

‡

I had for some years been a member of the board of *Tribune* newspaper and on entering Parliament quickly joined the Tribune Group of MPs. Although Tribune had lost much of its left-wing verve, I chose not to join the Campaign Group, which had broken away in the early 1980s as part of the split between 'soft' and 'hard' lefts, between 'Kinnockites' and 'Bennites'. But the Tribune Group was in an even worse state than I had suspected. It was inactive with irregular and pointless meetings. Just about everyone who was not in the Campaign group, or on the Party's old right, seemed to be a member, and Tribune had clearly lost any sense of purpose as a forum for the left to discuss and organise.

After Labour lost the 1992 election – our fourth defeat in a row – new blood was injected into Tribune. Friends like Roger Berry and Richard Burden (both also ex-Young Liberals) and Michael Connarty from the Labour Co-ordinating Committee joined. Although none of us wanted Tribune to become an oppositionalist group to the leadership, we did want it to be a source of vigorous policy debate, pamphleteering and new ideas. I was pressed to become its secretary and I did, even though I was worried at being too new for the post.

Neil Kinnock had quickly resigned as Party leader after taking a terrible battering in the Tory media, which was grossly unfair, not least because he had done an enormous amount to make Labour electable again. Radicals like me in the Tribune Group supported Bryan Gould to succeed him against the favourite, John Smith, who was from the right of the Party. Leaving aside the 'hard' left, there were now three serious strands of thinking on Labour's future. The first, represented by John Smith (who was easily elected leader), was pragmatic and non-ideological; he was a reassuring figure from Labour's mainstream who looked more authoritative than Neil Kinnock, but he showed little sign of being willing to square up to the scale of the challenge Labour faced to avoid being almost permanently out of power. Second was a growing strand around the up-and-coming stars Gordon Brown and Tony Blair, impatient with Smith's caution, known as 'modernisers'. Third was the strand in which I felt most at home: we accepted Labour had to change (as we had done ten years before in the Labour Co-ordinating Committee) but were insistent on retaining the Party's commitment to policies of equality, social justice and democratic reform.

These strands played themselves out in growing tensions within the Tribune Group. Roger Berry (a professional economist) and I wrote a Tribune pamphlet urging a more expansionary, Keynesian, economic policy than that adopted by Labour's front bench. Gordon Brown, now Shadow Chancellor, was insistent on making a break from the 'tax and spend' agenda the modernisers felt was the main reason for our 1992 defeat. Although Brown went ballistic and tried to prevent it being published, we held our ground and willingly made some amendments to the text suggested by his team. With the backing of the group, the pamphlet was published, albeit against Brown's wishes. Instead of forcing a confrontation, why didn't he simply disassociate himself from it, Roger and I wondered? After all, we weren't arguing for nationalisation of the commanding heights of the economy, merely reasserting Labour Keynesianism. In any case he was in the leadership, responsible for the Party's economic policy, and we were only new backbenchers.

But for Brown the problem was that it was a Tribune pamphlet and he was a member of Tribune; he couldn't tolerate any dissent from his position. He asked me to come and see him in his office and, after a few opening pleasantries, rounded on me in a bullying rant. I stayed calm, arguing my case, astounded at his behaviour. I had always respected him enormously. He had an instinctive feel for Labour's history and values. We had been in touch as far back as 1969–70 when he was a coordinator for the Stop The Tour campaign in Edinburgh. Like Robin Cook, Brown had a colossal brain and he was also extraordinarily hard working and politically astute. In retrospect I was wrong and he was correct that Labour could not win a modern election on our overtly Keynesian platform. But there was no need for intimidation. It was counterproductive too. More adept senior politicians, more secure in their own skins, would have sought to persuade, to find common ground and to neutralise such dissent. It showed him to have a fundamental political flaw. Two years later in 1994, when Brown was considering standing to be Party leader, I was asked whether I would back him. Sorry, no, I said, not after what I had seen of his behaviour at close quarters.

After John Smith's election in July 1992, Robin Cook, who had been Smith's campaign manager as he had for Neil Kinnock in 1983, asked me to be on his frontbench team. I was surprised, but Smith vetoed the idea. Robin was disappointed, explaining that Smith thought I was 'too independently minded'. But I hadn't expected the offer in the first place and was content in my emerging role in Tribune. Roger Berry and I also wrote another pamphlet criticising the whole architecture of the euro as enshrined in the European Union's Maastricht Treaty. We were both fervently pro-European and accepted the case for the euro in principle, but believed that it was designed in such a way as to enforce a rigid, right-wing monetarism on European member states. (When the euro came under severe threat after the global 2008–9 financial crisis, many of our arguments seemed relevant again.) However, this time the Tribune Group refused to endorse publication so we went ahead anyway under the emblem of the *Tribune* newspaper, the board of which had now elected me as its chairman.

Because the modernisers were insistent that Tribune's radical stance was unacceptable, tensions within the Group were now rising. At the November 1993 annual general meeting, where officers came up for election, I faced opposition from a more centrist candidate, Janet Anderson. There was a huge turnout, and people not normally present at Group meetings, including Gordon Brown, Tony Blair and Peter Mandelson, suddenly appeared with the purpose of voting me out, which they narrowly succeeded in doing by thirty-seven votes to thirty-four. Although disappointed that Tribune would now revert to its formerly passive role (which indeed it did), it had become very difficult to take it, the new direction many of us felt was needed, so I was phlegmatic about the coup. However, I had also issued a statement saying that it was disappointing that the Tribune tradition of Nye Bevan and Michael Foot had seemingly been abandoned. Janet Anderson was surprised when I wished her all the best when we bumped into each other in the Strangers Bar later. My political principles may have led me into adversarial stances, and I would give as much as I got in debate. But by temperament I had never been an adversarial personality. Perhaps because my own roots were almost literally in life-and-death politics, and I had experienced both political setbacks and successes, most parliamentary intrigues did not seem worth all the fuss and frenzy that consumed too many Labour colleagues and led them to become almost more opposed to each other than to the Party's opponents. Furthermore politics invariably involves not just high-minded principles but low-minded scheming, and I never had either much stomach, or much expertise, for the latter.

‡

The following year my role as a British MP took me back to the land of my childhood. It was April 1994 and I was an international parliamentary observer for South Africa's first-ever democratic election, with Nelson Mandela standing for President. With a sense of hope and excitement, I was collected from Johannesburg Airport by the Welsh political journalist Max Perkins and his television crew. They were making a programme about the election around my return and, as we pushed our baggage trolleys out, my Labour colleague Diane Abbott, Britain's first black woman MP, remarked: 'I suppose this will be a very emotional return for you, Peter.'

Almost immediately, it was. The last time I had seen Poen Ah Dong and Aubrey Apples was when they waved us a tearful goodbye into exile at Pretoria railway station in March 1966, when I was sixteen. Now aged forty-four, tears were shed again, at Poen's house in the coloured township of Eersterust outside Pretoria. The TV crew had already been on reconnaissance for a few days and went ahead to knock on Poen's door as I waited until beckoned to walk in and be filmed. Climbing out of the car I was suddenly overcome with surging emotion and had to check myself.

'Welcome home to the new South Africa,' Poen greeted me warmly with a big hug. With him was Aubrey Apples, now blind, as well as scores of relatives, young and old. The children and grandchildren were lined up to greet me, some proudly bearing the names of my mother and father. Poen said that, if he hadn't been asked to keep the meeting low key due to concern for my safety from apartheid supporters, the whole township would have turned out in a welcome.

Afterwards, there were only a few hours to spare before I had to rejoin the team of parliamentary observers for the first official briefing. So we went quickly to try to find our old house at The Willows which had played such an important part in my parents' activism and was just a few miles away. However, the surrounding area to the front and side had been completely altered by three decades of suburban property development. Eventually – there it was: the distinctive pair of linked *rondavels* (circular thatched homes) seemed to have been preserved in time, although the grounds were markedly different and the swimming pool a great deal smarter than our leaky old one.

There was the front door which I had opened to a Security Police officer bearing my mother's banning order. The familiar *kopje* behind had been declared a protected area. I looked up, searching for the tree off which a stone thrown by the Security policeman had bounced as he was chased up the hill by my father thirty years earlier. Now the bush and scrub looked innocent and fresh in the tranquillity of the sun. Pretoria was full of memories and, driving back, it was absolutely extraordinary seeing Nelson Mandela posters up in the middle of the city. Mandela smiling from lamp-posts in Pretoria of all places! Not for the last time I wondered: was this really happening?

But out there somewhere the old South Africa still lurked. A bomb planted by the white extremists of the Nazi-like AWB exploded outside the African National Congress's headquarters near our hotel in Johannesburg, killing and maiming ANC activists, candidates and passers-by. It happened shortly before we arrived and I carried my bags to the hotel through debris and milling crowds. Police and military were everywhere. Thankfully, however, such terrorism was not repeated: rather, it was apartheid in rigor mortis.

After a briefing on our duties as observers, the HTV crew drove me to see Hugh Lewin, back at home after many years in prison and exile, and now heading up the Institute for the Advancement of Journalism, which specialised in training blacks. Hugh spoke of hearing excitedly in prison of the rugby tour demonstrations, of the hated 'young traitor Hain' who was leading them, and of the boost to the political prisoners the news had been.

The atmosphere was relaxed and optimistic, and I was beginning to feel at ease, going that evening on an impromptu visit to a cabaret bar in Johannesburg's Market Square with Diane Abbott, who would not have been allowed into such a venue in years past. The audience, mixed race and young, laughed together at the white comedian, a sharp observer of the absurdities of the old South Africa, who asked to meet me afterwards. But if the Market Square bar could have been in any modern metropolitan city, Alexandra township the next morning was an antidote to all illusions. Still an appalling slum covered in rotting rubbish, with dusty tracks, shanty dwellings, rudimentary sewerage and little running water, it was right next door to Sandton, one of the plushest suburbs in the world. Yet, despite Alexandra's squalor the election atmosphere there was still infectiously buoyant.

Then it was off to the Wanderers, headquarters of the newly constituted United South African Cricket Board, to meet Ali Bacher. 'You were right, Peter, I was wrong', he said generously as the cameras rolled confirming how the 1970 tour cancellation had been a watershed. At the stadium there was a sign saying spectators who ran on the pitch would be prosecuted – a poignant point for me to be filmed. Alongside Bacher's, Khaya Majola, now director of cricket development in the townships, had his office. Assisting Khaya was Conrad Hunte, the great West Indian opening batsman of the 1960s, out on an English-sponsored coaching programme for young players in the townships. I told Conrad I'd seen him at Nottingham when we went up to the Trent Bridge test match in 1966, and reminded him that he had written during the height of the STST campaign as a member of Moral Rearmament complaining that I was too 'militant'; he laughed in embarrassment.

Back in Pretoria that evening there was a reception at the British Embassy. The Ambassador, Anthony Reeve, was modern, informal and astute – a contrast to the useless ex-colonial gents we knew in the early 1960s and who were obstacles to change rather than facilitators. An Afrikaner woman introduced herself from 'foreign affairs' in the South African civil service. 'It's a real privilege meeting you,' she said, 'you have done so much for us.' Apparently I was no longer 'public enemy number one'.

The next day, the eve of poll, a *Daily Mirror* photographer took me to the Carlton Centre for Nelson Mandela's final campaign press conference. The lax security worried me: if I could get in without a pass, what about somebody with malevolent intent? But all was well: Mandela presided over the event with his usual saintly, benevolent authority, patient but clear, grave though occasionally mischievously witty.

At the *Mirror's* instigation I sent a note up to the ANC's press spokesman, Carl Niehaus. Would there be an opportunity to be photographed with Mandela? I was beckoned up at the end. There was a scrum with photographers clambering around him and I felt embarrassed that the *Mirror* man seemed to be most responsible for this. Then, unexpectedly, we were ushered into an ante-room and I found myself alone with Mandela as he rested. We chatted amiably for around ten minutes. He was tranquillity personified, even oddly downbeat: 'Peter, I suppose I should be jumping for joy. But I just feel stillness. There is so much responsibility, so much to do.' It was almost as if he too couldn't quite comprehend that this historic moment had arrived at long last, and it was a privilege just to be with him. Everybody – from the media to his personal staff – treated him as something extremely precious: the special 76 year-old President in waiting, who held the whole country's future in his hands.

‡

The driver allocated to me was Desmond Khoza, a professional book keeper who had lost his job, and also a well-informed ANC supporter. At the introductions, he turned round and gave me a hard look in amazement – his face breaking out into a big smile. 'I can't believe it's you. After all these years, how wonderful to be driving you,' he exclaimed, enquiring after my parents, whose activities he had followed in the 1960s. They, unknown to me, were also voting – for the ANC – having discovered that their old South African identity cards were acceptable. They queued up joyfully with hundreds of others outside the Methodist Central Hall in Westminster, one of three polling stations in London.

On that historic Wednesday morning, 27 April 1994, we left the hotel promptly at 6 a.m. for Orlando West and East, the homes of Sisulu and Mandela, in Soweto. From the car we could see the gold mine dumps looming in the early mist. Desmond Khoza came from Orlando so we had no difficulty finding polling stations despite being given lists of rather inadequate addresses – worryingly typical of the rudimentary organisation around the election. Arriving at our first polling station at about 6.30 a.m., half an hour before it was due to open, there were hundreds, maybe thousands, already queuing up, their mood calm and expectant. More were streaming in out of the morning haze as the sun lifted. It was soon evident that the democratic niceties were being almost painfully respected, the calm seriousness with which the polling officials handled their first-ever democratic election engagingly moving.

Because Desmond was an official driver for international observers he was able to jump the queues and vote first. He waited anxiously to have his hand stamped. Then, as he put his ballot form in the box, he turned to catch my eye, smiling, part triumphant, part astonished – before leaving the polling station with a broad grin, punching the air in excitement. Hardly able to accept that, in middle age, he had actually voted for the first time in his life, he told me he had been worried in case his ballot paper might be snatched away at the last minute. An old woman – perhaps in her nineties –was led shuffling away after voting, a smile of eternity gracing her weathered face, as young men bounced confidently out in their trainers, giving high fives to friends. After all those years, all the bitterness, the killings, the violence, the lives wasted away in prison, here it was happening, amazingly right in front of us: constitutional apartheid being exorcised.

However, the logistical problems were immense. Some polling stations were not opening until midday because they didn't have elementary equipment like stamps, the hand spray for identifying those who had voted, ballot papers and so on. Was this a deliberate ploy in such an obvious ANC stronghold, I wondered? Over in Orlando West one polling station was surrounded by outside broadcasters, radio and television, including some from the BBC, who quickly grabbed me for interviews. President de Klerk had just been to vote there. But the station was due to close shortly because of a shortage of ballot papers – no doubt conveniently after, rather than before, de Klerk's media staged appearance. At a nearby polling station I bumped into the Progressive Party champion, Helen Suzman, clutching makeshift voting equipment and stationery she had purchased herself: 'This process must not be allowed to fail, Peter,' she said determinedly as she bustled away.

In Soweto, where multiple murder and mayhem was a daily occurrence, crime and violence simply disappeared for those few days. Even the police were friendly. White policemen, sporting machine guns, welcomed me as an election observer and even allowed a memento photo amongst them. Happy and relaxed in the sunshine, they expressed relief that it was going peacefully as they guarded the very democratic process which was ending their brutal history of repression. The next day we went to Alexandra township and to the white suburbs Edenvale, Lombardy East and Rembrandt Park. It was as interesting and moving an experience in another way, as blacks and whites queued together for hours, chatting for the first time as equals. The ANC polling agent Shantie Naidoo couldn't believe her eyes. Nor could a grey-haired white National Party city councillor, schooled in years of apartheid rule. 'Are you *the* Peter Hain?' he asked in amazement. He stuck out his hand, gave me a warm handshake and asked for my autograph. Not so many years before, he'd probably have had me knee-capped. I ended up signing autographs for other whites. The new South Africa was stepping forward with a verve and excitement that was hard to believe but wondrous to behold.

The next day was an anti-climax because we should have been observing the counting. But the chaos around the election meant that voting was extended in some areas, KwaZulu and Northern Transvaal for example. The election administration had been shambolic – a sad contrast with the beautiful process of voting itself. Watching the wall-to-wall television coverage with a racial mix of presenters was another sign of dramatic change, as was being invited into the studio to do a South African TV interview for the first time.

Finally on the Saturday morning I travelled to observe the counting with fellow Labour MPs Bob Hughes and Paul Boateng, to Benoni where Bob, chairman of the Anti-Apartheid Movement, had been at school. Virtually nothing was happening when we arrived in an Indian township at 9 a.m. However, we were able to see the ballot papers being unfolded for reconciliation purposes and turned upside down. It was possible to get an idea of the vote: seemingly over ninety per cent for the ANC. By now my initial anxiety had evaporated in the euphoria and I was relaxed when people recognised me and came up to chat. One ANC agent, a black woman in her sixties, who had been with Trevor Huddleston when Sophiatown had been cleared in the late 1950s, suddenly threw her arms round me and kept saying 'thank you'. Yet people like her had suffered all those years and, whatever contribution we'd made from safety abroad didn't really seem to compare.

How did the white presiding officer think it would go? 'An ANC landslide.' What did he feel about that? 'No problem – actually it's a relief, having apartheid lifted off our backs.' Such equanimity from a former military policeman who had seen action in the Caprivi Strip along the border with Namibia and Botswana, a notorious flashpoint where the white military had committed atrocities against infiltrating guerrillas. This boded well. His courtesy and helpfulness notwithstanding, we could hardly observe any serious counting because of procedural delays and mix-ups. So we returned to the hotel and then went down to the ANC headquarters nearby, picking our way through the remaining glass and rubble from the bombing. There by pure chance we bumped into Walter Sisulu, standing around in the foyer like anybody else; the vice president of the ANC, vital mentor to Mandela, had lost none of his earthy humility.

My last look at the election was on television before flying out. With many results now in, the ANC was standing at fifty per cent and rising. It was an incredible lump-in-the-throat feeling to watch the citadels of white power falling as the votes piled up. Although I had no illusions that an election observer could really know what was going on, our presence was an important deterrent to any potential wrongdoing. It was a privilege to have been a tiny part of the process, to observe spellbound as all the years of struggle finally bore fruit.

The presidential inauguration took place on 10 May 1994 at the grand neo-classical government offices, the Union Buildings, which lord it over the city from a perch on the hillside. VIP dignitaries sat in the sun on the terraces that step down the hill. On the broad lawns below, where I had played as a boy, a multi-racial crowd of over 50,000 waited expectantly for the swearing in of South Africa's first black President. Watching on TV in my House of Commons office, it was another miracle moment for me as, at 12.16 p.m., Nelson Mandela rose: 'In the presence of those assembled here, and in full realisation of the high calling I assume as President in the service of the Republic of South Africa I, Nelson Rolihlahla Mandela, do hereby swear to be faithful to the Republic of South Africa, and do solemnly and sincerely promise...'

Towards the end of his inaugural speech, the new President declared: 'Never, never and never again shall it be that this beautiful land will again experience the oppression of one by another and suffer the indignity of being the skunk of the world.' The 4,000 assembled VIPs rose spontaneously to their feet for an ovation in a moment of genuine emotion. And, as the cheering died away, from a ridge across the city came the roar of helicopter gunships, jet fighters in acrobatic flights trailing the new South Africa flag, swooping in to salute to their first ever black Commander-in-Chief, when once they had shot up and bombed his people.

‡

'MANDELA'S BOKS': the banner brandished six months later in the crowd for the South Africa–Wales rugby international at Cardiff Arms Park said it all. For my parents and me, invited guests, it was a thrill to see Chester Williams, the black Springbok winger, scoring tries for his country. A week before, on the eve of the tourists' match against Swansea, I joined the new sports minister, Steve Tshwete, at the top table. In 1969, when I had been organising to disrupt the Springbok tour, he had been organising rugby matches as a political prisoner with Nelson Mandela on Robben Island. I also found myself a guest of honour at a dinner welcoming the South Africans at my home ground in Neath, The Gnoll, savouring the moment with Arthob Petersen, Coloured executive committee member of the new, united South African Rugby Football Union.

(A year later, on 15 November 1995, the Springbok captain Francois Pienaar shook my hand enthusiastically at an official reception for his World Cup-winning team in the High Commission building, outside which we had held so many protests and vigils.)

Yet, while the South Africans had embraced the new, non-racial rugby era, for a good few of their Welsh, Scottish and English hosts, the Springboks' return was – after an inconveniently indecent interlude – 'business as usual'. They had been just as happy to welcome the old racist South Africa, and seemed not to have absorbed the lesson of history: that apartheid would not have been defeated without uncompromising opposition, including rugby isolation. My old Welsh opponent Wilf Wooller was unrepentant at a pre-match reception in Cardiff: 'That bastard Peter Hain – thank God he's a socialist,' he fulminated. (Some progress: he used to denounce me as a 'communist' in the Stop the Tour days.) Amidst the celebrations, I took the opportunity to remind British rugby that, by failing to take a stand early enough, it helped ensure that generations of young black and Coloured rugby players never had the chance to play for their country. There was a debt to redeem: to ensure that young blacks in the poverty-stricken townships got the facilities and the opportunities to play and to tour – unlike their fathers, grandfathers and great-grandfathers.

On such occasions, the moments to savour continued to pile up for all anti-apartheid activists as we greeted each other in amazement. In July 1994, I had been invited to Lord's by Ali Bacher as a guest of the visiting South African team for the first test since 1965 and couldn't help celebrating South Africa's win. However, when I climbed up high in the stand to the BBC commentary box for a long lunchtime interview on the history of apartheid in cricket, a number of old gents eating and drinking from their hampers made clear their displeasure at my presence. Following me up, my teenage cricketer son Jake observed: 'They still really hate you, Dad.' A few weeks before I had volunteered to welcome the South African cricketers at Heathrow Airport; where some in the English cricket establishment were unhappy, the South Africans were delighted to see me, including their coach Mike Proctor, another world class player banned from international participation because of our protests.

The following year, in July 1995, the first-ever tour by the Soweto Cricket Club took place, the team of youngsters appropriately captained by Khaya Majola. One of their matches was near my home in the Neath Valley, against the leading village club Ynysygerwn, of which I was patron. The tourists were to say afterwards that it was the highlight of a most successful tour. Ali Bacher came down and I also invited Tom Cartwright, now a constituent, who had been replaced by Basil D'Oliveira in 1968, adding to the sense of history coming full circle. The Mayor of Neath put on a pre-match lunch and civic reception and the day ended very late with celebrations, presentations and Khaya Majola, a big man in every sense, crying on my shoulder. Welsh songs from the Onllwyn Male Voice Choir competed with the singing from the Soweto players, who had earlier performed an ANC *toi toi* (jive) and chant as they left the field. The match was drawn on the last ball, the teams sharing 444 hard-fought runs. 'There I was wondering who I wanted to win, when Nelson Mandela swooped in and made it a draw,' I quipped at the post-match presentations. It had indeed seemed like divine intervention. However, the Soweto boys were visibly apprehensive when a police car roared up to the clubhouse, siren on and lights flashing in the dark – until they realised it was a prank: the smiling police officer was the batsman who had plundered runs off them earlier.

I was present at another historic occasion in London on 29 October 1994 when the Anti-Apartheid Movement, for nearly forty years the leading such group in the world, wound itself up. The ANC deputy general secretary, Cheryl Carolus, who had flown in overnight from Johannesburg, paid ringing testimony to the AAM's work. There were tributes from the veteran Labour MP Joan Lestor and from AAM stalwarts, including Ethel de Keyser and Abdul Minty. Bob Hughes, Labour MP for Aberdeen North, had carried the movement's banner as its chairman for many crucial years. Dick Caborn, Labour MP for Sheffield Central, had been its treasurer, at one point helping rescue the organisation from near bankruptcy. Mike Terry, executive secretary, had worked tirelessly and selflessly during the critical period since the late 1970s. In a simple ceremony, and to a standing ovation, the three of them lifted the AAM's banner and folded it up: job done in supporting the struggle inside and maintaining the pressure for sanctions and boycotts outside. As Abdul Minty remarked: 'The AAM was a movement committed like few others to bringing about its own early end.'

We had steadfastly maintained our strategy against an onslaught from apartheid apologists. The hypocrisy of Conservative MPs still rankled with me, such as John Carlisle – nicknamed the 'Member for Pretoria Central' – who had shamelessly backed the Nationalist government, and accepted generous 'freebie' trips from its front organisations. It rather stuck in the craw to be present as many of these Conservative MPs queued up to be seen with Nelson Mandela when he visited the House of Commons, including Margaret Thatcher, scuttling down to the front, who had notoriously denounced him as a 'terrorist' only a few years previously. But history had vindicated the AAM and all who supported it.

‡

I was an established British MP. My family was British. By now my parents had British grandchildren and had active roots in their south west London community. We had never expected to return to South Africa and my parents still had a residual apprehension about going back. Partly this was out of fear of what they had fled from. Partly it was that they had buried so much psychologically in leaving South Africa, so what effect would going back have on them? But the sheer exhilaration of the election convinced me a holiday for the whole family was a must, and I persuaded them to go.

The whips understood the special circumstances and I got permission to extend the traditional Westminster Christmas recess. Mom and Dad – now excited though also still nervous – my wife Pat, sons Sam and Jake, sister Sally, her partner Arthur and baby daughter Connie went as a group. My cousin Liz had arranged to greet us but, totally unexpectedly, VIP limos waited, indicators blinking on the airport tarmac in Cape Town for a surprise welcome in the fresh early morning sun.

Later, visiting the city's Waterfront marina, we could see the old railway tracks on the dockside where, twenty-nine years before, we had arrived under Security Police surveillance after our Berlin Corridor-type journey from Pretoria to board a ship for Britain. It was hard to imagine those dark days as we lunched, seals lazily bobbing at the quayside. Up the majestic Table Mountain by cable car we looked out over the beauty of the Cape Peninsula, surely one of the sights of the world. 'The fairest cape of all,' said Francis Drake. And, yes, there beyond the Atlantic breakers, shimmering in the haze, Robben Island, where Nelson Mandela and so many others had spent the prime of their lives.

Mandela now sat astride his nation almost God-like. Even whites, fearful before the elections, now worshipped him. 'Isn't our President simply wonderful,' they would say. *Our* President? We encountered a touching tribute to Mandela's extraordinary influence at a *braaivleis* (barbecue) at the home of Andre Odendaal, whom I had first met during my secret 1989 visit. Andre, a white Afrikaner involved in the anti-apartheid struggle, told how his mother had for several years refused to recognise his marriage to his Asian wife Zhora, a fellow activist, or to meet her and their mixed-race children. Then came the months after the election. Slowly the fear ebbed as Mandela mutated from Satan to saviour. Blacks weren't going to burn her out of her farm in the Afrikaner hinterland after all. She invited his family to visit, though not yet at the farm (a mixed marriage would still shame her in the eyes of her white neighbours). They should book into a nearby hotel and meet in the car park. He stood there with her grandson in his arms. She paused, then reached for the small baby, cradling it gently as her own. Suddenly she seemed to emerge from a trance, asking to meet Zhora, who had remained discreetly in their car. As we enjoyed the *braai*, Grandma was upstairs babysitting – Andre's first Christmas with his mother since the marriage. Although she was still fearful of meeting me, Andre insisted on introducing us as she rocked the baby to sleep.

It was as if a great millstone had been lifted. Whites could for the first time be themselves, at ease with the world. I was reminded of their friendliness and old-fashioned courtesy: it was always there, but obscured by complicity in the brutality of apartheid. The old South Africa we had left had been descending relentlessly into a pit of human depravity. The new one was buoyed by an infectious optimism from whites and blacks alike – though in those early times they too were caught by the same sense of wondering whether it was actually true.

It was difficult to find anybody who admitted to ever having supported apartheid. And of course most whites had just gone along with it, turning a blind eye to the misery and the oppression while enjoying the immense privileges. Over ninety per cent of whites never visited a township, choosing not to know, rather like Germans who lived near Nazi concentration camps. But there seemed to be a desire to exorcise guilt. Some of our relatives had kept a studious distance when my parents most needed support in the dark early 1960s. Now they gave us generous hospitality, a small example of the healing process that was such a moving feature of the new country.

Nearly 600 miles eastward along the coast from Cape Town, past long sandy beaches and turquoise sea, lies Port Alfred on the Kowie River where my mother was born and where we had idyllic summer holidays swimming, boating and fishing. They say 'never go back'. And Port Alfred, like the country, had changed a lot in thirty years. The yuppie marina seemed out of place. But the Kowie was as we had remembered it, especially upstream where it was protected by a nature reserve. The wide, expansive beaches remained a delight. 'It's not right. We should never have been forced to leave all this,' said my mother, tears streaming at the emotion of her return to her childhood home on the banks of the river. Her parents had died there during our absence and she had not been allowed back to attend their funerals.

Also nostalgic was our return to nearby Grahamstown and the school, much the same as before the War, where she won a 'deportment girdle' for 'good behaviour and standing up straight'. The English colonial feel of the town had been engagingly preserved. But it was startling seeing blacks and whites in the same queues in shops and banks, and the odd black family in restaurants and pubs. Later on our travels it was also pleasantly strange to enjoy mixed-race swimming on previously segregated beaches (on one occasion amidst a school of dolphins surfing in the waves).

Christmas Day 1994 was like an action replay of my childhood: sunburning weather by half past seven in the morning, pre-lunch drinks on the lawn and roast turkey on the veranda. We spent it with Peter Brown and his family at their farm, Lion's Bush, in the Kwazulu-Natal midlands north of Pietermaritzburg (where I'd lived as a toddler). A longstanding friend and Liberal Party veteran who had recruited my parents, Peter was celebrating his seventieth birthday as we arrived – a reminder of another talent wasted. He should have been in government, but he too was imprisoned, then successively banned from the 1960s onward. The peaceful atmosphere was striking. Political violence appeared to have vanished just eight months after the election, yet barely ten miles away at Mooi River there had for years been scenes of awful carnage between rival Zulu supporters of Inkatha and the ANC.

On the drive up from Natal to Johannesburg, we stopped at Ladysmith, scene of a famous 118-day siege during the 1899–1902 Anglo-Boer War, and found the home where we had lived for a couple of years in the early 1950s. By late afternoon, Johannesburg was in sight, the yellow glint of its gold mine tips visible through the baking heat haze. Another group of old friends embraced us in a welcome-back party. One said how the 'stop the tour' sports protests in 1969–70 had been 'decisive' in rocking whites into accepting change. 'The government must have bitterly regretted kicking out the Hains,' she chuckled. The goodwill amongst blacks remained remarkable. Alan Paton's warning from a black priest in his seminal book *Cry, the Beloved Country* – 'I have one great fear in my heart, that one day when they turn to loving they will find we are turned to hating' – seemed not to have been borne out.

The only upsetting thing was the ubiquitous wave of crime and muggings which had now invaded white communities where under apartheid it had been confined to black areas like Soweto, long a murder capital of the world. However, another old white friend brushed this aside: 'It's just redistribution of wealth. What else do you expect with sixty per cent plus black male unemployment?' But in the plush Jo-burg suburb where we lodged with friends, every home seemed to be guarded by security gates and burglar alarms. Whites travelled only by car – and even then were vulnerable to hijacking at gunpoint. Although South Africa had been liberated from constitutional apartheid, the poverty and destitution was much, much worse than when we lived there. Over seven million blacks – a quarter of the total black population – subsisted in squatter settlements ringing the white cities. On the Cape Flats, we were shown the latest grim squatting areas, not by accident named 'Beirut' and 'Vietnam' by their inhabitants.

In the Kruger National Park there were a delightful few days with one of my parents' struggle friends Jill Wentzel. Nwanetsi camp, isolated on the Mozambique border, gave a real feel of the primitive African bushveld: hyena and baboons patrolling the perimeter to a cacophony of birds and Christmas beetles. My parents were spotted emotionally holding hands outside at dawn soaking up once more the smell and sounds they loved, recalling what we had given up. The experience made them admit something which – in order to avoid the limbo life of an exile – they had repressed for a quarter of a century: how sorely they missed their old homeland.

And then the *pièce de résistance*. Some of the black activists who had struggled alongside them in Pretoria, suffering much worse harassment than we did, celebrated our return after thirty years. Poen Ah Dong and Aubrey Apples turned out with dozens of their relatives and gave my parents a special rendition of the national anthem, '*Nkosi Sike Lele*'. When we knew them, they lived in shacks. Now we partied at the sumptuous family home of Poen's daughter Mee Ling, in Pretoria's exclusive Waterkloof Glen. She would never have been allowed to live in such a 'white' area in the old days, and it would have been illegal to hold such a multi-racial party where liquor was served – certainly unthinkable that two white Afrikaners happily barbecued a lamb for the predominantly black guests.

At our home town, Pretoria, our old schools were much the same. At Boys High my father pointed out the spot where, as a banned person, he had had to watch me play cricket from outside the school fence. Hatfield Primary School honours board still bore the name 'P. Hain' as head prefect in 1962: the gold lettering had survived even my denunciation by the media and by government ministers in the early 1970s. At the Union Buildings my mother pointed out where she'd been spat upon by civil servants during a picket. Now all was at peace in the morning sunshine, the new flag fluttering proudly overhead. Once the seat of white oppression, it now housed Mandela's office.

The Old Synagogue, which had acted as a court when my mother had attended Mandela's trial in 1962, and where she and my sisters had met his wife Winnie, was now boarded up. But she couldn't help breaking down outside the Supreme Court, where our friend John Harris had been sentenced to death, and Hugh Lewin jailed for seven years. The prison where my parents had been jailed, and where in the old days blacks were hanged at the rate of over a hundred each year, was hidden behind a new, less threatening, facade. It made me wonder what all those agents of the police state who had intimidated, tortured and killed in the name of apartheid were doing with themselves these days. Were we passing them by as we walked in the city centre?

Although that holiday, following the secret visit and then the election, meant I had returned three times, my emotions still churned. And I had only spent my childhood there. However, my parents had lived there for about forty years, the last extremely fraught, and they had to adjust to returning home all in one breathtaking go, experiencing both the delight and the turmoil of old friends and old places that carried such deep meaning. Although thrilled, on their return to Britain they were for several months not quite themselves, extremely unsettled.

Having fought to defeat the Old South Africa, we found ourselves unapologetic evangelists for the New One. The people are hospitable, the weather warm, the food and the wine a delight. Nowhere else in the world can be found such a rich variety of animals, birds and flowers, and such breathtaking variations in landscape, with an infrastructure that makes visiting so effortless, whether in the Mediterranean-type southern Cape, the hot humid littoral of Natal, or the dry heat of the Transvaal highveld. The country, for so long a pariah, was now at last able to reveal itself, in Alan Paton's immortal words, as 'lovely beyond any singing of it'.

‡

If 1994 was a momentous year for South Africa and therefore for our family, it was also to be an important one for the Labour Party and therefore for my role as an MP.

That May the Party leader, John Smith, who'd had a successful couple of years, suddenly died of a heart attack in his morning bath. He was at the height of his powers as a politician, skilfully making the Party seem at ease with itself while taking tough decisions. I had picked up rumours before a scheduled meeting of the Welsh Grand Committee, and it was quickly adjourned, the House of Commons going into mourning for one of their own, a popular figure, signalling that a common bond of humanity and camaraderie can and does cut across the Party dogfight.

But, politics being politics, through the genuine sense of grief and shock we all felt in Labour, questions immediately arose about Smith's likely successor. Walking down from the Welsh Grand through the Members' Lobby I bumped into Michael White, respected political editor of the *Guardian*. The next day he reported my off-the-record views as the verdict of 'a senior Tribune MP': Tony Blair would be leader with John Prescott his deputy. There was little doubt in my mind Tony would win it, and when I later bumped into him in a corridor for a chat I told him so. Despite our differences, we always had good personal relations. Ironically I was on my way at the time to see Robin Cook to say I would back *him* if he stood to provide a platform for the credible left of which he was the de facto leader. He toyed with the idea, and invited a close circle of friends to a meeting. 'There's only one serious question,' he asked of us each directly, 'Can I win?' We would have liked him to stand, but had to be honest with him: nobody could beat Tony Blair. Cook decided he was better off trying to have some influence from the inside, though along with the rest of us he had few illusions how much this would count if the Blair/Brown/Mandelson axis got control of the Party as it was about to do. I felt more comfortable on the outside and voted for Margaret Beckett for leader and John Prescott as deputy, both also representatives of the credible left.

Blair won at a canter, with Prescott his deputy. The two could not have been more different. Blair, modern, debonair, highly articulate, media friendly, travelling ideologically light, and the chippy Prescott, with mangled syntax, working class and Labour to his fingertips. The media gave this 'dream ticket' a favourable welcome, the mood in the country going with 'New Labour' and against John Major's tottering and increasingly shambolic government. Blair was indeed the man of the moment.

He soon set about forming his shadow ministerial team (underneath the shadow Cabinet, which was by rule elected by Labour MPs). Isobel Larkin my researcher, who had very good antennae, picked up a rumour that I might be given a junior Northern Ireland post, and Diane Abbott told me the same thing. I never heard anything more myself and certainly nobody from Blair's camp approached me, nor did I ever encourage the notion, as I thought it improbable. I had other priorities as chairman of *Tribune* newspaper and one of a loose group of Labour MPs associated with Robin Cook – including Clare Short, Derek Fatchett, Roger Berry and Richard Burden – who went under the label *What's Left?* It was to be the title of a *Tribune* newspaper pamphlet I wrote and published in the early autumn of 1994, a critique of the 'modernisers' and a polemic for the 'credible, serious' left as we considered ourselves. The pamphlet was reprinted and made the newspaper some much-needed money.

That August, Steve Richards, then political editor of the *New Statesman,* published an interview with me in which I described the Party leadership's attitude to our core vote as being 'gratuitously insulting'. Although some Party critics felt I was too fond of a catchy phrase, it did accurately convey what most Party members and traditional supporters felt, and caused a considerable stir. On this occasion, as on other similar ones in later years, I felt somewhat schizophrenic: uncomfortable about the row but acting out of conviction. The leadership and many MPs may not have liked it, but as the deputy leader, later to be Deputy Prime Minister, John Prescott, some years later told me when giving me a ticking off on another such occasion: 'At least you are always talking about Labour ideas, Peter. You are a thinker and a campaigner. You never brief against or attack colleagues like others in the Party do – I'll give you that.'

Where Blair was absolutely right was in jettisoning Old Labour baggage, including being seen as anti-business and antagonistic to 'Middle England'.

He was also correct to force the Party to engage with a broad section of people and not simply with itself as it had always been prone to do. But I could never accept that in the laudable mission to make Labour electable, our values and our idealism had to be downgraded. Furthermore, Blair's 'New Labour' mantra defined itself *against* the Party rather than *for* an agenda that could be seen as distinctively Labour. I set my views out in a book published in 1995, *Ayes to the Left* (the title a play on words bellowed out by the Speaker of the House of Commons before votes: 'Ayes to the right, Noes to the left'). I popped in to see Tony Blair and gave him a personal copy, to which he responded by giving me his recently published collection of speeches which he quickly inscribed with the words: 'For Peter in admiration, Tony'. His wife, Cherie, later told me, a twinkle in her eye: 'I have put a copy of your book by his bedside to make sure he reads it.' I don't know if he ever did.

Meanwhile, I had become increasingly established in Neath and in Wales. My constituency office under Howard Davies quickly developed a reputation for first-class advice and assistance and something of a centre for the community and for the Labour Party. I had also developed a new agenda for the South Wales Valleys, long in decline after the progressive closure of mines, and organised a well-attended conference in Neath's Old Town Hall, September 1992. One of the policies was to replace the old pit villages in Valleys like those in my constituency with 'industrial villages'. These would be high-tech clusters, using modern communications, locating jobs and skills in what were rapidly becoming green and attractive places in which to live and locate.

In August 1994 the National Eisteddfod, a week-long annual celebration of Welsh language and culture, came to the Neath Valley, just up from the village in which I lived. I had learnt enough Welsh to give welcomes and say thank you, both at meetings and when canvassing in Neath communities with many Welsh speakers. So I resolved to make a statement of my support for the language at the opening ceremony by welcoming it as the local MP. Although Howard, a native Welsh speaker, was dubious because the event was a pinnacle of achievement for those proficient in the language – poets, writers, singers, musicians – I persevered. A local Labour member, Caryl Chiswell, a retired teacher and highly proficient, agreed to tutor me. I wrote out a four-minute address in English which she then translated. In an iterative process in which she coached me over a few months, changing certain words and phrases into ones which she felt I could more easily deliver, I gradually became more confident. I had written my own phonetic assists on the text and she recorded a version herself on a tape which I used to improve my delivery. It had to be

---

*   *Ayes to the Left: a future for socialism* (London, Lawrence & Wishart, 1995).

first class, nothing less would do. Although Welsh is a very difficult language to learn – especially for someone like me who had never found languages easy – I had one advantage: the South African accent has some cross-overs and I therefore found certain Welsh inflexions easier than, say, someone from England would have done. The Eisteddfod leadership was very supportive and as the event opened I was welcomed onto the platform, notes in hand. To my relief, Caryl's expert coaching did me proud, the loudest of several ovations coming when I passed on thanks from Nelson Mandela for the work of the Wales Anti-Apartheid Movement.

The truth is I had found my home in Wales. I liked the people, their banter, their warmth, their strong sense of family and community, and also their more traditional standards of upbringing which chimed with mine. I shared their commitment to sport, which was hard wired into me from childhood. Perhaps because the Welsh feel outsiders compared with the English, I felt more comfortable being absorbed into Wales. After twenty years as the local MP, my parents, sister Sally, niece Connie, eldest son Sam, daughter-in-law Paula and four grandchildren were also living in the Neath Valley.

One particular Welsh cause to which I was politically committed was devolution. Devolving power was the essence of my own 'libertarian socialism' and I readily agreed to speak at a conference committed to a Welsh Parliament in July 1994. However, with two MP colleagues who also spoke, I was censured from the Welsh Labour Executive. A referendum facilitated by the then Labour government in 1979 had been badly lost by four to one, with the Labour Party in Wales deeply split and Neil Kinnock leading the No campaign. The scars still remained in both the country and the Party. Yet by the time I came to Wales there was a new momentum for devolution – perversely encouraged by the Conservative government, which (despite being opposed to devolution) was arrogant and bitterly unpopular.

When the Caerphilly MP, Ron Davies, became Shadow Secretary of State for Wales in 1992, I was one of the few Welsh MPs willing actively to help him take forward the push for devolution within Welsh Labour. He was a convert, also having been an active No campaigner in 1979. Despite being a consummate political operator, he was not trusted by many Welsh Labour MPs, especially the older ones who were more devolution sceptic, and this made his task even more difficult. However, I gave him my total support, over the next few years helping him win successive elections to Labour's Shadow Cabinet. There is no doubt that, without his determination and (at times highly stressful) dedication to drive this forward, Labour would not have gone into the 1997 election as clearly committed to establishing a Welsh Assembly.

In 1994–5, Ron – who had made a point of welcoming me even before I

was elected an MP and had backed me during my Tribune Group tribula-
tions – had asked me to become campaign officer, a new post in the Welsh
Shadow ministerial team, which I was happy to do even though some of the
old-timers amongst the Welsh MPs raised an eyebrow at apparently premature
promotion. I had not interpreted the role as anything more than using my
campaigning experience to help Ron and the Welsh team.

Campaigning during the Monmouth by-election a few years before that,
the Liberal Democrats had a pushy poster team and their colours were all over
a newish council estate in Abergavenny. They attracted me like bees to a pot of
honey, and an old woman came to the door.

'Sorry to bother you, wonder whether you might vote for Labour,' I asked.

'Yes, love, always do.'

'Thanks very much – but do you mind me asking why you have that Liberal
poster in your front window?'

'A nice young man asked if I would do him a favour and allow him to put
it up. So I did.'

'Could I ask you another favour then?'

'Of course, love.'

'Would you mind if I took that poster down for you?'

'Please, that would be *very* nice of you.'

So I did, then paused. 'Would you mind if I put a Labour poster up for
you instead?'

'That would be lovely! Thank you very much.'

I managed to return to our campaign HQ with a dozen Lib Dem posters
similarly retrieved and replaced.

Although playing my part in attacking the Tories as part of the increasingly
effective parliamentary campaign Labour was mounting against John Major's
shaky administration, and despite remaining on good terms with Tony Blair,
I was still expressing public scepticism about the New Labour project. So in
autumn 1995 the phone call from Tony's communications director, Alastair
Campbell, came as a real surprise. Years before, I had been friendly with
Alastair when he was a journalist with the *Mirror* group, and we had worked
together on a campaign against unemployment which its papers backed. But
now he took me by surprise. 'Peter, we are going to make an honest man of
you,' he said. 'Tony wants to see you about joining the team.'

I was later shown into Tony Blair's office where he explained his purpose.
'We are entering a key phase in the run-up to the general election,' he began. 'I
want you to help us. You are talented and we cannot afford to waste any talent.
I want you to go into the Labour Whips' Office.'

Me? A whip? I must have looked astonished, and he hurriedly added. 'It will be good for you. You will learn a lot, can earn your spurs and build trust within the Parliamentary Party where there is a lot of suspicion about you. If you do well, then I can move you up.' He also explained how he would have wanted to bring Ken Livingstone in too, but that Ken's behaviour had never permitted that. 'I may not have liked everything you have said or written, Peter, but you have never been aggressive or personalised your criticisms like Ken has.'

I had no doubts about accepting his invitation. Tony had been willing to bring me inside and, despite the reservations I still had about New Labour, winning the next election mattered almost more than anything else to my Neath constituents who had been ravaged, first by Margaret Thatcher and then by John Major. Most important, I never had been an 'all or nothing' person.

CHAPTER SIX

TO BE OR TO DO

The first day of May 1997 was quite different to my last general election, in 1992, when my blood had run cold listening to the BBC radio headlines at ten in the morning. 'Early polling in Sussex is very heavy,' the newscaster had reported. Sussex? True blue. It was my first inkling we had lost – even the usually reliable BBC 'exit poll', declared just after voting had finished that night, wrongly predicted a narrow win for Neil Kinnock.

But not in 1997 – except in under-estimating the scale of victory: a Labour landslide for Tony Blair and for me a 27,000 majority, Labour's biggest ever in Neath. The campaign had been a breeze. A discredited, tired, embattled Conservative government was swept from power on a pro-Labour, pro-change tide. Door after door, high street shopper after shopper, responded with enthusiasm. It was a joy to be Labour that spring.

During 1995–6, I had knuckled down as Robin Cook's foreign affairs whip, tasked with sorting out a more coherent operation on Europe. It was a bit of a hospital pass by the Chief Whip, Donald Dewar, and his consummate deputy Nick Brown (deliberate, I thought – to test me out). By dint of hard work, including persuading reluctant colleagues to turn up to Standing Committees A and B where European legislation was regularly enacted, I had managed to pull it off, enjoying both the responsibility and the challenge.

Tory government Ministers, used to sailing through badly attended committee sessions, suddenly faced grief as my colleagues appeared for votes or even intervened in the proceedings. I decided (and was encouraged) to break the whip's usual vow of silence. Given a steer by a wise senior colleague, I developed a technique of spotting an obscure paragraph in a European directive or report and asking what it actually meant. Typically this threw the government into total panic. Used to reading out from a brief, the hapless Tory Minister, invariably ignorant of the technical detail, would cast a desperate eye at Foreign Office civil servants as he waffled away. Soon there was a fresh Labour *esprit de corps* as we had some fun at the government's expense. (When, a few years later, I was a Minister handling such committees, I warily prepared myself for such mischief – mercifully it never came.)

My other task was to draw up a document for more coordination between our European MPs and the Parliamentary Labour Party. This involved much consultation, and I presented my conclusions to Jonathan Powell in mid-1996. 'A good job of work,' he commented, then moved unexpectedly to the merits of Tony appointing a separate Cabinet Minister for Europe, instead of the normal middle-ranking Europe Minister of State under the Foreign Secretary. I hadn't given the proposition any thought, but Robin Cook was alarmed when I mentioned it: Europe was a big part of his portfolio and he was damned if he would let it go. Although there were good arguments both ways, much the same territorialism was shared by his Labour successors in office, in 2006–7 ending in a serious spat between Foreign Secretary Margaret Beckett and Geoff Hoon, appointed Europe Minister with a seat at the Cabinet table.

Whips' duties normally confined me to Westminster. But, unusually, several of us were put on a Labour parliamentary trip to Dublin in January 1996, including a liquid visit to the local distillery where I enjoyed my first taste of Paddy Irish whiskey with enthusiasm. Later we climbed out of our minibus for a lunch with the British Ambassador, uncertain where to go. One colleague worked herself up into a real huff. Looking around haughtily, she lighted on a scruffy, nondescript woman who happened to be standing nearby but appeared not the slightest bit interested in us: 'Outrageous. Should be someone to greet us. I'm a British MP!'

The woman simply blanked her, muttering: 'Piss off, madam, I'm Special Branch.'

In August 1996 in Papua New Guinea, one of our hosts abruptly fell into his dinner plate fast asleep, snoring away. Embarrassed colleagues tried unsuccessfully to shake him awake, but he was not for disturbing until an hour later he jerked up, food all over his face.

My only really hairy experience during a parliamentary visit was in Nigeria in June 1993 as an official Commonwealth observer in the presidential elections. Outside Port Harcourt, the Ogoni people had been in regular conflict with Shell Oil, which had a huge operation drilling for oil and gas with the full support of both the Nigerian government and the regional Rivers State government. But local people insisted that they were not benefiting from the massive wealth extracted at considerable environmental cost. Flaring of gas, oil spills and local degradation spawned the Movement for the Survival of the Ogoni People, which demanded local autonomy and control of a fair share of the revenues from their resources. (On 10 November 1995 an internationally known Ogoni activist, the playwright Ken Saro-Wiwa, was hanged by the Nigerian junta for his role in the struggle.)

The presidential contest was between the outsider, a charismatic wealthy businessman, Chief Moshood Abiola, and the candidate favoured by the junta, Bashir Tofa. At a briefing with senior opinion formers in Lagos the view was

Tofa would win. But I was picking up a very different reaction from drivers, cleaners, our armed police protection officer. Abiola was the clear favourite amongst the people fed up with the junta.

My escort in Ogoniland was an anxious senior Foreign Office official, Peter Young. As we drove between polling stations, at one point witnessing a running knife fight between rival gangs of supporters, he beseeched: 'I don't want to lose an MP!' Feelings were starting to run high as the day wore on, with polling heavy. Our High Commission Land Rover came to a halt driving through a village, blocked by people, curiously staring at me through the windows. By now Young was beside himself with worry. The locals did not seem too aggressive but I feared they could become so if our vehicle just ploughed on through them. So I opened the door and climbed out to chat, explaining who I was and what we were doing. They were excited and interested; the crowd pressing in around us by now expanding fast as news of the novelty spread. Then suddenly there was a hush. The crowd parted and a smart young man in a white suit and hat appeared as if out of nowhere, to my additional astonishment handing me a business card: the youth leader of the Ogoni Movement. We chatted amicably then drove off to waves and cheers.

Abiola won – most thought decisively. But it was academic: the regime annulled the result because their man had lost and detained Abiola; sadly, he died in prison five years later in December 1998. However, my last memory of that visit could not but be comical. Waiting to take off at Lagos Airport – a High Commission staffer having checked our bags onto the plane because otherwise they might have disappeared – a great rush of people made their way across the runway, dodging between aircraft landing and taking off: men, women, children, grandparents, heaving bags in the tropical heat. They all arrived at a plane and paused to catch breath before boarding – only to find it was the wrong one. Suddenly, a shout and the whole group turned, picking up bags, skirts and babies, and sprinted several hundred yards in another direction.

I had enjoyed the whip's job – both working with my old friend Robin Cook, and organising Labour colleagues. Tony had set on a pattern of placing people in the Whips' Office first. More is learnt there about what goes on underneath the radar and what makes the Commons really tick than in any other role: I would highly recommend it to any MP interested in a frontbench role, albeit with one qualification. Amongst MPs are talkers, thinkers and organisers. Some are surprisingly disorganised – though pointed in the right direction or given a platform, they can perform, maybe even brilliantly. To be an effective whip you have to be an organiser.

To illustrate this role I was asked to fly to Cape Town for a few days in November 1996 by friends in the African National Congress. Then two years into Nelson Mandela's new government, the ANC's former freedom fighters were finding it hard to adjust from struggling against the state to running it: where they had been steeped in distrust of authority, now they had to deliver the ANC's legislative programme. The Chief Whip, Arnold Stofile, had been a key sports activist when I made my illicit 1989 visit. Now he wanted to put some order into the engaging chaos of the ANC Government Whips' Office, and my reputation as an anti-apartheid leader was judged a good basis for being listened to. Other British whips might have been distrusted as 'colonial' figures.

I arrived punctually at the Constantia farmstead venue, but the whips were on 'African time'. Nobody turned up for at least an hour. Good start. When they drifted in, many seemed pleased to meet me but others seemed uninterested, even resentful at being asked to turn up. Stofile introduced me as a 'comrade' and we swapped stories from the struggle before I took them through how we organised our Whips' Office. Whipping is more about good organisation to deliver the ANC's objectives than the caricature of discipline and dark arts, I stressed. The meeting's mood changed from sceptical albeit courteous indifference to real interest.

'You mean you have to pressure colleagues to turn up and vote?' one incredulous whip asked. 'But they might be busy on other things.'

'Nothing matters more than getting government legislation through, so other things just have to wait,' I replied. It turned out her main duties involved allocating car parking spaces, and I tried unsuccessfully to persuade her that should be undertaken by officials, not by whips. She retorted that ANC MPs had not been getting their fair share until she took charge of the permits herself. Gradually our cultural gap narrowed and soon questions and points were being fired at me from all sides, Stofile later confiding it had been a real help in focusing energy and effort on the real priorities of whipping for government.

‡

Late in July 1996 I was in the shower when Tony called and had to be fished out, dripping, by my wife Pat, to be appointed a Shadow Employment Minister under David Blunkett – another friend (though not as much of an ideological soul mate as Robin). When the reshuffled team was reported in the *Financial Times* the next day I was described by a 'Blair ally' – presumably Alastair Campbell – in football parlance as 'inside left, not outside left', and the 'acceptable face of Labour radicalism'.

My first task was to help soothe trade union leaders at the annual Trades Union Congress in Blackpool. Most knew me because I had always made a point of attending as an MP, just as I had when I was a union research officer. This time I found myself in the middle of a huge media fuss provoked by my Shadow Employment colleague Stephen Byers. Close to Tony, and seen by journalists as speaking *ex cathedra*, Byers had lunched with journalists over fish and Frascati in a Blackpool eatery, the Seafood Restaurant. It was meant to be one of those candid, off-the-record occasions, but the story was explosive: Byers had mused about ending the historic union link with Labour, before heading back to Westminster.

As the only member of the Labour Employment team in Blackpool when the storm broke, I had a hurried chat with David Blunkett. He was livid, but also ambivalent as he did not want to damage his own position by attacking such an intimate Blairite as Stephen. I was the only one there to do media interviews and was in a strong position to rebut the story without criticising Byers since he had given no direct quotes: the Labour–trade union link was part of our heritage and would stay, I said firmly, while privately making it clear to everyone that I totally disagreed with Byers. Speaking at a fringe meeting I was also able to confirm, with Robin Cook's prior agreement, that we would immediately lift the ban imposed by the Conservative government on trade union representation within GCHQ, the listening centre of the British intelligence services.

Part of the Blairite frontbench team, yet not a Blairite, I continued to tread a careful path, trying to stick to my principles without breaking ranks, and enjoying ferreting out new statistics and facts which demonstrated with carefully placed press coverage the paucity of the Tory employment record and the chronic job insecurity felt by millions of low-paid workers.

I also continued to press my argument for a participatory Labour Party, against the increasingly dominant Blairite thrust of tight centralised control and favoured insiders. With fellow frontbencher Derek Fatchett and our Tribune colleague Jean Corston, I wrote an article for the *New Statesman* on the eve of Labour's 1996 conference advocating much greater membership involvement in policy making. In January 1997 *Tribune* newspaper published a pamphlet by Derek and me entitled *A Stakeholder Party*. It cheekily borrowed Tony Blair's phrase from his speech about the economy a year before and applied it to how Labour should be run, with members, trade unions and MPs in participating properly in policy direction. If this had been done, perhaps Labour in government would not have provoked such – ultimately debilitating – disillusionment amongst Party members and supporters.

‡

By now, however, with an election just months away, all was focused upon winning. The Tories had virtually thrown in the towel. Still stuck in my mind was a riveting remark by the Hendon North Tory MP, John Gorst (a veteran of the Grunwick dispute), on a visit to Angola. More than two years before the general election, he had told me that he would lose his seat (regarded as comfortably Conservative) and that we would win a big majority across Britain.

In May 1997, that is exactly what we did. After his own constituency count 300 miles to the north, and a phone call from the Tory Prime Minister, John Major, conceding defeat, Tony Blair flew down to London as Prime Minister designate in the early hours of Friday morning.

Robin Cook told me he was so determined to be in London ready for when Tony appointed his Cabinet that he cadged a lift on a private flight down in the early hours from his constituency outside Edinburgh. I made do with driving up as soon as I could. Adrenalin tends to carry you through election night, the early-hours count and then into the day itself – though a shower is a useful wake-up. I always slept like a log the night afterwards.

Having arrived at my London home, I watched on television as Tony Blair swept joyously into a flag-waving Downing Street, carefully choreographed and packed with cheering supporters. Soon he was followed in by his senior team – Gordon Brown, Jack Straw, Robin Cook and others – who walked back out as new Cabinet Ministers. Checking he would be part of the Cabinet – because you never knew what twist there might be – I called Ron Davies on his mobile to find he had just arrived at No. 10, with his special adviser to be, Huw Roberts, long experienced in Welsh public affairs. (More than a decade later, Huw confided: 'Ron was very excited waiting to go in, but strangely subdued on the way out. Hours later, driving back to Wales, Ron said: "Rhodri Morgan won't be on the team." Huw was both astounded and conflicted because Rhodri, a close friend and neighbour, had actually recruited Huw to work for Ron.)

Knowing nothing of this, that night I wondered where, if at all, I might figure in the remaining, lower ranks of government. I was not to find out until the weekend was over. These are moments in limbo, hanging about, waiting for the call and wondering if it will happen at all. As the ministerial appointments rolled out, some with a bit of spin indicating favourites, I put in a call to Sally Morgan to find out where I stood. A friend from Labour Co-ordinating Committee days and Tony's political secretary, she was at the heart of the appointments process and assured me 'you will be OK'. But almost the whole of the ministerial team had dribbled out and I had virtually given up into Bank Holiday Monday when Tony finally called in the evening.

'I want you to go to the Welsh Office,' he said.

The Welsh Office? Although pleased at being a Minister, I was staggered. 'But there are no vacancies, Rhodri Morgan and Win Griffiths are going there surely?' I replied, aware of all their hard work in the Shadow Welsh roles.

'There is an element of substitution,' Tony was delphic, sounding uncomfortable. 'I think you can do a really good job there because you are a good campaigner and I need you to ensure we win the referendum.'

'I'll deliver it for you,' I promised, still taken aback, muttering 'Thank you'.

Almost immediately Downing Street began briefing that mine was one of the 'inside left' appointments in the new government and that I was to take charge of the Welsh referendum campaign. The latter was widely welcomed in Wales because it indicated to Yes campaigners that the Prime Minister was serious about winning, when he had often seemed lukewarm about devolution.

With the media now reporting the news, I began getting congratulatory phone calls from friends. Incomprehensibly, however, neither Rhodri nor Win had yet been contacted – they like me had been in limbo all weekend and still remained so. I assumed I would be a third minister alongside them in the new Labour team under Ron. Others thought the able but low-key Win might be the fall-guy. But then the truth dribbled out, astonishing everyone in Welsh public life: Win was in, Rhodri out.

Surely not? He had been a dead cert. I was immediately worried about replacing the talismanic Rhodri – me an outsider, he the proverbial Welsh insider. I reflected on my new and totally unexpected situation – both an exciting opportunity and a real predicament.

As a bewildered political class in Wales took stock, it was rumoured that, when they had served together in the opposition Energy team, Tony had found Rhodri chaotic and disorganised. According to the well-informed political journalist Andrew Rawnsley, Tony had been put off after staying the night at the rambling, untidy Morgan family home to the south of Cardiff and observing the family dogs licking breakfast plates.

I called Rhodri immediately to say I was as bemused as him. He sounded shell-shocked and uncomprehending, thanked me for my courtesy and stoically wished me all the best. We had worked closely together, notably in a small Welsh group which Ron Davies led during by-elections, known as a crack campaign team. Although I was not to blame, I knew he felt pretty bitter. Ron professed equal surprise when we spoke later, then quickly moved on: 'I am allocating you the best portfolio, the economic agenda: education, industry and transport.'

By now the evening had gone into the night and I was called by Judith Cole, my new private secretary, who, sounded flustered when I said I would be arriving early in the morning – apparently the practice under the Tories had been for more civilised mid-morning starts – but she quickly arranged a driver to collect me.

‡

A favoured phrase of an older, senior colleague from my Young Liberal days stuck in my mind: 'Some in politics want to *be* somebody, others want to *do* things.' I was determined to *do*, not to *be*. It was nice to be a Minister and nice to have the convenience of a driver. But I had never been interested in status and was suspicious of those who were. Despite ritual accusations from the left of 'betrayal', I felt I had not so much compromised my principles on joining the Blair team as accepted the constraints, which meant I was no longer a free spirit. I had already accepted the collective responsibility, the adjustments and the pragmatism that come with the privilege of serving in office. That did not concern me – or, nearly two years earlier, I would have refused a frontbench position and remained on the back benches. However it made me even more determined to seize the opportunity to drive through changes.

That Monday evening, my family and friends phoning with excited congratulations, I drew up a list of priorities beginning with abolishing the unpopular, right-wing Tory policy of nursery vouchers. Most new Labour Ministers had been preparing for this moment having shadowed the posts they now occupied. But I was starting from scratch and followed my political nose. I had heard of civil servants filling up the day with appointments and visits to keep Ministers conveniently busy, and was determined to set my own agenda from the outset. To his credit, Ron was happy to let me get on with it. He was excellent at delegating and was determined to focus single-mindedly upon delivering his personal mission: historic devolution for Wales.

Next day, Tuesday 5 May 1997, I was given a friendly though carefully formal welcome into Gwydyr House, the small London office of government in Wales, most officials being Cardiff based. The building opposite Horse Guards Parade in Whitehall was old fashioned and comfortable. In earlier life it had dispensed compensation to slave owners (the mind boggles) after the abolition of slavery. Judith Cole, herself new to the Private Office, was nervously attentive. She presented me with a small dossier entitled 'Briefing for Incoming Ministers', including a draft White Paper on Devolution and details on an early Referendum Bill. I set it aside to read in due course as she was taken aback to be presented with my priority action list.

It was soon apparent that, while scrupulously professional, the Welsh Office officials were pleased to be serving Labour Ministers. The Tories had got stuck in an anti-devolution, anti-Wales rut, typified by John Redwood's arrogance as Secretary of State. He never slept a night in Wales, never learnt the national anthem and was almost single-handedly responsible for all Welsh Tory MPs losing their seats: Wales in 1997 became for the first time a Tory-free zone. He was also notorious for a right-wing gesture of 'sending' £100 million from the Welsh block grant back to the Treasury. (Actually, officials confided to me, they ensured it never was 'sent back', he was merely allowed to trumpet that it had been.)

My Tory predecessors also had an old-fashioned style. I was told that most hardly if ever came into the large, 2,000-strong hub of the Welsh Office in Cathays Park, Cardiff. When in Wales they worked via red boxes in their constituencies: they decided policy by paper and submission, rather than by engagement with officials – totally the wrong way around for thorny problems especially. I quickly changed the practice and soon officials came blinking nervously into my office as if on alien territory. Then I realised that everything came to me via the departmental director, Education for example. The policy official doing the work on a document would pass it up the line to maybe four or five superiors until eventually the director would come and discuss it. So I made what was seen as a 'revolutionary' reform: everyone directly involved, including the most junior official who may have done the spadework, was invited to meetings where we thrashed out policy. Obvious perhaps, but a big culture change and one that came increasingly to be valued.

I also insisted on being called by my first name – if anything an even bigger shock to the system. Most officials found it very hard to break the habit of a lifetime, some never did.

'Hullo Derek, June, Richard, Huw, please call me Peter.'

'Yes, Minister.'

Eventually, they would manage to spout out 'Peter' as if their mothers would disapprove. I was to find this throughout government, even when succeeding some Labour colleagues, and despite the Prime Minister putting out a new 'call me Tony' edict to Whitehall. I arrived on the first day as Leader of the House of Commons in 2003 to 'Good morning, Leader!' Everything in the Private Office was 'Leader' this or 'Leader' that. Maybe my predecessors enjoyed that grandiose eminence. I thought it preposterous. Despite insisting on my real name, it took a week or two to drag it reluctantly out of them.

I got on especially well with my new driver, Mick Smith. A proud working-class Londoner from Stockwell, Mick was straight talking and totally loyal. He would ensure all the proprieties of ministerial car use were respected, but where he was able to, went the extra mile in making it easier to combine a busy job with family and other responsibilities. We had a good gossip and laugh daily; it helped that he also supported Chelsea Football Club. Mick was to stay with me throughout my twelve years in government, moving together between different Whitehall departments.

In 2010 David Cameron's new Conservative government made a mistake they would live to regret when, donning hair shirts to appease rapacious media populism, they (allegedly) abolished ministerial drivers on austerity grounds. Some of this was hypocritical because red boxes could not be taken on the London Underground or bus and needed to be driven, while hapless Ministers went by bus or tube. Relatively speaking, the driver service cost a pittance and it lifted so much pressure from the job, making it so much more efficient. I always worked hard in the car, devouring red boxes or cramming in reading, and could not have done my various jobs as effectively without that indispensable driver support.

I was also lucky not to suffer car sickness, even on long hours of twisty journeys up and down between south and north Wales, sometimes frustratingly stuck behind tractors or caravans. Tony Blair, like some other colleagues, was not so fortunate and was unable to read or work on papers; he tended to make telephone calls, talk to officials or snooze. Joining him on a drive from the back entrance at No. 10 to catch one of the Queen's flights from Northolt Airport, I noticed he was not wearing a seat belt. 'Tony, it's against the law. You must put it on,' I said. He gave me a funny look and then did as he was told. In my second year as a Welsh Minister I had launched a television-based campaign with the police to 'belt up in the back', and did not want a media story about ministerial hypocrisy.

It was exhilarating to have the opportunity to implement Labour policies and values, to spread opportunity in education, to promote public transport, to work with the business community to try and drive up skills and entrepreneurialism from its low base in Wales. The sheer breadth of the portfolio gave enormous scope for creativity – officials having to work harder than ever.

There was also an early run-in with No. 10. Because Wales was relatively small compared with England, we were ready to abolish nursery vouchers in my second week; indeed missing that window would cause logistical problems in achieving early implementation. I wanted to press ahead because it signalled early intent that Labour was going to be radically different. But England and Scotland weren't ready, No. 10 wanted a coordinated announcement and Alastair Campbell called to ask why I was being 'difficult'. I explained patiently the real reasons behind our timing. Ron firmly backed me up and officials saw it as a cathartic moment when No. 10 finally relented: under us the Welsh Office was no longer to be cravenly subservient to London diktats.

The new policy was launched before a packed media in a Cardiff primary school and greeted with widespread enthusiasm from parents, teachers and

Labour members. Media handling needed careful attention, because the Press Office was still stuck in the John Major doldrums, ponderous, bureaucratic and unimaginative. Good and relevant pictures were of the essence. However, as an enterprising photographer manoeuvred me into his favoured position in a classroom, I took a precautionary glance over my shoulder: there was a large 'Willy Wonka' banner draped there. It paid to be constantly conscious of the tricks of the paparazzi, just as I was meticulous about refusing to chat after radio or TV interviews until microphones had been taken off. Imprinted in my mind was the furore when John Major had chatted informally after an interview about the 'bastards' in his Cabinet to the top television political editor Michael Brunson.

Much of what I did as a Welsh Minister was popular, partly because people wanted big change from eighteen years of right-wing Conservatism and because we were in the honeymoon period for a fresh government. But some decisions ruffled feathers. Extending Welsh as a required school subject for an additional two years to age sixteen, GCSE level, provoked criticism from Conservatives and communities living near the English border. (Within years it was regarded as normal.) I also took on vested interests in driving through a Labour manifesto commitment to rationalise education for sixteen-year-olds and over by requiring school sixth forms, further education colleges and training providers to cooperate and offer their students much better and wider choices of academic or vocational courses.

Back in Neath, there was pride at the constituency's first MP to become a full government Minister (my predecessor had been a whip). There was an excited cheer when I arrived a little late to the Party's general committee meeting just after the election, in hand my red box, symbol of government. After all the Tory devastation to local communities, the mine and industry closures, the mass unemployment, the poverty, *we* were in power at last.

A year later, it was an especially joyous occasion when Nelson Mandela visited Cardiff in June 1998 to address a European summit hosted by Tony Blair. He was granted the Freedom of the City and I was deputed to escort him from his hotel. The ceremony in Cardiff Castle was majestic in the sunshine, the packed crowd was expectant, a queue of VIPs sweltering in the unusual heat. But he ignored my guiding arm and stopped when a group of primary school children caught his attention, and began conducting them to sing 'Twinkle, Twinkle Little Star'. Cardiff that day experienced a vintage Mandela performance, singing and dancing with the children, and electrifying his adoring audience. He met my father again for the first time since they had been together in South Africa in the anti-apartheid struggle forty years before. 'Are you still causing trouble?' he asked. And, seeing the former

Labour leader Neil Kinnock, in the second row of VIPs, he boomed: 'Hello, Neil. Why are you hiding from me there at the back?'

‡

However, the referendum to establish a Welsh Assembly came first. Officials had done an impressive amount of preparatory work. Legislation combined with Scotland had to be taken quickly through Parliament to achieve September polls. Ron tasked me with heading a communications team to explain the government's position: a novelty for me running a campaign on behalf of, rather than against, the government.

One of the things I tried always to do in my political life was to think several steps ahead. A year before, even though I was not in the Welsh Shadow team, I had conceived of and helped set up the Yes for Wales campaign. It seemed self-evident that the referendum campaign would need to be carefully prepared, well in advance. There was little trust between Labour and Plaid Cymru, the latter still blaming us for the devastating defeat in 1979 when the Yes vote was barely twenty per cent. They considered Labour's new pro-devolution credentials suspect and there was deep antagonism to Plaid in Labour's ranks which I shared, especially after my bruising by-election campaign where they had played it very dirty.

But, I had worked with political opponents during both the Stop the Seventy Tour and the Anti-Nazi League campaigns, amongst others, and Ron Davies was happy for me to go ahead without formally authorising it. Terry Thomas, who had helped me in the Neath selection and was a key figure in the Welsh Labour Executive, didn't like the idea at all. But I managed to persuade him not to try and block it, by suggesting the initiative did not need Labour's official blessing.

On an unusually scorching Saturday in July 1996 at an annual summer party held at our home in Resolven in the Neath Valley, I broached the subject privately with Leighton Andrews, an old friend of over twenty years from our days in the Young Liberals (and later Labour Assembly Member and a Welsh government Minister). An astute and experienced operator, Leighton was ideal to drive the Yes campaign forward, and he was gratify-ingly keen. Our task was formidable, however: to achieve a swing from the disastrous 1979 campaign of fully thirty per cent – a psephological record buster. And in order to do that we had not just to bring together and build trust between individuals from disparate backgrounds, but also to do so in some secrecy within the goldfish bowl of Welsh public life where everybody seemingly knew everything.

To form an initial steering committee, I concentrated upon people I knew personally and who I considered might actually do some work. By the time we were ready to convene the first meeting, a reasonably strong group had come together.* Plaid Cymru, however, remained difficult. Their former leader, by now a peer, Lord Elis-Thomas, dismissed out of hand the idea of participating in a Yes campaign; he was still scarred by 1979 and contemptuous both of Labour's ability to deliver devolution and of the limited powers proposed. Also surprising was the refusal of Adam Price, subsequently an MP and leading figure in Plaid. He had helped research and draft a document produced for my Valleys conference in 1992. 'My Party wouldn't approve if I got involved,' he said when I called him. The attitude of these two Plaid figures was irritating and disappointing: so much for their commitment to devolution. After all, *I* was the one taking the real risk in pushing forward with the venture, many of my Welsh Labour MP colleagues and the leadership of Welsh Labour – Ron excepted – disapproving of such collaboration. (Tony Blair's team were, however, pleased when I briefed them, especially that we had obtained backing from senior business figures.)

Later, however, Plaid's leader, Dafydd Wigley, and the Party's whip, Ieuan Wyn Jones, were much more supportive and, when they saw which way the wind was blowing, Elis-Thomas and Price eventually jumped on board. Years of campaigning had taught me that where action is required some prefer to posture. Another disappointing recalcitrant was Nicky Wire of the Manic Street Preachers. Highly political and a socialist, he was pleased to hear from me when I phoned, but refused to be one of the public figures for the campaign because he didn't consider Labour's devolution plan radical enough – he apologised to me when it was all over.

Meanwhile the general election had been won and we were busy as Ministers. Ron Davies skilfully masterminded the devolution project, which absorbed almost all his time, managing both the governmental process and the Wales Labour Party – the latter requiring deft politics, with some members of the Party Executive and some MPs still lukewarm to hostile.

That July 1997 there was an encouraging opinion poll for the Yes campaign, showing the No vote had fallen from 37 per cent to 27 per cent, while the Yes vote had risen from 34 to 39 per cent. However, there was also a setback. Government advice determined that we would not be able to have an official public launch of the White Paper, *A Voice for Wales* – even though it was a government document, printed for Parliament in the nomenclature of a

---

* For an excellent, insider's account of the campaign see Leighton Andrews, *Wales Says Yes* (Bridgend, Seren, 1999).

'Command Paper' and funded by the Welsh Office. Obtuse advice stated that a launch might constitute 'campaigning'. A curious contortion: apparently the document could be published in the normal way provided nobody knew about it. Despite readily supporting the devolution project, Welsh civil servants were incredibly myopic about anything smacking of 'campaigning'. This was deeply frustrating because my communications strategy had been premised on government resources delivering widespread attention for, and distribution of, the document. The civil servants' case was that a Welsh Assembly had not yet been endorsed by Parliament – there had not yet been a Devolution Act – so there was no authority for government funding to promote it.

The only solution was to find a way of launching it separately. So I called Leighton Andrews and asked whether Yes for Wales could organise a big launch. He was immediately receptive though daunted by the extra responsibility and the extra cost for what was a thinly resourced campaign. However, even that was in question until the last moment, because No. 10 became typically nervous, worrying about media attention focusing solely upon Celtic constitutional issues which had nothing to do with England. There was also discussion with the Cabinet Office as to whether Wales or Scotland should launch first. I had tense phone calls with Alastair Campbell and Peter Mandelson before we were cleared to proceed for the launch on 22 July. Ron Davies, flanked by Win Griffiths and me, made a statement to Parliament and then we rushed off to Cardiff. Fortunately Leighton Andrews had delivered a highly impressive event in Cardiff Castle attended by more than 200 people including many prominent figures and celebrities, helping create a real campaign buzz. I had ensured *A Voice for Wales* was available through newsagents and it became by far the Welsh Office's best-ever seller.

That was not the only piece of official obstruction to be overcome. Well into the summer, Parliament was in recess; most Ministers and MPs, tired after the long pre-election build-up followed by the campaign itself, had gone away on well-deserved holidays. However, our Welsh team was hard at work and there was an impasse in late July when sticklers both in Cardiff and somewhere in Whitehall refused to countenance a door-to-door drop of the government information leaflet I had overseen, summarising *A Voice for Wales*. Apparently it might influence the referendum outcome: outrageous! So the government couldn't even explain its own policy to citizens. This after all my careful preparation – including persuading Tony Blair's communication expert, Philip Gould, to undertake valuable focus groups to guide our message.

Frustrated because officials wouldn't budge, I phoned Peter Mandelson, Tony's fixer as Minister Without Portfolio. He was also bewildered and frustrated in a distracted sort of way – other more pressing matters of state were evidently on his mind. However, he helpfully suggested circumventing the official blockage by convening a Cabinet committee – the usual mechanism for Ministers to broker an agreement if civil servants could not, or were unwilling to, do so. There was no certainty I would win my argument, however, because Ministers would turn up briefed by the same network of officials that was blocking me. There was also some grumpiness in the system: not exactly the most convenient time of the year to call Ministers and key officials together.

The Cabinet Office, which opens off Whitehall and backs onto No. 10, seemed a great deal sleepier than usual when I arrived from Wales and walked down the corridor alongside the still preserved old brick wall from a tennis court used by King Henry VIII, and into Meeting Room 'A', where Cabinet committees usually convened. Peter Mandelson was in the chair and invited me to make my case. Several other Ministers read out from briefs which regurgitated officials' arguments about the proprieties of spending money on 'propaganda' close to a referendum. I replied forcefully that the Government was entitled to explain what its new creation, the Welsh Assembly, *was*. Nobody else would do that and there was a great deal of public confusion. The leaflet would not explicitly advocate a Yes vote. It would simply place objective information before the public.

Then it was revealed that Scottish Ministers were putting an equivalent government leaflet out quite late, just before the official campaign period began. So Scotland was doing what my officials were telling me Wales could not! Mandelson's summing up was masterful. 'The Prime Minister strongly backs this referendum. Peter has made a compelling case. The leaflet should go ahead, but with two provisos: it needs to be distributed sooner rather than later, allowing a short interval before the referendum campaign actually begins, and the content needs to be cleared through officials.' The meeting over, he winked conspiratorially at me as he swept away to mind the shop, and I returned to Wales having achieved all I wanted but ruminating on a day or more lost in frustrating civil service standoff.

Meanwhile the Yes campaign was beginning to get lift-off, encouraged by another poll showing seventy-one per cent believed a Welsh Assembly would pursue policies better suited to Wales's needs. Rather overlooked, I thought, was a more ominous finding: fifty per cent thought it would increase the cost and bureaucracy of government – already shaping up as one of the No campaign's main arguments with a populist appeal.

The No activists were a mixed bunch, chaired by the Bank of Wales chief, Julian Hodge, and dominated by Conservative Party members, but including some Labour supporters. Because they were unable to match the by now glittering array of public figures, celebrities, Labour, Plaid Cymru and Liberal

Democrat politicians, it was too easy to under-estimate them, especially since the No campaign was also much less visible on the ground. In Neath for instance, they were virtually anonymous compared with a broadly based and enthusiastic Yes campaign. I had asked Hywel Francis to chair as someone on the Welsh left with a long and respected pedigree (and from 2001 Labour MP for Aberavon).

I was especially anxious to make a strong Labour appeal to Labour voters – the majority in Wales, whose support was critical – and back in May had argued: 'We say to each and every Labour supporter, this is a loyalty vote in your new Labour government. Do not side with the Tories in undermining such a crucial part of our programme by voting No or by not bothering to vote at all.'

The Yes campaign was to be indebted to some deft work by leaders of the employers' organisation, CBI Wales. Elizabeth Haywood, its director, supported by chairman Ian Spratling, managed to ensure Welsh business stayed neutral in the campaign – a dramatic change from 1979 when it was vociferously in the No camp. It was also an advance on Scotland, where the CBI remained opposed. Both Ron Davies and I had been working hard to engage with Welsh business, and the Yes campaign was doing so too.

Although Ron remained sublimely confident about the inevitability of victory, I was becoming less certain the more I campaigned on the ground. I was out there every day through August, increasingly worried that not enough doors were being knocked on. Local residents personally contacted could be persuaded – though usually only after a lengthy conversation. But the campaign was not reaching anything like enough people. Leighton Andrews, doing a magnificent job coordinating the Yes campaign, was receptive to my concerns. But Ron felt I was too pessimistic. 'I can feel it in my bones, the public are with us,' he insisted. But he was necessarily preoccupied with high-level activity amongst Welsh opinion makers where the mood was positive. I was on the streets and it did not feel like that at all – the argument could be won, but often only by individual contact.

One experience came to haunt me. I organised a 'Valleys Tour' into our Labour heartlands, and set off in mid-August in a minibus full of Cardiff University students, a media phalanx in tow. Our first stop was Pontypridd on market day, always packed with locals and visitors from all over the Valleys. We arrived to an enthusiastic welcome from local Labour members and I set off to meet and greet. The response was warm, people friendly, hands shaken, leaflets readily accepted: excellent. Then I lighted upon a small group of women pensioners chatting over a cup of tea. 'Hello love,' they smiled in warm recognition, 'we are all Labour, all behind you.' Great, I thought, only too conscious of half a dozen TV crews, photographers and print journalists around me, scrutinising a real 'live' conversation. I thanked them, dished out leaflets, and reminded them to vote Yes on referendum day.

'No, definitely not. We don't want independence.'

Their mood suddenly turned grumpy, the media crowding in excitedly to capture the moment. 'YES CAMPAIGN REBUFF' – I could already imagine the ensuing coverage. So I sat down with the women and took them patiently but firmly through the argument. 'Oh – it's not about independence then?' Their mood lightened. A few long, hard minutes later and they were smiling again. 'We'll all be voting Yes then! Good luck, love.' I said goodbyes, immensely relieved. The episode formed the core of the day's media reporting – about how they had been won around. Yet the Yes campaign did not have anything like the capacity to reach all our target voters in the face-to-face manner Pontypridd market had demonstrated was clearly needed. Crisscrossing Wales, and joining up with small groups of activists, I was finding it harder than any other campaign I had been involved in for thirty years.

However, by the end of August, it seemed as if we might have turned the corner when popular rugby international Neil Jenkins and Manchester United star Ryan Giggs declared for Yes, along with Catatonia star Cerys Matthews and the chart-topping Welsh band the Stereophonics. A new poll put the Yes vote up to 42 per cent and No on 22 per cent, though the level undecided was still worryingly high. Campaigning in Merthyr Tydfil on Saturday 30 August, I felt the tide was at last flowing our way, the scepticism I had been encountering gradually vanquished by the growing momentum behind the Yes campaign. I went to bed much more confident.

It was to be a fateful night. In the early hours of the morning, I was woken at my home in the Neath Valley by an agitated phone call from my House of Commons secretary, Jill Hays: Princess Diana had died in a car accident in Paris. It was shocking: she was a national icon, and Tony Blair later caught the national mood perfectly with his description the 'People's Princess'. I could not get back to sleep, sensing immediately it would also have a profound impact on the campaign. Out of respect and in keeping with the mood of national mourning, the government decided to suspend campaigning for a week, the Yes and No campaigns following. Absolutely the right course, but it froze the Yes campaign just at the moment we were starting to get real traction with voters. Just when people were starting to focus on what having their own Welsh legislative voice could do for Wales, their attention was dramatically wrenched away.

No sooner had activity resumed than we were rocked by a poll showing the Yes vote had slumped to 37 per cent with the No vote right up behind on

36 per cent over a quarter remained undecided. There were just two weeks left until polling day on 18 September 1997, and I went knocking doors up the Garw Valley in deepest Labour Ogmore where nobody seemed to have heard of the referendum. But after a few hours almost every other window was plastered with Labour Yes posters, the association of Labour with Yes and Tories with No being the main motivation rather than the case for an assembly, which few understood. This was simultaneously encouraging and alarming because it depended purely on a level of doorstep contact we were still not achieving. Daily Yes and Labour press conferences were almost falling over each other, meetings of the faithful were happening every night, and new celebrities were being added. But all this gave a false sense of momentum because in Labour heartlands – Neath excepted – the ground operation was patchy to say the least.

Ron remained confident and – in public – so did I. But I continued to warn both him and Leighton Andrews about my concerns. However, there was a big boost from a decisive Yes vote in Scotland (timed deliberately a week before ours), enabling deployment of a pre-planned slogan, 'Scotland Voted Yes – Don't Let Wales Get Left Behind.'

‡

The Monday before the referendum, some Yes campaigners, Ron included, were reassured by the latest opinion poll: 37 per cent Yes, 29 per cent No. I continued to worry about those 'undecided' who had risen to 34 per cent from around a quarter before, and about the crude but simple message of our opponents – 'No to more cost, No to more politicians, No to more bureaucracy'. Ominously, the poll found 61 per cent believing the extra cost of the Assembly should be spent instead on health and education. Leighton Andrews, above all, was acutely aware of the brutal realities of a closely fought campaign and had taken all these arguments head on and rebutted them, as well as getting effective messages out. But, night after night on television, the simple fear message of the No campaign kept pounding away against our optimistic, idealistic message of Wales walking tall with its own democratic voice.

On a visit to Neil Kinnock's old seat, Islwyn, the reception was disturbingly cool. But on voting day in Neath I got a fantastic response. The cosy town centre was abuzz with positive vibes, people calling out 'We are with you' and raising thumbs. Drivers tooted their horns. After all the work I had done from Anglesey to Newport, from Pembroke Dock to Deeside, it was intensely moving being home again witnessing everyone rallying wonderfully to our cause. Instead of the usual dank Valleys weather, it was a magnificent day right across Wales, perfect for our upbeat campaign.

But one Neath citizen worried the life out of me. I called out as he walked past: 'Hope you are voting Yes today,' and he turned back. 'Something for you to know, Peter,' he said, 'I was in the voting booth, pencil in hand and it kept wavering between Yes and No. I didn't know what to do. In the end I thought: what does Labour want and what does my MP want? They're both Yes so I'll be too.'

Across the nation, feedback to Leighton Andrews in the Yes headquarters showed a patchy picture, with Cardiff bad. That night with my son Sam I joined Ron Davies and our ministerial team at the College of Music and Drama in central Cardiff, where the result was to be collated and announced. We had decided to adopt a low-key media approach. But I could hardly rebuff the media scrum demanding an interview when I arrived. Although cautiously optimistic, I deliberately reduced expectations by saying we had a mountain to climb after the terrible drubbing of 1979. Some senior Yes campaigners thought I was 'profoundly demotivating', but I had had more personal contact with voters across Wales, prided myself on my nose for the mood on the doorstep, and the blunt truth was I didn't have a clue about the outcome.

In the ministerial sanctum at the college, the mood was tense and expectant. Plaid leader Dafydd Wigley arrived, very downbeat, Liberal Democrat leader Richard Livsey a little more positive. It was to be a rollercoaster night, our mood up at the first result from Wrexham where the loss was not anything like as bad as expected. A quarter of a mile away, the Yes campaign party was gloomy as activists returned from nearby areas to report a negative vote. To boost morale Leighton Andrews announced a positive tip-off from the experienced Bridgend Yes campaign leader, Carwyn Jones (twelve years later to be First Minister). A cheer went up at this bellwether signal from a town that crossed over from the more sceptical east of Wales to the more positive west.

There had been media speculation that Ron Davies might have to resign if the vote was No; somebody was infuriatingly briefing against him. Labour colleagues Rhodri Morgan and Kevin Brennan arrived to urge him not to do 'anything daft like that'. However, Rhodri warned him about 2 a.m.: 'We're going down tonight and there are going to be some terrible recriminations in the Party.' By now Dafydd Wigley was in tears. A Welsh Office official involved in the count told me she was emigrating: 'I am so disgusted with my Wales.'

During the campaign I always thought there was an unreal optimism, and some of the people riding that wave were now slumped in defeat. Then the Neath result came through. It was a stonking Yes – at over two thirds, the biggest percentage anywhere in Wales. Friends in the Neath count reported some voting boxes from former pit villages like mine, Resolven, were 80 per cent Yes or more. I was elated, struggling to keep the emotion surging inside me at this massive backing from my own area.

At around 2.30 a.m. I was smuggled out through a back door of the college to avoid the media throng desperate for interviews none of us were willing to give, and was driven to the Yes hotel party. I wanted to thank the Yes campaigners who had been magnificent, while also reminding everyone that ours was a campaign of hope against fear, of democracy against elitism, for the people against the establishment. As I entered I got a standing ovation to chants of 'Neath, Neath, Neath' – the monosyllabic anthem of my local rugby team. Leighton Andrews later wrote: 'Peter delivered a fighting speech ... But he seemed strangely downbeat, unwilling to suggest a victory was likely. His speech enthused the crowd however, and the chants of "Neath, Neath, Neath" were repeated as he left.' I was whisked back to our sanctum at the college, again dodging the media. 'I couldn't make the figures add up any longer,' Andrews recalled, telling his wife he thought we had lost by 1,500 votes.

By now the Yes leaders were in the doldrums, and starting to discuss how they could clear campaign debts. People were distraught. It was nail-biting waiting to hear our fate. Then I wondered down a corridor and almost bumped into a bustling official clutching a piece of paper. 'We've done it!' she muttered. I could hardly grasp the news. How? It seemed too good to be true. I went to find Ron Davies, who had been preparing to accept defeat, making speech notes, his stoic calm suddenly transformed as he excitably asked for the result to be checked and double checked. Surreally, on a TV in the room the BBC was reporting that we had been defeated when we knew that wasn't the case – or was it?

Shortly afterwards the result from Carmarthen was officially announced, a huge win. (But not as large proportionately as Neath, I was careful to remind everyone...) The majority was bigger than anybody had anticipated, and just enough to tip the overall result into the very narrowest Yes by 559,419 votes (50.3%) to 552,698 (49.7%). In our sanctum there were delighted hugs and congratulations all around, the relief palpable, if disbelieving. Dafydd Wigley's tears of despair turned to ones of joy and he and Richard Livsey were invited by Ron up onto the platform with Win Griffiths and me, all hoisting our arms and holding hands in triumph. 'Good morning,' Ron paused, 'and it's a very good morning in Wales.' At the Yes party, pandemonium broke out. Many people had meanwhile gone to bed depressed we had lost and woke up to a miracle that we had won.

Privately, however, Ron dismayed me with his schizophrenic attitude, both greatly dependent on my steadfast support and loyalty, and yet also jealous, according to his special adviser Huw Roberts. Despite being a good communicator, he envied the media coverage I obtained while also being only too conscious this was vital to securing his own policy objectives, both in the referendum and across government. He also seemed insecure about the good relationship I enjoyed with No. 10 despite my record of (at times outspoken) independence of mind. He disliked and distrusted Peter Mandelson and was in turn distrusted by Party officials in London and in Wales. When Mandelson decided he was coming to Cardiff for a high-profile referendum visit, Ron deliberately boycotted it and deputed me to welcome him. (To be fair to Ron, Mandelson was also unpopular with Yes campaigners and with Labour supporters.)

Yet, months after the referendum, he privately encouraged some media to speculate that I might succeed him as Secretary of State when he secured his ambition to become First Minister in the new Assembly. This, even after I had disagreed with his opposition to the Party's policy of 'twinning' two seats for Assembly candidate selections so that Wales could proudly be the first legislature in the world to be made up of more women than men.

Tony Blair once said to me that Ron could 'lie without blinking'. I had experienced that too. A complex man, yet someone I still admired at the time, not least because of his commitment to devolution and his aversion to New Labour fundamentalism. There is no question he was the man for the hour. Ron would rightly be recognised as the architect of devolution.

As an outsider who had become a Welsh insider – a Pretoria boy turned Neath man – I felt privileged to have been part of changing history.

‡

A year later, and almost twenty-three years to the day since my bank theft arrest, Tuesday 27 October 1998 proved the second most surreal day of my life.

I had come into work at the Welsh Office in Whitehall around 7.30 a.m., expecting to catch an early word as I habitually did with Ron Davies before the day took off. These could be most productive moments because he would invariably be reading the newspapers, and thinking things through before the bustle and pressure on the ministerial day started. But to my surprise he wasn't there.

The story really began the day before at our offices in Cathays Park, Cardiff, at the usual Monday early morning meeting to take forward the devolution agenda. We had both been busy and I hadn't seen him for a while, so suggested it would be good to get together in Parliament that evening. His favoured way was a curry with lashings of wine and beer, preceded by a short session in the House of Commons Strangers Bar. He was enthusiastic – then, mid-morning, popped into my office clutching a typically lousy speech by officials for a business audience that lunchtime. As the Minister for Business, I made some suggestions, he scribbled a few notes, and we again confirmed that we would see each other that evening. I reported the commitment to my private secretary, and then took a train up to London, assuming Ron was meanwhile on his weekly self-drive. Perhaps, I speculated, to claim the generous mileage rates then applicable to MPs – only later discovering his private secretary was seriously concerned because (despite having a hands-free mobile phone) he was often out of contact for several hours. That Monday evening I bumped into Nick Ainger MP, Ron's parliamentary private secretary, who asked: 'Where's Ron?'

It was all rather curious, but I thought nothing much more of it. Until, in the office early next morning, when I enquired as to Ron's whereabouts. His principal private secretary, June Milligan, appeared flustered. His car had been stolen, she said. My immediate thought was: as a Minister things go OK provided your roof doesn't leak, a member of your family hasn't been injured, the car doesn't break down, or any of those ordinary daily-life experiences don't occur – then you can just about keep the show on the road as ministerial life goes relentlessly on. But, if only one of these things happens, then everything goes off the rails. Poor Ron, I thought, he's got the whole pressure of the job and this has happened to him. June also indicated that maybe a red box had gone missing, which worried me: Ministers are not allowed to let a red box out of sight because of sensitive Cabinet papers.

Upstairs in my own office I asked Judith Cole, my private secretary, to check on the phone how things were going, which she did intermittently as I got on with my own work. Mid-morning she came in looking shocked: 'Alastair Campbell is sitting in the private office outside Ron's door.' I was amazed. The Prime Minister's communications director would not normally come into a Cabinet Minister's office – contact would usually be by phone or at No. 10.

Meanwhile I was busy, although I remained concerned, asking Judith to keep in touch. Then the phone rang around about one o'clock. It was Anji Hunter, Tony Blair's government relations director and, like Alastair, a friend. 'Would you come straight over?' As it happened I was free to do so. However, she wouldn't give any explanation. 'I need to see you right away. I have been trying to reach you.' Odd – because I had been in my office all morning and if Downing Street wants to reach anyone anywhere, its famed switchboard – 'switch' as it is known – can normally do so very quickly.

I walked the few minutes straight across Whitehall, and was immediately met by Lance Price, formerly of the BBC and deputy to Alastair Campbell. 'The reason you are here is Ron Davies has resigned.' I was flabbergasted. 'You must be joking,' I blurted out. Why? All sorts of questions raced through my mind. I couldn't think of any possible explanation. Ron was so committed to the job, that he'd suddenly resigned was just mind-boggling.

Then Lance quietly explained: 'He had a homosexual encounter on Clapham Common.'

Even more astounding. Over the years we had worked together, both in government and beforehand, the Welsh devolution project had become the all-consuming purpose of Ron's life and he had battled through tough opposition. That he would just throw this away was inexplicable. Equally inexplicable, however, was the thought that he'd had a homosexual encounter. Those of us who knew Ron well – or thought we did – had witnessed him laddishly leer at women. Although he always insisted that shortlists in the Welsh Office for important posts had women on them, when in male company, he was very much 'one of the boys', almost unreconstructed. I knew he had an awkward marriage and, wondered, if anything, whether he might be having the odd affair. But the notion of him being a closet gay man seemed completely out of character.

I was told that the Police Minister and Cardiff South MP, Alun Michael, had been appointed his successor, and that Tony had considered appointing me. Meanwhile I remained sitting at Anji Hunter's desk, having been asked to do evening TV interviews explaining the government's position. Various people came in and out of her office to chat as I hung around.

With a moment to myself, I picked up Anji's phone and called Rhodri Morgan, who was similarly transfixed in astonishment and turmoil. In strict confidence I told him I was inside No. 10 and that he should try and speak to Tony Blair as soon as possible about replacing Ron as Labour Assembly leader. 'It's really, really important you do that,' I urged.

Confronted with a problem or new challenge, I always tried to think – what's the next step? Having resigned as Secretary of State, there was no way Ron could stay on as Labour's candidate for First Secretary of the National Assembly for Wales, an election due the following May. Rhodri, who had stood against Ron in a bruising campaign for the leadership in the summer, was the obvious replacement, but I was worried that Tony Blair (who had already dispensed with Rhodri and appointed me instead) might not want this. So I suggested that he speak to Tony before the die was cast. He immediately understood the necessity. I called a few other people, including my agent in Neath (Howard Davies) to tell them what was going on but swearing them to secrecy, not knowing the set-up in Downing Street and whether calls were monitored, as Ministers' calls put through by their private offices always were.

I had been stuck in Anji's office for several hours when Alastair Campbell walked in, after briefing Westminster journalists on the extraordinary news, soon the top item of the day. He filled me in and then asked who I thought should be our Candidate for First Secretary. I replied immediately: 'Rhodri,' explaining firmly that he had only narrowly been defeated by Ron and was hugely popular in Wales.

'I don't think that's going to be acceptable to Tony. We can't have him in that post. It's too important,' he replied.

'Well, I think it would be the right decision and Rhodri would be good at it.' I argued with him, explaining the probable repercussions I could foresee for Welsh Labour to which No. 10 were apparently oblivious.

'If it is not going to be Rhodri, who do you think it should be?' Alastair then asked.

I thought for a second. 'I strongly disagree with Tony. The consequences could be serious for us in Wales. But if that's the way it has to be, the obvious choice is Alun Michael, because he is Secretary of State for Wales, just as Ron was when going for First Secretary.'

'Would Alun really want to do it? His whole focus has been on Westminster, not on Wales.' Alastair, apparently without knowing it, had put his finger on a problem of perception which I had feared and which was indeed to dog Labour for the next year.

Then it was resolved that in fact Alun Michael would be put up to do the media interviews, and I went back over to find the Welsh Office also still in trauma. The only thing predictable about being in government, I was discovering, was its unpredictability.

That evening I bumped into Nick Ainger. We both stared at each other in total amazement. Jon Owen Jones, who had replaced Win Griffiths in the summer reshuffle, and who had previously been the Welsh whip, said whips usually knew everything about everybody, but he had also been dumbfounded.

My next task was to get on with my new boss, Alun Michael, which wasn't necessarily straightforward, since we had been on opposite sides in battles in the Tribune Group five years before when he had voted to get rid of me as secretary. However, I tried always not to bear grudges – life was too short – much to the frustration of Howard Davies, who maintained I was too 'soft' with colleagues and others who might not have my interests at heart.

During the Neath by-election, Alun had been my campaign manager and done a terrific job. Afterwards he had gone out of his way to help induct me into Parliament, helping obtain my identity pass and asking the Serjeant at Arms Office to find a locker for me – the sort of advice immensely helpful to a new MP being initiated into the strange ways of the Commons. I was always indebted to him.

Next day, the usual early morning meeting in the Secretary of State's office had Alun sitting in Ron's old chair. When he asked about the leader of the Assembly – First Secretary, or First Minister as it was subsequently termed – I was clear: 'Rhodri is the obvious choice, the Party will want him. But Tony has ruled that out, so there's only one person who can do it, which is you.' Alun – clearly unsure because it would mean resigning as an MP – said he'd think about it.

But by the following week he had agreed with Tony to go for the job and I was their preferred choice as his campaign manager in the ensuing Party election. Would I do it, he asked? Yes, I replied, because I thought that it was important to give him all the support that I could especially since he had supported me in the by-election. He hadn't invited this turn of events, was in some ways also a victim having suddenly been presented with a career-jolting ultimatum. He was still vulnerable and his other junior Minister, Jon Owen Jones, was noticeably sceptical. Many of my colleagues on the left of the Party and a number of my friends, including my closest confidant, Howard Davies, were subsequently critical of me for so readily agreeing. I just didn't see there was an alternative. What sort of deputy abandoned his boss? Alun was in an impossibly difficult situation.

I had no illusions about the obstacles of competing with Rhodri, who was an enormously popular figure in Wales and whom I had advocated for the job. Alun and I were to have a good working relationship in the ministerial team, where I gave him my full support and he reciprocated. He had been by all accounts an able deputy in the Home Office but doing the top job is very different and he seemed continuously buried under a mountain of work. Around his desk would sit piles of files on the floor containing unanswered correspondence or submissions he had not got around to signing off. Quite unlike Ron, he was submerged in the detail rather than a man for the big picture. He would make obsessive minor corrections to press releases or grammatical changes to the letters drafted for his Ministers rather than letting others pick up on those minutiae.

The Yes campaign had been tough enough. But it was almost a doddle compared to the one to get Alun elected. Rhodri was the Party's favourite and feelings ran very high – my first real taste of being denounced by colleagues on the left. I had asserted my independence of mind in government. But this was different: for the first and only time in my life, I was campaign chief for the establishment candidate.

Alun eventually won – narrowly – by 52.68 per cent of the electoral college to Rhodri Morgan's 47.32 per cent. He was a clear winner amongst Labour MPs and the trade union executives but, ominously, amongst Party members, Alun lost heavily by 35.5 per cent to Rhodri's 64.5 per cent. I felt no sense of joy – only of a necessary job done, of an obligation delivered. The result was announced on 20 February 1999 and Rhodri's wife Julie Morgan MP, for whom I had campaigned in the 1997 general election, confronted me as we emerged from being told the result in an upstairs room in St David's Hotel, Cardiff. 'You should be ashamed,' she said angrily, brandishing her finger. I fully understood, but still campaigned for her in subsequent elections: personal emotions flare up and down but politics goes on.

Instead of being a popular champion for Wales, I now attracted some bile, including from some Neath constituents. Many of my friends across Britain were also critical. But I have always put a premium on loyalty to colleagues, and did not see how I could fail to support Alun in his campaign after he had supported me in mine. I agonised over the choice but in the end it came down to choosing between two able Welsh Labour figures who had different strengths and weaknesses.

When, immediately after the contest, Peter Mandelson congratulated me on Alun's win, I told him how tough it had been. 'Very character forming for you, Peter,' he replied with an ironic smirk. Be that as it may, remaining a government Minister had its downsides, involving difficult personal choices, and this was most certainly one of them.

‡

During the first election campaign for the Assembly in May 1999, and standing as Labour's candidate for his Caerphilly constituency, Ron Davies was under the delusion that he could still become First Minister. As the campaign chief, I had to admonish him for spinning stories to the media in which he indicated he was waiting in the wings to take over as leader in case Alun did not win a seat in the 'list category' of Assembly Members where he was standing.

Late on election night I bumped into Ron by chance at the Cardiff centre where the media were based. We had both finished doing interviews and he beckoned me furtively over to a dark corner. 'What's your Plan B?' he asked. I pretended not to know what he was getting at.

'You know – if Alun isn't elected. You *must* have a Plan B,' he said impatiently. 'The Welsh Labour Executive needs to be convened right away. I have done the figures and I know they will elect me as his replacement.' He listed some of the people, including Welsh trade union leaders whose support he claimed had been pledged in that eventuality. Sadly he had lost the plot. Weeks before some of the very same people had tipped me off about Ron's manoeuvrings and told me that, contrary to Ron's claims, they had not the slightest intention of backing him. But I did not tell him that. Nor did I mention that I did indeed have a 'Plan B', which I had privately got agreement for at No. 10 and from the Welsh Party general secretary, Anita Gale: and this was to do the precise opposite. If Alun had lost, we would indeed have convened the Welsh Executive and installed Rhodri as leader by acclamation.

Defeating Rhodri also had consequences for Labour in that first election to the new Assembly. Alun was widely perceived to be a candidate 'imposed by Blair' from London and Labour suffered a serious backlash, losing traditional Labour strongholds to the Nationalists, such as Rhondda and Islwyn. That also meant a difficult start to the new legislature, with Alun's leadership always in question, including from his own Labour Assembly group, most of whom had supported Rhodri. Eventually, after a difficult nine months leading a minority Labour administration, Alun lost a crucial motion and resigned. Rhodri replaced him and went on to be a popular leader – almost a father figure of Wales – for ten years. Eventually Tony Blair finally acknowledged that he had made a mistake – as he had in trying to prevent another popular Labour politician, Ken Livingstone, from being elected Mayor of London. New Labour 'control freakery' came at a huge cost in lost support and lost faith in the Party.

‡

Post devolution, in the summer of 1999, the *Western Mail*'s marvellous cartoonist Mumph had me playing 'battleships' with my ministerial colleague Jon Owen Jones, a spider weaving its web in the still air behind us. It was – as Mumph's cartoons on Welsh public life always seemed to be – uncannily accurate: capturing perfectly how we had almost nothing to do for a few weeks in this post-devolution interregnum. The Assembly had assumed our executive functions and the new Wales Office was being adapted to its new legislative role where one less Minister would be required. Having worked at breakneck pace for three years, it was disorientating. I had loved the job, it had been a real privilege helping deliver devolution. But, my task completed, I was keen to move on – to where, who knew?

It was mid-afternoon on the last Wednesday in July 1999 when our Whitehall sleuth in the Welsh Office put his head round my door: 'The reshuffle's finally started.' Five jumpy hours later and my pager vibrated: 'Call Kate Garvey at No. 10.' The Prime Minister's vivacious diary secretary asked if I could come over. By this time, I had departed for my London base in Putney and so a telephone call was fixed.

'Is that Mr Hain? Downing Street switchboard here, can I put you through to the Prime Minister?' A few clicks, a long pause and a friendly greeting. 'Peter, I want you to go to the Foreign Office. It's a huge job. The Middle East peace process. The Indian sub-continent. Derek Fatchett [who had died tragically] was one of the government's stars when he did it. It's a great opportunity for you.'

I was delighted at promotion to one of the most senior posts under the Cabinet – and one close to my heart. Another Downing Street switchboard call and Robin Cook was on the line with a warm welcome. It's hard to keep a secret in Wales and I soon had to fend off questions from Welsh journalists since Downing Street were not confirming the appointment until they were ready to. My new private secretary, Frank Baker, was mystified when I was put through to him. Geoff Hoon had been his new Minister for a few months following Derek Fatchett's sudden heart attack and Geoff didn't even know he had been moved. He was meeting Ministers in Israel and was woken up at 1 a.m. by the Prime Minister to be told he was now Europe Minister. Reshuffles are like a jigsaw puzzle: one appointment impacts upon another as people are contacted, moved and sacked in a complex process of person management, joy and tears.

The next morning I called in early at the Welsh Office for a rushed goodbye and gave a bottle of Glenfiddich malt whisky to my, by now, ex-private secretary, Judith Cole. At the door of the Ambassador's Entrance to the Foreign Office, off St James's Park behind Downing Street, there was a shout 'Peter', and I turned as journalists waiting outside No. 10 clattered down the steps, cameras running.

I had wondered whether the mandarin culture of the Foreign Office would be much stiffer than the informality I had cultivated in Wales. But Frank Baker was modern, easy to get on with, a football fan like me – and we quickly agreed to operate on first-name terms.

During an exhilarating couple of days in the old seat of Empire at King Charles Street, I was plunged straight into a meeting with the Pakistanis about the Kashmir conflict and delivered an evening speech about reconciliation between Islam and the West to a packed room where seven European nations ratified the Treaty of Locarno in December 1925. Friday's morning papers had thirty-year-old pictures of my rebellious youth organising anti-apartheid protests. My two sons, now the same age as I was then, didn't rate as very cool the flares and the floppy hairstyle.

Others too were enjoying the irony. A courtesy visit from the Indian High Commissioner began discussing Mahatma Gandhi's youthful experience in South Africa when he developed his philosophy of non-violent direct action. My new officials commented that it was actually an advantage having a Minister with an ex-colonial background. New Labour, New Foreign Office? A meeting with the Israeli Ambassador went well too, especially as I discovered that his son had the excellent judgement to be a Chelsea fan. Over the years in government that followed I would often use football – or another relevant sport – to break the ice and establish a cordial relationship with a new diplomatic or ministerial contact.

A good part of the Welsh Office in Whitehall could be fitted into my grand new rooms overlooking the rear of Downing Street and Horse Guards Parade. But the computer seemed Victorian and I searched for a quill pen icon on the screen. A promise was made for a new internet-linked PC, but to cable it in involved digging up the august floor.

In his grand room, Robin Cook sat me down with a map of the world and rearranged responsibilities provisionally allocated by the office. 'It must have been like this dividing up the world in the days of Empire,' he said mischievously; to my surprise, Robin evidently enjoyed the pomp of the Foreign Office. But, after the blow of Derek Fatchett's death, it was as if he had a soul brother again in the noble building. He made me Minister for the Commonwealth, on top of the Middle East, the environment, human rights and the United Nations. Against the advice of officials, he also added nuclear non-proliferation: 'We share the same stance on nuclear disarmament and I know you will do what I agree with,' he told me. To my delight, I became Africa Minister too. The South African High Commissioner, Cheryl Carolus, was thrilled, and there was a lump in my throat when I called by to see her in the gaunt grey edifice off Trafalgar Square outside which we had demonstrated so often in the apartheid years.

CHAPTER SEVEN

MAKING A DIFFERENCE

While dozens of us had been waiting anxiously by our phones for the Downing Street call during that reshuffle in late July 1999, my new Foreign Minister colleague, Baroness Scotland QC, had no idea she was in the frame. Her five-year-old son Jack answered the household phone and reported a strange man in a cabinet wanting to speak to her. Surely it was a ruse? No, she was told, the Prime Minister wanted to see her right away. 'Sorry,' she replied, 'can't do. I'm interviewing nannies.' However, later that evening, she did see him and was astonished to be offered a Foreign Minister job – only having to consult her husband (like her a high-flying lawyer) on whether the family budget would survive a huge cut in her income. One of the nicest people at the top of Labour politics, her charm and decency came with a steely intellect.

It was good working under Robin Cook again. We had both become senior figures inside the government without ever fully becoming insiders. No. 10's relationship with Robin was warily mercurial – his abilities were admired and he had a strong base in the Party, but he was treated with a certain detachment. Within months of taking office in 1997, he had been hit by tabloid revelations that he was having an affair with his Commons secretary Gaynor Regan. Ambushed by Alastair Campbell while waiting at Heathrow Airport for a holiday flight with his wife, he was brutally advised to make a choice there and then. He chose to divorce (later to happily marry Gaynor).

Although Robin was never someone you could get close to, it was perhaps his own bruising experience that helped him give me some sound advice when I told him that my wife Pat and I had separated after nearly twenty-five years of marriage. He was supportive and suggested that I put out a short press statement announcing the separation. Both Robin's press spokesman, John Williams, and Alastair Campbell were helpful and the ensuing low-key media stories were sympathetic, accurately reporting us as victims of pressured government life. But having to bare ourselves to the public was still uncomfortable, especially for Pat. In grubby tabloid style, the *News of the World* sent a reporter to Neath in a pointless pursuit to interview almost every woman Labour activist who had been seen campaigning with me. There were also repeated but unsuccessful attempts to doorstep Pat – unpleasant at an emotional time; to her credit she maintained a disdainful silence. The tabloids had nothing to print and the advice I had received was correct – get a factual story out first rather than be subject to rumour, media exposure and inevitable invention.

We were proud of the way we had brought up our two sons Sam and Jake (then in their early twenties). Pat had supported me in my political activity and I had reciprocated both in sharing responsibilities for our boys and by encouraging her in her own interests. But the pressures of 100-hour working weeks in government had brought to a head what in retrospect was always a fault line. Despite having married into it, she was never really comfortable with the all-absorbing life of politics and (I felt perfectly reasonably from her standpoint), began spending more time with friends in London. Although immediately following the separation there were strained months between us, we were later able to divorce amicably and remain friends, helped by both of us falling in love again and remarrying: in her case to Ian McGarry, a mutual friend of twenty years, former Putney Labour activist and general secretary of the actors' union Equity; in mine in June 2003, to Elizabeth Haywood, whom I met when she was still director of the Wales CBI, and who, despite the pressures of politics, gave me a private life full of joy and contentment.

Robin Cook, however, was not a team player. He had four of us working to him but had little interest in ministerial team meetings which I always found indispensable in government. Despite being politically close, I found him an enigma. He was excellent at delegating which was marvellous because I could really drive forward policy and activity. But when one of my responsibilities escalated right up the media and diplomatic agenda – as happened on Zimbabwe and Sierra Leone – he simply took it over without discussing it with me. Of course it was his prerogative to lead on the top issues – but I did feel that he might at least have taken my advice and been more collegiate. Instead he relied on his formidable brainpower, political acumen and ferocious ability to devour a brief.

The contrast a couple of years later when Jack Straw succeeded Robin was stark. Although there was never the same close political trust I had with Robin, Jack would readily seek my views and had regular team meetings. Despite being one of the most experienced in the Cabinet, in the first six months of his tenure Jack was uncertain in the job and I helped him out on numerous occasions, often springing to his defence when journalists suggested that he was not up to it. When I volunteered advice on a policy issue, Jack would consider it carefully and more often than not take it, sending minutes out to that effect – all of which made a Minister like me feel valued, and encouraged greater confidence and authority from officials as well. Nevertheless, on my departure from the Foreign Office in 2002, he briefed to the media that at least in my successor he would no longer have a Europe Minister 'playing lead violin'. I always found Jack approachable, whereas it was difficult to get through Robin's private office to see him. So, when we discovered Robin was around, my principal private secretary, Frank Baker, would call his private secretary to announce I was on my way into his grand office, knocking politely first; Robin was invariably delighted to see me and would happily break off from what he was doing, leave his desk, and sit me down on one of his luxurious sofas for a productive chat. He was politically inspiring, brilliant in so many ways, a pleasure and yet also a problem to work with.

‡

Within days of arriving at the Foreign Office, Robin had gone off on holiday with other Ministers, cheerfully telling me I was in charge. Though aware that he could have been contacted by mobile telephone, I threw myself into the job, revelling in the responsibilities.

Almost immediately there was a crisis in the small west African state of Sierra Leone. I arrived one morning in early August 1999 to be told that five British soldiers and other UN peacekeepers were being held hostage by a rebel faction. They had been driving through the Occra Hills about forty miles outside the capital, Freetown, to collect several hundred children and young women abducted during a brutal eight-year civil war notorious for mutilations of babies and children.*

Immediately aware that the capture of British citizens would become a hot issue, I called an emergency meeting, determined to rescue them. 'How quickly can we get a team in?' I asked. Two to three days by scheduled civilian flights, apparently. I was amazed at this lackadaisical reaction: the government would be pilloried. 'I want a team to fly out later today – including the SAS.' Officials looked startled and sceptical. However, they came back later to report that this was indeed now going to happen. Not for the first or last time, that for me was what being a Minister was all about: as far as is possible running events – not being run by them.

Anxious to stay out in front of the story and to demonstrate we were in charge, I gave interviews, refusing to comment on media reports that the team included elite Special Air Service commandos that had freed hostages in past missions. The team, I told BBC radio on 6 August , was not a 'gung-ho' mission

---

*   The previous year Sierra Leone had been toxic for our government. The Foreign Office, my predecessor as Africa Minister included, had been hauled to account over alleged official collusion in arms shipments to the Sierra Leone government by British 'military consultants' Sandline International which breached United Nations sanctions.

but 'contained all the expertise from military to police negotiating skills and Foreign Office personnel, to negotiate the safe release of these hostages. We want this resolved peacefully and quietly if that is possible.' Although I did not want media hype over the SAS, it suited me that the rebels holding the hostages would inevitably learn about the feared soldiers. A few days later the hostages were released unharmed.

However, within a year, and after intelligence that Freetown was in danger of being taken by rebels again, Tony Blair backed our recommendation and scrambled about 700 British troops there. They were backed up by planes, helicopters and warships carrying 800 marines. It was a unilateral British initiative with international blessing, successfully repelling the rebels, establishing order and rescuing a United Nations mission near to collapse. By the time our forces withdrew, the Sierra Leone government had been helped to train soldiers able to deploy right across the country.

Our intervention was widely praised. We were treated as heroes by the locals and one of Bill Clinton's senior officials, with whom I had been discussing the idea of a United Nations 'rapid reaction' capability, told me enviously: 'You guys have got a rapid reaction reach like nobody else.' After Kosovo in mid-1999 – when British intervention was decisive in stopping ethnic genocide – Sierra Leone further emboldened Tony Blair. Causing consternation in an unsighted Foreign Office, he had set out the case for 'humanitarian intervention' in a notable speech in Chicago on 22 April 1999. I backed the idea, seeing intervention, ideally by the UN or other international organisations like the European Union, as potentially progressive in the cause of international justice. It could avoid catastrophes like those which occurred in Bosnia and Rwanda when the world stood by in the early 1990s in the face of horrific genocide and ethnic cleansing. However, the doctrine was to prove fateful over Iraq.

‡

Success in Sierra Leone was followed by failure with Zimbabwe. I had joyfully welcomed President Robert Mugabe's landslide election win in 1980, majority rule having replaced racist white minority rule for the first time. But Mugabe had become increasingly autocratic and corrupt, using state violence against opponents and the media. Our government's relations with him deteriorated badly: Tony Blair could not stand his abuses, seeing Mugabe as a dangerous blot on his Africa focus – the strongest of any modern British Prime Minister. My predecessor Tony Lloyd had a bad meeting with Mugabe, who remarked that he preferred Margaret Thatcher's Tories to Labour: they had given him an easier ride.

He was due over on a private visit to London – mainly so his wife Grace could pursue her hobby as a serial luxury shopper – and it was fixed for me to meet him at his hotel, St James's Court, near Westminster. My officials were keyed up – maybe we could get a diplomatic breakthrough, reporting that Mugabe's people were intrigued that a supporter of their liberation struggle with my anti-apartheid history now spoke for the old colonial power. I was more doubtful, but if I could establish a relationship maybe something positive would come of it.

We met on a Friday evening, 29 October 1999, Mugabe accompanied by his Foreign Minister Stan Mudenge. Formally polite at the outset, Mugabe began complaining about 'British interference', Labour's 'lack of understanding' and 'colonial attitudes'. Always expensively turned out in perfectly pressed suit and tie, Mugabe had a preening ego which smacked of deep insecurity (such a contrast, I couldn't help thinking, with Nelson Mandela's easy, self-deprecating humanity). We kept talking but getting nowhere. He had a moan about Tony Blair and his Ministers, and I quipped that I was from Africa, with a record of liberation struggle solidarity. 'Yes, yes, Peter,' he patted me on the knee, smiling for the first time. 'We know you are different, we know you are one of us. Maybe we can do something together in future.' The mood of the meeting eased, both sets of officials looked relieved, smiles all round. Professional diplomats live or die by diplomacy, and they were hoping my credentials had achieved a fresh start. I gave him a copy of a political thriller set fifteen years earlier: *The Peking Connection*, about a nuclear link to apartheid South Africa and which sympathetically featured Mugabe. Afterwards my camp was upbeat.

But the very next morning, the prominent gay rights activist Peter Tatchell attempted a citizen's arrest of Mugabe, accusing his regime of condoning 'murder, torture, detention without trial, and the abuse of gay human rights'. As his motorcade left the hotel, four protesters forced the President's car to a halt. Tatchell opened the rear door and grabbed the startled Mugabe by the arm: 'President Mugabe, you are under arrest for torture,' he announced. 'Torture is a crime under international law.' However, police soon arrived and manhandled Tatchell and his colleagues away, detaining them in Belgravia police station until, seven hours later, Mugabe had completed his Christmas shopping at Harrods and his plane had departed for home.

Although I couldn't help admire Tatchell's ingenuity, when I heard of the incident I was full of foreboding. Mugabe will go mad, I thought. He duly did. I had already exchanged amicable conversations with the garrulously thuggish Stan Mudenge, but when he called me a few days later, it was obvious the protest had unhinged Mugabe. 'My President wants an apology. He believes you tipped off the protesters.' The accusation was so bizarre as to be risible. But, within weeks, Mugabe was in full flow, accusing me of orchestrating the whole thing. His homophobia now rampant, he publicly accused Tony Blair of having a 'gangster government' of 'gay Cabinet Ministers'. Stan Mudenge attacked me for a 'pre-conceived and pre-meditated agenda of demonising and ostracising Zimbabwe's leadership' and, even more absurdly, denounced me as a 'racist'. Still later Mugabe came out with the wacky allegation that I was 'Peter Tatchell's wife'. (Tatchell pithily responded that I was 'far too New Labour' for him.)

Meanwhile Mugabe's militia had embarked upon violent land seizures, attacking white farmers and driving them off. Five white farmers were killed in March 2000 and nearly 800 farms earmarked for expropriation – even though, at the outset of his rule in 1980, Mugabe had actively encouraged white farmers to stay. The attacks were done in the name of redistributing land from white settlers who in most cases had owned it for generations, but for every one ousted around a hundred black workers lost their jobs. Our government had earmarked £37 million for land reform in Zimbabwe. But it needed to be well managed, transparent and legal, and Mugabe's land grab was the exact opposite. Tragically he handed all the farms to his cronies and soon weeds were spreading over the once fertile fields. Mugabe's policies led to mass rural unemployment, widespread starvation and a reliance upon imported food and food aid – this for a country which was once the beautiful bread basket of southern Africa.

I became more and more furious about Mugabe's wanton destruction and vicious attacks on his own people.* He unleashed militia on the opposition MDC and rigged the parliamentary elections of June 2000. In the 2008 presidential elections, it was a measure of the desperation of his people and their bitter opposition to his tyranny that they turned out in defiance of Zanu-PF violence to defeat Mugabe in the first round of the contest. Only the threat of even more murderous brutality prevented the victor Morgan Tsvangirai from assuming the presidency as the people had voted.

What particularly angered me as Africa Minister was that Mugabe had prostituted the ideals of the freedom struggle which he had once led with distinction. They were the same ideals of democracy and human rights I had fought for in the anti-apartheid movement, and that Nelson Mandela and his comrades had sacrificed so much for. I also felt strongly that, where I had once condemned white tyranny, consistency demanded the same stance over black tyranny.

---

* For a chilling account, see Peter Godwin, *The Fear* (London, Picador, 2010).

Black victims of Mugabe sent me messages applauding my outspoken stance, saying their morale was boosted by knowing they had support, not just from right-wingers happy to side against a black dictator, but from the left and from someone with a credible record of support for liberation struggles. One, Sekai Holland, was international officer for the MDC, whom I had first met during the 1971 Springbok tour campaign in Australia where she lived in exile from Ian Smith's racist regime. She urged me to maintain my stance; this despite being savagely beaten, her life constantly endangered.

But it became fashionable amongst white liberal commentators – including some British newspaper Africa correspondents – to argue I was playing into Mugabe's hands. This was naive in the extreme: Mugabe needed no excuses or alibis. He was set on his dictatorial path. I preferred the messages of encouragement from Mugabe's victims rather than listening to snipings from armchair observers. Our friend from the early 1960s in South Africa Hugh Lewin had lived in Zimbabwe and was also supportive, as was his journalist partner Fiona Lloyd, a Zimbabwean. Hugh told me what was happening under Mugabe was in some ways worse than under apartheid when, although the judicial system was rigged against you, the odd case could still be won; that seemed impossible under Mugabe.

I was fortified in the knowledge that Nelson Mandela was equally contemptuous. Speaking at a United Nations event in Johannesburg in May 2000, Mandela gave vent to his anger with Mugabe when he referred to those African leaders who 'once commanded liberation armies ... [and now] despise the very people who put them in power and think it is their privilege to be there for eternity. Everyone knows well who I am talking about.' He never once disagreed with my position when we discussed Zimbabwe; on the contrary he gave me every encouragement. He was, however, circumspect over his own government's sadly pusillanimous role. At a private meeting in his London hotel in 2002, his frustration was all too evident, and he started to spell it out – then, abruptly, dismissed the subject, waving his hand: 'Peter, you must speak to my President,' he said evidently concerned that he was tempted to breach his self-imposed protocol of loyalty to his successor.

Mandela remained tormented by the havoc and terror unleashed by Zanu-PF. In July 2008, with Zimbabwe almost destroyed and Mugabe clinging on to office despite losing the presidential election, Mandela denounced 'the tragic failure of leadership in our neighbouring Zimbabwe' at a fundraising dinner in London. During his own presidency, Mandela's relations with Mugabe had been poor, the prickly Mugabe openly resenting a much bigger liberation hero than himself, and Mandela abhorring Mugabe's rising despotism and self-serving corruption.

My old comrade and now President of South Africa, Thabo Mbeki, was especially culpable. His government toadied embarrassingly to Mugabe, when they could have pulled the plug on the tyranny. Pretoria supplied electricity and other vital strategic necessities. Yet it chose not to exert serious pressure. Some of the arguments deployed were frankly embarrassing, echoing the specious propaganda of apartheid apologists. 'Outside interference' was condemned, sanctions against Mugabe 'would hurt the masses'. Other arguments were insulting: we had no right to criticise a former liberation leader, even one now a tyrant; as a Minister now representing the old colonial power, I was out of order. There was speculation that as an old liberationist, Mugabe was regarded by his peers in the traditional 'African chief' sense as the most senior, and they deferred to him.

On an official visit to South Africa in early January 2001, I questioned the strategy adopted towards Mugabe by the southern Africa leaders: 'Constructive engagement seems to have failed.' The South African *Sunday Independent* put a front page spin on the story and the South African Foreign Minister Nkosazana Dlamini Zuma wrote a furious letter of protest to Robin Cook which she then leaked. Although having a large chip on her shoulder, we had got along fine until this attack, and she deserved credit for being the country's first ever woman Foreign Minister. (In a poignant footnote to this episode a few weeks later when I was unexpectedly reshuffled, she and her officials anxiously sought reassurance that my move was not a consequence of her complaint. It certainly was not, as will be seen later.)

I also warned in the interview that failure to deal firmly with Mugabe would rebound upon neighbouring states. Indeed foreign investment into the region slowed and refugees flooded across the border, mainly into South Africa, triggering ugly attacks from indigenous residents which tarnished the rainbow nation's reputation. Zimbabwe blighted Thabo Mbeki's noble vision of an 'African renaissance' based upon democracy and good governance. And I met potential foreign investors who were even put off doing business in South Africa, fearing contagion because of the failure to bring Mugabe to heel. Although I remained on good terms with the South African government, Mbeki included, it remained a big disappointment that they had failed to live up to Nelson Mandela's – admittedly exacting – standards.

‡

There was a constant and perfectly understandable clamour from all officials to visit their country of responsibility, happily filling the diary, with seventy-four countries under my wing. But there was no way I could make a difference on all of them. So, apart from covering the ground with as many visits as possible – flying more than 250,000 miles in just over eighteen months – I decided to focus upon conflict resolution. Zimbabwe was clearly a failure by that yardstick, but elsewhere there were some real achievements.

Foremost was an international treaty to ban 'blood diamonds'. As I studied daily intelligence reports, it was very apparent that the illicit trade in diamonds was fuelling conflict, especially in Sierra Leone, Angola and the Democratic Republic of Congo. Typically, rebel groups would forcibly capture control of alluvial diamonds in the silt or mud of river banks. They would then trade these for arms and other necessities for their murderous activities. Everybody in the legitimate diamond trade knew this was going on, but turned a blind eye.

The pressure group Global Witness and Canada's UN Ambassador, Robert Fowler, had been trying to expose the bloody trade, but I was the first Foreign Minister to tackle it. The initial reaction from diamond companies and countries was one of horror: global publicity over 'blood diamonds' could destroy consumer confidence in the jewels and damage jobs. My initiative was condemned by companies like De Beers and the World Diamond Council and there was worried diplomatic traffic from the southern Africa diamond producers – South Africa, Botswana and Namibia. Given Antwerp's centrality as a trading centre, the Belgians were in a panic, the Israelis, Russians and Indians also fretful about the impact upon their own trading operations. No. 10, concerned about a diplomatic and business row, asked to be kept in the loop.

But I pressed on. Eventually, the tide started to turn, as the main companies, traders and African countries were persuaded of the advantage to them of cleaning up the trade. The so-called 'Kimberley process' was initiated to negotiate a solution. It took nearly two years of talks and pressure before we finally secured a United Nations international treaty, the Israelis and Russians being the most resistant until I made it clear they would be seen as culpable if the process collapsed. It was also no coincidence that the rebel forces in Sierra Leone and Angola were subsequently defeated. Diamonds could still be 'a girl's best friend' but only if not covered in blood.

‡

Angola had hardly been on the Foreign Office's radar, so when I determined upon making it one of my priorities, there was some grumbling amongst officials: it wasn't in the Commonwealth and had a corrupt government, so why bother?

My interest went way back to the anti-apartheid struggle. South Africa, together with the CIA, had sponsored a brutal civil war by arming and funding the rebel UNITA forces of Jonas Savimbi against the once Marxist MPLA government, an old ally of Nelson Mandela's ANC. In 1995, I was selected for a parliamentary visit to the country. It had been all but destroyed, the aftermath of the still simmering civil war starkly evident in towns with buildings blown apart and burnt out tank wrecks everywhere. Once a thriving country, with enormous mineral and oil resources, highly fertile, with an abundance of food for export to neighbours, it was now a basket case. Starvation and poverty were rampant. Limbless people begged in the streets and children stepped accidentally on landmines planted across once lush fields by Savimbi's militia.

We were flown on a diminutive United Nations plane deep into rebel territory, landing on a small, remote dusty airstrip in the bush, consignments of heavy arms visible in foliage beneath camouflage covers. As we climbed out, several smart, shiny limousines roared up, incongruous in the primitive surroundings. Savimbi's staff jumped out, wearing dark suits and welcoming us in American-accented, well-spoken English; doubtless as intended, they seemed more sophisticated than most government representatives we had met, who spoke little or no English. We were whisked off to a hall in the small town of Bailundu and asked to wait. Time dragged – deliberately, we wondered? – then Savimbi suddenly made a grand entrance, immaculately dressed in a crisp white uniform and matching military cap, brandishing a silver-topped cane. He gave us a little speech in fluent English, then deftly fielded questions, only becoming irritated when I challenged him about his collaboration with apartheid South Africa. Afterwards he worriedly sought me out to persuade me he was a 'true African' – more Africa's Pol Pot, I thought.

Now I was in a position to make a difference on Angola as Africa Minister. Since it was not a priority for either No. 10 or the Foreign Office, I was able to change the policy of Her Majesty's Government on my own. Previously Britain had sat on the fence between a notoriously corrupt government and Savimbi. That was not good enough. People power was unable to assert itself in a civil war fomented by Savimbi's homicidal forces. We now did all we could to defeat Savimbi, and had an immediate impact: I was informed about his operatives discussing what to do about 'that man Hain', and complaining I was 'causing big problems' by targeting their UNITA movement. I issued instructions for Britain to help identify Savimbi's whereabouts, and in February 2002 he was trapped and killed by Angolan forces in remote eastern Angola. Mission accomplished, even if seeing photographs of his bloodied corpse made me wince.

Before that, Thabo Mbeki had taken me aside at an Africa–Europe summit in Cairo and sought to persuade me to back off. 'Whatever his activities, Savimbi is an African,' Thabo told me. 'The MPLA are mesticos' – the term given to those of mixed African–Portuguese blood.

'But Savimbi was sponsored by apartheid and he has been destroying Angola for years,' I retorted.

'Yes, of course. But you must understand, Savimbi represents an important African majority in Angola,' he said. I nodded politely, but resolved to take absolutely no notice and to push on regardless. Although I held no brief whatsoever for the corrupt MPLA governing elite, Savimbi needed to be destroyed to enable an alternative politics to assert itself and Thabo's spurious attempts at Africanism cut no ice against Savimbi's primitive fascism. After Savimbi's death, Angola began to recover, restoring the shattered towns I had witnessed.

During a visit to Angola as Africa Minister in 2000 the red carpet was rolled out, our Ambassador delighted that at last Britain was seen as a player. But despite a warm welcome from President dos Santos in the governing elite's luxurious enclave just outside Luanda, I encountered stiff opposition in getting permission for British Airways to schedule Luanda as a prime business destination. It seemed to me a no-brainer – the airline then most valued by business sending out a message that Angola was now open for business. But, despite warm encouragement from the President and his Foreign Ministers, the Angolan civil aviation body was having none of it, a key official clearly in hock to Air France, which had none of BA's scruples in its dealings locally. Eventually, however, there was a concession: BA were allowed the singular honour of one weekly return flight, when many more could have been filled, since oil was now fuelling high growth. Senior BA executives said they would never have got the route without my clout with the Angolan government.

‡

Another conflict zone focus for me was Sri Lanka. Torn apart by a gory civil war between the majority Sinhalese and the minority Tamils – the latter's military wing, the Tamil Tigers, specialising in suicide attacks way before Islamic jihadists adopted them – it seemed to cry out for political dialogue rather than military conflict. The Tigers' leader, Prabakaran, had a reputation for blood-stained fundamentalism, and the organisation itself was proscribed in Britain. But I insisted to a nervous Foreign Office on meeting the Tigers' London-based political negotiator, Anton Balasingham. The only concession was for the encounter to be private and on neutral ground – a London hotel room rather than the Foreign Office. The Sri Lankan government would have gone ballistic had they found out. It proved a useful ice breaker. Drawing on both

my experience of Welsh devolution and southern Africa liberation struggles, I
floated the notion of devolved autonomy for the Tamils within the state of Sri
Lanka, rather than the independent nation the Tigers were fighting for. It had
a sympathetic reception. Later I met Norway's impressive interlocutor, Erik
Solheim, who was delighted to know that British policy had now changed and
we would be actively supporting his mediation efforts. Our previous studious
neutrality was tantamount to siding with a government that would not be seen
'treating with terrorists'.*

Then, in November 2000 I paid an official visit to Colombo, capital of
Sri Lanka. Visible everywhere were high-level security checkpoints and armed
guards on the lookout for terrorist attacks by the Tamil Tigers. Centrepiece
of the visit was a speech to a packed audience at the British Council entitled
'Peace through Change: the British Devolution Experience' which focused
upon lessons from the Northern Ireland conflict. My message – conflicts could
not be solved militarily, and political negotiation, even with bitter enemies,
was necessary – was not universally welcomed. There were angry questions
and protesters outside carried placards stating 'Peter Hain Mind your own
Business' and 'Your peace moves will not be tolerated here'. The veteran
Foreign Minister, Lakshman Kadirgamar, with whom I had a cordial meeting
and a smiling handshake for photographers, later denounced the speech. But
the opposition leader, Ranil Wickremesinghe, gave it an enthusiastic welcome.
A year later he negotiated a ceasefire after winning the general election and
took forward a peace process (which, however, sadly did not survive the return
to power of the party who had rejected my overtures during the visit).

‡

As Middle East Minister I had initially to overcome suspicions by Israelis
and the Jewish community in Britain that I was too pro-Palestinian, having
spoken up for Palestinian rights as early as 1970 when a Young Liberal leader.
Then their cause was nothing like as well known or well supported as it later
became, and many in the Jewish community saw the issue in 'for us or against
us' terms. Aware of this, and explaining that at the beginning he had faced a
similar problem, Robin Cook introduced me to Michael Levy, well-connected
in the Jewish community, a Labour peer and Tony Blair's personal envoy to the
Middle East. Michael, who had made his wealth in the music business, now
devoted an enormous amount of his time and energy to fundraising for the

LEFT With Mom and Dad, as a baby, Nairobi 1950.
RIGHT Child in the heart of Africa with Dad and puncture, the Congo 1951.

LEFT Pietermaritzburg, 1953.
MIDDLE My mother, Adelaine Hain, speaking in Lady Selborne township, Pretoria 1962.
RIGHT Adelaine Hain banned from attending Sally's birthday party, so inside looking out, 1963.

LEFT Tom, Sally, Peter and Jo-anne in Pretoria, 1964.
RIGHT With John Harris's baby son David, 1965.

LEFT Anti-apartheid activists: Adelaine and Walter Hain, Pretoria 1964.
RIGHT In Pretoria Boys High School uniform, 1965.

LEFT ABOVE Hain children representing banned parents at farewell activists party, Pretoria 1966.
LEFT BELOW Family into exile: on board ship at Cape Town docks, March 1966.
RIGHT Protest leader, 1970.

Being carried from 10 Downing Street after Young Liberal protest in spring 1969.

LEFT Acquitted outside Old Bailey, April 1976 bank theft trial.
RIGHT With Pat and newborn Sam, August 1976.

LEFT Protesting with small sons Jake and Sam, 1979.
RIGHT With Ralph McTell and Julie Christie, Putney 1983 election.

Protesting outside South Africa House with my mother Adelaine Hain, 1987.

LEFT Secret visit to Johannesburg, December 1989.
RIGHT Neath by-election, March 1991, with John Morris MP and Alun Michael MP.

With Howard Davies (right) at Betws Mine in South Wales, 1994.

With Nelson Mandela on the eve of his election as President, Johannesburg 1994. © George Hallett

LEFT Beside my desk in the Foreign Office, 1999.
ABOVE Africa Minister, outside Pretoria, 2000.

Speaking at the United Nations Security Council in New York, 2000.

LEFT Married, 14 June 2003: with Dad, mother-in-law Zaidee, Elizabeth, father-in-law Douglas and Mom.
RIGHT With Nelson Mandela, Elizabeth and parents, July 2003.

LEFT Meeting soldiers in Belfast after riot, September 2005.
RIGHT Belfast graffiti, 2005.

Secretary of State for Wales with Shirley Bassey, 2006.

ABOVE LEFT With Prince Charles, Camilla and Elizabeth, Belfast 2006.
BELOW LEFT With Rhodri Morgan, celebrating the Royal Assent for Government of Wales Act, July 2006.
RIGHT Speaking at the Labour Party annual conference, 2009.

Northern Ireland settlement 2007: Gerry Adams and Ian Paisley. © Steve Bell.

Party – raising around £100 million from individual donors, amounts never before achieved by Labour. He also acted as an unpaid, volunteer diplomat for Tony Blair, travelling the world at his own expense. We became good friends and he gave me sound advice and loyal support.

With his help I was soon accepted for what I was: a Foreign Minister recognised by Israelis as an honest and even-handed broker, becoming trusted by both sides, albeit with known Palestinian sympathies and contacts going back decades. My low-key visits to the region provoked none of the controversies of more senior figures like Robin Cook, Jack Straw and William Hague. However, unlike in Angola, Sri Lanka or even Zimbabwe, I had no illusions that the UK was anything more than a bit player. America was the dominant influence, and its administrations were over-influenced by the powerful US Jewish lobby, which had funded the state of Israel for decades. It was frustrating because the solution to this old conflict was obvious to all: an independent Palestinian state alongside guarantees of security for Israel.

However, I was dismayed by the lack of leadership shown by the Palestinian leader, Yasser Arafat, at the crucial summit hosted by President Bill Clinton at Camp David in July 2000. Having carefully set the summit up, the Americans made a real hash of it. Nevertheless the Israeli Prime Minister, Ehud Barak, came with a comprehensive offer on all the key Palestinian demands: territory, refugees and an independent state. However, it gave virtually nothing away on Jerusalem, the iconic religious capital for both Jews and Arabs, and this proved a fatal stumbling block for Arafat, Barak retreating into his shell, later to be swept from office by the right-wing Ariel Sharon. From Barak's and Israel's point of view, the offer was generous and indeed risky. Yet Arafat had refused to engage.

Later I spoke with Barak's chief of staff, Danny Yatom. 'The trouble with the Palestinian leadership is they never understand that when they reject a deal, the next one (when it eventually comes) is always worse,' he told me, going back over the history. This bluntly savvy perspective, though typically Israeli-centric, was uncomfortably plausible in a context of Israeli supremacy over the Palestinians. Although I had no illusions about the hard-nosed self-interest of Barak's proposal, the years of fighting, death and destruction which followed seemed to vindicate my instinct at the time that Arafat should have negotiated, done the best deal he could, and lived to build upon it.

But liberation leaders are not always power brokers. Some (unlike Nelson Mandela or even Gerry Adams) cannot transform themselves from being outsiders to insiders when the opportunity arises. Arafat was one such – a sad conclusion for me as a steadfast backer of justice for the Palestinians and a critic of Israeli intransigence, before, during and after becoming Britain's

Middle East Minister. Terje Larsen, a brilliant Norwegian diplomat active in the Oslo Process, agreed with me that an historic opportunity had been missed by the Palestinians, albeit on a deal which fell well short of their aspirations and necessarily was bound to do so, given the balance of forces ranged against them.

Several months afterwards, at a meeting in the Prime Minister's office in Tel Aviv in August 2000, I tried to persuade Barak to reopen negotiations. An ebullient character, mercurial but easy to talk to, Barak saw me only at Michael Levy's request; somebody at my level would not normally have been given access. The big dividing issue was not Palestinian statehood and territory, but Jerusalem – and specifically the Al-Haram al-Sharif/Temple Mount. This iconic centre remained the focus of intense religious conflict between Israel and the Islamic world, between Jews and Muslims. According to Judaism, their sacred temple was underneath the Temple Mount structure, on the side of which was the Wailing Wall. On top sat the Al-Aqsa Mosque together with the city's symbol, the Dome, which contained the rock from which the Prophet Mohammed was believed by Muslims to have ascended to heaven. The site was therefore contested between Jewish and Muslim faiths who both claimed primary historic and spiritual ownership. Arguably it was even more sensitive than the division of Jerusalem into Palestinian quarters and Israeli ones.

I suggested to Barak a possible solution which we had been working on: an agreement to share sovereignty, with the Al-Haram al-Sharif/Temple Mount vested in God or some kind sort of higher authority, possibly the United Nations. He was quite interested in the idea, exploring it thoughtfully. Previously he had insisted publicly on full Israeli sovereignty over the whole structure – completely unacceptable to Arafat and which would have caused uproar across the entire Islamic world. But this option seemed to him to have the potential for a compromise. 'Well, where there's a will, there's a way,' he told me. Although he contemptuously dismissed Arafat as a leader who didn't have 'balls', after I had pressed him further, he encouraged me to carry a private message that talks could reopen over this proposition for the holy site.

I was driven at once to Gaza, also encouraged by Arafat's foreign representative, the able and decent Nabil Shaath. He was excited by the news and told me: 'Our President [Arafat] should listen seriously to this. But he doesn't trust Barak. You have credibility with us; see if you can persuade him to.' I did try, at a meeting in Arafat's office. But he seemed curiously detached and distracted, in one of his gloomy moods I had been warned about; you never knew if he was putting this on for foreign Ministers or whether he genuinely was in a total depression – probably a mixture of both. I persisted, trying to get his attention by talking him through our proposition. Suddenly Arafat's whole manner changed. He became animated and interested. 'Do you really think Barak is willing to move down this road?' he asked. 'Yes,' I replied. 'If you offered to meet, maybe we could get something going again.'

Shaath was pleased at Arafat's response, confiding that, despite persistent efforts, he had not been able to persuade him of a similar course. I relayed this to Barak by phone at his home a few days later when I got back to London, and said that they should have a meeting, that there was considerable potential. I had also passed on a similar message to Dennis Ross, the American negotiator, and to the American Ambassador in Tel Aviv.

You don't have to be bosom pals to be able to negotiate successfully. Throughout history, when conflicts have been resolved, the leaders involved may not have liked each other, but tended to respect each other. On the substance, Barak and Arafat were tantalisingly close to reaching an agreement. But they remained totally contemptuous of each other. Barak told me: 'You know you can never trust Arafat. All he is interested in doing is strutting around, meeting world leaders; he will never get down to serious negotiation. He will never take responsibility for tough decisions and provide strong leadership to his people.' Arafat on the other hand was equally dismissive, telling me a number of times: 'Barak is a military man. He's not a politician. You can't do business with him because he doesn't think politically. He makes mistakes the whole time. He won't get to grips with the politics.'

Yet if only these two had been capable of engaging, a deal was there for the making. I knew that from talking to them, and by getting into the detail. There was also a huge area of agreement between their teams of negotiators. As always, however, in deep conflicts, when you get to the final stage of closing gaps, those gaps may be small but they remain significant. Furthermore it seemed to me at the time that the Americans were making a serious pig's ear of it all. That was also Michael Levy's view. We both argued that we should try and mount a British initiative.

But nothing came of it. Arafat seemed to enjoy the status of being photographed abroad with Prime Ministers and Presidents, but (as I saw again in a frustrating meeting with Tony Blair at No. 10) without being willing to engage in the substance of give and take. By the time he died four years later in 2004, the Palestinian cause in dire straits, he was widely seen as an obstacle to a settlement, instead of, as before, a leader bravely willing to take risks for peace.

Being driven between Israel, Gaza, the West Bank, Lebanon, Syria and Jordan, I was struck at how small this fraught region is. They live cheek by jowl. What enormous potential there would be for economic cooperation if the conflict could be ended! Israel, by far the most technologically advanced, could benefit by outsourcing to its lower-cost neighbours, and they could benefit from the resulting rise in wealth and prosperity. What a crying shame they were instead locked in battle, Israeli intransigence and seemingly knee-jerk aggression driving their own beleaguered nation into isolated ignominy.

One initiative nearly did make progress, however. In mid-2000, on a visit to Damascus, the capital of that most inscrutable of autocracies, Syria, I carried a secret Foreign Office proposal drafted by two bright officials, Philip Hall and Christopher Prentice. It was something of a freelance operation, as we had not had it cleared by No. 10 and I had not discussed it either with Michael Levy. It concerned the Golan Heights, captured by Israel from Syria in the 1967 'Six-Day' War. Strategically valuable to Israel, the Golan was a serious obstacle to any rapprochement between the two countries and had become a symbol of their continuing enmity. At its feet was the strategic Sea of Galilee, providing about fifteen per cent of Israel's water supply. Plenty of formulations had been tried and had failed to provide a basis for resolving the dispute. Our new proposal was to identify a band of territory that encompassed an equal area of both sea and shoreline. This would be an international free zone, perhaps United Nations policed and controlled, and to which both Syrians and Israelis would have full rights of access but which would not concede issues of sovereignty or control to either.

The Syrian Foreign Minister, Farouq al-Sharaa, whom I had met before in New York, had a reputation as a hard-liner, but he was both surprised and pleased to discuss the proposal. He immediately made arrangements for me to see the leader designate, Bashar Al-Assad, being groomed by his dying father, who had ruled the country with an iron fist for decades. There was much hope that Bashar, a young, Westernised surgeon who had lived in London for years, might break with the Ba'ath Party stranglehold and open the way to a more pluralist Syria with both political and economic reforms, perhaps working with the young, more modern leaders of Morocco and Jordan. But that proved a forlorn hope. In our private meeting I found him open and articulate if an innocent to politics. Perhaps for that reason he was quickly captured by the Party and state apparatus, to Syria's great loss. Soon afterwards bitter conflict – which was to last years – once again broke out between Palestinians and Israelis and nothing more was heard of the proposal, though the Israelis seemed to have learnt about it almost in real time, such was their intelligence capability. (Sadly also Bashar turned into an even more brutal dictator than his father, culminating in the slaughter of thousands of his own people following the 'Arab Spring' of 2011).

‡

During the same period I could not help becoming increasingly hawkish and militant over Saddam Hussein's tyranny. He governed arbitrarily and cruelly with a casual indifference to human life, eliminating everyone in his way. He shot dead a colleague in a Cabinet meeting and had his son-in-law murdered.

He subjugated the human rights of fellow Iraqis using all the instruments of torture, imprisonment, assassination, ethnic cleansing and cultural repression. He persistently targeted Iraqi Kurds and Shiite Muslims, most shockingly using chemical weapons both against the Kurds at Alhabja in spring 1988 and against Iranians during the Iraq–Iran War in 1986. It is estimated that throughout his tenure Saddam orchestrated the murder of as many as three million Shiites, including indiscriminately slaughtering 148 children and adults in the summer of 1982 after a failed Shiite assassination attempt. Although there were plenty of candidates, nobody in the modern world could compete with Saddam as a contemporary Hitler.

He was also a threat to the region and maybe beyond. He had invaded Kuwait in 1990, wreaking havoc and destruction and setting oilfields alight in retribution against allied armies forcing him to withdraw. He had provoked a bloody eight-year war by invading Iran in 1980 with horrific casualty levels: nobody is certain of the total, but estimates range from half to one million dead, between one and two million wounded, with about 2.5 million refugees. He also attacked Israel with scud missiles in January 1991. The Middle East remained a powder keg, autocrats were the norm and the one democratic nation, Israel, was routinely intransigent and had a record of ruthless violence, but nobody acted with such ferocity towards neighbours as Saddam.

I had also been blooded over Iraq by facing an aggressive campaign against sanctions imposed by the United Nations after Saddam's Kuwait invasion. They were designed to contain his threat and were focused upon strategic equipment. But Saddam had astutely deflected the impact onto his own people, forcing *them* to suffer from sanctions applied to his regime while his *own* coterie lived a life of luxury on smuggled food, fuel and goods. With callous indifference, he exploited the sanctions regime so that ordinary, innocent Iraqis became the victims and liberal/left opinion in Britain reacted in horror, not against the unscrupulous perpetrator Saddam, but against our government, which backed the sanctions. I found echoes of the old right-wing propaganda from the 1970s and 1980s that sanctions against the apartheid regime 'harmed the black majority'. But this time the arguments were coming from many on the left who had been alongside me in revealing how specious those apologists for white South Africa were.

Robin Cook was vilified and protesters soon rounded on me. I became a classic target for the left for 'betraying' my record on human rights and justice. On 20 January 2001, the newspaper I had read since a teenager, the *Guardian*, carried a vicious 'Janus' cartoon. It was a portrait of me facing both ways: one in student garb toward my anti-apartheid record, the other in suit and tie seemingly allocated sole responsibility for the death and deprivation of Iraqi citizens; the cartoon added: 'Pull tab to turn coat.' This hurt deeply, but I had faced smears all my political life – although from the right and not, as on this occasion, the left. Most significant, none of the protesters provided any credible alternative whatsoever. Effectively they were throwing in the towel against Saddam, inviting him to gas or torture even more of his own long-suffering citizens or to invade another neighbour. Too many were fellow travellers with the dictator. My Labour MP colleague George Galloway (with whom I had worked closely in the 1980s on the Labour left) was especially vitriolic. But then he exposed himself in 1999 when he spent a Baghdad Christmas with Saddam's deputy, Tariq Aziz, later convicted of war crimes. Earlier Galloway had met the tyrant himself when, in front of television cameras, he fawned: 'Sir – we salute your courage, your strength, your indefatigability.' Many thousands of Saddam's victims meanwhile lay in unmarked graves.

I believed this obscene dictator had to be opposed uncompromisingly. The fact that he was now under attack by Americans who had previously propped him up made no difference to me. Too many on the left supported everything the United States opposed almost as a matter of principle. I instead tried always to assess each situation on its merits according to the values of justice and human rights which had always motivated my politics. I had opposed Saddam when the US and Britain were backing him in the 1980s and I still did: appeasement of oppression was the real crime against humanity, and here were my leftist critics behaving as appeasers.

In the year 2000/2001 (when I was still Middle East Minister) the UN was making up to $17 billion available to Iraq for the purchase of humanitarian goods. This was more than Egypt, Syria or Jordan had to spend in equivalent areas (for example health, education, housing). Yet my critics never asked why the people of those countries did not suffer the same privations as the people of Iraq. Was it not Saddam's brutal indifference to the condition of his people which he manipulated for the gullible abroad? The Iraqi people continued to suffer because the regime deliberately under-spent the UN relief money made available for its people's needs. For the last six months of 2000, Iraq ordered no medicines through the UN's oil-for-food programme and put on hold $1.1 billion worth of goods vital to alleviate popular suffering. Yet Saddam's regime was actually exporting food and medicine. By this time we had helped ensure that sanctions were better targeted than they had been. Food, medicines, agricultural, educational and water and sanitation goods could easily be exported to Iraq simply by notifying the UN. In Kurdish northern Iraq, where Saddam's writ did not run, the same sanctions applied, but the situation was much better – health indicators had actually been improving, and infant mortality rates were lower than before the sanctions were imposed.

Both Robin Cook and I had worked hard to take resolution 1284 through the UN Security Council to increase the flow of humanitarian goods into the country. The resolution also offered a way out of sanctions by allowing for their suspension in return for cooperation with UN weapons inspectors. But our critics failed to unite with us in calling on Saddam to take up this offer – and instead aligned themselves with him in opposition to the UN, so perpetuating the very humanitarian plight they were protesting about, and abandoning Saddam's victims to their fate.

Meanwhile I had become increasingly worried about the regular intelligence reports from MI6 that showed Saddam was proceeding covertly to resurrect his weapons of mass destruction (WMD) programmes. He resolutely refused to allow weapons inspectors into the country, supporting our belief that he had stockpiled WMD – chemical, biological and potentially nuclear – and would pose a major threat to peace in the region again.

While in public taking a tough line and robustly rejecting criticism – including at a lecture in Cardiff where protesters aggressively heckled and harangued me – I was privately trying to find a solution to the impasse, regularly meeting Middle East leaders with whom I got on well. 'We Arabs like you, Peter,' the Foreign Minister of Morocco, Mohamed Benaissa, told me once. The Omani Foreign Minister, Yusuf Bin Alawi, and the Qatari Foreign Minister, Sheikh Hamad Bin Jassim Bin Jabr Al-Thani, were desperate to resolve the situation and we were in regular touch. When they asked what they could do I urged them to act as intermediaries with Baghdad. They carried messages: if Saddam allowed the weapons inspectors in and lifted his block on UN food and other aid, I would press for sanctions to be lifted within six months in line with UN resolution 1284. But we would not be hoodwinked. He had to act first.

Washington under Bill Clinton's presidency took an extremely hard line and, although I got on well and worked closely with his people, they were decidedly lukewarm about these initiatives. Foreign Office officials were also nervous and cautious, warning that Saddam would exploit such contacts for propaganda purposes and might see them as a sign of weakness on our part. Unsurprisingly it soon became clear to me that the Iraqis were trying to manoeuvre a situation to gain a diplomatic coup rather than to do a deal allowing weapons inspectors in – reinforcing in my mind that Saddam had something to hide. So I let the initiatives wither, while always showing willing, as when William Morris, secretary general of a charity, the Next Century Foundation, tried to mediate; I had first met him ten years earlier during my selection as parliamentary candidate in Neath where he lived. He later recalled: 'People of good conscience were trying to avert war, but it was futile.'

However, invading Iraq was the last thing on my mind during this time, though I had believed, long before my term as Middle East Minister, that it was a catastrophic error for the international forces not to have gone all the way to Baghdad in the Gulf War after they had pushed Iraqi forces out of Kuwait in February 1991. They should have finished the job off by toppling the evil dictator, as could have been achieved relatively easily, with international and indeed Arab support, saving much bloodshed and chaos to follow. Unlike others on the left, I was never a semi-pacifist. From my father's active service in the Second World War with a South African infantry battalion, to my support for the ANC's liberation struggle, I had resolved that armed action was often necessary.

However, being on the front line of controversy over Saddam in 1999–2001 was as nothing compared with being sucked into a far worse Iraqi vortex – and one that did lasting damage to our Labour government and all who served in it, me included.

‡

The first news of Al Qaeda's 9/11 attack on New York's World Trade Center came as I was waiting in Brighton for Tony Blair's speech to the annual Trades Union Congress. By now Europe Minister, I was looking forward to the speech as it would be an olive branch to the trade unions, arguing how vital a role they played in society, something close to my political heart, but not previously to Tony Blair's.

Then I bumped into Colin Brown, respected political correspondent of the *Independent*. He was no longer interested in the speech. 'Something really bad has happened in New York, don't know what it means yet,' he muttered. It was around two in the afternoon as we gathered around the nearest TV to see the shocking pictures of airliners being deliberately crashed into the Twin Towers – memories of taking my two young boys up in that long lift journey to the top twelve years before flashed through my mind – and I thought immediately: this is going have a seismic political impact.

Huddled together with other Ministers watching live TV, we got word that Tony Blair had abandoned his prepared speech, instead substituting a short one before haring off to Downing Street. As always on such big occasions, Tony was at his best, delivering a perfectly judged, short, sombre but passionate address about the threat of this new kind of terrorism, judging almost instantly the enormity of the attack's implications for the world.

By now it was clear Al Qaeda was responsible, so I made my apologies to our TUC hosts and cadged a lift off Liz Symons, Foreign Minister in the House of Lords, and sped back to London. 'How significant a moment is this?' she wondered. 'It changes everything,' I replied instinctively, as we talked through the implications with her husband Phil Bassett, formerly a top journalist who worked for Tony in Downing Street.

Tony Blair and his senior Ministers met immediately in the emergency Cabinet committee, COBRA, putting contingency arrangements in place. It was a frenzied time and I found it difficult concentrate on my main work as Europe Minister. A day or two later I was asked to undertake a whole series of media interviews by No. 10, which I hadn't expected. Tony Blair and Jack Straw had done the main news media, but I was asked to come in underneath and do more forensic programmes like the BBC's *Newsnight* and *Any Questions?*, followed up by weekend programmes which necessitated withdrawing from my constituency surgeries and, unusually, staying up in London that weekend. I was quickly embroiled in doing one broadcast interview after another and a few weeks later at the Labour Party conference in Brighton, No. 10 asked me to do wall-to-wall interviews, as well as BBC TV's flagship *Question Time* and the comparable Jonathan Dimbleby programme on ITV.

I also decided it was important to address the left, natural *Guardian* readers like me, where there was a lot of concern, especially about the US approach of raining cruise missiles down here, there and everywhere. So I wrote articles for the *Guardian* and the *Independent* pointing out that the left had never been afraid to fight just causes, for instance in the Spanish Civil War aiding those opposing fascism, or Michael Foot pamphleteering against appeasement of the Nazis. In a more contemporary context it was the left that supported liberation struggles in southern Africa even though they involved violence. It created quite an interesting debate.

Although George Bush was widely distrusted by the British public and indeed international opinion, Tony Blair, rightly in my view, expressed complete solidarity with the American people, arguing that Al Qaeda could strike anywhere in the future, including London, Berlin, Moscow or Beijing. Tony's leadership helped assemble an extraordinarily broad coalition, not just in solidarity with the Americans, but in support of a military response backed by the United Nations. It also helped ensure the response in Washington was much more cautious, targeted and surgical than might have been the case amidst the domestic pressures for a reckless lashing out against Afghanistan and Osama Bin Laden. In that respect Tony Blair's role was historically pivotal. This was very evident reading the secret transcripts of the conversations between Blair and Bush and between Jack Straw and the US Secretary of State

Colin Powell. Tony also successfully pressed in a private memo for evidence to be produced about those responsible for the 9/11 attack, before any action was taken. In their conversations you could sense George Bush almost (but not quite) coming of age in international affairs, when his instinct was for right-wing unilateralism.

Nevertheless there remained an insuperable problem, the burning sense of anger and grievance that the Islamic world felt about the treatment of the Palestinians above all, but also about atrocities against Muslims in Chechnya. It was very apparent to me, following the collapse of the Middle East peace process, that on the street in places like Cairo the Palestinian issue had become 'Islamicised' especially after the right-wing Israeli Ariel Sharon, then the opposition leader, provocatively staged a walk on Al-Haram al-Sharif/Temple Mount, the sacred Jerusalem site for both Muslims and Jews. His irresponsible gesture unleashed a tidal wave of anger throughout the Islamic world, playing into the hands of Bin Laden and his followers.

So it was all the more remarkable that the Islamic world and the Arab countries stood so solidly in support of the international coalition's invasion of Afghanistan to destroy Bin Laden's base there. Equally – and again under Tony's insistence – London and Washington resolved to assemble a humanitarian and political coalition to resolve some of the problems in the area, as well as deal with the immediate terrorist threat. Tony made an extraordinarily powerful speech on 2 October 2001 at Labour's conference which got huge attention, beamed live in the US and Britain. He skilfully projected the whole effort to eradicate international terrorism within the context of a 'New World Order' based on stability, cooperation and community – the complete opposite of American parochialism and unilateralism, but listened to in the US because nobody had stood more solidly by George Bush's side.

Asked to step in as the main speaker for the Chancellor, Gordon Brown, at a Fabian Society conference in January 2002, I argued in front of a big audience for a new 'progressive internationalism' which not only confronted terrorism and intervened militarily where absolutely necessary, but also put international justice, democracy, human rights and tackling climate change right at the top of the agenda.

Meanwhile George Bush and his neo-con Defense Secretary, Donald Rumsfeld, had started making bellicose noises about Iraq almost as soon as they took office in January 2001. Now their focus was upon Afghanistan where the Taliban government had provided Al Qaeda and its leader Osama Bin Laden with a terrorist base. Within months an American-led invasion backed by our government had toppled the Taliban and driven Bin Laden out from the capital, Kabul, and into the impenetrable mountains on the Pakistan border. Although deeply uncomfortable about being in alliance with Bush's neo-cons, I had no doubt about the necessity for this invasion and for British participation.

But, by the time I had joined the Cabinet a year later in October 2002, Bush and his coterie had bafflingly switched their focus from Afghanistan – which was to prove catastrophic for the mission there and to drag us deeply into a quagmire in a country which had over the centuries successfully repelled all invaders, including the British, most recently humiliating the Soviet Union.

Instead, the momentum towards war with Saddam was gathering, Bush making specious claims of a non-existent link with Al Qaeda. In those early months Tony Blair had the full support of the Cabinet, despite all our deep misgivings about Bush and his aggressive neo-con foreign policy. Tony had led the diplomatic drive to get a UN Security Council resolution requiring Saddam's compliance with its international obligations. Although there was some sceptical questioning from Clare Short and Robin Cook, nobody disagreed with his strategy of trying to get a second United Nations Security Council resolution authorising military action against Saddam. Jack Straw regularly briefed us on the progress of the negotiations at the UN, as did Defense Secretary Geoff Hoon on the general military situation and build-up of forces. By January 2003 there were around 200,000 US and British troops around the Iraqi border – a clear and present threat to Saddam that he should comply.

Then, on 30 January 2003, Robin Cook, really for the first time, expressed his deep reservations during a Cabinet meeting. He was, as always, authoritative, given he had been the Foreign Secretary dealing with Iraq for four years. He argued that Saddam Hussein had been contained by the previous strategy of sanctions and weapons inspectors between 1991 and 1998 until the weapons inspectors were ejected. He said it was important that the chief UN weapons inspector, Hans Blix, be given more time and that his position should not be prejudiced by any pre-emptive action. Under intense pressure and with troops gathering on his border, Saddam had finally agreed a few weeks earlier to let Blix and his team into Iraq, though the regime was making every effort to hinder them.

Robin argued that we had been successful at keeping Saddam in his cage. But although that was true, I found myself increasingly disagreeing with my old friend, recalling the virulent attacks we had both suffered about the sanctions policy. The fact of the matter was that Saddam was still in power. Nothing had changed. He was still – at least as we firmly believed from our intelligence – either developing or building or preparing further WMD programmes. His appalling human rights record inside the country was still continuing and his ability to threaten other countries remained. I sympathised with those in Washington and elsewhere who were arguing for a new approach, saying we couldn't continue with a failed sanctions policy and the impossibility of getting cooperation over weapons inspectors, as Jack Straw argued very convincingly. The Cabinet discussion was more a taking of views. There was no cut and thrust where somebody had a dispute with someone else; you put your points, the PM listened, and at the end he summed up.

Tony Blair was working flat out to achieve the second UN resolution, using his influence with Bush to persuade the distinctly unenthusiastic neo-cons to stick to the UN route. It was clear from reading the confidential Foreign Office briefings from Washington that, without Tony Blair's insistence, Vice President Cheney and Defense Secretary Rumsfeld would have got their way for unilateral US military action.

The entire Cabinet had assumed all along that the French President, Jacques Chirac, was characteristically posturing in refusing to back the second UN resolution, authorising military action to enforce the first one. (Frustrated at their behaviour, I once unwisely described the French as 'contemptible', causing a minor diplomatic flurry.) Tony was convinced Chirac would sign up in the end and I knew from my own experience that getting agreement at the UN could take months. But then the situation changed dramatically for the worse when the French dug in and began to lobby Security Council member states actively against a second resolution.

The mood of the Cabinet on the 17 March was sombre. Robin Cook's chair was empty; I couldn't help staring at it. The start was delayed as Clare Short was in Tony's office being persuaded she should stay; nobody knew whether she would, until she bustled in looking tense. Tony dramatically reported that Saddam had failed to comply with his obligations to cooperate imposed by the first UN resolution, and that Chirac was effectively exercising a veto against any sort of UN resolution imposing a deadline for either cooperation or military action. We were on the brink of war. He asked Peter Goldsmith, the Attorney General, for his view on legality. We all turned expectantly, but Peter was crisply concise: given the circumstances, military action was lawful. That was to become, to say the least, highly contentious in the debate which raged for years afterwards.

I made three points. First it was important that we worked closely with backbench MPs because they were under considerable pressure. They had given undertakings to their constituencies that they would not back action without United Nations authority, and now they were going to be asked to do so. Second, it was very important that we ensured the French were put in the dock and not us. Public opinion was now on the move and French intransigence was pretty critical in that. I knew from my Europe Minister experience that, rightly or wrongly, France and the French were not popular with public opinion. Their obstinacy could help us make our case. Third, that opinion in my Neath constituency, which was predominantly working class, was increasingly supportive of action, with families having troops stationed out there already, whereas in more middle-class areas – more 'New Labour' if you like – that was not the case; there were nods of agreement around the table.

So the Cabinet agreed to go to war, calmly and solemnly. I remember thinking: history is probably like this – you make decisions which have momentous consequences, without either being casual or sitting on the edge of your seats. Instead we had adopted a course which seemed the logical conclusion of the preceding weeks' events.

The following day, Tony was at the top of his game at an emergency Parliamentary Labour Party meeting, the biggest I had ever attended. The mood was electric as he delivered a compelling and powerful speech. He was also at his eloquent best opening a dramatic emergency debate in Parliament on 19 March, obtaining a clear mandate by 412 to 149 votes – our main worry being that of those voting against, 139 were Labour – one in three of our colleagues. Although we gained no credit whatsoever from those opposed to the invasion, it was the very first time that a British government had troubled to seek Parliament's authority for war. Previously wars had been declared by Crown Prerogative without recourse to Parliament.

In the debate there was a terrific and impassioned resignation speech by Robin Cook which won wide respect. Privately and decently, he had consistently questioned the strategy, canvassing my support soon after I had joined the Cabinet. At one point I phoned him while he was travelling on Eurostar, urging him to stay. Even before Iraq, Robin had become pretty alienated from the whole Blair government, and had been deeply wounded when unexpectedly sacked as Foreign Secretary immediately after the 2001 election. He told me that, if he had known a move from Foreign Secretary was on Tony Blair's mind, he could have prepared for it and made a graceful exit rather than be humiliated. His departure was deeply disconcerting, making me question my motives for staying. But the truth was I disagreed with Robin on Iraq so there was never any question of following him. There was another issue. Although I flatly disagreed with our policy on some other issues, the advantage of staying in the government was to fight your corner or advance other causes passionate to you.

However, Clare Short's behaviour was very different from Robin's. She did an explosive BBC radio interview attacking the whole policy even though she remained a member of the Cabinet. She had mounted no real critique at Cabinet meetings. Although vocal in raising mainly humanitarian issues, she seemed content with reassurances by Tony. The contrast with her public utterances was stark: as if she had all along disagreed in Cabinet. I didn't like the way that she denounced what we were doing over Iraq in public without arguing that case in the Cabinet as Robin had done. She would insist on the United Nations being involved, which we were to a very large extent achieving. She would insist on preparations for humanitarian relief, which we were doing anyway. So she seemed to win the arguments on those points because they were already the view of the Cabinet. All the time she was getting a lot of kudos in public for articulating what was virtually the anti-war position against the Cabinet of which she remained a member.

I was disappointed to see how an admired friend – one with whom I had worked very closely on Labour's left, on the board of *Tribune* newspaper for instance – ended up. Her eventual resignation from the Cabinet undermined her credibility even with anti-war supporters, because it came so late. One of the warmest and most passionate people in politics, she diminished herself by becoming personally vindictive and bitter towards Tony. Sadly, she was to resign from the Labour Party she had loved and which had once loved her too.

‡

I had discussed the build-up to war regularly with 'C', Sir Richard Dearlove, chief of the Secret Intelligence Service (SIS), popularly known as MI6, with whom I had worked closely as Foreign Minister and got on well. We were all frustrated at the inability to discover WMD, which everyone was emphatic Saddam possessed. I was informed that Saddam had for months been moving a lot of his WMD and dispersing them in anticipation of UN inspectors coming in. When they eventually arrived, a couple of tip-offs given to Hans Blix's weapons inspectors – who were constantly under Iraqi surveillance – led to venues where there was evidence that things had been moved very quickly beforehand.

A key bit of intelligence in Joint Intelligence Committee briefings was that significant elements in the regime would switch very quickly should Saddam be toppled. The common assumption that the regime would stand and fight to the last drop of its blood was therefore invalid. That intelligence at least proved to be absolutely right: the army didn't fight to the last man and the regime very quickly splintered and dissolved.

Polls taken at the time of the invasion showed Britain split right down the middle – even three months afterwards, an ICM poll in June 2003 showed 48 per cent in favour compared with 40 per cent against. Nevertheless it was extremely uncomfortable. A large majority of Labour Party members were against their government, many thousands leaving the Party in disgust. Members were demoralised and divisions between the trade unions and the party leadership deepened. My own close family flatly disagreed with me. My parents were implacably opposed, perhaps the main political disagreement I had ever had with my Dad, who in so many ways was my mentor. Elizabeth disagreed (she thought we should be toppling Mugabe instead). My sons Sam and Jake had a go at me. So did virtually all my political friends and close colleagues. Nelson Mandela phoned me, more angry than I had ever known him, almost breathing fire down the line: 'A big mistake, Peter, a very big mistake. It is wrong. Why is Tony doing this after all his support for Africa? This will cause huge damage internationally.'

I felt resolute, but it was a period when the tension between ideals and realities was more stretched than at any time I was a Minister. Almost the worst to handle was the fuming public criticism for coat-tailing President George Bush and his arrogant, right-wing administration. Most people in Britain, left, right or centre, deeply distrusted Bush and his coterie. His Defense Secretary, Donald Rumsfeld, who regularly put his foot in his mouth, seemed to glory in cantankerous public statements that might have appealed to a right-wing back yard in America, but alienated the rest of the world and embarrassed not just us but Bush's allies. The Bush neo-cons flouted international treaties and refused to support the International Criminal Court. They were contemptuous of the UN, spurning multilateralism for unilateralism. They were opposed to just about everything I stood for in democratic politics.

That churned over and over in my mind, especially since one of my formative political experiences had been opposing American intervention in Vietnam. However, friends and close relatives, with whom I continued to share the same values and beliefs, were not willing to confront the very hard choices that come with being in government. They had the luxury of being outsiders. I was now the insider with all the associated responsibilities – and made to appear an ogre as well. But, although there were several times like this when my 'outside in' transition had severe downsides, I clung to the belief that there were opportunities in government to make a difference too – and not many politicians had those opportunities.

Notwithstanding almost universal public perception, Tony Blair also found it very difficult dealing with the Bush regime, and would freely volunteer this in private. His foreign policy adviser and later our Ambassador to Washington, the much respected David Manning, once told Ministers when I was in the Foreign Office: 'America is our closest ally and our most difficult friend.'

Nevertheless I felt we had taken the correct decision, while fully respecting that others vehemently disagreed. I subscribed to Tony Blair's argument that unless we dealt with Saddam, he would never obey the international community's wishes, never accept the authority of the United Nations, and that that was really serious for the future of the world. I emphatically believed he posed a real and very dangerous threat, specifically in the Middle East. I also agreed with Tony Blair's position that it was really important that the US, and especially an administration under a right-wing Republican like George Bush, wasn't isolated, particularly by those who didn't subscribe to its neo-con ideology (and we certainly didn't).

If that were to happen, the US would become even more unilateralist. If the US felt it had to act alone to defend its 'national security', then the world would be an even more dangerous and unstable place. Britain's support for, and cooperation with, the Bush regime's policy on Iraq, despite all our misgivings and despite genuine, sometimes fierce, divisions in private over particular strategies and tactics, was vital in preventing that from happening. Despite his 'poodle' tag on Iraq, Tony Blair fully endorsed the Kyoto Agreement on climate change, the International Criminal Court and the Comprehensive Nuclear Test Ban Treaty – all stances opposed by Bush.

But, in the end, Iraq was near fatal for Tony Blair and for our government. It destroyed trust in Tony and in Labour, and caused a mortal breach between our Party and its progressive base in British politics. It became almost pointless arguing that I had acted in good faith, based upon the evidence I had been shown and my own deep hostility to Saddam born from both my values and ministerial experience. People simply saw it all as a big lie. Yet I acted honestly. Why, when I accepted the good faith of those who passionately disagreed, could they not accept my good faith? I wasn't 'fellow travelling' with Bush. I wasn't 'sucking up' to Blair. I had very good reason to think Saddam still had the very WMD he had used before – a view also held by all foreign intelligence services, whether or not their governments backed the invasion.

Of course I also had my doubts, and hated being in de facto alliance with George Bush and his reactionary neo-cons. I felt betrayed by the incompetence of the Americans: they had a war strategy, but not a post-invasion peace strategy. It was a catastrophic American error to abolish the entire Iraqi state on the grounds that it was a Saddam institution – when most people, like state employees under the Nazis, are not ideological, just getting by and doing their jobs. The international coalition should have utilised the skills and experience of Iraqi local and national administrators, not carelessly dismantled the whole structure, in the process both alienating wide layers of the now unemployed population and producing anarchic service delivery and incompetence which simply accentuated that alienation.

But, by the end of my time in government, people had simply stopped listening to the legitimate Labour case for war. When the intelligence was subsequently revealed to have been totally false, nobody was even interested in my explanations any more. To rub salt into these wounds, early in 2011, a main source confessed to having deliberately lied about crucial evidence given to his German handlers and quoted by US Secretary of State Colin Powell to the UN Security Council (much to Powell's anger and consternation). Motivated by a desire to get rid of Saddam, the source, an Iraqi, was familiar to me from his codename in intelligence documents: 'Curveball'.

‡

After Iraq, all our foreign policy achievements seemed to be forgotten – much as Nelson Mandela had foreseen in his phone call to me. Yet I was proud of our record. We had secured an international treaty to ban anti-personnel land-mines, the Comprehensive Nuclear Test Ban Treaty, the International Criminal Court; we had led the world in tackling climate change, and in trying to 'make poverty history' by trebling Britain's overseas aid budget and cancelling debt which crippled poor nations.

We reformed arms exports legislation to prevent exporting military equipment which might be used for either external aggression or internal repression; Ministers like me had to scrutinise each application according to strict criteria. This was a world away from the Tories who had scandalously sold British arms to almost anybody, their nemesis coming with the prosecution of directors of Matrix Churchill. A Coventry company, it had been caught exporting a 'supergun' to Saddam in flagrant breach of UN sanctions, but with the covert backing of Tory Ministers. When this government complicity was exposed in their 1991 trial, it collapsed, triggering an official inquiry by Lord Scott which reported in 1996.

I was also proud of our achievement negotiating the UN Nuclear Non Proliferation Treaty in May 2000 in New York – another example of how ministerial initiative and political values could make all the difference. In the build-up to the UN conference the usual stalemate seemed likely. Negotiations always polarised between the 'P5' nuclear weapons countries (five permanent members of the Security Council) and the non-nuclear states. The 'New Agenda Coalition' – formed two years before and composed of Brazil, Egypt, Ireland, Mexico, New Zealand, South Africa and Sweden – wanted full disarmament. I never saw the point of going to events just to go through the diplomatic motions and resolved in advance to try and make some progress if possible.

Once there, I got chatting to my old friend Abdul Minty, formerly secretary of the British Anti-Apartheid Movement, and now South Africa's chief negotiator, telling him that, if their New Agenda Coalition had some flexibility, I was keen to get the P5 to do a deal. And I repeated this to other countries in the non-nuclear coalition who seemed sceptical until they realised I was serious. My officials, used to stonewalling, were also wary. But they quickly saw the opportunity once they realised I was determined, especially since they knew from Robin Cook's mandate to me that I was acting with his authority even though I had not formally consulted him in advance. Effectively I changed UK government policy in line with my own values and Robin's. The result – against all expectations – was a deal: the other P5 countries including the US swung behind Britain and it was unanimously agreed that all countries of the world would work towards the global elimination of nuclear weapons. The P5 had conceded that objective for the first time while meanwhile retaining their capability and as a result the New Agenda Coalition had been able to move the non-nuclear states away from their previous insistence on immediate disarmament.

As Minister for the UN, I enjoyed chairing Security Council meetings on African crises when the UK had the presidency – once startling members by beginning a post-lunch session bang on time. Our excellent Ambassador, Jeremy Greenstock, quickly exploited my enthusiasm. Sometimes I was on a ridiculous treadmill, catching what was then the 8 a.m. British Airways flight, and landing seven hours later at JFK Airport in New York for 10 a.m. local time, to be rushed to a Security Council meeting at 11 a.m., then straight back that evening on the 'red eye' flight arriving at Heathrow the next morning around seven.

Foreign Ministers in equivalent countries, France for instance, had the benefit of their own private planes, as I ruefully noted in early August 2000 when departing from Arusha in remote, rural Tanzania after Nelson Mandela had persuaded foreign leaders to attend peace negotiations to resolve the conflict in Burundi. The day before, landing at night at the little Kilimanjaro Airport, I asked what the large contraption was by the main runway. 'President Clinton's portable landing gear for Air Force One,' came the laconic reply. Now that was style! When we all departed, my French counterpart hopped on his own plane while I cadged a lift on a UN plane to Nairobi, then waited five hours in the middle of the night before taking a commercial flight to Tel Aviv. It wasn't possible to sleep and I arrived in time for breakfast and a shower before setting off for meetings with Israeli Ministers and Palestinian leaders. Tiring, yes, but exhilarating too.

‡

On my way to give a lecture on the future of Africa in the evening on 23 January 2001, there was a call from Anji Hunter, Tony's director of government relations. I had managed to identify a suitable opportunity in a black township in the Cape Town area for her teenage daughter to do voluntary service on an AIDS project. The conversation then turned and Anji sounded very depressed about Peter Mandelson's predicament. He had once again become embroiled in an issue of ministerial propriety after admitting he had made misleading statements over the passport application of the controversial Indian billionaire Srichand Hinduja, but denying he had done anything wrong. However, it looked to the press and others as being a direct trade-off for the Hinduja brothers' contribution to the controversial and ill-fated Millennium Dome project which Mandelson had helped deliver. 'Tomorrow's papers are going to be awful. Things don't look good for Peter,' Anji volunteered, surprising me: I had thought the media furore would blow over. However, the next day, he was indeed forced to resign, unfairly I thought.

The same evening I was scheduled to address a group of NGO leaders about the main themes of my new pamphlet, *The End of Foreign Policy?*[*] Intractable international problems defied traditional diplomatic solutions, for example 'mad cow disease', which had spread from Britain across Europe; recent devastating floods in Mozambique; or a computer virus sent out by two students in the Philippines which had disabled ten million computers worldwide. Each reflected a new kind of world shaped, not by old clashes of ideology or power, but by more complex forces which could blight the twenty-first century. How effective could a domestic government campaign against HIV/AIDS be when in 2000 three quarters of British victims were infected while travelling in Africa? How could we mobilise against global warming or illegal drug use, when the cause was not some hostile power's ambition or greed, but millions of individual decisions mainly by Western consumers?

No single government department could on its own deal with climate change, drug trafficking, or intensifying competition for water and fish. The problems were joined up, so government must be joined up. Previously, responsibility for foreign policy resided in an elite group of specialist diplomats. But tensions arising from declining water tables in the Middle East, collapsing fish stocks in the Atlantic and persistent drought in East Africa could not be solved at the conference table. This task required the specialised skills of all

---

[*] Peter Hain, *The End of Foreign Policy?* (London, Fabian Society, Green Alliance and Royal Institute of International Affairs, January 2001), with a foreword by Robin Cook. The Finnish government ordered scores of copies and remodelled their Foreign Ministry around its recommendations.

government departments – and the committed and innovative involvement of non-government actors in business and civil society.

Successful international policy would in future centre on 'convergent' policy solutions by joined-up governments forming new partnerships both domestically and globally. Perhaps, I suggested, Foreign Ministries would become Departments of Global Affairs – as the concept of 'foreign' became ever harder to define. In the process we would see an end to traditional foreign policy and the evolution of a new foreign policy based upon global linkages and embracing global responsibility; a foreign policy for a world in which there is no longer any such place as 'abroad'.

I concluded with the wry comment: 'For a Foreign Minister to contemplate "The End of Foreign Policy" may seem like inviting redundancy.' Hardly had I settled down to a lively discussion than my pager went off with a message to ring Downing Street. I had no inkling of the purpose when Tony came on the line. Sounding upset and drained by the resignation of his close confidant Mandelson, he soon came to the point: 'Peter, you've done a great job at the Foreign Office, especially Africa. I don't want to move you, but things have developed today and I want you back in domestic politics. I'm sending you to the Department of Trade and Industry to take Helen Liddell's job as Minister of State for Energy and European Competitiveness. There are some big domestic problems to be solved in Energy before the general election. I need you there.'

Tony brushed aside my concern that this might be construed as a demotion from what was one of the biggest Minister of State jobs in the government. 'No, no, no, it's a huge job. We are in a critical time with the election coming and I really need you to sort the problems.' My mind was in something of a turmoil as I went back to the NGO gathering, not revealing what had happened. Then my pager went off again to call Downing Street and by now my guests were getting suspicious. This time it was Sally Morgan, Tony's political secretary. 'Tony wants you to know that this is a big step forward for you,' she said. 'And I will make sure that Alastair briefs to that effect.' Which is exactly what he did.

So that was that. After all that had been achieved, the arbitrary cascade of a reshuffle caused by the Mandelson resignation had caught me in its wake. When John Reid had been moved from Scotland to replace Peter in Northern Ireland, Helen Liddell had been moved from Energy to replace him. A few days later Anji reassuringly called to explain that once Tony, Jonathan Powell and the Cabinet Secretary, Richard Wilson, had realised that there were knotty and urgent issues in Energy, Wilson had suggested my name. That was some consolation, because I had enjoyed the Foreign Office enormously and regretted the move. Early the next morning I said goodbye to my shocked private office, which had the reputation for being the happiest in the building. A really nice touch was an unexpected handwritten note from Sir John Kerr, the Foreign Office's brilliant permanent secretary: 'You were quite the best thing that happened to us.'

CHAPTER EIGHT

BRITISH OUTSIDER IN EUROPE

While still Energy Minister immediately after our second landslide win in the general election on 5 June 2001, Downing Street asked me to go to Luxembourg for a European Council of Ministers meeting. My task: to negotiate a tricky employment directive which Britain had been delaying. It imposed obligations on companies to consult employees before deciding on closures and redundancies. I had to brush up on the detail, because I wasn't the Employment Minister and did not really agree with the delay stance, though I could understand Tony Blair's desire not to give any offence to business on the eve of an election.

By building relationships and negotiating hard, I managed to prevent the council proceeding by majority vote against us as it was likely to do. Instead we achieved an agreed position which granted to Britain a seven-year phasing-in of the directive. Even though I was obliged to concede rather more than my remit had originally intended, No. 10 was pleased. By the time I arrived back in London, however, a reshuffle was well under way. Jack Straw was the new Foreign Secretary, replacing Robin Cook. I had no idea whether I would stay at Energy or what would happen to me, so asked my trusty driver Mick whether he had any news: it was a reshuffle rule that ministerial drivers were usually in the know. 'Europe Minister,' he replied authoritatively. 'We have to go immediately to see the PM.'

That was a real surprise. Although firmly pro-European – having voted Yes against many on the left in the 1975 referendum on whether Britain should stay in Europe – I had rebelled in 1992 over the Maastricht Treaty and written a pamphlet arguing that the architecture of the euro was too right wing and was not sustainable.[*] But at least the drive in to Whitehall gave me time to think about my response. That Tony was prepared to trust me with such a big and highly charged portfolio was encouraging, and I formulated two requests of my own.

'Up to now we haven't had really good Europe Ministers. My fault, I suppose, because I appointed them,' Tony said ruefully in his No. 10 den, Jonathan Powell there too. 'I think you could really make us influential, like Pierre Moscovici,

---

[*] See also Peter Hain, *Ayes to the Left* (London, Lawrence & Wishart, 1996), chapter 5.

the French Minister.' When I asked him about progress on the euro, he brushed it almost disinterestedly aside, coming back to the Moscovici benchmark. So instead I asked if he could make me a Privy Counsellor – a position not enjoyed by my predecessors. I had decided to ask because it signalled a seniority that automatically but not exclusively came with Cabinet membership. I also asked for a special adviser because of the toxic politics of Europe in the media and Parliament. He and Jonathan looked at each other. 'Don't see why not, but Jonathan, check out the SpAd position: are there any for Ministers under the Cabinet?' (A few weeks later I was sworn in as a PC but told the SpAd post wasn't possible – hardly a surprise but worth the try.)

On the way out from seeing Tony, Alastair Campbell sidled up. 'You and Jack: two sceptics on the euro,' he winked mischievously – and hardly had I left Downing Street than this line was being carried by broadcasters, appearing also next morning in the newspapers. The notoriously Eurosceptic *Sun* reported 'a senior source' as saying: 'By appointing Peter and Jack, the PM has shown there must be bloody good arguments why we should join the euro.'

I drew up a list of priorities before my first full day back in the Foreign Office on Tuesday 12 June 2001, this time in a different, even grander, room designated for the Europe Minister. One was to see Gordon Brown early because I felt that we had to end the corrosive tension, backbiting, briefing and counter- briefing between the Foreign Office and the Treasury. Acolytes of Robin Cook and Gordon Brown had been fighting a spin battle through the media, damaging the whole euro debate and harming the government.

Gordon, it turned out, was keen to see me the next day at 11 Downing Street, but when I knocked on the door there was no answer. Eventually a policeman came over and suggested going into 10 Downing Street and then through the connecting corridor. There was nobody in. We were in charge of the place. James Morrison, my principal private secretary, and I hung around bemused. Long minutes dragged by. Then there was a noise, the front door opened and a rather scruffy, tie-less man – a messenger – came in. 'How are you all then?' he said casually. 'The Chancellor's going to be along in a couple of minutes.'

Gordon bustled in, apologising for the long delay, immediately relaxed, took his jacket off and sat himself down in a chair, congratulating me for getting the job, saying it was 'really good news'. We talked a bit about the election, why the turnout had been so low, why the campaign had been an odd one, and how the Tories might develop. Then he ushered our respective private secretaries outside so that we could talk one-to-one. I hadn't had a proper conversation with Gordon since he had shouted and threatened me over economic policy nearly ten years earlier. Now he was charm personified – a side to his personality many never saw. After some general chat, I came to the point. 'I really need as Europe Minister to work closely with you. I don't want any of the damaging nonsense that's gone on between the Foreign Office and the Treasury.' He nodded but didn't say anything. 'On the euro I just want to know where I'm going because no one is telling me. Tony gave me no steer about the euro at all even though I asked him.'

'The most important thing is that we calm everybody down and that we get the discussion on a proper basis,' Gordon replied. The shock defeat in the Irish referendum on the Nice Treaty on European enlargement on 7 June 2001 was especially worrying him. He then went into a long exposition on how he'd spent four years getting the economy right, achieving economic stability, low interest rates and the independence of the Bank of England – all of which had been very successful but which had involved some extremely difficult choices, especially early on. And his clear dilemma – the thing that was haunting him – was that if the wrong decision was made at the wrong time, then Labour's hard-won reputation for a strong economy and rising living standards could be destroyed by a shockwave, taking us back in the public's mind to 'Old Labour economic incompetence'.

He then added, as if trying to convince me: 'Look, I'm committed to the single currency. It's something I believe in and in the right circumstances it's going to be good for Britain, no question about that. But this decision can't be made on the basis of just setting a deadline and then going for it. It's got to be on the basis of economic convergence, and the five tests which we've set out.' (I had hastily looked them up the previous night just in case I got tripped up: they covered economic convergence, sufficient flexibility, financial services, jobs and investment.) He then went into a semi-academic analysis of the dilemmas involved, the problem of the pound being too high against the euro. If you brought it down too quickly that could have an inflationary effect which would then force the Bank of England to put up interest rates. Clearly, manoeuvring all the economic indices into position to achieve euro member-ship would be incredibly difficult. But, he added, he was planning a statement to Parliament with a carefully considered analysis alongside it, setting out the basis for a full economic assessment with a roadmap to potential euro entry.

This made me reconsider the manner in which Labour had positioned the argument on the euro. Instead of its advantages to companies in reduced trade and currency exchange costs, we had to show the ordinary citizen voting in a referendum that the euro was in their personal interest. The argument could not be won by single-currency enthusiasts: it had to be something a majority felt was going to be good for their mortgages, their jobs and their future security.

Gordon concluded by saying he'd enjoyed the meeting and I subsequently learnt from the private secretary grapevine that he had been delighted that I'd asked to see him. It reminded me again how important personal chemistry is in the workings of politics and high office – something which you neglect at your peril – though it cannot solve all the problems and inevitable tensions. Two days after the meeting, I decided to deliver a 'cool it' message through an interview requested by the *Financial Times* and discussed beforehand with John Williams, the Foreign Office chief press officer recruited by Robin Cook, who was always a source of excellent counsel. Far from cooling it, however, the interview provoked some chatter, typical in the notoriously and stridently anti-European British media.

By which time I was in frozen Gothenburg attending my first European summit. There my main function seemed to be doing television and radio interviews though I methodically introduced myself to other Europe Ministers, some remarking pointedly that I was the fifth Labour Europe Minister they had dealt with in four years. I also faced the new experience of being placed under siege by anti-globalisation protesters involved in running battles with police around the summit – I'd been involved in a few of those myself in a previous incarnation.

‡

However, it was very evident that our whole communications strategy on Europe was not what it should have been. The language used by our government was fine up to a point – 'at the heart of Europe', or 'strong in Europe', stressing the need for 'economic reform in Europe'. But it didn't really engage with people's fears and concerns, rife in the dominant anti-Europe media – such as 'losing sovereignty'. It was also pretty impenetrable, because European Union *aficionados* submerged themselves in arcane technicalities, such as:

> The Antici Group considers that agreement at the next Council is crucial for the following IGC, so the troika and the PSC must be consulted to get consensus amongst the Presidencies especially over an extension of QMV in the second or third pillars, but then again CSFP could be affected by action in the first pillar if the Commission intervenes through conciliation given Parliament's right to co-decision with the Council.

Taking advantage of a lecture *Progress* had asked me to deliver, I changed the planned theme to 'plain speaking on Europe', later reproduced as a pamphlet.*

---

* Peter Hain, *Plain Speaking on Europe* (London, Progress, 17 July 2001).

James Bevan, one of the very few civil servants I ever found who could write excellent speeches, helped draft it. (Most officials churned out slabs of boring text full of information but with no narrative. My test for a speech draft was always: 'Would you really want to listen to this stuff yourself?')

On sovereignty, for example, my argument was we weren't really *losing* but *sharing* it, as we did within the United Nations and NATO. In those two cases Britain gave up rights to pursue foreign and defence policies unilaterally, in return for greater strength and safety in numbers. The draft had to be cleared, not just inside the Foreign Office, but also with No. 10 and the Treasury. I had another long chat with Gordon Brown, who made various suggestions, but he was pleased with the overall argument, as was his influential special adviser Ed Balls. So I was able to ensure that Foreign Office and the Treasury stuck together, preventing the media from playing their old games.

On the euro, I had drafted a passage on which James Bevan commented electronically: 'I really don't think you should put anything about the euro in the speech, because the Treasury won't like it and everybody will get terribly excited. JB' But I stuck to my guns because a plain-speaking speech on Europe could not avoid such a crucial issue as the euro. BBC's flagship *Today* programme interviewed me after they had been emailed the text. But they had mischievously opened up the 'track changes' feature to reveal earlier drafts. Their presenter Sue MacGregor excitedly probed me on the 'mysterious JB' – a silly thing to do because the speech contained a big section on the euro although their bemused listeners would never have known that. Caught on the hop because I had no idea they had a tracked-change version, I made light by replying: 'Maybe it was 007.' It was so typical of *Today*, the BBC and the media generally, to turn a substantial argument on Europe into a trivial and contrived process story.

My next focus was upon 'big bang': 1 January 2002 when euro coins started circulating in the twelve member states. Some thirty-four million trips would be made by British citizens to euro-zone member countries during 2002. Even though some of these would be multiple trips, around half the population would be feeling, seeing and using the euro. So this was an opportunity to engage in more sensible debate about something practical instead of something unknown and therefore worrying. I suggested producing government leaflets for travellers, explaining the euro in objective, factual terms. Resisted by my officials on the basis that the Treasury wouldn't like it, I persisted, winning the backing of John Kerr, head of the Foreign Office. In fact Ed Balls was so keen, he wanted the Treasury emblem alongside the Foreign Office one. So did the Department of Trade and Industry.

Alastair Campbell hadn't really appreciated the significance of the date that coins would first circulate. He had been enthusiastic about the 'plain speaking' speech and we had a brain-storming session. 'Off the record, Alastair,' I asked, 'Do you think we will go for the euro referendum or not?' He looked thoughtful and then replied: 'Well, I think on balance Tony will go for it, I think he is going to want to really grab it by the throat and go for it. Probably in this parliament – but it's a close-run thing.' This was highly significant because he was both close to Tony and personally cautious about the whole European project.

In early September, Peter Hyman, highly regarded in Downing Street and a longstanding staffer for Tony, explained that he was keeping an overview of Europe. Thinking back to the Yes for Wales campaign, I suggested convening a small group to do some serious planning for a potential referendum. He was keen to get Tony's communications guru Philip Gould involved, but was concerned about my suggestion of involving Peter Mandelson: 'When Peter is involved there tend to be leaks, and he tends to become the story, obscuring the main objective,' he said. I later bumped into Philip Gould at a Labour Party reception. Despite having a certain reserve that I wasn't a New Labour insider, he'd always been very friendly, not least because as a teenage demonstrator he'd run on cricket and rugby pitches when I was leading anti-apartheid protests thirty years before.

A few days later Philip came into my office, excited about preparations for a referendum, but worried about its winnability. He thought there was enormous opposition, fear and ignorance, and that we would be getting into very dangerous political waters, fanning prejudices and fears that New Labour normally managed to dispel. When I pressed him hard, he thought a referendum could just about be won, but that it would be really difficult. However, he also thought that Tony was likely to do it: 'It's just the sort of thing Tony will just do. He'll just go for it. If he does he will be confident he can win it.' My sense was that the most likely date for such a euro referendum would be spring 2003, after the coins had circulated for a full year with people having become accustomed to using them. However, Gordon Brown's very real reservations remained, especially since under Labour the British economy had been doing quite nicely, thank you, outside the euro-zone.

Roger Liddle, Tony Blair's Europe policy adviser, suggested I have a proper chat with Peter Mandelson. My relationship with Mandelson had been difficult as a backbencher, but he had been supportive of me as a Welsh Minister and we remained mutually cordial. Although I well understood why many Labour members were paranoid about him as a master of the manipulative dark arts, he was also probably the most gifted and skilled operator in modern politics. His flaw was almost to cultivate a Machiavellian reputation which partially led to his two resignations from the Cabinet. When we met he was very worried about my 'cool it' message on the euro, but subsequently referred to me publicly as Tony Blair's 'very effective Europe Minister', adding privately with mock concern: 'I hope I'm not doing you any damage by praising you, Peter.'

At the same time, travelling around the capitals of Europe, meeting leaders of other member states and candidate countries, it was very evident that everybody wanted us in the euro. Equally, there was a sympathetic acceptance of our acute difficulties, and the loss of the Irish referendum was salutary – 'if you don't know, vote no' the dominant theme of that campaign. Dick Benschop, the Dutch Socialist European Minister, bright and likeable, told me: 'Our government has been very understanding about your predicament on the euro. We won't lock you out of any economic decision making, for which there is a lot of pressure amongst the other euro-zone member countries. In fact Britain is being kept in the loop far more than strictly speaking the provisions of the euro organisation allow. But if we get the feeling you are not going to go for a referendum this parliament, we will just have to concede to the French in particular, who want to proceed on key economic decisions without you.'

‡

With exaggerated hyperbole, one euro official described it as the biggest event of its kind in the history of the world. On just one day, 1 January 2002, 300 million people changed their currency. In the Netherlands the entire army was deployed to ship the new coins and notes throughout the country. There was huge interest in the British media, much of it eagerly anticipating 'chaos'. But although I'd already acquired a reputation for speaking out in plain terms about the coming euro and the case for Britain being in it, I didn't want to get caricatured and stereotyped as 'Mr Euro' by the *Sun* and the *Daily Mail*. So, instead of being photographed spending euros as Alastair Campbell had originally suggested, I decided to do selective interviews, the main one for the *Independent* with Andrew Grice, their excellent political editor. He got a lead story focusing on my remarks that a lot of British shops were going to take the euro – including the high street store Dixons, even though its chairman, Stanley Kalms, was fiercely anti-euro. Kalms didn't want the rest of Britain to have it, but he was quite happy for his own company to trade in it. I said I would prefer European visitors to spend their euros to the full value of their purchasing power in British businesses, rather than giving the commission to the money changers in Paris or Berlin.

This all created quite a stir and on New Year's Day I was up early in

Gwehelog, Elizabeth's house in the Monmouthshire countryside outside Usk. It was a bright morning, snowy and frosty, a couple of broadcast vans from the BBC and Sky waiting. I did the *Today* programme flagship slot at about ten past eight, wondering who on earth was listening at that hour on New Year's morning – then settled down to help prepare for our brunch party. A little while later the Press Association rang wanting to 'take the story on'; obviously there weren't many stories around. But, wary of high-voltage euro media coverage, I took the precaution of asking what PA had reported me as saying from the *Today* interview.

'We are saying you said it was inevitable that Britain would go into the euro,' the reporter said.

'But I never said it was inevitable,' I replied indignantly.

'Oh, so you are now denying you said it was inevitable,' he countered ominously.

Lo and behold, the next story PA put out was me denying that I had said euro entry was inevitable – when I had never even hinted at that on any of the broadcasts that morning. And then to compound the felony some of the newspapers reported the next day that I been 'slapped down' by Gordon Brown and the Treasury – all of this between just after 8.10 on New Year's morning and around 10 a.m. when PA called me to follow up *Today*. The idea that Gordon, after a Scots Hogmanay, had phoned me in this early morning slot was complete fantasy, but it was symptomatic of the overblown, over-hyped media spin about the euro.

Although the *Sun* and the *Daily Mail* despatched journalists all over Europe to discover little old ladies sobbing as they had to cope with the new currency, none were to be found. The changeover itself was an amazing success. It also illustrated perfectly the usual British pattern: first, saying something won't happen and then, when it does, saying it's going to be a failure and then, when it's a success, desperately trying to catch up. And it reflected Britain's schizophrenic relationship with continental Europe since the Second World War, something Hugo Young describes so well in his book, *This Blessed Plot: Britain and Europe from Churchill to Blair*.

Immediately after the launch of the euro, opinion polls showed a rise in public support for Britain's entry. I talked to Digby Jones, director general of the CBI. Much like me, he was a pro-euro realist who claimed attitudes within industry were changing on what was a desirable rate for British entry. Everybody agreed that the pound was too high. A stronger euro was needed before Britain could safely enter. But whereas three years ago his members had told him Britain should enter on 2.65 Deutschmarks to the pound (the old benchmark), now they thought they could cope with 2.95, because the British economy was stronger. (Ironic, that, since 2.95 was the target rate at which we joined the Exchange Rate Mechanism – a rate far too high and which led to our humiliating exit.) The dilemma was that there seemed no prospect of the euro strengthening – and if, as markets expected, the euro appreciated after British entry, that would leave us short changed.

Over an interesting lunch with fifteen economists and business people convened by Merrill Lynch, every one of them disagreed about the rate at which we should enter. It was quite extraordinary. Adair Turner, another former CBI director general who was also with Merrill Lynch, told me he thought the markets would take the pound and the euro to where they ought to be once the government had made our position clear.

During a rare opportunity for a one-to-one with Tony on a small jet returning from a European summit in early spring 2002 I had asked him directly about the timing of a referendum: 'It's got to be in this Parliament,' he insisted. He was absolutely clear that the politics of it necessitated that. It was a question of getting the economics right and obviously squaring Gordon Brown. Although I was struck at Tony's determination to proceed, this was before Iraq, after which his political position in both the Party and the country was much weaker.

Meanwhile I had talked discreetly to key pro-Europe individuals about raising funds for communications research, focus groups, opinion polling and detailed research to be conducted by Philip Gould. But substantial funds were required and the operation had to be done very carefully. We didn't want damaging exposure about organising a 'shadow' euro campaign when it was never my intention to undermine Gordon Brown, who would have felt that the credibility of his economic judgement had been called into question. I rather doubted he would have approved of the enterprise, yet the preparatory work was necessary whatever the eventual timing, which he would effectively determine. So it all had to be done at arm's length.

I got Peter Mandelson involved, who in his political acumen and antennae was head and shoulders above everyone else. He paged through a copy of the *Sun* full of anti-euro material, saying how cleverly it chimed with the focus group work, and how much it was in tune with the anti-euro sentiment in the population. But, despite being the best qualified to run a Yes for Europe campaign, he would also have become the best target for opponents – which he readily acknowledged. Nevertheless I couldn't envisage running a Yes for Europe campaign without Peter Mandelson involved in some key way.

Pro-euro business figures raised £200,000 remarkably easily and they commissioned some in depth public attitude research. Peter Hyman joined me for an interesting presentation by Philip and Stan Greenberg, the legendary

American pollster and communications expert who had worked for the Democrats. It showed that, although the euro referendum was certainly winnable, it would be really tough. I then discussed with Peter Hyman, Philip Gould and Peter Mandelson whether we should launch a Yes for the Euro campaign quite independently from the Labour Party and certainly from the Government. It could be modelled on the Yes for Wales referendum campaign that I had initiated back in 1996 with the help of Leighton Andrews, whom I also involved in this project. I envisaged a very lean organisation without a formal constitution or membership or any of the costly administrative paraphernalia of a permanent body like Britain in Europe. We talked about doing this in the middle of 2002.

The dilemma was how to maintain control over an organisation that had to be independent of Labour. I also talked to Pat McFadden, between jobs as one of Tony Blair's special advisers and doing freelance work at the time. A tough, canny Scot who had worked for John Smith before Tony Blair, he was well respected. But he didn't think he could approach people whose expertise he needed unless Gordon Brown was privy and approved. Otherwise there would be a huge bust-up if Brown's camp found that a No. 10-sanctioned initiative was under way. When I spoke to Sally Morgan, now Anji Hunter's successor as director of government relations, and formerly Tony's political secretary, she was very uncertain. Pat McFadden had warned me from bitter personal experience: 'If it came to a bust-up between Brown and Blair you often get hung out to dry' – which made me even more concerned not to get into that position. Although Blair's people – Hyman, Gould and others including Mandelson – were keen, in the end it was me who would take the rap. Since Sally Morgan later told me she couldn't get Tony Blair's agreement for approaching Gordon Brown, preparatory work would have to be done on a much more discreet, more limited basis, with Pat McFadden sitting in his room at home drawing up a strategy – which is was how things were left in the spring of March 2002.

The whole episode left me with mixed feelings. Although I had never been a euro-fanatic, Tony's people were keen and, to be frank, both trying to tackle an insoluble problem and the sniff of another difference-making campaign drew me forward. I had tried to act as an honest broker between the Blair and Brown camps, yet I wasn't at all bereft when the project died a death.

‡

Back in the late summer of 2001, shortly after I became Europe Minister, it became evident that a number of European countries and others were keen on a 'Convention on the Future of Europe'. Its aim would be to design a new political architecture following the biggest ever enlargement of the European Union, taking in ten new countries in 2004 with Romania, Bulgaria, some ex-Yugoslav countries and conceivably Turkey to follow. The existing structures, which had been designed for the founding six countries, were creaking at this total of twenty-five and rising. They were simply not up to the job of connecting Europe with its citizens on the one hand and delivering efficient and effective policies on the other. Our initial stance towards this idea of a convention was deeply sceptical – typically outsider British. Why is this necessary? What purpose would it serve that an intergovernmental conference couldn't achieve on its own? (One was due in any case in 2004 to address precisely this post-enlargement question.)

We were especially worried about its provenance: European MPs and other 'federalists' trapped in the 'Brussels bubble' – elements not under the control of national governments. Through the summer into the early autumn of 2001 we tried to oppose the convention. But when it became apparent that it was going to happen anyway, that the highly federalist Belgian presidency was determined to press ahead regardless, we then switched tack to say that there ought to be a decent interval between the end of the convention and the beginning of the required intergovernmental conference, allowing for consultation, and for a firebreak before serious treaty negotiations.

Initially we felt we should keep our distance from it, with governments not implicated in the final outcome as they would certainly be if they were directly represented. We tried to think of somebody who could represent the government, but who would be at a convenient distance rather than a serving minister. Driving with Tony Blair to the airport after his press conference in Belgium at the Laeken Summit in December 2001, I suggested Peter Mandelson. But he carried a certain amount of baggage and Tony clearly was of the same view. So I talked to Jack Straw. We canvassed different names, but none of them seemed to measure up.

In January 2002 I found myself in the southern part of the Czech Republic, at a meeting of the Visegrád Group – Europe Ministers from the Czech Republic, Slovakia, Hungary, Poland–and ourselves. It was freezing as I arrived late in the evening for a dinner with some rather nice Czech wine in the gothic cellar of a remote country château. We discussed our respective approaches to the convention. 'We certainly won't be represented by a Minister. We're going to keep a certain distance,' I said.

When I got back to my hotel, news was breaking of a wide-ranging interview I had given in the *Spectator* to Anne McElvoy. The magazine, edited by Tory Boris Johnson, had typically spun and hyped a quote that 'we have the worst railways in Europe', and given it to right-wing papers, the *Telegraph* and *Mail* running it as front-page leads. Anne had first tried to get me to say something on the euro, to tease out some new phrase that they could blow up into a story – something of a media sport. But I wouldn't play ball. Instead she said: 'Here you are, this independently minded person, you're not a clone, do you have *any* disagreements with government policy?'

'Well, every member of the government, even the Prime Minister, has disagreements with government policy,' I replied defensively. 'But when you're in government you don't talk about them in public.'

But she kept needling away until, finally (and mistakenly) I gave in, revealing what I had often said in private: that we had neglected investment in public transport. 'We should have invested earlier; it is like turning an oil tanker around, which is why we have the worst railways in Europe.'

I went to bed realising there would be some damage limitation to undertake. The next morning media phone calls came in, left, right and centre. There was a frenzy about whether I had been licensed by the Prime Minister or not, whether I was attacking the embattled Secretary of State for Transport, Steve Byers, and all sorts of other nonsense. The truth was more mundane: it had been an aggressive interview and I had answered a straight question in a straight way; moreover what I said was true. John Prescott tried to get hold of me, doubtless to blow a fuse. He was always very direct: he would deliver some expletives on the PM's behalf and then forget about it. But the two of us couldn't get through to each other. That suited me: when he eventually made contact in the late afternoon, I suspected his temper would have subsided, as indeed was the case.

Then, out of the blue, Downing Street rang my private secretary Sarah Lyons to say that I was wanted – for a serious bollocking, we both thought. But it was Jack Straw on the line. Passing off the rail row as a bit of a nothing, he left me dumbfounded: 'I have just come out of a meeting with Tony. He wants you to serve as the government's representative on the Convention on the Future of Europe.' Why the about-turn, and why me, I asked? 'Tony now thinks that the convention is going to be much more significant than we wanted. He is worried it might get out of control. You have the authority, are a good negotiator, he trusts you.'

Interesting that Tony once again had maintained a strategic grip on the real issues despite the media frenzy that from day to day swirled around No. 10, and in this case the obviously unwelcome and annoying conjunction of the railway story with the predicament of Byers, one of Tony's confidants. I went ruefully back into the Visegrád meeting, and reported: 'Britain's policy last night that we weren't going to put a government minister on the convention has changed.'

‡

My appointment was a matter of stress to the Foreign Office because it meant that I was effectively doing two jobs, even though they overlapped. So, for example, on a visit to Cyprus in July 2002, I did some convention business along with Greek–Turkish issues on the island. But we did have to make tough decisions about Europe visits, because convention meetings in Brussels were over a couple of days every fortnight and sometimes more frequently. There were also key working groups which I attended conscientiously, the small team occasionally depending upon an RAF plane from Northolt Airport because otherwise I couldn't physically make the meetings in Brussels in a sensible and efficient manner without damaging other government duties. On one occasion I was driven onto the tarmac at Brussels, climbed in, and within a few minutes took off. I landed at Northolt, got into the car, was driven into London, attended a key meeting, then went straight back out again to Brussels.

Convention sessions were held in the plenary hall of the European Parliament building, with over 200 delegates and alternates. Back rows were usually packed with officials and journalists. You tended to speak for only three minutes, with an alternative arrangement for so called 'blue carding' where you could catch the chairman's eye and speak for one minute if you had a particular point to make in response to other things that had been said. I tended to speak quite passionately where others read their material into the record almost civil servant fashion. Our team observed that my speeches were listened to more than most. I usually stood up so as to be heard and seen where other delegates sat. I also tended refer to what others had said – more a reflection of the British parliamentary style of debate.

Hardly any other governments were directly represented at the opening of the convention and Tony Blair's foresight was vindicated because I was the most senior. Hard work and the huge professionalism of the Foreign Office team meant British influence was much greater than we could have dreamt of on a body which we had initially opposed, pursuing an agenda for a new 'European Constitution', which we thought daft, and which was full of 'Brussels bubble' types. A year later Tony startled a planning meeting by insisting: 'In its long-term impact upon British interests the convention could be more important than Iraq. That will be over in a period, but the future political architecture of Europe will remain with us for generations. The outcome has to be a success for us or else it will poison Britain's relationship with Europe.' He'd also said to me privately that he thought that it would define whether it might be possible to win a referendum on the euro, which he was still keen to hold.

I very quickly started to network systematically through meetings, breakfasts, lunches and dinners, and to brief myself up on the arcane complexities of European treaties and constitutional procedures, which inhabited a different world with its own language and own culture, baffling not just to citizens, but to MPs – or even Europe Ministers. The inaugural session was marked by a grand speech from former French President Valéry Giscard d'Estaing, chosen as the Convention President with Tony's backing over the respected former Dutch socialist Prime Minister Wim Kok, because France and Britain, despite perpetual tensions, fundamentally agreed on Europe's institutional architecture, that is to say a Europe of nation states not a federal super-state; Tony thought it significant that all the small countries and 'super-statists' wanted Kok.

The convention was a melting pot of egos, interests, ideology, high principle and low pragmatism. Most were suspicious of any British government; many saw us as a block on their European dreams. I put a pro-European but tough nation state position, placing us quite well, and spent considerable time and effort building personal relationships, trying to show respect and humility while also demonstrating steel and inventiveness.

By the summer of 2002, several months in, European and British newspapers were reporting the British team as the most proactive and successful, despite resistance from many European MPs and indeed the European Commission.* There was sterling work by my 'alternate', Patricia Scotland, now a Minister of State in the Lord Chancellor's Department. Her forensic legal grasp, formidable intellect and personal charm worked wonders.

We both found that others – notably the Irish, Danes and the Swedes – often came in sheltering behind us to get an agreed position once we had put our heads above the parapet and taken any flak. We broke fresh ground in accepting the idea of a new European Constitution when Jack Straw made a strong speech arguing that, contrary to the attack from Conservatives and other Eurosceptics, what mattered was not the idea of a European Constitution – in their many thousands of words and hundreds of pages the various EU treaties constituted one anyway – but what was in it. Indeed there were advantages in a simplified and clarified single text, making it obvious to its citizens what the European Union was all about, where its powers lay, how its competences were defined as against those retained by member states. We also broke new ground in endorsing the principle of a single 'legal personality' for the European Union. This meant that the EU would be an internationally recognised entity, simplifying international negotiations, which typically required separate

---

* For an excellent analysis see Peter Norman, *The Accidental Constitution* (Brussels, Eurocomment, 2003).

agreements on trade and aid with the European Commission, and then on foreign and security policy with the European Council.

By now I was very much the convention insider, and could sense some discomfort from Germany and France who suddenly replaced their delegates with their respective Foreign Ministers, Joschka Fischer and Dominique de Villepin. I had formed quite a good friendship with Fischer as Europe Minister since we both had radical backgrounds, in his case on the far left. German lessons provided by the Foreign Office brushed up my thirty-year-old 'O' level, and I greeted him in his language when he arrived to much attention on the convention floor.

'I'm here because *you* are here!' he replied in his excellent English, 'I hear you Brits are running the agenda. That's why I've come.'

But in practice neither he nor de Villepin was able to make up ground because their global duties meant they couldn't put in the time that I did, any more than Jack Straw could have done. Other countries who similarly reshuffled their representatives with big hitters had the same problem. I had spent months building relationships and these were really important in the European political culture.

Although, by the autumn of 2002, we were quite well placed, a lot of heavy lifting was still required to secure our objectives. An absolute priority for Tony Blair was to get a full-time President of the European Council, instead of a six-monthly rotating presidency where each country took a turn, chairing the Council, speaking for it, negotiating the agenda and driving it forward. He wanted the job to be full time, elected by heads of government to give the European Council and therefore the European Union real strategic direction both in foreign policy and in domestic policy. Council meetings were often chaotic as I had seen for myself at the Laeken Summit. One country would come in with its own pet subjects and go off in one direction and then another country would come in six months later and veer off, if not in the opposite direction, at least in a new one. This was not a serious way to run Europe, nor for Europe's voice to count in the world or to be effective in driving through the reforms needed in economic policy or foreign security and defence policy.

I explained this to the US Ambassador to Brussels when briefing him on the British perspective, and his eyes lit up. 'President Bush was over recently for the US–EU Summit, and asked "Who is the top guy for me to deal with?" I replied: "Well, there is the President of the Commission, the President of the Parliament and the President of the Council, but the President of the Council's six-month term is about to expire so it is equally important to meet his successor." By this time the President's eyes had long glazed over!'

Europe had no answer to the famous 'Henry Kissinger question': 'To whom in Europe do I pick up the phone?' Yet paradoxically, the very people who wanted a stronger Europe – in the Commission, the Parliament and the smaller nations – saw a powerful President, representing member governments, as a threat to their own influence.

'But surely you want Europe to be a powerful voice dealing with America, China, India, Russia?' I would argue. 'How can you expect that to happen without a strong head who can speak for the governments, who can deliver as nobody else in Europe can?' Because they were hostile to the influence of member state governments, these Euro-federalists were not willing to will the means – an ironic reversal of roles, with Britain, the so-called 'backmarker', a frontrunner in wanting a *stronger* Europe than they did, albeit a markedly *different* one.

The smaller countries wanted a more powerful and elected Commission President instead of an elected full-time President of the Council, which they saw as a 'big-country fix', since France, Spain and Italy backed our proposal. Significantly, however, the Danes were won round. Their Prime Minister began by being opposed when they assumed the presidency in the second half of 2002. But by the end of it he announced that he had been converted to the idea of a full-time post because as a serving Prime Minister he found it almost impossible to be an effective EU President at the same time – especially with the two traditional tours of capitals prior to each of the two European Councils during a presidency. This involved visiting fifteen countries twice in six months; with an extra ten countries after enlargement, that would become completely unrealistic. We also managed to win the case for national parliaments to have a veto over European Commission proposals if they infringed the principle of subsidiarity – that is if they encroached upon areas reserved for national parliaments.

Much to the surprise of other delegates I was seen as creative and proactive rather than stuck in traditional 'British outsider' scepticism, and this enabled me to win backing for what remained our very clear red lines. On social policy for example, a working group that we tried to resist was set up very late in the day to meet in January 2003 under the chairmanship of the genial Professor George Katiforis, a Greek socialist with particularly good English but with anti-British instincts because of our traditional stance on Europe.

Likeable with a folksy style, he once told me: 'You are not at all like the British.'

'That's because I am not really!' I replied.

Precisely because I did not have any of the social and class trappings associated in European eyes with being British, being an 'outsider' helped me to become a Convention 'insider'.

There was a painstaking Whitehall- and Treasury-dominated procedure to clear the text for my speeches, but I often departed from these agreed texts on occasions when I judged it politically wise to do so. Although that caused some unease, when I was able to win outcomes in line with my negotiating mandate, such unease went away. On social policy, I posed the choice in deliberately ideological terms, rejecting both an American free market model (which many wrongly associated with Tony Blair), and a highly regulated and costly labour market. I was very positive about wanting a Europe of social values, social justice and full employment, but argued strongly that the way you could achieve this was not to impose more and more business regulations, which protected only those with jobs, but to generate the flexibility and employability which created new job opportunities. We'd been particularly successful at this in Britain under our Labour government, compared with continental Europe's dreadful unemployment record. That argument was won inside the group but there remained a question of whether they would come back to fight another day by demanding qualified majority voting (QMV) on social security and taxation and employment law, which would have been a deal breaker for us. I formed quite a good a relationship with Amelio Gabaglio, the general secretary of the European Trades Union Congress, somebody who also viewed the British with suspicion, understandably since we were always on the opposite side on employment and social policy. He unofficially conceded privately, during some bargaining, that he wouldn't press the case for QMV if we were very forward on social justice and full employment policy, which I was more than happy to agree. The result was a positive outcome nobody in Whitehall had thought possible.

Another working group, established in the late autumn of 2002 on common foreign and security policy, was strategically very important for us because there was a big move from within the Commission, the European Parliament and some member states, especially the smaller ones, to put it under the control of the Commission and, therefore, indirectly under the Parliament. There wasn't any way that Britain was going to accept our foreign and military policy being run by Brussels. Fortunately France was in exactly the same position despite our traditional rivalry and the poison generated by Iraq which loomed large over the convention. A key proposal was to 'double hat' the High Representative appointed by governments through the Council with the External Relations Commissioner to form a single Foreign Policy Representative. This was a sensible idea but to whom would the new post be accountable?

Javier Solana, the High Representative, formerly Spanish Foreign Minister and NATO secretary general, influential and charismatic, explained in exasperation how in Bosnia, he had needed a vehicle in order to implement a peace-keeping operation in line with agreed European policy. But he didn't have the Commission's resources to purchase the necessary vehicle and so had to persuade a major car manufacturer to donate one. Similarly when he went to New York or Washington he was not able to use the Commission officials based there to support his diplomatic activity because they were not allowed to serve the Council – also plainly ridiculous. So there was a case for bringing the two jobs together. However, the danger was that the Solana role would cease to be operational because it would just get locked into all the Brussels-based Commission bureaucracy. Even more dangerous, it might effectively lead to a back door takeover by the Commission of foreign and security policy from governments in the Council.

I believed the best way to get what we wanted was to support the 'double hat' proposal, but on our terms only, and persuaded both Jack Straw and Tony Blair to back this. But it meant being quite blunt in one session of the working group: 'The truth is that of the entire European Union of fifteen countries, only Britain and France – perhaps with Spain, Italy and in certain limited circumstances Germany and the Netherlands – have any serious defence forces or any serious military capability that could be deployed to carry out peace-keeping operations or involve Europe in foreign policy implementation. And we are not about to hand over control of our soldiers to countries whose own soldiers are not making a contribution.' My argument was listened to attentively if not willingly. The other issue which was a key one for us was maintaining unanimity in the European Council for common foreign security policy decisions. There was a big push from some of the smaller states, European MPs and to some extent the Commission for more qualified majority voting. This was a no-go area for us. It would have meant ceding foreign policy decisions to Brussels when vital national interests were at stake. To break the impasse, I made a new proposal whereby the Council could agree by unanimity to go to qualified majority voting on a particular foreign policy development, welcomed by Jean-Luc Dehaene, chair of the working group, the former Belgian Prime Minister. A formidable expert and tough operator, he saw it as creative way out of the potential log jam.

‡

In the middle of all this, on 23 October 2002, my parliamentary assistant Phil Taylor paged that Estelle Morris, Secretary of State for Education, had suddenly resigned. Although I loved the Europe job, and had made huge progress in the Convention, I knew from previous experience that, once a reshuffle started, you never knew where it might end. My private office, worried I might be promoted, became even nervier when next morning there was a call from Downing Street enquiring as to my whereabouts. I was asked to go to see the Prime Minister via the Cabinet Office in Whitehall to avoid the media now gathered outside No. 10. My staff were depressed and tearful, almost as if there was a bereavement; we had all grown close, even by the standards of my other private offices. Sally Morgan, Tony Blair's government relations director, suggested I wait in her office. I could hear to-ing and fro-ing, recognising the voices of Jack Straw and John Reid. Stuck reading the papers, time ticking by, I wondered what was going on. Then Wales's Guto Harri, a BBC political correspondent, called on my mobile (I'd kept it switched on despite No. 10 regulations). He'd heard that I was going to be promoted to the Cabinet, but to what? 'No idea,' I replied truthfully – without admitting I was actually in Downing Street.

Getting restless, I turned on Sky television. There I saw that Charles Clarke had been promoted to Secretary of State for Education, leaving the chairmanship of the Labour Party – one of the jobs I'd been tipped for. A few minutes later Sky's political editor Adam Boulton, standing about forty yards away from me outside in Downing Street, said John Reid had gone to be Party chairman from Secretary of State for Northern Ireland. Ah, I thought, there is only one person to replace him: Paul Murphy, the current Secretary of State for Wales, since he'd been a number two in Northern Ireland under Mo Mowlam and was widely believed to be the key backroom negotiator for the Good Friday peace agreement. Maybe I could be taking over his Wales job? Then Guto Harri phoned again: 'Congratulations, Secretary of State for Wales!' Minutes later Sky reported it too. I hadn't even been offered the job, but was hearing about it from broadcasters after what must have been a briefing by Alastair Campbell.

I meanwhile resolved to press Tony Blair to keep my job on the convention because I had been able to make considerable progress. I needn't have worried because no sooner had he told me I was indeed 'going to Wales' than he somewhat tentatively added: 'But I want you to stay on the convention.' He was both pleased and relieved at my enthusiastic agreement. So was Jack Straw, my convention team and the European department of the Foreign Office, who had been pressing this strongly. However, it did require considerable dislocation and upheaval – Sarah Lyons moving to a desk in the cramped Wales Office, with some complicated IT modifications needed securely to access the Foreign Office intranet.

‡

At meetings he periodically convened on the convention, Tony had a short attention span, understandable for a Prime Minister. I always spoke briefly, making key points whereas my successor Denis MacShane would meander and quote *Le Figaro* or what was in that morning's other European press. Jack Straw would often speak to enormous and somewhat eccentric detail, with lots of historic references, which clearly irritated Tony; you could see him stop listening in Cabinet meetings too. It was also quite obvious that Jack was in a more sceptical position than the Prime Minister and was proud of it. I was more on the same European wavelength as Tony. I also knew what was practically deliverable in the convention compared with unrealistic expectations from some Cabinet colleagues; I sometimes quietly recast my remits while still securing our bottom lines.

The convention was full of larger-than-life characters. Despite his aristocratic aloofness inimical to my own background, I couldn't help being impressed by Giscard d'Estaing. Especially for a 78-year old, he had a formidable grip on policy detail, though not necessarily (his own secretariat indicated to me) a huge appetite for work. A shrewd and wily operator, he would take no prisoners, often summing up at the end of a convention session in his peerless way saying what he thought, whether or not that had been the consensus – in one case, much to my frustration and irritation, and quite contrary to views expressed from the floor, stating that there was support for extending qualified majority voting on taxation instead of the unanimity rule which protected British interests. But generally his strong leadership was helpful: his support for a full-time President of the Council for instance. His chairing of the convention proceedings was patrician, on the one hand courteous to a fault, genial and witty, but on the other hand sharp – very much the great man, the rest of us his subjects, even though he treated ministers, myself included, with a polite old-fashioned sense of deference. Where I addressed all others by their first names, I always deliberately called him 'Mr President'. He liked that.

To schmooze Giscard, Tony Blair invited him to a special dinner at No. 10, remarking ruefully that he should come more often because the fine Bordeaux retrieved from a Whitehall cellar for the occasion was in a different class from standard No. 10 fare. To get to the small upstairs dining table, Giscard had to navigate, somewhat bemused and sniffy, through toys sprinkled over the floor belonging to the Blairs' baby son, Leo. Tony flatteringly, but doubtless for an ulterior purpose, told Giscard that I was 'one of the smartest politicians around'. The dinner was a success in winning Giscard's backing for our main objectives, though I felt Tony was far too accommodating on some other issues and I had to retrieve the situation by meeting Giscard a week later to reinforce our red lines. As we stood on the steps at No. 10, waving Giscard goodbye and joking about Leo's toys, I mentioned my first grandchild, Harry, then several months old. Tony turned to stare at me for an age, shaking his head, saying nothing, as if musing: 'We are a similar age, I have a tiny son and you are a grandad?'

Giscard's indispensable right-hand man was John Kerr, the convention's secretary general. The former Foreign Office chief had a forensic eye for detail as well as a strategic grasp of geopolitics. A chain-smoker, Kerr was cunning, tough and careful not to display any pro-British bias. Where Giscard was grand and sweeping, Kerr spotted all the plots before they were even hatched and expertly managed the drafting of the new constitution.

The two convention vice presidents were also important. Giuliano Amato, the former Prime Minister of Italy, likeable, constitutionally highly adept, knew the treaties inside out, upside down and sometimes argued at a level way above most in the convention, certainly me. A good person to work with, I could have frank discussions with him. He was also the father figure of the Socialist group, meetings of which were a complete waste of time. He sat at the top table, sporadically raising his pronounced eyebrows. Our eyes would occasionally meet as if to say 'What on earth am I doing here?' He once said to me: 'You know, when I was Prime Minister I really enjoyed the job because I was able to do all sorts of different things. But now, morning to night, it is Convention, Convention, Convention.' For most of us the convention was a huge commitment, but for Amato it had taken over his life.

The other vice president was Jean-Luc Dehaene, whom the Tory government had once blocked for Commission President because of his super-state ambitions. I got to admire his grasp of the issues, his intellect and political skills. We worked well together – an unlikely alliance with a super-state advocate. I flew over to Brussels to have a productive working lunch with him, just Sarah Lyons and I in a thirty-seater RAF plane – the only way we could accomplish the visit. The venue was a tasteful Flemish club which he explained he had set up because he felt somewhat isolated by the dominance of the Walloons. Business in Europe was often done over dinner, lunch or breakfast, with plenty of time allocated. Convention lunch breaks typically lasted well over two hours, which always rankled with me; I would have preferred to get away earlier: how un-European!

Another larger-than-life figure was Íñigo Méndez de Vigo, a conservative Spanish MEP. A big engaging character, he was adept at moving lightly around where he needed to. On behalf of the President of the European Parliament, he convened an informal group of a dozen movers and shakers who met at each convention session without officials, for dinner on the twenty-sixth floor of the Hilton hotel. The food and wine was mundane, but the room had a marvellous view of Brussels, on a summer evening quite spectacular. We were able to get to know each other better and to explore informally where there might be a consensus between very disparate views. I tried to be both constructive and frank about what Britain could and could not accept. As we built trust between us, the Hilton group became a useful vehicle for moving forward.

Joschka Fischer's appearance enabled me to move the Germans away from their frustrating super-state alliances. On 24 April 2003 I took him through all the main issues, including taxation and social security, where our two countries were at loggerheads.

'Peter, the problem for us is we pay all the EU bills and other countries take advantage,' Fischer argued.

To which I replied: 'You want us to pick up your high social costs and make us uncompetitive.'

It was clearly in Germany's interest to get more qualified majority voting on taxation so that they didn't have to keep funding the European Union's budget as they had traditionally done, but he was sympathetic to my argument. On defence I asked how on earth he was involved with the Benelux countries in some kind of separate parallel defence arrangement when none of them had any real military capability. He just shrugged and said: 'There are only three European countries that matter on defence: Germany, France and Britain in reverse order.' And on the argument as to whether Europe should be a defence partner or a counterweight to the USA, he said: 'This is a real problem. If you are a partner you are taken prisoner by the USA. If you are a counterweight you will be ignored by the USA.'

Joschka was always fascinating, with a broad sense of history and ideology. I found our bilaterals especially useful because he was always much more creative than his officials, who looked uneasy as he conceded point after point since he had a much more realistic political perspective than the integrationist rigidity of the German Foreign Affairs Ministry.

As relationships strengthened in this way, those who might have started off hostile began trying to reconcile their own objectives with what they knew were our bottom lines. We also assembled different alliances on different issues – for instance Spain, Italy and eventually Germany supporting Britain and France on a full-time President of the Council; Ireland, Sweden and Denmark backing us on maintaining national vetoes over tax and social security. The British Conservative MP David Heathcoat-Amory unwittingly boosted my credibility in the convention, because he was so extreme in his fierce Euroscepticism, appearing continuously to strain at the leash to get out of Brussels, not just to get back home, but to pull Britain out of Europe too. If that was what our Labour government was up against, convention delegates would tell me, rolling their eyes in disbelief, we had better help you. I had an especially good relationship with the Spanish, but to get their support for maintaining a national veto on tax and social policy, I backed their insistence on reopening the voting distribution for countries under the Nice Treaty, which they felt strongly penalised them. My concession was made without consulting officials and John Kerr was, unusually, beside himself, berating me. Tough – because my deal with Spain was important to getting what we wanted in the end.

The British media remained unremittingly virulent, fed by visceral Conservative attacks. 'Blueprint for tyranny' screamed a front-page *Daily Mail* headline on 8 May to its six million readers:

> Stealthily and slyly, a European constitution is today being created that will destroy Britain's independence, indeed its very identity ... the end of every-thing we understand by the terms British and Britishness. There will be no more national sovereignty, no more meaningful election to Westminster, no freedom independent of our European partners.

A week later, the *Sun* bellowed to its nine million readers 'Save our Country' over a front page emblazoned with the Union Jack and pictures of the Queen, Admiral Nelson and Winston Churchill. 'In 1588 we saw off the Spanish. 1805 we saw off the French. 1940 we saw off the Germans. In 2003 Blair surrenders Britain to Europe.'

European newspapers – some resentfully – reported the final outcome on 13 June for what it was: 'a triumph for Britain', some also name-checking me for a 'personal coup'. Needless to say, I preferred the European judgement!

‡

On 9 June 2003, Gordon Brown made a statement to the House of Commons giving the government's decision on whether the five tests had been met to enable Britain safely to enter the euro. Several weeks before, Cabinet Ministers had been sworn to secrecy and given a weekend to read eighteen dense Treasury studies, averaging 200 pages each. They included abstruse jargon: 'hysteresis' apparently meant that if an economy had a shock, then it didn't necessarily return to its original equilibrium level. There was no way I could absorb all of the thick texts over a weekend. So I relied mostly upon the summaries. They covered the whole lot of very interesting stuff – including labour market flexibility, the euro and the cost of capital, the pound–euro equilibrium rate, effects on the City, trade, the housing market, prices, modelling statistics and modelling transition, fiscal stabilisation, impact upon business and the United States single currency.

They demonstrated Gordon Brown's brilliance, both intellectually and strategically, the way he anticipated and thought things through, inside out and upside down. He had set up the debate in a very effective way. It was quite clear that it wasn't going to be a Yes and I wasn't unhappy with that. I didn't think that it was politically possible to join then, and the study showed that Britain wasn't economically in the right position either. Convergence was happening, we were getting closer and closer, in terms of business cycles and interest rates and all the rest of it, to other European economies and it was a question of continuing on that trend. Each member of the Cabinet then had a series of separate meetings with Tony Blair and Gordon Brown. Mine was on 20 May 2003 and I drew up a little checklist, noting that labour market flexibility had increased since 1997 (a key part of meeting the five tests). Flexibility in the real wage rate had increased since 1997 and, on key issues like the impact on the City, entering the euro was neutral. In terms of trade it was a clear benefit.

So I decided to focus on main points – a fairly relaxed occasion, joined by Helen Liddell, the Scottish Secretary, and Paul Murphy, the Northern Ireland Secretary. Helen immediately attempted to demonstrate an economics expertise, perhaps parading her credentials for a future Cabinet promotion. She spoke authoritatively and had clearly got to grips with the subject in great detail. But it seemed to me that she was missing the real point. I argued that we had to develop a political strategy of getting from where we were as a result of these studies and the final economic assessment to come, to where we wanted to be, which was to join the euro. First, it was absolutely vital for our political credibility with the pro-euro business community, the pro-euro section of British public opinion and above all for the rest of the European Union, that we made it crystal clear we were on the road into the euro. Second, we had to keep the option open of joining in this parliament. Third, members of the Cabinet should be free to argue the case, for which we needed a core script. Fourth, there should be a Referendum Bill in the next Queen's Speech signalling our intention to join, but with a commencement order that would allow us to set a date later when the time was right.

Gordon scribbled away in his own inimitable fashion and Tony seemed generally pleased. I thought it was altogether a useful exercise of collective Cabinet consultation. On Saturday 31 May I again flew back into Heathrow from Brussels to find in my red box a copy of Gordon Brown's economic assessment – another thick tome. As everyone expected, it showed conclusively that we had been making significant progress in all five of the economic tests but that there was insufficient convergence. It made me question whether other countries in the European Monetary Union were fully convergent either, and whether this would continue to be an excuse for us not joining. If we had greater convergence than some existing members, perhaps we were setting our standards too high, or they too low? When I went to a second meeting with Tony and Gordon, again at No. 10, this time just with Paul Murphy, I decided to make these points in a note which I handed over. They seemed quite pleased, though perhaps they were just humouring me. I asked whether Britain was doomed always to set higher hurdles than everybody on joining – something I had discussed a few days previously with Charles Clarke, the Education Secretary.

There was a consensus at the Cabinet meeting on the euro on 5 June, lightened by John Prescott's quip: 'The best thing about this whole exercise of Cabinet consultation is that you two have got together,' pointing to Tony and Gordon. But when there was talk of holding a referendum on the same day as a general election, I reminded everyone that the Electoral Commission had appeared to bar that. Tony seemed unhappy about this, others mumbled. 'Why should we take our orders from the bloody Electoral Commission?' Prescott interjected angrily. 'Bunch of bloody tossers.' I said that the force of our case for a delay would be compelling, but 'only if the various courtiers in No. 10 and the Treasury don't over-brief on either side'. There were some eyebrows raised balanced by nods. I also pressed for a very close and early dialogue with the trade union movement over proposals for regional flexibility, in particular regional pay bargaining, because that had the potential for pulling the trade union movement even more against the euro, with significant unions detaching themselves from the pro-euro position that had been won by John Monks, general secretary of the TUC.

I added that when it came to the referendum, it would come down to trust. 'Post Iraq, we are in trouble with the electorate on trust but the public would be really struck by the Prime Minister and the Chancellor being prepared to take a risk. People would be impressed that we were not doing something for short-term popularity reasons but because we thought that it was in Britain's long-term interest.' There were lots of nods, especially from Tony. Although I did not reveal this, I was drawing on the private polling by Philip Gould and Stan Greenberg when I had been Europe Minister. I was heartened: at last we had a clear 'Yes but not yet' strategy which, if presented properly, gave us the platform, based upon the economic framework and five tests, to confront the great bulk of Eurosceptic opinion in the country. I could not have been more wrong. Instead it proved to be Labour's last throw of the euro dice because another big European row was about to engulf us.

‡

The well-financed anti-European campaign for a referendum on the Constitutional Treaty was now in full cry. Tony had resolutely resisted this, arguing as I did that it was not like the euro – or even British entry when Labour had called a referendum in 1975 to seek retrospective endorsement for a Tory decision to take us into Europe. But Tory opportunism was boundless. They had delivered the Maastricht Treaty, which established the euro – immeasurably more momentous than the Constitutional Treaty, part modest reforms, part bringing into a single, accessible text the many separate treaties which almost required a PhD to fathom.

Nevertheless pressure for a referendum was intensifying. Inside the Cabinet a faction headed by Jack Straw and Gordon was furiously lobbying Tony to concede. Once at a meeting at Chequers I had witnessed Jack quarrelling with a grimly frustrated Tony like a dog at a bone; he wouldn't let go. In the media it proved almost impossible to argue the merits of the new draft treaty amidst the strident clamour for a vote. Then the French President, Jacques Chirac, called a referendum, and Tony, judging the French would probably lose it, so breaching the requirement for unanimity in treaty endorsements and rendering superfluous a British one, somersaulted and conceded one too.

He told the House of Commons on 20 April 2004:

> The question will be on the Treaty. But the implications go far wider. It is time to resolve once and for all whether this country, Britain, wants to be at the centre of European decision making or not; time to decide whether our destiny lies as a leading partner and ally of Europe or on its margins.

He had decided 'to confront head on' what he stated was 'partially at least, a successful campaign to persuade Britain that Europe is a conspiracy aimed at us rather than a partnership designed for us and others to pursue our national interest properly in a modern, interdependent world.'

Although it left me rather high and dry, Tony's decision lanced the anti-Europe fury. In a referendum in May 2005 France overwhelmingly and unprecedentedly rejected the Constitutional Treaty. Three days later so did the Netherlands. It was dead. But my work was not. Intensive negotiations stripped out the self-aggrandising clutter from the draft treaty, including the whole concept of 'new Constitution'. All the key convention reforms I had toughly negotiated remained: a good deal for Britain which resulted in the Lisbon Treaty, signed on 13 December 2007, and entered into force on 1 December 2009. My fifteen busy but fulfilling months in Brussels had been worth it after all.

However, having accepted the full-time President representing member governments, the European Union in a typical fudge then gave a new lease of life to the rotating presidency and rejected a strong candidate with a global reach, Tony Blair, for a nondescript one, Herman Van Rompuy. Tony would have offered the very strong leadership Europe needed when the eurozone slid into crisis in 2011. Instead, its leaders delayed and dithered, deepening the crisis.

‡

Very soon after I had taken over as Minister for Europe in June 2001 it was evident that Gibraltar was going to be a big issue. I discussed it with Jack Straw and found that we shared a common perspective. In his previous job as Home Secretary he had been very concerned about dodgy practices on Gibraltar – money laundering, tax evasion, drug trafficking and crime. Jack's desire to do something about Gibraltar coincided with my gut instinct that it was ridiculous in the modern age for Britain to have a colony on the tip of Spain nearly 2,000 miles away. Two years before I had jointly bought a small *finca* with friends just up the Andalucian coast, and had got to know and admire the Spanish, Elizabeth's great fluency in the language (she was often mistaken by locals for a fellow citizen) adding to our enjoyment. 'We've really got to try and sort this if we can,' said Jack refreshingly. 'It will also help our strategic relationship with Spain.'

So I decided to make my first visit as Europe Minister to Madrid, where I was introduced to their Europe Minister, Ramón de Miguel, a cultured man with an impressive hinterland, sense of history, and a long track record of diplomacy in Africa and elsewhere in the world. I had been fed dark warnings that, when talking about Gibraltar, he would become very heated. But we got on fine.

Ramón was accompanied by high calibre, tough officials: Carlos Basterreche, a Basque, and Ricardo Dietz Hochleitner, a details man, and despite some German ancestry a traditional Spanish hardliner. I said I wanted to take a decisive step forward on Gibraltar, and that my own African roots made it easy for me to understand the strength of feeling about a bit of Spain being British; or a little bit of England trying eccentrically to cling on to Spain. We would have felt the same way about the Isle of Wight, though in Gibraltar's case an isthmus formed a physical connection to the mainland. They seemed nonplussed as if I'd rather spoiled their standard script.

Around the same time Peter Caruana, the Chief Minister of Gibraltar, visited me in London, saying we'd met before and he had followed my career. A theatrical character, who liked ten sentences when one would do, he was intelligent and, unlike Jack, I rather warmed to him. Both of us had a feeling we could do business, and an official visit was soon arranged.

In early September 2001, I flew with Gibraltar Airlines, the owner recognising me and urging me to be 'brave': the business community was frustrated by the uncompromising stance of local politicians and residents, he said. I leapt at his offer to sit in the cockpit as we landed, excited on a beautiful morning at spotting familiar sights: the mountain top town of Ronda, Malaga, Marbella, Estepona and maybe even our small *finca*. We came in low over the sea – exhilarating, seeing the runway loom, rushing up as we landed.

I had decided not to do a press conference because I didn't want to be cornered. Over Gibraltar anything you said was exaggerated in triplicate, the slightest nuance becoming a huge fuss. Instead, I'd placed an article in the *Gibraltar Chronicle,* the daily morning paper, a bible on the Rock. The status quo was not sustainable, I argued; there had to be a process of normalisation, everybody had to change – Gibraltarians, Spanish and British. That set the tone for a successful visit. After a formal ministerial meeting, I had lunch with Peter Caruana in a pleasant restaurant on the waterfront – on my own as he had insisted, confessing to a congenital, perhaps understandable, suspicion of Foreign Office officials, who he thought manipulated Ministers. Caruana was not to know that suited me fine. Emyr Jones Parry, then the Foreign Office political director and later NATO and UN Ambassador, whom I trusted implicitly, advised me to meet on a one-to-one basis, and ask Caruana what he thought a final settlement might look like.

So I did just that. Caruana gave an intriguing, thoughtful and encouraging response: 'An Andorra solution would be worth looking at,' he said. Andorra's status is essentially one of co-sovereignty between Spain and France, expressed through the King and the Bishops, though it has its own autonomy and its own representation to the United Nations and in the European Union. I responded enthusiastically and we had a productive discussion in which he was, however, at pains to stress the need for caution, insisting there had to be a long and familiar list of confidence-building concessions from Spain, such as freeing up border controls and air access – matters which had for so long caused such antagonism towards Spain. Madrid had good reason to believe, however, that Gibraltar would simply pocket such concessions and remain inflexible on the constitution.

Caruana then took me on a wander down Main Street, something traditionally done by visiting British Ministers. I was immediately recognised with 'don't sell us out' exhortations. When I later saw the former Chief Minister and Labour Party opposition leader, the crafty but likeable Joe Bassano, he also gave me a long lecture about never selling out. An old class warrior, he was somebody who you sensed would never change. We had good-natured discussion which included his experiences when living in London as a Labour activist. Joseph

Garcia, leader of the small Liberal group, was more extreme than Bassano. Other opposition groups were similarly hardline, stuck in the past, reciting a mantra of independence, anti-Spanish and anti-British too.

It reminded me at the time of hardline unionists and loyalists in Northern Ireland. Although they craved their British identity, Britain was more a protective umbrella for what in their case was 'Ulster first and last'. Of course, Gibraltarians had very good cause to be angry, frustrated, suspicious and fearful because Spain had acted in a particularly ham-fisted, aggressive and reactionary fashion towards them over the years. But most Gibraltarians simply wouldn't think creatively about a future of opportunities rather than threats – which made Caruana's task almost impossible.

A few weeks later I decided to go out to Spain for further discussions with Ramón de Miguel and his team, hosted by our Ambassador, Peter Torry, who smilingly reported that as a young rugby fan he had 'hated' me during the Stop the Springboks campaign but now accepted 'the error' of his ways. More significantly, he'd never experienced such a dramatic change for the better in relations between Madrid and London. Having again talked to Emyr Jones Parry beforehand, I decided to surface a co-sovereignty proposal. Essentially, I explained, it would mean Britain and Spain sharing sovereignty, with Gibraltar having much more autonomy, getting rid of all the colonial nonsense and also overcoming all the obstacles that affected normal daily life – border controls, restrictions on telephone access, lack of easy diversions to Malaga of incoming plane flights to Gibraltar Airport in bad weather and so on. Having broken the sovereignty log jam, the Spanish were really up for all sorts of ideas and were no longer obstructive on any of Caruana's 'confidence building' measures. My officials concurred that this meeting proved to be a dramatic breakthrough.

Shortly afterwards I briefed Peter Caruana on the Madrid meeting, telling him: 'Gibraltar gets more power, more sovereignty in terms of your own decision-making structures – things you've wanted for a long time – and you as a Chief Minister become a more powerful figure by obtaining powers currently determined by the British Governor acting on behalf of London. All the frustrating obstacles and the intimidation preventing normal life on the Rock will go. But the co-sovereignty has to be part of that. If it isn't then we are stuck with the status quo. I want you to be part of negotiating all the detail. You can shape the outcome and protect all your interests.'

Caruana listened politely. Then all the creativity and flexibility he had first demonstrated in our productive lunch a month earlier expired in a puff of traditional Gibraltarian obstinacy. 'There is no prospect of me doing that, no prospect of me agreeing with such an approach,' he said. But, I reminded him, he had set me off on the co-sovereignty model through his Andorra idea.

'Well, I might be willing to go along with something like that but only subject to all sorts of conditions,' he conceded, explaining with passion that he had to maintain the confidence of his electorate, he could not go out on a limb. A least one of his predecessors had been drummed out of office for showing the slightest flexibility. His whole demeanour changed, no longer a figure able to cut through ancient prejudices and lead from the front, taking his people into an immeasurably better situation, as I thought he had the potential to do.

Instead Caruana began slipping into an oppositional mode, breaking the trust I thought we had established by chatting to the media. There was bad blood between him and our officials, who were astonished at my patience and contemptuous of his bombastic theatrics. Jack Straw dismissed him as a 'grandstander'. By this time I was about the only person in the Foreign Office with whom – despite everything – he had good relations. He saw me as different from the mandarins and Ministers he was used to. A Mediterranean, melodramatic, emotional lawyer who talked the hind leg off a donkey, he could be pedantic and pompous but I found him quite engaging.

On the Rock there was a manic and contradictory refusal to take part in the so-called 'Brussels process' – initiated by the Tory government under Margaret Thatcher in 1984 as a way of getting Madrid, London and Gibraltar to try and resolve matters – while simultaneously and incessantly demanding that their voice be heard. But, minus Caruana, we went ahead anyway with what proved to be a very successful meeting in Barcelona, with the Foreign Minister of Spain, Josep Piqué, and Jack Straw. Having prepared carefully with pre-meetings, we cracked the whole issue and laid out the ground for a deal which would entail co-sovereignty, maximum self-government for Gibraltarians, and full cooperation from, economic assistance from, and joint Spanish representation at the European Union rather than the traditional London–Madrid stand-off on Gibraltar.

A fantastic new deal for Gibraltar was in the offing – but there was no sign that the Gibraltarians were remotely interested in it. They were stuck, wanting to remain where they were, yet schizophrenic because they didn't like where they were. Under the deal they would remain British if they wished and the deal would be subject to a referendum on the Rock. Their cherished British way of life would be unchanged – except for the better because the sense of being under siege from Spain would disappear. Objectively it was hard to see why they were so irate – both refusing to engage yet frantic that we were pressing ahead without them.

However there was cross-party help from Lord Garel-Jones, Europe Minister under John Major. A Spanish speaker with a Spanish wife, he had a house in the country to the west of Madrid to which he retreated each weekend. Wily with a somewhat furtive air, he was always plotting, ever the operator: you could imagine his previous incarnation as Tory deputy Chief Whip. One evening he suddenly appeared in my Commons ministerial office wearing a dirty old raincoat saying what he'd been up to, a fag hanging out of the corner of his mouth. He also tended to arrive in the Foreign Office as if he was still the Europe Minister. My office had its own private toilet across the corridor and I was minding my own business one day, opening the door when I was startled to bump into him coming out on the way to a meeting with me. 'At the appropriate time, if the going gets rough, I will say publicly that this is what we were trying to do under the Thatcher and Major governments,' he assured me. Lord Howe, Foreign Secretary under Mrs Thatcher, also rang me to say that he wanted to support us and said he was writing a helpful article in *The Times*.

Tony Blair proved steadfast mainly because he attached great importance to a close relationship with Spain and Italy in that order. 'Spain is very important for our economic reform agenda in Europe, for which we don't have that many allies. France and Germany for example can be very difficult. We need an alliance with Aznar [Spanish PM] primarily.' He saw the whole Gibraltar question on a much wider canvas of Spain as an emerging power in Europe, close to ourselves in driving forward a common European agenda, both of us united in opposition to a European super-state, but cooperating together on an intergovernmental basis at the core of Europe. Tony didn't want Gibraltar as an obstacle to that important agenda.

‡

Caruana was not only unwilling to go out on a limb at home – so rigid, inflexible and reactionary was opinion on the Rock – he was also bolstered by shrill support in the British conservative media and amongst an influential group in Parliament. There were MPs – Labour and Conservative – who acted and spoke as Government of Gibraltar apparatchiks. Once, when I had to answer a Commons debate in Westminster Hall on Gibraltar, the chairman (rather belatedly advised by the clerk) asked the MPs present to declare their interest. They all stood up to a man declaring free trips to the Rock, some barely concealed holidays. One right-wing Tory backbencher, Andrew Rosindell, was out of the Ark. 'Why can't you just reintegrate Gibraltar and make it part of England?' he asked.

It was hardly surprising, therefore, as the winter of 2001 drew on, that Caruana continued playing hard to get. He wrote a long, detailed, lawyer-like letter to Jack Straw, setting his conditions for joining the negotiations in 'safety and dignity', doubtless expecting the traditional flat rejection from Madrid. Instead he was granted unprecedented concessions by the Spanish government, giving him virtually all he wanted. But when it quickly became clear that, for Joe Bassano and others, Caruana's participation in the very direct negotiations they had all long demanded would be a hanging offence, he understandably if frustratingly refused to come.

But they had not before dealt with Foreign Office Ministers like Jack Straw and me who were not going to be pushed around, jump to attention, or fall over every time they said no, or issued another one of their histrionic demands. So I began to consider a fresh approach. We would quietly continue the official-to-official negotiations with Madrid, which were going very well under the leadership of Emyr Jones Parry, not at all the caricature of a toffee-nose, instead probably the best negotiator in the Foreign Office. But I thought back to Northern Ireland when the then British Prime Minister, John Major, and the Irish Taoiseach, Albert Reynolds, signed the joint Downing Street Declaration in 1993, aimed at breaking a negotiating impasse. It was a water-shed and eventually led to Tony Blair's Good Friday peace settlement in 1998. Given that Caruana wouldn't come to the table and that the negotiations with Spain were going very well, I proposed we outflank Gibraltarian intransigence with a joint British–Spanish declaration. It would be contained within a White Paper to be endorsed by vote both in the British Parliament and the Spanish *Cortes*. Madrid was enthusiastic and we proceeded to iron out legalities and details in a growing consensus around a substantial and detailed document.

Despite his obstinacy I continued to talk with Caruana over the phone from time to time and then early in 2002 had him to a pleasant lunch at Lancaster House with two of his deputies, explaining the plan we had in mind based on four pillars. The first was the preservation of Gibraltar's traditional way of life, from a pint of beer to British citizenship. The second was full cooperation by Spain, an end to all the aggravation suffered by Gibraltarians which had even included stopping football matches, dog shows and pigeon races. The third was full self-government and the abolition of the Governor – the full devolution of powers Gibraltar had long sought. The fourth was co-sovereignty; although I had conceived of this concept myself, I later discovered that it had been floated under the Tories, though never openly pursued with Madrid. Caruana and his colleagues fully acknowledged the enormous opportunities of such a deal for the Rock but remained trapped by obduracy at home.

However, I didn't tell him that there were still three big red lines to be resolved. The first was our insistence on retaining full British jurisdiction over NATO's strategically important defence base. The Spanish argued that would imply British sovereignty over what was effectively forty per cent of the territory. But they readily conceded there must be full British operational control. So the question was how to formulate that. The second red line was Madrid's demand that this co-sovereignty settlement should be an 'interim' one towards the Spanish claim to the sovereignty they had painfully ceded in the War of Succession 300 years ago. As I told Ramón de Miguel, this 'slippery slope' to full Spanish sovereignty was impossible for us. I wouldn't have agreed to it, we wouldn't have got Parliament's backing and certainly we wouldn't have got it through a referendum on the Rock. The third red line was the Spanish proposal that they should identify Gibraltar in their constitution as a defined region of Spain, which was again unacceptable. Madrid's problem was one of political optics: they knew full well that Spanish sovereignty was out of the question but alleged that if they were to shelve their historic claim they might not get it through *their* Parliament. I didn't buy that because the socialist opposition – whom we kept privately informed – supported our objectives. Nevertheless we kept negotiating to find a solution to these three obstacles, the Spanish Foreign Minister Piqué arguing that they would have to be elevated to Prime Ministers Aznar and Blair to resolve.

I didn't often get face time with Tony and grabbed the opportunity on 15 February 2002 when I flew with him on a small RAF plane for a day trip to Rome to attend an Italian–British summit with the Italian Prime Minister, Silvio Berlusconi. Because of Berlusconi's right-wing policies and his colourful reputation, the summit attracted controversy. I was offended by Berlusconi's politics but nevertheless intrigued to meet him as my job required. At a palatial venue we had three hours of discussions mostly on a terrace over a sumptuous lunch, food piled lavishly high in a small mountain between the two teams. Berlusconi seemed surprisingly progressive about Africa. But, in the middle of talking about European economic reform – the main purpose of the event being to agree an alliance against the Franco-German one which had dominated European politics for generations – he egocentrically lurched off into a rant about Italy's judges. 'They are all communists! I am not a criminal,' he complained to a bemused Blair, who smiled considerably but said nothing.

On the flight back Tony was enthusiastically on board over Gibraltar. 'It is really important to get a better future for Gibraltar, to secure a better relationship with Spain and to remove it as an obstruction to our relations within Europe,' he said. He was contemptuous of Gibraltarian attitudes and insistent upon making a deal which could move the whole situation forward. Subsequently, he told Parliament of his full support for an agreement around co-sovereignty.

Meanwhile the Conservatives were ramping up their opposition, Michael Ancram, the Shadow Foreign Secretary, leading the attack. Ancram opportunistically turned his back on the pragmatic stance taken by his party in government, and effectively acted as a crude mouthpiece for Caruana and Gibraltar.

Caruana, having first failed to derail the Brussels process talks, had also failed to prevent us proceeding with our planned joint agreement, and now pressed forward with his own referendum. However, he was unaware that the draft agreement envisaged a second stage of dialogue and negotiation, engaging directly with the Gibraltar government on the detail before proceeding with legislation. Once residents on the Rock had a chance to read in black and white the huge advantages to them, perhaps attitudes might change. Some in the business community, including the prominent and influential Gaggero family, could see the enormous economic potential, so much so that Caruana pressured them not to meet me. Although a number defied his edict and came privately, many pulled out, aware of the intolerance that would be shown in the claustrophobic community on the Rock.

One leading business figure came to me with an exciting idea of a 'Euro Hub'. It was to turn Algeciras harbour and Gibraltar into probably the most important container and harbour port in the whole of southern Europe, ideally placed for both the Atlantic and Mediterranean. He knew that this would not be possible unless we got an agreement with Spain. I used this example to explain the enormous potential a co-sovereignty agreement offered to various groups and individuals from the Rock, including a trade union delegation. But most were hostile to our position, sometimes vehemently so.

The next stage of the strategy was to get European Union backing and I suggested a supportive statement by the European Council, which was achieved at its meeting in Barcelona in March 2002. It also promised to underpin a settlement with additional European Union finance – potentially tens of millions of euros to develop the airport for the whole of southern Spain and the Euro Hub project. Then, after I spoken to a number of key MEPs, the European Parliament overwhelmingly adopted a supportive resolution against lonely opposition from the Tories. So there was a whole set of building blocks – all that was needed was to reach a final agreement. I set in place preparations for the planned White Paper (containing an appendix covering all the familiar issues from opening up Algeciras harbour to making the airport a major strategic one for the region) to be flown out by an RAF plane and distributed to the 25,000 people of Gibraltar immediately it was published so that they knew exactly what was proposed rather than the spin their weak politicians would put on it.

By this time I had become a hate figure on the Rock, the target of angry posters and speeches, taking me back over thirty years to the time when I was stopping apartheid rugby and cricket tours. Yet Gibraltarians were also schizophrenic. On the one hand they wanted the great bulk of what the agreement promised – particularly an end to Spanish aggravation and significant new opportunities – but immediately I pointed out that we had already secured all these and more in the negotiations, they just pooh-poohed them, returning to express an intense and bitter hatred of co-sovereignty. Objectively, this knee-jerk reaction made no sense at all. In modern Europe with open borders, with no change in their lifestyle – except for the better – with their British identify safeguarded, they would each have much more freedom and security from an historically predatory Spain. They remained rigidly wedded to their idea of 'Britishness' in a totally artificial sense, both because they would remain British citizens if they wished anyway and because sovereignty cannot be exercised in any realistic way unless there is an ability to do so – and, in many crucial ways, the 'sovereignty' of those on the Rock was hemmed in by Spanish intransigence.

On 18 April 2002 I flew to Madrid for a full day's negotiations on a draft text. It was a really tough negotiating session over our three red lines. I had a text on the defence base which I was willing to share. But I didn't want to fall for the Spanish negotiating trick of revealing your hand when you hadn't closed off the other matters. We expected a thorny and inconclusive outcome to the meeting. How wrong we were. During six hours of intense and difficult talks, including as ever a splendid lunch, I was tougher than I'd ever been with the Spanish – not gratuitously so, but simply to make it clear that if they wanted the prize of an agreement, our red lines had to be respected. I conceded some minor word changes. Then, to our astonishment, as the evening arrived, we realised we had a full agreement including on the defence base, where they had been trying it on (senior Ministry of Defence officials later shown the text were delighted with it). They conceded a referendum on Gibraltar would have to occur (their worry had been establishing a precedent for the Basques) and accepted co-sovereignty could not open the door to full Spanish sovereignty.

We shook hands not quite believing our governments had managed to come together on Gibraltar for the first time in 300 years. Ramón de Miguel was delighted. However, I noticed that Ricardo Dietz Hochleitner, his hard-liner who had been uneasy throughout the session, looked stunned. We rushed off to catch our flight back, celebrating with a beer at the airport, still pinching ourselves over a glass of champagne on the plane. 'You played it brilliantly,' said Emyr Jones Parry – praise indeed coming from him. Jack Straw was also pleased.

However, there was a final twist when we landed in London. I got into the car and switched on my mobile to find a message from Peter Torry, the British Ambassador: Dietz Hochleitner had got straight to the Foreign Minister,

Josep Piqué, and the whole thing had begun to unravel. José María Aznar had wobbled at the last minute. Carlos Basterreche had phoned Stephen Wall, the PM's Europe adviser while we were in the air, to apologise and explain. Just as we were surprised to have concluded the agreement that day, now it was being tantalisingly vetoed by Madrid, its conservative, nationalist government getting cold feet at the last moment. I was deeply disappointed and so was Ramón de Miguel: we had negotiated toughly and in good faith. He soon phoned himself, embarrassed, apologising profusely. Several years later, he said ruefully to me, shaking his head: 'Aznar and Piqué made a huge mistake of historic proportions.' He appreciated the supreme irony that it was Madrid which came to the aid of Caruana.

Things went downhill after that. A week later we got a sudden summons to Downing Street to discuss Gibraltar. Although Tony had backed us fully all the way, he was clearly relieved to have been let off the hook by Aznar because he had had an angry delegation from pro-Gibraltar Labour MPs. 'We are not going to be able to strike a deal at this moment because the Spanish aren't ready for it. Trying to reopen their historic claim is not on. We should just park the agreement, allow things to settle down, allow opinion in Gibraltar to realise that co-sovereignty is the way we are going, and allow Spain to realise that this deal remains on the table.' Jack and I tried to argue with him but to no avail.

With the Gibraltarians realising there was an impasse and cock-a-hoop, Jack felt he had to visit the Rock, where he was almost violently attacked by a baying mob, rescued just at the point when the visit almost ran out of control. Although badly shaken he admirably returned even more determined to proceed with my proposal to publish what we had agreed because, despite containing several key elements on which Madrid had resiled, it would confront Gibraltarian paranoia head on. By demonstrating that a British government was no longer prepared to be blocked by their unreasonable obstinacy, publishing would fundamentally change the political landscape. The Gibraltarians would never be able to go back, because from that point co-sovereignty would be the established terrain from which to move forward.

At one point Tony looked as if he was willing to publish as we both recommended – then, right at the end of May he made it clear he wasn't. Because Madrid had resiled, Tony didn't want Gibraltar interfering with the difficult European debate due to come to a climax over the year ahead, both over the euro assessment and the outcome of the Convention on the Future of Europe. Gibraltar had the capacity to stir a lot of anti-European sentiment.

However, Jack Straw and I still had one card to play. In a surprise statement to the House of Commons on Friday morning 12 July 2002, he announced:

'After twelve months of negotiations, we are now closer than ever before to overcoming 300 years of fraught history and securing a satisfactory outcome to a process established nineteen years ago by the Conservative government. We and Spain are in broad agreement on many of the principles that should underpin a lasting settlement. They include the principles that Britain and Spain should share sovereignty over Gibraltar including the disputed territory of the isthmus; that Gibraltar should have more internal self-government; that Gibraltar should retain its British traditions, customs and way of life; that Gibraltarians should retain the right to British nationality, and should gain the right to Spanish nationality as well; that Gibraltar should retain its institutions – its government, House of Assembly, courts and police service; and that Gibraltar could, if it chose, participate fully in the European Union single market and other EU arrangements. We had hoped to reach agreement with Spain by the summer, but I have also made clear many times that no deal is better than a bad deal. There have been distinct 'red lines' throughout this process.' The Tories and the usual suspects on our own back benches were livid, repeatedly interrupting with shouts of 'shame', 'surrender' and 'sell-out', their own interventions full of bluster. Beside himself with rage, Peter Caruana was apoplectic that we had had the temerity to place the co-sovereignty policy of Her Majesty's Government on the record in Parliament.

Although deeply disappointed to have come so tantalisingly close to an historic breakthrough, I felt proud of trying to make a difference, trying to get to the bottom of such a difficult and sticky problem rather than just coasting along the traditional diplomatic route. I don't regret what we did or the personal flak that I took in ensuring that, at the very least, co-sovereignty will always remain part of the future political architecture for Gibraltar. In time, I believe, serious thinking on the Rock will come to see it not as a threat but as a liberating opportunity.

Caruana's much-vaunted referendum took place on 7 November 2002 with a resounding No vote of 17,900 (98.48 per cent) to 187 (1.03 per cent), on a turnout of 87.9 per cent. It was a curious affair because there was no deal on the table to assess – simply defiance of the very notion of co-sovereignty without knowing what it meant in a draft treaty which had not been revealed. It was also despite what Peter Caruana had admitted to me in a friendly chat in a reception after the Queen Mother's funeral earlier that year.

'Actually co-sovereignty will make no practical difference to daily life on Gibraltar except to make it easier and better,' I told him.

'I agree with you, Peter,' he replied. 'But that's not the point!'

A telling response, revealing in a nutshell why the whole issue was so bedevilled by myths, history, emotions and prejudice.

When I became Secretary of State for Wales in October 2002, the *Gibraltar Chronicle* ecstatically greeted my promotion with a front page headline: 'Hain booted out into Cabinet.'

‡

Whether Britain can ever become a true 'insider' and leader in Europe is doubtful, so long as our deeply ingrained scepticism always seems to triumph. Even Tony Blair's government – the most pro-European ever – was in a constant battle with the media and with a large section of the public. And we weren't assisted at all by the frustrating habit of the 'Brussels bubble' to indulge in constant navel contemplation: self-indulgently looking always to integrate rather than to deliver, in the process opening up a gulf between its citizens and undermining Labour's pro-Europeanism.

I still want Europe to play a powerful global role. The European Union contributes over half the world's overseas aid. We negotiate as equals with the US over international trade. But our foreign and security policy has been largely ineffectual. My memory of attending European Foreign Ministers' councils was of various countries' Foreign Ministers stating their points, rushing outside to repeat them in ringing tones to the waiting microphones, telling domestic audiences what they wanted to hear, but finding afterwards that nothing would come from an agreed resolution. For Europe to punch its weight in global diplomacy will require a mindshift from '*resolutionary*' diplomacy to *serious* diplomacy.

The full-time President and single Foreign Representative in the treaty which did eventually emerge from the convention could help position Europe to be a serious global force: not so much a rival for the US as a force to be reckoned with by the US. For the foreseeable future, the US will be the only super-power. But China will increasingly assert itself, not just economically as it already has, but diplomatically. So will India, with Russia remaining an important force. In this emerging multi-polar world Europe has a crucial and potentially pivotal role to play, I hope, as a force for progressive internationalism.

CHAPTER NINE

MANDARINS, MINISTERS AND MEDIA

Nobody had taught me how to be a Minister. Although during the 1997 election campaign I had read Gerald Kaufman's instructive if somewhat satirical book,* I relied upon my own experience, instincts and political values. Crucially important for an incoming Minister is to have a plan. Otherwise, the rivate office, diligent and supportive though I found all of mine, quickly takes over, filling the diary and prompting busy hours of worthily processing papers and shuffling between meetings. Most important is to arrive on the first day with a sense of political priorities, even if the detail needs to be filled in. Otherwise even the most able Ministers find themselves running to keep up.

Many in our ministerial cadre, particularly though not exclusively below Cabinet level, seemed more captured by their departments than not. However, Charles Clarke was a notable exception. In 2000, when we were both Ministers of State, he in the Home Office, I in the Foreign Office, we had a meeting to discuss getting retired police officers to help with the transition from military peacekeeping to local civilian security, especially in African conflict zones. My officials had been frustrated by lack of cooperation from their Home Office counterparts and recommended a ministerial meeting to resolve the impasse.

Often on such occasions, a ministerial colleague would regurgitate their brief and the meeting would end, with officials happily going off to do what they love doing: reflect, write a fresh paper and prepare for another meeting. But Charles arrived, plonked his burly frame on my office sofa, eyed up the grand old colonial surroundings, and politely interrupted my opening remarks. 'Peter, I have looked at this carefully – and I completely agree with you!' His officials looked more startled than mine. 'Now shall we tell them all to work out the details as quickly as they can, and let's discuss some politics.' As the room emptied, we reflected upon what proved to be a common perspective on the shortcomings and successes of the Blair government and how to make it better. How refreshing it was to deal with Charles – a huge talent and a good man, if at times rather too brusquely self-confident for his own good.

It is pointless being a Minister unless you are prepared give political leadership. Although the legendary *Yes Minister* television series, where civil servants

---

* Gerald Kaufman, *How to Be a Minister* (London, Faber & Faber, 1997).

run rings around their hapless Minister, comes uncomfortably close to the mark, my experience was rather different. Officials, I found, valued strong political leadership and direction – Ministers who knew their own minds – provided they were willing to take advice. The best private secretaries ensured delivery of my ministerial decisions while keeping a wary eye for propriety and telling me things I might not want to hear. The best officials had a 'can do' rather than a 'can't do' attitude, and if the civil service only adopted that motto as the norm it would be massively more efficient and immeasurably better at delivery.

Occasionally officials would have to carry out decisions with which they disagreed. For instance, in 1998, after a complicated negotiation to resolve a previously intractable problem to establish a much-needed new European rail freight terminal at Cardiff, the permanent secretary, Rachel Lomax, threatened she would require a 'Direction' from the Secretary of State if we wanted to proceed against her advice – a pretty serious matter. Although we got on well and I admired her as a breath of fresh air in the rather old-fashioned 'can't do' culture in the Welsh Office, I thought she was plain wrong. So I pressed on, accepting minor concessions which allowed her to back down gracefully, and the freight terminal went ahead.

In contrast to my old friend from Labour left days, Chris Mullin, who seemingly detested being a Minister,* I felt it was a real privilege being in government, constantly reminding myself of the debt I owed to those many unsung heroes of the labour and trade union movement who leafleted and knocked doors whether in the wind, rain, heat or cold. But, by comparison with the Foreign Office, the Department of Trade and Industry when I arrived in January 2001 had a slightly backwater feel – strange for such an important department. Few of the officials, though mostly good to work with, were of the same calibre. On the other hand, it was stimulating to be thrust straight back into the thick of domestic politics. My new remit concerned bread- and butter-issues affecting my constituents. With votes at stake, fellow MPs were much more closely engaged than most were on foreign affairs.

My in-tray was bulging with unresolved problems. The compensation scheme for former miners injured at work was a mess. Its remit had been established by a court judgment and officials took refuge in that whenever I challenged a policy or procedure. Bristling with lawyers, the scheme was a bureaucratic nightmare. Terrible press coverage in the regions and nations, focusing upon personal stories of anomalies and injustices aplenty – as I knew only too well from my own coalfield constituency – meant I had to sort out the politics as well as reform the scheme.

---

*   Chris Mullin, *A View from the Foothills* (London, Profile Books, 2009).

Pretty soon it was evident what reforms were urgently needed, including speeding up and simplifying the medical assessment and payments procedures. Officials were very reluctant to take these forward until they realised I was insistent. My approach was to be firm but simultaneously to maintain good relations with each key official, showing respect and sympathy while forcing them to accept change. Throughout my twelve years as a Minister, I don't recall shouting at anybody. Officials who had made a mistake – and there were some howlers – were invariably distraught, their professionalism stained. What was the point of throwing a tantrum or screaming at them? That wasn't me anyway.

While driving necessary reforms, I decided the best way to deal with hostile local or regional media was to undertake regional tours to coal community areas. I asked my press officer to fix an advance interview (normally with the Westminster-based correspondent of the relevant regional newspaper, who was usually keen to get a story). This was a technique I adopted first as Foreign and then Europe Minister, in those cases with London correspondents. The aim was for publication on the morning of my visit. Journalists liked being 'ahead' of the story and for me it served as an agenda setter. (In 2002 on a visit to Stockholm, the Swedish Foreign Minister, Anna Lindt,* told me her Prime Minister had commented admiringly on a prominent interview in the main morning paper. He was curious as to how I had achieved it: the local media normally took no notice of a routine visit by a Europe Minister).

On these mining tours I tried to present myself as a 'change' Minister, accepting not all was right and expressing a determination to reform, disarming critics but being careful not to criticise my predecessor. The *South Wales Argus*, for instance, had been running an aggressive campaign with searing stories of former miners sick, in pain, waiting for their money. To the paper's delight and surprise, I backed its campaign, pledged to put things right and congratulated the paper for persuading the government. Within several months we had turned the issue around, the payments had started flowing and the media began to report former miners receiving their cheques (some as large as £100,000). By the time the general election was called four months into the job, Labour MPs like me were able to go onto the front foot and publicise achievements for the miners rather than be stranded on the back foot over criticisms.

During this period, and against official advice, I fixed to meet Arthur Scargill, by now a nostalgic miners' leader rather than a contemporary one. The issue was payments owed to women workers in pit canteens after an

---

* Tragically she was murdered in a Stockholm department store in 2003, perhaps the brightest European star of her generation.

equal pay ruling bringing them into line with male pit bath attendants. For over twenty-four years, Scargill had refused to negotiate seriously because he considered the amounts being offered derisory. But, after all this time, the women wanted a settlement and I wanted to deliver it. Scargill came to my office, cutting a rather sad figure, his eyesight failing. Perhaps because we had known each other before, and because I treated him with respect, he quickly began to talk turkey. I suggested we converse one to one, my officials nervously filing out. The basis for a settlement was soon clear and I showed him possible figures under which the women would receive an average of £12,000, some as much as £40,000, in lump sums, because the department had set aside funding. He later tried to wriggle out of our agreement – he preferred being oppositional to negotiating the best possible outcome – but I decided to pay out the money anyway and gave the *Daily Mirror* the story before he put his negative slant on it. Labour was acclaimed for righting what I described in the media on 25 April 2001 as a 'long-running injustice'.

Another urgent problem dumped upon my lap by the Prime Minister was a month to ensure the smooth introduction of ultra-low-sulphur petrol (ULSP) to coincide with the Budget. However it was soon apparent to me that this was not possible. Significant bottlenecks and shortages would be likely at hypermarkets, politically contentious on the eve of a general election widely talked about for early May. The last thing we could countenance was a price rise at the pump, especially after disruptive fuel protests six months before.

There were several possible options, the one I came to favour a price reduction on all petrol on Budget day, but with that reduction phased out when ULSP became universally available, probably in mid-May, and alone attracted the reduction. Downing Street was understandably breathing down my neck and I prepared the very detailed note they asked for, canvassing several options and recommending the one I thought best. But the Treasury were not happy about us putting these three options to the Prime Minister: it was their prerogative to do so because they had sole responsibility for tax matters. So I had to indulge in some subterfuge with Geoff Norris, Tony's business adviser, who suggested along with Stephen Byers, my Secretary of State, that I remove the three options from the formal note that went over to the Prime Minister, which seemed pretty pointless to me, because he wasn't getting the clear advice which he had requested. Instead I copied the original note with my favoured recommendation to Norris separately so that he could then put it with a covering note on the formal paper for the Prime Minister, ensuring he was fully in the picture. I then wrote a note to Gordon Brown at the suggestion of his special adviser, Ed Balls, analysing the situation but saying that these duty issues were a matter for him. All the proprieties were respected, the

Prime Minister got the information he needed while the Treasury felt its nose hadn't been put out of joint. Such were the manoeuvrings necessary to overcome egos and 'departmentalitis' rife within Whitehall, the Treasury by far the worst offender.

Replacing the flawed and outdated 'electricity pool' with a more modern system of determining the price paid to electricity generators was a further hot potato. The reform would undoubtedly make for a better system, but it was hugely complex matter and Downing Street was naturally concerned to avoid a consumer price hike on the eve of an election. Stephen Byers was very cautious, and the decision had been repeatedly postponed. However when I realised that the market was anticipating a lower forward price on the basis of the reform – without which prices would leap – it seemed like a no-brainer. The problem was to get the detail right, which required considerable attention. It was a case of focusing on outcomes, not getting bogged down in impenetrable technicalities served up by layers of experts (and which, to be frank, I hardly grasped). Once I was clear in my mind about the central choices, I recommended to a somewhat sceptical No. 10 and Secretary of State that we press ahead. Although I was relieved that they backed my judgement, it was still rather a gamble whichever way it went, though the fact that doing nothing would certainly trigger price rises proved decisive for me. Fortunately, the transition to the new system went like clockwork. My only strong regret was that the design (which it was too late to change fundamentally) tended to penalise small and mostly renewable energy generation.

‡

Maintaining a grip on the ministerial brief involved striking a balance between the routine and the significant. My twelve years in government suggested several lessons. Around 80 per cent of the pile of papers and files in your in-tray or red box were straightforward and could in principle have been handled by the departmental machine. You needed to keep a weather eye on this bulk because it might contain elephant traps, plain mistakes, or in the case of letters to MPs what I called 'piss-off' messages couched in turgid prose by drafting officials blissfully oblivious to the impact. You couldn't simply sign off this material even if tired or late at night. However, for me doing the job successfully meant focusing laser-like on the twenty per cent where a difference really can be made. I also 'did my red boxes overnight', keeping on top of the workload, leaving more time to prioritise and focus on the politics.

Once in the Cabinet I was entitled to two special advisers (SpAds): political appointees required to comply with civil service rules. They were essential to drive forward my political objectives, keep in touch with the media and to ensure officials were not acting as a drag anchor. The role of SpAds attracted much irrational chatter and criticism in the media – and by opposition parties until they got into power, realised the indispensable benefits and appointed the same number as we had done. The most effective had sharp political antennae, prepared to be tough on my behalf and yet able to get on with officials, some of whom resented the role.

I was fortunate in my choice of SpAds, all able, hard working and loyal.* Phil Taylor, with me almost throughout, was one of the best, dedicated, super-bright, with an acute political brain and a nose for coping with the spin of the modern media. He could be confrontational – sometimes 'hard cop' to my 'soft cop' – which provoked complaints from officials (and the odd one from Ministers in my teams). But his record of achievement was clear, for instance helping me to drive forward reform across sleepy departments in Northern Ireland resentful of ministerial direction. However, the longer we were in power, the more I noticed the tendency for new SpAds of Cabinet colleagues to be technocratic rather than political: a big mistake, perhaps reflecting how Labour became increasingly managerial rather than missionary. It was also curious how most – but not all – of the SpAds in the Welsh government after devolution operated in an almost apolitical manner.

‡

One of the delights of being Energy Minister was prioritising renewable energy in a way that had not been the case before. As a committed 'green', this was close to my heart and one incident had a broader resonance for the minister–mandarin relationship. Officials recommended I accept an invitation to visit a dynamic company called Solar Century, specialising in solar and photovoltaic panels. I happily agreed, mentioning we would need to generate media coverage to signal increased government commitment; yes, yes, nodded officials. A fortnight later when I asked what we were going to announce to ensure the visit made an impact, the answer was nothing. In that case, I was not going. This provoked consternation. If there is one thing officials prefer over writing papers for Ministers, it's arranging visits for Ministers. I stuck to my guns, sensing the stand-off might produce action. 'But there is no money available to announce more government support for solar,' they pleaded. I still wasn't shifting.

---

* At different stages, Andrew Bold, Matthew Burchell, Joe Carberry, Dan Lodge, Claire McCarthy, Rob Philpot, Greg Power, David Taylor, Phil Taylor.

Finally, with the as yet uncancelled visit embarrassingly close, officials came to see me. They had discovered surplus funds in an obscure research unit burrowed away in the depths of the department. A couple of scholarly-looking types were ushered in, seeming surprised at being allowed out, telling me they had never met a Minister before. We were, after all, able to announce an additional £3 million of support for domestic solar installations. The visit went ahead to acclamation in the renewable energy sector and the green movement that maybe our government was after all on their side – an incremental advance in the fight against climate change.

Five years later as Secretary of State in Northern Ireland, I ensured the installation of the first marine current turbine in the UK. It was sited in Strangford Loch to take advantage of the fierce-flowing currents there. But like many things new, there was a mother and father of battles with environmental officials who did all they could to foil the project. Only determination and Phil Taylor's relentless eye for detail in overcoming various blocking manoeuvres by officials ensured it was eventually installed.

Another personal ministerial cause was complementary medicine. Our first son Sam was born with eczema. Later, he developed asthma too. At first, we relied on conventional treatments. Various creams were prescribed and a steroidal spray. But they didn't work. In fact, the spray seemed to make him worryingly and unhealthily even more dependent on it. So instead, we turned to complementary medicine. And, with the help of homeopathy and tight restrictions on the sort of food that he could eat – avoiding in particular gluten and milk products – both ailments went away. This experience will be familiar to some parents whose children have health problems. Indeed, 90 per cent of patients seeking homeopathic treatment only do so after the failure of conventional medicine to achieve results. We had reached a point of desperation, and I only became a true convert to complementary medicine after seeing the difference it made to my son, subsequently becoming a regular user myself.

Although one in five Britons use complementary remedies of one sort or another – from reflexology and aromatherapy massage to nutrition and osteopathy – civil servants and the medical establishment remained deeply resistant. I unsuccessfully tried as a Welsh Minister in 1997–9, and then as Secretary of State for Wales from 2002, to persuade Welsh Labour Health Ministers to advance the cause. Yet a report published in 2005 by Christopher Smallwood highlighted a wide range of available research and case studies demonstrating the value of alternative medicine. In one of the case studies, 85 per cent of patients reported an improvement in their condition, with more than half showing a marked improvement.

Furthermore, the Smallwood report highlighted the potential of complementary healthcare to reduce costs to the NHS. In one example, when patients were treated with complementary therapies, there was a thirty per cent drop in GP consultations and a fifty per cent saving on prescriptions. It was a serious piece of research, written by a hard-headed economist with a tough-minded and independent approach.

Yet the medical establishment remained stubbornly conservative – as defenders of the existing paradigm have always done throughout the history of science, until, that is, a new way of thinking has proven its worth. I recalled from my university studies how Thomas Kuhn described this phenomenon in his book.* In all scientific disciplines, the conventional paradigm stubbornly survives, its expert advocates defending it bitterly to the very end against the upstart alternative, until suddenly it is overthrown in favour of that very alternative.

However, neither I nor any supporters of complementary healthcare have suggested that it should somehow supplant all conventional treatments. For many serious diseases, like cancer, only conventional therapies are powerful enough to provide the life-saving treatment. The same is true of serious infections and limb breakages. But complementary therapies used in conjunction with conventional medicine can both aid recovery and enhance the overall wellbeing of the patient. For example, breaking a leg requires surgery, but taking mineral supplements and homeopathic remedies like arnica can support the patient's own healing process, and enhance the effectiveness of conventional treatment.

Frustrated at resistance from government colleagues and officials, my opportunity to do something came in Northern Ireland when I was Secretary of State between 2005 and 2007 and quite literally in charge of everything there. For the first and only time in twelve years as a government Minister, I had the power to integrate complementary and conventional medicine within the NHS.

Against sniffy resistance from officials and medics, I established a special £200,000 fund for a two-year pilot enabling GPs (if they chose) to refer patients to complementary therapists for free treatment on the NHS. This was a substantial amount given the small population there, and equivalent to around £6 million across England. The results were very clear. Sixty-five per cent of participating GPs thought their patients' health had improved. The same proportion reported they had seen their patients less often since their referral. Fifty-five per cent of patients took fewer painkillers and 45 per cent less conventional medication. GPs also reported sharp reductions in patient

---

*   Thomas S. Kuhn, *The Structure of Scientific Revolutions* (University of Chicago Press, 1962).

use of other NHS services. Patients were assessed by their GPs to be generally better and the costs for the NHS were significantly lower. My pilot had wider benefits for the economy, as 64 per cent had less time off work. The patients themselves were even clearer. According to an official report in May 2008 for Northern Ireland's Department of Health, 80 per cent of patients recorded an improvement in the severity of their main symptom and 73 per cent an improvement in their level of activity associated with the main symptom. About 80 per cent said their general health, wellbeing and physical health had improved.

The report also recommended extending the pilot more widely right across Northern Ireland, but sadly this did not happen. When I argued in Cabinet during a health policy discussion that we should encourage complementary medicine on the NHS, Tony Blair was interested and supportive. But the then Secretary of State, John Reid, replied dismissively as if it was a middle-class fetish: 'Peter's proposal sounds more like Islington than Islwyn.' Later on, and just before he was moved from being Secretary of State for Health in 2009, I persuaded Alan Johnson to launch a similar pilot in England. But after his departure it was long-grassed by officials and only reluctantly resurrected when I also persuaded his more sceptical successor Andy Burnham to progress it, until the idea once again disappeared when Labour lost the election in 2010. The Northern Ireland pilot remained the first government-led example of the successful integration of healthcare on the NHS in the UK (a handful of local health trusts did allow it). I felt both sectors could and should co-exist in the NHS, with the patient the winner.

‡

Integrated healthcare generated a strong alliance with His Royal Highness the Prince of Wales. Prince Charles was the most prominent advocate, and we quickly found common cause when we met at Highgrove, his home in Gloucestershire, on a formal introduction as Secretary of State for Wales. It was an unlikely alliance between the heir to the throne and a Cabinet Minister who had never been a monarchist.

Prince Charles always replied to my regular notes to him on the state of Wales. Sometimes he sent letters in his own handwriting and I got used to his observations in thick black ink spread over several pages, headed 'Dear Peter' and signed 'Yours ever, Charles'. One of these expressed his upset when I left government: he wrote that I was the one Cabinet Minister he had encountered over the years who fully understood how important a role integrated health-care could play, including assisting people who suffered unnecessarily under the conventional system. He also expressed the hope that the Northern Ireland pilot scheme might continue and expand.

I always found him easy to talk to, even if his manner sometimes seemed from a past era. But I could not bring myself to obey mandarin guidance to call him 'Sir' or 'Your Royal Highness'. Better not, I found, to call him anything during our conversations. Despite our very different backgrounds, we always got along well. He had a good sense of humour and was well informed, if from an establishment perspective. Her Royal Highness the Duchess of Cornwall was good company. Eyes twinkling, she had a mischievous streak and very evidently made him happy, as Elizabeth and I saw when they kindly invited us on our own to dinner at his London residence, Clarence House. They were interested to hear that I had used homeopathic remedies for malaria and yellow fever on ministerial visits to Africa instead of the usual prophylactics, and about how my private secretary had contracted shingles after a jarring car accident; sceptical initially, but desperate for something to work because none of the conventional medicines had been effective, she was only cured after a friendly practitioner in my Neath constituency recommended a herbalist in Ireland.

Prince Charles did, however, have one major disagreement – over hunting with hounds. Legislation to ban it was taken through Parliament in 2004 while I was Leader of the Commons. Although strongly backed by animal lovers, it was highly controversial. During one of our conversations, the Prince suddenly brought up the subject, explaining his support for hunting, very exercised. 'It's a great British tradition,' he said, leaning forward, and confiding plaintively: 'Do you know, the best thing is when I join everyone afterwards at the local pub. It's my only real opportunity to meet *ordinary* people *properly*.'

As a Pretoria boy I was brought up to be polite and show respect, but not to fawn or bow. Instead I tried to find a point of proper communication beyond the habitual small talk members of the Royal Family have to endure as they meet thousands of strangers on their public engagements. I was full of admiration at how accomplished and natural were most of the Royals at this, knowing something of the pressures involved at my far less exalted level as MP and Minister. In 1999 I was asked in Robin Cook's absence to accompany the Queen to Maputo, capital of Mozambique, which, unusually for a former Portuguese colony, had just joined the Commonwealth. It seemed like her entire household was along too, numerous ladies in waiting and flunkies bearing double-barrelled names and looking disapproving. At the official dinner, stranded on the top table, the Queen at times looked lonely and bored, flanked by President Chissano and his over-awed young teenage daughter. Sitting next to the daughter I discovered she was taking school exams the next day and leant across to mention this to the Queen; evidently relieved, she began delightedly chatting with the daughter, worrying whether she would be in bed on time.

In 2000, the Queen attended a Commonwealth reception. The secretary general, Chief Emeka Anyaoku, made a special point of welcoming my parents, who had also been invited. Mom and Dad, both republicans, had accepted invitations on the basis they wouldn't be required to meet the Queen. But, mischievously, I told her they were present and she asked to meet them in an ante-room where she was receiving certain guests; they were dutifully well behaved, as they were greeting Prince Charles. Also present was Meredith Burgmann, then a senior parliamentarian in the New South Wales legislature, but when we had first met in 1971 also a militant in the anti-apartheid struggle; she was representing her country, Australia, just as I was my country, Britain; we enjoyed the irony together.

The Queen never ceased to amaze me with her patient serenity, diligence and willingness to engage. Throughout my time in government she was hardly a young woman, yet coped extraordinarily well with a relatively punishing schedule. She was pretty sharp at keeping abreast of events and politics, often using informal chat after Privy Council meetings to catch up, enjoying a bit of political gossip. On occasion, she also revealed a wicked sense of humour. As traditional, after disrobing at the end of the 2003 Queen's Speech and before departing, she shook hands with the Lord Chancellor, the Lords Chief Whip and Leader of the Commons, lined up in a little row and live on television. When it was my turn I tried to lighten what was a stuffy ritual by asking her about sitting on the throne in the Chamber and receiving the speech, handed to her by the Lord Chancellor from a special pouch. What would she have done if it had been empty? She paused for a second then, gave a conspiratorial smile: 'I would have had a cunning plan!' TV commentators and viewers wondered what the 'off-mike' amusement had been about. Her sense of mischief was also evident in Buckingham Palace at the retirement party for her private secretary, Sir Robert Janvrin, not at all the caricature of a stuffed shirt. In a witty speech he said how difficult it had been to find a suitable time to fix the occasion since the Queen was always so busy. 'And whose fault do you think *that* is?' she interjected, guests collapsing with laughter.

One of my duties as Secretary of State for Wales was to supervise recommendations to the Queen for the award of honours for Welsh citizens. At my first meeting with First Minister Rhodri Morgan and the Welsh Assembly government's honours team in December 2002, I argued – and Rhodri backed me – for Catherine Zeta Jones to receive an honour as Wales's leading international actress and Oscar winner. Over subsequent years I pressed her case repeatedly at biannual meetings about honours, but always the exasperating response came back: 'She's too young' or 'She hasn't done enough'. It baffled me. What were these old fogies, the so-called 'great and good' sitting on the Cabinet Office committees which drew up final lists for the Palace, *thinking*? Was there a prejudice against her because she was Welsh? Various English figures from the entertainment world seemed to get honours at the drop of a hat. Finally, totally frustrated, I suggested to Rhodri just before he stood down as First Minister in December 2009 that we pen a joint letter advocating her case. It was the last letter he signed before leaving office. And it seemed to have done the trick, because she duly received a well-deserved OBE in 2010. If we hadn't done that, I doubt she would have been recognised by the Queen, who was of course oblivious to the manoeuvrings.

The Queen had, it seemed to me, one the most tiresome duties to perform swearing in new Privy Counsellors or Cabinet post holders (every time you moved a Cabinet job or were newly appointed after an election the same routine was followed). Half an hour before my induction at the Palace on 18 July 2001, I had a rehearsal at the Privy Council Office at 2 Carlton Gardens. The induction procedure seemed medieval and probably was. The full ceremony was normally at Buckingham Palace (though it could be at Windsor Castle, Balmoral or Sandringham if the Queen was in residence). First you moved before the Queen and knelt awkwardly down on one knee on a footstool covered in maroon velvet and either swore on the Bible, or in my case affirmed, loyalty to Her Majesty. Then you stepped forward and knelt again on a second, slighter higher footstool and took her outstretched right hand in your right hand and kissed it (brushing your lips rather than giving her a smacker), before standing, stepping back and bowing or curtseying. When I recounted this to Neil Kinnock, he hilariously regaled me with the story of his own rehearsal: 'A camp retired admiral took me through the procedure. As I knelt down before him and made as if to kiss, I looked up and thought "No way!"'

The annual opening of Parliament by the Queen provided another inside view of the weird and wonderful ways of the British establishment, the House of Lords resplendent in pageantry. As Leader of the Commons (which had the associated title of Lord Privy Seal) I had a ringside seat with a dose of participation. On Wednesday 26 November 2003, at precisely 11.07 as instructed, I joined the Lord Chancellor, Charlie Falconer, in walking down to the foot of the Sovereign's Staircase to greet the Queen as she stepped down from the Royal Carriage. Her horses were whinnying and stamping quietly inside the Sovereign's Entrance to the Lords as she was conducted by the Lord Great Chamberlain and the Earl Marshal to the Robing Room. I then walked up to await my allotted spot in the Sovereign's Procession.

Ahead of me was a pantomime of bizarre figures I had no idea existed including: Fitzalan Pursuivant Extraordinary, Rouge Dragon Pursuivant, Maltravers Herald Extraordinary, Clarenveux King of Arms. Everyone else was wearing brightly coloured robes and, as I walked through the Royal Gallery dressed neatly in my normal dark blue suit, the great and good amongst hundreds of special guests seemed to stare and say to themselves: 'What's *he* doing here?' There again they probably didn't even notice this outsider because there were so many much more exotic insiders on parade. Behind me were the Sword of State and the Cap of Maintenance (title given to the Leader of the Lords, the first black peer to hold the title, Valerie Amos, looking regal in her red robes). Then came 'The Queen's Most Excellent Majesty' followed by, amongst many other notables, Lady of the Bedchamber, Gold Stick in Waiting (Princess Anne), Master of the Horse and the Captain of the Honourable Corps of Gentleman at Arms (Bruce Grocott, a government whip also impressively imperial in red robes and bronze helmet).

Were we in office but not in power? The grand occasion seemed to summon up that age-old question for Labour governments.

As an outsider I was not born into the pernicious British class system, and perhaps that helped me to move more easily between the very different people my role in government required. My day might begin with a royal encounter in London and end with a rowdy dinner attended by a politically incorrect speaker at one of my constituency rugby clubs. I had a good relationship with Prince Charles but also excellent ones with the leaders of protest movements. I found myself happy in the company of business leaders but also had excellent relations with trade union leaders. In Northern Ireland, holding receptions at Hillsborough Castle – by tradition there were plenty of these – I invited for the first time groups of nurses, cleaners, bus drivers, postal workers and engineers, instead of only the usual Ulster landed gentry. Although contemptuous of much of the British establishment and its toffee-nosed conservatism, I never felt cowed by or inferior to it – but then again was never fully accepted into it (which suited me fine).

My 'outsider' background did, however, come in useful in another way. Unusually for somebody in my middle-ranking position, international leaders and ministers knew me from having also been university students of the same generation in Britain at the time of the Stop the Tour campaigns in the late 1960s and 1970s. African leaders, especially, knew of my anti-apartheid role and that helped to form good friendships. After the death of the Queen Mother there was a memorial reception on 30 March 2002 in the Locarno Room at the Foreign Office which I was deputed to host until the Foreign Secretary and the Prime Minister arrived from the Westminster Abbey funeral service. I found myself talking to the Prime Minister of Saint Vincent, the President of Iceland

and the Prime Minister of New Zealand. As students each had participated in demonstrations alongside me, or had been involved in the anti-apartheid movement. When Tony Blair came over from the funeral, I mentioned this to him as an icebreaker and he enjoyed the irony, remarking to our gathering: 'I guess you were all arrested together then, were you?'

‡

Towards the end of 2001 political commentators and correspondents started talking me up as a rising star in the government, for example the veteran columnists Anthony Howard of *The Times* and Alan Watkins of the *Independent on Sunday*. Although pleasing, I was very conscious that fortunes in politics, particularly at this level, rise and fall – sometimes unexpectedly and swiftly – and tried to remain chilled rather than obsessed about my ministerial career.

Then I was driving back from a summit with the Prime Minister in February 2002 when he took a call from Alastair Campbell. It was to discuss what to do about the resignation of Jo Moore – who had been hounded as special adviser to Steven Byers ever since her notorious 'a good day to bury bad news' email on 9/11 – and the simultaneous resignation of Byers's communications chief, Martin Sixsmith, formerly a senior BBC journalist. There was a huge media furore, Tony Blair clearly at something of a loss. He said he couldn't really understand why the media were just so deranged, since it was another row which was totally peripheral to the central thrust of government policy but nevertheless encouraging a growing impression of self-inflicted unpleasantness around his administration.

Tony suggested to Alastair that they should put up for media interviews a Minister who 'had reached the top of their time and their place in government, not an up-and-coming Minister'. He had in mind somebody like Jeff Rooker, who was unlikely to be promoted, but was nevertheless a very effective Minister of State. When he put the phone down, he turned to me and said: 'I had thought of suggesting you do it, but like Charles Clarke, you're both up-and-coming and I don't really want you engaged in a battle with the media, because it would put you at odds with them at a time when that is not healthy for either of you or the government.'

On Thursday 12 June 2003 I was out in Brussels negotiating the final stages of the draft constitution for the new European Treaty after a gruelling couple of days. The previous weekend the papers had been covered with speculation about a Cabinet reshuffle. When I'd asked Sally Morgan about it, she'd indicated it might be on that Thursday, but Tony was incredibly busy so that might not be the case. Clearly something was up, however, and I wondered whether it might involve me after reports that I could be promoted.

I was busy at the time in detailed convention discussions, speaking at the plenary and in between taking Wales Office business as well by mobile phone. Then it became evident from text messages that a reshuffle had already started around midday. Phil Taylor called with the startling news that Alan Milburn, the Health Secretary, had resigned. I was amazed because he was authoritative in the Cabinet, very close to Tony and positioning himself, I thought, to take on Gordon Brown in a leadership race to succeed Tony. Indeed his special advisers had been briefing the newspapers to that effect quite consistently and he was not afraid to confront Gordon in the Cabinet. Then Tony called and I left my seat to stand on the fringe of the convention arena. He said that he wanted me to become Leader of the Commons, both a surprise and a delight to be given such a senior post. He added, however, that he wanted me to stay on as the Secretary of State for Wales – and took me aback when he referred to a new Department of Constitutional Affairs taking in the Wales Office under Charlie Falconer.

I had no idea this was coming, and immediately asked whether I'd still be answering Welsh questions, whether I'd still be taking Welsh legislation through the House of Commons. Tony didn't have a clue and hurriedly said: 'Speak to Andrew Turnbull.' The Cabinet secretary came through ten minutes later with a less obscure picture, namely that the Wales Office would come under the Department for Constitutional Affairs. However, I would stay as Secretary of State, I would head my own office, and for the purposes of policy, parliamentary and political business, nothing would change. I would remain in charge. But for the purposes of personnel matters and back office services, Wales Office staff would come under the permanent secretary of the new Department of Constitutional Affairs.

Meanwhile the news started to leak out. As usual, Downing Street had been briefing. But this time they made a spectacular bodge of communicating the reorganisation, provoking a great commotion in Wales and amongst my Welsh MP colleagues. At one point it appeared that the Secretary of State's post had been abolished, that Wales was being summarily transferred into a department under an unelected peer, Lord Falconer. The Wales Office was in turmoil, not least because staff huddled round the television first heard about it from Sky TV's Adam Boulton, who actually announced news of the office's abolition, adding: 'To be honest, they've had that coming.'

For a government supposedly excellent at communicating, this was another example of abject failure – especially if, as later transpired, it had been considered over a period rather than cobbled together at the last minute. It was further evidence of Tony Blair and his team never really giving Wales proper respect and attention, contrary to Scotland where the Secretary of State's role was pretty minimal because all primary legislation had gone to the Scottish Parliament. The role of Secretary of State for Wales remained crucial, then responsible for all Welsh primary legislation.

There was also an impression to the media of a government in some disarray at the centre, with a major Whitehall reform done on the back of an envelope. The historic post of Lord Chancellor was yanked out, creating a Lord Speaker to preside over the Lords and establishing a Supreme Court, with an independent judicial commission to appoint judges instead of the Prime Minister. These radical and progressive reforms were very welcome to reformers like me, but the whole thing was rushed out without proper explanation or expert attention. Perhaps the post-Iraq invasion fiasco was infecting No. 10's operation more deeply.

‡

All this, together with the concluding session of the European Convention, happened immediately before Elizabeth and I had planned our wedding on Saturday 14 June, in Neath. To maintain our privacy, she bought the ring without me and, since to have registered our marriage in a close community like Neath was out of the question, we did so surreptitiously in Wandsworth, near our London flat. I described myself as an author, not untrue but not fully true either, because the notice had to be displayed publicly for fifteen nervous days in February and we hadn't yet even told any of our relatives.

It was a lovely sunny day, Elizabeth rather surprising our respective mothers by (quite rightly) refusing to make the conventional vow of obedience in the local register office. The reception afterwards in the nearby Towers Hotel had been planned by my sister Sally and Elizabeth. Tables were named after South African freedom fighters, including Nelson Mandela, Walter Sisulu, Donald Woods and John Harris, especially movingly for our family and his adult son David, one of our guests. Nelson Mandela kindly sent a card and there were other South Africans there, including a surprise, our old friend and former political prisoner Hugh Lewin.

Elizabeth spoke first with great humour, setting the tone for a fun day: having been proposed to by the Secretary of State for Wales she ended up marrying the Leader of the Commons. I said I may be Leader of the House but not of *our* house. The atmosphere was terrific, with our good friend, the top Welsh broadcaster Roy Noble acting as master of ceremonies with his unique colloquial humour and inexhaustible supply of anecdotes about the Welsh

Valleys. He called in half a dozen people for short witty speeches, including Jake, my youngest son, who voluntarily rose to say how proud he was of his Dad, welcoming into the family Elizabeth – whom he called 'Queen Liz' – in a beautiful and moving little speech. It was a relaxed, enjoyable occasion, capped by a rasping vignette from the Welsh comedian Max Boyce, a constituent from up the valley in Glynneath, who ribbed everybody, not least me.

‡

Three days later I had to reply to an opposition censure motion on the reshuffle, my speech fortunately going down well despite being necessarily confrontational because we had to knock them back hard. I was concerned, because as Leader of the House I had also to be seen to speak on behalf of the whole House, not just the government. It was time of plaudits on my promotion, my marriage and the success achieved at the European Convention, with nice messages, including from friends in the media.

How quickly it can all change at the top, because this high was succeeded by a definite low. A few days later I was due to deliver the second annual Aneurin Bevan Lecture on 20 June. It had been months in planning on the chosen topic of Labour's historic role to bring about greater equality, given topicality by Peter Mandelson's remark that New Labour was 'intensely relaxed about people getting filthy rich'. The gap between rich and poor had been opening up, those at the very top receiving spectacular rises, even though we had done more to tackle poverty than any government, with a statutory minimum wage and tax credits to top up low wages and help support children. Additionally, more middle-earners – including nurses, class teachers and police constables – were being dragged into paying the top rate of tax. They were also still paying national insurance, which was capped, enabling the very rich to escape paying what amounted to an extra 10 per cent tax; those on £1 million paid a marginal tax rate of 40 per cent, those on £35,000 a marginal rate of 50 per cent. However, with all that had been happening, there was no time to consult or clear the speech and it was finalised in a rush, pitched in relatively low key, modest terms, asking a question: should the squeezed middle get a fairer deal financed by those at the very top contributing more without damaging the culture of risk taking and enterprise so crucial to generating wealth and economic success?

My special adviser Phil Taylor pre-briefed the *Daily Mirror*, which, unbeknownst to me, gave it tabloid hype: TAX THE RICH on the front page with new tables inside showing the impact of 50 and 60 per cent tax rates. I awoke in a hotel in Ewloe, north Wales, where I was on a ministerial visit, astounded to find the breakfast broadcasters leading with the story, their spin that as a senior Cabinet Minister I was demanding higher rates of tax and was on a collision course with the Prime Minister and the Chancellor. No. 10 and the Treasury were reported denying any knowledge of it and Alastair Campbell phoned around about quarter past seven. 'The media are neuralgic. What's it all about, Peter?' He was understandably grumpy, even though Phil had told No. 10 about the *Mirror* the night before. He suggested I went on the *Today* programme to try and knock it down. They took me immediately by phone from the hotel bedroom. I was firm with John Humphrys, a legend at adversarial interviews, asking why you couldn't have a sensible debate about these matters. That's all I was asking for. I hadn't suggested any specific tax rates and I was not interested in a return to the old days of tax-and-spend and punitively high tax levels (the latter points Alastair had urged me to make).

My mobile phone together with that of my Welsh press officer Alan Cummins rang incessantly in the media frenzy. Phil Taylor, by now heading back to London, was also plagued with calls. There was pandemonium, the media spinning wildly, determined that this was a government split story, insisting that I was advocating 50 or 60 per cent rates of tax despite my insistent denials: these were never in the speech text. The whole story just took off in a dreadful fashion. Sally Morgan came through saying that Tony was cross and would probably be phoning me; he later did so from Greece where he was attending a European Council meeting, with British journalists there only interested in one story: the 'tax bombshell' at home. 'You need to close this down and rewrite the speech,' he said (Tony left the rants to Gordon Brown and John Prescott). 'Be careful what you say this evening. We mustn't seem to be advocating high tax rates.' At the same time I could tell he had some sympathy for the humble question I was asking about middle incomes being treated rather unfairly.

Soon Gordon himself came through, belligerent and saying that this was playing to a Tory agenda, because they had been making a noise about too many middle earners getting into the 40 per cent tax bracket. I didn't agree with him, because in truth we had gifted the Tories an opening which we should have addressed. However, it was perfectly fair for both Tony and Gordon to insist that could not be done through an off-the-cuff speech which had not been cleared and had unexpectedly taken off like a rocket.

The key during such a media firestorm is to try to remain calm. Travelling further westward to Anglesey, I agreed to do a number of interviews for BBC, ITV and Sky, who turned up with outside broadcast units at Wylfa nuclear power station, which I was visiting. But I refused to get into their obsession with what might have happened earlier that morning between myself, No. 10

and the Treasury, and instead focused on fair taxes under Labour and unfair taxes under the Tories – not the interview they wanted but the one they got.

Meanwhile the speech had gone over to No. 10 and the Treasury and sections of it were filleted with Phil Taylor liaising as I was driven on the five-hour journey to south Wales to deliver the lecture. I was happy with the new lines that our manifesto had stated that we wouldn't raise income tax rates and that it was not my intention to suggest otherwise. But the first draft that came back from No. 10 was unacceptable, and I refused to deliver it. In these circumstances you had staffers operating under the general authority of the Prime Minister, but with their own agendas, fretting and sometimes misjudging the situation. Finally I did clear a redraft amidst frustrating patches of bad reception through mountainous mid-Wales, arriving in plenty of time on a sunny evening in Cardiff for a quick look at the revised text before I rose to speak. A pack of journalists were waiting with around six outside broadcast units. Ironically the first Aneurin Bevan lecture had been delivered by Gordon Brown.

Without all the media spin over the day, I doubt it would have received much coverage, if any. I rose, cameras clicking, the speech running live on Sky and the BBC News Channel, poking fun at the journalists and then delivering a long and serious lecture on our achievements as a government in the context of Bevan's views and his values. Although it went down pretty well with the audience, I didn't do any further interviews and didn't take any questions because I knew that journalists in the audience would be obsessed with the issues of process that fascinated them rather than any of the issues of substance that I was trying to address.

The Saturday morning coverage in the tabloids, especially the *Sun* and the *Mail*, was absolutely appalling – even going back to the 'Hain the Pain' anti-apartheid days over thirty years before. But I had phone calls from backbench colleagues like Richard Burden who said they were really pleased and when I got into the Commons lobby to vote – always a useful way of touching base – a number said 'Well done'. Reaction in the Labour Party, in Neath and the trade unions was enthusiastic.

The whole episode was obviously quite a shaker. The credibility I had earnt inside government over the European Convention especially was undermined. On the other hand I'd clearly struck a chord with the public, which made it especially uncomfortable for the government. Messages of support poured in from all sorts of different people, rich and poor. The following Sunday at my local gym in Neath, a swimming attendant, working part-time to top up his pay as a teacher said: 'I've only just gone into the 40 per cent bracket, and I don't understand why, on about £35,000 a year, I should be doing that.' My instinct that there was a real unfairness problem was confirmed by a *Daily Telegraph* poll which specifically put the questions I had asked. By two to one, there was overwhelming agreement with me that those on high incomes should contribute more and middle-income earners less to avoid entering the 40 per cent tax level. There was also public antagonism to the way that I had been 'slapped down' over what many people saw as a legitimate debate. Some in the media tried to have it both ways by criticising Gordon Brown and Tony Blair for suppressing debate when it was media spin which had turned a mild few questions into a political mega-controversy. Virtually only the *Financial Times*, the *Independent* and the *Guardian* played it reasonably straight, the *FT* with a remarkably supportive editorial. But the truth was you could not discuss issues, especially tax, in the fraught cockpit of modern media frenzy – which I should have known.

The following week's Cabinet meeting was not very comfortable. Tony asked me to pop into his room beforehand to explain that he wasn't having a go at me, but would tell the meeting that we had to find a way of having sensible discussions without these going ballistic. When the Cabinet convened he did this, very fairly. 'It is really important that we don't act in a way that could be divisive and that there are no surprises sprung on people,' he said, 'because the media are out to get us at the moment over Europe, Iraq and other matters. Everybody around the Cabinet has been in the position where you suddenly get blown out of the water by the media.'

Even the most message-cautious and careful Minister like Jack Straw faced periodic controversy over Iraq, for instance. There was some discussion around the Cabinet table and John Reid, turning to me, said: 'The point is that we had two Cabinet ministers for the previous year [he was referring of course to Clare Short and Robin Cook] who were actually briefing against the government and attacking the government from the outside. Peter obviously wasn't doing that. He was making the point that we needed to have a proper strategic discussion inside the Cabinet about such questions, which we only very seldom do.' An interesting observation because John was especially close to Tony, and he and Gordon were old foes.

Afterwards, David Blunkett, the Home Secretary, made a point of asking me personally how I was feeling. 'Pretty bruised and upset,' I replied. 'Well, don't worry, my old mate,' he said, 'there is a real problem about being unable to have a proper political debate, and we are trapped by it as a government. On the one hand you can't really have open debate about such a sensitive tax issue. On the other hand there is a clear mood out there that there ought to be something more put in front of people on such crucial issues than the slanging match on the *Today* programme and the spin journalism and confrontational debate that inevitably follows.' He also made a very public point of coming to our London wedding party; no other Cabinet colleague showed.

For the next few weeks I tried to let the fracas settle down. Within a month it had virtually disappeared as a story, as Tony Blair had told me it probably would do. It was a crazy game, this Cabinet politics: quite mercurial, up one moment, down the next, a 'rising star' in the media, then on your way out. Particularly since I had a high profile there was a fair amount of envy within the Cabinet: from both colleagues and competitors. Some were angry about the tax affair, others were irritated or saw it as a leadership bid plot, which was pure fantasy despite some loose journalist chatter. (People from time to time suggested to me I stand for leader, but I never considered that a possibility.) It was cynically seen as a bit of political positioning, notably by Jack Straw, under whom I worked amicably as Europe Minister. He had a private go at me but I stood my ground and said it had been a bit of a cock-up (I had been told by friendly Foreign Office sources that at the European Council meeting in Greece, Jack was overheard saying how this was a 'big moment' and that I 'had to be watched'). To be fair to Jack, however, he would say to your face what he felt and then move on.

However, Gordon Brown's people briefed aggressively against me. Ironically the day before the Bevan controversy, I'd seen him in Cabinet and thanked him for the pager message that he and his wife Sarah had sent us on our wedding day. Indeed he'd joked that he'd read that I'd turned my pager off and that they were worried that I hadn't got it. Gordon's values and labour movement instincts were closer to mine than Tony's. But he was not an easy person: you were either for him or against him. A formidably, and at times ferociously, strong-willed politician of exceptionally high intellect, it was often difficult to have a proper give-and-take discussion with him. He didn't easily accept a contrary view. Quite unlike Tony, Gordon seemed insecure about his dealings with colleagues.

‡

The experience of waking up in the morning and being blasted out of sight by broadcasters made me even more focused than I had been before on the problem of political spin.

Regardless of party, what I called 'the political class' was in a real bind through our failure to communicate anything properly or intelligently via a rapacious media. Being at the top of government, it was striking how little anything in print or broadcast by political journalists resembled reality and how much spin there was on most of their stories. Even the most highly respected political editors were under tremendous pressure to get a story that would create a news item, hopefully be reported by the *Today* programme, be picked up by fellow journalists and help to shape the day's news agenda. The best would sometimes be exasperated that what they judged were genuinely important stories no longer made it into even quality broadsheets, such was the modern media fad for personality, tittle-tattle and internal party conflict in reporting politics.

Top journalists have become, not spectators or observers, but players themselves. Instead of watching the game, they are on the pitch interfering and helping shape its direction and its outcome. Instead of following the agenda, the media are increasingly setting it. Instead of reporting, political journalists are increasingly spinning.

Intense competition means even broadsheets hugely over-hype. As I consistently experienced, sub-editors often wrote headlines and introductions which bore little resemblance to quoted words – and then the BBC and Sky transmitted this hype or spin as fact. The media has become a 24-hour, rolling, non-stop machine, with producers and editors of broadcast bulletins or newspapers crying out for a new angle to 'take the story on'.

Politicians respond with media grids, texts, tweets, emails and pre-briefings of announcements – anything to wrestle back control of the frenzied news agenda – so journalists respond in kind by running leaks of half-developed government policies. With a reputation from the outset for tight media control and spin – in contrast to John Major's failed administration – our government wanted both to announce our policies and control the reporting. As I saw at close quarters, Alastair Campbell was brilliant at this task. But he became so aggressively phobic about his former profession of journalists that he ceased to be as effective. I remember finding him in his office in No. 10 one day wearing a baseball cap emblazoned with 'media scum'. 'I hate the tossers,' he said cheerfully.

A 'Westminster bubble' inhabited by the political class and Westminster journalists conducts debate in way and on terms that have little relevance to the average citizen. What people want from the media are facts and views on which to make up their own minds, not to have to peer through the fog of spin by the political cognoscenti. Increasingly, highly intelligent people from outside politics told me they just do not believe anything that is being reported any more. They do not like the way every attempt at open debate is turned into a split or the way that every microscopically different ministerial word becomes a gaffe. They want to see, hear and read the merits of interesting ideas by Ministers or Shadow Ministers instead of all sorts of angles and spin and process minutiae – endlessly fascinating and exciting to the incestuous

Westminster bubble but boring and dull to everyone else. The truth is most voters are more interested in reading or hearing about how our policies are likely to affect their lives – for better or worse – than they are in reading about the latest story of a political aide of whom they have never previously heard or a bit of process to which they are indifferent.

The Westminster bubble is also obsessed with who's up and who's down – everything is interpreted as a personal rivalry, not because there could possibly be a genuine thought-through policy debate going on: even within the Cabinet. I was first in the media spotlight during anti-apartheid campaigns in the late 1960s and 1970s. But I had never before experienced so much made-up journalism, invariably amazed at what I read about myself. As a Cabinet Minister, I was known for plain, straight speaking, answering questions not ducking them. It got me into the odd scrape. But then even the most cautious, on-message politician has been there too: it comes with the job these days.

The media cannot have it both ways – we cannot be both 'control freaks' and then, when we loosen up, be accused of having 'lost control'. When Ministers all sang from the same hymn sheet we were accused of being boringly controlled by No. 10. Yet when we went 'off script', the government was 'adrift' or 'split', the PM either too weak or too intolerant. The way the Westminster bubble behaves is insulting a public that wants intelligent debate. We need to tap into that evident appetite for grown-up political discussion.

On topical policy issues – like Europe, student fees or Iraq at the time – there was a real appetite for serious, intelligent information, debate and opposing views and tough questions asked of politicians. I never had any problem as a government minister being put on the spot by John Humphrys of *Today* or Jeremy Paxman of *Newsnight*. In a vibrant democracy, government ought to be challenged and scrutinised, especially by journalists. But we are now into an entirely different game where the media become part of the story they should be reporting objectively, completely alienated from, and alienating, the public, turning off viewers, listeners and readers from politics by the million, and spreading cynicism so corrosive to democracy.

I wrote an article about this for the *Independent on Sunday* at the end of July 2003 and gave a speech to a seminar at the Institute for Public Policy Research which provoked a lively interest from senior journalists present, reflecting a growing recognition of the problem amongst serious commentators and some broadsheet editors. Commentators, notably Nick Jones along with Steve Richards of the *Independent*, both formerly of the BBC, were also fiercely critical of the way that BBC journalism had developed, often on an unsourced basis and highly spun.

That this was dangerous was revealed in the private polling that Philip

Gould presented to a Political Cabinet that July. It showed that there was a tremendous trust gap between the government and the public, with the public turning off politics entirely. And this was not only to do with Iraq going sour at the time. Philip made the point that this was precisely the agenda of the right and would pave the way for a Tory return because if you could disillusion voters, the optimistic and progressive politics that Labour represented would be vanquished and the door would open to the right's cynical form of politics with progressive voters staying at home. I was very concerned that voter turnout was falling, voter distrust increasing, voter switch-off happening on a huge scale. It was, I felt, a complicated phenomenon, not only to do with the Westminster bubble and the way we operated, but that in advanced democracies, there did not seem space in people's lifestyles for the kind of political interest that is so vital. I always thought politicians exaggerated the extent to which the average person was interested in day-to-day politics. But this was something much more fundamental. We were part of a systematic turning off of a whole generation of people who once took an informed, if not active, interest in the political process. And this was six years before the MP expenses scandal which was massively damaging to the credibility of politics.

It is the way that we in the Westminster bubble engage with people that is the problem (and by 'we' I mean politicians *and* the media). If we don't crack this then we will all go down together – politicians and political journalists alike. Because the lower voter turnout falls, the less editors are going to feel that they have to cover politics at all. And that spells redundancy for all of us – democracy included.

Most politicians of all parties are decent people motivated by a desire to do good. Equally, most journalists went into their profession to report, and often uncover, the truth. There is a fine tradition of investigative and campaigning journalism that must continue – including by broadcasters. Many genuine scandals have been exposed, and suffering and abuse ended, because of excellent journalism. But we can both contribute to a better balance. Government can do more to cut out the spin and cut down on the packaging. And the media can do more to report substance and content. It is high time politicians stopped trying to be journalists and journalists stopped trying to be politicians. We need a new deal.

CHAPTER TEN

FROM HORROR TO HOPE: NORTHERN IRELAND BREAKTHROUGH

Elizabeth was angry. 'After all you have done for him – and he gives you Northern Ireland! Next time I see Tony, I'm going to give him a piece of my mind.' (And, several weeks later, on a train to Cardiff, that's exactly what she did to a sheepishly nonplussed Prime Minister and an embarrassed husband.)

My trusted special adviser Phil Taylor was depressed: 'The one job we don't want is Northern Ireland,' he had said beforehand. But I didn't agree. In fact I was delighted. The chance at last really to make an historic difference in one of the most difficult jobs in Cabinet. It immediately seemed to me this was exactly why I had made the long journey from the outside to become a Cabinet insider.

Tony had been rather diffident when he called the day after the general election in May 2005. 'We need to sort Northern Ireland and I think you are the person to do so.' And, almost before I replied 'Thank you', he hastily added, as if sugaring the pill, 'You know you will have your own castle: Hillsborough.'

He need not have bothered. I had heard from friends in government how much they had enjoyed the official residence of the Secretary of State – evidently quite a spread. But I felt a bit insulted. I had never been into all the trappings of office. My own castle? Sod that, I thought. Maybe it was my non-British upbringing because it was hardly an incentive. I did not need one. (But that did not stop me trying to soften up Elizabeth with the prospect.)

Frankly, I was surprised, and not at all dismayed: just privileged to be trusted with one of the jobs closest to Tony's heart, and on which he had expended more energy and more political capital to greater effect than any British Prime Minister before him.

‡

Almost immediately when I was appointed that Friday evening, our lives changed fundamentally – more than at any time in my eight years before as a Minister. There was the normal introductory call from my new private secretary and also from the permanent secretary, Sir Joe Pilling, who explained that I would now have 24-hour personal armed security. Could I be available for a briefing tomorrow morning, a Saturday? Of course, I said. In that case my new protection team would arrive to pick me up. I would be unable to go anywhere or do anything outside my home without their continuous accompaniment. Not even to pop out for a newspaper or to see my grandchildren, I asked? No.

The only obstacle to my briefing arrangements was that I had a seat with my son Sam and three-year old grandson Harry to enjoy the thrill of my team Chelsea hoist the Premiership Cup as the new champions after their afternoon match in nearby south west London. No problem: I could start the briefing in my new office, go to the match, and then come back again and complete it.

As I had found from the outset in government, it is important to be, and to be seen to be, in political charge from the moment you meet your new team of officials. I had decided to invite Claire McCarthy, a dynamic young Labour national press officer, to join Phil Taylor as my other special adviser; we had first met years before when she was a campaigning Labour student in Wales. Realising she would be having her first decent night's sleep for weeks after a hectic campaign, I delayed calling her until 9 a.m. and offered her the job. Still drowsy and startled, she nevertheless agreed and we arranged to pick her up two hours later on the way into my new office.

Then the protection team arrived at our London home in two vehicles: an armoured Jaguar and a 'back-up' Range Rover. Polite and insisting always on calling me 'Sir', they explained their procedures. I would always travel in the back of the Jag immediately behind an armed Metropolitan Police officer in the front passenger seat alongside a specially trained driver. The back-up would have two armed officers, driver included. Part of a larger team assigned to me which would rotate through the week, they would always escort me once I left my front door unless I was in my office or working in Parliament.

Elizabeth had dreaded their ever-presence, 'like having people at the bottom of our bed', she would explain; although I sympathised, I knew we could cope. I am a pretty phlegmatic person who had adjusted to change all my life. Although the team, required to maintain a professional distance from their charges, were considerate, friendly and totally discreet, there was no privacy – and Elizabeth found this impossibly difficult when deeply upset after her father's death in 2006.

However, we gradually found there were also advantages, like being able to have a drink out on social occasions and never having to worry about the route to a destination or arriving on time. I soon discovered shared interests like motor racing and of course football, especially with Billy, whose Dad had been a professional footballer. The irony was enjoying full-time protection from the 'Met' which had, in my previous life of protest, kept a decidedly wary eye on me.

I had decided to do interviews for the Northern Ireland media around midday and had rehearsed my lines with officials over the phone and then when I got in to my new office. I wanted to be seen to take charge right away, so television, radio and press turned up for a brief statement and questions, the eyes of my new protection officers eyes roving constantly as I stood in front of the cameras on the pavement outside my new office.

The rather nondescript but pleasant modern office building overlooked the Thames. It was next to MI5's headquarters just down from Parliament. Although the world of security and intelligence was familiar to me from my years in the Foreign Office, this was much more intense. There is so much to absorb on entering a new post that I had developed a habit of focusing on the big picture and learning the detail on the job, rather than getting bogged down memorising the voluminous facts put before me.

The team of senior officials gathered to meet me were as always pleasant and respectful, as we sized each other up. Sir Joe was the chief 'securocrat' in the immortal words of republican leaders like Gerry Adams. A small man, he would sit quietly in key meetings, biding his time before making a penetrating point. Cunning and sharp, he would slip around the office hardly noticed, all seeing and all knowing from his long experience in the department.

‡

Since my first fact-finding visit in 1972 to Belfast and Derry as a young radical at the height of the 'Troubles', I had retained an interest in Northern Irish politics. That was the year when the greatest number of people were killed – more than 500 – and many more wounded. I could still recall sharp images, like walking past a woman on a pavement in Belfast as she pushed her baby in a pram, soldiers crouching within feet, guns pointing in all directions: the ordinary incongruous amidst the extraordinary. In the old walled city of Derry I had been ushered quickly into a car with a couple of young 'Provos' – Provisional IRA members – and driven off for a 'chat', wondering whether I would ever be seen again.

Although I had never had any truck with the IRA, my anti-colonial upbringing made me sympathetic to the political aims of Irish republicanism, though certainly not the violent methods. During the mid-1980s I increasingly felt that the British strategy in Northern Ireland was going nowhere and, with Labour MP Clare Short, had helped launch a 'Time to Go' campaign. Its objective was for the government to set a target date for withdrawal and meanwhile to promote negotiations for a political settlement. It was broadly based, in contrast to the predominant Irish solidarity campaigns on the British left which I found sectarian and uncomfortably close to being IRA fronts. I was, however, introduced to the Sinn Fein leaders Gerry Adams and Martin McGuinness at the time, who told me they wanted a political settlement, even if the IRA were still active.

But it had been nearly twenty years since 'Time to Go', I had not been involved since, and in any case the whole political landscape had changed fundamentally, making my days of activism long irrelevant. The ground-breaking Good Friday Agreement of 1998 negotiated by Tony Blair had opened the door for the very first time to a power-sharing government between unionists, nationalists and republicans at Stormont, the gaunt parliamentary buildings just outside Belfast city. Long known as 'a Protestant parliament for a Protestant people', it had seen a period of local rule before this collapsed amidst a crisis in October 2002.

Given my pedigree, I had to be very careful to overcome unionist suspicion – strong with *any* British Secretary of State, from whom they automatically expected 'betrayal', but in my case potentially greater still. Tony had indicated that none of my predecessors had got close enough to Ian Paisley, the fiery, veteran leader of the Democratic Unionist Party. So I resolved to do so.

As I read and listened my way into the job, it was evident to me that at least two things had to change. First, the government had to start treating Paisley and the DUP with proper respect: they were outsiders and had always said 'no'. I needed to get them to become 'insiders', able to say 'yes' by assuming the responsibilities that always come with leadership. They would not do that if they were continuously being treated with disdain as 'the problem', 'the troublemakers'. The electorate had put them on top so it was pointless hankering after the days of 'more reasonable' politicians like David Trimble. (Actually a notoriously prickly person to deal with, despite his undoubted political courage.) So I resolved at the outset to treat Ian Paisley as the First Minister in Waiting. 'You will have to deal with the problem when you are in charge, Ian,' I would say if he lobbied me on a local issue. He would deny a willingness to accept the post, while chortling knowingly.

Second, I had to change the weary pessimism amongst my officials and in the opinion-forming classes of Irish politics, North and South. The success of the Good Friday strategy of Tony Blair and Irish Prime Minister Bertie Ahern had been built around a core agreement between the then leader of Ulster unionism, David Trimble, and John Hume of the nationalist Social Democratic and Labour Party (SDLP). Although intransigent opponents over the years, they were then both the leaders of Protestant and Catholic communities, and constituted a new 'centre' of

Northern Ireland politics which provided the platform for Good Friday and power sharing.

However, Paisley's DUP had been grumpily dissident within the all-party devolved government. They had gone along with, rather than signed up to, Good Friday. Paisley had refused to enter the government, deputing subordinates to become Ministers. Meanwhile Sinn Fein, with the IRA still in play though on ceasefire, were semi-detached, and allegations that they had used their positions in the government to retrieve sensitive information and 'spy' on opponents led to the collapse of devolved power and resumption of British direct rule in 2002.

But I faced a completely different set of political outcomes after the 2005 general election. Trimble had lost his parliamentary seat, and his once mighty Ulster Unionist party clung on with a sole MP, vanquished by the DUP. Ian Paisley was now the leader of unionism. Similarly, Sinn Fein had overtaken the SDLP as the largest party speaking for Catholic, nationalist opinion. The 'centre' had been marginalised, the 'extremes' were now the top dogs. The conventional British wisdom, pursued from John Major's time as Prime Minister and successfully achieved under Tony Blair, that a settlement could be built around a core of centrist parties, was in tatters.

That explained why people I met around Westminster or Stormont in those early weeks of office – from civil servants and MPs to journalists – was gloomy. The more so because, only eight months previously in the autumn of 2004, a comprehensive attempt at a new power-sharing agreement, this time involving unprecedented discussions with the DUP and Sinn Fein, had failed after coming close to fruition. This setback was compounded in December 2004 by the IRA's heist at Northern Bank in Belfast when armed men stole £26 million – the biggest robbery in the history of the United Kingdom. 'How can I trust them again?' Paisley later privately said to me. 'We had made real progress towards an agreement around the comprehensive proposals, then, weeks later, they go and do *that*. Just as well we did not get an agreement or I would have been skinned alive.' I understood his point exactly.

More grief in every sense had come from the brutal murder by a member of the IRA in February 2005 of a republican, Robert McCartney, who had been drinking in a Belfast pub. He had been knifed by a fellow drinker after an argument and, immediately afterwards, with their customary efficiency, the local IRA went in and 'cleansed' the pub of any incriminating evidence. The murder provoked outrage, not least in the local nationalist community where a spirited campaign for justice was launched with great bravery by McCartney's sisters. For Ian Paisley, amongst many others, it underlined the folly of brokering an agreement with Sinn Fein. Although the murder had not been officially sanctioned by the IRA, if this sort of pure gangsterism and criminality still infected the organisation, how could a deal be done with republican leaders, Paisley asked me?

Despite the prevailing pessimism, however, I felt optimistic. The more I looked at it, the more I felt that having the DUP and 'the Shinners' in charge could be a positive. Drawing on my South African experience, I recalled how the deal there was eventually done between the two most polarised groups: the Afrikaner politicians who were the architects of apartheid, and the leaders they had imprisoned: Nelson Mandela and his comrades. Over the years, repeated attempts by the West to court centrist groups – including Mandela's Zulu rival, Buthelezi – had proved futile. And although the two situations were very different, in Northern Ireland there was also no force of any real significance more extreme on either side of the DUP and Sinn Fein. If we could get them to agree, it really would stick where the centre parties had been unable to make it do so. I started to articulate this thought as I got to grips with the politics and built relationships with the key politicians – albeit as something of a lone voice for optimism amongst the seasoned, sceptical peace process practitioners around me, Tony Blair included.

‡

Another novelty amongst the many in the job was having my own jet to 'clipper' me over the water. A contract with a private company which leased rock star Chris de Burgh's plane meant a jet was even available at four hours' notice to cover emergencies. I quickly realised the job would have been impossible to do without it, especially as I remained Secretary of State for Wales too. There were to be frequent trips to Belfast, London and Dublin, often in the same day, mostly from either the Royal Air Force's Northolt Airport west of London, or Cardiff Airport.

So, on the Monday morning after I was appointed, I was driven out to Northolt bound for Belfast and my first official visit as Secretary of State. Unusually (because she had a busy professional life running a small company) Elizabeth accompanied me so that we could be photographed together in a planned walk-about in Belfast city centre. (Northern Ireland society is strong on family and marriage.) Our cars were nodded through by Northolt's military security at the airport gate and we drove straight onto the tarmac, an RAF officer saluting and helping with our luggage as we climbed aboard the waiting small jet.

The small jet terrified the living daylights out of my special adviser Phil Taylor, a nervous flyer – his paranoia confirmed when it took off and a pile of

documents cascaded into his lap. Elizabeth spent most of the journey calming
nerves during the smooth flight, the early summer weather fine as we swept
down over Belfast Loch. However, Phil was vowing never to get in the small
plane again as it swung about alarmingly before suddenly settling about ten
yards up and making a perfect landing at what is now called George Best
Belfast City Airport. Our fresh Northern Ireland police protection team was
waiting in an armoured Vauxhall saloon: Alan – a Manchester United fanatic
– and Ali – a Leeds United fan. Football as usual was an effective icebreaker.

It was a short drive into a very different Belfast from the one I had first
seen thirty-three years before. The city was booming, shiny new buildings
everywhere replacing bombed hulks and a busy main shopping area thronging
with people who in years gone by would have scurried about furtively fearful.
The car pulled up alongside a scrum of journalists, television cameras and
photographers. Constantly aware of my new protection officers hovering, I
made a short statement of my pleasure at doing the job and my determination
to promote a political settlement, followed by a stream of questions from a
variety of media characters I was later to get to know very well. Elizabeth,
herself an accomplished media performer, adroitly made sure she was in the
right place for the pictures the media wanted of us, yet leaving me the space
to do the politics. We posed alongside a placard from that morning's *Belfast
Telegraph* with a huge caption 'Hain takes up the reins' which made the next
day's paper. But, ever sharp, Phil thwarted a cunning attempt to manoeuvre
me in front of a nearby tanning centre; Westminster journalists had given me
a 'permatan' nickname, a relic I suppose of my African upbringing. Then I
introduced myself amidst the media buzz to intrigued shoppers, all of whom
seemed friendly enough. After any number of election visits to many a town
centre in Britain, I was used to chatting to complete strangers, and the walk-
about was judged a success.

Then it was straight over to my office in Stormont Castle, in the middle
of the large estate which also housed the parliament building and government
departments. Somewhat fairy tale in appearance, albeit with a fully modernised interior, it meant that I now had four ministerial offices: the partner one
in London, and the two Wales offices in Whitehall and Cardiff. None of my
predecessors had ever shared the job with another Cabinet post. I was introduced to an additional set of staff, again making it clear I wanted to operate on
first-name terms, which many found difficult, and that I needed a computer
with email installed on my empty desk.

Elizabeth had meanwhile been driven over to our official residence, the
much vaunted Hillsborough Castle, twenty miles south of Belfast, expecting
to catch up with her work until I joined her that night. Instead she was briefed

on the running of Hillsborough and asked her preferences. She rather threw civil servants and staff by explaining she had no intention of giving up her independent career in Britain and taking up permanent residence, which is what they clearly expected.

Hillsborough was indeed a new experience, when I realised I would have a housekeeper, Olwyn McCarthy, who would cook for me, and the castle's charismatic head honcho, David Anderson, both of whom had presided over many Secretaries of State before me. Their jobs together with the other staff were to make my complicated life as easy as possible: food and drink would be provided whenever needed, informally or formally, and clothes and rooms cleaned. Never having had an ostentatious lifestyle, I was determined not to change my attitudes, but simply make use of the facilities and staff all schooled over the years to enable me to do the complex and difficult job before me. I did, however, make two requests which were immediately granted: to have a computer installed on the desk in the so-called 'dressing room' behind my large new bedroom, and a couple of gym machines placed in a nearby empty room so I could get regular exercise while I was there.

We found the building itself – an Edwardian country house – stately but not at all staid. It managed to combine the functions of homeliness, together with being an office, a venue for almost daily public receptions, and the scene of high-level political meetings. A 'kick your shoes off and curl up on the sofa' kind of house, yet also the official residence of the Royal Family when visiting Northern Ireland; we were shown the Queen's luxurious en-suite bedroom, with the Duke's bedroom adjoining.

Because of the years of security and political turmoil, there was a long tradition of having a duty minister always in residence, either the Secretary of State living in the castle itself, or one of the three junior ministers, who could stay in a spacious attached apartment. On duty weekends this meant family or occasional friends could also stay. However, on such occasions we cooked for ourselves, mostly in the small kitchen next to the dining room upstairs in the living quarters, or if lots of people were staying, downstairs in the huge, clunky kitchens from where staff normally served official dinners or receptions. We especially enjoyed having most of our close family over for Christmas week, which Secretaries of State traditionally spent at Hillsborough. The first time, in 2005, I converted the Throne Room (where the Queen bestowed honours from her ornate chair of state) into a temporary football pitch with a pair of children's portable plastic goalposts to play with my grandson Harry. Hillsborough was both comfortable and enjoyable, especially in good weather when we would walk the huge and beautifully maintained grounds, aware that security cameras carefully placed to deter intruders followed almost our every move; a point I always carefully mentioned to others in case of any cavorting.

Although rather strange at first, the life I was now living quickly settled down as I adapted to the constant travel and found ways of working almost continuously, doing red boxes in the back of cars, on the plane, late at night or early in the morning – and somehow finding time for Elizabeth and our families. Combined with constituency duties, my working week averaged a hundred hours. Over the next two years, I was going to need every one of those hours and more to achieve my hope of settling the bitterly tangled conflict which for centuries had plagued my new fiefdom.

‡

One of the first crucial changes I made was to insist on being present at every one of Tony Blair's meetings, especially with Gerry Adams and Martin McGuinness, whom he had cultivated and customarily met on his own with Jonathan Powell, his chief of staff, an indispensable cog in the negotiating process. Well before getting the job I was aware that successive Secretaries of State had been excluded from all but the most routine of these meetings, almost relegated to a bit part in the grand scheme of the peace process; Mo Mowlam reported making the tea at one summit. I could not see how my job could be properly done on that basis. My Northern Ireland Office staff thought I was wasting my time, but Jonathan came back to agree that it made sense. At the first major meeting in No. 10, Adams and McGuinness were surprised to see me alongside Tony and, very soon, word spread. Tommie Gorman, renowned reporter for Irish TV, remarked to me that all concerned had noted the significance of the change, as did DUP and Sinn Fein leaders.

Adams and McGuinness were the most professional and tough negotiators I had encountered in politics. Well read and meticulously prepared, they were courteous and straightforward, a similar political generation to me, also schooled in the radical turmoil of the late 1960s, though in their cases moving into the IRA. I was briefed that they remained members of the IRA Army Council, effectively the organisation's Politburo. I got on with them well, they were informal with a good sense of humour and would invariably end telephone conversations or leave meetings with a 'God bless'. Often I would see them on their own, but sometimes with a larger group including Gerry Kelly, who had been imprisoned for his part in the Old Bailey bombing in 1973.

They had travelled a long and hazardous journey from IRA commanders to principal political strategists for a democratic peace settlement. I well

understood that they had to keep their republican hinterland on board, a notoriously difficult task given the long history of splits in the IRA, some viciously
violent. Adams was haunted by the memory of Michael Collins, the IRA
leader assassinated from within his own ranks in 1922. This followed Collins's
agreement to the Anglo-Irish Treaty the year before, which partitioned Ireland
into what was to become an independent republic in the south, with the north
remaining part of the United Kingdom. My task was to work with them to get
the IRA finally to end its war and with Sinn Fein to sign up to support policing
and the rule of law – all objectives unthinkable to anyone who knew the bitter
terrain of Irish politics and history.

In meetings Adams and McGuinness occasionally played 'hard cop, soft
cop' (if that is the correct analogy, given their history). Adams especially was
not averse to irony. Early on, when I pressed him on something he knew full
well – that the IRA's Northern Bank robbery had been hugely damaging to the
process – he airily denied its involvement. 'You know what it's like to be falsely
accused, Peter. You were charged with a bank robbery once!' he said, only half
in jest. 'But I was innocent!' I replied. 'They all say that, don't they?' came the
instant retort. If I pressed him too hard he would also have the odd dig at my
radical background, as if I was betraying it – this I smiled at and ignored, for
it was obviously one of their negotiating ploys. He knew that I knew what he
was up to.

Bespectacled and tall, with greying black hair and a bad back, Adams often
seemed tired. There was a sense with him that if we did not succeed in getting a
settlement in this phase, then he might have little more to offer, as if the whole
long journey had exhausted his generation of republican leaders, now edging
into their sixties, and anxious that their children and grandchildren did not
have to go through the same arduous experience. He would occasionally disappear to his retreat in Donegal to recuperate. Like the other leaders I was dealing
with, I always tried to find a point of human contact beyond the tensions of
the politics. That was less easy with Adams, though he could expound at length
about his love for shrubs and trees, and how he was husbanding new plants in
his garden. Once, during a lengthy interlude in negotiations at Hillsborough
Castle, he explained how he had walked its gardens and come across some
shrubs he fancied, surreptitiously digging one out and placing it carefully into
his car boot to transplant back home. What the IRA bodyguards, who always
drove him around in an oldish grey Mercedes, made of this he never said.

Martin McGuinness, wiry, also well mannered and polite and always
asking after family, made the two-hour journey back to his wife at their home
in Derry at the end of every day in Belfast. Unlike Adams, who was rather
disdainful about anything sporting except Gaelic football, McGuinness like

me was a keen soccer fan. He would report on Derry City's progress and, like I did, watched big matches on television if he had the time. Incredibly for a hardline Irish republican he was also a big fan of the English cricket team, able to recite match statistics and comment expertly on each of their batsmen or bowlers. England's victory over Australia in the Ashes series in 2005 especially enthralled him, and we marvelled at Welsh fast bowler Simon Jones's then novel 'reverse swing' technique.

Once, after my then political director, Jonathan Phillips, and I had had a good meeting with Adams and McGuinness, the former raised a local constituency issue. I replied: 'Don't worry about it, Gerry. I'll ask Jonathan to look at this personally, I know you trust Jonathan.' McGuinness looked me in the eye and said: 'Peter, we don't trust any of you. Don't think for a minute that we trust any of you!' It was not said in an unfriendly way.

Two months into the job, on 7 July 2005, bombs went off in London on the Underground and in a bus, planted by Al Qaeda-aligned jihadists, killing fifty-two people and injuring over 700. Elizabeth frantically tried to make contact on jammed phone lines and when she finally did and heard I was on my way to Northern Ireland commented with unconscious irony: 'Thank God you're going to Belfast – at least you'll be safe there!' But first there was a hairy drive with portable flashing lights on the armoured Jag as we mounted pavements and went the wrong way up streets to get out of gridlocked London. A planned meeting with Adams and McGuinness took place that afternoon in my office at Stormont Castle which usually had Sky News on a TV in the corner. We found ourselves watching the pictures of the carnage, both of them shaking their heads in horror. The irony of such condemnation and genuine sorrow from two leaders of an organisation which had itself staged bombings in London, albeit nothing like as serious, seemed lost on them. Adams did, however, insist that government support for the invasion of Iraq was badly mistaken and simply invited the horror we were all condemning.

Despite our friendly relations, neither of these two Sinn Fein leaders were averse to the occasional rough tactic. When I was insisting in late 2006 that they would have fully to support the policing and justice system, they both complained to Tony Blair and Jonathan Powell about me in terms which implied the PM should have no confidence in my continuing role as Secretary of State. Although I was not too concerned about this, my officials were momentarily worried in case I might find myself circumvented by No. 10 as my predecessors had sometimes been. But Tony and Jonathan saw this for the ploy it was – one occasion at least when Adams and McGuinness were ignored.

Around the same time, at the end of an especially tense meeting in the conference room at Hillsborough Castle, the two asked to see me on my own. We found ourselves squeezing into a small box-like room and they aggressively insisted that my pressure upon them risked sabotaging the whole process and they would ensure my role as Secretary of State was terminated by refusing to deal with me. Although the incident was physically threatening, I politely and calmly stood my ground and they departed without the usual friendly 'God bless'. I did not take this personally because I knew that their mission to win over their republican grass roots from a lifelong hostility to policing and the law was proving horrendously tough. Had they deliberately planned to intimidate me or did they simply blow up amidst the tension? I stood my ground and, after a sticky few weeks, our negotiating relationship resumed on the same professionally cordial basis – nothing of that kind ever occurring again.

Ian Paisley and his fellow DUP leaders were an entirely different kettle of fish. Ian I found to be a real gentleman with old-fashioned manners of the kind with which I had been brought up; perhaps why we got on so well. Like Adams and McGuinness he had moved on, and appeared to have mellowed from the ranting bigotry of his past. With a sense of humour I warmed to, he was extremely shrewd, hugely popular and wary of the British embrace. He suggested early on that I meet his key compatriots over dinner in Hillsborough. 'My men are very suspicious of you, Peter, and I want you to get to know them better.' He always referred to them as 'my men', and with two exceptions indeed they were. We had a convivial though dry evening – they did not countenance alcohol. I had no illusions that their suspicions had been entirely stemmed, but Paisley confided later that they had warmed to me. 'A good thing,' he said.

Putting Paisley and me together – high Presbyterian and inveterate agnostic, right-wing veteran and left-wing upstart – might have seemed a combustible cocktail, but we got on very well. Despite our numerous arguments, I sensed he wanted to do a deal if it was possible – though on terms which seemed on the surface to be insurmountable.

I decided to invite him and his family to celebrate his eightieth birthday at an official dinner at Hillsborough, and he was delighted. The castle's full banqueting table was engulfed by tiny grandchildren and adults to his huge enjoyment, reminding me of my own close and extended family.* Paisley's wife, Eileen, was a formidable force and renowned hardliner. 'You know, she was in

---

* Ironically my involvement in this happy family event meant I did not get a frantic mobile phone message from Elizabeth when she had pulled herself from our wrecked car, upside down on the M4 motorway in Wales after aquaplaning at night in a flash flood; an example of the strain between public and private life.

politics before me,' he said proudly of her election as a local councillor well before he was. The first Christmas we spent at Hillsborough, I invited them both to tea. After some family talk, Paisley and I adjourned to the Lady Grey Room for a bit of informal negotiation, leaving Elizabeth gallantly playing host to a one-way conversation from his wife who presented her with a booklet of her religious writings.

Escorting him on his own from the castle a few months into the job, I asked whether he could conceive of being First Minister. 'Yes, Peter,' he said, rather to my surprise, 'but only for a while. I want to see my people safe, then step down.' Reporting back to my astonished officials the next day, it was evident this was the first time he had given such a signal. Once, during a visit to his Antrim constituency, I invited him to join me in a Catholic primary school he had never before set foot in, and paid tribute to him before incredulous teachers.

Paisley's son, Ian Junior, was, I increasingly realised, very important to the settlement I wanted to achieve, though publicity addicted and a target of huge jealously amongst his colleagues. 'Untrustworthy, a loose cannon, trouble with a big T,' my officials and some of his DUP seniors warned. But I could not help liking him and acknowledging that it was very difficult making his own way as a politician living in his father's very considerable shadow. Moreover I realised that Ian Junior – like me a motor sport fan – was an influential gatekeeper to the 'Big Man' as Paisley was colloquially known, someone who was on top of the detail his Dad floated over and intensely loyal. About a year into the job, and initially against the advice of my officials and that of the DUP deputy leader, Peter Robinson, and his close associate Jeffrey Donaldson, I began seeing Ian Junior privately, often at Hillsborough, which was near his own family home.

Robinson and Donaldson were both supporters of my football team, Chelsea, and I was able to get them invited to a few matches. Although with a somewhat abrasive public image and reputation as a hardliner in previous years, Robinson was the brains behind the DUP, an extremely astute tactician with a tight grip on the Party machine. He was often frustrated both at the endemic reluctance of his Party to progress negotiations and Paisley's penchant for the big picture and indifference to textual nuance for which Robinson had a specialism. We would have regular and very frank meetings, often in my Westminster parliamentary office, which he could come to without anybody else noticing. These were invaluable conduits for both of us to test out ideas and strategies.

Amongst their DUP colleagues, others also had an importance, especially Nigel Dodds, once Paisley's political assistant before being elected himself, and seen as a drag on progress towards an agreement, with a hatred of Sinn Fein that sprang in part from being attacked once when visiting his severely disabled son in hospital. I also tried to get closer to Dodds and, as time went on, he might join Robinson and Donaldson at their invitation for informal talks. However, he was always cautious and, I sensed, someone happier to lead from behind rather than the front. There was only one person who would be capable of leading the truculent DUP into a power-sharing government: the man who had always said 'no' – Paisley himself.

There were of course other important figures in the complicated tapestry of Northern Ireland politics. Mark Durkan, talented leader of the SDLP with an enviable facility for phrase making, was understandably resentful of the way Sinn Fein had elbowed his Party out of the way in the Catholic community. Consequently he and his colleagues had an irritating tendency to be oppositional where under John Hume in previous decades the SDLP had been such a bravely constructive force. The same was true of Reg Empey, the Ulster Unionist leader, a somewhat erudite figure. Ironically the most liberal and centrist of the parties, the Alliance, had in David Ford a pernickety leader quick to take offence at some imagined slight and in many ways the least flexible of them all. His prickliness was in massive contrast to the genial and garrulous David Ervine, loyalist leader of the Progressive Unionist Party, to the paramilitary Ulster Volunteer Force what Sinn Fein was to the IRA. Despite his murky and violent UVF history, he was by miles the most progressive of any of the unionist politicians, actually closer in his working-class politics to Sinn Fein, and with socialist-leaning values much in common with mine.

Although all these politicians had to be catered for as part of my weekly diet in and around Belfast, the most important by a long way for getting a settlement were the two Paisleys, Robinson, Adams and McGuinness. But how to get them together when the DUP would not even acknowledge Sinn Fein members as people, let alone as politicians with a mandate?

‡

In Northern Ireland there was always a crisis around the corner, and my first came in the person of Sean Kelly, a well-known IRA figure called by unionists 'the Shankill butcher'. He had been convicted with fellow IRA members for bloodily bombing a fish shop in the loyalist Shankill Road in the mistaken belief that loyalist paramilitaries were meeting in a room upstairs. But with 400 others he was let out of prison under the Good Friday Agreement early release scheme for republican and loyalist paramilitaries. Every individual so released under special licence had to avoid violent, paramilitary or illegal activity or risk suspension of their licence and reimprisonment.

Late one night in mid-June 2005 at Hillsborough I was working on a red box when, without any prior notice, a submission marked 'secret' came to the top of the files left for my attention. It recommended revocation of Sean Kelly's licence and presented evidence of him apparently orchestrating young republicans clashing with loyalists as trouble erupted outside a pub after a televised match between the Catholic-supported Glasgow Celtic and the Protestant-supported Glasgow Rangers football teams.

I immediately knew this was a hot potato. Damned if I agreed the submission because it would destabilise an imminent peace move by Gerry Adams to disarm by the IRA. Damned if I did not because the submission came with evidence and a recommendation from both the police and prison services. If I ignored or countermanded it where would that leave my credibility? Maybe I was being set up with a deliberate test as to whether I could be trusted with the security of Northern Ireland and the security agencies of which I was now in charge? So I accepted the recommendation, albeit with considerable foreboding. Lo and behold, a few days later the DUP's Peter Robinson and Jeffrey Donaldson let slip that they had been aware that the process for Kelly's licence suspension had been activated weeks before and that the recommendation would come to me. So DUP leaders, often uncannily well informed from within the police, knew all about it well before I did.

Next morning, I summoned the permanent secretary, Joe Pilling, and political director, Jonathan Phillips, and told them of my decision. But, I added, I would not tolerate anything so serious again just turning up in my red box without proper discussion of the implications, and I made clear my suspicions. I gave the same message to the Chief Constable, Hugh Orde, all of them accepting my strictures that officials well down the line, perhaps merely seeing the issue as one of due process, would have to refer matters higher up to their superiors before setting in train proceedings that could only have one outcome under the legislation: the decision I confirmed.

The Saturday afterwards, as news broke of Sean Kelly's rearrest, I got an angry call from Gerry Adams. 'You must know every republican will see Sean's arrest as proof the security forces are trying to destabilise the republican movement. How can I do what I have promised to do – deliver the end of the IRA's war – when you do this to me? You are somebody who understands the Northern Ireland situation maybe better than any of your predecessors. You know how damaging all this will be at such an important time. Where is your evidence? My information is that Sean was trying to restrain the disorder, not to organise it. You are going to have to let him back out. I am going out publicly to say this.'

Although I replied that the evidence provided to me was clear, and that others contravening their licences had also been reimprisoned, I privately agreed with Adams. I had been equally unhappy about the *fait accompli*, though I could not say so. Subsequent discussions with him, Martin McGuinness and Gerry Kelly, underlined not just their anger, but also their intense frustration. Just when they were engaged in turning around hardline IRA and Sinn Fein supporters to produce an historic renunciation of violence, their refuseniks had an issue to leap upon. Inevitable strong complaints to No. 10 and Dublin led Tony Blair and the Irish Foreign Minister to ask me how on earth this had happened. Although they accepted my explanation and my officials swung into action strongly to back me up, I was momentarily concerned about damage to my credibility. In fact both saw it as just another of the many blips with which over the years they had become far more familiar than me, and which somehow had to be got through. 'We will have to sort this,' Tony said in the margins of a Cabinet meeting, and I agreed. But turning it over and over again in my mind, I knew that to have done anything else would have torpedoed the due legal process of both letting prisoners out and reincarcerating them if they breached the terms of their release.

Subsequent meetings with Adams and McGuinness made it crystal clear they needed Sean Kelly out to deliver the historic IRA statement. So I took advice from Joe Pilling and Jonathan Phillips that this would only be possible if the IRA's statement ending their war was unequivocal. If it was, a carefully choreographed sequence of procedures, including a submission from Pilling to the prison governor, could produce Kelly's release.

On 20 July Adams called me asking for an urgent meeting, giving me sufficient confidence to ask for a slot at Cabinet the next day where I reported that the IRA statement was imminent. But, I added, never take anything for granted. The last period of conflict resolution is always the most difficult; people who had travelled miles always found it hardest to cross the last few feet. I recalled that more people than ever in South Africa's history had been killed in the four years between Nelson Mandela's release from prison and his election as President.

Later I flew back to Belfast when the general officer commanding the British Army in Northern Ireland came in to see me. A straightforward military man, he wanted to dismantle both watch towers and fortifications near to the Irish border in South Armagh because they were no longer serving their surveillance purpose. Furthermore, he was only deploying four per cent of his 10,000 capacity to provide back-up to the police and maintain security, which was simply untenable at a time when the military were over-stretched in Iraq and Afghanistan. He wanted to run down the number of soldiers faster than originally planned, even though the total then stood at a third of its peak during the height of the Troubles. Welcoming this, I asked him to delay any action until after the IRA had made its intended statement.

Events were coming nicely together, confirmed by a call on my mobile from Gerry Adams, who said our meeting the next day had to be very private, my political director, Jonathan Phillips, joining me alone and any report given to Jonathan Powell in No. 10 and not copied more widely. On Friday 22 July 2005, Adams came into my Stormont office with Martin McGuinness and laid out his plan. He was tense, though as always determined. The IRA would make a statement, not to curry favour with the British government, but because they wanted to do it. It would be such a decisive, historic move that even for him to discuss it with me beforehand was potentially treasonable to the IRA. That being so, it had to be followed by immediate progress on longstanding Sinn Fein demands, including speedily winding down the British military presence and its surveillance stations and the release of Sean Kelly, which had now become an important bit of leverage for both of us. He wanted meetings with both British and Irish Prime Ministers the next week and, subject to achieving satisfaction of progress from our side, would show me a copy of the IRA statement the day before it was issued. The scene was set for a potentially momentous week – except that nothing was ever certain in Northern Ireland.

‡

Our mood was optimistically tense, and survived an unexpected scare when I was bundled into a military helicopter at Bessborough Army base and flown over South Armagh's 'bandit country' to see the soon to be dismantled watch towers. The helicopter was incredibly noisy, its interior stark and functional. Just before we took off, another officer jumped in and, without explanation, attached a steel rope to his belt, hooked it onto a vertical metal pole set in the middle between our seats, pulled the sliding door shut and squatted on the floor. We took off and swooped up and over the mountains, instructions coming thick and fast through our ear sets: 'Watch tower one o'clock, watch tower eleven o'clock.' Then, to my shock, the officer on the floor leant over and pulled the door back – just like that. There I was staring down into an abyss as we circled a watch tower, the seat belt hardly offering any comfort as we zoomed repeatedly up and down, leaving me gripping my seat plain terri-fied. On the way back I was offered repeat performances, but said that I had seen quite enough, thank you very much.

We flew into the police and Army base in Crossmaglen, for decades an IRA stronghold and inaccessible by road to police or soldiers. Out of curiosity, I decided to walk out into the town escorted by the soldiers, my protection officer Ali chasing frantically behind when he realised what I was up to. Nobody took much interest and the town seemed peaceful enough in the sun. As we flew back, it was hard to conceive the murder and mayhem which had long poisoned the beautiful rolling countryside. Large new houses in spacious grounds sprouted like mushrooms across the terrain below: proof of sudden wealth, much of which I was assured came from paramilitary criminality.

After we had got back Gerry Adams came on the line saying he wanted to see me around midday the next day, 27 July. Despite our run-in over Sean Kelly he wanted to show me a copy of the IRA's planned statement, which he had earlier indicated to Tony Blair would be unconditional, with all armed volunteers instructed to pursue only peaceful and democratic activities, and their weapons decommissioned.

An hour after he was due at Hillsborough Castle, Adams had not arrived, so I called him. 'You have waited eight hundred years for this moment, so you can wait a few more hours. Don't hassle me,' he said with cryptic jocularity. You never could tell with him whether the delay was unforeseen or whether he was happy for us to continue kicking our heels.

It was a warm summer's afternoon when he eventually arrived with Gerry Kelly at about half past two, in an open-neck shirt with rolled-up sleeves, sandals and a Bluetooth earpiece linked to his mobile phone. I showed him into the Lady Grey Room, the scene of many an important *tête-à-tête*, including between George Bush and Tony Blair on the Iraq War, a photograph of which adorned the corner. Adams sat in 'Bush's' chair and I occupied 'Tony's'. Jonathan Phillips and Gerry Kelly made notes behind us. Relaxed though utterly focused, Adams said somewhat elliptically that he was having a problem with the Irish government which had to be sorted out.

'My instructions are to show only Tony Blair and Jonathan Powell a copy of the IRA statement,' he said. 'I am passing it to you exclusively and I don't want it shown to the Irish government. They can stew in it. I have to have Sean Kelly out and both governments have to agree to welcome the statement. You must know we are acting in good faith and we respect your good faith.' Adams was, however, practised at squeezing every last item out of a key moment like this, and was well versed in the art of brinkmanship. 'The problem is the statement will not issue from the IRA until Dublin agrees over this outstanding issue between us.' I couldn't help savouring the irony of Adams discovering the Irish were proving more crotchety than the British.

Almost as he said this he broke off as a call from the Taoiseach, Bertie Ahern, came through on his mobile, and Adams told him: 'I can't deliver photos of the decommissioning of IRA weapons. We have got to assert the independence of the international decommissioning agency [the IICD]. Photos are impossible.'

Then he paused, as if savouring the moment, and handed over a copy of the IRA statement for Jonathan and me to read. In old-fashioned typing on several plain white sheets of paper, I quickly realised it was indeed the cathartic statement promised. The IRA was ending its armed struggle from four o'clock in the afternoon the next day – 28 July 2005 – all its armed units were instructed to dump their arms, and must engage in purely peaceful and democratic activity, and not in any other activities whatsoever (code for no continued criminality). IRA representatives were also authorised to decommission weapons, not only in front of the IICD, but also for the first time independent Protestant and Catholic clerics.

There was, however, a typical Adams twist when he insisted on no photocopies of the statement, which he wanted sent by secure fax to No. 10. Instead Jonathan Phillips was forced to copy over 1,000 words in longhand, which he considered a deliberate last minute humiliation of 'the Brits' by Adams. More than an hour was wasted as Jonathan carefully transcribed the statement onto a word processor in our small office and then printed it out for faxing. Adams was clearly allergic to a leak by email, though apparently ignorant that an email via the government intranet was a lot more secure than a fax sent necessarily on an open line.

The tension built amidst the ongoing argument with Dublin which was being much more hardline. Their insistence on photos of the decommissioning was apparently a requirement from the deputy Prime Minister, Michael McDowell, leader of the coalition partner party. Telephone calls flew in and out, and at one point I could not get through to Jonathan Powell or Tony Blair. They were in a meeting of COBRA, the emergency committee chaired by the Prime Minister because of intelligence on another Al Qaeda London bombing the next day; just as one terrorist threat was expiring, another was replacing it.

It was now late afternoon and time was marching rapidly on, threatening a procedure carefully pre-agreed with officials to comply with judicial protocol required to action Sean Kelly's release. I had to have seen the IRA statement, whereupon the permanent secretary, Joe Pilling, would send a carefully prepared email advising me to release Kelly, noting that my decision of 15 June to suspend Kelly's licence had been finely balanced, and circumstances had now changed with the IRA statement, and therefore I could exercise my powers to release him.

But I was not prepared to trigger this until I knew for absolute certain that the IRA statement would indeed be made the next day as Adams planned. And the Taoiseach was not backing down over the photos of decommissioning because otherwise his coalition government might be at risk – something I did not believe, by the way; his intransigent deputy could be placated some other way. So Adams would not budge. He sat in the sun on a bench on the terrace outside the Drawing Room with Gerry Kelly, taking mobile phone calls, munching fruit and cake supplied by the Castle's staff. Impasse.

The evening crept in, and the sun lighting up Hillsborough's flower beds and manicured gardens began to recede. A chill rolled in. Unless I had a resolution by eight o'clock, Maghaberry prison, where Sean Kelly was being held, would be locked up as always for the night and he could not be got out that evening as had to happen. Then Adams came rushing in. What sort of mobile did I have? His was running out of juice. Could he borrow my charger? I retrieved it from my briefcase upstairs and handed it over saying I wanted it back.

His phone now stuck on the end of my cable continued to ring incessantly, the conversation sometimes in Irish. But still no resolution. The Taoiseach had been watching horse racing all afternoon and so contact with him – including from a fretting Tony Blair in London – was at best intermittent. Another logistical complication: my plane was sitting on the tarmac and the city airport closed early at night. With forty-five minutes to go before the eight o'clock prison deadline, I decided to indulge in a bit of brinkmanship myself, telling Adams that I was leaving unless we got a result; once I was up in the air, I could not be contacted to authorise the release. He responded by asking Gerry Kelly to drive straight up to the prison and wait outside, worrying that Sean Kelly (who knew nothing at all of these manoeuvrings) might imagine he was being abducted from his cell to be killed by the British secret service, such would be his likely confusion and probable state of paranoia following his sudden incarceration six weeks earlier.

A minute before eight, with my bags packed, the car engine running, Adams found a way through, stating on his mobile to the Taoiseach's adviser in Dublin that if he could be given an assurance his boss would stand by his previous public position that photos were unnecessary, then he would authorise the IRA statement to be given next day as planned. All sealed, I issued my command to the prison governor to release Sean Kelly, pre-prepared emails and letters having kicked in just before. The Taoiseach's truculent deputy would just have to lump it. Job done, though with no sense of triumph in the regal décor of the Lady Grey Room. Adams didn't do celebrations with Brits – to him, outsider or not, I was just another Brit. I shook hands, saying goodbye. 'God bless,' he replied with a whimsical though tired smile.

Within minutes of an astonished Sean Kelly being collected from his cell and walking out to be greeted by Gerry Kelly, Sinn Fein must have told the media and his release led the news overnight with the IRA statement anticipated. I knew unionists would be furious – as indeed they were. But no matter, that could be managed. We had a few glasses of wine on the jet over to London. The IRA's long and bloody war was finally over.

‡

The morning of the statement, I made calls to my predecessors explaining what would happen. Each probably allowed themselves a 'He's a lucky bugger, why not on my watch?' thought, though all were full of congratulations, including Mo Mowlam, upsettingly slow and frail as she complained at having to toddle around at home on a zimmer frame, her health deteriorating rapidly. It was hard to imagine this of such a formerly vivacious and charismatic figure, admired by so many. Within weeks she had sadly fallen and died.

I also saw Ian Paisley to brief him personally on the detail. He came in from his 'holidays' (which as far as I could tell involved being based in his London flat and preaching daily to branches of his church around East Anglia). Dressed in a light sports jacket and tie – *very* informal for him – and pleased to be pre-informed, he was relaxed, chatty and in witty mode. A few weeks before, at one of my ebullient receptions in the Wales Office, he had turned up unexpectedly with some MPs. I introduced him to my decidedly reluctant Dad, who was similarly aged, but with diametrically opposed politics. Instinctively I broke the ice by telling them that as old jailbirds they had much in common. Paisley loved that and chortled aloud with the rest of the packed room when I specifically welcomed him in my speech, referring to the 'two jailbirds'. It was fascinating dealing with the 'Big Man' in these one-to-one sessions and, after I had shown him out my experienced officials remarked approvingly that he evidently liked me.

However, Paisley was in decidedly different mode a few days later. On 3 August a furious delegation which he led came to see me, the two women Assembly members refusing to shake my welcoming hand. Peter Robinson was at his bombastic best. They had simply banked the IRA statement, typically finding fault with some its wording, and were on the warpath. Three issues were toxic: the release of Sean Kelly, the disbandment of the Royal Irish Regiment (Northern Ireland's home-based soldiers who had carried the brunt of security for nearly forty years) and the dismantling of the South Armagh watch towers. All three essential measures but all, I knew full well, seen by unionists as a kick in the teeth. With the exception of Sean Kelly, these moves had been publicly announced as a result of government agreements years before. 'But we had no advance warning of any of it,' they complained. Well, if Ian Paisley had been First Minister with the rest of them in government they would of course have been properly consulted, maybe another reason why he should get into government early, I responded politely but firmly. They didn't like that at all.

Later that day Paisley came back with a delegation of unionist victims, including relatives of those killed by Kelly and his colleagues in the Shankill atrocity. I always sympathised during these encounters because the suffering and bitterness was so palpable, and politely tried to explain my position, promising to meet their longstanding demand to appoint a commissioner for victims, which they welcomed. Paisley had helped me enormously with this meeting by popping in minutes beforehand on his own with good advice not to try and shake their hands as I normally did. I knew that I must now invest even more time and effort in him and his DUP colleagues if we were to get them to play ball in the way we had so far managed to achieve with Sinn Fein.

One of the crucial measures for the DUP was indeed a new victims commissioner, which had been promised by my predecessor Paul Murphy but was beset by the inveterate Northern Ireland problems of selecting someone acceptable to all sides and defining who was a 'victim'. Unionists were offended by the notion that victims of those killed by the security forces could be equated with victims of terrorism. Republicans argued that for grieving relatives a death was a death and that there was a war going on.

With my officials, equally keen to make progress, I devised the idea of an 'interim commissioner' who would consult widely and report on the remit and role subsequently to be undertaken by a full-time commissioner chosen according to the normal public appointments procedures. Because I would simply be tasking a suitable individual to report to me, I could just choose someone appropriate without the normal process of advertising and open competition. Government ministers tasked individuals all the time with specific reports or projects, so there were plenty of precedents.

I then asked Paisley for suggested names, stressing the individual needed to be capable of inspiring confidence across the community divides. I would not consider, and nor did I imagine he would ever contemplate himself, some DUP protégé or party figure. His first suggestion was indeed unsuitable, but then Paisley suggested Mrs Bertha MacDougall, a retired head teacher and widow of a Royal Ulster Constabulary policeman shot in the Troubles. She was interviewed by senior officials and recommended to me as a very strong candidate with no DUP connection. I saw her myself and found her ideal: capable, softly spoken but determined and shrewd, and evidently only too well aware of the sensitivities of the role.

I knew I would be criticised whatever I did about victims and whomever

I chose. But I had never shirked tough decisions in the past and certainly was not about to do so now. There are ministers who prefer a quiet ride and manage the in-tray without changing anything, and I never saw myself as one of those. I was never reckless. But I was prepared to take risks to do the right thing. I had come to the job to get a political settlement and I was very clear in my own mind that, without building trust with Paisley and implementing at least some of what the DUP called 'confidence building' measures, that would not possible. Furthermore, neglect of victims had been a running sore which needed attention.

So, with all the necessary due process undertaken by my civil servants, I decided to appoint Bertha MacDougall and announced her name at a press conference where she demonstrated the quiet toughness and competence she must have had as a head teacher, despite never having faced the media before. But, as I anticipated, the balloon went up immediately, the SDLP whinge-ing that it was a 'biased' appointment to placate the DUP. Sinn Fein were hardly enthusiastic, but their leaders understood my thinking. The SDLP were in their usual oppositional mood, currying favour with the prevalent senti-ment that saw anything 'not for their side' as something 'for the other side' and therefore automatically to be opposed. But I stood my ground and, as she got on with the job, groups across the divide were soon impressed with her impartiality and especially, as a victim herself, her instinctive sympathy, even with IRA-linked victims groups. The truth was I could not have chosen anyone better.

However, nobody had anticipated that one of Northern Ireland's judges would wade in behind the critics. There was a lucrative lawyers' industry for judicial reviews, which had become a form of politics by proxy. In the absence of functioning democratic politics, the courts were perpetually called upon to settle political grievances which would never be given the time of day in Britain.

Instead of simply dismissing out of hand the judicial review reference for the sectarian political ploy it was, Judge Paul Girvan flamboyantly treated it all very seriously indeed. As 2006 went on, my senior officials spent an inordinate amount of their precious time and resources delving into the small print and appearing as witnesses in court. It was a pantomime absurdly given credence by Judge Girvan. I happened to bump into one of his recently retired superiors at a social occasion and found him as incredulous as I was. Meanwhile Bertha MacDougall was quietly and effectively completing her task. A year on, with the legal proceedings still in full flow, she had finished her report to general acclaim from all but the most jaundiced.

Meanwhile, inch by inch, I was making progress on the peace process. Then, even more unbelievably, Judge Girvan decided to ask the Attorney General to investigate whether I had somehow prostituted my office and perverted the course of justice. The media lapped up the ensuring furore, in their insatiable appetite for process over substance. With my officials I thought the judge off his rocker, a view privately expressed to me by the Lord Chancellor, Charlie Falconer, who was equally bemused.

I was determined not to allow this irritating side-show distract me as much as it was my permanent secretary, now Jonathan Phillips, and the head of the Northern Ireland civil service, Nigel Hamilton, whose integrity was outrageously being questioned by Judge Girvan's high-handed and idiosyncratic behaviour. Eventually, the Attorney General's report dismissed it all, albeit with some pointed remarks about matters of detail in the civil service process around the case. The Appeal Court was similarly dismissive of his charges except on a procedural technicality. Having had run-ins with judges during my time as an anti-apartheid protester, I did wonder whether some history explained the eccentricity of the judge, or even whether in common with other high earners he had been unhappy about my reforms of the property tax system which raised rates for larger houses. 'No, that's just Northern Ireland for you,' people would remark with a knowing smile.

So it certainly was, when I was invited to confirm the promotion of the said Justice Girvan to become the Right Honourable Lord Girvan in Northern Ireland's Appeal Court. A document forwarded from Buckingham Palace with the Queen's official seal and signature 'Elizabeth R' awaited my imprimatur for the appointment to proceed. Pondering the document in my red box at Hillsborough on Christmas Eve, could I in all honesty agree to this when Justice Girvan's legal capabilities seemed so flawed? It was a momentary rather than serious thought. I knew full well that would provoke an even greater fuss and, just to be sure, called Charlie Falconer, who was actually on holiday in the Caribbean. 'I agree with you, not a wise thing to do,' he said amused. Nevertheless promoting someone who was going out of his way legally to damage me seemed a novel obligation.[*]

‡

Assuming my duty as Secretary of State to maintain order over controversial unionist parades by the Orange Order was something of a poacher-turned-gamekeeper role. The summer marching season had long provoked violence as Orangemen clad in sashes with bands banging drums paraded through

---

*   See Afterword, p.455.

nationalist and republican heartlands which felt intimidated. The Twelfth of July commemorating William of Orange's 1690 victory for Protestantism over the Catholic King James at the Battle of the Boyne was a notorious flashpoint. I perfectly understood why unionists asserted their right to commemorate their culture and history; I equally understood why long-oppressed Catholic communities found routes through their own streets and past their own houses extremely provocative.

By a mixture of good fortune, sensible policing and hard work by Sinn Fein leaders, we had just about got through the Twelfth of July without the normal bloody clashes. However, only after I had personally intervened, taking early morning calls from Gerry Adams and mediating a solution with Hugh Orde, a no-nonsense and politically astute Chief Constable whom I came to admire. (And who should really have been promoted to run the Metropolitan Police in 2009 and then again after the 2011 riots, but that's another story.) It was fascinating sitting in the police/army operations room called 'Gold Command' with live visual coverage of the flashpoints, especially in Ardoyne, a nationalist stronghold in West Belfast. In a couple of conversations with Gerry Adams I mentioned in passing that I had just seen him trying to calm both republican protesters and policemen; he seemed coolly unimpressed.

But that was July 2005 and the sting in the tail of the marching season came with the Whiterock Parade in September. To any outsider the fierce dispute over the route seemed so arcane as to be preposterous. It centred around whether the marchers should go through a gate which was iconic for them but incendiary to Catholics, or whether they would march up to the gate and then detour round to exactly the same point.

Bitter it certainly became on the day, as if all the good work over the summer had been for nothing. After much argument and consultation, the independent regulatory body, the Parades Commission, had made a determination on the route, and there was uproar amongst unionists. Ian Paisley was his old bellicose self, thundering on about 'serious consequences' on the day; he had past form inciting disorder and then being absent at the scene of the crime. Having been listed as a speaker at a protest rally, he wisely did not show up.

Our worries that loyalist paramilitaries would be active proved uncomfortably accurate. Soon the parade turned into a straight fight with the police backed up by soldiers. Unusually, Orangemen clad in their sashes joined in. Elsewhere police and army formed lines to stop loyalists breaking into republican communities to trigger sectarian conflict of the old twisted kind. Many police were injured as the desperate events then took a sinister turn. Masked gunmen from the Ulster Volunteer Force opened fire on police officers, firing hundreds of rounds, mainly at armoured Land Rovers – a frightening ordeal of bullets clattering onto the vehicle, causing a huge din for officers crouched inside. It was a minor miracle nobody was killed.

I was briefed by Shaun Woodward, my Security Minister, and later spoke to some of the police involved, having decided to change my diary and fly over on the Sunday evening so I was visibly seen to be in charge and could visit the police first thing on Monday. I was briefed by senior officers and met some of those who had been attacked on the front line, the media covering my show of solidarity.

Then I was shown secret video footage of the whole day, especially of the gunmen who fired off their rounds and ran quickly down alleyways into the gardens of nearby houses. There, waiting women, children watching, grabbed the balaclavas and handed over fresh clothes so the gunmen could escape, leaving their weapons to be gathered and hidden by fellow male conspirators. None of them knew they were being watched live and recorded. There on the screen in the darkened room were grim scenes from the 'old' Northern Ireland returning to haunt the new one which had been stepping hesitantly into a brighter future.

The bloody sectarian conflict of Whiterock now loomed ominously over all the progress made with the IRA during the summer – almost as if unionists and loyalists felt aggrieved at how the old republican enemy was getting all the plaudits, and were determined to demonstrate that, albeit in a twisted attention-seeking way, *they* still counted too.

Fortunately it wasn't all bad, however. Wiser counsels in the unionist community had also been shocked, quickly realising that their cause was in real danger of being discredited. Scenes of Orangemen with their emblematic sashes fighting police they had always seen as 'their own', with gunmen firing in the background, became symbolic of a wider unionist malaise, suddenly pitched onto the side of the very lawless violence they had long associated with republicans.

I decided to move quickly, establishing contact with moderate elements within the leadership of the Orange Order, and privately pressurising the DUP, who had publicly been in semi-denial about Whiterock. On the one hand they condemned the violence but on the other refused to accept culpability for the whole confrontationalist build-up in which they too had been complicit. However, whatever he was saying in public to keep on side with the Orange Order, Ian Paisley was privately very worried, as he confided to me.

I also started to make overtures to the leaders of the loyalist paramilitaries. This was highly controversial, not least because many of their followers had just been in open warfare with the security forces. But, again, both my South African insight and belief that people on the outside had to be brought in if at all possible, convinced me I should be prepared to take the political risk of talking to the enemy of the moment. After all, I reasoned to my officials, that was exactly what had been done with the IRA many years earlier. It was more difficult with the loyalists because their main organisations, the Ulster Volunteer Force and the Ulster Defence Association, had become more criminal than political. Whatever their original motivation and residual political rhetoric, both groups had degenerated into gangsterism. But there were still important politically orientated elements and, over the months that followed, I worked hard to seek these out, eventually meeting individuals who almost came blinking into the sunlight as they walked into my official rooms: 'men who are normally in uniform' as Mary Madden, my excellent community outreach official, put it. I attracted some public criticism, mainly from the DUP and the SDLP. By contrast Gerry Adams knew exactly what I was doing and was supportive, Sinn Fein still hankering after a longstanding dream of theirs: a working-class alliance across the divide with loyalists.

The other change I made was to the Parades Commission. I had become convinced that its approach was far too legalistic. That may well have been necessary in times when there was no dialogue between the opposing forces on the ground. But the end of the IRA's war had changed the mood fundamentally. Republicans and nationalists were more up for negotiating and there was less of a 'thou shalt not pass' rigidity towards Orange parades. A new chairman of the commission was due to be appointed, and I made it clear I wanted someone who could negotiate and not just issue legally enforceable route determinations; instead of being an almost automatic substitute for proper negotiation these should only be issued in the absence of an agreement.

My officials recommended as 'appointable' two candidates for me to interview informally and choose between. Their preference was the one with long experience in public administration. But I chose Roger Poole, formerly a modernising trade union officer with a reputation as a problem solver, and who had spent most of his adult life as a negotiator, even though my officials considered him the riskier choice. The decision was more than vindicated as Poole was totally to transform the context for parades, my officials delighted. This was to be an example of when a Minister really could make a difference: in twelve years of government I saw too many instances where Ministers took the cautious line, and simply allowed the official machine to trundle on as it would have done without them.

This approach paid off because I was invited early in 2007 as the first Secretary of State to visit the headquarters of the Orange Order. It was an interesting occasion, not least when their reputation for being right wing was confounded. I was proudly shown an old photograph of the Orange Lodge branch in my childhood home of Pretoria. It had voluntarily disbanded in the 1930s after refusing to abide by the pre-apartheid colour bar confining membership to whites. 'We don't see you as a typical Brit, Peter,' one of the Orangemen present confided.

‡

In late September 2005, the Independent International Commission on Decommissioning (IICD) confirmed that all IRA weapons had 'been put beyond use'. The IICD worked from, amongst other things, estimates from the Security Service and were satisfied that the IRA had decommissioned all weapons under their control.

Towards the end of the year, six months into the job, I had begun to sow seeds for what I believed was a relatively small time frame for securing an overall settlement. I pointed out, especially to Paisley and his colleagues, that we faced uniquely favourable circumstances. Tony Blair and Bertie Ahern were two Prime Ministers who knew the process and the key individuals like the back of their hands. But Tony had indicated he would be stepping down, probably in 2007 – the same year as Bertie faced the uncertainty of an Irish general election. Sinn Fein and the IRA had moved everything on exponentially – though they still needed to sign up to support policing and the rule of law, which was historically and politically an even tougher hurdle for them than ending a war which hadn't been practised for a decade.

But, I argued privately to the DUP, Northern Ireland Assembly members faced re-election, also in 2007. They had already been elected once before, in 2003, to a body which was suspended, and I couldn't see the public accepting the charade of voting a second time for something which did not exist. None of the DUP politicians faulted the logic. So I began saying this publicly and, unusually for almost anything any Secretary of State might say, nobody contradicted me. Newspaper editorials across the divide agreed, and journalists started to question politicians about the implications of a time window just eighteen months wide. I then added, again without dissent, that I would cancel the due 2007 election if there was no settlement by then.

The DUP hated the gauntlet being thrown down in this way. Soon they were to hate it even more when I determined upon another stratagem popular with the voters, in fact almost wildly popular. I would not be prepared to keep paying for long the salaries and generous allowances Assembly members received if there was no progress towards a settlement. 'You are bullying us, Peter,' Ian Paisley thundered at me. 'The Ulster people will never stand for that.' The problem, he knew full well, was that in this instance the people *would* stand for it, especially when I started saying in speeches and interviews that Assembly Members were the only citizens who did not have to turn up at work to get paid.

This was meat and drink for the media. Soon they were running stories about the size of the Members' salaries (not large, but much larger than local average earnings), together with all the allowances for staffing and offices, car mileage and subsistence for overnight stays away from their constituencies. The Members hated this and hated me for doing it to them, grimacing as they conceded I was right. Peter Robinson quietly told me approvingly it was causing real consternation in the large DUP Assembly group, and also to party officials and leaders since another element of the public funding involved was paid directly to the parties to enable them to organise their Stormont activities with support staff, in the DUP's case amounting to hundreds of thousands of pounds a year. Robinson could not say so publicly of course, but he felt it helped 'reformist' elements like him who wanted a settlement against the large body of refuseniks in his party. Inside information also indicated that my threat had caused deep concern amongst the families of DUP Assembly Members, understandably worried about how they would pay their mortgages.

Effectively they were being pressured from a tangent never before tried, and which might well not have worked years earlier, before Assembly Members had become a semi-permanent political class with all the trappings and lifestyles of modern democratic politics – save for a functioning legislature. However, the strategy was not without risks. If they really called my bluff and I was forced to close down the cross-community political class, the breadth of which – from hardline republicans to hardline unionists, all under the same roof – had never before existed in Northern Ireland, that would create a worrying political vacuum.

The next innovation was to reform domestic policy in a way no Secretary of State had done before. My predecessors had generally taken the view that, in the absence of a locally elected government, radical changes in domestic policy – education, health and so on – would be mostly consensual. Meanwhile they would focus all their energies on the peace process – leaving the civil service effectively in charge. Most of my energies were also concentrated on the peace process, but I rather enjoyed the opportunity to run the place myself. There was no other job in Cabinet, aside from being Prime Minister, where you effectively governed a whole country, in charge of everything from agriculture to security.

Despite civil service resentment (and sometimes resistance) I had my Ministers – David Hanson, Shaun Woodward, Angela Smith, Maria Eagle, Paul Goggins and David Cairns – embark upon a radical reform programme, for instance reducing hospital waiting times for operations from years to months. I was also able to pursue my own agendas including a new renewable energy fund. We adopted policies to strip out huge layers of bureaucracy, for example cutting excessive numbers of local councils from twenty-six to seven, which was unpopular with the politicians, though not with the voters. Abolition of the eleven-plus exam – which determined whether a child went to a top grammar school or was left behind in a secondary modern – was unpopular with unionists but not with nationalists and republicans.

Reforms to make the property tax system fairer by increasing charges for higher earners and reduce them for lower earners brought the middle classes out in revolt. This was despite Phil Taylor helping to devise a scheme for me, unique in the UK, where bills were not just linked to house value but income as well, and with wide-ranging exemptions including those in education and training and those leaving care until they were twenty-one. The introduction of water charges, from which Northern Ireland residents alone in the United Kingdom were exempt, brought out almost the whole population in revolt despite devising a way of protecting those on low incomes, also uniquely in the UK. With her proverbial dry wit, my private secretary only half-joking maintained she would have to send her pensioner mother out to stack shelves in a supermarket.

My public rejoinder to a continuous torrent of complaints was: 'I believe these policies are in the public interest. But if you don't like them, you know only too well what the solution is – replace direct rule ministers with elected devolved government.' I practically incited them to make me redundant, and my radical domestic policies became important levers in the political process – in the end to some extent decisive.

But it wasn't all heavy politics. I spent considerable effort using my international motor sport contacts to try and get Rally Ireland – the event which spanned the border and was a small symbol of unity across the divides – into the World Rally Championship calendar. As part of the promotion and lobbying, I agreed to be 'co-driver' (navigator) for Billy Coleman, a famous Irish rally champion long since retired. A lovely man well into his sixties, he was a farmer in Cork and we had some fun going as fast as we could. Near disaster struck however, when the rally promoters failed to fill the petrol tank sufficiently and we ran out of fuel on a remote track somewhere in the Tyrone countryside, a former IRA stronghold. Until the rally's safety helicopter arrived half an hour later, there I was stranded by the roadside, my armed protection officers frantic with worry and miles away. The IRA of old in the Northern Ireland of old would have rubbed their hands in glee at the sight of a hapless British Secretary of State, a sitting duck in their territory.

‡

As 2006 came in, I was keen to get the Assembly up and running again because that would be the way to get all the parties working together and thereby to build the foundations for a subsequent political settlement. However, this looked impossible. Ian Paisley and his colleagues were keen to have a 'Shadow Assembly' so they could be seen to be doing their jobs and to use it as a platform for their views. But they would not tolerate a fully fledged Assembly with powers devolved since that, amongst other things, meant participation in government with Sinn Fein. By contrast Gerry Adams would not accept the 'sop' of a 'Shadow' body: it had to be the real thing or nothing. Deadlock.

Eventually, after tortuous negotiations, stand-offs and mini-crises, we came up with a formulation that might just about carry the day: neither a 'Shadow' nor a fully functioning Assembly, but an 'Interim' one, with committees covering different problem areas which could 'prepare for government'. It would exist from 15 May 2006 through to 24 November 2006: the deadline I set for an Executive to be formed and power to be devolved. None of the parties was entirely happy with this, but all could just about live with it, and I took emergency legislation through Parliament to establish this new creature, which opened without fuss as planned for the first time since it had become moribund four years before.

I had taken powers of direction over the Assembly, including choosing the new Speaker, Eileen Bell of the Alliance Party, her two DUP and Sinn Fein deputies, and determining the agenda and order of proceedings for the opening session. Although surprising for an independent legislature to tolerate my potentially dictatorial powers, these had the support of the parties who did not want it to fail on some as yet unforeseen but all too familiar stand-off. They trusted the British Secretary of State (whose presence they all otherwise resented) to hold the ring and take decisions where they were incapable of doing so themselves. In other words they wanted me, an 'outsider', to fall back upon: an ironic, almost semi-colonial relationship, but one I was happy to abide by if it delivered the desired outcome.

The 24 November deadline, I repeatedly insisted, was for real. I wrote in the *Belfast Telegraph*: 'Setting a deadline is not an attempt to threaten anyone or to bully anyone or force anyone into a place they don't want to be. But it is time for the political caravan that has been touring for years and years to find a permanent place at Stormont.' If the deadline was not met, I would pull the entire Assembly down together with all their pay and allowances – the public willing me on, and unionist politicians seething that, for once, *their* voters were on *my* side. Upping the ante in this way was high-wire strategy, and there were rumblings amongst the old hands, including some of my Tory and Labour predecessors, that it could all fall over. My calculated risk also put my credibility at stake. The DUP – resenting as they put it 'holding Ulster to ransom' – seemed determined to break the deadline for its own sake, though privately Peter Robinson and even Ian Paisley perfectly understood that I was helping them to achieve progress by ensuring for the first time a serious down-side to saying 'no'. All the other parties were sympathetic to my approach, albeit surly about threats over the pay and allowances. At least Tony Blair and Bertie Ahern were fully behind me – though I had no illusions that, if it went pear shaped, I would carry the can, not them: the time-honoured privilege of the boss.

Just before the Assembly reopened for the first time in nearly four years on 15 May 2006, there had been a government reshuffle. Beforehand I had indicated to Tony Blair that I did not want to be moved, because I wanted to finish the job of achieving a political settlement and thought I could. He made a point of speaking to me privately afterwards and saying that he was sorry about the circumstances because he had wanted to give me an even more senior post (Jack Straw had just been demoted from Foreign Secretary and some of Tony's advisers had said in the past I would be an ideal person for that job, though whether that had been on his mind, who knows).

There was a restrained buoyancy as Stormont came out of cold storage and reconvened for a brief opening, all the politicians anxious to present a dignified image to an electorate increasingly impatient with their squabbling: 'Get on with it or get out' was the view on the street. There was little appe-tite for point-scoring plenary sessions and, instead, Assembly members once more started meeting in committees to discuss policy, which was all on the record. However, the DUP still did not acknowledge Sinn Fein and stuck by the pretence of only speaking through the chair (the reality was rather more complex). I was relaxed over outbreaks of bad temper – especially between Sinn Fein and the DUP – because the very fact the parties were engaged in an 'interim' form of legislative politics was a real advance.

In early July, my trade union hinterland came in useful when I took the precaution of taking some advice on employment law before writing to the clerks at Stormont asking that staff of all MLAs and all the parties be given three months' notice that their employment would terminate after 24 November if there was no deal. The media were briefed that staff in any doubt about their masters' intentions to settle should be looking for other jobs. Stormont was abuzz with worried assistants conferring about their fate and Assembly Members throwing dark looks in my direction.

‡

Meanwhile the ticking time bomb of traditional republican hostility to supporting policing and the rule of law continued, and I constantly discussed how we could resolve it. Sinn Fein privately insisted that it was incendiary amongst their rank and file; however, it might, just might, be possible if they had the certainty both of participating with the DUP in government and a timetable for devolving justice and policing to that government. The DUP insisted that was out of the question unless Sinn Fein had signed up beforehand – the process once more stuck between a rock and a hard place.

Then came an episode symbolic of the contradictions and ironies of this endgame period. The popular loyalist leader David Ervine suddenly died after a massive heart attack, his funeral a huge occasion. My presence was warmly welcomed and there was a surprise attendee: Gerry Adams. He had asked my advice about going and I had said it was a great idea. But he was understandably nervous, his bodyguards even more so – everyone only too conscious of the history of bloody feuds between their two organisations. He was acknowledged and treated with courtesy, leaving afterwards immediately in front of me, tensely walking between grim ranks of the Ulster Volunteer Force parting for us in the overflow outside. I had fixed for Security Police to cocoon his party, just in case: IRA leader of old protected by hated agencies of the Brits, loyalist paramilitaries barely an arm length away, bristling though respectful.

Sinn Fein had to change their position on policing, I knew only too well, if Ian Paisley was ever seriously to contemplate a deal. During increasingly productive and warm private meetings with him, Paisley was indicating he wanted to make an agreement if he possibly could. But he added: 'I just cannot deliver it without them backing policing. And I won't try.' In public he would refer to 'Sinn Fein-IRA', in private to 'them' or 'the other fellas'.

All the parties supported the devolution of policing and justice from London to Belfast – in principle. But Paisley's DUP was extremely wary about timing, and could not countenance the notion unless republicans were fully signed up to law enforcement. How could Sinn Fein participate in government without supporting policing and the judiciary which would, in devolved mode, be accountable to that very government? A pretty compelling argument, I felt, and made that clear to Gerry Adams, Martin McGuinness and Gerry Kelly.

Equally, a compelling argument for republicans was that they could not countenance signing up for policing and justice administered and controlled by the very British state whose legitimacy in Northern Ireland they could not and would not accept, indeed were founded to destroy. What helped was that the IRA were shown by independent monitors to have been delivering, not just on their commitment the previous year to end their war, but to get out of criminality as well.

As the summer ended, Assembly Members came back to their committees, intensely aware that time was running out. The countdown was on for the decision end-date, 24 November 2006. A deadline, I reminded them, which, for the first time in the process leading up to, and after, Good Friday in 1998, had been deliberately put in legislation. There was no wriggle room. Whether I subsequently liked it or not, it was set in statute, and Parliament would be contemptuous of any DUP attempt to come back and ask for new legislation to move the date: if there was no progress, the Assembly would come tumbling down.

‡

Despite the dull grey rain, the pretty and historic Scottish university town of St Andrews brought back fond memories for Tony Blair, on the drive to the summit. 'I met some nice girls here,' he said wistfully, 'And, over there, that pub,' he pointed out of the window, 'that's where I played in our rock band.' Unusual, that, because Tony was never really sentimental or nostalgic about the past. He always wanted to 'move on', to look to the future.

With the deadline fast approaching and still no sign of a deal, we had called the summit between 11 and 13 October 2006 to bring things to a head. Getting everyone under one roof, even if they were not all talking directly to one another, seemed the best way forward to concentrate minds. Like everything else we were trying, it was risky. Expectations were roused. If it failed, that would be a severe setback.

Everything was in place for a success. Independent monitors had been issuing reports every few months, their latest confirming that the IRA had committed itself to an exclusively political path. The summer parading had been the best and most trouble-free for decades, the new chairman I had appointed delivering dialogue of the kind which had never occurred before. Ian Paisley had just met the Catholic Archbishop of the whole island of Ireland – something he had always refused to do. The day before we all arrived at St Andrews I gave interviews and wrote press articles encouraging the politicians to seize the opportunity: 'We can't continue this endless merry-go-round of virtual politics, in which for four years now Assembly Members have been acting as fully fledged legislators when they aren't legislating or doing their jobs.' I had seen Ian Paisley on his own before this and he had seemed remarkably positive.

This summit – like European ones I had attended as Europe Minister – had a certain, claustrophobic life of its own. We were all bunched together under the same, very large, roof of the Fairmont Hotel, a luxury clifftop resort overlooking the Fife coast and set in a 520-acre estate. Everyone walked about in self-important groups. I chatted to all and sundry. DUP delegates would march past Sinn Fein members without acknowledging they were even there. Yet they had sat together facing us in the same room at the brief formal opening session on the Wednesday afternoon when we all arrived.

It was slow to begin with, as Tony Blair and Bertie Ahern saw each of the party leaders in turn, the foggy, wet weather outside adding to the downbeat atmosphere. The next day was completely different, dry and bright, though progress again seemed very slow. Suddenly a frisson of excitement: the two Prime Ministers and their security entourages were seen heading for the coast in the sunshine, Tony striding out and Bertie scampering at his side. I remembered from European summits that Tony walked at a tremendous pace.

Then, the evening drew in, gloom settling on everyone. We were stuck. The DUP weren't shifting as Paisley had indicated they might, and the media sensed their pre-summit scepticism was being vindicated. Tony asked me to go and explain this to all the delegations. I eventually tracked down a Paisley-less DUP coming buoyantly out of their small meeting room.

'How's it all going?' they asked jauntily.

'Terrible,' I replied, 'it's going to crash. We are making arrangements to bring forward transport right after breakfast.'

Peter Robinson, normally sphinx-like, looked startled. Some of his colleagues went white with shock. 'You aren't serious?'

'Of course I am. And you are the problem. You won't budge. Everyone else has been flexible. Still, if that's the way it has to be, I will immediately put in place arrangements for the Assembly to be pulled down.' I stated this in a low-key and matter-of-fact tone, obviously resigned to failure. I was playing it by instinct because Tony had not asked me to be so blunt. But I felt we had reached the point when everyone had to stop going through the motions.

My astute parliamentary aide Dan Norris MP together with others later thought this a crucial encounter of the summit. It certainly did jolt the DUP back to their senses. They couldn't posture any more. It was for real.

Paisley was informed and Peter Robinson, the key negotiator, was spotted in late-night talks near the hotel bar with the Irish deputy Prime Minister. I conferred with Tony and Bertie over a few beers, with our officials grabbing a seat in his hotel living room wherever they could perch. Then I went to bed, like everyone else wondering what lay ahead of us.

Waking up early as I usually did, I decided to go and see Tony. He was up, barefoot in track suit bottoms and T-shirt, scribbling away, the ubiquitous Jonathan Powell hovering. We took stock. Tony thought he had found a way through. Maybe. It had come down to policing, as I always knew it would. Paisley and then Adams came and went. So did the others.

Then, with what we thought was an outline agreement to hand, much of it pre-drafted, each delegation came down the corridor to see me, and I took them through the detail. Paisley seemed calm, though some of his previously intransigent colleagues were subdued as if being denied their familiar NO reflex. I pointed to the fact that all Sinn Fein Ministers would have to swear allegiance to policing and the rule of law before becoming Ministers, something Paisley had confided in me was the key for him: 'If they swear this before God in public, that's what we need.' The other side of this coin was Sinn Fein's demand: a commitment to the devolution of policing and justice within two years.

Inch by inch, as the morning passed, we seemed to be getting there. Then there were the inevitable last-minute hiccups. Gerry Adams dug his heels in over a commitment to legislate for equality for the Irish language, pressing Tony Blair, who turned to me, eyebrows raised, in that 'What the hell do I do now?' way of his. I was pretty forthright. I had experience in Wales where the language was spoken by twenty per cent of the population. In Northern Ireland, it was under one per cent. Furthermore, in the event of devolution, responsibility would pass to the Assembly. How could the government legislate for the language over their heads? Adams still pressed hard. Apparent to all was the irony of 'the Brits' forcing the language on the Irish against the wishes of an Assembly in which the unionists had a blocking majority. Constitutionally and politically it was nonsense. But Adams was insistent, so we put some words in anyway.

Meanwhile time was marching on. We were all due to gather in a final plenary session, then to make an announcement on a stage in front of a specially prepared backdrop signalling 'The St Andrews Agreement'. The choreography was vital. Media deadlines had to be met, people had to catch planes for other commitments. Yet we were still not absolutely sure we had everyone fully signed up. Adams was still jibbing at the text. Ian Paisley Junior scurried in with his very own last-minute demand: something over a planning application for a luxury hotel and golf course on the Antrim coast next to the Giant's Causeway, a United Nations World Heritage site.

Tony seemed transfixed. 'Let's just all go to the plenary and announce it,' I urged, 'we can't keep messing about. None of them are going to back off now.' Unless, that was, we prevaricated and let them unravel our carefully stitched-together series of compromises. Then we would be back to square one. There is a moment when you just have to go for it, I argued. Jonathan Powell and Tom Kelly were with me. We hustled a hesitant Tony out towards the plenary, the media waiting.

It was just as well we did call their bluffs. All the delegations filed in, and sat down on their best behaviour, the atmosphere expectant. As we waited for the Prime Ministers, I joked across the room with Paisley and Robinson, some of their colleagues stony faced behind them. It was a jovial yet digni-fied occasion, given engaging poignancy by presentations for Paisley and his recently ennobled wife. It was their fiftieth wedding anniversary. Bertie Ahern gave them a specially preserved and polished bowl carved from a huge walnut tree at the site of the Battle of the Boyne, such an iconic event in unionist folklore. Paisley was visibly moved and almost overcome by the generosity of the gesture. 'Thank you very much. Thank you. This is a great day for Eileen and I – and a great day for democracy too.' The significance of the last bit was noted by all, Adams acknowledging it, McGuinness smiling broadly.

It was a typically Northern Ireland outcome. If there wasn't yet full agree-ment about the agreement, there was no disagreement either. Tony Blair's overnight genius was for the two Prime Ministers to 'call it' and to present the agreement to the parties, on the understanding that none would disagree. Four days later a new Programme for Government Committee would meet at Stormont to discuss priorities for the new Executive, with Paisley and Adams sitting together for the first time. I would take emergency legislation through Parliament the week before the deadline on 24 November and the same day the Assembly would meet to nominate First and deputy First Ministers. In early March 2007 there would be fresh Assembly elections, giving a mandate for the parties to enter government together. On 26 March power would be devolved. But if it went badly wrong at any stage, my ultimatum to pull the Assembly down would take effect.

After media interviews, we left quickly. I wanted to get Tony out soon, before he could be nobbled. Gerry Adams came pounding past me in the hotel looking furious. 'Where's Tony?' he said. 'He's gone,' I replied, sparing with the truth. He had 'gone' from the meeting areas but was elsewhere in the hotel and I was about to join him for the drive to the airport.

My jet – diverted to Belfast on its way to Cardiff – was packed, not just with the Paisleys and Ian Junior, who had asked to be taken back to Belfast for a celebration of their anniversary, but with Peter Robinson and Martin

McGuinness too. I wondered how they would all be squeezed in together: hardnosed in silence perhaps? But no. As I joked and chatted, a sort of banter even passed between the Paisleys, Robinson and McGuinness! Funny how, when you got even Northern Ireland enemies together, they had more day-to-day life in common than divided them. What passed between them was all rather indirect and deniable of course, but another hopeful if surreal pointer to the future.

Meanwhile our team was quietly jubilant. The summit had exceeded our hopes and certainly confounded the media. The St Andrews Agreement, Tom Kelly told me, was 'probably even more significant than Good Friday because the DUP is inside the tent'. There were no wild celebrations, however, because too much could still go wrong.

‡

It all nearly did, four weeks later, on Friday 24 November 2006, the original deadline, now the all-important occasion for nominations for First and deputy First Minister 'designates', namely Ian Paisley and Martin McGuinness. Expectations were high: the 'Transitional Assembly' had gathered for the first time, the media in force, outside broadcast vans surrounding Stormont, live coverage scheduled, the politicians excited, some more grumpily so than others.

But there was at least one major stumbling block which could bring it all crashing down on day one. With Sinn Fein still not signed up for policing as they had promised at St Andrews because Paisley had reneged on meeting in the Programme for Government Committee, the DUP were in a sour mood. Paisley had himself agreed to be nominated, but 'his men' were distinctly unhappy.

As I had directed, the Speaker opened up proceedings and all went reasonably smoothly, everyone on best behaviour, all too conscious that they must be seen by the public to be doing their jobs. Then the much-anticipated moment: the nominations of Paisley and McGuinness. I was watching it live on television and the tension was palpable: what exactly would happen?

Reading somewhat haltingly from my script, Speaker Eileen Bell said that there were nominations for Paisley and McGuinness, and she understood these were agreed. There was a rumble of dissent amongst the DUP ranks, and Paisley rose seemingly about to thunder an Ulster 'NO!' Then, as if by divine intervention, there was a confusing commotion and alarms went off. The Speaker stood up before Paisley could speak and announced suspension of the sitting after an apparent attack on the building.

Providence had it that, minutes before, a loyalist paramilitary, Michael Stone, had tried to burst armed into the chamber, seemingly to kill Adams and McGuinness with half a dozen bomb devices. He had previously been convicted for randomly murdering three mourners at a 1988 IRA funeral as he ran into a Belfast cemetery firing a pistol and lobbing hand grenades. Stone had been released early in June 2000, under the terms of the Good Friday Agreement. Bizarrely, he later described his Stormont act as 'performance art replicating a lapsed terrorist'. Assembly security staff tackled and disarmed him, and the building remained evacuated for the rest of the day, Members going off for the weekend.

However, I still had a crisis to manage. Gerry Adams and Martin McGuinness quickly demanded to see me, frustrated that Paisley had reneged again, this time on accepting nomination. Paisley must correct the situation, they demanded, and I could not disagree. Half an hour later Paisley and Robinson trooped in at my request.

'We are in a serious position, Ian,' I said. 'Everyone is saying you did not agree to be nominated for First Minister. In that case I will have to pull the Assembly down. The legislation leaves me no alternative. What are we going to do?' Paisley was calm but evidently worried. 'Can you issue a press statement to clarify the position?' I asked.

He reached for his pen and wrote out a short statement which Peter Robinson amended. It confirmed what he had said at St Andrews, namely that it was his intention to accept the nomination for First Minister, after the election on 7 March and provided that all the conditions agreed at St Andrews for Sinn Fein to support policing had been met. Just what I wanted: we were back in business – but it had been perilously close to collapse.

My brilliant press chief, Dennis Godfrey, a Belfast wordsmith with a wicked wit, described how the whole business of Paisley agreeing to be nominated was like a 'spot the badger' moment from a live 'Badger Watch'-type programme beloved of the BBC.

Ten minutes a night with the camera trained on a bush.

Suddenly there is a flash and the voice of authority says: 'That's it! We've seen the badger! Let's catch the magic moment again.' There is a slow flash and what looks like a thumb print on the lens.

The next day: 'Did you see the badger last night?'

'Yes, I think so.'

Two days later: 'That was some badger the other night.'

'Yeah, and did you see the teeth on it?'

‡

Much of my Christmas–New Year break at Hillsborough that year with our extended family was spent on the phone, shuttling between Sinn Fein, the DUP and Tony Blair, by now on a family break in Miami at a large house owned by one of the Bee Gees. The media constantly moaned about 'freebies' from friends who lent him their retreats. But he could not escape on a package holiday somewhere. Apart from the family, he had to have with him a small office and a full complement of armed protection officers.

The familiar catch-22 was still paralysing progress in Northern Ireland. Adams would not call a special Party conference, an *ardfheis*, to endorse policing until his Executive, the *Ardchomhairle,* was clear that the DUP would stick to the St Andrews timetable for devolving policing. The DUP would not give such a commitment until they were certain that Sinn Fein was genuinely delivering on policing. All sorts of formulas for Paisley to make a statement enabling Adams to convene his *Ardchomhairle* were tried, in an interminably frustrating process.

When Tony answered the phone for about the sixth time one day, I sympathised that his wife Cherie must be exasperated. 'I think she wants to nuke Northern Ireland,' he said wryly.

Finally, Adams decided simply to convene his *Ardchomhairle* anyway – a bold step. I had kept assuring him Paisley would deliver on sharing power if he delivered on policing – but it was a huge risk for him: '*You* may be convinced, Peter, but how can *I* be really sure?' he quite reasonably asked. Still, the log jam was cleared.

An increasingly exhausted Adams went on a punishing schedule of daily meetings with local republicans right around the country to win support for his strategy and, right on the eve of the election, the *ardfheis* finally backed him.

‡

But the election campaign did not fulfil the parties' expectations. Instead of being dominated by the usual issues of violence, security and age-old divisions, the people united together on one issue. 'All they want to talk about is your water charges!' a bemused Paisley confided in me. 'They just want us to get into government and put an end to them.'

I reported back to Tony, for whom the familiar kaleidoscope with which he had grappled for ten years was being shaken. He hadn't bargained on my policies on water charges or banning academic selection for high schools or stopping all discrimination against homosexuals coming up trumps in this way. Indeed he had sniffily referred to my agenda for a 'socialist republic of Hain'. Now he was obviously delighted.

Both the DUP and Sinn Fein strengthened their dominance in the elections, a vindication of Paisley's willingness to countenance sharing power, and Adams's support for policing, both against the wishes of their respective fundamentalists. The day afterwards, Paisley was ebullient when I travelled up to meet him in his constituency: 'Get in there and do it, Big Man, the people kept telling me,' he confided with enthusiasm. His previously refusenik son Ian made sure the visit went well and that the waiting media had a good photo opportunity of us together. It was clear that this was a family ready to take power, ready to say 'yes' for the very first time.

Still, it wasn't easy finally to get them over the line, and there were more histrionics to come. Having often been the despair of Peter Robinson and the reformers in the DUP, Paisley had now leapt over them, and they resented him meeting me on his own. 'He's almost being reckless,' Robinson moaned to me. Suddenly they had switched roles, with Robinson, the likely successor, more hawkish. 'We cannot take the majority of our party with us if we devolve power on 26 March,' he insisted. The date which I had deliberately put in the legislation was not achievable. 'It would split the Party. We have to go past it – into May,' he argued, 'then we will go into power with Sinn Fein.'

'But how can anyone be certain of that?' I asked. 'Nobody will believe you will ever do it.' There was always a macho 'Ulster says NO' element to the DUP and I was not going to succumb. I dug my heels in, taking the precaution of going privately to see Tony Blair, as I wasn't entirely sure he would stand firm, though Jonathan Powell and Tom Kelly were totally with me. I asked Tony directly whether he would back me on this. 'Absolutely,' he replied. 'This is the moment when it will either happen, or it won't. You have my full support.'

At a frantic series of meetings with the DUP Tony was as good as his word, making it clear that the deadline had to be met. I was talking to Robinson, Tony was talking to Paisley, we were both talking to Adams and McGuinness. As the deadline loomed, we were all desperately trying to find a way through. Then Robinson, the master party strategist, decided to call a Saturday meeting of his Party Executive just two days before the Monday deadline.

On the Friday, I jetted back from Belfast to No. 10 for a final meeting at Paisley's request. His DUP delegation was a little larger than usual, including the previously recalcitrant Nigel Dodds. Gradually, reluctantly, a possible solution emerged. Tony was reassuringly firm on the deadline, but then made an ingenious suggestion. Since we could not agree to extend it into May the only way forward was if the DUP could get Sinn Fein's agreement to do so.

That meant the two parties meeting formally for the very first time over the weekend to negotiate a mutually acceptable agreement, with a public meeting between Paisley and Adams on the Monday deadline day.

Then, just as we were making progress, a message was rushed into the room. Iranian Revolutionary Guards had taken British sailors hostage in the Gulf, and Tony had to deal with the crisis, leaving me to continue the negotiations. The mood was positive, if tense, as the DUP knew the deadline was otherwise set in statute, and the Assembly would fold. Eventually, Tony returned and we finally agreed on the detail, albeit without any sense of celebration; the DUP didn't do those. A recommendation would be put to their Executive the following day, and Robinson and Dodds would lead for their side in an historic first negotiating meeting with Martin McGuinness and his colleagues. They would try to agree the way forward – exactly what Tony had been striving for over the past decade: face-to-face dialogue at last between the two old enemies.

I immediately phoned another of the outstanding officials at the Northern Ireland Office. Only days before, I had promised Clare Salters we were sticking to the deadline so there would be no more emergency Bills for her to draft. Although it was late Friday evening, she was at her desk with her team. 'A grovelling apology, Clare, we need a Bill by Monday,' I told her. 'No problem, we have already planned for this and will work all weekend,' she replied, explaining that if it had not gone through Parliament and received Royal Assent by Tuesday night, the Assembly would indeed fold, needing another election to be restored.

The Saturday proved to be an odd combination of tension and exhilaration. Elizabeth and I were at Hillsborough Castle, but there was not much I could do. The ball was now well and truly in the court of the old protagonists, and we went for walks in the grounds, albeit with my mobile phone ringing constantly. By mid-afternoon, news came through that the DUP meeting had backed the leadership, so that was one big step forward. Now would the other steps follow?

I made my office at Stormont Castle available for the meeting between Sinn Fein and the DUP, wondering whether it would fail. My key officials lurked in the background providing practical assistance as needed. It was a novel experience, for previously our presence was always necessary to achieve progress in separate meetings with both parties, holding them in sequence so we could carry messages and effectively facilitate negotiations by remote control. Now we were out of it: exactly what I and my Labour predecessors had dreamt of.

In fact this piece of Saturday night history could not have gone better. As leading figures from both sides told me afterwards, 'we found we had

much more in common as people from Northern Ireland than we thought.'
My political director, Robert Hannigan, introduced them to each other and
then left them to it. The ice breaker was the live European 2008 qualifying
football match on television between Northern Ireland and Liechtenstein, in
which Northern Ireland triumphed 4-1. I got an excited call from my private
secretary, Mark Larmour: 'They have the match on TV. We can hear them
all repeatedly interrupting themselves to cheer on the team.' Each of the four
pizza take-away shops he had called to order food thought he was hoaxing
with an order for Stormont Castle. Finally he persuaded another outlet to
deliver: 'If you say that's where it is, we'll be there.' However, DUP hardliner
Nigel Dodds got food poisoning. He had to leave sick and in agony, but then
popped his head back around their door: 'Don't think I am leaving for any
other reason,' he anxiously reassured Sinn Fein.

‡

Seasoned sceptics – broadcasters, politicians, civil servants – rubbed their eyes
in disbelief. There, on the deadline day, the morning of Monday 26 March
2007, Ian Paisley sat serene in Stormont next to a beaming Gerry Adams, the
pictures transmitted across the world.

But it almost never happened. Not because of negotiating disagreements –
but because of the seating plan. Paisley would under no circumstances sit on
the same side of the table as Adams, whereas Adams insisted on doing so. I
obviously wanted them both next to each other for photographs and television
pictures, a vital symbol of the settlement and for history. Robert Hannigan
came up with the brilliant idea of a diamond-shaped arrangement so that the
two of them sat on either side of the same end. For all the world they were
sitting next to each other but Paisley was able to hold true to his position: not
on the same side of the new table hastily assembled overnight.

There was an element of magic about it for me. I had throughout, and
often alone, believed we could do it, and now was nearly the culmination of
all I had worked for, something most thought would never, ever happen. The
next day I rushed the Bill through both Houses of Parliament and the Queen
signified her assent. Now in prospect was a still more important date: devolution day on 8 May 2007 when Ian Paisley and Martin McGuinness would
become First and deputy First Minister.

To general surprise, they quickly developed a good working relationship –
they became known as the 'Chuckle Brothers'. But before they could take power,
I was to receive the very first letter they had jointly signed: please could they take
over my offices at Stormont Castle? Never had an eviction notice been so gladly

received, I quipped publicly, and arrangements were made for the outsider to move elsewhere on the government estate to make space for the new insiders.

In the weeks that followed – and before I was reshuffled to another Cabinet post – there were other tasks to fulfil. But none were the equal of Devolution Day, when a smiling Paisley and McGuinness took over power from me. A joyous occasion when a new Northern Ireland was born, it went off without a hitch, the sunny day signifying the hopes of all. My parents, now in their eighties, had been specially invited over, and I proudly introduced them to all the leading figures including Martin McGuinness's Mum, a small lady up at Stormont for the first time in her life and equally proud of her son. Prompted by my fiercely supportive private secretary, Mark Larmour, I just followed both Prime Ministers in to the First Minister's room to be photographed with Paisley and McGuinness. 'I wasn't expecting you to be here,' Paisley winked at me. (Nor was anyone else.)

After their ten years of work, all the public credit naturally went to Tony Blair and Bertie Ahern. Others directly involved (including my senior officials) saw it differently. The veteran Irish TV political editor Tommie Gorman generously said: '*You* were the man who did it, Peter. You came as an outsider and brought a whole new strategy. You had the balls to front them all up and the courage to keep going. Without you it wouldn't have happened.'

Not that everything had been resolved. Graffiti in a republican neighbourhood of Belfast still proclaimed – HAIN IS INSANE; in a loyalist one – SINN HAIN. A loyalist painter responsible for starkly sectarian, vivid murals of balaclava-clad gunmen had been asked to join a project to transform these into ones more fitting in the new era. But despite personally approving of the project, he spurned all approaches to participate, explaining: 'I am not a very good painter. I can't do faces, only balaclavas.'

CHAPTER ELEVEN

POLICE, SPIES AND LIES

Security Police hostility became a constant in my life from when I was about ten years old in South Africa. Then in Britain as an anti-apartheid leader I was again targeted by police, Special Branch and intelligence services. So it was to say the least novel, from the moment I was elected MP for Neath in 1991 and faced aggressive protests from defeated Plaid Cymru activists outside the election count, to receive full and courteous cooperation and support from local police officers and the Chief Constable. We quickly formed close working relationships.

Ten years later in September 2001 MI5 was forced to open many of its secret files for the first time after an independent tribunal accepted that a blanket ban on releasing information was unlawful under the Data Protection Act. After media revelations about old MI5 files held on members of our government, the head of MI5, Stephen Lander, came to see me at the Foreign Office. Low key and courteous, he confirmed there had indeed been such a file on me and I had been under regular surveillance. However, he was at pains to say, I had nothing to worry about because the file had long been 'destroyed' when I had ceased to be of interest. What an anti-climax! It would have been good to see it. Furthermore, he was anxious to impress, I had 'never been regarded by the Service as a communist agent'. So that was alright then.

‡

Since MI6 (sometimes known as SIS) had also been interested in me as an anti-apartheid leader, I was intrigued to find myself working very closely with the Service in the Foreign Office between 1999 and 2002. My private secretary would place 'folders' on my desk every morning containing reports from the Service, the Joint Intelligence Committee and GCHQ; read and initialled, they would be put in a safe or returned. Foreign Office staff handling these were obliged to be security cleared – or to undergo Developed Vetting, known colloquially as 'DV'd', a very intrusive investigation of personal background. But that did not happen to entrusted Ministers. I wasn't even given briefings about complying with the Official Secrets Act – it was just assumed I was fully trustworthy and that I had read the Ministerial Code, which requires official secrecy compliance. However the seriousness of the material and the privileged access was warning enough to be utterly discreet.

As well as Africa, my brief covered highly sensitive countries in the Middle East and east Asia. So there was a great deal of fascinating material. Some of it was little more than well-informed journalism or high-grade gossip. But there were invariably real nuggets, including invaluable insights into the thinking and plans of foreign governments and their Ministers which helped shape policy and diplomatic judgements. Relatively early on, I was visited by a senior MI6 officer who identified three codenames for highly placed British informants ('sources') within countries of concern. I paid even closer attention when these codenames were flagged.

With GCHQ, it was clear that capability was not the real issue. What mattered was identifying and processing information of real value and in real time amongst the mass of material which could have been, or was, gathered. GCHQ officers were professional, enthusiastic and keen to have a Minister both interested in their work and willing to make use of it. On visits to GCHQ in Cheltenham, I was shown examples of intelligence directly supporting what I was trying to do, giving me important and encouraging insights into how effective my efforts were.

Often, on overseas visits to Africa or the Middle East, briefings from local SIS officers gave real insights. Officers from the Service would also meet in my London office from time to time to update me or to help me make policy assessments.

Within months of becoming Foreign Minister in July 1999, I had grown exasperated at the wealth of reports of private planes flying in arms supplies to African conflict zones – Angola, Sierra Leone, Democratic Republic of Congo – and flying out 'blood diamonds' received in payment. This murderous traffic was fuelling war and destroying communities. Flight schedules were repeatedly changed to avoid discovery, enabling arms – missiles, small and heavy weaponry, bombs, anti-personnel mines, munitions – to be landed at dusty airstrips in the bush. Typically, the arms would be picked up in Ukraine, Bulgaria or Moldova, officially bound for, say, Burkina Faso or Rwanda. The end-destination would not be filed and the routes would suddenly alter as the planes 'disappeared' for a day or more.

Determined to try and break this bloody trade, I called a high-level office meeting. 'What are we going to do about all this?' I asked. 'We know when the planes are flying and where they are aiming. We have got to stop this.'

'Yes, Minister, but we mustn't do anything to compromise our sources – they are risking their lives for us.'

'Well then, why don't we just shoot the planes out of the sky?' I asked

'But that would be against international law, Minister!' came the startled objection.

So you are telling me we cannot do anything? We know exactly what's going on. Some of these arms are being supplied via Monrovia to the RUF terrorist group in Sierra Leone and then being fired at our own British troops. How can we just keep collating all this data, informed up to our eyebrows, and do bugger all to use it while our soldiers are attacked and death and destruction goes unchecked elsewhere?

There was silence. I wasn't happy. Officials were busily engaging in what all mandarins love – writing lots of papers, calling meetings, indulging in *process* – but, frustratingly, there was no action at the end of it. I reflected on the stalemate and then resolved to play the only card I felt I could: name the individual arms traffickers in the House of Commons. Protected by parliamentary privilege – which meant no MP speaking in the House could be sued – it was a prerogative to be used sparingly and with integrity. But the immediate reaction from officials was negative. The usual excuses were paraded. Such data had never been used this way before – blah, blah.

Instead, prompted by my principal private secretary, Frank Baker (an excellent 'can do' official), I talked directly to the head of MI6, Richard Dearlove, who was encouragingly sanguine. So, it emerged, were his senior officers – with case officers positively enthusiastic.

Eventually, after considerable chasing, I had full clearance. I drafted an appropriate question and approached friendly MPs to table it for the next monthly Foreign Office Questions session. Fortunately they were placed sufficiently highly in the list to be certain of being reached, and I had my text well prepared and rehearsed. But when the big day arrived Frank Baker and the Africa director, Ann Grant, asked for a private word. They had become trusted friends as well as being first-rate officials, and wanted to make sure I was prepared for every outcome: 'You are aware that by going ahead there could be repercussions for your career?' But I had never before allowed 'my career' to get in the way of what I thought was right, and I wasn't going to do so now – especially since the Foreign Office had fully cleared what I would say.

However, there was only any point in the initiative if it got extensive media attention and the Foreign Office press team said they would not handle it out of concern about potential libel repercussions if they made or took calls not covered by parliamentary privilege. This was bogus. It could and would have been handled on background – I was the only person on the record. Disappointed, I replied that in that case I would do it myself and, on the morning of Questions, finalised calls tipping off key journalists. There was a lot of interest, though I didn't have the same journalistic reach as my official press team.

Then, a couple of hours before I was due to stand up in the Commons on 18 January 2000, there was a phone call from Sherard Cowper-Coles, Robin Cook's private secretary. 'On further reflection, the Foreign Secretary thinks you should not proceed. Better to have another look and maybe do it next Questions.'

'But this is ridiculous, the whole thing has been agreed for weeks!' I replied. Then I played my trump card: 'In any case I have already told the media, as I had been advised to do by officials. Robin wouldn't want an even bigger story about blocking me, would he?' Taken aback, Cowper-Coles immediately saw the merit of my rejoinder and promised to call back. He never did. Actually I doubted whether Robin really had issued this instruction or he would have called me himself, and he sat happily beside me as I spoke in Parliament.

As it transpired, the whole episode went like clockwork. The story spread around the world, provoking infuriated and bellicose threats from those I had named. Some were put out of business. In the Foreign Office afterwards I couldn't find anybody who disagreed. Moral of the story: be decisive, prepare carefully, but then stand your ministerial ground.

In the Commons on 18 January 2000 my words were recorded in the Official Report:

> It is vital that private individuals and companies engaged in breaking the law by deliberately breaching UN sanctions on UNITA are stopped. I can inform the House that we are referring to the UN sanctions committee today, and its expert panels, the details of three such individuals, which we hope they will be able to follow up. It is widely known in the region that Jacques 'Kiki' Lemaire flies in diesel fuel, landing on UNITA airstrips in a Boeing 707 or Caravelle aircraft. Tony Teixeira has been supplying diesel fuel to UNITA, again flying it in by plane. Victor Bout, who runs an air transport company, has flown in arms to UNITA. It is also believed that Bout owns or charters an Ilyushin 76 aircraft, which was impounded in Zambia en route to Angola last year.

The Belgian investigator Johan Peleman, working for the United Nations, was delighted at my initiative. Later on I stepped up pressure against Bout and again used parliamentary privilege to attack him on 7 November 2000, this time also referring to African governments which it was clear were complicit:

> Sanctions busters are continuing to perpetuate the conflict in Sierra Leone and Angola, with the result that countless lives are being lost and mutilations are taking place. Victor Bout is indeed the chief sanctions buster, and is a merchant

of death who owns air companies that ferry in arms and other logistic support for the rebels in Angola and Sierra Leone and take out the diamonds which pay for those arms. All the countries that are allowing him to use their facilities and aircraft bases to ferry that trade in death into Sierra Leone and Angola are aiding and abetting people who are turning their guns on British soldiers, among others, in Sierra Leone. It is important that they stop doing that. All the governments named, including some Presidents and senior Ministers, have been complicit in that barbarous trade, and it is vital that they cease it immediately, comply with UN sanctions and help end those wars.

With the enthusiastic backing of a task force, we were able to target Bout relentlessly. On one occasion it was arranged for a new helicopter Bout was ferrying out to Angola to be impounded in Slovakia because it was in breach of UN sanctions. I also fixed with the Crown Prince of Abu-Dhabi and head of its armed forces, Sheikh Mohamed bin Zayed – with whom I had formed a good relationship as Middle East Minister – to close down Bout's operation in Sharjah. But Bout – a former KGB officer – still enjoyed protection high up in the Kremlin. All efforts to persuade the Russians to block his murderous activities came to nothing. Later, Douglas Farah and Stephen Braun, authors of a book on Bout, recorded:

> Hain's 'merchant of death' tag stuck, a dark sobriquet that became synonymous with Bout's growing perch atop the international arms trade ... Hain's one-man 'name and shame' campaign proved as effective in its own right as the United Nations' painstaking efforts to document the Bout network's arms routes. Hain's rhetoric demonised Bout as the enigmatic fueller of Africa's ills while Johan Peleman and his UN colleagues provided damning evidence.[*]

Bout was also supplying Al Qaeda and the Taliban in the Afghanistan conflict. And, according to Farah and Braun, in February 2002 a British agent sent an encrypted message that Bout was on one of his planes taking off from Moldova bound for Athens where he was establishing a new hub. Plans were made for his arrest, but shortly after the encrypted message was sent, his plane veered abruptly off its flight plan and disappeared for ninety minutes. When it reappeared and later landed, British agents boarded the plane, but Bout was no longer amongst the passengers. Somebody with access to that encrypted message had tipped him off. He surfaced in Congo a day later and subsequently returned safely to Moscow. (Long after I had ceased to have ministerial responsibility, the Royal Thai Police arrested Bout in

---

[*]   Douglas Farah and Stephen Braun, *Merchant of Death* (Hoboken, New Jersey, John Wiley & Sons, 2007), p. 178.

Bangkok on 6 March 2008 – the culmination of a sting operation set up by the US Drug Enforcement Agency. On 2 November 2011, a New York court found Bout guilty of attempting to sell heavy weapons to a Colombian rebel group.)

Working productively with our intelligence services on the basis of accurate evidence they had painstakingly collated encouraged me to admire their professionalism and dedication. Perhaps that was another reason why I was later to see little reason to disbelieve the fateful and damningly inaccurate intelligence on Iraq in 2003.

‡

Having worked closely with MI6, I soon found myself switching to do the same with MI5, first as Leader of the Commons and then as Secretary of State for Northern Ireland from 2005.

Soon after I was appointed as Commons Leader in June 2003, a senior MI5 officer (and later director general), Jonathan Evans, asked to see me and said they were concerned about the possibility of a biological or chemical attack on the House of Commons. There was particular concern about the prime time slot at Prime Minister's Questions on Wednesdays at noon. With most of the Cabinet and Shadow Cabinet present in a packed Chamber, the occasion would present a sensational coup for Al Qaeda, perhaps surpassing even 9/11.

Part of the solution, MI5 believed, was for a glass security screen to be installed sealing the Commons Chamber from the public gallery. But they had unsuccessfully sought to persuade the Speaker and senior Commons officials about this. Apparently Robin Cook had also been resistant before he resigned as Commons Leader several months earlier.

After further probing about the level of risk of this type of attack, it didn't take me long to decide. Notwithstanding resistance from the parliamentary establishment (who were mostly hidebound by tradition), it seemed a no-brainer. Imagine if I did nothing and there was such an attack? Quite apart from the horrific consequences, to have been warned and done nothing was immeasurably worse than to have tried and failed to persuade a reluctant Parliament (which my shrewd principal private secretary, Glynne Jones, considered likely).

He was correct about the official obstruction. Michael Martin, the Speaker, was flatly against a screen. So were the so-called 'men in tights' – the senior Commons officers who ran the place wearing comically ancient garb. And not just those – many MPs were equally unhappy about putting up what they saw as a barrier between visitors in the gallery and their MPs.

However, after protracted negotiations – including MI5 chief Eliza Manningham-Buller speaking to senior MPs on 'Privy Council' (confidential) terms – and much harrumphing, I finally persuaded the House of Commons Commission to install a £600,000 temporary screen over the Easter recess in 2004. After having a chance to see how unobtrusive the screen was, I was then able to get the House to vote on 22 April for a permanent screen – which was finally erected over a year later in September 2005. My necessary role as the security hard man of Parliament might have seemed counter-intuitive – it certainly was to me.

Security around the Palace of Westminster remained a nightmare, and my otherwise good working relationship with Michael Martin became strained, until events were to conspire to overtake him and others blocking change. Early in the morning of 20 March 2004, two members of the environmental activist group Greenpeace climbed the famous clock tower housing Big Ben to demonstrate against the Iraq War. Then, on 19 May 2004 purple flour was thrown by members of the campaign group Fathers 4 Justice at Tony Blair as I sat next to him during Prime Minister's Questions. In the split second that I felt something move behind me, I wondered whether this was indeed the very lethal powder attack I had taken action to thwart – though simultaneously confused as to why the screen had not stopped it.

In fact the protesters had been sitting in front of the screen as supposedly trusted guests of a peer, having won special tickets at a charity auction. The House was immediately suspended and the Chamber evacuated. If it had been ricin or anthrax, we had agreed a procedure to lock MPs inside the Chamber while they awaited decontamination; otherwise lethal spores could have been spread outside, infecting others too. Quite probably MPs would also have been forced to undress in front of each other.

In interviews afterwards as Commons Leader, I said the protest was a 'wake-up call' and a 'very embarrassing lapse', adding that the attack could have been ricin or anthrax, and killed large numbers of MPs. I requested an urgent meeting with MI5 officers and used the incident to drive forward a £5 million upgrade of security at Westminster. Careful to add that we needed 'to strike a proper balance between proper security and the rights of public access to Parliament and its members', I insisted that Commons security needed radically improving. 'Frankly there has been a very old-fashioned culture around the House of Commons for far too long, not just from many of the authorities involved, but also from MPs,' I said.

‡

However, the parliamentary security saga was far from over. Making the traditional weekly Commons Leader statement on a Thursday covering forthcoming business, I found myself prominently defending legislation to ban hunting with hounds. Although happy to do so, this issue which aroused such passion amongst Labour Party supporters had not been one I had ever prioritised.

Critical votes on the Hunting Bill were due on 15 September 2004 and I was involved in negotiation with militantly anti-hunting MPs like my old friend and fellow Chelsea fan Tony Banks. They were unhappy at a two-year delay in the commencement date of the ban, aimed at taking it well beyond the imminent general election, and allowing all concerned to plan ahead. Meanwhile Tony Blair had a rough weekend in his constituency, besieged by hunters; Hilary Armstrong, the Chief Whip, also had a difficult time. Tony fulminated to the Cabinet about the 'strategic mistake' of a full ban which he had never been keen on in the first place. But I was able to persuade him that there would be a huge revolt against him by Labour MPs if he prevaricated at this late hour. In the end the Party united around an eighteen-month delay on implementation, and there was a very clear and decisive parliamentary majority for it.

However, the day of the hunting debate became submerged in an extraordinary protest by huntsmen. The House of Commons Chamber was invaded, apparently for the very first time since the seventeenth century. There was uproar as television pictures exposed embarrassing and farcical responses from Commons security officers. The Serjeant at Arms waltzed into the Chamber after the young huntsmen, his sword swinging wildly from his waist, as middle-aged doorkeepers ran in desperately and rugby-tackled them. I was chairing a session of the Modernisation Select Committee upstairs when I noticed on a monitor screen that the sitting had been suspended without explanation. Word quickly came that there had been an interruption and when I realised what was happening I asked to vacate the chair and rushed downstairs. The Commons, sitting for the first time in September, resembled a building site. Corridor floors were up and cupboards gaped wide open in the ancient building, exposing all sorts of works and maintenance normally done in recess.

I invited myself into a meeting with Commons clerks, a shell-shocked Speaker, Michael Martin, the Serjeant at Arms, Michael Cummings, and the Chief Whip, Hilary Armstrong. 'This is very serious. It will underline the dreadful state of House of Commons security in the public's mind,' I said, reminding everyone it came on top of the purple flour and Big Ben protests. I insisted on decisive action and leadership. The Speaker – proud to be the first working-class Glaswegian to occupy the venerable position – was somebody I liked and got on with. I despised the snotty class prejudice directed at him. He was in his own terms a quietly determined moderniser grappling with the Commons' frustrating fiefdoms. I had many private conversations in which he made clear what he was doing and I supported him. But I could see that the shock of the hunting invasion had left him almost paralysed. Although I sympathised, I urged him to make an urgent statement when the sitting was reconvened so he appeared to MPs and the media to be in command. But he decided instead to leave it until after the first main vote, which was due to take place around an hour later.

When I came in for that statement, he was sitting in the chair and I had a private word, alarmed to discover that he was still reluctant to say anything at all. He said, nodding his head sadly: 'Peter, I'm just, I'm just, absolutely uncertain what to do in this terrible situation.' He kept repeating 'a terrible situation'. I replied gently but firmly: 'Michael, I really think it is imperative that you are seen, as the head of security, to stand up and take charge of this matter and give confidence that we are moving forward to tackle the breaches and to make sure that they can't occur again.' This was especially necessary because the Serjeant at Arms had told me that it was 'an inside job' of some kind. The protestors knew exactly what they were doing. They had come from an upper committee corridor dressed in building gear which they then stripped off, entering the Chamber via a little-known back staircase from which they were able to burst past the doorkeepers.

Eventually he did make a statement late that day. It didn't carry much conviction or authority, but nevertheless assured the media and MPs that he was going to come back with a response to the situation. Along with the Commons authorities he was understandably devastated by the whole episode. It was as if events were conspiring to destroy Parliament's comfortable clubbiness, its obscure rituals and its insider ethos. Although I made an effort to be respectful of such traditions, I was never enamoured of them; I never truly felt an insider, seduced into the club like so many MPs. My main concern was how dreadfully it was playing on television. Excitable reporting worldwide pictured the huntsmen bursting into the Chamber with the 'men in tights' looking absurdly incompetent. It also showed exactly what I had been arguing for months: the desperate need for modernisation.

When the Cabinet met the day after, on 16 September 2004, I recommended seizing the opportunity to impress upon the Commons authorities and traditionalist MPs the need for radical reforms which I had so far been thwarted from implementing. I wanted a professional full-time director of security, answerable to both Houses, but covering the whole of the Palace and with operational authority, working in direct contact with the Security Service and the Metropolitan Police. The Home Secretary, David Blunkett, came straight in: 'Peter is absolutely right; we have got to make sure that he is given all the backing he needs. The Security Service and the Met have been tearing their hair out about the unwillingness of the Commons to reform.' There was a long supportive discussion. My predecessor John Reid said that he had been very worried about the building works that had been carried out in the September period: 'Some of the people involved could be fitting out the House for blowing it up Brighton-bomb style. There could be a situation where people were coming in and lining the corridors where floorboards were being lifted and cupboards opened, with timing devices which might go off later.' But when John Prescott vigorously backed me and added: 'We've got to take control,' I responded with an important qualification: 'It's much more difficult than this, John, because the House of Commons is a separate and constitutionally sovereign body. The government cannot just establish an iron grip over it.' Tony summed up saying that if the House of Commons would not shake itself up then government would have to do it. He was encouragingly firm in backing me.

Fortified, I went to make the weekly statement about next week's business – only to find that the Speaker had, unilaterally and without consulting me, decided that we would not be able to discuss security matters during Business Questions, which I thought was an appalling misjudgement. Perhaps he was seeking to thwart my prepared statement calling for radical reforms. But it was a big mistake not to allow MPs to ventilate concerns, and there was considerable cross-party disgruntlement. It reflected both his own lack of self-confidence and his determination to keep hold of security matters, not to allow them to be seen as the responsibility of anybody else.

Well aware that the vacuum the Speaker had so clumsily contrived would encourage the media to turn the story into one of ridicule and weakness, I decided to issue my planned Commons statement to the media – just as well because it immediately started running strongly and supportively, to be followed through in the next morning's papers, preventing both the government and Parliament from being panned and mocked. I knew only too well that I would be ruffling the Speaker's feathers and those of House officials – and indeed they made that quite clear in sniffy complaints to Glynne Jones. That was a pity. I hadn't sought to make enemies. But this was an occasion for being decisive and, if I had kowtowed to their sensitivities, we would all have been lambasted. By publicising a reform package, we had all been protected from even greater criticism.

My concern was reinforced on my way back home by train to Neath, when there was an urgent phone call from Phil Taylor, my special adviser. He had been tipped off by the *Sun* that one of their reporters had posed as a waiter in the House of Commons and they had pictures of him serving the deputy Prime Minister, John Prescott. The *Sun* had got him into the Commons for over three weeks on false references which were not even checked and with a false identity which was not even followed up by the normal security procedures. Their reporter had even taken a fake bomb in to the Commons with him; if it had been the real thing, Parliament could have been blown up. The *Sun* wanted a reaction immediately before their deadline, and I gave them a couple of paragraphs, dictated to Phil, saying that the newspaper's escapade had done the House of Commons a favour. The *Sun* ran it very prominently the next day, delighted with my reaction, which the editor had not expected. But, when we spoke by telephone, the Speaker was livid: 'How can you congratulate the paper for breaching our security?' he asked. Clearly he didn't get it. Earlier that morning, in a BBC radio *Today* interview with John Humphrys, I laid out a series of reforms, making it clear, however, that we didn't want a fortress Parliament and that the public needed to have access to their MPs because it was 'their democracy'. We had to strike a balance between security and access: we didn't want the government taking over House of Commons security, but the police and the Security Service needed operational authority. It was essential to move forward, we couldn't continue to drag our feet.

‡

On Saturday 25 September 2004, Elizabeth and I woke up with a jerk at six in the morning to the sound of banging on doors, pebbles thrown at windows, shouting and screaming, and a hunting horn bellowing through an opened letter box. It was pitch dark outside. Our home was isolated near the edge of a forest, high at the end of a lane leading up from the village of Resolven. (The year before Home Office experts had come down to check on security and said breezily that it was so vulnerable we might as well not bother.) Shadowy figures rushed around, how many we weren't sure. The sheer din was frightening enough, Elizabeth terrified that they seemed ready to burst into the house, perhaps threatening our lives. We scrambled for a phone, and called up the police on a special number. But they were unable to come up for at least half an hour. Stay inside, the inspector said. My first inclination was to try talk to them, but he insisted we stay inside.

After what seemed like an age, both of us creeping around the house, and occasionally people outside spotting us and shouting in agitated excitement, the police finally arrived, the duty inspector saying he was surprised that the protesters didn't want to let the police through. 'They mean business,' he said grimly, summoning reinforcements. It was lighter now and we could see hunting banners in the garden. Meanwhile more and more demonstrators were arriving, demanding the government stop their plans to ban hunting with hounds. (Ironically, until this incident, Elizabeth had rather sympathised with them.)

Although the presence of the police officers inside stabilised the situation, it remained menacing. The inspector, who had been up all night, was about to keel over with tiredness until Elizabeth calmly made him scrambled egg for breakfast. There was lots of to-ing and fro-ing. Gradually more and more police arrived, forcing the demonstrators back off the property, and closing the gates at the end of the drive. Whenever I stepped outside or showed my face, it worried the police because the huntsmen were both above on the bank behind the property and down the side. Then I wasn't able to flush the toilet; our taps didn't work either: somebody had cut the water off. The stopcock was hidden outside the gate up the hill where they had amassed – but under a rock and quite hard to find. Someone must have done some pre-planning. I later learnt that one protester had felled a tree in an attempt to block the lane – but it had fallen the wrong way: into, not out of, the forest.

Suddenly a prominent Transport and General Workers Union organiser, Andy Richards, came bounding up to the front door. Burly and overweight, he was sweating profusely after climbing up the long steep hill from the village. I was astonished, though moved to see such a good friend. How on earth had he got in, I asked? 'I walked smiling through the crowd as if I was one of them and then showed my T&G union card to the police on the gate,' he winked. He had heard about the demonstration on the radio, and decided to come and help out. 'Do you want me to phone the boys and get them to come and sort this lot out?' he asked, eyes narrowing. No, I replied immediately. Although grateful for the offer of solidarity, which exemplified the best of the South Wales Valleys, we needed to come through this with some dignity and a sense of dialogue, not confrontation if at all possible.

Hours dragged by. It was frustrating because we were due to leave for Labour's annual party conference in Brighton by about 11.30 in the morning. But by midday it was very evident we weren't going anywhere: hundreds were blocking the narrow lane out. Although I told officers I was very happy to go outside and talk to the protesters as they had demanded from the outset, it was equally obvious that they were waiting for all their supporters to arrive from various parts of Wales, some far away it seemed. The police took the view it was better to let them calm down, let everybody arrive and make their point. Seasoned in protester motivation, that made sense to me.

One option, the police had half-heartedly suggested, was to be driven out forcibly, crushing through the demonstrators who had placed their cars to blockade us in. But I was worried about people being hurt, transferring sympathy from us as besieged householders to the demonstrators. So we just sat it out. Meanwhile I called Lyn Harper, my agent and longstanding friend. He hunted himself, didn't agree with the ban, and was close to the local Banwen Miners Hunt and its master, whom I had met amicably the day before. Could he use his influence? He arrived in the village, sized up the situation and knocked on my sister Sally's door in the village asking to use her phone. But, though she knew him well, she wouldn't let him in because he was also a hunter!

After what seemed like an age, the protesters appeared to be getting bored and the police were able to negotiate for their leaders to come and talk to me in return for dispersing. They had invited television and radio stations, press reporters and photographers jostling in the lane, and demanded that we all had microphones so our conversation could go live. I wasn't being grandstanded like that and, eventually, they did agree to our discussion being filmed from a distance without microphones, after which they could do interviews and disperse. I arranged chairs in an arc for the cameras, put a little table out on the drive and, because we had no mains water, placed some mineral water for them on a tray so that it looked hospitable.

When they trooped in to see me, the conversation was formal and strained and they wouldn't take the glasses of mineral water. Fairly aggressive and hostile, they made their points clearly and calmly. Proud to be working class, they claimed to be Labour supporters. One argument from an ex-engineering shop steward struck me forcibly:

> This is my life. I take my hounds out in the morning, I go to work, and immediately I come in I take them out again. I love them. That's the way I want to live my life. If you take that away from me, what have I got left?

True to their pledge, they did disperse. After eight hours of siege, we were finally able to drive out for Brighton under police escort, passing a few walking demonstrators with placards, peacefully chatting. The police car zoomed us towards the motorway at well over the speed limit. After I had turned down their offer to take us out in a police car with outriders, an unmarked white Volvo followed us until the Severn Bridge.

As a former protester now being protested against, the episode left mixed feelings. It was unpleasant and I felt guilty that Elizabeth had been frightened. But I could also understand the huntsmen's motives. Although I had never been party to targeting opponents in their homes, my anti-Springbok protests would also have been intimidating to the players.

But that was not the end. A month later, on 27 October, I travelled to Oxford to address a meeting of the University Labour Club. Although I had done such meetings on my own for years, Phil Taylor was concerned and decided to come too. On the train we got news that there were a number of huntsmen gathering outside Balliol College, and we asked for the police to be contacted in line with advice to Cabinet Ministers. But when we arrived there were no police in sight. So I climbed out of the cab very quickly and rushed in through the porter's gate before the demonstrators had realised I was there. Frustrated at missing me, they jostled and punched Phil instead. Labour Club members immediately surrounded me as we walked through classic Oxford quadrangles to a small lecture room. I waited inside while they checked people coming into the meeting against their own membership list. Tension was running high, with shouting outside from hunt demonstrators still determined to confront me.

Soon police officers from the local armed response unit arrived, incongruously bristling with machine guns. By coincidence their unit been in the vicinity and they were apologetic that no police had come earlier. As if he had some premonition, one officer insisted on standing right alongside me as I rose to speak – rather disconcerting and something that had never happened in thirty-five years of political meetings. Hardly into my speech a man suddenly jumped up from a seat near the front, screaming and throwing three eggs which splattered against my suit, luckily missing my face. Much more alarmingly, he stormed forward with a snarl, fists raised, clearly intent on violence. Almost as he reached me he was tackled to the ground by the armed officer near my side, two other officers jumping forward from their seats to help drag him away. I finished my speech, Labour Club members too shocked to ask questions, and was whisked away in a police car. The officers took no chances with a group of demonstrators waiting for me at the station, slipping me through a back entrance onto the train with an officer accompanying me all the way to Paddington. My embarrassment at all this police resource being diverted was swiftly dismissed: 'Sir, no way will we lose a Cabinet Minister.' (That was exactly the view of the South Wales Chief Constable, Barbara Wilding, who also assigned armed officers to protect me.)

At the Cabinet the next day, 28 October, Margaret Beckett raised government websites advertising ministers' public speaking commitments – an open invitation to the Countryside Alliance and hunt protestors to plan ahead. I described my experience the night before, Tony Blair looking shocked. It was quite clear that something needed to be done, and the moment I arrived in Neath railway station late that night, a couple of plain clothes police officers were waiting. They drove me home and stayed the night in a car parked outside, to be relieved at seven o'clock the next morning by another team who came with me into Cardiff where I was due to address a Disability Wales conference. Hunt protesters were waiting, barracking noisily outside despite people in wheelchairs going into the meeting. But the protection team got me in with no difficulty. For the rest of the weekend I had a close protection team around the house and wherever I went – even to the gym or to take my grandson Harry out. We travelled in their car, it was easier that way.

‡

This strange life moved on almost seamlessly when I was appointed Secretary of State for Northern Ireland in May 2005 – except that police protection was now ubiquitous, even on trips abroad. Sometimes it seemed absurdly unnecessary, for instance during a question and answer session in a pit village primary school in my constituency. Because any visit anywhere was routinely preceded by a protection officer reconnaissance, I invariably arrived to high anticipation as the children excitedly sought a glimpse of the armoured Jaguar or even maybe a gun (they were allowed a push at the heavy car doors but the guns remained firmly out of sight).

Perhaps the most marked difference in the new job was working with the Security Service (MI5), with whom I soon developed a good relationship, seeing regular reports analysing developments in the IRA and loyalist paramilitaries, their threats and their politics. These were based on sources whose identity was properly never revealed to me, though some were obviously very well placed.

MI5's chief, Eliza Manningham-Buller, was cheerfully shrewd. A lady of up-market conservative stock, we could hardly have come from more different backgrounds. But she was straightforward, had no airs or graces, was easy to deal with and, as I found right away, had a good sense of humour.

'What coffee would you like?' she asked at our introductory meeting

'Decaf please.'

'You *are* good! I need a double espresso to kick-start my mornings.'

'No, I'm not that good. I drink too much wine with evening meals and at social occasions.'

'Charles Clarke [the new Home Secretary] offered me red wine at five-thirty in the afternoon! I told him I don't drink,' she retorted mischievously. When she attended my Secretary of State parties held in MI5's atrium, I drew both the venue and her presence to the attention of guests, with a good behaviour warning; she took it in good spirit.

Having first worked together on the same side in the parliamentary security fiasco, she was very frank both about the work of her service in Northern Ireland and the severe limitations they faced in neutralising the jihadist threat in Britain because of the difficulties of penetrating its amoeba-like cells. In an early briefing, she had told me pointedly: 'You are the most vulnerable of any UK Cabinet Minister. Unlike the others who have intelligence responsibilities, you are all the time dealing face to face with people on whom we have intelligence.' That was good advice because I was sometimes in conversations or negotiations informed by secret knowledge which could not be inadvertently or unknowingly revealed as that might compromise the existence or maybe the source of key intelligence.

‡

The seamy side of spies was shockingly evident in the murder of Pat Finucane on 12 February 1989, one of the most disturbing problems I had to wrestle with because evidence of state collusion was strong. A respected Belfast solicitor who had often represented republicans during the height of the Troubles, he was brutally shot dead in Belfast, while eating Sunday lunch at home in front of his wife, who was wounded, and their three children. His murderers, two loyalist gunmen, sped away in a red Ford Sierra taxi driven by Ken Barrett, a high-ranking member of the paramilitary Ulster Defence Association (UDA) who eventually pleaded guilty when put on trial in September 2004.

However, this was not just another of the many grisly loyalist murders. Barrett was also a Special Branch agent and in 2002, the BBC's *Panorama* programme broadcast secretly recorded interviews with him describing meetings with his paramilitary commander and a senior Royal Ulster Constabulary officer where he was instructed to kill Pat Finucane; with IRA terrorism widespread, similar encouragement had been given to loyalist terrorists to kill republicans.

Two other UDA members, William Stobie and Brian Nelson, were also RUC Special Branch agents. Stobie had collected and hidden the weapon after Finucane's murder, yet Special Branch both failed to inform investigating police that Stobie was an agent, and failed to pass on relevant intelligence. Nelson supplied the gunmen with the intelligence needed to identify and locate Finucane. He had also been recruited by the Army's secret Northern Ireland intelligence unit, the Force Research Unit (FRU), a team of army officers tasked to recruit and train double agents within the paramilitary organisations. In evidence to the official Stevens Inquiry, Nelson said his army handlers knew that Finucane was a target.

The FRU's commanding officer in the 1980s was Brigadier Gordon Kerr (then a colonel, known as 'Colonel J'). He told the extensive inquiry by former Metropolitan Police chief Sir John Stevens that the FRU sought to persuade the UDA through Nelson to switch from killing ordinary Catholics to killing active republicans instead; the UDA through Nelson would be supplied with the necessary information on targets by the FRU.

Pat Finucane had republican sympathies but he was a lawyer, not an activist, still less an IRA member. Yet, as the Stevens Inquiry concluded in 2003: 'There was a collective failure by the security forces to prevent, or properly investigate, Mr Finucane's death.' Canadian judge Peter Cory's *Collusion Inquiry Report: Patrick Finucane*, revealed in April 2004 that various security forces had been keeping files on Finucane, and in 1988 these files recorded plans to kill him.

But the question was: what to do about this? Having seen much of the detail, I was determined not to be party to any cover-up. It was an horrendous killing and justice had certainly not been done. The Finucane family had fought bravely for many years to get the truth out into the open and wanted a public inquiry. But they would not accept one under the 2005 Public Inquiries Act because evidence from the security forces could be given confidentially. The reason for this restriction was to enable the security forces to provide key evidence without compromising sources or methods and therefore their ability to continue confronting terrorism. Although I also wanted the truth to be revealed, I was satisfied there was no alternative to the 2005 Act: it was the only vehicle available. I had also seen how public inquiries in Northern Ireland had cost hundreds of millions, made millionaires out of lawyers and taken years, without satisfying the families of victims or the communities which had demanded them.

After both the horror of their ordeal and the long fight to seek the truth, I sympathised with the family's deep distrust of anyone in authority. Had I been in their position, I probably would have felt the same: state collusion had helped kill Pat Finucane; why would the state, even nearly twenty years later and under my direction, come clean? Despite my record over the decades, despite my sympathetic assurances to them which went way beyond the normal civil servant lines of my predecessors, they simply saw me as another Brit. There seemed no prospect of resolving this stand-off.

But surely there *had* to be? I tried to think laterally. What about a government apology, on the record in the House of Commons? Might that bring closure? On 3 August 2005 I considered a draft for such an apology: 'Information suggests strongly that those in service of the state either encouraged others to kill Mr Finucane, were indifferent to the threat to his life, or at the very least, failed to take sufficient steps to save his life. The government therefore apologises unreservedly for any activity, wilful or negligent, committed by those in service of the state which may have aided or abetted his murder.'

Tony Blair, Eliza Manningham-Buller and Northern Ireland's Chief Constable, Hugh Orde, backed my approach, as did my senior officials.

However, we had to obtain agreement from the Ministry of Defence since 'Colonel J's' FRU was in the frame. I talked informally to my colleague Des Browne, the Secretary of State for Defence and a former Northern Ireland Minister, who knew of the Finucane case. This was followed up by a formal meeting in his office. But the MoD was concerned about a precedent being set and vetoed the proposal. Not for the first time its lumbering bureaucracy buried its head in the sand and a shocking stain on Britain's record in the Troubles remained.[*]

‡

One of my duties was to sign warrants necessary under the Regulation of Interception Protection Act. These authorised phones, computers, properties or vehicles to be bugged, and replaced the haphazard arrangements which had existed when my own phone was bugged during my days of radical protest. Usually an official would come by appointment for me to sign a bunch of pro forma warrants which explained the background, purpose and necessity for an individual or individuals to be so targeted. However, in an emergency I would be telephoned – sometimes in the middle of the night – for authorisation.

It was a fascinating task which I undertook with diligent enthusiasm, sometimes also signing or agreeing warrants for one of my Cabinet colleagues – usually the Home Secretary – if they were unavailable. On occasion these calls would involve live plots. Frequently, warrants were needed to prevent Real IRA or Continuity IRA bombs, murders or robberies. Both groups were heavily penetrated but they were still dangerous.

Amongst the hundreds of warrants I was asked to sign, I recall refusing only two. One was a particularly hazardous operation to attach a bug to a car which if discovered would have been embarrassingly exposed to the media. The other I considered both unacceptable politically and of dubious value. However, neither of these refusals altered what became a close and trusting relationship with MI5 officers whose dedication I admired and who were always keen to show me around their various bases and demonstrate their technology.

We did, however, have a constant argument about the necessity to shift coverage and activity to the 'dissident' IRA groups and away from the Provisional IRA – there was a certain 'dead weight' in surveillance of the Provos. Although understandable given their violent history, things had changed dramatically

---

[*] However, in November 2011, the Prime Minister, David Cameron, apologised to the Finucane family and the Secretary of State for Northern Ireland, Owen Paterson, followed with a statement to Parliament.

and I felt much greater priority should be attached to targeting the dissident groups – a view borne out in subsequent years when their brutal and criminal activities became even more dangerous.

In May 2006 there was a bizarre allegation by a journalist that Martin McGuinness had been a high-level British informer for the past two decades and maybe even when he was an IRA commander in Derry in the 1970s. The story raged for a bit and then blew over. Furiously denying it, McGuinness believed it was a deliberate attempt to sabotage his role in the political and peace process. When I expressed my sympathies, he was frustrated that there was little he could do. As I had found over the years, journalistic standards are not what they were. Mud can be thrown, lies spread and stories run under lurid headlines – a paragraph of rebuttal somewhere later, if you were lucky. The standard official line on speculation about the identity of a British spy was always to say: 'We never confirm nor deny such allegations.' But I took the trouble to check and, when I was asked about it on BBC's *Question Time* soon afterwards I did not contradict the official line but went out of my way to signal my utter disbelief.

‡

During mid-2006 there was another bizarre lie – this time directed at me. Peter Law, the Labour Welsh Assembly Member for Blaenau Gwent, and highly popular locally, had been denied what he considered his rightful inheritance: standing to be Labour's Member of Parliament for the same constituency. It had been decided (with my forthright support as Secretary of State for Wales) that the selection of our candidate would be from an all-women shortlist. Experience showed that this was the only method of changing the appallingly low level of women MPs; Wales had a particularly bad record. The decision was bitterly resented in the community and the local Labour Party split, some leaving the Party, others boycotting the selection.

Those members participating chose Maggie Jones. Although Welsh born, she had lived in London for decades, and was a national trade union officer and former national chair of the Labour Party. She was therefore portrayed as 'London imposed', provoking even greater resentment. (She was also a close friend from Putney Labour Party days and had been my 1983 election agent. But I had absolutely no influence over her selection: she was judged the most capable of the women who had applied.) The media had a field day and when Peter Law announced he was resigning from Labour and standing as a 'People's Voice' candidate, he triggered a process culminating in his victory in the 2005 general election: no small achievement, because Blaenau Gwent had been rock solid through the days of Nye Bevan and Michael Foot, who had successively represented the Labour citadel.

However, Law had been the MP for under a year when he tragically died from cancer. Even as his coffin lay in the family house, local figures including his wife Trish began astonishingly asserting that I had offered him a peerage to persuade him not to resign and stand against the Party. With local feelings raw over his death, the story took off – given sustenance by the national Labour controversy which led to a police investigation over what became known as 'loans for peerages': that undeclared loans to help finance Labour's 2005 general election campaign were given in return for promises of a place in the House of Lords. Despite my strenuous denials, the Welsh media simply ran the story anyway. I was furious, especially with Welsh journalists whom I knew well. They ran the story because it was 'a good story', when it was simply a lie.

True, I had got on well with Law over the years and in 2004 I did have several phone calls seeking to persuade him not to stand. But the idea of offering him a peerage was preposterous. I didn't have the power to do that and would never have entertained it. Most frustrating of all, Law was now dead – the one person who could have squashed all this nonsense. However, the truth did not get in the way of the story and it almost took off nationally when the Plaid Cymru MP Elfyn Llwyd used parliamentary privilege to name me. He hadn't even troubled to check with me first and knew as he stood up in the Commons on 4 May 2006 that I was at my father-in-law's funeral in Devon. No matter – why should conventional parliamentary courtesy and a family death get in the way of a sensational smear? (Llwyd was later forced by the Speaker to apologise for misleading Parliament.) Then, just as Westminster journalists began focusing upon what had previously been a Welsh story, the truth finally, albeit inadvertently, prevailed. Six months earlier ITV Wales had done an interview with Peter Law which they had 'forgotten', and in which he had cheerfully derided the allegation: 'I have to say that's all very colourful and wishful thinking. No one ever offered me a job in the House of Lords and no one ever offered me any other jobs. So I mean that's all theoretical and it's fairyland stuff.' Having run excitably for a fortnight, the story came to a shuddering halt.

‡

Late at night in July 2005, my mobile phone rang. A telephone interception was needed on a suspect for the bombing of London's transport system three weeks earlier. Ironically, he was located in a house a couple of miles away from our London home; I immediately agreed. Around midnight, as I was about to fall asleep, there was another call concerning three more people – also London bombing suspects – who had either phoned the flat or were also in it. Then around six the following morning, my phone rang again: one of the people arrested as a result of an interception I had authorised had ominously shaved all his bodily hair as if readying for a suicide attack, and the surveillance needed to be widened.

A year later, again shortly before falling asleep in our London home, I was called by the Home Office security unit. Regular briefings had confirmed worrying levels of Al Qaeda-linked activity. But now another house in London was being watched where it was believed a cell was planning a terrorist act and might have a 'dirty bomb' stored there. They had a further request; could I leave my phone on all night and could they call back at any time as it was a very serious situation? They called twice, in the early hours and then at about six in the morning. Later that day they thoughtfully called again to say the plot had been foiled and to thank me. Throughout, London had slept blissfully unaware of the threat – still less of the efforts to thwart it.

‡

They say all political careers end in failure – and that was certainly the way it felt when I was forced out of the Cabinet on 26 January 2008.

The surreal saga which led to my resignation had begun two months before. On 29 November 2007 Claire McCarthy, special adviser in my new role as Secretary of State for Work and Pensions, took an early morning call from the London *Evening Standard*. Had the Prime Minister's chief fundraiser, Jon Mendelsohn, made a donation to my campaign for the deputy leadership of the Labour Party?

That campaign had finished five months before and my organisation long wound up. So I called Jon, a respected friend, to check. He had made a donation to my campaign alone and he was angry that he was being chased from pillar to post. The media were in full cry after revelations that a businessman, David Abrahams, had channelled Party donations through two employees to conceal his identity. The Leader of the Commons, Harriet Harman, had unwittingly accepted a similarly illicit Abrahams donation to her winning deputy leader campaign. The Party general secretary, Peter Watt, had been brutally – and I thought unfairly – sacked by Gordon Brown. Like others in the Cabinet I had observed all this engulfing helpless colleagues, never imagining it might involve me too.

However, as I gave the information to Claire to pass on, a more troubling thought occurred to me. Had Jon's donation been registered as required with the Electoral Commission? This registering obligation had not crossed my mind for many months. But since I hadn't recalled the donation, I hadn't recalled registering it either. So I also asked that we check the Electoral Commission website. Ominously the donation wasn't on there.

At my insistence, our campaign had been rigorous about registering all donations over £1,000 within thirty days of receipt as was required. 'In the end it is money that destroys politicians,' I remember telling my campaign team. 'Make sure everything is straight up.' It was a frenetic period, rushing to and fro negotiating the Northern Ireland political settlement, campaigning in the Welsh Assembly elections and fitting in political visits for the May–June 2007 Labour deputy leader campaign.

Now, all these months later, that ill-fated campaign long forgotten, and a big new Cabinet job absorbing my attention, there was a sick feeling in the pit of my stomach. How could the Mendelsohn contribution have been overlooked? The very last thing I wanted was to get caught up in the media storm raging around what was now a police investigation into the Abrahams donations.

There was only one thing to do, I hurriedly decided. Tell the Electoral Commission – and the Parliamentary Commissioner for Standards because there was also a requirement to register donations with him. And tell the media too. In the furore around loans and donations to the Labour Party, there had been leaks from a suspected Conservative supporter who worked for the commission. Better to bring it to public attention myself, however much I dreaded becoming part of the bigger story.

So that's what I did, explaining that, due to an administrative error, it had not been registered and that I would now be doing so. No tabloid sensationally exposed me, no political enemy exposed me: I 'shopped' myself to the authorities and the media – and a lot of good *that* was to do me.

Because, although my Mendelsohn press statement was accepted by journalists and opponents for the oversight it was, I realised the next day that it was only the tip of the iceberg – the beginning of the nightmare to follow. When I examined the Electoral Commission website, it was obvious other donations must have been omitted. Why? I was perplexed. It was clear that our system for declaring donations had failed.

‡

At the first opportunity on Monday afternoon, 3 December, I arranged to meet the Prime Minister to explain the situation. Entering through the Cabinet

Office rather than the front door in Downing Street so as not to attract attention, I was filled with trepidation. Although I had transferred my loyalty to him as leader, I always felt Gordon needed, rather than wanted, me in the Cabinet; whereas for Tony it was the reverse. Furthermore, donations scandals were swirling around No. 10, all hangovers from the Blair years. Now another of his Cabinet was adding to his problems.

However, Gordon's manner could not have been more decent and supportive. He railed against the 'fucking stupid position' our own legislation to clean up Party funding after the Tory years of anonymous Hong Kong billionaires had placed us in. 'When we stand for election to Parliament, MPs have agents who are legally responsible for complying with the rules. Under our own law only *we* are! It's madness. Especially for an internal Party election.' His only concern was that I had not got the whole picture sorted out before telling the media. 'How long will it take? You don't want media speculation to grow,' he warned with what proved portentous prescience.

I then went immediately to see the Electoral Commission, telling Lisa Klein, director of party and election finance, accompanied by Robert Posner, legal counsel, about my predicament, and that I wanted to make a full declaration. Lisa Klein made three points in reply. I needed to make a full review to ensure completeness and accuracy. I should keep her apprised of the time frame. And the Electoral Commission 'would keep a proportionate response at this end without pre-judging what isn't before me'. Although there was nothing hostile in her manner to signal the draconian response the commission did take, I remained suspicious of leaks and so issued a second public statement stating my intention to provide full details of the further donations I had realised had not been disclosed.

On Friday afternoon, 7 December, I called Lisa Klein to say that Mendelsohn had just confirmed his bank had retrieved the cheque for his donation from his personal account and it was 'in the post'. She thanked me and added: 'I've some good news. You have declared some donations you didn't need to because they were £1,000 or under. In the statement you are preparing for us you are not obliged to declare these unless you want to.' Apparent evidence that, far from seeking to conceal donations, we were being over-transparent. Her manner was one of having bigger fish to fry – the Abrahams donations and others.

However, there were daily media calls to ask when I was submitting my full return, a sense of closing in on a Cabinet prey. Finally, with Christmas having caused further delays, we were able to piece together the whole picture and I was ready to make the full declaration to the Electoral Commission on 10 January 2008; to be transparent in view of intense media pressure I issued a full public statement.

When I handed over the documentation to Lisa Klein and Robert Posner at the Electoral Commission's headquarters, I took with me John Gould, my experienced solicitor from Russell Cooke whom I had been advised to engage. What transpired astonished him. Having clarified one or two details linking the bank statements to the payments, Klein and Posner appeared almost uninterested. Instead Klein said: 'Can we put our pens down and talk to you about reforms we think are necessary in the legislation?' I was a senior Cabinet Minister and they were seizing the opportunity to lobby me.

> The problem we face as the regulator is we cannot impose a penalty proportionate to the scale of the offence. We can only either deliver a ticking off or bring in the police to prosecute. We would like to be able to issue a fine or some other civil penalty like for a parking offence.

'That sounds pretty reasonable,' I replied, as the conversation ended cheerfully. My solicitor was baffled at the encounter, which he considered unprofessional. They hardly asked me any questions, and there was nothing in their demeanour to suggest the unprecedented action the commission subsequently took against me.

‡

Over two weeks elapsed before they passed judgement. Lisa Klein phoned with a few perfunctory enquires over accuracy of electoral addresses and such-like; some minor corrections were made, in one instance a home address replaced a work one. But never at any time did she or Posner take up my offer to be questioned about anything that might be troubling them. I was therefore encouraged to believe the commission had no substantive concerns. I had brought the problem to their attention in the first place. I had been open and truthful all along. I had acted in good faith throughout. There seemed every reason to suppose I would be treated the same as everyone else who had inadvertently broken the rules.

I could not have been more wrong. Journalists were indulging in one of their feeding frenzies and the persistent media assault was wearing. TV crews and photographers spent a fruitless night outside an address I had not lived at for eight years. Then, having discovered our address in a large complex, they were thwarted by a loyal supporter, a British African, on the front desk. He called to say 'the paparazzi' were outside, enabling Elizabeth and me to slip unnoticed via a side entrance to be picked up by my loyal driver, Mick. 'Just as well they weren't there snapping us, I'd have run them over,' said Mick, angry at my treatment. 'A lot of good that would have done me, Mick!' I replied.

I tried to remain resolute. I had been through a lot in my time and I wasn't going to be beaten now. But people who didn't follow the detail weren't aware that I hadn't pocketed the money, merely that entirely legal donations had been reported late: so they thought I was just another politician caught in a 'money scandal'. That was the thing I hated most.

Gordon Brown, though privately supportive, made it worse by saying in a TV interview that I was 'guilty of an incompetence'. Technically true perhaps, but appallingly, and perhaps lethally, clumsy. When the 'incompetent Hain' headlines duly ran, I was livid. That was something I had never been accused of. Was he cutting me loose, I wondered? 'Sorry, Peter, it didn't come out quite right,' he later half apologised.

I had seen the media onslaught against other Cabinet colleagues – David Blunkett, Peter Mandelson, Tessa Jowell and, later, Jacqui Smith – and recalled phoning David and Tessa to give my support and express solidarity. But I never imagined I might join them in becoming a quarry. As more than one political editor shamefacedly told me later: 'When the story runs, it may be garbage, but we still all have to follow it.' I just kept going, my family, friends, local party, constituents and MP colleagues backing me or speaking up for me. Tessa and David both called to offer encouragement. Leigh Lewis, my permanent secretary at the Department for Work and Pensions, was very robust and so were senior Cabinet Office officials: I couldn't have wished for better, not least because I had seen other senior civil servants settling scores when an obviously unpopular Minister was on the rack. Other Party colleagues kept their distance, even some I had steadfastly supported as Ministers. The old adage – 'you find out your real friends in a crisis' – certainly held true.

‡

While I was being hounded, those who had committed the very same offence of reporting donations late were not. Some of the amounts were very large, including £64,000 for Boris Johnson in his successful London Mayor campaign. Ironically, even the MP who spoke for the Electoral Commission in Parliament, Peter Viggers, was himself nearly three years late in reporting a sum of £3,000. Between 2001 and early 2008 when I registered my full list, over £4.5 million in donations had been reported late by political parties without any action being taken, let alone a prosecution being brought. Over the same period fully 600 donations from MPs were reported late, with not a squeak against any of them by the Electoral Commission. Between 20 February 2008 and 30 June 2008 there were 172 donations, totalling £783,574, which were reported up to seven years late by MPs, including by the Tory leader, David Cameron, and the Liberal leader, Nick Clegg.

Then there was the example of Tory Shadow Chancellor George Osborne. He somehow escaped his obligation under the 2000 Act as a 'regulated donee' by failing to report £500,000 of donations to his private office from City barons exposed by the *Mail on Sunday* in early January 2007. This was at the same time as I was being harassed. Although the Conservative Party did report it, my solicitor advised, he should have done so too. Additionally in August 2007, when a guest on a yacht during a Corfu holiday, Osborne had solicited a donation from a Russian oligarch, despite the rule that as a foreign national the latter was not eligible to make political donations. Osborne's suggestion that any donation could be channelled through a British-based company was also against the rules.

The commission turned a blind eye to all that, as they did to the Midlands Industrial Council, a group called Coleshill and other shadowy Tory front bodies and individuals channelling hundreds of thousands of pounds worth of anonymous funds to the Party in direct contravention of the Political Parties, Elections and Referendums Act 2000, which expressly outlawed conduits.

None of my donations were foreign or indeed impermissible. If I had contravened the law on the much less serious grounds of being late in reporting that, then hundreds of other MPs had done the same. As my former agent in Neath, Howard Davies, later wrote angrily in the Welsh national paper, the *Western Mail*: 'So why one rule for Hain, another for everyone else? We think he is a scapegoat.'

Apart from my mistake on failing to ensure all donations were registered within the required thirty days, a contributory factor at the end might have been my media tactics. When he kindly phoned during the saga David Blunkett offered some sage advice. 'In retrospect I made the mistake of not following my instinct, which was to get out in the media and explain myself,' he said of events that led to his second resignation from the Cabinet. 'I allowed myself to be controlled too much by No. 10. Don't do that, because you have nothing to hide. You have done nothing dishonest.' However – despite David's warning and my own best instincts – under pressure from Gordon Brown and his team (joined by my solicitors, who felt it would was prudent to stay silent while the Electoral Commission was deliberating), I felt obliged to say nothing. The contrast was made with George Osborne, who despite being harried over his 'yachtgate' incident, nevertheless did some broadcast interviews. I was not providing any explanation, as if I had something to hide, seemingly cornered – which is certainly exactly how it felt when the media descended to camp outside our house in Neath on the Saturday after I had made my full report.

I had a worried phone call from a Labour friend: 'You are being hung out to dry.' With the 24-hour news programmes carrying despatches from reporters baying outside the house, I sat down at my computer and drafted a statement. But then came hours of frustrating delay as Gordon Brown insisted on clearing it personally, instructing me to say as little as possible and take no questions. All the time news bulletins, annoyed at the delay, built the statement up into a drama.

After I delivered it live to camera, Tories, joined by frustrated journalists, quickly seized upon my failure to answer questions as proof I had something to hide. By nature an optimist, I was engulfed by a pessimistic sense of inevitability.

‡

Two weeks later, on Thursday 26 January 2008, I came into work early as usual, this time a little anxious because Lisa Klein had promised I would be told where I stood. I was in the middle of a key meeting in my departmental office with Ministers and officials on something I had been keen to tackle – simplifying the tangled benefits system – when I was beckoned to take a call from my solicitor. John Gould was incredulous: 'The commission have called in the police to investigate for the Crown Prosecution Service.'

I was dumfounded: the police? Unprecedented: why? Ulterior motives, sinister designs, the very injustice – all flashed through my mind. But I knew in that instant I would have to resign. In dark moments over the preceding weeks I had wondered whether it might come to this. But I had been sustained by the truth: if I was guilty of anything it was being too busy on my Cabinet duties to ensure the procedures I had insisted upon for reporting campaign donations were followed at the end, as they were at the beginning.

That fateful phone call signalling a possible prosecution gave me a real sense of *déjà vu*. After becoming an insider of sorts, now I was back in familiar territory: the outsider battling against an establishment apparently determined on making me a victim again. How else could the extraordinary behaviour of the Electoral Commission be judged? Even media and political critics were astonished by the unprecedented police referral. So why did the EC do it? It was clear from the way they had blatantly lobbied me that they wanted a change in the law as late donations continued to pile up by the million. That they had never bothered to accept my invitation to question me further before making their decision suggested their minds were set: they were making an example of me.

Although sympathetic, Gordon Brown was clear I had to resign when we spoke by phone. I numbly agreed, and we arranged for an exchange of letters, an obviously pre-planned reshuffle later executed smoothly.

Along with the bank theft fit-up, it was without doubt the worst thing that had happened to me in my forty years in politics. The very idea of being mixed up in what the media portrayed as a 'money scandal' offended all my values and upbringing – indeed everything I had stood for. Many people had disagreed with my politics – sometimes violently – but not even my enemies had ever seen me as self-seekingly corrupt, because I wasn't. The whole saga sapped away at my political morale as never before.

Elizabeth was a tower of strength – though her anger had to be restrained as she would cheerfully have 'clocked' anybody she perceived as responsible: from the commission, to Gordon Brown, to the media. But, even more unfairly, she soon became a victim as well. After a successful five years of growth and expansion, her search and recruitment business had run into difficulty and needed recapitalising. Negotiations for a takeover by a larger 'headhunting' company were proceeding smoothly despite a typically disgraceful story on 20 January 2008 in the *News of the World* when the media were in full cry. 'Hain's wife in sleaze probe' screamed its headline. It was based upon a total fabrication: that contracts won under tender by her business for public appointments came courtesy of my influence as a government minister. In fact, as Sue Gray of the Cabinet Office told me, Elizabeth was known to be 'scrupulous' about turning down any public sector work in any government department where I was a Minister. The rules would in any case have made any attempt by me to exert any influence impossible. No matter – mud could be slung, with the help of a rent-a-quote Welsh Conservative MP David Davies, who told the paper: 'We cannot allow the government of Britain to resemble that of a banana republic where lucrative contracts are given out to friends and relatives of the powerful.' He also gave the story legs by referring the matter to the Parliamentary Standards Commissioner for investigation. (Long after the story had come, gone and done its damage, the commissioner dismissed the complaint as a nonsense – but, in the usual way of the media, that was never reported by the *News of the World*.)

I felt even angrier about this than I did about my own treatment. Politicians like me are hardened to expect attacks. But why should my wife suffer when her career had long been established quite independently of me? She had been a prominent businesswoman in her own right long before we even met. Then, if anything, she had to pursue her career *despite* me and my high political profile.

Elizabeth nevertheless concluded the take-over negotiations and went for a celebratory drink with the managing director and finance director. 'We will just need to run it past the chairman,' they said, 'It should be a formality; we enjoy his full confidence and he backs our judgement.' But the chairman

Googled Elizabeth and up came the *News of the World* story. 'Don't want any media focus on our company,' he explained, vetoing the deal. It was too late in the day to begin new investment discussions elsewhere, so she put her business into voluntary administration and thirty people lost their jobs – harrowing and humiliating as she lost not just her business, her own job and her reputation, but her own savings invested in the company.

Both of us felt traumatised – in my case, coupled with rage and guilt that she should have suffered such unwarranted collateral damage. In the long months that followed, I felt a sourness about politics which I had previously seen as a mission, even a calling. Only a determination not to allow reactionary enemies to win kept me driving forward to clear my name.

We were fortified by fantastic support from my Neath constituents. Their disgust almost matched mine. Part of me felt like hiding away. But I knew I had to get out proudly and proceed with my duties both in Parliament and above all in Neath. Mansel Jenkins, a local pensioner, buttonholed me while we were showering in the local gym: 'You hold your head high, Peter. Don't let them make you ill,' he wagged his finger pointedly. A few weeks later, when I went out knocking on doors to support our local council candidates in the run-up to the May elections, I would be recognised and go through my usual routine requesting support for Labour, concluding with a thank you. But before I could go, there was invariably a poignant new end to the encounter.

'And how are *you*?'

'Well I have had a bit of a rough time recently.'

'Yes, I *know*! They are just trying to victimise you. It's outrageous. Everybody knows you have done nothing wrong.'

It was an extremely touching 'Neath against the world' expression of solidarity.

Equally moving and totally unexpected was a personal, handwritten letter from the Prince of Wales. Presumably without having any more knowledge than a well-informed reader of *The Times* and assiduous listener to the BBC Radio 4 *Today* programme (which he was), the Prince grasped intuitively the essence of my surreal predicament. On 27 January 2008, he wrote:

> I can well imagine what you must be feeling – but I couldn't bear witnessing the appalling time you were put through by the media in their most self-righteous mode. I think I can probably imagine the kind of thing that happened to you when you have so much to do and have to rely on others to take care of these things for you. All of us who have offices understand this. However, I just wanted to send you much sympathy at a most difficult time and to say how greatly I have appreciated your help and understanding over several projects of mine. I hope

you can make the most of this enforced period of 'exile' and I can only send you both my warmest good wishes and sympathetic thoughts. Charles.

I replied personally on 2 February:

> Your letter meant a tremendous amount to both Elizabeth and I and it really brightened up our weekend. You seem uncannily to have grasped the truth about the unbelievable sequence which has enveloped me and catapulted me out of office with a police investigation of all things.

Glynne Jones, my principal private secretary as Leader of the Commons and then Secretary of State for Wales, also kindly wrote: 'What an honour it has been to know you and work with you these past years. You are without doubt one of the most honest and generous people I have ever met.' Tony Blair also sent a generous, handwritten letter.

'I am sure you will be alright,' everyone kept saying. But I was far from certain. After all I had been the victim of one precedent – the police referral – who knew, I could be the victim of another by being prosecuted. That prospect was not just frightening, it was downright bizarre because not a penny went to me, not a penny came from taxpayers, there was no fraud, no foreign, improper or illegal donations. My offence was voluntarily to own up to donations being reported later than the thirty-day deadline.

I also had a call from the chairman of the Welsh Rugby Union, David Pickering: 'We still want you and Elizabeth to be our guests at the international on Saturday.' He brushed aside my protests that I was no longer Secretary of State. And, at the pre-match luncheon, the president, Dennis Gethin, concluded his customary witty speech singling me out amongst the guests for a special welcome to rousing applause. (Nearly forty years earlier in the middle of the Springbok campaign, any notion even of my presence would have invoked horror.)

All these and many more expressions of support fortified me as the police investigation dragged on and on. Encouragingly, however, the investigating officers were clearly frustrated at being diverted from what they told potential witnesses – donor friends and former campaign workers – was 'real crime'. My former Northern Ireland protection officers were openly contemptuous of the investigation: 'Everyone in the Met knows this is balls,' said one. Meanwhile legal bills were mounting despite my solicitors graciously doing all they could to keep costs down.

It was scant consolation that my resignation had lanced the boil, and the media moved on to something or somebody else. Tellingly, a few weeks afterwards, I was on the BBC's *Jeremy Vine Show*, to talk about Ian Paisley's decision to step down as First Minister of Northern Ireland, and the producer asked off air, perplexed: 'So, remind me, why *did* you resign then?' A bloody good question, I thought.

The police exercise was at huge expense (£250,000 according to one estimate), and all the witnesses had been interviewed by mid-summer; so had I, the officers considerately doing the interview at my solicitors' office rather than forcing me to go to a police station. Then, frustratingly, there was a further delay as all my former campaign staff and some donors were reinterviewed. They were each asked whether they were members of the Labour Party. That seemed odd – nobody knew at the time why, including the police, except that the Crown Prosecution Service had requested this.

‡

Eventually, ten months after I had resigned, my solicitors received a call from the CPS on the afternoon of Wednesday 3 December – their decision would be given to me on the Friday morning, 'at the same time as it was made public'. Great – so I wouldn't know about my fate before the media. Those thirty-six hours were nerve-racking – especially since I couldn't alert anyone or the whole media circus would have kicked itself back into life with speculative stories. Elizabeth did, however, tell close relatives the night before – something I was to regret, because my mother, now aged eighty-one, became so stressed that she had a small seizure, causing her to be hospitalised for a brief period, making me even angrier at our predicament.

When I got the phone call that Friday morning, it was both a relief and a puzzle. The case against me had been dismissed. I turned from the phone to give Elizabeth – both of us still full of pent-up anxiety – a hug, and, to my immense embarrassment burst into tears, the tension finally erupting. She was on her way to a job interview in case she suddenly became the sole breadwinner. But then the conundrum: the CPS had found that I wasn't even legally responsible for declaring the donations on time in the first place! Our campaign was a temporary Labour Party 'members association' as defined in the Act (hence presumably the late queries about the Labour membership status of campaign staff and officers). Others carried the legal duty to check and register donations. The CPS concluded: 'Mr Hain was not the "regulated donee" and nor was he the person responsible for dealing with donations.' Not only was I mistaken in believing that this legal duty fell upon me, so too was the Electoral Commission – which, mind-blowingly, did not even understand the law it was meant to regulate.

I quickly finalised a brief media statement, and phoned a few key journalists, determined to get my version out first: 'I chose to leave government to clear my name and I am pleased I have now done so. I said all along that reporting some of the donations to my 2007 Labour Party deputy leader campaign late was an honest mistake. Now everyone knows that it was. After ten months in limbo while the inquiry took its course, I now look forward to tackling again the issues of social justice, human rights and equality as I have done for all forty years of my political life, both outside and inside government, from anti-apartheid protester to Cabinet Minister. I am especially grateful to my Neath constituents who have given me wonderful support during a difficult period for my family and I.' Next day the *Guardian*, as if repenting for being part of the malevolent media spin at the start of the year, gave generous space to my clearance and kindly even wrote one of their trademark 'In praise of' editorials about me. The rest treated the story in a routine, semi-statutory fashion. Whereas the frenzy about my resignation had led many front pages and broadcast bulletins, my exoneration – still less the fact that I bore no responsibility for reporting the donations – hardly rated a mention. (Three years later, the prominent BBC journalist Andrew Marr confessed to me that, until he found himself a media target over a 'super-injunction' to keep an affair secret, he had no idea how awful it was to be on the receiving end of his profession.)

‡

So what is the fundamental conclusion that I draw from this sorry affair? It is that the unintended consequence of well-meaning legislation by Labour to clean up political funding in the flawed Political Parties, Elections and Referendums Act 2000 was to draw the police into politics. My case caused some of the Act's worst features to be removed or changed under successor legislation in 2009. But we would be going down the American road if judges and police were constantly dragged into politics. If a politician or party commits a criminal offence – such as fraud or theft – then remedies have long existed under the criminal law.

It is vital that our democracy is free of corruption and that funding of parties is clean. But the police have better things to do than hunt down politicians in a media frenzy where the truth gets lost for breaches of rules that can be enforced more sensibly. And those MPs who have been too ready to call for police involvement need to understand that any momentary political advantage over an opponent might come back to haunt them by undermining politics itself.

CHAPTER TWELVE

CABINET LIFE UNDER
TONY AND GORDON

Walking up Downing Street to attend my first Cabinet meeting in October
2002, my mind went back more than thirty years to spring 1969. Then I
had made the same walk as one of a group of Young Liberals protesting against
Harold Wilson's 'In Place of Strife' legislation to restrict trade union rights. In
those days you could wander freely up to the door at No. 10, and we duly sat
down, unfurling banners. I was photographed being carried off by a couple of
constables, one holding my collar, the other my feet, to be dumped unceremoniously on Whitehall. This time police nodded me through the anti-terrorist
gates with a 'Good morning Sir' smile.

Just across the road in Whitehall I had arrived on the steps of the Wales
Office, to be photographed holding aloft a statuette of Nye Bevan which had
sat on the mantel shelf of my office as Europe Minister. This time I placed it in
the grand office of the Secretary of State for Wales, asking also that my framed
poster of Nelson Mandela be hung in place of an old masterpiece to some
sniffy disapproval: two political heroes to keep an eye on me as they would
do for over seven years as a Cabinet Minister. I greeted familiar officials from
when I was last a Welsh Minister – except this time I was in charge, albeit of
a small department. It was exciting because I loved working for Wales and my
Neath constituency was thrilled.

Attending Cabinet for the first time was quite an experience, welcomed
warmly by the Prime Minister to 'hear, hear', after being handed a diagram
showing exactly where to sit: right down at the end of the table, signifying
bottom in the Cabinet pecking order. The longer I spent in the Cabinet under
Tony Blair, the further my allotted place was moved up alongside the 'big
three'; Chancellor, Foreign Secretary and Home Secretary, who sat right opposite the PM. There was a similar choreography for photographs of the whole
Cabinet taken upstairs at No. 10. At our last photograph under Tony in 2007,
the Lord Chancellor, Charlie Falconer, sat next to me on the front row: 'At
this rate you will be the next PM!' he ribbed. 'How do you say "bullshit" in
legalese?' I replied.

Tony Blair had a reputation for Cabinet meetings which were dull
and short – and certainly not the traditional mechanisms for building

collective responsibility. If that was the case earlier in his government, it certainly wasn't so now. Tony presided over Cabinet meetings with an easy informality, everybody on first-name terms. Apparently listening to contributions even if distracted at times, he invariably summed up decisively, with an impressive insight into the *politics* of any policy issue or situation. His command of the whole government agenda was formidable, sometimes leaning back to mutter to Jonathan Powell, a constant presence in the chair behind him.

Even when the going was very rough, Tony's Cabinet meetings were buoyant in a kind of jolly way, sometimes perhaps with an underlying nervousness. For instance on 5 February 2004, when he was being assailed on Iraq, the media in full cry, the Westminster bubble bursting with indignation and demanding his head, he walked in smiling with his usual mug of tea, in shirt and tie (he never wore a jacket in Cabinet), sat down and said cheerily: 'Good morning, everybody.' The rest of us spontaneously responded 'Good morning, Mr Blair!', as if in a primary school assembly acknowledging the head teacher, to raucous laughter. Again and again I was struck at how steadfast Tony was in driving ahead strategically and keeping focused, despite all the daily swirling political crises, battles, arguments, conflicts – and tensions with Gordon Brown.

The rule I adopted for myself, and observed by most but not all Cabinet colleagues, was to speak only when I felt I had something significant to say. About a month after joining I began: 'Colleagues told me that Cabinet meetings were boring – but I haven't found that at all.' To general laughter Tony feigned shock: 'Who told you that?' But when we broke, a number came up to me and said: 'They used to be, but they have changed a lot in the last year or so.'

Cabinet meetings were very useful occasions to do a bit of networking and negotiating. Colleagues tended to arrive early and meetings rarely if ever started on time. Tony followed tradition with Thursday mornings, Gordon switched to Tuesdays. I would usually arrive five to ten minutes early and nobble various Cabinet ministers and colleagues that I needed to do some business with, or simply have a chat.

Especially during various inquiries into the Iraq War, there was much chatter, including by the odd ex-Cabinet Secretary, about Tony's style of 'sofa government' – vastly exaggerated in my experience. The idea that his Cabinet colleagues were a bunch of patsies who could simply be ignored or rolled over was preposterous. We included some strong-willed, experienced characters. Yes, Tony had an informal manner and I always found him approachable – it was one of his most appealing characteristics. Yes, he ran the Cabinet as a tight ship and, yes, difficult decisions were often thrashed out on the sofa in his small office privately, the most sensitive with his senior colleagues John Prescott, Gordon Brown or sometimes Jack Straw. As I found, Tony would also resolve awkward policy matters bilaterally with individual Cabinet Ministers. None of that was possible in an open Cabinet meeting and nor, at least from my reading of the literature as a student of political science or accounts of Margaret Thatcher's government, was that unusual. In truth, post Second World War, there had been a steady and probably inevitable drift from 'Cabinet government' to 'Prime Ministerial government'.

Gordon Brown sat right opposite Tony, normally head down staring intently at his pile of papers and scribbling away. He spoke only occasionally but when he did it would be fast and rather dour. His pre-Budget briefings were delivered with machine gun velocity, so I had to scribble down key points frantically, frequently let down afterwards when trying to decipher my appalling handwriting. Gordon's economic analyses were formidable and often very interesting; in 2004 for instance he reported that the developing world's share of manufacturing exports had changed from less than 10 per cent in 1980 to 25 per cent and would be 50 per cent within twenty years – a dramatic change in the balance of economic power in the world, with five million jobs due to flee Europe and America and other industrially advanced countries. But Gordon also seemed curiously semi-detached from the rest of the Cabinet which otherwise had a good feel: people of a similar generation pretty comfortable with each other. Gordon seemed set apart, rather aloof, yet a powerful brooding presence.

John Prescott was Tony's night-watchman, or Cabinet enforcer, chairing key Cabinet committees where sensitive issues were often resolved. In these or in full Cabinet, he would often sum up at the end of important debates and lay it on the line, as he did on Iraq for example, saying 'This is the position and Tony must be backed'. A grumpy character with whom you could agree and enjoy a good relationship, but nevertheless find surly to the point of rudeness, his eyes continuously switched distrustfully. Angry with colleagues who leaked and briefed, he was more frustrated than any of us with Blair–Brown tensions. He was a prickly customer with whom I got on reasonably well, albeit with a slight edge to our relationship – perhaps because I was not horny handed enough, as he carried his working-class background around with a big chip on his shoulder. Nevertheless we were from the same part of Labour politically and he was grateful in my early Cabinet life for some background work on the fire fighters' dispute through my union contacts.

Margaret Beckett was a long survivor, having been a Minister in the Callaghan government in the late 1970s. A tough, shrewd operator with a good grasp of a brief and sound political instincts, I always found her straight and a good colleague to work with. She tended to speak infrequently in Cabinet but did so to a purpose which really added something. By contrast Jack Straw spoke a great deal. There was always a foreign policy item on the Cabinet agenda but he would intervene across subjects as one of the Cabinet heavyweights, authoritative if with a tendency to over-detail as a self-confessed 'anorak'; he had an amazing memory for facts and figures and historical references. But some saw his contributions as nerdy and eccentric, albeit often engaging.

I got on well with Charlie Falconer. Decent, sharp, open and enjoying Tony Blair's close confidence, he was very useful to the PM when things needed smoothing over. Of the others, David Blunkett spoke periodically and always commandingly. Some thought that as Home Secretary he was too initiative-taking and attention-seeking for a job which frequently required avoiding publicity not generating it. But I constantly marvelled at David's grasp of detail and his command, not just of his tough portfolio, but right across the political and policy agenda. Although he relied on Braille briefs, he had a phenomenal memory and sense of the politics of the moment.

Our good relations went back to our 1980s days in the 'soft left' – though David had since moved much further than me over into the centre, to become a trusted Blairite. At one crucial Cabinet committee on identity cards in Old Admiralty House, chaired by John Prescott, David was thwarted by what he believed was a Brownite plot. I had been sitting next to him and he was steaming as we dispersed. I tried to calm him down as he took my arm to be guided to his car. 'I am resigning. I can't do my job with Gordon and John undermining me the whole time,' he said, incandescent. 'I'm going right round to see Tony.' As soon as he was in the car, I rang Sally Morgan. She was grateful and Tony talked him out of resigning.

Alan Milburn saw himself as Tony Blair's successor. His acolytes made that plain and, since he was one of the original Blairites, that made a lot of sense. He spoke in Cabinet outside his health brief frequently, thoughtfully and with a good degree of authority – somebody that I hadn't at first expected to be as impressed with. He was an on-message figure (and sometimes outrider) for virtually anything No. 10 wanted saying, and made no bones about disagreeing with Gordon Brown in open Cabinet discussions. His sudden resignation in June 2003 to spend more time with his wife and young children was a shock, especially as there had been were stories that he was standing up in Cabinet against Gordon. It was also a big blow to Tony Blair, who had now lost another close confidant along with Peter Mandelson and Stephen Byers. That left Tony with people like Charles Clarke and me who, though loyal to him, were more independent spirits and, in my case at least, not true New Labour believers.

Some colleagues said hardly anything, though Gareth Williams (Lord Williams, the Leader of the Lords) gave a heavyweight and witty weekly report on business in the Lords before his sudden death in September 2003 left a big gap. Also listened to closely was Alistair Darling, who made short but impressive political observations on issues outside his brief, perhaps one of the most under-rated members of the Cabinet, I thought, in my early years. Charles Clarke would intervene sparingly outside his brief, usually with good points. John Reid became more formidable the longer he was in the Cabinet, earthy and often amusing, a genuine intellectual with a remarkable historical grasp, occasionally revealing his Marxist schooling. He always had something interesting, and intelligent to say. A tough personality and not easy to get close to, he had something of the Stalinist about him. He was nevertheless a very effective and consummate operator. When I took over as Leader of the Commons, I found he had been trying to reverse a lot of Robin Cook's modernising reforms which I then progressed.

Clare Short would butt in whenever she fancied and Tony treated her with a benign tolerance, almost deferring even if she was often abrupt to the point of rudeness. Her ballsy interventions irritated other colleagues, some looking to the ceiling as if to say 'Here goes Clare again'. Patricia Hewitt spoke very well, with interesting and original points, but too frequently and at length, sometimes irking Tony. Despite disagreeing over nuclear energy, Patricia and I worked closely together on the 2003 Energy White Paper when Margaret Beckett and I were able to change its original pro-nuclear stance without rancour. Often when you got disagreements in Cabinet, special advisers would brief journalists hungry for split or personality clash stories, some also originating from advisers in No. 10 or the Treasury. John Prescott, who chaired the energy Cabinet committee, congratulated us all on a difficult issue having been resolved without the public leaking and acrimony unhappily all too frequent in our government.

Accepting a Cabinet position means accepting collective Cabinet responsibility. But I also tried to maintain my independent spirit, while respecting colleagues in charge of other portfolios and trying to say the kind of things inside the Cabinet that I was prepared to say outside. Below the top four or five, my hinterland meant I was better known than most colleagues – compounded by being trusted by No. 10 to communicate a very clear message and to engage in media debate for the government in a way that some other Cabinet Ministers weren't, especially on difficult issues like Iraq, Afghanistan and Europe. Although relations with Cabinet colleagues were cordial, I was aware with some more than others that there was a certain reservation and jealousy about my profile and tendency to say publicly what I believed.

‡

'Political' Cabinets saw party officials replace civil servants and were important to consider more strategic and Party issues, and there was a priceless moment on 12 January 2006 when we concluded our Cabinet meeting for a coffee break before a session of the Political Cabinet. However, there was no coffee to be found and we somewhat grudgingly resumed.

Then the door burst open and Vera, a No. 10 veteran who normally organised tea and coffee, came bustling in. Slightly aggressively she looked around: 'What are *you* all doing in here?' As the room burst out laughing Tony, nonplussed, explained. But she wasn't having any of it. We never got our coffee; instead she took it upon herself to lecture us on perceived leniency towards sexual offenders: 'We're all against this, I hope you lot are too,' provoking renewed laughter. So never mind the TB–GB's, *that's* where the power really lay in No. 10. Completely unfazed, she left us still coffee-less and Tony told how, shortly after the 1997 election, he had met senior trade union leaders. Vera was invited in to take coffee orders. She looked fiercely around the table as if she rather resented giving them anything, pronouncing: 'Well, you lot have never done anything for *me*!'

Tony Blair was always very crisp, focused and interesting at these political sessions. When he took over Gordon Brown tried his best but somehow we never really escaped the gloom and drift which steadily engulfed us under his premiership. Under Tony meetings would typically begin with a polling presentation from Philip Gould, under Gordon from Deborah Mattinson. However, neither Tony nor Gordon was willing to confront the remorseless erosion of our political base the longer we were in power.

Not that these issues weren't raised. For instance on 8 November 2002 Robin Cook said that he thought that politics was being decoupled from the state and that we ought to be on the side of the citizen not the state, otherwise we would not win the public over. He thought there was widespread alienation and that this was damaging us politically - something I strongly agreed with, as did David Blunkett, who said that there was a sense of social disintegration and an attitude of 'Sod politics, we can't do anything about it' which was very damaging to a progressive government like ours. Jack Straw said that we needed to provide much more ideological leadership to the Labour Party membership – a familiar theme of his in private conversations as well and which I shared – that the Party was pretty discontented and we were not really taking them along. Tony listened to all this, seemed to absorb it, but nothing really changed: he had set his New Labour course and sailed on.

Nearly three months later, at the Political Cabinet on 24 January 2003, similar themes emerged. Jack Straw argued that as Cabinet Ministers we were being driven around in our cars the whole time and could easily get out of touch so we needed to redefine our ideology and our way of communicating. Robin Cook similarly thought that we were now seen as the establishment and that we needed to find a way, as Margaret Thatcher had done, of being in power while continuously challenging the establishment. I thought that our biggest enemy was the Tories, but the biggest immediate threat in election terms, especially in local elections, was the Liberals, and we were ceding too much political territory to them. (Tony never really accepted my argument about the Liberal threat, nor did Gordon: for them the Tories were always the main worry. Yet the Liberals were to prove increasingly dangerous for us and, frustratingly, we would not prioritise a strategy for dealing with them.)

I also worried that people had pocketed our achievements – they simply took for granted economic stability, low unemployment, low inflation, low mortgages and low interest rates; these were seen as being part of the furniture and we weren't necessarily getting much credit. We needed to get out of the debates obsessing the political class and the Westminster bubble and engage directly with people. We had lost the ability to talk to the party and the trade unions. I said I'd really noticed that when I'd given a speech recently at South Shields, David Miliband's constituency. Party members didn't realise what we had achieved and we had to find a way to explain those achievements in passionate language which Party members understood and which were related to our values. I always tried to do that because far too much of our language as Ministers was technocratic and managerial; New Labour had drained us of passion and values.

This January 2003 session coincided with an interview on the *Today* programme by Jack Straw's son Will, who as president of the Oxford Union attacked the government's policy for introducing student fees. Jack was in the position of having to apologise for his son. I sympathised because I sometimes had to explain away an elegantly argued letter in the *Guardian* or *Tribune* from my Dad criticising the government.

Again, at a Political Cabinet on 10 June 2003, I felt we never really faced up to the decline in our support, especially following the Iraq invasion. Philip Gould reported that 64 per cent of the public thought that country was going in the wrong direction and only 28 per cent the right one. Although, reassuringly, 68 per cent thought the economy was stronger, Hilary Armstrong, Chief Whip, said that around fifty Labour MPs were seriously disaffected and a larger number were alienated from Ministers. I agreed with Jack Straw that our predicament was more serious than Philip had suggested; that the Party was in a bad way and that we had got into a habit of picking unnecessary fights with Labour MPs and members. That was nearly seven years before we lost office – by which time these problems were even more entrenched because we had not addressed them

I added that we were suffering from differential turnout from our own supporters which could mean our poll lead would not translate into votes. Nevertheless our recent Labour victory in the 2003 Welsh Assembly elections demonstrated that our recent reform to enable easier postal voting had increased turnout of Labour voters. I was also worried that too many people on middle incomes were being squeezed by paying the 40 per cent tax rate – an argument which got me into serious trouble when I made a speech on this a week later. Subsequent discussion was notable for identifying a new political phenomenon. Iain Duncan Smith, the Tory leader, had been written off along with the Liberals as a serious governmental alternative, and so voters were what colleagues described as 'free agents' and 'dissenters' amidst a sense of social fragmentation which also had serious implications for our political base.

‡

The controversial introduction of fees for students illustrated both the hard choices facing Cabinet Ministers and the fault line in our government: the serious divide between Blairites and Brownites. Cabinet on 10 June 2003 was one of the occasions when that divide surfaced starkly. Gordon Brown, backed by Alistair Darling, was very sceptical about raising necessary additional finance for universities by charging students tuition fees, and Jack Straw said sharply that decision making at the top of the government was dysfunctional and needed to be sorted out; he was admirably blunt at times.

Charles Clarke was in the lead as Secretary of State for Education. Virulently anti-Brown, to the point of recklessness sometimes I thought, he was a person who told it straight and I respected him for that; if he disagreed with you he told you so without rancour. Like me, he didn't bear grudges, though we were totally different in that he had a reputation for being quite a bruiser and didn't suffer fools gladly. On the other hand he was an astute politician with a self-confident capacity to absorb policy briefs and wasn't afraid of taking big decisions.

For a strong supporter of universal benefits like me, this was a very difficult issue, and it unquestionably contributed to alienating a generation of young people from Labour. However, its purpose was to raise extra funds to make our universities world class (in stark contrast to the dramatic hiking of these fees to £9,000 a decade later by the Coalition to fill the gap left by their 80 per cent cut in teaching budgets, so transferring the great bulk of the cost from taxpayers to students and families).

Several arguments were compelling to me. Even after introducing the initial annual fee of £1,000, students would only be contributing £1 for every £14 of university funding by taxpayers, the majority of whom had not enjoyed the privilege of a university education and nor did their children. Second, university graduates on average enjoyed much higher earnings later in their working lives, so making a contribution themselves seemed fair. Third, if there was a choice about raising extra tax revenue for education, then surely the priority should be on even greater early-years support than we had managed as a government? That could be life-changing, including whether youngsters ever got the opportunity to go on later to university.

Charles's proposal was to allow universities to charge fees and to recover the cost retrospectively when graduates found jobs and then only according to their incomes. Backed by Tony, he had a fierce argument with Gordon Brown, who favoured a graduate tax. Although they agreed on the necessity to charge fees and both favoured financing the extra income for universities initially through extra borrowing (subsequently to be recovered from graduates in work), they disagreed on the mechanism.

Charles also believed students should repay only the total they had incurred in fees – a case put to me in a surgery in the former pit village of Crynant one Saturday morning by an articulate daughter of a former miner; she argued impressively that she was quite willing to contribute to the cost of her university education, but felt it would be unfair to pay more than that cost. Whereas Gordon's policy was to levy what would have been a very small increase in the rate of tax for graduates; his was the more progressive in the sense that richer students would pay more over their lifetimes. But it confounded my Crynant student's case (which I reported at a Cabinet discussion, Tony referring warmly to my example in his summing up).

Charles operated in a consensual way with Cabinet colleagues, involving them in the decision. He phoned me several times as he did others, both to test the water and to explain his case. By contrast, Gordon operated almost as a loner supported by a few Brownites. He never placed a practical alternative before us, or spoke to potential supporters like me. In the end Charles, with Tony's active backing, did succeed in beating off Gordon's position, which was extremely unusual on a fiscal issue. My decision was made easier by Charles offering to devolve student finance to the National Assembly for Wales. It provoked some turbulence amongst my Welsh Labour MP colleagues who saw me as too pro-devolution and worried about the implications of different systems operating in Wales and England. (By 2011 they were grateful when our Labour Welsh government was able to adopt a different stance and refused to raise fees to £9,000 as the Tory–Lib Dem government did in England.)

Although levels of student debt were manageable when fees were low under Labour, when they rose astronomically under the Tory–Lib Dem government, high debt became crippling. To leave university with a debt of perhaps £50,000 was a huge disincentive especially to students from average- or low-income families. I therefore came to believe a graduate tax would be a much fairer, more progressive policy.

‡

Another – and this time much more personal – insight into the raw meat of Cabinet politics came over Welsh devolution. The 22 July 2004 Cabinet meeting was the last one before we were off on our summer holidays, the cloud from Iraq seemed to have lifted a little and colleagues were in a good mood. Very important because I needed their backing for my paper on more devolution for Wales – and I wasn't sure I would get it.

A commission on Welsh devolution had proposed replacing Wales's limited form of devolution, which still depended a great deal upon prior parliamentary approval, with what amounted to autonomous Scottish-type law-making powers, including varying income tax. It was the product of a deal the Liberal Democrats had demanded from Rhodri Morgan in the coalition administration between 2000 and 2003, and was chaired by the Welsh Labour peer Lord Richard.

I was faced with a difficult challenge of management, my experienced private secretary Simon Morris gloomy about finding a solution. I had long favoured full law-making powers for Wales. But my able deputy Don Touhig was a renowned devolution sceptic, reflecting his Gwent Valley background. There were difficult discussions with Welsh Labour MPs hostile to any more powers going to the Assembly. A dinner was arranged by Don and our Welsh whip Nick Ainger with all the Welsh Labour Ministers – Paul Murphy, Secretary of State for Northern Ireland, Alun Michael and Kim Howells – and David Hanson, Tony Blair's parliamentary private secretary and therefore with the ear of the PM. As I had anticipated it had all the appearance of an ambush. But Richard's package was undeliverable – especially proceeding straight to a Scottish-type settlement without a referendum when the existing settlement had been endorsed by one in 1997. When I readily agreed a referendum was essential, my colleagues seemed satisfied – even relieved because they saw it as a blocking device. On the Commons grapevine, the word quickly went around that peace had broken out in the Welsh Group of MPs. What they had not appreciated, however, was that I was formulating a different plan.

I had to carry my parliamentary colleagues while delivering the extra powers for Rhodri – or else, with a tiny majority, his position would become untenable. It was a tricky circle to square, and few thought it possible, including Tony, who was personally supportive but politically sceptical: with Iraq, Europe and all the other issues on his plate, his view was 'Don't bring me a problem, bring me a solution'. I gradually built an agreement with Rhodri, who had been initially frosty when I insisted a referendum was needed, grimly interpreting it as a block on our mutual aspirations for the same reason that some of my Labour MPs did: that a referendum was not winnable.

Despite our recent history Rhodri and I rubbed along well, even if we were never close. He had an amazing memory, able to recall almost photographically facts, incidents or individuals, a renaissance man with a remarkable hinterland of knowledge and interests, from sport to academia. Passionate and encyclopaedic about Welsh rugby, he could either be 'down the pub with the boys', pint of beer in hand with an endless fund of funny stories, or hold his own in an erudite dialogue with an economist. However, it was always difficult to get him to focus in meetings as he would easily wander off, enjoying being master raconteur just as much as the rest of us enjoyed listening to him – though not always in tightly timetabled ministerial meetings.

Eventually, I proposed a two-stage way forward and persuaded Rhodri to sign up. The first stage would be for Parliament to release extra powers desired by the Welsh Assembly by Order in Council rather than by primary legislation – a faster track which in the event delivered seven times the extent of powers to enable the Assembly to legislate. The second stage caught everyone by surprise. The mindset was for a 'pre-legislative' referendum. I came up with the concept of a 'post-legislative' referendum. The advantage for me was that full law-making powers would be on the statute book, ready to be enacted when it was judged best to call a referendum, calling the bluff of sceptical colleagues.

All my policy preparation and political negotiation with colleagues completed, I put a paper to PD, the policy devolution committee chaired by Charlie Falconer, the Secretary of State for Constitutional Affairs, with whom I had worked closely on this whole matter, which normally would have been settled at that level. I was pretty confident of it going through with the support of Charlie and other colleagues including David Blunkett. I had supported them on various tense issues, especially of a Blair–Brown variety, and now received supportive responses. Although himself a devolution sceptic Paul Murphy acknowledged that if he'd still been in the job of Secretary of State for Wales he would have had to manage it much as I did; his backing was crucial amongst Welsh MPs as was that of Don Touhig, admirably loyal despite his severe reservations.

When I arrived at PD the week prior to Cabinet on 22 July 2004, Andrew

Smith, sitting next to me, said: 'I guess this will only be five minutes, will it?' But then John Prescott breezed in, planted himself down and launched a tirade about how it was opening up the whole of the devolution question right across the English regions and in Scotland. This was despite the fact that I had taken special care to meet John on numerous occasions early on and I thought I'd squared his support. The only way out was to take it to the full Cabinet.

Calmer afterwards, John told me he would accept a Cabinet decision to move forward on Wales provided there was also backing to look again at regional English government powers; he was irked that some of the Welsh Assembly's powers were not being given to the English regions – on transport for instance. I spoke to a range of allies in the Cabinet and also saw Tony Blair. He had bigger things on his mind and, looking to his summer break, told me cheerfully: 'I am more interested in my bucket and spade than this issue becoming a huge controversy.' At the meeting, I explained that I had consulted backbench Welsh MPs and had gone to great lengths to consult Cabinet colleagues through PD and there had been pretty tough negotiations to get us all in the same place. I added that I supported John's views on regional government for England.

However, contrary to his assurance that he'd give me a fair wind, John Prescott insisted that the English regions were being discriminated against. He didn't like Richard's proportional representation and tax-varying powers – neither of which I was proposing, as a matter of fact. But that was beside the point because, as often on such occasions, John was pretty incoherent, though you usually got the drift of his argument. Paul Murphy said my proposal was in tune with Welsh Constituency Labour Parties and MPs. David Blunkett backed me too, reciprocating my support for him on a number of Cabinet issues. Gordon Brown was also supportive, though not fulsomely like David had been – Gordon rarely exuded warmth towards Cabinet colleagues. Others whom I'd supported on their issues backed me too; this was quid pro quo time.

To my relief, when he summed up, Tony was clear: I had the support of the Cabinet. He was concerned that we went forward on a consensual basis which he thought I was doing 'very effectively', adding that he'd changed his mind on devolution: he'd been pretty lukewarm about it before it had been implemented, but now thought that it had lanced the boil of nationalism. Interesting: a Prime Minister who had presided over more radical constitutional change than any British PM for perhaps a century had come retrospectively to accept it.[*] Afterwards John was not at all resentful: he had got his

---

[*]   See Tony Blair, *A Journey* (London, Hutchinson, 2010), p. 253: 'Though not passionate about it [devolution], I thought it inevitable.'

point on the record. When I reported the outcome to Simon Morris in the
Wales Office, he was both relieved and flabbergasted: 'I don't know how you
have managed this.' I wasn't too sure either.

‡

However, securing Cabinet backing proved by no means the last hurdle.

Under John Prescott's leadership a regional government referendum took
place in the North East of England in early November 2004. Campaigning
there I was worried about the outcome. A pre-recorded telephone message
went out by mistake at 2 a.m., 4 a.m. and 6 a.m., waking people up to hear:
'This is John Prescott urging you to vote Yes in the referendum. Please press
a button if you have any questions.' A lot of people did exactly that and told
him what they thought about being woken up in the early hours. However, I
doubted that was the only reason for the decisive defeat, with the vote going
nearly four to one against establishing a regional government in the North East,
much the same as when Wales had first had a referendum in 1979 on establishing an Assembly. Intensely disappointing for me as well as John because I
always felt that, without devolved powers to the English regions, the UK's
asymmetrical devolution settlement left 'the English question' unanswered and
Labour vulnerable to a reactionary Tory agenda of English MPs alone voting
on English-only legislation.

It also made John even more resentful about more Welsh powers. At the
first Cabinet after the election, on 12 May 2005, my successor as Commons
Leader, Geoff Hoon, presented the Queen's Speech due the following week.
He said one of the reasons why we were so well prepared for the legislative programme that session was because of all my work – nice to have it
on the record. But when he mentioned the Government of Wales Bill and
the White Paper which would precede it, John Prescott jumped in. Though
acknowledging I had been scrupulous about using the Cabinet process to
achieve consensus, he said we shouldn't just 'lob this through'. Then Jack
Straw also intervened, saying that while campaigning in Wales he had been
struck that performance on hospital waiting times by the Assembly was 'truly
appalling' and it would be 'ridiculous to start giving them more powers'; we
should be saying instead: 'If you don't deliver on policies like health you
don't get more powers.'

Thank you very much, I thought. Neither of them had bothered to raise
any concerns with me beforehand. Tony, clearly disconcerted by these big guns,
started to say something that implied we could put it off. 'Excuse me ,Tony, can
I have a say?' I quickly interjected, others bursting out laughing. I explained I'd

had difficult negotiations with Rhodri to pull him back from positions which were unachievable and undesirable. I really needed the Cabinet's backing. I'd gone through all the proper Cabinet processes. This was a crunch point for me. I couldn't be expected to do my job as Secretary of State for Wales effectively if I was sabotaged now. John, looking rueful for once, decently said that he didn't really have a quarrel with the policy. 'OK then,' said Tony, changing his mind, 'let's proceed.'

However a final battle still had to be fought. A week before the Cabinet meeting on 24 November 2005, I'd got wind via my excellent new Wales principal private secretary, Glynne Jones, who had transferred over from the same posting to the Leader of the Commons, that Geoff Hoon was trying to ditch the Bill to make space for extra emergency terrorist and council tax legislation. This would have been absolutely catastrophic, and probably cause Rhodri's Welsh government to fall.

I therefore embarked upon on another full-scale lobbying exercise with No. 10 and Cabinet colleagues, many of whom I had backed over difficult decisions – like identity cards, hospital trusts, student fees, and terrorism laws – and now needed that reciprocated. When we got to the meeting Geoff began by saying 'something had to give' in the legislative programme, pointing out that Bills were missing their target dates for introduction and that he had been discussing with me deferring the Wales Bill to make space. It was clear that the Bill had to proceed but if there was some way of shortening it, that would be helpful.

I had tried to talk him out of this shortening nonsense the day before when he was clearly confused about the whole architecture and purpose of the Bill, which I found surprising in somebody who was a constitutional lawyer. (Geoff had clearly been wound up over the legislative programme by the same officials in the Cabinet Office who used to try it on with me.) But Tony immediately came in and said the Bill 'was absolutely essential'. (I'd also talked to him the day before and got Rhodri Morgan to call him.)

That enabled me to begin in a deliberately conciliatory way. 'I imagine if I had still been doing Geoff's job I might have been discussing this matter with myself as Secretary of State for Wales,' producing a laugh and easing the tension. Before leaving Cabinet I made a precautionary check with the minute takers (former officials of mine as Commons Leader) that they would record Royal Assent would be needed eight months later by July 2006 as I had stipulated. Eventually, the Bill was enacted on time – one of my proudest achievements (only the Conservatives voted against).

‡

The Cabinet meeting on 9 September 2004 was our first one back after the summer recess and followed newspaper frenzy – with familiar briefings from the Brown and Blair camps – about whether Alan Milburn would be brought back and what this would do to the Blair–Brown relationship. Eventually Tony had appointed him to lead the forthcoming general election campaign – something Gordon had thought was his baby. Just before the Cabinet convened we were escorted upstairs for a Cabinet photo and I was struck that eight people had left since I had joined under two years before.

We all took our allotted spots, with a vacancy into which Gordon eventually sidled up looking like thunder. It was comical to observe how he manoeuvred into position between Tony to his right and David Blunkett to his left. He refused to walk up in the normal way, face towards the seating position, turning around before sitting down. Instead he turned around before he got anywhere near and backed in, his body language signalling extreme awkwardness and hostility towards Tony, no greeting or small talk, angling towards David and never uttering a word to Tony. The photographer told Gordon to cheer up and smile, the rest of us doing our cheesy grins. He was clearly livid about Alan's return and the briefing that had surrounded it about him being sidelined over the election campaign.

I found myself walking downstairs to the Cabinet Room with Gordon afterwards and asked him how he was feeling. 'What do you think?' he muttered, tight lipped though friendly. 'The problem is we have not solved a whole lot of problems and those problems have to be solved.'

However the Blair–Brown saga was soon to begin an entirely new phase. On the final day of the 2004 Party conference, I had a session with Tony in his heavily guarded fourth-floor hotel room, security having been stepped up post Iraq to create what was effectively a fortress on the seafront in Brighton. My purpose as Leader of the Commons was to discuss the content of the Queen's Speech on 23 November.

It was a good meeting, he was totally focused and there was never a hint of the drama to follow. He wanted something on drugs and on counter-terrorism; the message had come from No. 10 that he wanted separate Bills. But I explained that, for business management reasons, this would only be possible if he was willing to lose some very good legislation. We only had maybe ten weeks of legislative time before he called a general election which everybody expected on 5 May 2005. The solution, I put it to him firmly, was that he could get what he wanted with clauses in the same Bills. He saw the point immediately. Clearly once you discussed it with him the rigid edict from Downing Street melted away and common sense prevailed. An example of needing to stand your ground from time to time and going to the top person rather than just accepting instructions from officials or political advisers lower down.

I also explained that I was well down the track with the content of the Queen's Speech, which would follow the election so that our third term would begin with big issue momentum, unlike in 2001. Alan Milburn came in midway through the discussion and planted himself down as if he was part of the furniture. His people were briefing that he was effectively deputy Prime Minister, something that had enraged John Prescott and above all Gordon, who saw himself as the Prime Minister in waiting. It was quite clear from the chemistry between them that Alan was very much in favour and seen as the up-and-coming man. Tony seemed in rude health, full of restless energy, brimming with ideas to take the country forward.

So it was astounding some six hours later at home in London, to be called by Phil Taylor that there was a rumour going round that Tony had a serious heart problem, was going to go into hospital, maybe would even retire; I couldn't believe the latter but Phil was usually on the ball and later signalled that key broadcasters had been summoned for a TV interview that was going out at ten o'clock. Then Number 10 called and Jonathan Powell said that Tony was going in to have a small routine operation to correct an irregular beat in his heart that wasn't at all life-threatening but needed to be done; he had had a well-publicised heart flutter some ten months previously. He should be out the next day, and would be travelling to Africa the following Tuesday. He added that Tony would announce that he would do a full third term, subject to us winning an election, but would not contest a fourth term and would stand down in time for a successor to fight the general election, perhaps in 2009 or 2010.

You might think you were in the loop, but you really weren't and nobody else was either. Gordon Brown hadn't known about it, nor had any other Cabinet Minister with the possible exception of Alan Milburn, whose 'friends' (code for himself or aides) were saying that he would contest the premiership when a vacancy occurred and that he was being lined up as Tony's successor by both Tony himself and others. Alan saw more of Tony, even as a backbencher after his resignation in the summer of 2003, than did most Cabinet Ministers. Although able and a televisual presence, he had a very limited base in the party; the trade unions were deeply hostile and they had a third of the votes in the leadership electoral college.

Gordon, I readily acknowledged, was in pole position, miles out in front of anybody else. Equally he was an ambivalent figure, provoking both fierce support and fierce opposition. He was a bully and if you didn't toe his line you got hammered in the media by being briefed against by his team, as I had experienced. Some of his people regarded me as a threat, others were supportive and friendly. But Gordon's own political personality meant that you were either for him or against him. I was neither. I admired him. He was a formidable Chancellor and one of the towering politicians of his generation. But he was often dogmatic and got things totally wrong – for example, his notoriously miserly 75p increase on the state retirement pension early on in government which was rightly seen as insulting by many pensioners. His most catastrophic error was in his last Budget in 2007 when he abolished the 10p lower tax rate we had introduced, causing consternation amongst traditional Labour supporters, numbers of low earners losing money. (When I queried it at the Cabinet meeting immediately preceding the Budget he airily assured us there would be 'no losers'.)

I was doing the Party's anchor role for the Hartlepool by-election coverage the night of Tony's bombshell announcement on the ten o'clock news. So I found myself the first Cabinet Minister commenting on the Prime Minister's decision, with No. 10's enthusiastic encouragement. Trying to douse down the excitable media questions, I added that in typical Tony fashion he had invented a new British constitutional doctrine of the fixed term. Nothing novel: many other world leaders, the Presidents of France or the US, were elected on fixed terms. He was right to declare that he didn't want 'to go on and on', Margaret Thatcher's fateful phrase which famously helped trigger her downfall. It was a typically audacious Tony Blair statement, catching everybody by surprise and shifting the whole political landscape in a fundamental way. I didn't think he could have gone into a general election, as I put it, standing to retire rather than to govern; he had to show that he was ready to govern, though not 'to go on and on'.

Fortunately, the Hartlepool by-election was a comfortable Labour victory, as I had sensed the previous week when campaigning, despite a strong challenge from the Liberal Democrats, renowned street fighters in by-elections, tough, aggressive, exploiting any weakness in an opponent's armoury. As in the Birmingham Hodge Hill by-election the previous July, where we had also held off a very strong challenge, Labour's strategy was hard-hitting and aggressive, too much so for many Party members and MPs. However, I thought it was spot on. Targeting the Lib Dem candidate's shortcomings and their Party's policy opportunism was absolutely right because if you didn't take them out, then they took you out: that was the lesson of the Brent East by-election in September 2003. There we had allowed the Liberal Democrats a clear field to campaign right over the summer, to identify every broken paving stone and exploit every local grievance. We had responded instead with a standard, complacent campaign that appalled me. Now in Hartlepool the Lib Dems had been relegated to fourth position.

I managed to get through the night's TV commentary and fell asleep at half past three only to be jerked awake at ten past seven by *Good Morning Wales* wanting to do an interview, having noticed that clips had been running in the morning bulletins from what I had said during the night. A small example of Cabinet life: very little sleep, very little chance to gather your thoughts.

However, despite the best face we all put on it, Tony's statement did begin two years of counting down, factionalism and pressure by Gordon's camp for what they also saw as the 'handover to which he was entitled'.

In his memoirs,[*] Peter Mandelson agonises about the collective failure of the Blair–Brown New Labour triumvirate of which he was part to stem the poison circulating incestuously between them and their camp followers. They were responsible for both the birth and death of the government – and, yet, he writes plaintively, 'it should not have been like this!' A fine thing to say after it was too late. Blair–Brown factionalism proved corrosive to Labour's mission and vision. It was part of why we lost touch with millions of our natural supporters and those won to us so dramatically in 1997.

But although the day-to-day arguments with colleagues can seem to take up all your time, they aren't the real story of government. We were one of three great British governments of the progressive left since 1900 – and, at least until the global financial crisis of 2008, arguably the most successful of all of them. But if it had been less about Blair–Brown feuds and more about our political vision, it could have been so much better.

‡

Meanwhile, despite opposition from Jack Straw and No. 10, I had travelled to the US on a private visit in August 2004 in the run-up to that November's presidential election – the only Labour Cabinet Minister to show open solidarity with the Democrats, who were baffled and hurt by what they saw as the Blair–Bush love-in. John Kerry was the Democrat candidate and I had a series of meetings in New York and Washington with those at the heart of his campaign, including Susan Rice, US Africa Minister when I was doing the job for Britain, and subsequently Barack Obama's UN Ambassador. A rare honour was when Harold Evans and Tina Brown threw a packed party to welcome me.

These links with Democrats helped over the next couple of years when, as Northern Ireland Secretary, I had to grapple with a conflict that had long attracted the attention of US politicians influenced by the powerful Irish American community. Enlisting backing from a senior US politician could

---

[*] Peter Mandelson, *The Third Man* (London, HarperCollins, 2010).

help make progress, especially those close to the republican leadership, some of whom had seen the IRA's struggle against the British almost as equivalent to the struggle for American independence.

Hilary Clinton – then the recently elected Senator for New York – was the most impressively briefed despite all her other policy expertise and interests. Meeting Senator Edward Kennedy was also special. Northern Ireland was a cause close to the heart of the Kennedy family, and he was friendly with Gerry Adams – well placed therefore when I asked him to deliver a tough message to Sinn Fein to sign up to support policing and the rule of law. The walls of his study were covered with family pictures. There were also busts of both his assassinated brothers. Later, in what sadly proved to be one of his last such visits, I was delighted that he accepted my invitation to Belfast as a guest at the ceremony to mark the settlement in Northern Ireland.

That 2004 presidential election saw a nail-biting finish with John Kerry appearing to lead through the day, some of his people buoyantly texting and phoning me. But the religious right had meanwhile been queuing up to back George Bush, who won comfortably. With their extremist views, these fundamentalist Christians were nearly as horrifying as Islamic fanatics; their influence on the world's most powerful country was profoundly disturbing. I was very disappointed with the outcome as was the whole of the Labour Party. Tony Blair put his best face on it – he had always expected a Bush victory and therefore during the campaign maintained studious neutrality which I understood, but Labour MPs were deeply depressed.

When the Cabinet met two days after the election, Tony said that he would now press even more strongly for Bush to promote the Middle East peace process, trade justice and an end to US protectionism. (But, although Tony was never gung-ho about Bush, he was vastly over-optimistic. On none of those key issues did we get any of his hoped-for progress.) I raised the lessons of the campaign, both the innovative techniques that I had seen on my visit and the politics: especially the role of security in the campaign, asking if we could have a proper read-across and analysis because the Tories always followed the Republicans and the latest techniques in the US were usually some years ahead of politics in Britain.

‡

Early in March 2005 I reviewed with Tony, Sally Morgan and Jonathan Powell my different approach to the Leader of the Commons job: to get a real political grip on the legislative programme, which the very talented team in the Cabinet Office had long regarded as their provenance; their ethos was that it should not be 'too political'. I did not agree and had in Phil Taylor a special adviser similarly enthused and also keen on, not to say possessed by, the minutiae of getting the legislative programme right. Such was the determination of the Cabinet Office team to exert control that you needed your SpAd to sit in on the working groups of officials and to insert the *politics* into what otherwise became *process* – at the end of which the Leader was presented with a *fait accompli*. Phil was a 'making a difference' SpAd as I liked to think I was a Minister and demonstrated an extraordinary appetite and energy for the task, generating simultaneously both resentment and admiration from the officials.

We both saw the opportunity to get stuck right into the politics of the whole government agenda in a way that virtually nobody else, apart from the PM, could do. Yet, I discovered, the process seemed designed to push through a continual sludge of off-the-shelf legislation from departments, some which would have been offered up to Ministers regardless of the party in power. At meetings of the Cabinet committee on the legislative programme, some Ministers regurgitated their civil service scripts with little if any explanation as to why their Bill really mattered to the government's political agenda.

Instead of just accepting Bills that came though this sausage machine, I would challenge departments to come forward with alternatives. I also tried to forestall manoeuvres to frustrate progressive reforms, for example over civil partnerships for same-sex couples. Despite insisting that it should be a priority for the 2003 Queen's Speech, officials were adamant that it could not and would not be ready in time, suggesting the following year as more appropriate. My concern was that, just as with age of consent legislation, this might require the use of the Parliament Act to overcome resistance in the House of Lords – so any delay now would effectively rule out delivering what we had promised before the election. We held our nerve and insisted the Bill be brought forward. And it was. Particularly rewarding was being able to welcome the first ever civil partnership in the UK in Belfast in 2005 while I was Secretary of State for Northern Ireland.

Another important reform was to make much greater use of pre-legislative scrutiny, which Robin Cook had pioneered. Not only did extra time to scrutinise draft Bills lead to better legislation, but it could be a useful method of breaking a log jam, for instance on corporate manslaughter, which we had long promised but routinely failed to deliver. It was vital to ensure companies honoured their obligations on health and safety, not least in the construction industry, where eighty people had been killed the previous year. However, every week brought a new pretext for delay and in the end putting a draft Bill in the Queen's Speech was the answer, because all outstanding issues could be dealt with during scrutiny. Meanwhile, announcing it in the Queen's Speech established the commitment, making it all but impossible for any successor to row back – it became law in 2007.

Keeping a beady eye on the politics of every Bill was also important; for instance I blocked an animal welfare Bill clause which would have instituted a very crude ban on youngsters winning a goldfish bowl as a prize at a village fete: a recipe if there ever was one for a media assault on 'political correctness'.

Furthermore, our government like its predecessors had never properly communicated what we were trying to achieve through our legislative programme: instead of the usual collection of Bills listed A–Z, I grouped them into themes representing strong political messages. Also for the first time, we ran a communications operation around the Queen's Speech which had a proper strategy, involving our MPs and Party members rather as Gordon Brown always did so effectively with his Budgets. However, I was happy to accept some minor redrafting of my recommended wording for the speech itself to take account of Palace sensitivities that it should not be 'too political'.

As the 2005 election approached I was particularly focused on ensuring that we were able to hit the ground running legislatively afterwards. After the 2001 election very few innovative or exciting Bills were ready: most seemed either a hangover from before the election or an off-the-shelf filler. This time it had to be different. We would be a party entering our third term, unprecedented for Labour, and I was determined to do what I could to ensure the start of the third term had a reforming zeal that many felt had been missing since we first took office.

We therefore worked closely with Alan Milburn and his SpAd, Patrick Diamond, to ensure that legislation was already being prepared for anything in the manifesto requiring it. Departments found it exasperating. They were programmed to focus on the short term and their starting point was individual laws. We went to them with broad themes and issues that we knew concerned the public – work–life balance for example – asking them to work up measures that would make a real difference to people's lives.

At that March 2005 meeting with Tony I explained how we were turning the entire manifesto into a grid with every commitment requiring a law change prioritised and mapped to the legislation needed to deliver it. I also gave Jonathan Powell a note drafted by my private secretary, Glynne Jones; he enjoyed working for a Commons Leader who placed the office in such a commanding position on the legislative programme. Tony acknowledged the progress we'd made. 'I have always wanted it done in this way and will make sure that whoever does it in the future gets the same remit,' he told me. However, a senior official at the heart of the operation told me within a year after I was moved on to Northern Ireland: 'Matters have reverted to pre-Hain.'

‡

After the 2005 election numerous Party figures began lobbying me to stand for Labour's deputy leadership because John Prescott had said he would stand down when Tony Blair did. I was often reported as being 'ambitious' and in the sense that I wasn't just a political journeyman, that may have been true. But I saw things rather differently. I was less interested in a leading position than in the opportunity really to change things. Although privileged to be a senior Cabinet figure, I was nevertheless frustrated by our government's increasing drift away from fundamental Labour values. On equality, democratic reform, the green agenda and progressive internationalism, we had jettisoned the radicalism which motivated me and countless Labour supporters and which I felt was capable of mobilising popular support for a winning strategy. Standing for deputy leader would be a platform for such a positive alternative.

But then came a big shock. In early August 2005 Robin Cook suddenly died of a heart attack while climbing a mountain in his native Scotland. I was devastated because he was both a personal friend and a political mentor. Days afterwards, in a piece for the *New Statesman*, I wrote: 'When he was in the Cabinet, people knew they had someone right at the top who could speak and act for Labour's soul.' I added: 'Labour's left has regularly thrown up figures who could rouse a *Tribune* rally and warm the hearts of the faithful, but were never credible, leading figures in government able to deliver on difficult issues and appeal to a wider audience. Robin could both rouse and govern.' Without ever having anything like Robin's ability or stature, I saw myself in his mould. I flew back from a holiday in Spain to attend Robin's funeral in Edinburgh, a huge, fitting and moving tribute.

The same day Martin Kettle, the perceptive assistant editor at the *Guardian*, wrote an article on Robin's legacy featuring likely candidates for the deputy leadership. My name featured sympathetically but realistically. In retrospect perhaps I also got carried away with expressions of encouragement from senior trade union leaders like Paul Kenny, Derek Simpson and Billy Hayes, and politicians like Keith Vaz, some of whom like Paul backed me all the way, while others ended up backing rivals. Phil Taylor, supported by numbers of other friends and MPs, pressed me to get organised and prepared for a deputy leader campaign when it came, and at the TUC in September 2005 I was widely and warmly approached about it.

A year later on 11 October 2006, while we waited to fly up to Scotland for the St Andrews summit on Northern Ireland, Tony asked me how my campaign was going, the first time he'd mentioned it. 'Not too badly but early days yet,' I mumbled. 'I think you're well placed, you know,' he replied. On the plane I found myself sitting next to him on a seat marked Prime Minister. I got up to move: 'I don't think I should be sitting here.' Tony smiled mischievously: 'Well, you might as well get used to it, Peter!' He kept pulling my leg.

‡

Having announced back in September 2004 that he would be standing down as leader in this third-term parliament, Tony couldn't have expected anything other than continued speculation on the timing of his departure or indeed continued manoeuvring from Gordon and his camp to go earlier rather than later.

Following as anticipated dreadful local election losses on 4 May 2006, and speculation beforehand over whether Tony could continue as PM, there was a mighty reshuffle. Charles Clarke was ousted as Home Secretary after a furore when it was revealed that foreign nationals leaving prisons, instead of being deported as planned, were disappearing and could not be traced. He was very angry when I spoke to him later that evening. John Reid was moved from his favourite job of Defence Secretary to replace Charles. Brutally – though probably because Tony had lost trust in him mainly because of his manoeuvrings on Europe – Jack Straw was demoted from Foreign Secretary to be Leader of the Commons. Geoff Hoon was demoted from Leader of the Commons to be Europe Minister, sitting in Cabinet: rather odd treatment of a loyal Blairite. It was a ruthless operation and it didn't go to plan with Charles Clarke's resignation. Tony lost an important ally, especially in tensions with Gordon Brown. Charles was valuable to Tony because he was both supportive and gave frank private advice; a political heavyweight who I thought had been a good Home Secretary.

When the Cabinet reassembled the following week, 11 May 2006, there were a number of new faces and it had a different feel. Jack Straw immediately asserted himself in his new role of Commons Leader, stating bluntly that Labour MP attendance was a problem, that the Tories under David Cameron were now behaving much more effectively like we did in opposition and that we were behind the pace as a government. He indicated a serious fall in Labour MP morale, a collapse in camaraderie and teamwork, and disaffection from Tony's leadership. None of this was a surprise to me, though Tony and his team seemed to be in denial.

In retrospect they should have seen the writing on the wall from the final Cabinet before the summer recess on 20 July 2006. Israel's typically disproportionate onslaught on Lebanon had followed provocative rocket attacks by Hezbollah and the kidnapping of several Israeli soldiers. Our government together with the US effectively provided cover for the Israelis to blitzkrieg Lebanon, destroying hospitals, infrastructure and facilities without impacting upon Hezbollah's strength except to bolster its enraged local support. There was uproar amongst Labour MPs and Party members about Tony's unwillingness to at least distance himself from the Israeli action. Highly significantly David Miliband (Tony's former head of policy at No. 10) and also Bruce Grocott (Tony's former parliamentary aide, now Lords whip and a loyalist to the core), both expressed strong concerns, especially about where it might all end.

Although I felt exactly the same way, I didn't say anything because I knew that if I did it would be leaked. Lo and behold, both David and Bruce duly appeared in the media as unusually dissenting from the official Cabinet line. I did notice that Jack Straw maintained an absolutely rigid silence. Instead, as the Cabinet's serial note writer, he passed one to Tony which it later emerged stated: 'Don't take my silence as approval of this policy.' Later, in a remarkable but pointed breach of collective Cabinet responsibility, Jack wrote a strong open letter to his constituency (and particularly its Muslims, comprising some thirty per cent of his voters) in which he attacked Israel's response. It created big headlines everywhere.

We all went off for the summer with Lebanon, Tony's proximity to Bush and his seeming inability to influence the Israelis all toxic for him. Politically we were in quite a lot of trouble. But we never really discussed it. Political Cabinet meetings had been successively put off and I felt Tony was losing his grip, with Gordon waiting in the wings. After the August break it got even worse. Tony gave an ill-judged interview to *The Times* which spun it as 'Blair will go on'. It was the last straw. Nearly twenty Labour parliamentary aides and a junior Minister resigned, their open letter leaked and interpreted as a coup against Tony. Gordon Brown's hand was suspected.

I tried to play an even-handed role in broadcast interviews, praising Tony on the one hand as 'Labour's most successful PM ever' while stating that Gordon was the other towering Labour figure. I phoned Gordon to say that, judging by the reaction from my Neath Labour members, the furore was even more damaging for him. Although they were not natural Blairites they disliked disloyal plotting even more. Despite evidence to the contrary, Gordon denied any involvement. But I said bluntly that he needed 'to call off the dogs' or he would be the loser. He soon made a statement pouring oil on troubled waters, but not before his team had tried to persuade me to go on the *Today* programme over Lebanon. 'How could I do that when I wasn't Foreign Secretary?' I replied. Gordon never tolerated any Cabinet Minister even inadvertently straying into his patch, now he was asking me to do that to another Cabinet colleague!

The net result of all this turmoil was that Tony also gave interviews indicating that the imminent Labour conference would be his last as Party leader. The countdown to both his succession and John Prescott's was on.

‡

It seemed to come quite quickly. After the momentous establishment of devolved government in Northern Ireland on 8 May 2007, the campaigns for the election of the new leader and deputy kicked off. The leadership was a coronation: 313 Labour MPs nominated Gordon and only thirty-four refused (including Charles Clarke).

Six of us contested for deputy over six weeks, criss-crossing the country. Over the previous year I had worked with Phil Taylor on a very detailed set of proposals to fight the campaign on several broad themes. I felt liberated to have the opportunity normally denied by collective Cabinet responsibility to set out issues which I felt our government had been slow to tackle. I pledged a sustained effort to narrow the gap between rich and poor, including a focus on corporate excess at the top, not just lifting up a few at the bottom. Tony Blair had not believed the gap mattered. I disagreed. It was about the society we wanted to live in. It was about our values and about responsibility (which we always rightly demanded from those in receipt of state support, but seemed afraid to demand from those at the top). I also argued that the rising cost of living, including utility bills and public transport fares, was squeezing middle- and lower-income households. My manifesto set out proposals for a new Employment Rights Commission (expanding the role of the Low Pay Commission to enforce rights other than the minimum wage), and protecting the rights of temporary workers, on which the government was then dragging its feet. I also proposed that welfare-to-work policy should concentrate more on skills and training to increase employability rather than a treadmill of ill-fated job applications or at best a revolving door of insecure jobs.

Next, having helped deliver devolution in Wales and Northern Ireland, I was very conscious Labour had not addressed 'the English question'. My manifesto backed new more powerful English regional government and select committees for each region in the interim, as well as greater powers for local government. And I urged that we complete the unfinished constitutional changes of our first term and create a democratically elected Second Chamber and the Alternative Vote for the Commons.

Additionally, insisting tackling climate change should come right at the top of the political agenda, I called for Labour to espouse a new 'red-green' politics, marrying social justice with environmental justice both at home and abroad.

Too often green policies impacted negatively on those on lower incomes – for example higher fuel prices – whereas in Northern Ireland I had insisted in prioritising micro-generation for social housing, enabling families to sell energy back to the grid and reduce their bills.

Finally, I proposed a detailed blueprint to reform the Labour Party, including more influence for members over policy and a new formal role for supporters of the party who were not yet willing to be fully paid-up members. (Nearly four years later it was satisfying to be able to incorporate these ideas in the 'Refounding Labour' project that I led for Ed Miliband after his election as Labour's leader.)

All this was set out in a 15,000 word pamphlet;* no other candidate had such a substantive manifesto, though many adopted some of the ideas. But if the campaign was based on a clear set of values and a solid set of radical policies, the organisational machine underpinning it was soft. Despite being well resourced, with a website, leaflets and branding of high quality and an enthusiastic team of workers and volunteers, elementary mistakes were made during the short campaign. There was no coordinated ground campaign despite many hundreds of activists offering assistance, which meant that I did poorly on constituency party nominations, signalling weakness. As I subsequently found to lethal effect, the grip on spending and declaring donations collapsed in the later stages of the contest.

Despite this we had some early successes. I became the first MP to receive the required forty-four MPs' backing to make it onto the ballot paper, picking up further MPs as the campaign went on. I also received many more trade union nominations than anybody else, from the GMB to the building workers, mineworkers and train drivers. I might also have won the support of the biggest union of all, Unite. Their sixty-five member Executive Council convened to interview candidates and to decide whom to back. Carefully pitched, my speech went down well – according to those present, the best of all; though general secretary Tony Woodley afterwards told me I should have 'an Equity card' as if it was simply an act: it wasn't. Then the council voted – and I was the winner. Consternation between the duet at the top, Tony Woodley and Derek Simpson, who the year before had indicated backing for me but subsequently swung behind Jon Cruddas. They adjourned the session and nobbled council members during the break, arguing their leadership could not be embarrassed since they had already pledged support for Cruddas. Another vote was taken, and this time he won – my supporters on the council furious.

---

* *Rebuilding the Progressive Coalition* (London, Peter Hain MP, May 2007).

The deputy leader victor, Harriet Harman, was always going to be strong, her main message for a woman in the top two was appealing. But had the favourite, Alan Johnson, whom she narrowly pipped, not ran a complacent campaign he would have won. My earlier strength as the Cabinet figure with the broad support of the left and the grass roots was fatally undermined by two candidates pitching for that very same support. On top of his undoubted abilities, Hilary Benn had the great benefit of the iconic 'Benn' brand. At the eleventh hour he scraped late onto the ballot paper with the necessary minimum of MP nominations. Jon Cruddas also only just made it, but, despite having worked for Tony Blair, he was uncluttered by association with the least popular of our government's policies, and had a fresh and engaging appeal to the membership, also performing exceptionally well at our hustings. With Unite putting huge financial and organisational resources into his campaign and the left swinging behind him, I was squeezed out to come fifth. Paul Kenny, the shrewd GMB leader, had been frustrated with fellow leaders of the big unions: 'Only Peter has the seniority and Cabinet experience to be a big hitter,' he argued; 'whatever his qualities, Jon won't be that.' Kenny saw the choice in blunt terms: between the unions acting with their hearts or their heads.

However, even without all these factors and the strengths of my rivals, I still might never have won. Despite all my experience and work in the Labour and trade union movement, maybe I still remained a bit of an outsider. I had entered the race out of conviction – to try and change the course of our government, to bring us back closer to our roots and our values – but I ended up nearly facing a conviction. It was a searing experience, the biggest mistake of my political life. Elizabeth and my family had not wanted me to run at all, nor had my talisman, Howard Davies. Although they backed me to the hilt, I wish I had listened to them.

‡

Almost before we knew it, the end of June 2007 arrived with Tony's final Cabinet meeting. He made an elegant, as always perfectly pitched, self-deprecating speech, simply 'moving on' to the next stage of his life without apparent emotion. He was like that over big achievements and big moments, as I had discovered over Northern Ireland. Pre-arranged, Jack Straw and David Miliband gave the Cabinet's thanks to him and to John Prescott, and we gave them each a present.

Then Tony did his thanks and walked out with a wave and a smile, all of us spontaneously rising to clap him, looking around at each other and wondering 'What next?' It was a poignant moment and for most including me an emotional one too. Gordon's supporters doubtless felt elated. I didn't.

The day before, at his last appearance in the Commons, I was sitting next to him, having just completed Welsh Questions. Tony was in magisterial form, the House, extremely rough and bitter towards him in recent times, admiring. I thought he had no peer on big occasions. At Prime Minister's Questions he was supreme in his command of the detail and his way of soothing the House while delivering rapier-like attacks on the opposition with a certain charm. There was nobody, I thought, quite like him. He delivered a short final peroration which I could see he'd written out by hand, saying that he had never claimed to be a parliamentarian but always respected Parliament. He'd always tried to do the right thing, but whether it was a right thing was a matter for the country and for history to judge. He ended with a flourish: 'And that's it. The End.' Many of us had to suppress our emotion and the whole House did something which had never happened before – it rose spontaneously to applaud him, MPs across the parties clapping, to frowns from the clerks: *not* the done thing.

Despite Gordon persistently snapping at his heels, I was pleased for Tony that he was leaving in his own way, perhaps not exactly at a point of his own choosing, but at the top of his game, the Northern Ireland triumph still resonating. Yes, he had lost a huge amount of trust in the country and in the Labour Party. But he was still respected despite the venom he attracted over Iraq and, tellingly, still feared by the Tories. And, yes, he probably was near the end of that shelf-life the harsh, media-intrusive, modern political age gives even the most gifted and popular of democratic leaders. But to those MP colleagues who had long wanted him out, I replied: 'Tony is a class act.' And he was soon missed.

‡

Although looking forward to a fresh Cabinet challenge after settling Northern Ireland, I wasn't feeling exactly top of the world, my usual political optimism having been tempered by the disillusioning deputy leader campaign, which had also been gruelling coming on top of ten months' frantic work – the Northern Ireland process, then the Welsh Assembly elections and Party management problems forming a Welsh government since we had lost our majority.

After he had been sworn in as PM, Gordon formed his Cabinet, seeing most of us in the Prime Minister's Commons office, making a point of avoiding the media theatre outside No. 10. 'I want you to continue doing the Wales job and I want to make you a good offer of another job,' he said. 'But first of all I want to ask you about discipline because over the deputy leader campaign you courted the gallery. I can't have that in the government.' (Others also did, some including Harriet much more so, I thought, bristling.)

He went on: 'I think you've done great things as a Minister and I know you've got good relations with your civil servants and are thought of very highly by them.' Now *that* was nice. To my surprise I was now Secretary of State for Work and Pensions. 'I want you to do it because I know you're a fantastic campaigner, one of the very few we've got at senior level in government and we need a much more campaigning approach,' he said.

Then we had a slight disagreement. Explaining that we had too many millions on benefits costing the country billions, he said: 'I want you to bring down the age of a child at which lone parents are required to seek work below the existing sixteen years, not just to twelve as has been independently recommended, but right down to seven years – and I want you to do that as soon as possible.'

I didn't know the detail, but was immediately concerned. 'Fine,' I replied, 'but I just want to make one thing clear: you've always got to think of the children in these circumstances and seven is a pretty young age. Unless you've got affordable childcare available I don't think we should just force lone mothers out into work. But I'll see what's possible and maybe we could do a linkage to childcare.' He was a bit impatient about this, which worried me a little. (However, when I later took this policy forward, I made sure affordable childcare was part of the package.)

While waiting to go over to my new office I returned to say goodbyes to Northern Ireland staff, where I had formed good friendships. The permanent secretary, Jonathan Phillips, came in for a chat. Widely admired throughout Whitehall and in Northern Ireland, he unexpectedly volunteered that I'd done 'an outstanding job'. He didn't think the settlement would have been achieved without me – certainly not in the time frame achieved: 'You were the best Secretary of State I worked with.'

Why? I asked, not inviting further flattery but intrigued, wanting his insight. 'One of the things is your resilience. You are always determined whatever setbacks we got, the Sean Kelly episode, the judicial review, whatever it was, you just kept going, always cheerful, always determined on the right course – whether you were attacked or not. I've seen some of your predecessors either just beyond their wits' end with anger or depressed. You didn't seem to be at all. Also you had a good strategic grip and political feel.'

‡

It seems almost eccentric to recall this now, but Gordon Brown was once a popular Prime Minister. In his early months he dealt highly effectively, and with minimal fanfare, with three crises which immediately engulfed his new government: unprecedented and devastating floods, a bad foot-and-mouth outbreak, and a narrowly foiled terrorism attack on London. He hurried back from a bucket-and-spade family holiday in Devon to be in charge. Within weeks of the switch in Prime Ministers, Blair-supporting business people who had been deeply sceptical about Gordon were singing his praises to me. 'Not Flash, just Gordon', a tag then doing the rounds, encapsulated a somewhat surprised public mood.

In those early weeks, the only problem over which the government – but in reality the governor of the Bank of England – seemed rather less than deft was the shocking collapse of Northern Rock, the mortgage-based bank, in September 2007. The governor prevaricated and we were behind the curve, far too over-anxious as a Labour government not to nationalise the bank until finally we had to do so to protect the savings and homes of tens of thousands of people.

However, several weeks before that, out in Spain in August on our annual holiday, Elizabeth and I were invited to lunch with an astute friend from the financial services sector. He was deeply and unexpectedly disturbed about the state of the financial markets. I later recalled that as a premonition, first of the Northern Rock bankruptcy, which happened within weeks, and a year later of the much wider and horrific malaise which paralysed global banking and triggered the worst recession for eighty years. That all began from lending money to poor American households which they could not pay back – so called 'sub-prime' mortgages. So out of control were global bankers that nobody seemed to know they had purchased bundles of this 'sub-prime'. The write-offs alone from sub-prime lending were to exceed a mind-boggling $2 trillion dollars, equivalent to writing off the annual output of the entire UK economy.*

It all came crashing down on the world in the autumn of 2008. Meanwhile Gordon was contriving to convert the resounding success of his first three months into a crushing disaster. Riding high in the polls as the annual Labour conference neared in late September, Gordon and his closest advisers, including new Cabinet Ministers Ed Balls and Douglas Alexander, deliberately encouraged talk of a November general election. When Ed came to see me in my new post as Secretary of State for Work and Pensions and I asked about it, he replied:

---

*   See Gordon Brown, *Beyond the Crash* (London, Simon and Schuster, 2010), p. 266.

'If I were you, I'd be writing my constituency election manifesto.' Another new Cabinet Minister, Ed Miliband, in charge of the national Party manifesto, hastily arranged to see me, relieved I had loads of policy ideas, not just for my portfolio but more widely, some culled from my deputy leader campaign.

In Bournemouth at the conference, speculation was running wild. At a News International dinner for Cabinet Ministers, the company's luminaries Les Hinton and Rebekah Wade (later Brooks) extolled Gordon's virtues, Hinton especially excoriating about David Cameron. (That may seem unbelievable as I write this after the 2011 hacking scandal, but it is true.)

Gordon hadn't bothered to ask most of us about an early election and when chatting to Angela Smith, his parliamentary aide and formerly one of my Northern Ireland Ministers, I asked: 'Has any polling been done in marginal seats, especially London and the South?' No, was the worrying answer.

The clamour for an early election reaching a crescendo, substantial amounts were spent in preparation by Labour headquarters. But then Gordon abruptly back-tracked. Perhaps unnerved by a sudden poll surge by the Tories after their carefully staged conference promise to slash stamp duty on house sales – and perhaps worried he was unnecessarily risking being the shortest-serving PM ever – Gordon cried off, giving an exclusive interview to Andrew Marr of the BBC and thereby managing to offend other broadcasters camped outside No. 10.

The media were also angry at having been led up the garden path. 'Bottler Brown' was the happy chant from the Tories and their tabloid newspaper supporters including the *Sun* and others whose top people had been lauding him only two weeks before. All the old voter reservations and fears about Gordon came flooding back. He had, as I described it afterwards in a TV documentary, 'encouraged the train to leave the station without being sure of the destination'. Fatal. He never recovered. In retrospect an early election was probably our best chance of winning under Gordon; the Tories were panicking and clearly agreed.

Many of his Labour critics felt he had got his come-uppance, having been so desperate for the job for so long. They had never thought he could be a successful PM. But he was dealt a difficult hand. By the time he took over, our government was deeply unpopular and we were later engulfed by tumultuous events beyond his responsibility: the global banking crisis and the deeply corrosive scandal over MP expenses.

‡

Gordon's new Cabinet was less experienced and much younger; I was one of the oldest aged fifty-seven – disconcerting because I'd never seen myself as a 'greybeard'. His first Cabinet meeting was short but purposeful and it felt nice to be part of a fresh start. Yet it was also paradoxical because there didn't seem be a fundamentally different strategy. It seemed like change and continuity both at the same time.

At least at the beginning, his meetings were quite different from Tony's. He listened intently to colleagues, scribbling furiously with his bold marker pen, compiling a sheaf of notes. 'Is this what Cabinets used to be like?' Ed Balls whispered sitting next to me. Not really, I replied, though there was a similar informality with flashes of humour, the new Gordon even relaxed and witty. As time went on, the scribbling continued but he seemed to hunch dourly into his seat.

Apart from being part of the same New Labour generation, that was where the similarity with Tony's premiership ended. Although his work-rate could not have been surpassed, he seemed unable to delegate. Cabinet Ministers and permanent secretaries soon complained that they could not get decisions from No. 10. Tony somehow managed to juggle dozens of issues at a time, to be focused on the most pressing but to be sufficiently across them all to run a smooth and efficient ship. Gordon drilled down in forensic detail on the issue of the day, neglecting the many others competing for his attention.

At the beginning especially, his office was dysfunctional. Nobody seemed to have sufficient authority or self-confidence to give you an answer. Under Tony, you could call Jonathan Powell, Alastair Campbell, Anji Hunter, Sally Morgan or later Ruth Turner and they would either know Tony's mind or get back to you very quickly if they needed to consult him. Under Gordon, papers or verbal requests disappeared into a black hole.

I had a tortuous experience over new statistics due for publication appearing to show foreigners had taken an alarmingly high proportion of the three million new jobs created since we had been in power. Immediately I saw them I knew they would be incendiary, so I had a rebuttal and analysis for Gordon prepared and ensured key members of his staff were phoned to clear both the timing for releasing the figures and the best line to take. I spoke to his chief of staff, Tom Scholar, myself. Everything was agreed. By coincidence I was with Gordon the evening before the figures were released and thought of mentioning them to him; but he was rushed and the meeting was on Wales with Rhodri Morgan so I didn't. A mistake. With the story leading bulletins early the next morning Gordon called me around 6.30 a.m., fuming. He kept complaining: 'This destroys our employment record,' as if it was my fault. 'But I was told you cleared it,' I replied. 'No, no,' he stormed. However, Tom Scholar and others in No. 10 later insisted he did know when I angrily checked.

Gordon was also obsessed with publishing long documents. At DWP we put an enormous effort into producing ones on employment policy, the text painstakingly cleared over weeks. But the media rarely covered them and nobody read them. He also procrastinated over key decisions, for instance refusing to appoint Labour peers (except for a handful from outside the Party made Ministers), causing huge frustration to our leadership in the Lords and damaging Labour's influence. And yet, when it came to the G20 in April 2009 he was at his brilliant best, praised by fellow world leaders for almost single-handedly driving forward an agreement to save the global economy tumbling from recession into depression.

‡

Before I had been running a whole state in Northern Ireland. Now at Work and Pensions I was in charge of the biggest department with by far the biggest budget in Whitehall. By mid-December 2007, despite the donations night-mare starting to engulf me and losing sleep with worry, I was nevertheless able to make important policy progress.

My White Paper, *Ready for Work: Full Employment in Our Generation,* laid out a radical new strategy for getting people off benefits and into work. It expressed my own concept of an 'active' rather than 'passive' system of benefits which turned people into dependants and trapped them in a culture where they were ignored on benefit for life rather than encouraged and supported to get training and skills, leading hopefully to jobs. Of course some, severely disa-bled, mentally or physically, could not work. But I was very clear –and became even more so during my seven-month tenure at the DWP – that many people on benefits *could* work, provided they were actively supported and there was affordable childcare. It was our responsibility to encourage and find jobs for them to do so; their responsibility, indeed their duty, to take advantage of new opportunities. However, this was not cheap. It cost a lot of money, especially for people out of work for a while. The launch got quite a lot of coverage and was broadly well received.

At DWP I was also able to put into practice a belief first formulated in my radical youth: that change came through a combination of 'extra' and 'intra' parliamentary activity. Where ministerial colleagues might be indifferent to, and even sometimes contemptuous of, protesters or strikers, I wasn't. I had been where they were – maybe would return there some day after government. I tried to go the extra mile to bring outsiders in, with an open door to pressure groups, seeking wherever possible to find solutions, which rarely satisfied them fully but at least responded to their concerns. As a former union full-timer, I became a departmental 'boss' – successfully working in partnership with the trade unions, but firm where needed: for example in 2007 ensuring Remploy, the company which provided sheltered employment for disabled workers, had a viable future; also over civil service pay disputes in Northern Ireland and the DWP.

The first time I had been protested against was when Welsh college lecturers staged a picket to greet my arrival for a visit in 1998. An over-worried warning about the protest had been telephoned in advance. 'Drive straight past,' my jittery private secretary advised. I certainly wasn't doing that, and asked that our car pull up as I jumped out and had a chat, appreciated by the pickets. A year later I was able to switch budget spending recommendations served up by my officials and instead increase their pay.

My responsibilities at DWP in 2007 included health and safety at work, and there were protests by families of crane workers killed on site; again, I made a point of joining them to listen to their case. Around that time the building workers' trade union UCATT lobbied me about a disturbing jump in fatalities on construction sites, mainly workers in small firms where health and safety wasn't easily monitored. Against advice from officials I decided to call a 'summit' of employers, pressure groups and trade unions to agree a joint strategy to tackle the problem. It took some negotiating beforehand, and there was an annoying attempt to derail it by John Hutton, the free-market Business Secretary and Blairite outrider, who took it upon himself to complain I was 'hectoring businesses'. But he didn't understand the background. The event was a triumph, a wide cross-section of building employers participating constructively in the summit, seeing the venture as one in their own self-interest.

After being threatened by the militant Fathers 4 Justice group, who saw the DWP's policy over children of separated parents as discriminatory towards them, I persuaded very reluctant officials to change policy and open negotiations. I insisted the F4J leader withdraw his threat of violence first and began a difficult dialogue with the group in Wales where their people where less histrionic. That was, however, abandoned after I left the job, as was any serious follow-up to the building fatalities initiative.

‡

At DWP I had to grapple with a huge challenge. Over 140,000 workers had been 'robbed' of their pensions – a phrase which jarred with my officials but which I felt very strongly and passionately about. Their companies had gone bust, taking their pension funds with them. A few years before I'd met workers at ASW (Allied Steel and Wire) in Cardiff. I remembered one particular individual who had had nearly forty years of pension contributions and service in the company and was due to retire six weeks before it went bankrupt, losing every bit of his pension. The workers were not just bereft, they were also very angry: with us. For five years now they had been campaigning for equivalent compensation to that which was being offered to any workers who might face a similar predicament in the future, through the new Pension Protection Fund (PPF) which we had established and which was partly financed by industry-wide levies.

Before I ever dreamt I would have responsibility, I had spoken out in Cabinet on 12 February 2004 and had long felt that we were handling this scandal dreadfully. We'd gradually been dragged to offer eighty per cent of their pensions, but without equivalent conditions to those in the PPF. The workers demanded parity with the PPF and I couldn't see why we weren't granting it to them. We had eventually been pushed into the position when I became Secretary of State where we were offering £2 billion net present value, spread over sixty years, and it required around another £900 million to bridge the gap, also spread way into the future.

The pensioners had run an extremely effective and aggressive campaign, to which the Tories of all people had allied themselves. It was very dangerous for us politically – in fact bonkers. Most of the people affected were Labour supporters and trade unionists, amongst our core voters. Yet we'd alienated them to the point where some traditional Labour diehards were now even thinking of voting Tory. I went to visit a marginal seat in Hemel Hempstead in the autumn of 2007 and was ambushed by protestors, with an aggressive local Tory MP acting the bovver boy and carrying them all behind him.

However, Gordon clearly had a bee in his bonnet. I tried to talk to him round. But he wouldn't shift, any more than when he had blocked my predecessors funding a solution over the years as Chancellor. Extra funding identified by an actuary's report into residual assets in the failed schemes enabled us to reach tantalisingly close to a PPF-equivalent settlement but not to meet it. The gap frankly was not worth losing a political battle over. But Gordon was being pig headed.

Then the *Observer* carried a piece reporting a 'Cabinet split' between myself on the one hand and the Prime Minister and Chancellor Alistair Darling on the other. I'd been in consistent dialogue with Alistair and also with his Chief Secretary, Andy Burnham. But the person blocking a solution was Gordon. The story had been briefed by the Pensions Action Group, whose articulate spokesperson, Ros Altmann, was an expert on pensions, and had previously advised Tony Blair. She and her group had been running rings around the government and enjoyed the backing of the Tories. We had been tipped off the previous day about this damaging story. Gordon was out in Afghanistan and I rang the duty clerk in No. 10 and called Alistair to tell them that I'd heard it was coming and that it hadn't originated from me.

The media like nothing more than a government split story and followed up the *Observer* with gusto. When I went early to the Cabinet two days later on 10 December Gordon's private secretary called me in to see the PM. He was hunched in his office, which had been transformed since Tony left. A computer was on his desk, a big screen behind him which reflected up the words on his own PC. He glowered at me in a foul mood. 'I'm very unhappy about these leaks in the media, Peter. Government splits are terrible.' (He was a fine one to talk.) I told him I'd tried to reach him and spoken to Alistair to warn him, that it hadn't come from me, and that the Tories really had an open goal. But he wasn't listening. He went into an archetypal Gordon rant: 'You are weak. You are giving in to all their demands – whatever they want – and we can't afford it.'

I held my ground and stayed calm as I'd done fifteen years before under Gordon's torrent. 'Actually what I was trying to do was avoid a damaging political attack on you. Both as Chancellor and as Prime Minister, you are seen as the obstacle to a solution. The gap of affordability is very small. We have already committed over £2 billion and in July we committed to Parliament to match whatever the actuary's report identified in the residual assets.'

I insisted that we had to do this: 'If we don't we will be defeated in Parliament by the Tories and our own backbenchers. We've already lost a vote in the summer in the Lords and a defeat on the back of the actuary's report is a gold-plated guarantee. Politically we are in a really bad position because the Tories are allying with the trade unions and our core voters. In any case the financial argument for not doing it doesn't stack up.' I wasn't sure Gordon was listening to me. He continued to fulminate. 'You're acting like a pressure group. It's totally irresponsible.'

When I denied that I was the source for the leaks he went back on the attack. 'But your department's been leaking, your officials must have been briefing, because the media have some of the figures.' It was true that our officials had been in dialogue with the Pensions Action Group. But I explained that the figures were in the actuary's interim report a few months previously.

Still there was no meeting of minds as we went off to the Cabinet with Gordon still grumbling and now also concerned about Prime Minister's Questions the next day and the fact that he could be subject to criticism. Although I felt a bit battered, I was sure I was doing the right thing. I was going to stand my ground. If he wanted to get rid of me over this he bloody well could.

Later that day, travelling to Cardiff to make a speech as Secretary of State for Wales, I got a message to say that the PM and Chancellor wanted to see me that evening at eight o'clock. Impossible, I explained. No. 10 came back some hours later and said they wanted to see me at eight o'clock next morning, at a time when Gordon was normally focusing on Prime Minister's Questions, which he was due to answer at twelve.

I was driven back late from Wales and got into Downing Street early, well briefed about all the issues to find Gordon still in a bad mood, Alistair sitting quietly beside him. I was on the receiving end of a repeat rant: impossible situation, divided government, not a justified case, useless Ministers etc. And a fresh argument: the danger was the private sector would transfer all the risk to the state and that the Pension Protection Fund could be affected – a valid point, I replied, but still missing our fundamental predicament: 'The gap between us is very small. It just won't stand up in Parliament or to public scrutiny. We will be pilloried if we move significantly towards what would settle the matter, but then hold back on the last small bit.'

'Look,' I added in exasperation, 'if you instruct me to hold the line, I will have to do so. But you will be the political villain. It's *you* they will be gunning for, not me.'

Abruptly Gordon changed focus, turning to Alistair: 'Do you accept these figures of Peter's?' Yes, was the reply, the figures had all been agreed. Satisfied, Gordon seemed suddenly to come to his senses. 'OK then. It's really important we move to an early resolution of these issues.' We haggled over the detail but his mood had changed dramatically. Having finally taken the plunge, he was now very anxious for an early announcement and statement to Parliament.

My astonished officials had been certain I would be forced into an unacceptable compromise, but the victory was enthusiastically welcomed by the pensioners when I announced it on 17 December 2007. That day Gordon and I were together again at a Cabinet committee on Welfare to Work. 'You're a hero,' he told me.

'No, you are the hero for agreeing to it,' I replied.

'Everyone is telling me you are the hero,' he insisted. His jovial jesting was so different from his bullying the previous Tuesday and Wednesday. But that was Gordon for you.

Sadly for him and for us all, he was a well-intentioned, superhumanly dedicated and decent, but dysfunctional Prime Minister. Sadly for me, having achieved so much in rectifying that injustice and in resolving other key policy issues on my watch, I was out of the Cabinet a month later.

‡

Wounded by that saga I resolved to keep my own counsel on the direction of our government, remaining publicly loyal, relatively low key as a backbencher and instead enjoying writing my biography of Nelson Mandela and beginning to write this book. Neil Kinnock graciously told me that my behaviour had been 'exemplary' and that Gordon could not have asked for greater loyalty.

Colleagues kept saying 'You will be back', but I remained doubtful, especially when, in Swansea at the Welsh Labour conference in February 2009, Gordon either consciously or unconsciously delivered snubs deeply resented by numbers of delegates. He passed me over in the normal leader courtesies at the start of his speech. Then he added: 'I want to pay tribute for his outstanding leadership of the anti-apartheid movement to – Neil Kinnock!' Neil, used to plaudits as a former Labour leader, seemed taken aback and people turned to look at me in amazement. As if to compound it, Sarah Brown remarked to Elizabeth that I had 'not been loyal enough'. Elizabeth was furious. What planet were the Browns living on, we wondered?

However, a few months later, events took a dramatic turn. Labour was abjectly humiliated in the June 2009 local elections. In the European elections the same day we were beaten, not just by the Tories but by UKIP in England and in Wales by the Tories. In a carefully timed bombshell for the ten o'clock TV news after polls had closed, Tony Blair's former policy adviser James Purnell resigned from the Cabinet with a dignified but trenchant statement telling Gordon to 'stand aside to give our Party a fighting chance of winning'. Charles Clarke had indicated to me privately beforehand that something was afoot and there was speculation about others going too. Jacqui Smith and Hazel Blears had already stepped down.

With, we learnt later, Blairites Peter Mandelson, David Miliband and John Hutton moving swiftly to forestall any wider plot, I went to bed with my mobile phone switched off and was woken up early next morning by No. 10 in crisis mode calling on my home phone. Gordon's government relations director, Sue Nye, always friendly and supportive, came on the line, explaining she had been trying to reach me late the previous night. 'Gordon is minded to bring you back. He hasn't finally decided, so you can't assume anything,' she said.

'If he doesn't do so now, there won't be another time,' I snapped back, reminding her I had previously told both her and Gordon I would not accept a return at anything under Cabinet level. It was an unusually tetchy response for me. But frankly I wasn't being messed around after all I had been through. If Gordon wanted me back in the Cabinet, he could have me, but it wasn't the end of the world if he didn't – I had become accustomed to the advantages of a freer life.

Sue, ever calm and respectful, said she perfectly understood: 'But we need Sue Gray in the Cabinet Office to run over your parliamentary expenses first.' Although I understood why, I also felt it was a bit of a cheek. There had been no criticism of my expenses: not only within the rules, they also contained none of the excesses that so scandalised the public about too many other MPs. Sue Gray's check drew a predictable blank.

That took a few hours and meanwhile the Wales Office director and their chief press officer called to congratulate me on my return as Secretary of State. 'But I haven't been told that myself!' I replied. Hours later Gordon phoned to appoint me. I was indeed back. Although I felt very sad for my friend Paul Murphy, whom I was replacing yet again, the circle around the donations saga was finally closed. It had in any case been put well and truly into perspective by the MP expenses disgrace and was almost never mentioned again.

‡

Both before and after I returned to the Cabinet, Gordon's opponents continuously plotted against him. Even his previously loyal ally Alistair Darling had become totally frustrated and alienated.[*] Charles Clarke was the most persistent plotter. Although he had a burning contempt for Gordon as leader and PM, his motivation was genuine: 'I fear not just a defeat at the general election but a terrible one which will do lasting damage to the Party,' he told me in one of our regular chats. He was convinced that if Gordon departed we could at the very least mitigate the scale of that impending defeat and possibly even reverse it.

Charles was critical of me for returning to the Cabinet, and I knew that there was probably no chance of a Labour majority. But if we worked like mad we could minimise the damage, I believed. Furthermore I couldn't see how Gordon could be dislodged. For a start, there was no obvious successor. When I put this to Charles he responded airily: 'What we need is a contest. People will then come forward.' I was sceptical and told him so. The only circumstance in which I could envisage Gordon stepping down was if the whole Cabinet turned against him and installed Alan Johnson, who was the one figure I could imagine uniting the Party, acceptable to both Blairites and Brownites. But that wasn't going to happen. David Miliband was approached, gave mixed signals but declined. There were several half-hearted attempts to dislodge Gordon,

---

[*]   See Alistair Darling, *Back from the Brink* (London, Atlantic Books, 2011).

but, as I told the plotters – Charles and Margaret McDonagh included – I didn't see their schemes as credible; if they had been that might have been a different matter.

Instead, the Party limped forward gloomily. It was not as if we had run out of ideas or plans for the future: we were brimming with them. Before a Cabinet meeting on 9 December 2009 I asked the Cabinet secretary, Gus O'Donnell, about the comparison made by some commentators with the dog years of the John Major administration before 1997 when Gus had worked at No. 10. He confirmed what I felt: that our predicament was nothing like Major's. The Tories at that time were all over the place. There was no real energy, there were no new ideas. Our problem if anything was there were too many new White Papers and initiatives. Major was losing his majority in the Commons so could not legislate properly, and there was a sense of drift. Our problem was a very different one – and everyone knew very well what that was.

CHAPTER THIRTEEN

MISSION UNFULFILLED

Although Labour won the 2005 election with a clear majority, we did so with one of the smallest ever votes to form a majority government – just 35.2 per cent. We were saved by an unelectable Tory opposition and the sense that Tony Blair would win anyway; and I suggested at the time that the default position for the following election would be a hung Parliament. In 2009, and then in the run-up to the general election on 6 May 2010, I again argued this scenario to journalists, friends and political colleagues.

Before that election the Tory lead began to narrow, even more so after Liberal Democrat leader Nick Clegg's electrifying performance in the first of three TV debates in the campaign itself. Over four weeks, being driven several thousand miles all over Wales, political turbulence on the ground was very evident. Although there was a warming welcome from people often astounded to open their door to see a familiar TV face, I was in no doubt that, on the one hand many were fed up with Labour, on the other they weren't sure about the Tories.

While most in the Westminster bubble expected a Tory victory, I remained hopeful that – despite immense public hostility to Gordon Brown – we might see a repeat of the 1992 election, when voters switched at the last minute to keep an unpopular government they knew rather than an opposition they distrusted. I was wrong about that, but not surprised when the usual BBC election night exit poll pointed to a hung Parliament. As the night wore on it became clearer by the hour that the exit poll had been uncannily accurate.

Having planned for that outcome, I left the count straight after my comfortable Neath election win at three in the morning and was driven to London with my new special adviser David Taylor. We arrived at dawn at College Green outside Parliament, where the whole media circus was camped out in bright but chilly weather. Due to fulfil an interview request from BBC Wales, I soon found myself doing virtually every programme for every channel since I was the only Cabinet member on the spot.

My case was clear: we had lost the election, but the Tories had not won it. Labour should try to form a progressive coalition with the Liberals. The alternative was a right-wing Tory-led government. Soon my views were being reported prominently in news bulletins, the Westminster bubble excitedly digesting the implications of this unusual predicament.

A couple of years before – while, in rugby parlance, in the 'sin bin' out of the Cabinet – I had talked informally to a series of leading Liberal Democrats, some of whom, like Paul Tyler, I had known from my Young Liberal days long ago. Others, like Nick Clegg's chief of staff, Danny Alexander, I had not. We had talked about them supporting the Alternative Vote and a possible coalition afterwards in the event of a hung Parliament. It transpired Charles Clarke (also out of the Cabinet), with whom I had regular chats, was separately involved in a similar exercise. Charles thought a hung Parliament likely too, and had even had a private chat with senior establishment figures about the constitutional proprieties, including to whom the Queen would turn to form a government. Unsurprisingly, he took the view that Gordon would have to go. But we agreed neither of us would tell each other to whom we were talking and would not tell the Lib Dems we were liaising between ourselves. A group of Lib Dems were due to meet me over an evening meal at the south London home of one Lib Dem MP after the June 2009 European elections. But when I was invited back as Secretary of State for Wales, Paul Tyler called to say that it was not right to pursue the meal with a sitting Cabinet Minister.

Meanwhile, however, I got on well with Liberal MP Ming Campbell and we often talked about rugby (him a keen Scotland fan, me Wales). Respected for his foreign affairs credibility, he had had an unhappy spell as their Party leader before being been ousted, and we consoled each other over the trauma of our resignations. I explained my view that a hung Parliament was likely and that a deal with the Lib Dems might be on the cards based around AV. Ming was enthusiastic but very careful about relaying the message back to colleagues, and we took the precaution of exchanging mobile phone numbers. I told nobody about this. Trust is a rare commodity in the Westminster gossip factory.

I called Ming a few days before the election on 6 May and we agreed to keep in touch. Now, waiting between interviews outside Westminster, I pondered reactivating our 'back channel'. David Taylor nudged me towards the leading Liberal, David Laws, also doing interviews, but he wasn't interested in chatting. Staying up in London over the weekend there were frantic mobile phone conversations with Ming especially, who was desperate for a Labour deal. So too, it appeared, was Simon Hughes, who was in close touch with my former special adviser and good friend, Phil Taylor, who had known Simon for many years and was relaying messages back and forth. I also called Gordon Brown, hunkered down at No. 10; he encouraged me to pursue my contacts, as did Peter Mandelson, who was in direct touch with the Lib Dem leadership.

On the Saturday night, on my way back home by train after an evening meal with my son Jake in Windsor, where he and his wife Kirsten lived, Ming Campbell called, worried that – with Tory and Lib Dem negotiations apparently going smoothly – things were moving against a deal with Labour, and that Gordon Brown remaining PM was the main obstacle. I immediately called Gordon to tell him this directly, which wasn't easy, especially as Ming was an old friend of his.

Gordon responded testily: 'So who else do *you* want as Labour leader then?'

'Nobody,' I replied. 'I am just passing on what the Lib Dems are saying. Many still want to form a coalition with us, but you would have to go.'

It was a classic bit of Gordon bristle, but he calmed down when I also explained the Lib Dems would be more than happy with AV. When I reported the exchange to Peter Mandelson he asked: 'Did you really tell Gordon that? Very brave of you. How did he react?'

On the Sunday, watching my team Chelsea win the Premiership, I bumped into the Tory Shadow Minister Ed Vaizey, also a Chelsea fan, and there was a bit of banter between us. 'We are going to screw over the Liberals,' he said cockily. Speculation was feverish and the BBC's political editor Nick Robinson called during the match asking whether Gordon should step down. I refused to comment on or off the record; I was certainly not going to fuel such a sensitive matter. Instead I volunteered to be part of a small team Peter Mandelson was heading to negotiate with the Lib Dems; to my disappointment, Gordon turned down this offer.

However, Mandelson, ideally placed inside the ill-fated post-election discussions with Nick Clegg and his team, subsequently confirmed what I felt throughout: that, although Clegg was interested, and his Party certainly wanted a Labour deal, in the final analysis, he and his fellow 'Orange Book' colleagues were never really serious about it. We were more useful to get his Lib Dem elite a more favourable deal with the Tories – which is what they finally achieved over a couple of days of detailed negotiations. In any case, the parliamentary arithmetic was against a Labour coalition – we didn't have with the Lib Dems the majority they enjoyed with the Tories. But, as was soon very evident, Clegg was much more in tune with the Tory right-wing agenda of savage public spending cuts despite having denounced these only days before and indeed throughout the general election campaign.

‡

By Tuesday 11 May 2010 my Wales Office staff agreed it looked inevitable they would be getting a new Secretary of State. But then I was called to Buckingham

Palace to attend a meeting of the Privy Council. Making small chat as we gathered beforehand, it was one of those unspoken 'I know that you know what we all know' moments: the endgame was imminent, but here we were still performing our last dutiful functions as Her Majesty's Ministers. Peter Mandelson was inscrutable as Lord President of the Council, enjoying the pomp and going through the normal courtesies with the Queen before the rest of us were called in to stand in line as was customary.

The Queen peered at an agenda item requiring her to sign the Red Meat Industry (Wales) Measure 2010 and looked up quizzically at me. After the formalities, when she traditionally turned to us for a chat, she asked what it was about.

'To ensure Wales has the very best beef and lamb,' I explained.

'Well I had some lovely beef and lamb in north Wales during my visit a few weeks ago,' she replied.

'I am sure – and the weather was nice. I was up there campaigning during your visit.'

She nodded. 'We went by train. It's wonderful to take your home with you. Better than hotels,' adding wistfully, 'People cannot take us in their houses these days.'

She was in impish mood, smiling and enjoying a gossip. Talk turned to the 24-hour TV drama camped outside Westminster, Jack Straw moaning about intrusiveness of helicopter camera shots.

'Yes, they had television pictures from above of me going in my door!' Her eyes were twinkling. 'My press officer complained about my security. Actually I think it infringed my human rights!' She giggled, as we joined her in laughter.

A couple of hours later, I watched live television coverage as Gordon Brown drove to the Palace to tender his resignation to her. Disappointed but phlegmatic and unsurprised, I grabbed a few essentials from the office and returned home, only to be phoned and kindly invited back into the Wales Office first thing next morning to say farewell to staff lined up on the staircase, before my successor arrived several hours later.

'The only thing inevitable in politics is the end of a ministerial career' was one of my favourite quips in government – and now my twelve years as an outsider inside the centre of the Blair–Brown governments were over.

‡

In the year running up that fateful general election, Peter Mandelson was the Cabinet's most formidable member. I witnessed him at his peak as de facto deputy Prime Minister, trying to coax Gordon Brown and the rest of us to get up off our ministerial chairs and out of our red boxes to take Labour's fight to the people.

'You should all be out there taking more risks to stir up controversy – that's the only way to get media attention and expose the Tories; they are beatable, you know,' he urged repeatedly. Although colleagues would nod, they rarely if ever followed his advice.

Never natural buddies, I found myself agreeing with virtually all his arguments in the political sessions of the Cabinet, which became more frequent the nearer we got to the election. His analysis of the vulnerabilities of the Tories was masterful, his solutions and strategies likewise.

'We have the policies for the future, we have a past record to be proud of,' he would say, 'Now let's show some fight!'

Yet it was as if he was trying to prod a lumbering, sullen, depressed carthorse into becoming a surging stallion. Most of my colleagues thought we had already lost, some would say so privately. I had maintained for quite a while that we had everything still to fight for: a Labour majority was unlikely but we might still form a coalition to stay in power. In Wales I had formulated and led a 'Labour Fightback' campaign, ruthlessly prioritising key seats and mobilising party activists to great local enthusiasm; I unsuccessfully tried to get the strategy adopted in England too.

A friend inside the Party HQ 'war room' reported to me:

The election campaign never really got going. Staff were exhausted before the short campaign had even begun. Ministers were steering clear of the national campaign, focusing on their own constituencies. Press officers would call Ministers and ask them to do interviews or take part in campaign events and they would make excuses not to. It felt like many people had given up. Then came the Mrs Duffy incident. When she was interviewed after the encounter with the PM and said she would vote Labour after all, we thought maybe this was a turning point. It had been a good day and Gordon's walkabouts seemed to be getting good coverage on the rolling news channels. The atmosphere had lifted. Then a few minutes later that was all destroyed as Sky News started running the PM's comments as he sped away in the car with the live microphone still connected. We couldn't believe it. It was no one's fault – these things happen. But it felt like a real body blow. Staff were utterly demoralised.

Leading the campaign in Wales I had focused our message relentlessly around the danger of 'savage Tory cuts', appealing to anti-Tory but not necessarily pro-Labour voters to 'lend' us their votes in the critical Labour–Tory marginal seats.

But although the strategy worked well in Wales, and we did better than was predicted, Gordon Brown's leadership haunted Labour right across Britain. Brilliant but clumsy, he had lost whatever traction he once had with the voters. There was a No. 10 team of talent and decency, but no grip or clear direction because the man at the top did not facilitate that. A Party hollowed out of members and deeply in debt. A wider civil society and trade union movement, after years of being shunned, unwilling to galvanise us in support. A massively resourced Tory Party with the media in full cry backing it. Facing a cycle of change against our government, which was seeking to defy electoral history and secure a fourth term – and all that on top of the worst global financial crisis since the 1930s, for which voters blamed all sitting governments of whatever party the world over.

Given this, the 2010 defeat was perhaps inevitable. And indeed, our share of the vote at twenty-nine per cent was Labour's second lowest since 1922. But I remained, as I had been since my days of youth militancy, also frustrated by the left's oppositionalism. They knew only too well what they were *against*, but never really said what they were *for*, how they would fund an alternative programme, or how it could command public support and a majority vote at an election. They also played into the hands of the Tories, typified a month before polling day when the left-wing civil service trade union leader Mark Serwotka hit the front page with this gem: 'I have to say to you this – that if you judge a government by how it behaves as an employer, this is the worst government in the history of this country.' His members – their ranks swelled amongst the 800,000 additional public sector workers recruited under our Labour government – were about to find out just how much 'worse' it could get.

‡

In government the Tories, their many media supporters and their new Liberal Democrat converts, relentlessly traduced our economic record to justify the deepest, quickest public spending cuts in British history. To win again, it is vital Labour is successful in exposing that Orwellian rewrite of history and is successful in persuading voters that there is a serious, credible alternative.

In truth we had taken office in 1997 so determined on gaining a reputation for economic trust and competence that we even committed to standing by the Tories' public expenditure plans for the next two years and introduced tough rules for government spending and borrowing.

The origins of New Labour's mantra, 'No return to boom and bust', lay in the Tory boom of the late 1980s followed by the Tory recession in the early

1990s. For me its roots went deeper: to the experience of the Labour government of 1974–9. It was not just the politically disastrous 1978–9 'winter of discontent' that had worried me so much as Labour's 1974–5 salad days when high hopes triumphed over economic reality: 'The first months of the new government were characterised by our spending money which in the event we did not have,' according to Joel Barnett, Labour's Chief Secretary to the Treasury then.

So I had no illusions about the prospects for boosting public spending in the first years of our new Labour government, but remained optimistic about the future once we got the economy onto an even keel. Our initial restraint on public spending soon proved productive. By first cutting the public sector deficit and then turning it into a surplus for three years we cut national debt as a share of national income from over forty-two per cent in 1996–7 to less than 30 per cent in 2001–2, equivalent to a massive reduction of £175 billion today. This helped to build the platform of economic stability and delivered a decade of record investment in the public services as they were repaired from the dismal Tory inheritance of patients dying on trolleys in hospital corridors, collapsing education standards and 'the worst railways in Europe'. I felt Labour's historic mission was being accomplished and was proud to be part of it.

By June 2007 we had delivered an unprecedented decade of steady economic growth, low inflation and low interest rates which had taken UK employment to record heights. UK GDP per head grew faster than for any other member of the Group of Seven leading developed economies. Britain's national debt as a share of national income was lower than that of France, Germany, the USA, Switzerland or Japan, having fallen by six per cent since under the Tories in 1997 (worth some £90 billion by 2011). IMF figures showed that the UK's 2007 public sector deficit, at 2.7 per cent of GDP, was also low: the same as that of France and the USA.

The economic outlook seemed positive. The FTSE 100 share price index had hit a six-year high, reflecting optimism about the UK's economic prospects under Labour, and bank credit default swap spreads had fallen to an historic low, a sign of confidence in Britain's future in financial markets. Ministers like me began to believe that Britain had finally broken free from the cycle of boom and bust. Desperate to identify with Labour's success, David Cameron even agreed to match Labour's spending plans up to 2010 (suffering convenient amnesia when he subsequently denounced us for 'massive over-spending').

Then – quite out of the blue to governments the world over including ours – came the banking crisis, the global credit crunch and the worst recession for eighty years.

We responded by boosting public spending and borrowing to offset the catastrophic collapse in private sector spending. Total UK national output sank to 10 per cent below where it would have been had the economy stayed on its past growth trend, a £140 billion loss of national income. The effect of the automatic stabilisers – higher public spending as people lost their jobs and claimed benefits, and lower tax revenue as yields from taxes on incomes and spending fell – plus our £25 billion fiscal stimulus in 2008–9, and the £90 billion spent on bank bailouts, plunged the public sector into record annual deficits. But these were deficits which stopped a slide into slump and laid the basis for recovery from the biggest shock to hit the world economy in peacetime since the 1930s Great Depression.

Contrary to right-wing free market mantras and Tory/Lib Dem history rewrites, lower public spending and borrowing would have been no guarantee against the tsunami that struck the world economy in the form of the financial crisis of 2008–9. Ireland, Iceland and Spain had all run budget surpluses in 2007. They all had national debt lower as a share of national income than the UK. But they were still engulfed. The IMF has freely acknowledged that the worldwide increase in government borrowing urged upon the G20 by Gordon Brown and our subsequently much-vilified Labour government after the 2008 credit crunch staved off a global economic catastrophe.

However, the new Tory-led government embarked upon a massive and immediate tax and public spending squeeze. By rushing to reduce the public sector deficit it succeeded in turning a fragile but real recovery under Labour in 2010 into a faltering one under the Tory/Lib Dem coalition in 2011. That mistake has been made before. In the USA in 1936 President Roosevelt, under pressure to balance the American budget, cut back prematurely on his hugely successful 'New Deal', which, after the Great Depression, had caused the US economy to grow quickly for four years, slashing unemployment. Roosevelt was pressed to balance his budget within two years. Instead the US recovery went into reverse as the economy slipped back into recession and unemployment rose again sharply. Full employment was not achieved until the 1940s spending boom generated by World War Two, more than a decade after the financial crisis that had triggered the 1930s slump.

The big Tory deceit was that the deficit was caused by Labour's reckless spending and borrowing, the cuts therefore all Labour's fault. In fact irresponsible bankers caused the crisis. Before the banking crisis hit our economy like a storm, British government debt was low – lower than our inheritance from the Tories: we did indeed 'fix the roof when the sun was shining'. The low yields on UK government bonds before, during and after the credit crunch under Labour bore eloquent testimony to the fact that the international markets had full confidence in our government; they were not clamouring for the right-wing dogma subsequently visited upon Britain.

Labour's spending was in fact lower than in France, Germany, the Netherlands, Norway and Sweden, and was *never* 'out of control'. If it had been, the Tories would never have accepted our spending plans. But they did. Sometimes they even demanded we spend more. The Liberal Democrats always demanded we spend more all the time. Before the global financial crisis, government borrowing was far lower than in the Tories' last year in office, 1996–7. Although some of Labour's increased public investment could undoubtedly have been more efficiently delivered, it was absolutely essential to repair the public services and infrastructure that the Tories had shattered.

However, the sudden banking crisis showed that we had clearly adopted too lax a stance on financial regulation. Like much of the Western world we had allowed consumer spending to grow strongly, backed by rising household debt. We had allowed recklessly irresponsible bank borrowing and lending to become a law unto itself, untroubled by a flawed system of financial regulation. We had allowed market forces to have their head, and they had run amok, as the herd instinct took financial institutions like lemmings right over the edge. Today the casino side of banking still poses a deadly threat to economic stability, with bankers displaying the same temptation to take reckless risks in the belief that the taxpayer will step in to save them when things go wrong again. As they surely will because free market systems are inherently unstable and financial markets are prone to periodic failure.

Labour made another major mistake. I argued in government at the time for a more dynamic industrial policy, but it was against Treasury and New Labour orthodoxy. Stephen Byers as Industry Secretary undertook to be 'active but not interventionist'. His successor Patricia Hewitt in 2002 dismissed aid for industry as 'handouts', as if British industry were a bunch of *Big Issue* sellers. In 2003 her government document dismissed the whole idea of an industrial policy as 'protecting companies from competition and propping them up with subsidies'.

Things changed after the global credit crunch when Peter Mandelson took over and Labour adopted an exciting and radical strategy of 'industrial activism' to support the new industries of the future. In his book *The Third Man* he wrote tellingly in 2010: 'That is the problem with government. No sooner have you worked out exactly what your policies are, pointed everyone in the right direction, and started to make them work, than it's somebody else's turn.' Very true, but the problem with our government was that we should have had such a strategy from the very beginning, including when he was first Cabinet Minister for industry and business in 1999–2001. Then we might have encouraged a manufacturing sector better able to compete with the likes of Germany where governments *are* active, interventionist – and more successful.

Mandelson's 2009 statement recognised a role for state action in complementing markets, especially in respect of infrastructure, training and investment in innovation. It explained how public procurement could shape the business environment without seeking to substitute for markets, such as by encouraging the development of advanced petrol engines and electric vehicles. It showed how government can encourage investment in high-technology future jobs like low carbon, renewables, bioscience and the digital economy. It committed £1 billion to bringing government action to bear in areas where it could help to unlock potential, like offshore wind and carbon capture. By then Germany had created 250,000 jobs in its renewable energy sector while the UK employed only 16,000. The scope for government action to boost green jobs was and remains enormous.

The other area where New Labour weakened its resolve to act more boldly was in using tax policy to promote equality. Serious steps were taken to fight poverty. Labour left office having cut child poverty to its lowest level in a generation, taken a million pensioners out of poverty, and cut in-work poverty for two million families till the recession hit home. But we fell short of our aim to halve child poverty by 2010. The financial crisis and ensuing recession put that beyond our reach.

We always sounded reticent about redistribution, even when we were taking effective measures to reduce poverty: pensioner poverty (via the minimum income guarantee/pension credit and winter fuel payments), in-work poverty (via working tax credit) and child poverty (via child benefit, child tax credit and child trust bonds). We seemed slow to recognise both that the economic system was generating increased inequality by concentrating the income gains disproportionately amongst those at the top of the income tree, and that unequal societies tend to be unhealthy ones too, with more stress, more crime and less intergenerational mobility. We should also have led Europe in tackling evasion through international tax havens, in persuading the world to introduce a 'Robin Hood' tax on financial transactions, and made a decisive shift towards a genuinely progressive tax system.

Sadly, the Institute for Fiscal Studies found that income inequality increased during Labour's term in office, ending higher than in any year since the 1950s. The rise was smaller than that under the Tories during the 1980s and would have been even higher had it not been for our tax and benefit reforms. However, the fact remains that over the past thirty years incomes amongst those at the very top have powered ahead of everyone else as the share of profits and of investment income has risen. This seems to be true of most English-speaking countries though not of continental European countries or Japan. The credit boom may have masked the fact that middle-income households everywhere have been under pressure, by allowing them to spend more than they earnt. The bursting of the credit balloon exposed Britain's squeezed middle more than ever before and called into question whether their offspring could expect to enjoy the same standard of living achieved by their parents.

Britain still has nearly three million children, more than six million adults of working age, and two million pensioners in poverty; five million people on its social housing waiting list; and seventeen million citizens living with a long-term health condition (like a heart condition or asthma). There is plenty more for Labour still to do. Patience and persistence were vital to our success in the years 1997–2010. But being impatient for progress is what has always driven Labour forward – and we weren't impatient enough.

‡

In their book the journalists Polly Toynbee and David Walker analyse Labour's enormous achievements in government, as well as how and why we fell short. Their thoroughly researched verdict on the Blair–Brown era seems pretty fair to me: six out of ten.[*]

So why was this and how Labour can win in the future? The former No. 10 policy adviser Geoff Mulgan said that governments under-estimate what they can do in the long run and over-estimate what they can do in the short run. I recall only too well No. 10 'initiative-itis' where governing meant paying more attention to dominating the news agenda than to delivery (a bad habit copied by David Cameron and Nick Clegg). On crime, for instance, no sooner had one piece of legislation been enacted than another was hustling towards Parliament, implementation of the earlier one secondary. Additionally there were frantic drives to outsource public services – with, I argued at the time, no clear sense of Labour values guiding the limits of the market and the private sector.

Although, as Toynbee and Walker demonstrate, Labour did 'nudge the political centre of gravity leftwards – on public services, on income distribution and even on poverty', this was clearly not sufficient to prevent the Tories, with Lib Dems dutifully in tow, from using the excuse of the global financial crisis from 2010 to cut and destroy much of what we had achieved. New Labour was so in thrall to the zeitgeist of unstoppable market forces that we choked off the immense possibilities of fundamental change after winning three successive

---

[*]   Polly Toynbee and David Walker, *The Verdict* (London, Granta, 2010).

elections with clear majorities in an era where even Tory newspapers had no
serious alternative to back.

Although Tony Blair was in so many ways an amazingly accomplished
leader with an eerie sixth sense for the Tory underbelly, he and his closest
camp never experienced Tories on the *up* – for most of the time the Tories
were *down* the plughole. The Tories feared Tony, but too many natural Labour
supporters came to fear him as well. Although Labour's support is notoriously
and frustratingly fickle when the Party is in power, the blunt truth is that, of
the five million votes lost in government between 1997 and 2010, four million
were lost by 2005 under Tony.

Could he have won back sufficient support to stay in power again in 2010,
even if not in a majority Labour government? Quite possibly – because he
was certainly always going to be more electable than Gordon, and Cameron's
Tories still had a trust deficit. Nevertheless Blairites simply regurgitating New
Labour mantras and dumping all the blame upon Brown avoids their own
responsibility for the collapse in trust and the alienation of too many layers of
Labour's 1997 support.

I believed then and still do that there is a strong case for winning on a
more radical Labour agenda. The May 2010 election result suggested a core
'progressive' support at 49 per cent, according to Toynbee and Walker. This
assumes splitting and reallocating the Liberal Democrat vote, and adding
Green and Nationalist support: 'What the voting demonstrated was potential
for progressive policy, even at Labour's lowest ebb,' they argue persuasively. The
respected US Democrat pollster Stan Greenberg confirmed my own instincts
by demonstrating that British voters in 2010 strongly favoured more not less
financial regulation, more government not more free markets, and modest
tax rises instead of savage public investment cuts. That means a British public
more in tune with Labour's core values than those of any rival political party,
provided – and this is a big proviso – that the Party can win their *trust*. David
Cameron's failure to break through with a clear majority was proof of that.
Even in the most unpromising of circumstances for Labour, our ideology was
nearer to what the public wanted. As Toynbee and Walker argue: 'The Blairites
were wrong.'

This was my belief all along – that the Party needed to move beyond New
Labour, retaining the best of its components but jettisoning the worst: neither
going back to Old Labour's anti-business stance, nor accepting New Labour's
worship of markets and indifference to obscene bonuses and commercial
greed; neither going back to Old Labour's indifference to centralised public
bureaucracy nor accepting New Labour's readiness to privatise.

Although Labour in the future should never retreat from Tony Blair's appeal to Middle Britain, it was too often at a cost of ignoring white working-class concerns, especially over affordable housing and job insecurity. We should have empowered councils to build more many homes and ensured local people were prioritised; we should have regulated in favour of fairness and against incomers taking jobs on cut-price wages and second-class conditions. Failures over housing and job insecurity were the real reasons why immigration became the issue that dared not speak its name for Labour, haemorrhaging votes.

Although there should always be toughness on crime, anti-social behaviour and rule enforcement, our government often seemed too carefree about individual liberty in other areas. I never saw identity cards as the monster their opponents did – being asked to produce proof of identity is commonplace these days, identity theft widespread, and many other democracies have ID cards. But the ejection of a longstanding Labour Party activist Walter Wolfgang from the Party's 2005 annual conference using Labour's anti-terrorist powers when he was simply heckling epitomised for me an unforgivable indifference to civil liberties. We also failed to curb civil service zeal for frustratingly complex, overly bureaucratic regulation and service delivery. I recall well, just before I stood down as Secretary of State for Work and Pensions, beginning the task of freeing up local Job Centre Plus offices to get people into work without the entire paraphernalia of Treasury-imposed rigidities which strangled local staff initiative and dynamism, and which in turn later opened the door to the Tory–Lib Dem agenda of privatising welfare delivery.

Labour should always appeal to and mobilise that vital civil society constituency which used to be such an important part of the Party's periphery, but which became more alienated the longer we were in government. It represents the decent British majority, spanning faith groups and trade unionists, greens and community groups, human rights and Third World lobbies, anti-racists and women's organisations, united in a commitment to fairness and justice, key to revitalising Labour's historic mission. Labour must also become once again the party that attracts the idealism and support of young people, who became more disillusioned the longer we were in office.

And to achieve all that Labour needs transforming as a Party, because the standard political party model is bust. Membership has plummeted across the main parties. Whereas in the 1950s the proportion of the British electorate who were members of political parties was four per cent, now the figure is just one per cent. Labour's predicament has been made worse by the sharp collapse in the number of affiliated trade union levy-paying members from 6.5 million in 1979 to just 2.7 million by 2010. People are not 'joiners' any more in the way they used to be. That is why, through the 'Refounding Labour' project I led for Ed Miliband in 2010–11, the Party agreed to reach out to potentially hundreds of thousands of Labour supporters – people who wouldn't join, but who could be registered as supporters. That's what Barack Obama did to win in 2008 – he created a people's movement amongst those who never saw themselves as party animals but were with him, worked for him, and were vital to his victory.

These lessons were applied in a number of Labour constituencies which, according to the national swing, we should have lost, including Barking, Birmingham Edgbaston and Oxford East. They won against the tide because – through years of patient work in the community – they mobilised hundreds of *supporters,* and not just members, to campaign for Labour. They were at the heart of their communities and so people who would never have joined the Party delivered leaflets, persuaded neighbours, friends and relatives. They were Labour's invisible army in these constituencies: they went under the national political radar, and Labour won.

Together with another dozen constituencies they demonstrated what can be achieved by being in tune with the new politics. They denied David Cameron his majority. If – and only if – voters trust local Labour Parties, trust our MPs, trust our candidates and trust our councillors, they don't necessarily go with national trends in the way they used to. In an age of 24-hour news and the internet, politics may have become more global and national. But it has also become more local. Although the Liberal Democrats over recent decades partially understood this with their 'community politics', they also benefited by being uncontaminated with government. That is no longer the case, opening up a big opportunity for Labour: to re-establish the Party as the leading force for a wider progressive politics.

The key to Labour winning in the future is therefore to replicate the successes of Barking, Birmingham Edgbaston and Oxford East right across the Party, and at least to each of the 100 most marginal seats. The 'Refounding Labour' project is not just about creating a party fit for the digital era, and rooted in community organising, linked like an umbilical cord to local voters – it is also about *winning*.

To build a vibrant movement, Labour also needs to transform its policy making, because that is essential to rebuilding trust and support from members, trade unionists and voters. It is essential to open up our process of making policy, both to give Party members greater say and to enable supporters and voters to feed in their ideas, so that the Party leadership keeps in much closer touch with them than we did in government.

To win back the millions of votes we lost while in power, Labour also must learn from both its successes in government and its failings, advocating an agenda that is radical, empowering, internationalist and green, which mirrors Labour's soul with a renewed confidence in our values of social justice, equality, freedom and democracy. That agenda promises a Labour government capable of far surpassing the Blair–Brown era.

‡

Meanwhile there are several areas where new approaches are needed, informed by my roots coupled with my government experience in Africa, Europe, renewable energy and conflict resolution.

Although Labour focused upon Africa as no British government had done before, our mission remains unfulfilled. The body blow delivered against the global economy by the financial crisis arose from banking greed and bad regulation in the US and western Europe. But Africa suffered collateral damage – once again the victim of a centuries-old unequal relationship with the Western world.

Yet indiscriminate threats to the whole planet, mainly through global warming and climate change, mean a shared destiny for all nations, rich or poor. There is now a serious danger of a 'perfect storm', with every country affected, but Africa the main victim. Leaving aside terrorism, war and the proliferation of weapons of mass destruction, this 'perfect storm' has a number of components.

The banking implosion gridlocked private credit and investment, and massively cut Western government spending and investment, triggering a financial development crisis. Apart from the UK under Labour, most G8 countries failed to meet their 2005 Gleneagles commitment to double aid to Africa – leaving, according to the United Nations, a financing gap of up to $195 billion simply to achieve its Millennium Development Goals by 2015.

On top of this, rocketing food prices and an exponential increase in the demand for food has triggered an escalating crisis in food security. Water security is similarly a potential source, not only of strategic shortages, but also of conflicts between communities, regions and nations: it would not be a surprise to see water wars in future. In sub-Saharan Africa alone forty per cent of the population, or 330 million people, have no accessible clean water.

Add in extreme volatility in fuel costs – with oil prices very high and forecast to remain very high – and the scale of the challenge is daunting: seventeen of the twenty countries with the lowest electricity access on the planet are in sub-Saharan Africa, with only forty per cent of people in urban areas and a tiny 15 per cent of people in rural areas having electricity. All in all 585 million people in sub-Saharan Africa are surviving without any electricity. (That is fully 100 million *more* people than live in *all* the countries of the European Union.) Quite apart from the resulting misery and poverty, a huge number of

Africans are therefore without the essential prerequisite for any prosperous and stable modern society.

So what should be done? Absolutely key is harnessing Africa's abundance of solar, wind, tidal stream, and other sources of power to generate cheap and universally accessible renewable energy. That would not simply provide African communities with much-needed light and power. Crucially, it would also provide opportunities to generate sustainable and self-sufficient wealth and employment. Additionally green energy reduces emissions and thereby confronts global warming, in turn reducing serious African food and water shortages.

Without energy, health and social services are non-existent to primitive, educational opportunities extremely limited, and getting online impossible. Without radical change, the people of sub-Saharan Africa will be trapped in this vicious cycle, and Western aid will be constantly called upon like sticking plaster on a melanoma.

Europe needs to lead this change by investing in renewable energies in Africa. Although African countries increasingly look to China for investment, this has often been skewed towards China's ferocious appetite for minerals, with little or no transfer of technology and skills. So Europe should promote a true partnership with Africa, based on mutual benefit, transfer of knowledge, transparency, with the interests of the poorest at its heart.

Africa has the potential to go its own way with stand-free renewable energy and leapfrog costly grid-based generation as it has done so effectively in telecommunications through mobile telephony. With the help of EU investment, Africa – instead of a continent falling behind – could be a world leader in renewable energy, something which foreign private investors have not so far recognised. There is a huge investment opportunity in Africa, for instance in hydroelectricity, where only seven per cent of the potential energy resource is being utilised, and geothermal energy, where only one per cent is being exploited.

There has already been policy consideration in Brussels to cover the deserts, mainly the Sahara, with solar panels. Remarkably, more energy falls from the sun on the planet's deserts in six hours than the world consumes in a year. The Saharan desert is virtually uninhabited and close to Europe, which is potentially a huge market for renewable energy. As well as serving Africa's needs, the Sahara could one day realistically deliver fifteen per cent of Europe's electricity.

I would like to see a significant part of Europe's huge aid and development budget allocated to funding a substantial renewable energy investment programme in partnership with private companies. Although the Europe–Africa relationship has been one sided for centuries, global climate change is binding our fates together. We need each other more than ever before in the search for a 'perfect solution' to the gathering 'perfect storm'.

‡

Another unfulfilled mission is conflict resolution around the world, and our government provided a model for that. Most people simply take for granted the fact that Northern Ireland – isolated attacks by small paramilitaries aside – is now more at peace with itself than ever before, after a conflict created many centuries ago and sharpened by terrorism, brutal violence, terrible bitterness and prejudice. Yet the 2007 political settlement offered some guiding principles which underpinned the British government's strategy from 1997, and which could be applied to resolving conflicts elsewhere.[*]

First, our peace-making framework did not simply address ancient Irish constitutional divisions. It tackled human rights, equality, victims, and ending discrimination against Catholics in jobs and housing. It was these 'bread and butter' issues – and impartial policing, prisoner releases, decommissioning of weapons – which threatened the process on so many occasions. Dealing with them helped create more space for political leaders to be more flexible.

Second, one of Tony Blair's core beliefs was that people and personalities matter in politics, and that building relationships of trust, even where deep differences remain, is vital. So too is understanding, rather than being judgemental about, the pressures on the protagonists from within their own community or organisation.

Third, it is necessary to take risks. For example under the 1998 Good Friday Agreement releasing prisoners who had committed unspeakable atrocities: not easy – but essential to show paramilitary groups that a commitment to peace brought gains which could not be achieved by violence. In the early years of the IRA's bloody armed campaign, nobody in the British government could stomach talking with republican leaders, except in surrender terms, since they were regarded as completely beyond the pale after terrorist attacks on London and Birmingham, let alone within Northern Ireland; yet in the middle of all this bloodshed and mayhem, contact was initiated which much later on came to fruition.

Fourth, international forces need to be aligned. Tony Blair came into power to find a strong, confident Irish government, led by Bertie Ahern, and a US

---

[*] See Peter Hain, *Peacemaking in Northern Ireland: A model for conflict resolution?* (London, Chatham House, June 2007) and Peter Hain, 'From Horror to Hope' (Glucksman Ireland House Lecture, New York University, June 2008).

President in Bill Clinton who felt a strong personal attachment to Ireland and who was influenced by the large and politically significant Irish American community. Crucially, all three were prepared to work to a shared strategy, and each was prepared to be bold. This had never happened before and, as other parts of the world have discovered, these alignments of leadership and circumstance do not come along often: failure to seize the opportunity can mean condemning another generation to conflict.

Fifth, it is vital to avoid or resolve preconditions to dialogue. In the Middle East both sides have imposed preconditions effectively blocking any dialogue from beginning, strangling the peace process at birth. It is true that entering into dialogue – especially secret dialogue – with paramilitary groups carries risks. It did for British governments and it always will, but there is no alternative.

Sixth, it was Tony Blair's great virtue to grip and micro-manage the Irish conflict at the highest level, not intermittently but continuously, whatever breakdowns, crises and anger got in the way.

In the Middle East, efforts and initiatives have come and gone, and violence has returned to fill the vacuum. Fly-in, fly-out diplomacy has failed. Periodic engagement has led to false starts and dashed hopes. International forces have not been aligned and dialogue has been stunted. But Hamas and Israel cannot militarily defeat the other; they will each have to be party with other to a negotiated solution which satisfies Palestinian aspirations for a viable state and Israel's need for security.

Similar issues arise over the Taliban in Afghanistan, except that the complexities of warlords attached to the Taliban more for tactical reasons on the one hand, and the presence Al Qaeda leaders in the area on the other, make the whole process even more hazardous and complex.

In Kashmir, supporting efforts to take forward negotiations between Delhi and Islamabad is the imperative. Here, perhaps the lessons are also that a seemingly irreconcilable constitutional conflict can be addressed with ingenuity. The expansion of cross-border structures (and the planned devolution of policing and justice) was crucial to republicans agreeing to share power in what remained still a devolved part of the British state they disown. If India, Pakistan and the Kashmiris themselves can agree to an entity with soft borders and greater autonomy for Kashmiris on both sides of the 'line of control' between India and Pakistan, then maybe progress could be made while preserving the interests and longer-term objectives of each.

But the inescapable lesson of Northern Ireland is that deep conflicts will never be solved militarily. Either side may have temporary advances. But the solution has in the end to be political, and the mechanism has to be negotiation. Beginning the process on the basis of politics alone is what really matters – and I hope Northern Ireland will be an inspiration to those parts of the world that cannot yet even see as far as the starting point: that they too can one day enjoy the triumph of humanity in the long transition from horror to hope.

For Labour has always been an internationalist party: whether it be the unflinching Atlanticism of Ernie Bevin or Denis Healey, the passionate Europeanism of Roy Hattersley or John Smith, the unyielding anti-colonialism of Fenner Brockway and Michael Foot, or the courage of Jack Jones and George Orwell in fighting fascism in the Spanish Civil War. Unlike David Cameron, no Labour leader will ever have to endure the shame of apologising for the fact that in the struggle for freedom in South Africa their Party backed the wrong side. Indeed, my decision to join the Labour Party over thirty years ago was partly spurred by its commitment to the anti-apartheid cause and its belief that human rights are indivisible.

In our increasingly interdependent world, marrying that internationalist heritage to the progressive goals of the future is more important than ever: recognising that common interests and common problems can only be solved by collective action; that global security depends upon global justice; and that we must maintain the left's historic duty to defend human rights and promote democracy and greater equality around the world. Let's celebrate these values of progressive internationalism and resolve to put them at the heart of our foreign policy in Labour's next phase of government.[*]

‡

I have never seen myself as a 'politician's politician'. My transition from outsider to insider, from protester to Minister, ensured that. In the process I undoubtedly changed, moving towards the centre, but hopefully retaining my radical spark and values. I continued striving for the optimal outcome in causes most dear to me, but had to accept, like everything else in life, that's not always possible and that settling for *something* is better than achieving *nothing*. I also learnt a lesson which intuitively might seem obvious. Namely, that outside democratic government you are usually powerless but at least politics is more straightforward. Inside democratic government, you may be more powerful, but politics is immensely more complex and constrained: you are in office but rarely in command. Although political outsiders have both their own opportunities and limitations, so do government insiders. I found myself returning

---

[*] 'In Place of Foreign Policy; Progressive Internationalism', in *Rebuilding the Progressive Coalition* (London, Peter Hain MP, May 2007).

to the conclusion of my radical youth: the need for both extra-parliamentary pressure and parliamentary delivery, for both protest and government.

Personal attacks, media intrusion, lies and petty jealousies – all came with the territory. Yet I wouldn't have missed the opportunity to be a change-making Minister, just as I feel privileged to have helped end one of the great evils of our time: apartheid. But if our mission to be the great reforming Labour government of 1997–2010 remained unfulfilled, so does my personal one. There is much work still to do.

EPILOGUE

When Ed Miliband called me to talk about the leadership after the May 2010 general election, Gordon Brown was still in No. 10 and preparing to announce he would stand down if that helped the Liberal Democrats establish a governing agreement with Labour. But the Tories were talking increasingly purposefully to the Lib Dems about forming a coalition.

Ed explained that he would be the 'change candidate' for the Party leadership, keeping the best but changing the worst of New Labour – exactly what I felt was needed.

'I plan an insurgent campaign,' he said, sounding almost as if he were running to redefine the debate about Labour's future rather than to win, I thought.

'I am only willing to back you if you are out to win,' I retorted. I had been involved in too many idealistic leadership campaigns that had ended in honourable defeats. After the second worst result in Labour's history, I was only interested in a serious fight. Otherwise I might as well have backed his brother David – he, at least, was serious about winning the next election.

'Yes of course,' Ed replied hastily. 'I'm not just standing for the sake of it. I have thought long and hard. Standing against David is tough. But I think we have to change as a Party. We cannot succeed as New Labour Mark 2.'

Over the previous year I, like Alistair Darling, Alan Johnson and others in the Cabinet, had spoken to David about replacing Gordon as Prime Minister. David and I had always been friendly and he knew that I held him in high regard. But I talked things through with Ed and I liked what I heard.

David's campaign was up and running almost immediately once the result of the general election was known. He quickly signed up heavyweight support from almost the entire former Labour Cabinet – just four of us nominated Ed. The leadership battle was David's to lose. But though it was well prepared and well resourced, his campaign wasn't reaching out for a broader base; instead it was complacent with a tinge of machine arrogance, provoking resentment from several MPs.

Several years before, I had tried to get David to engage in dialogue with trade unions that were suspicious of him and also to spend more time meeting fellow Labour MPs, thus seeming less aloof in the Commons. But he made no progress with the unions, and the first time he made an appearance in the MPs' 'tea room', he just sat in a chair looking awkward instead of walking around chatting to colleagues, many of whom he had never exchanged a friendly word with. This attitude would come back to haunt him now and, significantly, some of the brightest of the new Labour intake – MPs like Luciana Berger, Rachel Reeves and Emma Reynolds, upon whom David would have been counting – swung behind Ed.

At an early campaign meeting with Ed I insisted on several key things that we had failed to achieve in my Deputy Leader campaign. First, there had to be absolutely rigorous reporting of campaign donations within the thirty-day deadline – this provoked amusement amongst colleagues who recalled the mess I had got into. Second, MPs who had nominated other candidates had to be asked early for their second and even third preferences (Wayne David was deputed to lead this task and did an excellent job). Third, we needed to prioritise obtaining early nominations from Constituency Labour Parties – again, something my Deputy campaign had badly neglected.

From a standing start, and rather ragged around the edges, Ed's campaign soon gathered momentum. He clearly performed strongest at a hustings session of Labour MPs – notoriously hard to impress. Trade union backing piled up. He had the momentum, but David was still the favourite, supported by a majority of MPs from the start.

It was a gruelling campaign as the six candidates pounded the country over five long months – a crazy schedule that could easily have been accommodated in six weeks. I had argued unsuccessfully with Acting Leader Harriet Harman for a short, sharp campaign to end just after the late July parliamentary recess, giving time for the new leader to settle in and prepare for the annual Party Conference and the big speech.

Another casualty of this long drawn-out process was the political debate over the economy, which Labour effectively abandoned, giving the new Conservative–Liberal Democrat government virtually a free hit. By the time the new leader was installed, the coalition had successfully pummelled the public with their propaganda that the global banking crisis was all Labour's fault and that there was no alternative to their programme of savage cuts and austerity. Only Ed Balls was able to make a serious critique, presciently predicting the disastrous stunted growth, increased borrowing and rising unemployment that resulted from this policy.

Two days before the leadership declaration, Ed called for a catch-up. 'You will win. It will be close but you will win it,' I told him.

'Do you really think so?' He sounded very doubtful, though I knew he had been working on his conference acceptance speech, assisted by my able former special adviser Phil Taylor.

As the six candidates walked in for the dramatic announcement to a packed and expectant Party conference, there was shock and turmoil on Ed's face. The candidates had just been told the result in strict confidence, but the outcome was obvious to all who knew Ed and it was clear as he made his first speech as Party leader that he was more conflicted by beating his brother David than immediately focused on the task in hand.

But, despite his deep admiration and affection for his elder brother, he had stood out of conviction. He firmly believed that Labour could not win again without changing in a way that David appeared unwilling to countenance. From the time he took that decision, his leadership displayed a toughness often underestimated by those impressed by his transparent decency and integrity.

Against all the odds Ed won for several reasons. He had an open, warm personality, offering both youthful freshness and governmental gravitas, intelligent yet approachable. People warmed to him. He talked like a real person, uncluttered by New Labour's grating technocratic jargon and on-message guff. He also came unencumbered by a label: neither 'Blairite' nor 'Brownite' caucuses piled in behind him. Indeed, he had often been a bridge between the two strong personalities, who spent far too much time competing against each other in government. That absence of the factional baggage so destructive throughout New Labour's life was seen as vital for the reassessment and renewal necessary to win.

Soon Ed was setting out his winning vision. No going back to Old Labour's anti-business stance, but a recognition that New Labour had an almost deferential policy towards markets, obscene bonuses and commercial greed. No retreat from Tony Blair's appeal to Middle Britain, but an acceptance that this was too often at the cost of ignoring white working-class concerns, especially over affordable housing and job security (the real reasons why immigration became the issue that dare not speak its name). A tough stand on crime and rules enforcement, but without New Labour's carefree attitude to individual liberty and its penchant for frustratingly complex bureaucratic regulation. In short, advocating a radical, empowering, internationalist and green agenda that mirrors Labour's soul with a renewed confidence in the Party's values of social justice, equality, freedom and democracy.

After his victory, Ed and his new team worked hard to win the loyalty of Party staff and his newly elected Shadow Cabinet, most of whom had not voted for him. In the first year some still seemed unreconciled and I felt the need to speak up in several Shadow Cabinet meetings about media briefings and leaks against Ed from certain colleagues, on one occasion referring to myself as 'Mr Grumpy' as I complained about their behaviour.

But steadily Ed asserted his authority, showing steel and vision, winning admiration for taking a stand on some important issues – such as bravely demanding senior heads roll at News International even before the full scale of the phone-hacking scandal was known. It was increasingly accepted that he and his Shadow Chancellor, Ed Balls, had called it right on the economy: that austerity at all costs would not deliver growth or jobs. His Commons performances became more and more authoritative. David Cameron – a consummate performer – was gradually exposed, revealing a tetchy, un-Prime Ministerial petulance when cornered.

‡

Ed Miliband faces a huge challenge if he is to defy conventional electoral wisdom and lead a one-term opposition to victory after the terrible defeat Labour experienced in 2010, but modern times defy psephological orthodoxy.

First, the Tories took office on a historically low base for a governing party. Their vote had been stuck over nearly two decades, inching up painfully slowly from a dreadful low of 30.7 per cent in 1997 to 31.7 per cent in 2001, then to 32.4 per cent in 2005 and finally to just 36.1 per cent in 2010.

In other words, despite facing an unpopular Prime Minister and a Labour Party that had lost the public's trust, mainly by virtue of being in office during the worst economic crisis for eighty years, not only did the Tories fail to win, they managed to gain a mere 5 per cent over thirteen years after a landslide defeat in 1997. Furthermore just 23.5 per cent or 10.7 million of the electorate actually voted for them. Apart from when Tony Blair led Labour and despite a significant population rise in the meantime, David Cameron achieved the third lowest number of Tory votes since 1931 and the lowest Tory percentage of the electorate since 1918.

Second, Labour under Ed Miliband quickly recovered around 10 per cent in the polls – overwhelmingly its natural voters, who had, stage by stage, defected after the introduction of student fees and above all because of the Iraq War, for the most part to the Liberal Democrats. These voters felt utterly betrayed by the Lib Dem leadership's enthusiastic embracing of a right-wing policy agenda that made Margaret Thatcher seem a moderate; they will very likely stay with Labour and not easily be wooed back to the Lib Dems.

Third, and perhaps most fundamental, the Tory/Labour duopoly of British politics seems broken. Its high point in 1951, when 97 per cent voted Tory or Labour, had collapsed to just 65 per cent in 2010 – a nadir resulting from the steady rise of other, smaller parties and a reflection of progressive disillusion-ment with British politics. Again, there is no evidence that this will easily be reversed and there are several reasons why, not least the increasing number and frequency of elections.

In the past people might only vote every four years or so in a general election and for their local council, often on the same day. Now there are five-yearly European elections, annual elections for multiple layers of local government in many parts of England, and elections every four or five years for devolved institutions in Wales, Scotland, London and Northern Ireland. As a Cabinet minister, it felt at times like being in a permanent election campaign – and now new Police Commissioners will be elected.

The more opportunities people had to vote for different bodies or posts, the more politically promiscuous they became. The Lib Dems were the main beneficiaries, but UKIP, Plaid Cymru and the Scottish National Party also enjoyed increased votes. Once people broke the habit of a lifetime by voting for neither Labour nor Tory, they were more likely to do so again and it became much harder to win them back, even at a general election.

Furthermore, some people started to vote for different parties at different elections. In Wales, for example, significant numbers voted Labour in a general election, Plaid for the Welsh Assembly and Lib Dem or Independent for their local councillor. People started to mix and match, enjoying greater choice and seemingly liking the idea of politicians having to work together.

Constituency boundary changes and the introduction of individual voter registration point to majority single-party government becoming the exception rather than the norm in future. That means Labour needs to fight harder than ever for every vote in order to win elections. But it also means the Party must accept that coalition politics may become a semi-permanent fixture in British parliamentary democracy, just as it has in local government. In which case, it is essential that coalition politics be enacted a lot better than under the Cameron–Clegg government, which made it a byword for broken promises. If it is the will of the people that no party should govern alone, they deserve a more mature approach to coalition government, and that means Labour radically rethinking the way the Party does politics.

By joining the Conservatives on an agenda that repudiated all their long-held claims to progressive credentials, the Liberal Democrats gave up, if not forever then for at least a generation, their niche as the 'anti-politics' party – and thus lost their ability to tap the growing reservoir of disaffected British voters. By promising to abolish and then instead trebling student fees they also lost the youth vote – rather as Labour did after Iraq. So the Lib Dems face a grim future. But, despite the recovery by Labour of some of its natural supporters, there is no reason to suppose that the two main parties will bounce back to their previous hegemony.

Some of the anti-politics vote the Lib Dems attracted will go elsewhere, in particular to UKIP and the Greens. The crisis in Europe and the fault line in the Tories will also mean UKIP are likely to poll well. As political scientist John Curtice has persuasively argued, 'the hung parliament brought about by the 2010 election was no accident. It was a consequence of long-term changes in the pattern of party support that mean it is now persistently more difficult for either Labour or the Conservatives to win an overall majority.'

So, even on a bad day, and doubtless after a relentlessly negative and well-resourced Conservative assault, Labour has everything to play for. On a good day the Party could well defy the odds and win outright in 2015. At the very least it is realistic to hope for Labour to be the biggest party, able to form a government. The question then is: with whom? It seems likely that the 'Orange Book' Lib Dem leadership – which hijacked their Party and took it into bed with the Tories – will be rejected by a membership desperate to restore the tradition of Asquith, Lloyd George, Keynes, Beveridge, Jo Grimond, David Steel, Paddy Ashdown, Charles Kennedy and Ming Campbell.

That assumes, of course, that there are sufficient Lib Dem MPs remaining after a probable battering in 2015. If there are, John Curtice is adamant that it will be in Labour's interest to leave open the option of a deal with the Lib Dems post-2015:

One of the lessons of the coalition negotiations in 2010 is that when the chips are down, preparation and prior contacts matter. In 2010, the Conservatives were ready and willing to do a deal, while previous contact had given Cameron and Clegg reason to believe they could work together. Labour, by contrast, was ill-prepared and internally divided on its willingness to strike a deal with the Liberal Democrats, while personal relations between key personnel in the two parties were poor. So while Labour will doubtless continue to mock and berate the Liberal Democrats in public, in private the party would be wise to keep the potential lines of communication open.

In that context, Ed Miliband's vision of Labour holds enormous attractions for those anxious to establish a government for the progressive, anti-Tory majority that has often been denied office in the last century.

This is a vision of a more equal, more just, more free, greener Britain: both pro business and pro worker; pro private competition and pro public services; pro state intervention and pro market efficiency; pro individual freedom and pro collective solidarity; pro active government and pro community empowerment.

‡

After the privilege of serving on Labour's frontbench for some sixteen years, twelve in government, and having led Labour to victory in the Wales-wide May 2012 council elections – our best results for nearly twenty years – I resigned as Shadow Secretary of State for Wales. I explained my reasons to Ed when we had met six months before.

I am a long-standing supporter of the Severn Barrage – by far the largest single source of renewable energy in Europe – and I believed that helping to deliver this through Parliament was the biggest difference I could personally make over the next few years, so I was keen to focus my attentions on achieving this goal. I also wanted the freedom to contribute much more on wider policy, including fighting the dire orthodoxy for austerity at all costs and notably on Africa, which remained close to my heart; therefore it was imperative that I free myself from the rule that allowed me to speak in Parliament only when the Secretary of State for Wales answered questions – about seven times a year.

I added that it was my intention to stand again as MP for Neath and to continue to fight hard for Labour across the country. And I told Ed that, should he wish me to do so in future, I stood ready to serve again.

AFTERWORD

MORE TROUBLE FROM JUDGES

Two days after the publication of this book in January 2012, it became apparent that my memoirs had stirred up some in the Northern Ireland judiciary.

The Lord Chief Justice thundered that my description in chapter ten (pp. 331–333) was an 'assault on the wider independence of the judiciary'. This was both bemusing and astonishing. For over two years as Secretary of State I had worked extremely hard to win the backing of Republicans for the rule of law and justice in Northern Ireland – something they had never recognised, viewing it as an alien import from the British state they had long sought to overthrow. Once this had been achieved, such was my confidence in the subsequent independence and integrity of the Northern Ireland judiciary that I later began the process leading to the devolution of justice and policing in 2010.

Now it appeared that I had inadvertently 'teased a judge', to use the words of *Daily Mail* commentator Quentin Letts (no supporter of mine), and this provoked a prosecution for contempt of court – a charge which carried a potential prison sentence. The medieval offence of 'scandalising a judge' was retrieved from the dusty shelf where it had lain for over a century and Biteback Publishing and I were soon in receipt of fulminating correspondence from the Northern Ireland Attorney General, John Larkin. Civilisation itself, it seemed, was imperilled by the irony and exasperation expressed in a single passage of this book.

Concerned that this storm in a teacup would lead to the Northern Ireland judiciary being widely ridiculed, I spoke privately to both the First Minister, Peter Robinson, and the Deputy First Minister, Martin McGuinness, members of the Northern Ireland Executive alongside the Attorney General. They were equally concerned, instantly seeing how the fledgling devolved judiciary could be brought into disrepute by a dubious adventure against a former Secretary of State when its primary function was to enforce the rule of law and deal with crime and terrorism.

Both Iain Dale, Managing Director of Biteback Publishing, and I were insistent we would not withdraw the offending passage or, as was even demanded at one point, the book itself. Whether or not the language I had used was too strong for some, for us this was a fundamental matter of freedom of speech. We had nothing to apologise for.

In that case, would some reassuring words suffice to end this madness, Peter Robinson wondered? This was a suggestion with which I was happy to comply. But an informal approach initiated by Peter's office brought an uncompromising response – the Attorney General was not for moving.

Some weeks later a trial date was set for 19 June 2012. There was universal incredulity amongst media commentators, senior British politicians of all parties and British judicial figures. A cross-party Parliamentary motion was tabled by nearly 150 MPs, led by former Conservative minister and Leadership contender David Davis MP and former Labour Home Secretary David Blunkett MP. The Speaker of the House of Commons was notably supportive, overruling advice from clerks to allow the motion demanding the Attorney General withdraw the prosecution. Asked by Blunkett at Prime Minister's Questions for his view on the matter, David Cameron indicated his own unhappiness, as, in private, did other Tory Cabinet ministers.

Across the water in Northern Ireland, Finance Minister Sammy Wilson demanded to know why taxpayers' money was being spent on what seemed to him a private vendetta. If the case went all the way to the Supreme Court, there was total confidence that the 'scandalising' charge would be rightly dismissed and confined back to that dusty shelf for eternity. In which case, the *Independent on Sunday* reported, it might cost the public £300,000 simply for the purpose of proving a point – hardly a trifling amount in a time of austerity and cuts in public spending.

Then my phone rang. It was a familiar voice on the other end, one I had learnt to trust and respect when Secretary of State, carrying an important but confidential message. If our solicitors could speak privately to the Attorney General's office, it might be possible to find a form of words that could produce a solution.

But what could that possibly be, I asked? After all, we had offered this informally through solicitors at the outset and I had subsequently attempted to do so again through the First Minister's office. But the reaction then had been intransigence and the launch of a full-scale prosecution.

However, that phone call did initiate a process which led the Attorney General to withdraw the prosecution on 17 May, just one month before the trial was due. The 'offending' text in the book remains unaltered for this and any subsequent editions. In a lawyers' letter agreed to coincide with the withdrawal of the case I said again what I had repeated right at the outset of the furore. Readers will see it below. The bizarre episode was over; free speech had been protected, common sense prevailed and faith in Northern Ireland's judiciary was restored.

And, shortly afterwards, Parliament moved to strike out 'scandalising a judge' from the list of criminal offences. Perhaps not quite what those responsible for initiating the prosecution had had in mind.

‡

'Whatever constructions and interpretations may have been put on the words in my memoirs, I certainly never intended to question Lord Justice Girvan's motivation in handling the Brenda Downes Judicial Review, or his wider capabilities as a judge. I simply disagreed with – and was exasperated by – the way he dealt with that particular case, coming as it did in the middle of immensely difficult political negotiations to achieve the final democratic peace settlement. I had never questioned his standing and motivation as a judge before that case, nor have I done since.

'My words were never intended to, nor do I believe they did, in any way undermine the administration of justice in Northern Ireland or the independence of the Northern Ireland judiciary – that very independence and integrity I worked so hard as Secretary of State to achieve support for from all sections of the community, including those who had previously denied it.'

Peter Hain

INDEX